...of finding out who...
...embers are on account...
...enerous way in which...
...d themselves to be prome...
...the various other form...
...ence of a teacher. W ba...
...son in unselfishness...
...ned! They had fondly...
...they had gone through...
...of amateurs exhibition...
II but now find themse...
...and mournfully mista...
...here is a rumor afl...
...have a concert. the...
...set, of course, is...
~~the~~ replenish the new...

D106494Z

L I S G A R

C O L L E G I A T E

I N S T I T U T E

1 8 4 3 · 1 9 9 3

JOAN FINNIGAN
EDITOR

Design & Production
Allan S. Sutton

Printing
Lowe-Martin Company Inc.

© Lisgar Alumni Association

Lisgar Collegiate Institute
29 Lisgar Street,
Ottawa, Ontario
K2P 0B9

Canadian Cataloguing in Publication Data
Main entry under title:
Lisgar Collegiate Institute : 1843-1993

ISBN 0-9697254-0-X

I. Lisgar Collegiate (Ottawa, Ont.) — History.
J. Finnigan, Joan, 1925- . II. Lisgar Alumni Association

L25.088L56 1993   373.713'84   C93-090394-3

But yet I treasure in my memory

Your gifts of charity, and young heart's ease,
And the dear honour of your amity;
For thee once mine, my life is rich with these.

George Santayana

As the current principal of Lisgar it is a privilege to write the foreword to this commemorative history of "The School." I feel not a little like Janus with one face looking back and deeply appreciating the legacy and tradition created under the leadership of men such as "Nosey" Stuart, John Dunlop and Wright Neil; the other face looking into a very uncertain future as the Ministry of Education announces its intention to radically alter the delivery of secondary education in Ontario.

Through the benevolence of the Ottawa Board of Education and my predecessors, over the past one hundred and fifty years Lisgar has evolved into a centre of excellence committed to Academics, Arts and Athletics. The significant role played by the school in the community, the city and the nation has been constant. The traditions of the school are perpetuated in its venerable and unique architecture, in the Memorial Hall with its Honour Roll lists, as well as through its orchestra, its yearbook, its athletic teams and the abiding loyalty of hundreds of alumni.

However, Lisgar is also a dynamic school keeping pace with a rapidly changing society. Lisgar's cosmopolitan image reflects today's Canada. The language department now offers Spanish, Japanese and Mandarin along with German, French, Latin and Greek. The Lisgar band has travelled to Finland, the orchestra to England, Wales and Vancouver. The school clubs are as diverse as Amnesty International, Women's Issues and Environmental Action. There are computer labs, multi-media labs and even computers for the composition of music. Our award-winning newspaper, *The Lisgarwrite*, compliments the *Vox Lycei*. Our International Student Space Simulation Programme, our Gifted Student Programme, our International Week are just a few aspects of today's vibrant Lisgar. The school's purpose has always been university preparation; our graduates today are found in universities world wide.

As we celebrate one hundred and fifty years of establishing traditions of excellence at Lisgar, it is somewhat ironic to realize that the Education Ministry's initiative in destreaming grades nine and thirteen will dismantle the structure and remove the focus of our present system. The future is uncertain but what Lisgar still possesses to counterbalance the contentious changes is a long tradition of stability, a well-preserved history and heritage, a deep rootedness in the community and an ongoing adherence to excellence in its staff and students.

We are the sum of our experiences; and our days at Lisgar had a large role in shaping us. I hope this book stimulates fond recollections of what many of us view as our most enjoyable days — our school days.

Best wishes to all members of the Lisgar Family

Alere Flammam

D. Ian MacDonald.

CANADA

PRIME MINISTER • PREMIER MINISTRE

I am delighted to convey my warmest greetings to the staff and students – past and present – of Lisgar Collegiate Institute and the readers of the school's historical retrospective commemorating its 150th anniversary.

This recollection of the many achievements which make up the history of Lisgar Collegiate Institute will no doubt fill present and former pupils with a sense of pride. One hundred and fifty years of dutiful service to the community, and indeed to the nation, are worthy of celebration. By honouring this tradition, you are ensuring that a lasting record of the institute and the many accomplishments of its alumni will long continue to offer inspiration to others.

Please accept my best wishes for a most memorable anniversary.

Ottawa
1993

On behalf of City Council and the citizens of Ottawa, I am delighted to have this opportunity to extend official City greetings to the Lisgar Alumni Association on the occasion of its 150th Anniversary.

As an alumna of Lisgar Collegiate Institute, this anniversary provides me with the opportunity to reminisce on memorable moments, enriching experiences, inspiring educators and unforgettable friends.

As the Mayor of Ottawa, it gives me great pleasure to acknowledge the Institute as a lively symbol of Ottawa's history. From the early days where it provided excellent education to the founding families of Ottawa — the Billings, Sparks, O'Connors — the Institute has always maintained an unrivaled reputation as one of the finest educational institutions of the region. Today, it serves all the communities of the National Capital and continues to be a professional source of high school education.

Jacquelin Holzman
Mayor

L I S G A R *1843 to 1893*

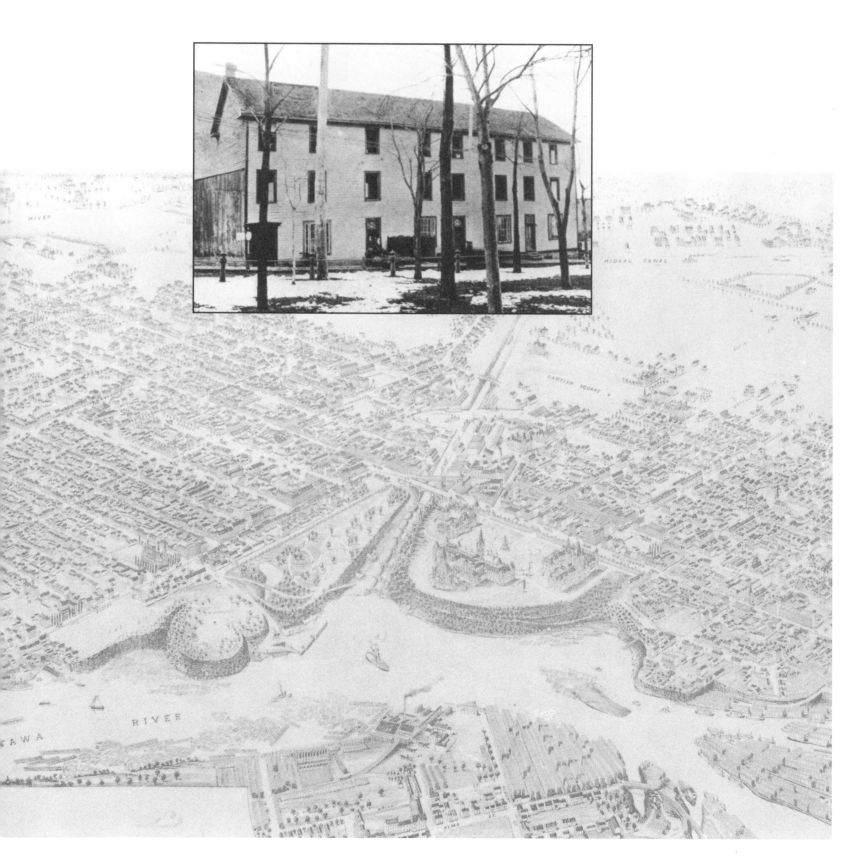

Previous Page:

Background Photo: Ottawa 1848

Foreground Photo: The Ottawa Grammar School from 1861-1874 as it was during Thorburn's time as principal, from 1862-1881, when John Macmillan took over.

INTRODUCTION
THE FIRST FIFTY YEARS

Long before the beginnings of recorded history, the site of the present-day capital of Canada was a sacred meeting place for tribes of Indians. Not only was the area around Chaudière Falls prehistorically established as an ossuary, but it evolved into a major fur-trading post as the Ottawas and Algonquins in huge flotillas swept down the Rideau and Gatineau rivers to their assignation with the mighty Ottawa River.

As a further archaeological layer, Ottawa City was spawned at the junction of these three rivers. Here, explorer Champlain and his party paused and portaged on their way westward to "La Chine" in 1613. By the end of the nineteenth century, Goldwyn Smith, English historian, educator, and critic, could describe the burgeoning settlement as a "sub-arctic lumber-village converted by royal mandate into a political cock-pit." In the period between Champlain's passage and Smith's arrival, the inhabitants of the emerging town site at the junction of the three rivers struggled to hold back the primeval wilderness with some of the attributes of civilization: stopping-places, churches, municipal buildings, prisons, hospitals, schools.

By the 1820s in the whole province of Upper Canada there were three hundred and fifty "common schools" with an attendance of eight thousand pupils, and in the eleven "District" and "Grammar" schools three hundred pupils. Many of the teachers in these schools were discharged soldiers or itinerant pedagogues from the United States, with the result that the education of these children was usually a matter for private enterprise.

In May 1843 the Dalhousie Grammar School was opened in the downstairs rooms of a rented frame building on the east side of Waller Street, a few yards south of Daly Avenue. Destined to become Lisgar Collegiate, one of the outstanding institutions of learning and quality achievement in the country, the elementary school in the previous two or three decades had been preceded by many brave and sometimes foolhardy attempts to bring reading, writing, and arithmetic to the children of Bytown's first settlers, new immigrants, canal builders, and a thin "upper layer" of professional and entrepreneurial elite.

In the spring of 1827 an itinerant American pedagogue named Fletcher opened one of the very first Bytown schools on Rideau Street but remained only a short time. The next year James Maloney from Wexford County, Ireland, opened a school near the Bywash, but soon afterward moved into a rough, scooped-roof log house at the corner of Besserer and Mosgrove streets. The school stood on the land that Colonel By considered integral to his canal building; he offered half a crown to buy Maloney's lot where the Basilica now stands. For reasons unknown, Colonel By did not take up the land and Maloney remained undisturbed until 1838, when he moved to 102 Clarence Street. There he remained for forty years, a fixture amongst Bytown's largely transient pedagogues.

BRIEF ARCHITECTURAL HISTORY OF LISGAR COLLEGIATE INSTITUTE 1843-1892

1843-1847

Dalhousie District Grammar School located in five locations:

1. Dwelling House (near Waller near Daly)
2. Wholesale Store
3. Carpenter's Shop
4. Retail Store
5. Boarding House

1874

Ottawa Collegiate Institute built on present site. Main entrance on Biddy Street. Principal's office was where library is now; library was where the present office is now.

1892

Four rooms added to South end, bringing building out to Lisgar Street. Front of building now on Lisgar Street. "1874" stone placed over the doorway.

In his *Recollections of Old Bytown* city clerk and writer William Pittman Lett (1819-92) leaves a graphic description of Maloney and his disciplinary methods:

> *A fixed star in the teacher's Heaven*
> *Since the old days of twenty-seven*
> *He taught and ne'er forgot the taws;*
> *The handle was just two feet long*
> *And well he trounced the noisy throng.*

James Maloney, "considered a man of good education and address," instructed his pupils in "Reading, Writing, Arithmetic and English Subjects." Furthermore, he managed the first adult night school, where it was said "Those of riper years can be carefully and expeditiously instructed in Reading, Writing, Arithmetic in all its various ways, and Book-keeping with Double and Single Entry, English Grammar, Geography with the use of Globes, Geometry, Algebra, Navigation, etc; all according to the precepts of the most modern and approved writers." Maloney's famous old schoolhouse was one of the few uncovered log houses still standing as late as 1923, when, like so many precious historical landmarks in the City of Ottawa, it was demolished to make way for "progress."

In 1830 J.R. O'Reilly and a Mr. O'Grady started schools east of the Rideau Canal, and a Mr. O'Leary one on William Street. On Cliff Street a school was opened by a Mr. Turner, but neither he nor O'Leary remained more than a year or two on the scene. James Agnew, also described by Lett as a "man of nerve and erudition," taught school in Bytown in the early years. In 1832 Lyman Perkins built at his own expense a little school where the first teacher, an American named Miss Kemy, taught twenty pupils.

In 1833 Hugh O'Hagan (later known as Hugh Hagan) came to Bytown from St. Mary's, Ontario, to open a school close to the corner of Sussex and Murray streets. Lett says he was "A man with learning, grace and mildness pictured in his face." About the same time, according to Lett again, Paul Joseph Gill, "a man with much tuition fraught, taught at the old creekside."

In 1835 James Moffat established his School for Advanced Scholars on York Street between Sussex and the Byward Market, obviously already a part of the commercial life of the town. Moffat soon had registered between fifty and sixty pupils, ten or twelve of whom were girls. At the same time a Miss Playter opened her Seminary for Young Ladies on Sparks Street near Bay and a Mrs. Motherwell ran a primary school on Besserer near Water Street, both of which we might assume were reserved for girls. Further opportunity for the education of Bytown girls was provided in 1838 when Mr. and Mrs. Cloran opened a girls' school on

St. Patrick Street, while at the same time on Wellington near Bay, a Mr. McKenzie, in from Perth, Ontario, opened a school for boys and Mrs. McKenzie one for girls.

From about 1835 to 1848 Peter Aikin Egleson taught in his own Academy on George Street North, and then went into the grocery business there. In 1837 the Reverend R. Short forged a new path when he opened "a school for both boarders and day scholars"; perhaps we might read between the lines here that a smattering of affluent parents up and down the Ottawa Valley required more sophisticated education for their children than that provided by the little red one-room schoolhouse on the concession line.

In 1838 James Fraser, who had teaching experience in both Quebec and Montreal and who had fought in the Rebellion of 1837, opened his school in New Edinburgh in a one-room house on John Street, a short distance from Sussex. In 1848 he moved to Bytown as assistant to John Wilson at the Duke Street School and was followed by William Stewart and then by David Wardrope, who left in 1849 to study theology at Knox College, and then by Duncan Robertson. In November 1840 R.E. Webster established a school "for those desiring to learn Greek, Latin, Philosophy, Reading, etc." Also in the early '40s Alexander Gibbs had a private school in Upper Town for tutoring students before they went on to study law.

In 1842 the District of Bathurst was divided, the eastern part being redesignated as the District of Dalhousie and, in 1844, a County Model School was opened at the corner of Queen and Duke streets on land presented by Captain Le Breton, after whom Le Breton Flats were named. The first principal was a Mr. Carey, described as "a genial kindly man" who later became an Anglican clergyman; his assistant, Mr. Healey, later opened a bookstore. Perhaps they were both early victims of "teaching burnout."

"The Scotch Kirk," as St. Andrew's Presbyterian Church was then called, was opened for divine service in 1828 by the Reverend John Machar, M.A., of Kingston. In 1832 Nicholas Sparks presented the Anglicans with the land on which Christ Church Cathedral stands today at the northeast corner of Sparks and Bronson.

During the summer of 1832 Bytown had been ravaged by Asiatic cholera and again in 1836 by a less virulent type. According to a pamphlet written in 1858 by Gertrude Van Courtlandt, wife of one of the first doctors in Bytown: "the first hospital in Bytown was a small wooden building situated on the bank of the river near the terminus of the Ottawa and Prescott Railway, being built in 1832 and intended for the use of cholera patients only. Subsequently, it was allowed to go to

decay and ultimately to be torn down for firewood by squatters in the neighbourhood."

The first in a long succession of newspapers in Bytown had already appeared on the streets: James Johnson's *Independent*, 1834, and Dr. Alexander James Christie's *Bytown Gazette*, 1836. William Lett because of his literary talents was editor of the *Ottawa Advocate*, a weekly founded at Aylmer by Dr. J.G. Bridges. Cartier Square and the Laurier Avenue Bridge were already landmarks when Captain Thomas J. Jones, born on the island of Barbados, had gone up the Rideau on the first passenger boat *The Pumper*, Colonel By and his officers having gone on up ahead aboard *The Union*. The first graveyard, Methodist, was opened on Sparks Street at the rear of Parker's Lye Works, considered a very appropriate location; prior to 1828 all bodies had had to go to Hull for burial and the new cemetery had to be considered a step forward.

On March 10, 1836, the men who would define the destiny of the forest industry in the Ottawa Valley, indeed, throughout Canada, the men who would accumulate the pre-income-tax fortunes that their descendants would live on for generations, gathered in Bytown to form the Ottawa Valley Lumber Association. It was an illustrious roster of names of the dynasties that would weave through the history of the Ottawa Valley, trailing behind them power, political clout, civic influence, and money: Joseph Aumond, Peter Aylen, Frederick Bearman, J.G. Bell, George Buchanan, Andrew Dickson, John Egan, Simon Fraser, Joseph Johnston, Robert Lang, J. McCrae, Alexander MacDonnell, Colin MacDonnell, Joseph Moore, T. O'Neel, Nicholas Sparks, Charles Symmes and William Thompson. Other early lumber operators on the Ottawa and its twenty-seven tributaries joined their peers in the Association for meetings at the Rideau Club: George Hamilton of Hawkesbury, Allan Gilmour of Gatineau Point, Robert Conroy of Aylmer, Boyd Caldwell and John Gillies on the Clyde and Mississippi rivers, Alex Barnet of Renfrew, John Supple and Peter White of Pembroke, George Bryson of Fort Coulonge. And there were others like A.H. Baldwin, John A. Cameron, Birch and Durrell, Thomas Cole, Robert Lock, W.W. Dawson, Jonathan Francis, H.M. Fulford, Robert Hamilton, Andrew Leamy, Charles and Ephren Mohr, David and Isaac Moore, John Poupore, Neil Robertson, John Ryan, Martin Russell, James Skead, James Wadsworth, J.R. Booth.

In his recollection of some of the old-time lumbermen of Ottawa and the Valley, the manager of one of Bytown's first banks wrote: "It was a rare treat to be present at Doran's Hotel during a casual meeting of the leading timber merchants on their return from Quebec City, and listen to their quiet banter. They were all superior men, possessed vigour of both body and intellect, and a healthy, friendly feeling of fellowship pervaded the whole company. Everyone enjoyed the emphatic discoursing of the argumentative Andrew Dickson of Pakenham, the rare jokes of Joesph Aumond, the quick wit of William Stewart, the quiet humour of George Lang, and the intelligent remarks of the pompous but kind-hearted Simon Fraser, of the Inverness Academy which he so fondly refers to as his 'Alma Mater.'"

As the timber barons acquired their fortunes, they tended to move from their mill towns to Ottawa, where they built their mansions—Daniel McLaughlin, James Skead, David and Isaac Moore—or they sent their children to school in Ottawa—Miss Harmon's School for Ladies, St. Patrick's School, Lisgar Collegiate. And so the names of the descendants of the timber barons were repeated in the school registers of the growing

town, on the athletic team lists as Ottawa became "the Sporting Town," and on the names of new streets— Booth, Gilmour, Sparks, Thompson, Skead, Kenney, Hurdman, Bronson, Blackburn.

The Shiners Wars between the English-speaking and French Canadian shantymen extending from approximately 1828 to 1838 had besmirched Bytown with an image of hooliganism, delinquency, and violence. The overwhelming lumbering influence upon the town—evidenced in lumber piles, lumber rafts, lumber slides, sawmills, piles of sawdust into which you could disappear, rough shantymen's hotels and stopping-places in Lower Town, shantymen's wild binges and frays—had led to Bytown's being dubbed "Slabtown." Not surprisingly, the elite of Perth looked down their aristocratic noses at the so-called

YOUNG, Sir JOHN, Baron Lisgar: second Governor General of Canada; b. 31 Aug. 1807, in Bombay, India, eldest son of Sir William Young, a director and large shareholder in the East India Company, and Lucy Frederick; d. 6 Oct. 1876, in Bailieborough, Ireland.

John Young was educated at Eton and Corpus Christi College, Oxford (BA, 1829). In 1834 he was called to the bar of Lincoln's Inn but never practised law. Elected to the House of Commons first in 1831 from County Cavan (his ancestral home), he served as a Conservative MP until 1855 and held two senior Treasury offices between 1841 and 1846, during Sir Robert Peel's administration. He succeeded to the baronetcy in 1848 and was Chief Secretary for Ireland, 1852-55. Created GCMG in 1855, he became in that year Lord High Commissioner of the Ionian Islands. The theft and publication of a dispatch in which he recommended an unpopular policy about their government led to his recall, though his administration was commended. As Governor General of New South Wales, 1861-67, Young, urged by the premier, nominated 15 new members to the upper house to secure passage of a regulation and was rebuked by the Colonial Secretary; he nevertheless completed his term. He became a KCB in 1859 and GCB in 1868.

Young was appointed Governor General of Canada and Governor of Prince Edward Island on 29 Dec. 1868 and, assumed office on 2 Feb. 1869. Shortly after arriving in Canada,

he commented publicly on Canada's independence within the empire and her freedom "to continue the present connection or in due time . . . to exchange it for some other form of alliance." There was nevertheless, he felt, greater loyalty to and respect for Britain in Canada than in Australia. He himself, however, found he now had less influence since his Canadian ministers decided measures in Cabinet before they came to him. whereas in New South

Sir John Young, Baron Lisgar, after whom Lisgar Collegiate was named in 1928.

"lumbering village," much preferring the social events and society of genteel Kingston and Brockville.

Somewhere around 1832 entrepreneur Thomas Mackay built a grist mill and a sawmill at the eastern edge of Rideau Falls around which New Edinburgh arose and became "quite a stirring place" when as many as one hundred farmers' wagons were seen moving about the site. Of these early mills Dr. Barker, editor of the Kingston *Whig*, wrote: "These mills are presumed to be the best in Upper Canada, not excepting those belonging to Messrs. McDonald of Gananoque."

To improve the health of the population of approximately three thousand inhabitants, Henry Bishoprick, in 1834, had opened a "Medical Hall" for the purchase of "Godfrey's Cordial," essence of peppermint, Cooper's

Pills, Syrup of Horehound, Winter's Vermifuge, "at Montreal prices"; also, fox and wolf poison, oils, paints, turpentine, pocket cutlery of all sorts, tortoise-shell combs, cacassar oil, and Butchart's Restorative Balsam.

A bad fire in a vacant wooden building owned by D. McKinnon on the creek side in Market Square, Lower Bytown, had led to a public meeting held in the Court House to form a Fire Club and purchase a fire engine with money raised by voluntary subscription. By 1837 the Bytown Benevolent Society had been established "for the purpose of relieving the suffering which the poor and destitute of the community might be exposed to from the scarcity and high price of provisions."

The official list of tavern keepers in the 1830s and '40s included Lucius Barney, Julius Burpee, Thomas

---

Wales he had been consulted by ministers before council meetings.

In Young's first year in Canada the disturbance led by Louis Riel broke out. As an appeasement he proclaimed an amnesty on 6 Dec. 1869. During the unrest the United States government barred the Canadian ship *Chirora* from the Sault Ste. Marie Canal on its way west; Young made a formal protest that it carried no military supplies and that American vessels, some armed, were freely using the Welland Canal. The ban on the passage was lifted.

During his term of office the Hudson's Bay Company territory of Rupert's Land was transferred to Canada, and Manitoba became a province in confederation. Originally scheduled for early 1869, the transfer was delayed by the rebellion until August 1870, and from April 1869 to that date Young had a key role as nominal lieutenant governor of Rupert's Land. During the Fenian raid into Canada in 1870, Young, according to Lord Dufferin [Blackwood] later, by a preemptory but judicious telegram to the adjutant-general, Colonel P. Robertson-Ross, prevented the summary hanging of captured American invaders.

When a delegation from British Columbia came to discuss confederation in June 1870, it was informed by Young personally of the desire of Canadians to have the colony join them. In 1871, the agreements for construction of the Canadian Pacific Railway to British Columbia were concluded. In that year also the Treaty of Washington was drawn up and signed. Prime Minister John A. Macdonald represented Canada on the commission in Washington and

fought diligently to protect Canadian interests. His independence annoyed the British commissioners and Lisgar (he had become Baron Lisgar on 2 Nov. 1870) added to their annoyance by communicating to them indiscreet remarks from Macdonald's correspondence with cabinet colleagues in Ottawa. Lisgar also complained to the Colonial Secretary of Macdonald's independence. Macdonald eventually agreed to secure Canadian approval of the unpopular Treaty of Washington if the British government would grant Canada a guaranteed loan of £4,000,000. Lisgar advised the British Cabinet that a much smaller sum would suffice. Nevertheless, Macdonald considered Lisgar the ablest of all the Governors General under whom he had served.

Shortly before his retirement Lisgar inadvertently failed to reserve a bill imposing discriminatory duties in Canada against tea and coffee from the United States. The Australian colonies then asked for similar rights, which the colonial secretary granted rather than risk displeasing Canada by disallowing its act. These protective tariffs meant an end to the British ideal of a free-trade empire.

Lisgar did not enjoy good health in Canada and resigned prematurely in June 1872. A man of ability, experience, and generally sound judgement, he died at his family home, leaving his wife, Adelaide Annabella Dalton, daughter of an Irish landowner, whom he had married 8 April 1835. There were no children.

Dictionary of Canadian Biography,1871-1880
(Toronto: University of Toronto Press, 1972).

Cochrane, John Johnston, Donald McArthur, Narcisse Paul, and William H. Thompson. Mr. B.S. Currier had taken a room at Julius Burpee's whence he made it known that he would insert "Artificial Teeth" and do the "Cleansing and Filling" for "Those that are decayed." Doran's Hotel had been the site for a meeting of the Justices of the Peace of all the townships "for the purpose of appointing a Building Committee to obtain estimates and Proposal for Gaol and Court House in Bytown."

A Rowing Club had been organized, a few of the gentlemen of the town "having procured an elegant Clyde-built six-oared gig named 'the Water Witch', with which they are practising and for which our splendid river [Ottawa] offers so ample an opportunity." There was talk of forming a Cricket Club.

The first Carleton Light Infantry had been mustering and drilling on Cartier Square for five years before the Dalhousie Grammar School was opened. Editor Christie of the Bytown Gazette described commanding officer Colonel Burke's first address to his men as "a speech replete with that chivalrous patriotism which glows in the breast of every true soldier."

In 1837 Christie's newspaper was keeping the town well informed. H.W. Knapp warned of his runaway apprentice, Miglory Velekat, an "indentured Apprentice to the Tanning and Currying Business," and warned that all persons "are forbidden employing, harbouring, or trusting him, under penalty of the Law." William Skead announced the opening of his "Sleigh, cart and wagon Manufactory near McLachlan's Mills at the Chaudière Falls." Knapp and Knowlton gave notice of dissolution of partnership in the furniture business; John McKinnon announced that he would lease the British Hotel; Robert Russell declared: "I will devote my time to measuring lumber"; and J.P. Weir advertised: "J.P. Weir, Steamboat Office, offers for sale Salt and Whisky; lots of it!" A branch of the Bank of British North America had been established "as a means of strengthening the British connection" and James Stevenson was the new manager of a branch of the Bank of Montreal.

The Union of Upper and Lower Canada had taken place in 1841 and Bytown attached great importance to the election of its first representative to the new Legislature. There should have been six hundred eligible voters but, because most of them lived on Ordnance lands bought in 1823 and leased to them, in reality only ninety Bytowners could vote. They were the ones who had bought land from Nicholas Sparks and Theodore Besserer. Three years later this injustice was overcome by legislation.

By 1843 the new Union Suspension Bridge over the Ottawa at Chaudière had been built to replace the one that fell in 1836. Lumberman Thomas MacKay, Scottish stonemason and contractor, had finished his eleven-room home locally known as "MacKay's Castle," situated in the heart of "MacKay's Bush" and destined to become the home of Canada's Governors General. Bytown had had its first public fair, opened its first marketplace and market building, constructed the first timber slide around the Chaudière Falls, and built the first mill to draw power from the Rideau Falls.

Despite the rough appearance and bad reputation of Bytown, its good citizens had their priorities straight, and by the 1840s, intent upon caring for the souls, minds, and bodies of its struggling inhabitants, they had already built the first churches, the first schools, the first hospital, and, in 1847, appointed the first librarian.

By 1843, the year that marked the opening of the Dalhousie Grammar School, young Victoria had been Queen of England for only six years. In a reign that was to last from 1837 to 1910, the longest in British history, she was to hold dominion over the complex, far-flung, and still intact British Empire; more profoundly, her period was to leave a characteristic and unique imprint on architecture and art, music and literature, manners and mores, sociology and science, philosophy and education. Indeed, Victorian influence, despite world-wide cataclysmic changes and upheavals, was to linger well on into the twentieth century.

When Victoria was crowned, her colony of Upper Canada was one of the newest parts of her Empire. There, the community of Bytown—which she later chose as the capital of the new country called Canada— had reached a population of five thousand and, along with Montreal and Quebec City, had become one of the centres of the enormously profitable timber trade, much of the timber being sent to England to build ships and, in particular, sailing masts for the British navy.

With its hodge-podge housing growth, willy-nilly streets, muddy roads, plank sidewalks, and general lack of gaslight for night travellers, the settlement could claim no Victorian refinements. But it was young and vibrant and growing, and this was the environment to which Lisgar Collegiate Institute, in its first decades, belonged; it was to reflect and parallel change and advancement throughout the nineteenth century. When Bytown was designated the capital of the new District of Dalhousie, it was decided that the town should have a grammar school like the ones in England. A five-member Board of Trustees headed by the Reverend S.S. Strong was organized to appoint a headmaster.

First principal Thomas Wardrope, M.A., came to the Dalhousie Grammar School fresh from the first graduating class at Queen's University. Ten years before, his parents had emigrated from Ladykirk,

Scotland, and settled in Guelph, Ontario. Thomas's brother, David Wardrope, left invaluable family memoirs in which he describes the passage over and the first back-breaking and often heartbreaking years of settlement in the new country.

David also gives an intriguing glimpse of brother Thomas's background to learning: "There were four of us boys, Thomas, James, David, and George. Then came Jane, our sister, born in 1828. Thomas was born in 1819. He was greatly in advance of us younger boys. Two reasons for that: 1.—he got more than his share of the brains at the start; 2.—they [the brains] were more cultivated by our parents, especially by mother. He [Thomas] could read when he was three years of age. He was sent to Edinburgh to college in his fourteenth year. These things made a great gap between him and the rest of us."

Wardrope, the scholar, arrived in Bytown only to find that no school existed. Surprised but not discouraged, he met with the School Board and an appropriate location for the school was selected. In May of 1843 the Dalhousie District Grammar School opened its doors.

Not even painted, the building that housed the school was a two-storey frame dwelling on what is now Waller near Daly. Classes were held in a one-room apartment on the second floor. The room was furnished plainly: backless benches, desks of uniform height for both the bigger and the smaller boys, and an immense, unpolished box-stove that provided heat from the centre of the room.

Since the school could accommodate only forty pupils, from its inception there was never a vacancy. Students came from Rockcliffe in the east to Britannia in the west; a few even came from outside Bytown and were forced to board. There was no discrimination: French and English, Catholic and Protestant, all learned together.

Instructing in the utmost simplicity, Headmaster Wardrope was at first aided by his younger brother, who died soon after the school opened.

After Wardrope left Dalhousie Grammar School in Ottawa in 1845, he served as minister at Knox Presbyterian Church, Ottawa, and eventually was elected Moderator of the Presbyterian Church in Canada. Wardrope was replaced at Dalhousie by the Reverend John Robb, M.A., who served until 1850. He in turn was succeeded by Mr. W.A. Ross.

In 1851 the school was renamed the Bytown Grammar School and was relocated to the northwest corner of Elgin and Albert streets in a building formerly used as a wholesale store. Five years later it moved again, this time to a carpenter's shop on Queen Street where it became known as the Ottawa Grammar School.

After being next transferred to a retail store on Metcalfe Street, the Ottawa Grammar School relocated in 1861 to a boardinghouse at the northeast end of Queen Street and remained there for over a decade. It was during this period that it began to acquire its enduring reputation of educational excellence. In 1873 on order of the Superintendent of Education, Dr. Egerton Ryerson, it became one of the seven grammar schools in Upper Canada to hold the status of collegiate institute. This title was attributed only to schools with four or more masters especially well qualified to teach the Classics, the Moderns, English, and mathematics.

It was also during the school's decade on Queen Street that an act was passed permitting girls to attend. While on Metcalfe Street, Principal H.J. Borthwick, M.A., had opened a private class for "young ladies who desired to continue their English studies." Eighteen students had enrolled in the two-hour afternoon class that was held daily and was taught by the principal himself. However, the 1871 Education Act meant that girls were more fully integrated into the school and the life surrounding it. It was reported that apparently feeling a need to appear more polite and gallant in the presence of "ladies," the boys demonstrated a more civilized manner under feminine influence.

Following the opening of the Dalhousie Grammer School in 1843 and the County Model School in 1844, in 1845 Miss Fraser and her four sisters, daughters of a Presbyterian minister from Lanark, opened a Ladies' College in the old Congregational Church on Elgin Street. That same year, four Grey Nuns sent from Montreal opened a Roman Catholic School in a small wooden house near the Basilica; it was to become the Rideau Street Convent. In 1849 the College of Bytown was incorporated in a wooden building in the garden of the Episcopal Palace; it was to become Ottawa University.

Through the influence of all its early entrepreneurial and English-speaking settlers and pioneers like the Wrights, the Symmes, the Holts, the Conroys, the Egans, the Forans, Aylmer very early was busily establishing institutes of learning for its children. The town had at least one academy in the 1850s; The *Citizen* of 1927 reprinted its advertisement:

"The directors of the Aylmer Academy beg leave to announce to the public and to parents and guardians in the district of Ottawa generally that they have fitted up Commodious Apartments in the Basement Story of the Town Hall, and have engaged Mr. P. Sheldon, a highly recommended and experienced Master, as Teacher. The directors will spare no pains in order to ensure that Youth entrusted to their care will receive a sound Classical and English Commercial Education. The Academy is now in full operation."

Reverend Thomas Wardrope, D.D. in a photo taken about 1870. Wardrope was first Head-Master of the Dalhousie District Grammar School. Born in Scotland of a clergyman father, Wardrope received his early education and began his studies for the ministry there. When he came to Canada in 1834 he enrolled at Queen's College, Kingston, where he remained until 1843 when he was appointed first Head-Master of the old Grammar School. Two years later he resigned to become first pastor of Knox Church, Ottawa. In 1891 he was appointed moderator of the General Assembly of the Presbyterian Church of Canada. In 1903 he attended the Diamond Jubilee of O.C.I. He worked for eight years, from 1864-71, as a member of the Board of Trustees.

Terms of Tuition per Quarter of 12 weeks, viz;
For common English branches, including History and Book-keeping, Single and Double entry, £150.

For Algebra, Element of Geometry, Natural Philosophy, Physiology and the rudiments of Latin, Trigonometry, Surveying Mensuration and the Greek and Latin Classics, £100.

PAYABLE IN ADVANCE

For further particulars apply to the Preceptor or to the undersigned Secretary Treasurer, Charles Symmes.

In the 1850s Mrs. Fitzgibbons was running her private school on Wellington Street in a stone row house just east of Fleck's Foundry. According to newspaper accounts of the time, Mrs. Fitzgibbons was "a fine French Scholar who taught the French language to adults and gave private tuition in French to students of all ages. The children of most of the well-known upper-town families went to Mrs. Fitzgibbons School in the fifties."

In the late 1850s and early '60s Alanson Cook, wealthy mill owner at North Nation and known as the "King of the Eastern Part of Ottawa Country," sent his daughter down to Ottawa to attend Mrs. Hackett's private school situated in a stone building on Queen Street, directly across from Dominion Church. A widow, Mrs. Hackett was a sister of W.P. Lett, city clerk and writer. Her girls' seminary attracted daughters of the wealthy throughout the Ottawa Valley.

By the 1870s specialization began spreading throughout Ottawa institutes of learning. In 1878 Professor D.J.B. Sawyer, at 28 O'Connor Street, opened Dominion College, a business college where penmanship was the premier subject. Professor Sawyer published his own textbook on penmanship in 1876, and in 1879 wrote a general book on the subject called *A Complete Exposition of the Pen Art*. He also published a magazine called *Pen Art World* as well as a copy book of his own design and copyright. His own superlative handwriting was said to be "just like copper-plate."

Charles Pope, a student at Lisgar in the 1870s, reminisced about his days at the Collegiate when it was still known as the old Grammar School and situated on Queen Street. In a *Citizen* article dated October 1938, Mr. Pope was quoted:

Far back in the distance of my early life—and if one so modest as this writer may quote from one of the greatest of British statesmen, "and upon a surface not yet ruffled by contention"—lies the memory of a homely edifice, a long brownish-yellow frame building with not a solitary pretension to architectural beauty.

With its clumsy desks—not innocent of the defacing jackknife—its old-fashioned unwieldy blackboards, and its benches as hard and unrelenting as Pharaoh's heart, it seemed out of harmony with the dignified name of The Ottawa Grammar School. But such it was; and it stood then, in 1869, and for many years after, where now the Russell Theatre rears its by no means aesthetic front. In emphasizing the duty of personal honour, the staff approached the great Arnold of Rugby. A case illustrative of the code of honour which prevailed among the boys of that time occurs to me at the moment; On a certain occasion during a recess, the school clock, remarkable for its unvarying inaccuracy as a timepiece, became the target for various missiles. Its venerable face for some time escaped injury but at last the inevitable happened and the clock was hopelessly smashed. Investigation, conducted with much solemnity, followed. But the culprit, realizing the enormity of his crime and fearing the condign punishment that would be meted out to him, shrank from the "open confession" which, we are assured, "is good for the soul." A boy, entirely innocent in the event, was about to be disciplined, but, at that juncture, regardless of the consequences, the successful assailant of the aged clock pleaded guilty to the by no means soft impeachment.

Therefore, on a certain December afternoon in the 1870s, a very small boy who had to exhibit a sufficient knowledge—or, in fact, any knowledge at all—of the fifth declension was "kept in after school." The day grew short and dark, as mid-winter days have a habit of growing, and, there being no means at hand for artificial lighting, the small boy was dispatched to a neighbouring house to procure a lamp.

He started bravely on his mission but forgot to return to the school until the following morning. How long the (im)patient teacher waited is not known to the small boy; but the lessons—the fifth declension was one—which he learned have not yet faded from his memory to this day. One of the lessons left a "marked impression" at that time.

* * * * *

In the year 1873 the Public School Board gave the salaries of the teachers a small boost. Whether a similar boost was given at OCI is not recorded, but the events that followed the raise and the statistics unveiled help to flesh out the history of teachers' salaries in Ottawa in the early days.

Immediately following the announcement of the salary boost, a letter to the editor from "An Elector" appeared in the Citizen protesting the increase. The Reverend H.J. Borthwick, the then new school inspector, took up the cudgels on behalf of the teachers. He wrote to the *Citizen*:

"Elector," says a higher rate is paid in Ottawa than in any other place in Ontario. Not if you look at it in the right way. The difference would be more than made up by the higher cost of living in this city. When the continual and just outcry of the Civil Service men and other salaried officials is for an increase of pay. Simply because in this city of dear living they find it difficult to make both ends meet.

Take my own office, every other inspector of the province is paid at a far higher rate than I have been—so with the secretary and other officials—but let it pass—increase or no increase, they can fight their own battles. But the poor teachers, the majority of whom are females, are in a manner, shut out from pleading their own cause.

I ask you, Mr. Editor, is £366 an extravagant salary especially when saddled with the condition of possessing a certain grade of certificates, to be got only after years of hard trial and study? The average of teachers' salaries in Toronto for 1871 was £357. In Halifax for 1871, £358. In Hamilton for 1872, £364, all places of cheaper living than Ottawa. It is strange, Mr. Editor, such a fuss is made about a slight increase to public school teachers' salaries.

The status of teachers in the community was a subject of discussion in the *Citizen* of March 23, 1929. In a little article headlined "Elevating Teachers" a *Citizen* reporter wrote: "Back in the 1840s, 50's and 60's, school teachers were regarded as more or less a necessary evil, not held in high esteem by the people who paid them salaries. They were very poorly paid."

For five years prior to 1855, Mr. Alex Workman, Ottawa hardware merchant, was the devoted local superintendent of the Ottawa public schools. In 1855, when he retired in order to devote more time to his business, he was given a farewell by the teachers. In his reply to them, Mr. Workman said: "During the five years of my service as a Local Superintendent of Common Schools in this city, I had, at all times, the welfare of the teachers in view while, at the same time, the mental improvement, the good morals and health of the pupils were not neglected. My desire was to place the teachers on that respectable footing [which] the importance of the duties that devolve upon them entitle them to."

The *Citizen* reporter concluded: "In these days [1929] when teachers have such a high standing with the public, it is funny to read remarks as those which Mr. Alex Workman made way back in 1855."

A group of modestly paid teachers and specialists at the early school. Top left; I.T. Norris, BA., a specialist in Junior Mathematics. Top right; W.A. Graham, BA., Junior English. Middle left; O.J. Joliffe, MA., Senior Classics. Bottom right; W.J. Skyes, BA., Senior English. Bottom left; D.A. Campbell, BA., Senior Science.

THE LYCEUM
THE LITERARY AND DEBATING SOCIETY OF THE SCHOOL*

The first literary society or debating club in connection with the old Grammar School is said to have flourished for a short time in the early 1860s. At the suggestion of Dr. Thorburn, who was then Principal, it was named after a similar organization in Edinburgh, the Philomathic Society. After a few years, however, it ceased to exist and any records that may have existed are believed to be lost.

After this, for a number of years there was no literary society in the school; but in 1878, largely owing to the efforts of Mr. Macmillan, the present society, the Ottawa Collegiate Institute Lyceum, was established. For the first few years of its existence the records are very scanty; indeed, it is not till 1883 that the present series of minutes begins. In an announcement of the Collegiate Institute, undated, but while Dr. Thorburn was still Principal (1878-81), the following sentence is found: "There is a Lyceum conducted by the students of the Institute, whose meetings are held on Friday afternoons. The exercises consist of readings, recitations, essays, and debates, and the meetings are presided over by one of the masters." In the earliest printed constitution, undated, but evidently in the early eighties, there is the following list of officers: President, J. Macmillan, B.A.; Vice-Presidents, Rev. T.D. Phillips, M.A., and A. Agnew, B.A.; Secretary-Treasurer, R.V. Sinclair; Executive Committee, J.T. Ross, G. DeH. Cunningham, S.W. Dyde, T.C. Boville, and G.A. Blair.

The... GILMOUR
BANK STREET,
OTTAWA, ONT.

FREEMAN I. DANIELS, Prop.

* Reprinted from W.J. Sykes, in *History of the Ottawa Collegiate Institute, 1843-1903* (Ottawa: The Mortimer Company, 1904)

The year 1883 marks a notable departure in the work of the Lyceum, namely the establishment of a printed paper called *The Philomath*. The first number of this paper is dated March 15, 1883. It was published twice a month, and eight numbers appeared: . . . *The Philomath* was a little four-page paper of which nearly two pages were taken up with advertising, a fact that reflects credit on its business manager, Mr. J.C. McLean, now of Montreal. The editors were C.J. Hardie, I.S. Heinrichs, and Miss Lothian. Mr. C.V. Campbell was distributing manager, and Mr. H.G. Todd attended to the advertising. From three to four hundred copies of each edition were printed. In the first number appeared an interesting article on "Our Old Boys." "Without premeditation or any attempt to exhaust the names of those especially deserving of mention, we give the following: *In Law*—Dr. Kennedy, and Messrs. Christie, Stewart, MacCraken, Hodgins, Greene, and Bishop. *In Medicine*—Dr. Allen, Dr. Wood, Dr. Grant, Dr. Stewart, Dr. Henderson. *In Business*—Messrs. Greene, Durie, May, Hay, Bate, Bronson, Perley. *In Teaching*— Mr. A.J. Bell, Mr. Smirle, Mr. Cowley, Mr. J. McJanet, Mr. T. McJanet. *In the Church*—Messrs. Bayne, Anderson, and Blanchet.

To these must be added the Sherwood brothers of whom the best known perhaps is Percy—now the chief of the Dominion Police.

Among the leading articles is a well-worded plea for a gymnasium, a plea that in 1904 would not be far out of place. Another article urges that school prizes be abolished; still another deals with the question of school fees. Under the heading, "School News," appear results of school examinations, names of the prize-winners in the school sports, and the accounts of the Lyceum meetings.

One feature of some of the meetings of these years (about 1884) was chemical experiments performed by the science master at that time, Mr. A. McGill, B.A., B.Sc., now Dominion Analyst.

Naturally the bare minutes give one a very inadequate idea of the actual work of the society, but an active and valued member in the early eighties, Mr. George Bethune, now of the Quebec Bank, Quebec, has contributed some interesting reminiscences that bring the early meetings vividly before us. He says:-

The Lyceum, or Debating Society, was instituted, if I remember rightly, in the fall session of '84 by a select few of the senior pupils, with the approval, and under the guidance of our beloved and respected Head-Master, Mr. Macmillan. Agreeably to our expectations, the juniors fell into line at once, and we had no trouble in filling the large room of the then Third Form with scholars of both sexes. I may say, without wishing to appear gallant, that much of the success

of the meetings can be put down to the lively interest evinced by the students of the gentler sex. At these meetings, which took place on each Friday after the close of the school session, the main interest of the proceedings rested in the various subjects of debate, which, comprising a fairly wide range of subjects, brought forth some really creditable efforts on the part of debaters. Some of our leaders in these oratorical encounters have since taken prominent positions in their chosen professions, among whom may be mentioned Percy Ryan, advocate and lecturer in McGill University, and Arthur Beament and Fred Magee, also members of the same distinguished profession.

To many of us, however, and more particularly those of the "female persuasion," the weekly appearance of the *Vox Lycei* was an event of paramount importance. Mr. Mark G. McElhinny, now a prominent dentist of Ottawa, and whose successor in the editorial chair I subsequently became, brought to the management of this literary infant, a capacity of no mean order, while we were indebted to our lady members for many a brilliant and witty contribution.

Such was the success of our first venture that in the following season, we organized a "Mock Parliament," which held its sessions in the Convocation Hall and, over whose deliberations, Mr. Nugent, as Speaker, performed his functions with dignity and impartiality. After a lapse of nearly eighteen years, I can recall with unmixed pleasure, the many instructive hours spent both in the humbler Debating Society and the more ambitious Mock Parliament, where Mr. Macmillan, Mr. Jolliffe, and Mr. Lafleur (Modern Language Master and later Professor at McGill) lent willing and patient ears to our boyish efforts.

Mr. Graham, the Premier of the Conservative Government was a fine specimen of our Canadian Scotchman, steady, canny, and pugnacious. But I think all those who flourished at that time, and are alive now, will agree with me that the palm as a speaker and natural-born debater must be awarded to Percy Ryan, the gallant leader of the Opposition, the promise of those early years has been amply fulfilled in his later achievements. We even strayed into the realms of Dramatic Art, and presented a historical drama in the Convocation Hall, the joint production of several of the senior boys, under the supervision of Mr. Jolliffe.

[Mr. Sykes continues:]

The years 1884-1888 were marked in the history of the Lyceum by special activity and interest. The debates were frequent and well-contested. The society [had shrunk in numbers], . . . as a consequence a member had more frequent opportunities to speak than at present. In some of these years one student would debate six or seven times besides speaking on matters of business and giving readings or contributing essays.

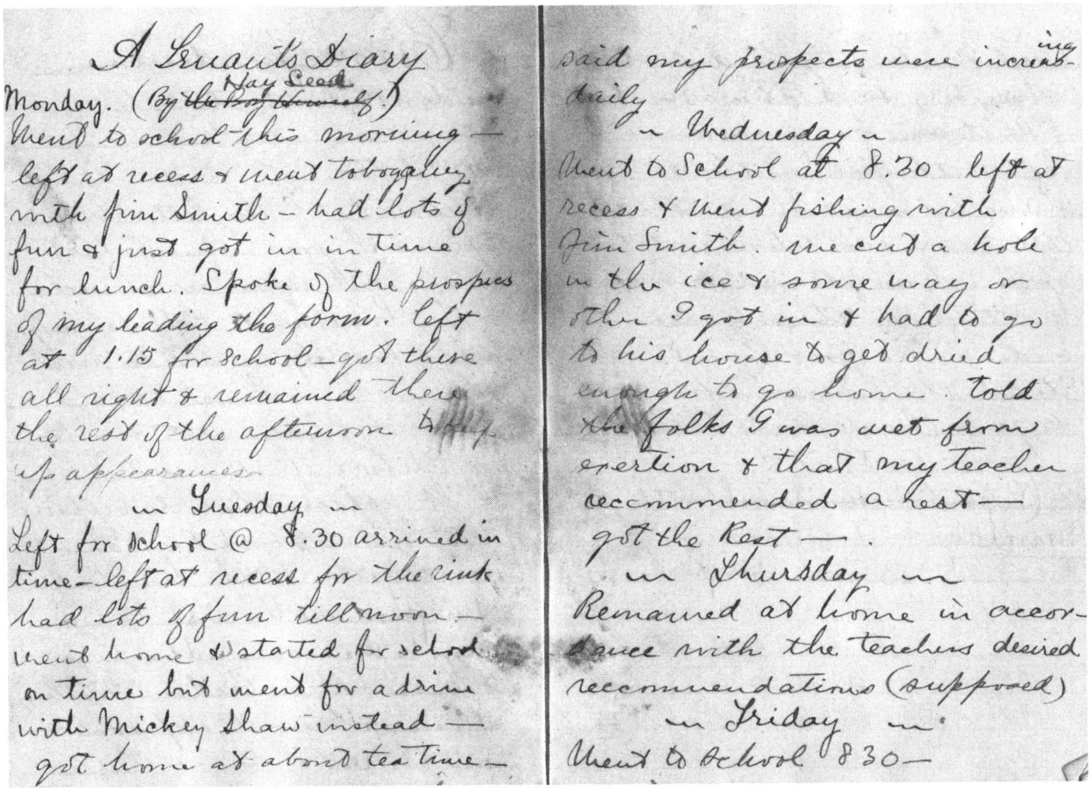

[Handwritten diary reproduction:]

A Truant's Diary
(By Hay Seed)

Monday.
Went to school this morning — left at recess & went tobogganing with Jim Smith — had lots of fun & just got in in time for lunch. Spoke of the prospects of my leading the form. left at 1.15 for school — got there all right & remained there the rest of the afternoon to keep up appearances.

Tuesday
Left for school @ 8.30 arrived in time — left at recess for the rink had lots of fun till noon — went home & started for school on time but went for a drive with Mickey Shaw instead — got home at about tea time —

said my prospects were increasing daily

Wednesday
Went to School at 8.30 left at recess & went fishing with Jim Smith. we cut a hole in the ice & some way or other I got in & had to go to his house to get dried enough to go home. told the folks I was wet from exertion & that my teacher recommended a rest — got the Rest —.

Thursday
Remained at home in accordance with the teachers desired recommendations (supposed)

Friday
Went to School 8.30 —

The Truant's Diary by Hay Seed from the first hand-written *Philomath* and *Vox Lycei*, Volume 1, Numbers 1-9, 1886.

Some of the programmes are worth special mention as showing how things were done "in the brave days of old." On May 7th, 1886, a public entertainment was given, the first part of which consisted of music and reading, and the second part of a play called "The Heirs," composed by Mr. G.H. Bethune, the editor of *Vox*. In the cast were Miss Hunter and Messrs. Bethune, Ferguson, Cummings, Beament, Ryan, Connor and McElhinney. This was a red-letter day in the history of the Lyceum. On another occasion the programme consisted of five readings and a recitation.

The year 1887-8 [September to May] was marked by the greatest activity in the history of the Lyceum: Of the weekly meetings, three deserve special mention. On December 9th, 1887, the Lyceum took the form of a mock parliament, with Mr. Charles Sparks as Speaker, Mr. F. Magee as Premier, and Mr. Percy Ryan as Leader of the Opposition. After some skirmishing in due parliamentary form, Premier Magee introduced a bill for Imperial Federation. The Leader of the Opposition moved that "the present House of Commons views with disapproval the fact that Your Excellency's advisers have betrayed the confidence hitherto reposed in them by the people of the Dominion of Canada, by submitting to their House of Commons a scheme which is foreign to the present needs and necessities; and that by so doing, this House of Commons recognizes such as a

Percy C. Ryan, Esq., B.A. Prominent in the Lyceum and an editor of the *Vox Lycei*. A medallist and scholarship winner at both Lisgar and McGill, Ryan was called to the bar in 1892 and practised in Montreal. He was appointed English Secretary to the Commission for Revising and Amending the Code of Civil Procedure and became lecturer on Roman Law and Civil Procedure at McGill University.

confession, on their part, of inability or want of inclination to deal with the practical questions with which is interlinked the future prosperity of Canada."

On March 2nd, 1888, a "Shelley" meeting was held, some items on the programme being an essay on the "Life of Shelley," readings and recitations from his works, and a discussion upon him, in which masters and pupils participated. . . . On May 18th, 1888, the decennial anniversary of the Lyceum was celebrated by an entertainment held in Convocation Hall. The programme was lengthy and well chosen, consisting of songs, choruses by the Glee Club, recitations, class exercises with Indian clubs and bar-bells, and an essay by Mr. Ryan.

It must not be forgotten that a Glee Club flourished during these years.

But no feature of the eighties deserves more emphasis than the founding and progress of the official organ of the Lyceum, the *Vox Lycei*. After *The Philomath* was discontinued in June, 1883, no attempt at journalism appears to have been made in the society for some years. In January, 1886 the *Vox Lycei* was started, chiefly owing to the efforts of Mark G. McElhinney who was its first editor. It was a modest little paper, written on pages of about four by seven inches and covering between fifteen and twenty of such pages. In the prospectus the editor stated the object of the paper:

Cover for the *Vox Lycei* of 1897.

To advance the interests of the Lyceum and of its members; therefore, the members should freely contribute to its pages.

Prose and poetry, wit and wisdom are alike welcome, providing they possess originality.

In particular the lady members, who then did not take part in debates, are invited to avail themselves of this means of taking a more active part in the work of the society.

The paper is to be "independent in politics and devoted to the advocacy of the cause of temperance and humanity."

The contents of the earliest volume of *Vox* do not differ widely from those of the *Vox* of today—verses, a story of some length, called "The Haunted College," and letters to the editor. Probably the editor then received more help from other members of the society than he does now. Someone writes to ask why no names have been added to the honor roll for three years.

How history repeats itself! There was a great deal of verse, most of it not up to the high standard of—say Alfred Austin.

There seems to have been in the eighties a rival society to the Lyceum—a Mock Parliament. On this as well as on the Lyceum a letter from an active worker in both, Mark McElhinney, throws considerable light. He says:

Interest in this Mock Parliament so demoralized the routine of school work that I believe [Principal] Macmillan stated that either the Mock Parliament or the Ottawa Collegiate Institute would have to go out of business. The Mock Parliament was thereupon dissolved.

No history of the Ottawa Collegiate Institute would be complete without mention of that Mock Parliament. Wm. H. Graham was premier, under whose rule I held a portfolio. I forget the cabinet list, but think that Fred A. Magee, T.A. Beament, and Wm. Hardie also were members. Percy C. Ryan was the leader of the opposition and was intellectually head and shoulders above the rest of us. N. Charles Sparks was one of the best men in the opposition.

During the term of '86, the Lyceum was a centre of great activity. The meetings were well attended, and the debates were original and full of vigor. Percy C. Ryan was the best informed and most powerful debater. W.H. Graham was a slow, impressive and effective speaker. Victor Campbell was also considered a heavyweight. Wm. Hardie, John McNichol, F.A. Magee, T.A. Beament, George Bethune, N. Charles Sparks, and Lorne McDougall were active workers. There was a tradition to the effect that the Lyceum had once possessed a paper called *The Philomath*. I have a dim recollection of seeing a copy. It had been defunct for many years. The *Vox Lycei*, of which I have the honor to have been the founder and first editor is, I believe, still in existence.

In the present system of education, a society such as the Lyceum is a saving element, preserving the individuality of the student from annihilation in the mad and useless rush for percentages in examinations.

[Mr. Sykes continues:]

After being edited by Mr. McElhinney and Mr. Bethune, the *Vox* fell into the hands of Mr. Percy Ryan. Part of his opening editorial is worth quoting as worthy to be a permanent aim of all future editors of the school paper. After announcing his intention to preserve the high standard of excellence the *Vox* had already reached, he amplifies as follows: "Nothing bordering on the vulgar will obtain entrance; slang will be carefully excluded. In regard to humor, which is by far the most dangerous department to manage, we are determined not to subvert the true literary standard of this paper to the outcome of rabid or senseless imagination. Genuine humor, however, will be appreciated and will find a suitable place in our columns. We intend to make the *Vox* a

First editor of the *Vox Lycei*, 1886. Mark G. McElhinney later had a long career as an Ottawa dentist.

literary paper. We shall not be content merely to uphold its past reputation, but our aim shall be to raise the standard of its literary worth. We appeal to the pride, the good sense, the generosity, and the genius of our school to uphold us in this resolve."

From the columns of *Vox* for this year (1887), we learn that a great election was held in the school. The Liberal standard-bearers were Messrs. Percy C. Ryan and Charles N. Sparks, while Messrs. W. Hardie and F.A. Magee represented the Conservative party. The number of *Vox* just before the election contains well-written election cards announcing platforms, making promises, and asking support; notices from the returning officer, J. McNicol, as to time and place of election, and the agents of the candidates also appear. Everything seems to have been done in due form—and the Conservatives won.

In the following issue of *Vox* appear cards of thanks, of which the most elaborate is that of Ryan and Sparks. From it we make these extracts: "'Tis better to have fought and lost than never to have fought at all." "We are proud to have had this chance of identifying ourselves still more closely with that large and heroic army of true Reformers who have lived at all times and in all countries."

With the fall of 1888 begins a new period in the history of the Lyceum. The former leaders, Ryan, Bethune, McElhinney, F. Magee, C. Sparks, Hardie, Campbell and others had gone, and new men came to the front—Blyth, Cross, McLean (S.J.), H.H. Horsey, and J.G. Gibson.

During this school year several matters of interest came before the society. In November 1888 the list of officers was extended to include a critic.

During this year ladies were first elected on the Executive. The former Executive of five was increased to seven, two of whom were to be ladies.

Of the programmes of these years two similar ones are worthy of mention. At present it is almost impossible to get anyone to read an essay before the society, but at each of these meetings, the reading of essays was the main feature. On February 21st, 1890, the following papers were read: "Digestion," by Mr. Gilmore; "Heat and its Properties," by Mr. McCurdy; "Etymology," by Mr. Jackson; "The Mineral Products of Canada," by Mr. Scott. In April of the ensuing year a similar programme was given, consisting in part of the following papers: "Jews in England," by Mr. Tarr; "The Life and Times of Edmund Burke," by Mr. F.B. Preston; "A Saxon Home," by Mr. Jackson.

It should be mentioned that during these years a prize was given for the best English essay, and that at these meetings the productions of the competitors were read.

Of this period, J. Goodwin Gibson, who took an active part in the various lines of work of the society, writes as follows:

Certainly the most interesting feature of the meetings in my first year was the *Vox Lycei*, edited by Bert Cross, who

The social reporter of the *Vox Lycei*, January to March 1889 gave this colourful account of the O.C.I. Carnival. These hand-written accounts were read out to the Lyceum audience.

I fancy wrote the greater part of it himself. I particularly remember the series of articles which he wrote under the nom de plume of "Kahwah." After he left, the *Vox* was conducted by an editorial board, of which I was a member for three years, and, though we had some good contributors, I do not think we ever had any humorist of the same calibre as Kahwah. His humor was vital and spontaneous, while that of most of our contributors was plainly artificial. I think he dealt largely with current events in the school, so that those early volumes if extant would contain much valuable historical matter.

In the opinion of Gibson, E.F.H. Cross, though not the founder of *Vox*, was, "under the *nom-de-plume* of Kahwah, one of the most fertile and productive poetical geniuses that ever contributed to its pages." The following doggerel is from Cross in the *Vox Lycei*:

MY FIRST DEBATE

I rose and stood upon my heels
*   On a splintery, wooden floor,*
And felt but like a speaker feels.
*   And looked towards the door.*

I stood upon my heels, I think,
*   Perhaps it was my head;*
If you had asked me at the moment
*   I never could have said.*

I gazed around about me; tried
*   About my theme to think;*
But the question would come to my mind,
*   Who taught the girls to wink?*

A boy in front then said to me:
*   "Speak out, don't be afraid."*
I looked down on him grimly.
*   And then no more delayed.*

"Mr. Chairman," loud I said it,
*   So that all the room could hear*
I got that far in safety, but
*   I felt then rather queer.*

"Mr. Chairman," I repeated
*   As I had said before;*
"Ladies"—how the girls all started,
*   As I said this with a roar.*

They looked upon me sweetly, ah!
*   No wonder I got red,*
And I turned my eyes away from them.
*   Then, "Gentlemen," I said.*

The gentlemen in answer gave
*   Each a feeble grin,*
And it seemed to me they muttered,
*   "Poor child, it is a sin."*

Oh! how I longed to take my seat,
*   But the speech was not yet made;*
And so I said I'll make it now,
*   And be no more dismayed.*

So I hurried on with my remarks,
*   And spoke as best I could;*
My argument was pretty strong,
*   But my notes were not much good.*

For they were written hastily
*   And scribbled in a hurry;*
And I could make but few words out,
*   For I was in a flurry.*

And when I paused to try and see
*   Why they were so affected,*
The audience grinned, as if to say,
*   "Ah! just what we expected."*

However, I got through at last,
*   And felt inclined to run,*
When everybody cheered so loud
*   With joy when I was done.*

Kahwah, *Vox Lycei*, 1887

[Gibson continues:]

Not many speeches made a lasting impression, but Herb Horsey's apostrophe to "Procrastination, thou art thief of time!" in his inaugural address as president will never be forgotten by those who heard it. In those days too Percy Ryan, then studying law in Montreal, used to come back to the Lyceum as a visitor and always gave us an eloquent harangue.

A rather off kind of performance was Evans Jackson's whistling solo. Whatever musical gifts he had were purely natural and usually exercised only for his own delectation; but he was persuaded to appear one night at the Lyceum. Though he did not know what bashfulness was, still there was to him something awkward in standing before an audience and whistling. So he hit upon the idea of fanning himself with a piece of cardboard, and so he stood fanning and whistling. Poor Jackson. He was man rather than boy, not long out from England and self-made—an earnest student, a writer of verses too, but compelled to eke out a living by delivering newspapers. This probably injured his health, for before long he was carried off by consumption.

Some minor changes in the constitution were the addition of the office of critic, first held by the Principal, and then by other members of the staff; and the election of a new president every month, so as to give more boys the chance of holding that office. Looking back I feel that the experience I got by being in the chair was the most valuable result of my connection with the society. The meetings were always conducted with a strict regard to the rules of Parliamentary

JAMES HOPE & SONS, Limited
61-63 SPARKS STREET, OTTAWA

BOOKSELLERS
STATIONERS
BOOKBINDERS
AND
PRINTERS

Established 1852

procedure, and points of order were hotly debated, which furnished better practice in speaking than the set debates. In such contests, it was generally felt that the girls held the balance of power. He who hoped to gain his point had to use not only cogent arguments, but all other subtle influences to which the feminine vote might be susceptible.

[Mr. Sykes continues his 1903 memoir of the *Vox Lycei*:]

Never, as far as we know, in the history of the society have there been better editorials than those written by Mr. Cross. The subjects are suggestive: "The Lyceum as a Literary Society," "The Lyceum as a Scientific Society," "The Lyceum as a Debating Society," "School Pride," "Ladies in the Lyceum." These subjects are treated seriously and thoughtfully in articles varying from five to eight hundred words in length. Notwithstanding the marks of immaturity in his writing, one cannot fail to be impressed with the promise of Cross's work.

Mr. H.S. Macmillan makes the following comparison between the Lyceum meetings of the later eighties and those of [the 1900s]:

I notice one respect in which there has been a decided advance since my time. I refer to the active part which the young lady students at present take in all of the work of the society. At that time the ladies assisted only in the lighter parts of the programme. They confined themselves strictly to music and recitation. It was considered a very radical move when two young ladies were appointed on the executive committee. The other offices were sacred to the sterner sex, and a young lady president was never dreamed of. A young ladies' debate at that time would have stirred the school to its very depths.

In the winter of 1889-1890, there were a number of good speakers in the school, whose fame attracted the YMCA debaters, and, as a result, a debate was held in the YMCA hall, where the Collegiate boys proudly vanquished their opponents. After the debate, the audience gazed in wonder while the enthusiastic O.C.I supporters took possession of the platform and gave their successful trio the famous "O.C.I bounce."

Prominent among the good debaters of that time were Percy Ryan, now a brilliant Montreal lawyer; O.E. Culbert, barrister, of this city; Herb Horsey, now in the Insurance business in China; E.F.H. Cross of Toronto; S.J. McLean, Professor of Economics in Leland Stanford University, California; and Gordon Lamb, whose eloquence was afterwards heard when he was a student at Toronto University.

It is a noteworthy fact that the O.C.I boys who had taken most advantage of the training afforded by the Lyceum work quickly forged to the front in the somewhat turbulent politics of the Toronto University Literary Society. The careers of John McNicol, Lorn McDougall, and S.J. McLean are examples of this, and that same training is now helping many O.C.I graduates in their more important life-work.

[Mr. Sykes resumes:]

In February 1892, a somewhat novel programme was presented. Nominations for mayor and aldermen (one alderman from each form) had been made at the meeting on the 19th, and on the following Friday the elections were held. Most of the candidates were elected by acclamation, but there was a stubborn contest for the positions of mayor and of representative of Form 11—a contest won by Messrs. R. Bell and W. Alexander, respectively.

During these years a marked feature of *Vox* was the leading editorial. Generally, it was serious in its nature and dealt with scientific or literary topics. For instance, the phonograph and the telephone are explained in two articles, while Chaucer, Ben Jonson, Ruskin, Wordsworth, and Carlyle are a few of the many literary men whose lives and works receive brief notice. No

The New Strap

We understand that two of the teachers of the institute have gone shares and purchased a new strap. We mention this fact because the strap is of a peculiar & unique character. It is a cat-o-nine tails. But two tails are gone. It is constituted principally of leather. It is not a trunk strap, nor a skating strap, nor is it made out of the ordinary leather — in fact it is by no means an ordinary strap. It is really an extraordinary strap. The teachers ... ably imported it from foreign parts. It appears to require a certain amount of usage in order to be kept in good condition & we need hardly say that it is kept in good condition. It is ... the common property of ... two teachers of the Institute. They treasure it. It is the delight of their hearts. It is not a razor strap but it is used for sharpening purposes. If any of our readers desire to make the acquaintance ...

From the days of hands-on crime and punishment comes this essay on the advent of the new strap at O.C.I. Hand-written in the *Vox Lycei* of March, November, December, 1889.

Page 1, Volume 1, Number 1, of the *Philomath* recorded an account of the magazine's inception.

At a meeting of the O.C.I. Lyceum on February 23, 1883, a committee consisting of Misses Lothian, Living, Macoun, Brown, Bowers, Farries and Robertson, and Messrs. MacLean-J.S., C.J. Hardie, C. Campbell, C.D. Fripp, C.A. Pinhey, O'Hanly, Heinrichs, McJanet, D. Campbell, W.E. Burritt, Todd, Williams, J.W. Ross, Jas. MacDann, Garland and Heney was appointed to edit a paper in connection with the Lyceum; and a motion was passed giving the aforesaid committee entire control of the paper, subject to the advice of the Principal of the Institute.

The committee met further on Monday, February 28, with Mr. C.J. Hardie in the chair. It was resolved to elect an editor-in-chief, or manager, and four assistants; namely—three editors, who shall read the proofs, and a Secretary Treasurer.

A committee, consisting of Messrs. Maclean, Hardie, Campbell, Burritt and Williams, was appointed to solicit advertisements.

doubt a certain amount of benefit was derived from all this, although most of these sketches suggest that an encyclopedia proved to be "a very present help in time of trouble."

THE *PHILOMATH* AND THE *VOX LYCEI*

The honourable traditions of the fourth estate began at Lisgar in February 1883 when the editorial staff released the first editions of the *Philomath* in handwritten volumes to the student body. These rare archival treasures, all nine volumes, are still held in the Lisgar Library.

Misses Living, Bowers, Farries and Robertson and Messrs Todd, Ross, Garland and Heney were appointed to canvas for subscribers to the paper.

On March 2, 1883, the name *Philomath* was decided upon by the committee and the Lisgar motto *Hic Pater in Genii Campus* assigned to the paper's masthead.

Philomath was printed using the facilities of the *Ottawa Citizen*. "The Citizen will print the cheapest of any, and their work is satisfactory," wrote the Secretary Treasurer. The printing of the first three hundred copies cost $9.50 and the second, $7.75.

The Executive Committee of the O.C.I. Lyceum, 1897. Back row, L. to R; R.M. Stewart, C. Baker, R.W. Kenny, W. Edwards, R.H. Armstrong. Sitting centre; T.A. Patterson, President. Sitting front; W.J. Sykes, Misses M.E. Young, H. Smirle, M. Stapleton.

The first issue of the *Philomath* was published on March 15, 1883. It consisted of four pages, two of which were taken up with advertising. The over six columns of reading material contained articles on "The Philomath," "Irish Affairs," "Old Old Boys," "Lotteries," and notes by the editor. Four hundred copies were printed.

The second issue was released on March 31. The third issue was released April 14 and contained an article entitled "A Plea for Canadian History." Five more issues were published, the last being the eighth issue, which was released June 27, 1883.

The handwritten issues contain every type of writing from editorials about schoolwork to poems written in French, English, Latin, and German. Several eloquent pieces stand out from this collection, such as Eugene Forsey's editorials one of which was reprinted in the 1992 *Lisgarwrite*, seventy years after its original publication.

The most striking aspect of these early publications is their similarity to those published today. Lisgarites appear to have belonged to much the same organizations throughout the decades, played many of the same sports, and shared the same concerns about politics, dating, and fashion. The main drawback of the handwritten *Philomaths* is the illegibility of certain authors' handwriting.

The handwritten editions were continued well into the 1920s, but none of those printed at the *Ottawa Citizen* seem to have survived.

A rivalry between the sexes is apparent in several issues from the late nineteenth century, in which the young men and women write sarcastic accounts of each other's fashions and habits. At this time most editors were male; females held the position of "Lady Reporter."

Between the demise of the handwritten newspapers and the appearance of the *Bull Sheet* in 1973, there may have been many abortive attempts to serve Lisgar students with weekly or monthly bulletins of "Town and Gown" activities and landmark events.

From the late William Hardy Alexander's reminiscences of his days (1890-95) at the Ottawa Collegiate Institute, reprinted in *The Citizen*, Jan. 29, 1938, we find the following:

"My mind leaps suddenly to a recollection of the journalistic ventures that graced the Upper first form in the second term of 1890-1891. It was Billy Askwith and 'Shanghai' Taylor who were responsible for the outbreak, I think, and very soon they had a little sheet (manuscript) circulating around the class every week which with its wit and humour served to make gerunds and gerundives and cube roots much more passable than in the nature of things they could otherwise have been.

"What the name of that paper was I have clean forgotten, but I remember well that Harry Link and I, whom fortune had made desk partners, determined to contest the field by issuing a rival publication which we named the 'Gab-Bag', though our opponents never deigned to refer to it by any other appellation than the 'Gas-Bag'.

"The rival journals lasted a considerable time, but Link and I succumbed when finally Askwith and Taylor brought out a 'Christmas edition' of their paper, all type-written. The printing press had triumphed over the manuscripts again.

"Those were the days when the O.C.I. football team used to play the second team from the University of Ottawa, and, if my memory serves me, the hearts of us little 'scrubs' were occasionally made supremely happy by victories, or at the worst, the games. Was it not about this time, too, that our school played the Kingston C.I. and were defeated mainly through the prowess of one Sliter, whom the Kingstons, rather unfairly as it still seems to me, placed upon their team. He was a rough player, but some of our senior students dumped him hard more than once."

In 1911 first editor McElhinney was required to do a twenty-five year retrospective on the inception of the *Vox Lycei*:

Perhaps George Bethune, Percy C. Ryan, and myself, had most to do with the matter, but it would be scant courtesy to forget that without the able assistance and hearty co-operation of W.H. Graham, Victor Campbell, Wm. Hardy, John McNichol, N.C. Sparks, F.A. Magee, T.A. Beament, Lorne McDougall, and others, our little venture had never been launched. There was solidarity about the boys at the Collegiate in our day, and the same probably exists as strongly as ever. We had our red-hot arguments, our disagreements, our individual opinions, and waged war continually, but none can say that any fought with ignoble weapons, and when it was a question of our school, we forgot all else and stood as one.

Our little paper had its lean weeks, for all are not equally inoculated with the germ of literary endeavour. At times the editor was forced to supply nearly all of the material for an issue, and make it appear by a variety of *nom des plumes* that the whole school was madly anxious to contribute. This is how we carried the interest over the lean weeks.

Regarding the aims and object of the *Vox*, such were set out in my prospectus as follows: "To advance the interests of the Lyceum and its members; therefore, the members should contribute freely to its pages. Prose and poetry, wit and wisdom are alike welcome, providing they possess originality." The lady members were invited to contribute and the paper was to be "independent in politics and devoted to the cause of temperance and humanity." That editorial menace to the souls of ambitious youthful contributors, the waste paper basket, had no place in our sanctum.

To my mind, the *Vox* is not to be judged by its feeble bugle-call, or its restricted and precarious existence, but rather by the spirit which called it forth and the answering spirit in the hearts of the school which sustained it. It was a little rootlet of progress trying to force its way through the stubborn soil of the time, a time which had become too self-congratulatory, and, as a consequence, bigoted in many ways. Educational methods looked more to the mass than to the individual. The supreme test was book-work. The medallist was the real thing. There was little attempt to encourage individuality, and independent thinking and working. The Lyceum and the *Vox* were an unconscious protest against the process of trying to force several hundred young human beings into one machine-made groove. Since school work did not furnish an outlet for all of our varied activities and requirements, we created such for ourselves.

Today, educational methods are different. You have manual training, nature study, essays to write on current subjects, scientific notes to make, and a hundred other little devices, calculated to bring out individual powers and arouse individual interests. Education and knowledge are no longer hopelessly confounded. The object of education is to awaken the mind to a consciousness of its powers and possibilities, and to the glory of productive thought and work. Once the awakening, all things will follow, and knowledge will be acquired as a means to an end.

EDITORS OF *VOX LYCEI*

M.G. McElhinney	1886	Carl Baker	1897
G.H. Bethune	1886	R.M. Stewart	1897
Percy Ryan	1886	C.I. Chubbuck	1897
J. McNichol	1887	B.T. Bolton	1898
F.A. Magee	1887	Harriette Smirle	1898
W. Macoun	1888	T.S. McMorran	1898-99
N.F. Connor	1888	Eilleen Clemow	1898-99
E.F.H. Cross	1888-89	J.G. Fleck	1899
S.J. McLean	1889-90	C.J. McEwen	1899
J.T. Blythe	1889	R.M. Timberlake	1900
J.G. Gibson	1889	R.G. Pushman	1900
H.H. Horsey	1889	D. Ross	1900
L. Lalonde	1889	Muriel C. Payne	1900-01
A.J. Kerr	1891	C.E. Hibbard	1901
W.J. MacDonald	1891	Ruth Orme	1901
A.W. Tanner	1891	G.E. Brennan	1901
F. Scott	1895	C.H. Payne	1902
W.H. Alexander	1895	G.P. Howlett	1902
R. Turley	1895	F.F. Dunlevie	1903
C.H.E. Askwith	1896	Helen McNicol	1903
C.J. Funnell	1896	H.B. Northwood	1903
W.M. Edwards	1897		

LISGAR CADET CORPS
1861-1870

The history of the Cadet Corps at Lisgar Collegiate Institute is closely intertwined with that of Canada. Beginning with the pre-Confederation threat of Fenian raiders and ending with the prospect of Fascist aggression during the Second World War the Victoria Cadets and the 94th Cadet Corps were ready to respond to direct and perceived threats to the sovereignty of Canada. Members of the Corps proved themselves first-rate soldiers in numerous military campaigns between 1866 and 1946.

In the early 1860s, during the Fenian Scare, there was a general call to arms in Upper and Lower Canada; consequently, "following the amendment of the Militia Act in 1862 to authorize the training of cadets in Canada, the syllabus of Normal Schools and many Grammar and High Schools was extended in 1865 to include military instruction." On April 15, 1866, the Adjutant General of the Militia in Canada, Colonel P.L. MacDougall, issued an order authorizing the formation of the Corps at the Ottawa Grammar School.

LISGAR CADETS
"ARMA VIRUMQUE CANO"
1861-1870

Brief Chronology

(1861 is generally regarded as the year of formation of the earliest school cadet units—No. 1 at College Ste-Hyachinthe, and No. 2 at Bishop's College School.)

1866 The "Victoria Cadet Corps Drill Association" authorized on April 15 by the Adjutant General of Militia, to be formed at the Ottawa Grammar School under Headmaster Dr. John Thorburn. At about the same time the "Ottawa Cadets" were organized at the Ottawa Classical and Commercial School.

1867 July 1, both Corps took part in military ceremonies inaugurating Confederation. November 7, at opening of first Parliament, fifty cadets from each Corps formed Guard of Honour for Governor General, Lord Monck.

(Victoria Cadets uniform was grey with green facings and black leather equipment, paid for by members themselves.)

1870 The Dominion of Canada Rifle Association allowed cadets to compete with militia in one match. Victoria Cadets won first three places! (Target shooting was strongly emphasized by the Victorias throughout the Corps' existence.)

Ottawa Collegiate Institute cadets at the turn of the century. According to Herb Beall, cadet historian, the first practice range was the Rideau Range on Laurier Avenue, the second Rockcliffe Park near the streetcar loop. Present day Connaught Rifle Range was the third site for target practice. Mr. Beall says that his uncle in the early 1900s as a cadet used the old Snyder muzzle-loader. This was superceded by the very accurate Martini-Henry, used for practice on Lisgar's Fourth Floor.

The Victoria Cadets
Head Quarters, Ottawa, 15th April, 1866

General Orders
Volunteer Militia.
No. 6.

"Victoria Cadet Corps Drill Association."

A Drill Association is hereby authorized at Ottawa under the direction of John Thorburn, Esquire, M.A., Head-Master of the Grammar School, to be composed of the pupils of schools and to be styled the "Victoria Cadet Corps Drill Association."

By Command of His Excellency the Right Honourable the Governor-General and Commander in Chief.

(Signed) P.L. MacDougall,
Colonel,
Adjutant General of Militia,
Canada.

"Nec quies gentium sine armis."—Tacitus.

Soon thereafter the "Veal Cutlets"—as they came to be known—began their biweekly drills under the direction of the head of the Civil Service Regiment, Lieutenant-Colonel Wiley, D.O.C.

Dr. W. Carden Cousens, writing in *A History of the Ottawa Collegiate Institute*, has the following to say about the origins of the cadet corps in Ottawa:

On the initiative of the Lieutenant-Colonel Wiley, Dr. John Thorburn organized The Victoria Cadets in connection with the Ottawa Grammar School of which he was the worthy Head-Master; and Rev. Thos. D. Phillips who occupied a like position in the Ottawa Classical and Commercial School organized "The Ottawa Cadet." These comprised seventy-five or eighty members in each corps.

School administrators and Civil Defence authorities worked in concert to ensure the success of the Corps. Lieutenant Colonel Wiley was assisted, Dr. Cousens goes on to tell us, in drilling his young recruits by John Macmillan, B.A.—teacher and future Principal of the school:

Captain Macmillan looked every inch a soldier and, in common with his subalterns, was very popular with the men under his charge, in whom he took a great interest. As he had served as colour-sergeant in company K Queen's Own Rifles while attending Toronto University, he possessed a thorough knowledge of military affairs.

Indeed, the cadets "so perfected themselves that they secured the reputation of being the best drilled corps in the city"; furthermore, the proficiency of the Cadet Corps was such that "the government became interested and furnished the corps with short military carbines, sighted up to 300 yards, for target practice." The cadets of Lisgar showed great aptitude on the rifle range and would go on to establish themselves as among the best marksmen in the world.

Ottawa, March 22nd, 1866.

Lieutenant-Colonel Powell,

Sir,—I beg leave herewith to enclose a list of the names of boys attending the Ottawa Grammar School and other schools of this city who have formed themselves into a Cadet Corps to be called the "Victoria Cadet Corps of Ottawa." It is under my supervision and Colonel Wiley is the drill instructor. We meet two days in each week, on the afternoons of Monday and Thursday from 4 to 5 o'clock. May I ask of you the favor of bringing the matter under the notice of the Government and of taking the necessary steps to have the corps gazetted.

I have the honor to be,
Yours very truly,
(Signed) John Thorburn,
Principal of Ottawa Grammar School

In 1867 I.B. Taylor, at the time Government Printer at Ottawa, presented a gold medal for marksmanship. The winners were: Charles Robertson, 1867; W.W. Proud, 1868; John I. MacCracken, 1869; John C. Grant, 1870.

Lieutenant-Colonel Wiley, D.O.C., the District Officer Commanding, a retired British officer who was credited with whipping into shape the first Victoria Cadets. Each member of the corps provided his own uniform but the government furnished short cavalry carbines sighted up to three hundred yards.

The service roll was as follows:

We the undersigned do hereby agree to organize ourselves into a volunteer military company to be called the 'Victoria Cadet Corps of Ottawa' and to serve under the provisions of class B of the existing Militia Law of the Province, under the command of the following officers, and to uniform ourselves according to the circular letter, dated Adjutant-General's office, Quebec, May 19th, 1860.

[W. Carden Cousens continues:]

The old stone armory on the corner of Sparks and Kent streets, was used as a hall of instruction for drilling the youthful but enthusiastic recruits, meetings being held twice a week.

On July 1st, 1867, Confederation was ushered in amid the acclaims of the people, and in Ottawa great preparations were made for celebrating the day. In addition to games and sports and a procession of the various trades-unions and industrial societies, there was a grand parade of all the troops in the vicinity, and "The Cadets," always in the van at such important events of the period, over one hundred strong, took part in the *Feu de Joie* and *March Past* of the troop, which terminated the most notable parade held at Ottawa up to that time. The companies taking part were the Prince Consort's Own Rifles, one battalion of regulars stationed at Ottawa at the time; the Ottawa Brigade Garrison Artillery, six companies; the Carleton Blazers, now merged

J. M. Currier, M.P. presented the Victoria Cadet Corps Gold Medal for competition at the rifle range by the two companies of cadets, the Victorias known as the "Veal Cutlets" and the Ottawas known as the "Dead Cats." In their first encounter J.H. Holt won for the Ottawa Cadets, 1886, but the Victoria Cadets won the next four years in a row, led by Harry Bate, Charles Robertson and A. Cotton.

in Duke of Cornwall and York's Own Rifles; the Ottawa Field Battery; the Victoria and the Ottawa Cadets. The *March Past* and the *Feu de Joie* were alike creditable to all parties concerned. And yet a greater honor was in store for them, and as patriotic youths, one which they esteemed most highly at the time. At the first opening of Parliament held at Ottawa in September, 1867, fifty men from each cadet corps acted as guard of honor to His Excellency Lord Monk, the Governor-General—the cadet companies lining the way from the Great Tower entrance to the doors of the Senate Chamber.

I shall now speak of the Metropolitan Matches. The first year the Metropolitan Rifle Association held its meeting at the Rideau Rifle Range. There was only one match open to the Victoria and Ottawa Cadet companies, distance 400 yards, seven shots. This was something new for the cadets as shooting previously had been at 100, 200, and

300 yards only (carbines being sighted to only 300 yards), so those competing had to procure the long rifle.

Pte. A. Cotton won first prize in this match with a score of twenty-six points. Pte. H. Gerald Bate and Pte. D. Robertson tied for second place with scores of twenty-five points each. In shooting off, to decide for the second prize, Pte. H. Gerald Bate made three *bull's eyes* and Pte. D. Robertson one *bull's eye* and two centres, Pte. Bate winning the second prize. (At that time *bull's eyes* counted four, *centres* three, *outers* two,) The prizes were $10.00 to the first and $5.00 to the second, and were presented, amid much cheering, to the winners by the Governor-General (I think), in the old skating rink on Maria street.

Soon their marksmanship became good also. At the annual meeting of the Dominion Rifle Association held at the Rideau Rifle Range, Ottawa, September, 1870, one of the matches at the short ranges was left open for competition to the cadets, distance 100, 200, and 300 yards, five shots at each. As a result of this invitation the cadets won the first four prizes, "The Victoria Cadets" winning the first three, and a member of the Ottawa Cadets winning the fourth. The commanding officer of the day offered to select a team from the cadets to compete against all comers. The challenge was not taken up. This officer expressed his confidence that the cadets would win at the short ranges.

The parade ground for the cadets was the campus in front of the old City Hall Square, and "a drill" always attracted a concourse of spectators—Colonel Wiley was very enthusiastic and proud of his protegés and of their progress. On one occasion while commanding and putting them through various evolutions before a distinguished assemblage, the Colonel was walking backward facing the men, who were ordered to advance. *By your right, quick march!* The words rang out quick and sharp as was wont with the Colonel, but as he moved backward he came in contact with a very large boulder over which he plunged and made a rather hasty descent to the ground. The pupils of the period all felt under a great obligation to the dignified Colonel for the interest displayed by him in developing their military instincts.

The cadet uniform was very becoming, and consisted of grey Halifax tweed with dark green facings;-grey forage cap, with dark green band and chin-strap of patent leather, leather ammunition belt and pouch; and a leather waist-belt; all provided at the expense of each individual member of the corps.

But the Government became interested and furnished the corps with short cavalry carbines (muzzle loading) sighted up to 300 yards. These served to increase the *esprit de corps* of the cadets, and active practices at the butts were carried on, the object of each boy's ambition being to become a member of the representative rifle team. Practices occurred in the early mornings from five to seven. At this period a silver medal we presented by J.M. Currier, Esq., M.P., for competition at the rifle range by the two companies of cadets, the Victorias and the Ottawas, both corps being known to the initiated as the "Veal Cutlets" and the "Ottawa Dead Cats." The teams were to be composed of six members selected by each side; ranges 100, 200, and 300 yards, 4 shots at 100 yards and 3 shots at the last two ranges.

Winners: J.H. Holt, Ottawa Cadets 1886; A. Cotton, Victoria Cadets 1867; Charles Robertson, Victoria Cadets 1868; H.A. Bate (Harry) Victoria Cadets 1869; H.A. Bate (Harry) Victoria Cadets1870

Great was the interest taken in this event, and the match came off on Saturday, September 26th, 1866, at "The Bluffs," a rocky ridge or promontory projecting into the Ottawa River, which now forms a portion of the beautiful Rockcliffe Park.

The competing teams were composed of six members of each corps of cadets, Victorias and Ottawas. Excitement ran high and the "fortune of war," ever fickle, wavered, the contest being a "neck and neck" one. It was finally decided in favor of the Ottawas by a bull's eye made by Harry Langton, one of that team, who won the match by two points.

John H. Holt made thirty points, the highest score, for the Ottawas, and was entitled to hold and wear the medal for the year.

In September, 1867, the return match was won by the Victorias, at the Rideau Rifle Range. In 1868, at the Rideau Rifle Range, the Victorias repeated their victory over the Ottawas and therefore became the owners of the trophy.

Attie Cotton made thirty-two points in 1867, and Charles Robertson thirty-four points in 1868, out of a possible forty points. These were the standard-bearers of their respective years. *Names of Teams: Victorias:* Private John I. MacCraken, Serg't Charles Robertson, Serg't Attie Cotton, Corp'l D. Robertson, Serg't G. B. Greene, Private J. P. Leslie; *Ottawas:* Serg't Harry Armstrong, Serg't W. C. Cousens, Corp'l W. Cassels, Private A. Todd, Private G. White, Private W. White.

A silver cup was also given by Captain McGillivray, a prominent volunteer officer and athlete, for competition among the members of the Victorias. This cup was won for two consecutive years, 1869 and 1870, by H. Gerald Bate and became his property. A gold medal was also very generously given by the late Mr. I.B. Taylor in 1867 (at the time Government printer at Ottawa) for competition amongst the members of the Victoria Cadets. It was won by Charles Robertson in 1867; by W. W. Proud in 1868; by John I. MacCraken in 1869; by John C. Grant in 1870. After this period there were no further competitions; the medal then became the property of John. C. Grant.

An incident occurred in December 1896 almost under the shadow of the school building in which the bravery shown by one of the (Lisgar) pupils attracted general notice, although the chief actor himself did not appear

Captain A. McGillivray, volunteer officer and athlete, presented a silver cup for competition in the Victoria Cadets. It was won for two consecutive years, 1869 and 1870, by H. Gerald Bate, and became his property.

to know that he had done anything out of the way. Just as the pupils were leaving the school in the afternoon, two boys who were skating on the canal broke through and went under the ice. Although the risk was great, Douglas Lyon at once volunteered to go to the rescue. A piece of old garden hose was found, and with one end of this tied to his waist and the other end in the hands of his comrades, Lyon went down into the freezing water under the ice to search for the two strangers. He succeeded in bringing one out, and twice again went down in futile attempts to find the other, only giving up when forced to do so by his assistants. Dr. Baptie and Dr. H.P. Wright, aided by masters and boys of the school, worked for a long time over the body that had been taken from the water but were not rewarded by any signs of life.

Although Lyon had not been able to save life, the bravery and singleness of purpose that he had shown were freely recognized. A gold watch, voted by the City Council, was formally presented to him at a public

Built in 1885 the Drill Hall has been a centre of the military life of Ottawa and a major presence in the life of Lisgar students whether they have been ordinary students passing by it daily or Lisgar Cadet Corps practising and drilling in adjacent Cartier Square. Two military units, the Governor General's Foot Guards and the Canadian Highlanders are located at the Drill Hall to this day.

meeting in the City Hall. In reply to the Mayor, who made the speech of presentation, Lyon expressed himself to the effect that he did not think he had done anything to make so much fuss about. Again, a medal was presented to him at a meeting held in the Rideau Rink. Finally, the facts of the case having been communicated to the Royal Humane Society, by Major Basil Bell, the medal of that Institution was awarded to Lyon. The recipient was at that time a member of the 43rd Ottawa and Carleton Rifles; so this last token was made the occasion of a military spectacle on Cartier Square, the Governor General, Lord Aberdeen, handing it to the hero in the presence of the battalion.

Douglas Lyon enlisted in the first Canadian Contingent for South Africa, and was with the Royal Canadians at Paardeburg and the other battles of that famous regiment. Upon his return to Canada he was again attending the Collegiate Institute when he was selected for service on the Canadian Contingent to the Coronation of King Edward VII.

There is no record of Victoria Cadets after 1870. Public apathy set in following collapse of the Fenian Raids.

ATHLETICS
1843-1893

"It is a good thing to have your minds trained and stored with useful knowledge, but there are better things than that. To learn honour, truth and right; to be manly and womanly; to be self-controlled and brave and gentle—these are better than all possible stores of learning."

With this specially chosen expression of the underlying philosophy and goals for athletics, set in the context of his time, Carden Cousens, one of the compilers and editors of *History of Ottawa Collegiate Institute, 1843-1903* and himself a renowned athlete, opened the chapter on Athletics and Cadets at Lisgar.

In Cousens' era in the last half of the nineteenth century athletic sport was considered to be a cognate of "military affairs," both combining to be a "marked characteristic of the young manhood of the city of Ottawa." The origins of the people, the climate, and the environment all contributed to "every man, young or old, taking an active interest in some kind of sport."

"The people, a mixture of vigorous races, French, Irish, English and Scotch, inherit healthy athletic and warlike tendencies. The hard frosts of winter, the dry bracing atmosphere of all the seasons, the exhilaration of life in the vicinity of a great river with its feeders of lake and stream and its broad valley of woods and rocky hills, all combine to make a physically and mentally active race."

The hand-written *Philomath* and *Vox Lycei* of 1886 contained an essay on the Value of Athletics, expressing opinions and sentiments as pertinent today as they were in the nineteenth century. This is excerpted.

One of the earliest reminiscences of sporting life at Lisgar came from Colonel T.D.B. Evans, C.B.A.D.C., commander of Canadian troops in the Yukon and in South Africa. He says:

"As far as I can remember, our sports in those days i.e. 1871-5 were played chiefly among our own school classes. One particular feature, I remember well, were the fights, usually arranged by the senior boys, between any two boys selected. The fights were always well conducted and took place in the old Russell House Yard. There was at least one fight per week and they were greatly enjoyed by all except perhaps the competitors, who usually had no choice in the matter."

Undoubtedly from the first year of its existence, on whatever served as schoolyard or "athletic field," the boys of the Dalhousie Grammar School must have played shinny and rounders, but there is no record of organized sports in the first twenty years or so.

"Sporting Notes" from the early sporting editors in the *Vox Lycei* record the struggling, haphazard beginnings of snowshoeing, baseball, cricket, and hockey clubs. From "Sporting Notes" of January 1889:

A report has got around that the O.C.I. have formed a Hockey club, and members of some of the city clubs have spoken to the Secretary asking for a practise match. We would like the boys to follow this sport out; they did so well in all their field sports last fall that we are sure they can show up well in this winter sport. The annual snowshoe race for the championship of Ottawa is about to take place at the end of this month. We have a Snowshoe Club in this school and we believe there are some good runners in it, we would like to see the club put one in for this race, as all the old city runners have retired, and they leave a good chance to win.

The question now is, when will we get any new exercises in the Gymnasium. Some of us have been in this school about two years and have never had a drill with the dumbbells. In the last two or three months some of our forms have not had a drill with the barbells, and even with the clubs never get beyond the first ten or twelve exercises.

By the time we meet again the skating rink will be going full blast, we wish it great success and trust that everyone will join in and push it on.

From the "Sporting Notes" on January 25, 1889:

"The second meeting to discuss the formation of a rink was held on Tuesday. The report of the rink committee was received and adopted. This report placed the expense at about $10.00 including $7.00 for the lumber, $2.00 for flooding and the rest for water, cleaning, construction, etc. The rink will be constructed in the boys' yard and will be about 90 x 100 feet in size. Work was commenced on Wednesday and the rink will probably be in good skating condition by next Monday.

"In the same issue two members of the rink committee, Gibson and Lamb, were reprimanded by the sporting editor, their general lack of contribution "by work or action" being described as "most disgraceful."

The "Sporting Notes" of that date also commented on other athletic endeavours:

The gymnasium has been patronized a good deal lately after hours. We believe that a number of pupils intend to petition the Board for a stove this winter. We hope this petition will be granted. It seems a pity that such a useful instruction, the one which can afford such profitable pastime to the pupils as the Gymnasium, should be closed to them all winter.

If the present snow continues and a little more arrived the O.C.I. Snowshoe Club should be soon organized.

The New Edinburgh Hockey Club would like a match with the Collegiate. We hope to oblige them in a few weeks.

A later *Vox* sporting editor reported: "The skating rink is progressing favorably as might be expected under the circumstances. We hope the pupils will turn out in full force to remove the snow. If the proper number of pupils got at it, we are confident that the rink could be clean in half an hour."

And further troubles: "There is some indignation at the procrastination of the fire brigade so frequently failing to fulfil their engagement to flood the rink. We would advise that the City fire brigade be no longer patronized by the Collegiate and that, whenever the school gets on fire, the job of putting it out be given to some other company."

A January 1889 *Vox* reported on the Snowshoe Club activities of the previous year: "Last winter the Snowshoe Club made two trips to Aylmer, where they had dinner and then drove home in the evening, all well satisfied with their trip. In these walks there was also an object. The 43rd Snowshoe Club [presumably associated with the military] went over the same ground and came home with the story they had done the distance of ten miles in two and a half hours, and that their record could not be beaten. The Collegiate boys went at it and beat it by some minutes, though their victory was disputed because they went by Skead's Mills while the 43rd went by Hull. We, however, think the Collegiate went over the longer distance."

The "Sporting Notes" editor in January 1889 had this to say about the Snowshoe Club again:

Thursday the 21st the first tramp of the Snowshoe Club. About twenty turned out, the club leaving the school at 4 o'clock with three of our football players leading, followed by a string of sports. They took a course along the canal bank 'til the head of the Deep Cut was reached, then branching off to the old head of the Rideau River they reached the rapids safe and sound, but with a broken shoe and scattered line. Following the Rideau for about a mile they then struck inland and having a very [blithe] leader they soon reached the Exhibition Grounds when all those feeling in condition entered for a half mile race. The race was won by "Jake" in the remarkable time of 7 minutes and 35 seconds with Tompkins second and Gibbens a good third. They then took South looking we suppose for a change in the climate which however they did not find, for, about a quarter to six a string of tramps about half a mile long and composed of twenty was seen heading for the O.C.I., some of them much the worse for trying to dispute the right-of-way with a barbed wire fence. However the school was reached and, after a song by the centre man and a chorus by the club, they broke up after enjoying the trek and with the best hopes of soon having another.

During the early 1870s a Cricket Club was promoted and captained by the Reverend T.D. Phillips, then mathematical master of the school. Mr. Phillips who later resided near Chicago, Illinois, was, from his youth up, an ardent lover of cricket; his name appears in the lists of the Upper Canada College teams from 1855 to 1858. For years he was one of the best-known Canadian players, and his cricket career extended over half a century. The old boys speak enthusiastically of the infinite trouble Mr. Phillips took in teaching the game and in instilling manly principles in the players. Matches were played between the club and various public and private schools, Cartier Square and the Rideau Hall grounds being alternately the scene of combat.

H.M. Ami, a member of the Committee for *History of Ottawa Collegiate Institute, 1843-1903* in his reminiscences as a former pupil of Lisgar wrote of some of the school's outstanding athletes in the 19th century:

Amongst the boys who were foremost in all out-of-door sports and games at the old Grammar School Tom Evans was a leader. Whenever snowball contests took place alongside and around the old building on Union Square behind the Russell House, from 1871-1874, it was always a pretty sure thing that Tom was at the head of one side—the winning side. In all other ball contests he was also foremost. Whether in attacking or defending a strong-hold—on the top of one of the Russell House sheds for example—he proved a general of repute.

The "old boys" had no playground of their own, and it was with the good will and permission of the dear old Chief of Police Langrell that we were permitted to play on Union Square right in front of the City Hall, then a modest wooden structure. But this was the spot where "Tom" fought his first battles, where he led victorious hosts against a real foe. The same ardour, vigour, determination, and pluck, which he displayed in the games and sports at the old school he displayed on the field of battle in the great North-West and in South Africa.

There are few of the "old boys" of whom we can be as proud as we are of Tom Evans. He is a soldier every inch of him. The military genius born in him pushed him forward and onward into difficult and responsible positions. He was always equal to any emergency, and with the bright career already won for himself, we look forward to even brighter deeds, whether in war or peace, in the defence and protection of our homes and the Empire.

Booth, C. Jackson, is a lumber merchant. Not a few of those who attended in the days of the old Grammar School of the Ottawa Collegiate Institute have gone into business and been successful. A large proportion of them have left the city for other parts of the Dominion, while others have crossed the international boundary line and are now successful merchants there. Booth has remained in Ottawa as a right-hand man to his father. When at school he was a leader of the athletics of the day. To him must be given the credit for introducing the Rugby game of foot-ball into the school [in] 1877. Previous to that time the foot-ball games were governed by no rules whatever, but the good old general adage: "Every man for himself and everything's fair" being applied without murmur or complaint. [With Booth] as captain and full-back of the Collegiate Institute "fifteen" in 1877 a match was played with the "Independents," which team was practically the Ottawas [Ottawa Capitals] and the O.C.I. boys won.

For many years after that, Jackson Booth was foremost in Ottawa foot-ball circles and figured prominently as full-back in the matches played in Ottawa, Montreal, Kingston, Toronto and Hamilton. From the O.C.I. Booth went to Queen's University, Kingston; he informs the writer of this sketch with what joy Principal Macmillan witnessed the defeat of the Independents or the Second Ottawa and the success of the Ottawa Collegiate Institute boys.

Former pupil A.H. McDougall in *History of the Ottawa Collegiate Institute, 1843-1903* provides a comprehensive record of Lisgar athletics 1889-1903:

A motley ghostly crew described as an early O.C.I. baseball team with admirers. On the back are written the names White, Lamplough, McDougall, St. Germain, T. Rooney, R. Slemon. Not dated.

In April 1889 a cricket club was formed, and shortly afterwards a baseball club. The interest in baseball evidently overshadowed that in cricket, for as many as five teams were at one time in existence among the students. G. MacCarthy and F. Code as captain and secretary-treasurer, respectively, assisted by W. Cummings, C. Taylor, and G. Murphy, managed the affairs of the baseball clubs in 1890. The team was defeated by the Normal School by a score of 12 to 2.

In March 1887 the existing clubs were united into an Athletic Association, with the following as its first officers: Hon. President, Mr. Macmillan; President, Mr. D.E. Smith; Vice-President, N.C. Sparks; Executive Committee, F.A. Magee, W. Hardie, R. Dowd, P.C. Ryan, S. Lawless; Treasurer, J. McNichol; Secretary, A. Spence; Assistant Secretary, W. Smallwood.

This general association, under different officers, continued in existence for two or three years when it was allowed to lapse. A period of separate clubs followed until, in 1899, the Athletic Association was reorganized. Since that time it has been in continuous existence. Principal Macmillan has been yearly elected honorary president, while the president and three vice-presidents have been chosen from the teaching staff. Mr. I.T. Norris, B.A., fills the position of president for the present year, 1903-04.

During the seventies and eighties sprinting, long-distance running, and other track sports were in vogue in all sporting circles. In more recent years general attention has been transferred to team games, such as foot-ball, and hockey, and interest in the former class has greatly declined. School athletics have naturally reflected the general tendencies of the times. This change in interest and the lack of suitable grounds have largely been the cause of the abandonment of the school sports that were held annually for many years.

The place and time of these meetings were the Metropolitan Athletic grounds and generally some day in June. Many curious and interesting reminiscences connected with the management of these affairs and with the contests that there took place might be given.

Mr. J.E. Wallace, the junior mathematical master, was nearly always called on to act as starter. Mr. Wallace besides being an excellent teacher and one of the best of disciplinarians was immensely popular with the pupils. When, in his smart, crisp way he had said: "Ready! Set!" and had snapped the pistol, everyone knew that the race was fairly and finally started.

Among those who acted as judges at different times were Messrs. P.D. Ross, T.C. Boville, A.P. Sherwood, A. May, Dr. Hutchison, Dr. Cousens, and various masters of the school.

The list of winners at the meeting of 15th June 1888, preserved by Mr. H.S. Macmillan, contains the names of a number of well known citizens of Ottawa.

Standing long jump—1, T. Birkett, 2, J. Taylor. Hurdle race—1, T. Birkett, 2, A. MacFarlane. Running long jump (under 16)—1, W. Kavanagh, 2. A. Anderson. Half mile race—1, N. Taylor, 2, W. Smith. Putting heavy weight—1, C. Chitty, 2, A. McFarlane. 220 yards race—1, C. Sparks, 2, C. Taylor. 120 yards race (under 14)—1, O.E. Culbert, 2, S. McDougall. 220 yards race (under 16)—1, W. Kavanagh, 2, H. Cole. 100 yard race—1, C. Sparks, 2, C. Moffatt. Running hop, step and jump—1, C. Chitty, 2, J. Taylor. 100 yards race (under 15)—1, L. Blackburn, 2, G. Robillard. Mile race—1, W. Smith, 2, C.T. Moffatt. Ex-pupils race—1, A. Macmillan.

This quarter mile championship race was decided to be no race as both of the leaders, C. Pratt and C. Chitty, fell, and were helped across the line.

The name of Evans Jackson is found entered for almost every event, as it continued to be for several years. Poor Jackson faithfully contested each race and never won a prize; he entered as a matter of course, or perhaps, of duty, and appeared to be just as happy as the winner when he finished a quarter behind in a mile race. The generous applause that greeted his performances was not all given in a spirit of derision as he had not an enemy in the school. His class-work and his poetic flights were entered into and carried out in the same spirit that controlled his sports. He died of consumption soon after he left the school.

One of the last meetings was held in November 1895. Notwithstanding the lateness of the date the meeting was a success. The championship on this occasion, decided by points, went to O.K. Gibson, the quarter mile race to Robert Kenny, the half mile to G. McKinnon, and the bicycles race to C. Henry.

Lawn tennis, in which the young ladies took the most prominent part, was an interesting feature of the games. Miss Florence Waddell won the championship for two years in succession. Miss Maud Whiteaves won the championship medal in 1891, and has since won many tennis prizes in both singles and doubles. She is now secretary of the ladies' club in connection with the O.L.T. Club. Among others who won the championship or other prizes were Miss. W. Masson (Mrs. Ide), Miss Stackhouse (Mrs. Grant), Miss Elizabeth Cluff, Miss Macfarlane (Mrs. Fairbairn), and Miss Muriel Church.

Among the old boys who have played, or will play the games with the O.L.T. Club are H.S. Macmillan, J.H. Larmonth, Norman Larmonth, David Finnie, J. Lorne McDougall, Jr., S. McDougall, T.S. McMorran, and F.A. Magee.

Mr. R.T. Shillington has supplied the following "reminiscences of sports at the O.C.I. twenty years ago":

At the time base-ball, and sprinting were the principal sports indulged in and the O.C.I. pupils were proficient in all branches. Their foot-ball team was really an excellent one,

composed of students who afterwards played with different university teams. Grant and Garrett, both of whom are in the ministry, Dr. T. Baskin, Dr. J.W. Shillington, both practising their professions in Ottawa, Dr. W. Graham, now one of the largest coffee growers in Central America, James McLaren, John McLean and Duncan McLean were among the most prominent. The base-ball team was one of the best amateur teams in this section at that time and rarely lost a game. The battery was composed of James McLaren, pitcher, and A. Code, catcher. McLaren is now one of our most successful financial men. [Timber baron] Code will be remembered as the man who first brought the Winnipeg, Victoria hockey team east to play for the Stanley Cup.

Mr. Shillington continues with a description of one of the most memorable foot races in which O.C.I. ever competed:

One of the most sensational foot-races ever run in this district was a mile race for the championship of the O.C.I. between Charles Lewis, now of the Merchants Bank, and Charles Bayne, who was some years later, when a medical student in his final year at McGill, accidentally poisoned. The first race ended in a dead heat and in the run-off, two weeks later, Bayne won by a magnificent burst of speed when just a few yards from the tape. The excitement was unbounded. The race was held on the exhibition grounds, and needless to say, studies were suspended, and all the students were there, together with thousands of citizens, including John Raine, Peter Duffy, and James Nutting, who were then the foremost sprinters in Canada. All declared that it was the best contest they had ever seen.

[McDougall continues:]

Dr. W. Carden Cousens won many prizes in 100, 120, and 440 yard races, both flat and hurdle. He was first in the handicap 100 yards at the Montreal A.A.A. [Amateur Athletic Association] sports in 1878, when the competitors included what were then considered some of the fastest men in America. His facility in getting over the maximum of ground in the minimum of time, aided by nerve and skill in stick handling gave him a place on the senior lacrosse teams of three cities in succession, Montreal, Toronto, and Ottawa. Any damage that the doctor, that was to be, then did to the noses or shins of his opponents has since been amply repaid to the human race.

The two brothers who now constitute the firm of Pratt and Pratt, barristers, etc., were both noted for fleetness of foot. Horace Pratt won five prizes, in his first year, at the Toronto University games. He won the 100 yard race in his first, third and fourth years. In his second year he came second in the classical 100 yards dash between Horace and Virgil [Horace Pratt and Virgil Lee]. After his return to Ottawa, he won many races including the 100 yards at the O.A.A.C. games and played on the team of the Metropolitan Lacrosse Club. Charles B. Pratt held the championship of the Collegiate Institute for two years. He was very fast for

Lisgar's tug-of-war team, 1890. Tug-of-war contests not only took place between schools but were popular events at every fair, Sunday school picnic and track and field meet. Unfortunately no names were recorded for these stalwarts.

100 yards and for the quarter mile and won many races at these distances, including the quarter at the O.A.A.C. sports in 1897.

Dr. Frank Hurdman was champion fast walker of McGill University in 1881 and 1882.

There does not appear to be any record of when or by whom the first rugby football club was organized in the institute. While the interest in races declined, that in rugby increased, and for years the latter has held, and continues to hold, the most important place in the calendar of sports.

An imperfect account of the teams and games of the different years, and the subsequent records of some of the players, is given below:

1888 TEAM:

J. McDougall, C. Chitty, C. Taylor, H.H. Horsey (Captain), E.H.F. Cross, W. Burns, T. McVeity, H. Hurdman, J.T. Blyth, F. Farries, J.G. Gibson, J. Robertson, E. Moffatt, Z. Lewis, G.

Parsons, W. Scott, W. Kavanagh, G. McCarthy, R. Bradley, A.J. Muckleston, and J.H. Larmonth.

Four matches were played, two with the second team of Ottawa College and home matches with the team of Kingston Collegiate Institute, all of which were lost. Of this team H.H. Horsey was afterwards for several years one of the stalwarts of the team of Queen's University that had so great a reputation as winners of championships; C. Taylor played on the Toronto team, and C. Chitty played lacrosse in Montreal and was president of the Montreal Hockey Club, when they were the holders of the Stanley Cup.

1889 TEAM:

F. Taylor, J. McDougall, C. Taylor, W. Kavanagh, J.G. Gibson, H.H. Horsey, G. Ridout, J.T. Blyth, H.S. Macmillan, and D. Cambie.

1890 TEAM:

F. Pratt, O.E. Culbert, H. Taylor, J.G. Gibson, H. Ketchum, W.A. Scott, G. Smith, L. May, R. Bradley (Captain),

A studio photograph of Lisgar's 1890 football team.

Members were Ford Pratt, O.E. Culbert, H. Taylor, J.G. Gibson, H. Ketchum, W.A. Scott, G. Smith, L. May, R. Bradley (Captain), W.R. Cummings, W.G. Black, S. McDougall, D. Cambie, W.R. Pallister, W.J. Macdonald. Ford Pratt became one of the outstanding hockey players of his time. R. Bradley performed outstandingly in both sports as well, playing on Toronto University and Osgoode Hall teams while he studied Law. H. Ketchum went on to be one of the star players of the Capital Lacrosse Club. S. McDougall played on the Ottawa Hockey team and W.R. Cummings on the basketball team of the Ottawa Athletic Association Club.

W.R. Cummings, W.G. Black, S. McDougall, D. Cambie, W.R. Pallister, W.J. Macdonald.

This team won from the second team of Ottawa City but was defeated by the second team of Ottawa College. R. Bradley, B.B., of the well known firm of barristers, made a noteworthy record for himself in both foot-ball and hockey. In both games he played on the teams of Toronto University, of Osgoode Hall and of Ottawa City. He also won prizes at the university for throwing heavy weights. Always a steady reliable player, at the critical moment of a game he often appeared to be possessed by an almost berserk-like rage as he rushed the ball, or the puck, on the opponent's goal. H. Ketchum was for years one of the star players of the Capital Lacrosse Club; O.E. Culbert played on the hockey team of Toronto University and afterwards on that of Osgoode Hall; S. McDougall played on the Ottawa Hockey Team, and W.R. Cummings on the basket-ball team of the O.A.A.C.

1894 TEAM:

S. Ross, R.M. Kenny, C. Henry, W.S. Curran, R. Turley, A.N.P. Morgan, A. Bailey, E.A. Taggart, F.W. Fee, A. Perkins, O. Bradley, L. May, R.W. Kenny, A. Cameron, and W. Hillman; Secretary-Treasurer, S.N. Chipman, later F.W. Fee.

A game with the second team of Ottawa College was lost by a score of 12 to 0.

1895 TEAM:

R.W. Kenny was Captain and R. Turley Secretary-Treasurer.

The O.C.I. team defeated the second team of the Ottawas, by 26 to 0. R.W. Kenny afterwards became quarter-back and captain of the Rough Riders, then as later champions of Canada. His capacity for "bucking the line" was only equalled by the way he could take punishment and smile sweetly on his oppressor for the time being. He has since been captain of the McGill University team and coach and rugby nestor of that institution.

1896 TEAM:

C. Ronth, O.K. Gibson, R.M. Kenny, C. Baker, A. Perkins, H. Christie, O. Klotz, A.H. Armstrong, D. Lyons, P. Ogilvie, W. Clarke, C. Young, T. Switzer (Captain), R. Shillington, A.J. Isbester; Secretary-Treasurer, O.K. Gibson.

C Baker became quarter-back on the team of the Royal Military College at Kingston, and is now an officer in the British army. C.A. Young has played on the hockey team of McGill; Richard Shillington on the Rough Riders, and the rugby team of McGill; and A.J. Isbester on the scrimmage of Toronto University, and with Buckman, another old Collegiate student, made up two-thirds of the Rough Riders' scrimmage that did so much towards winning for them the championship of Canada in 1902. O.K. Gibson and Isbester have both been on the hockey team of Toronto University.

1897 TEAM:

C. Young, C. Henry, T. Rankin, E. Hawkins, J.G. Fleck, E.J. Carson, W. McGuirl, Richard Shillington, H. Church, A. Bailie, H. Ralph, G. Church (Captain), C.J. Chubbuck, A. Maxwell, J. Aylmer; Secretary-Treasurer, C.J. Chubbuck.

This team won from the second team of Ottawa by a score of 3 to 0 but lost to Montreal High School by 10 to 5. J. Gordon Fleck played as quarter-back on the team of Toronto University and was manager of the team of that institution during the season of 1902.

1899 TEAM:

S. McCormick, C. Young, H.S. Macmillan, F. Musgrove, H. Kennedy, W. Chipman, A.H. Taylor, G.Pushman, A. Graham, C.E. Hibbard, J. McCormick (Captain), W.H. Dowler, F. Hammon, O. Stitt, G. Hare, G. Reiffenstein, A.A. Fraser; Secretary-treasurer, C.J. Keyes.

In this year, home and home matches were played with Renfrew High School, O.C.I. winning both, the first in Renfrew by a score of 9 to 5, the second in Ottawa 9 to 4. O.C.I. lost to Ottawa II (Seconds) by 16 to 1 but won two very hard matches from Montreal High School, in Montreal by 2 to 1 and in Ottawa by 4 to 3.

The Collegiate boys were invited to practise with the senior Rough Riders, during a part of this season on account of their second team not turning out. The following clippings

Lisgar football team, 1896; C. Ronth, O.K. Gibson, R.M. Kenny, C. Baker, A. Perkins, H. Christie, O. Klotz, A.H. Armstrong, D. Lyons, P. Ogilvie, W. Clarke, C. Young, T. Switzer (Captain), R. Shillington, A.J. Isbester; Secretary-Treasurer, O.K. Gibson. Baker became quarterback of the RMC team Kingston and went into the British army. Young and Shillington went to McGill and played on the hockey and rugby teams there. Shillington advanced to play for the Ottawa Rough Riders and Isbester, along with ex-Lisgarite Buckham was with the Rough Riders for the championship of Canada in 1902.

show how the boys faced this very unequal contest:"Those Collegiate youths would tackle a Wendigo."—*Ottawa Citizen.*

"It was surprising how those Rough Riders picked up after we started to practise with them."— *Vox Lycei.*

"Hammond says that Lamothe is the hardest man he was ever on."— *Vox Lycei.*

1901 Team:

J. Roberts (Captain), S. Fawcett, R. Léger, H. Smith, J. McCuaig, E. Brennan, A.H. Taylor, F. Hammond, D. Lyon, C. Cox, C. Ross, A. Mason, J.H. Stothers, J. Stephens, G. Chamberlain; Secretary-Treasurer, A.H. Taylor.

The senior team played a draw game with Renfrew High School, 10 to 10 and afterwards won from the same team in Ottawa by 11 to 4. They defeated the Tigers 2 to 1. The second team of the O.C.I. travelled to Brockville and played a draw with the St. Alban's School 4 to 4. They defeated the same team in Ottawa 15 to 0 and did likewise to a New Edinburgh team 8 to 0.

1903 Team:

P. Harris, C.G. Cox (Captain), A.H. Dion, C. Capreol, E. O'Brian, N. Kendall, A. Dick, O. Gallager, H.W. Dunnett, W.D. Herridge, E. McMahon, J. Knox, N. Reiffenstein, H.B. Northwood, J. Sifton, S. Dawson; Secretary-Treasurer, C.M. Ross.

This team was defeated on Thanksgiving Day by the Rideaus of Ottawa by 19 to 12, but won from Almonte, on October 31 by 12 to 0, and from the Sandy Hills of Ottawa on November 9th by 11 to 0.

Among the O.C.I. boys who have played on the Ottawa football team at different times are:—Dr. Basken, Dr. W. Carden Cousens, James Smellie, A.F. May, W. Schwitzer, George Bowie, H. Chesley, Fred Booth, Jackson Booth, E. Fellowes, Dr. H.M. Ami, H. Percival, W. Makison, H. Torrance, W. Torrance, D. McLean, Salter Richards, E. Taylor, L. Taylor, A. Ridout, Hamlet Allan, G. Bayne, H.H. Hurdman, John Roberts, T. Rankin, R.T. Shillington, Dr. J.W. Shillington, H.S. Macmillan, John McJanet, Arthur Pope, W.W. McKay, Col. T.D.B. Evans, A.M. Macmillan, J.E. Taggart, H. Buckman, G. Parr, John McLaren, Charles Armstrong, S. McDougall.

Lisgar football team, 1899. Members were; S. McCormick, C. Young, H.S. Macmillan, F. Musgrove, H. Kennedy, W. Chipman, A.H. Taylor, G. Hushman, A. Graham, C.E. Hibbard, J. McCormick (Captain), W.H. Dowler, F. Hammond, O. Stitt, G. Hare, G. Reiffenstein, A.A. Fraser; Secretary-Treasurer, C.J. Keyes.

In the hand-written *Vox Lycei*, January-March, 1889 the Sports Reporter in his Sporting Notes proclaims a new rule of scrimmage which he says will give "a light team an equal chance with a heavy one, and makes the game in all points more scientific."

The list of old boys, with their exploits on the field, known to local enthusiasts, gives good ground for the statement in the sporting notes of the Citizen of October 14th, 1900, that "the O.C.I. Foot-ball Club has been the feeder of the Ottawa seniors ever since foot-ball was first played in the city."

[McDougall continues:]

The next in interest to foot-ball in recent years comes hockey. Arrangements are generally made with one of the rinks in the city for certain hours during the week, although rinks have been constructed a couple of times in the school grounds. In the latter case they afforded more exercise in shovelling snow than in skating or playing hockey. Many of the boys are always members of outside clubs, and a comparatively small number can take advantage of the Collegiate organization; consequently hockey has not been a school sport to the same extent as has foot-ball.

In 1892, a team consisting of R. Bradley, O. Bradley, Macdonald, McDougall, Morgan, Scott and Whitton was twice defeated by Ottawa College, by 2 to 1 in the first game and by 4 to 1 in the second. In January 1895 the third form twice defeated the rest of the school, by 5 to 0 and by 10 to 0 respectively. The teams were:—Third Form, R.M. Kenny, O. Bradley, A.F. Chamberlain, O.K. Gibson, R.W. Kenny, A.J. Isbester and S. Ross. School:—McDougall, H. Ells, Henry, Holland, McKinnon, Schwitzer and Alexander.

In February, an O.C.I. team consisting of Alexander, R.W. Kenny, R.M. Kenny, Bradley, A. McDougall, Isbester, and Ross, played two games with the Thistles, losing the first by 3 to 1 and winning the second by 4 to 2. The Thistle team consisted of Hutton, Benson, Chamberlain, Gibson, Ells, Kavanagh and Henry. Again in March of the same year Alexander, R.W. Kenny, Holland, Bradley, Isbester, McDougall and R.M. Kenny defeated a team for the Governor General's Foot Guards by 8 to 2.

Between 1897 and 1901 Lisgar hockey teams played against Abingdon High School and Montreal High School in Montreal; C. Ross Co., Ottawa Legalites, Ottawa Bankers, Bryson-Graham & Co., all of Ottawa.

The match with the Bryson-Graham & Co. team in 1898 attracted great attention at the time. The Ottawa *Evening Journal* had offered a trophy to be given to the most popular hockey team in the Ottawa Valley, the winner to be chosen by readers of that paper. The contest had narrowed down to the O.C.I. and the B.G. & Co. teams, the latter at that time champions of the city league, when someone wrote to the paper asking about the record of the O.C.I. team and whether they could play hockey or not. The answer was an immediate challenge and a score of 10 to 0 in favor of the O.C.I. in the subsequent match.

The team of 1899 consisted of A. Graham, T.S. McMorran, C. Young, J. McCormick, A.A. Fraser, C. Scott, G. Reiffenstein and A. Proctor; that of 1900 of A.A. Fraser (Captain), A. Graham, G. Reiffenstein, C. Young, J. Roberts, F. Young, T. Sutherland, A. Mason, J. McCormick and S. McCormick.

A.A. Fraser afterwards played in the senior Ottawa team.

An O.C.I. team under the leadership of Mr. H.S. Macmillan has taken part in each of the basket-ball tournaments held by the O.A.A.C. [Ottawa Amateur Athletic Club]. Besides Mr. Macmillan, some of the players of note were V.O. Woodland, W. Johnson, W. McGuirl and H. Latimer.

Various ex-pupils of the Collegiate were prominent on the other teams, as W. Cummings, T. Rankin, F. Musgrove, and W.H. Lamb.

The team of 1903 consisting of H.S. Macmillan (Captain), S. Fawcett, O. Workman, J.W. Smith, J. Stephens, began their series in the city league by defeating New Edinburgh 5 to 4, and St. Patrick 25 to 15. After a very close contest they lost to the YMCA champions of 1902, by 15 to 13.

HEAD-MASTERS AND TRUSTEES

THE DUTIES OF A PRINCIPAL

The Principalship of a large Collegiate Institute is not a sinecure. The youth of our city are more difficult to control and guide, from the ages of thirteen to twenty-one years of age, than they are at any other period of their lives. Parents, on all hands, admit this—some openly, some with shame, and others with pride. The home authority is harder to maintain; the ambitions and buoyant hopes of our boys and girls are beyond immediate realization; they must be directed and controlled wisely, and to the Head-Master falls more than his fair share of this responsibility.

The duties of a Head-Master are very responsible, and many-sided. He has the discipline and organization of the whole school, the drawing up and adjusting of time-tables, the determining of the work of his several masters, and the meeting of the varied wants of students and parents. He is, in a sense a general manager and needs great executive power, in order to satisfy on the one hand the demands of the Education Department, and on the other the public. There is not only the student, but often the parents to deal with, and even at times to discipline. There is too, his relation to the many members of his staff and to each department. The law stands always as a Shylock demanding its pound of flesh, the Board pressing for care and efficiency, and an interested public ready at all times to give advice. There is worry in discipline, in time-tables, in problems of the school-task, in the failure of the students to reach the ideal. School-life is full of worry, and the Head-Master has the biggest share.

— Robert Stothers,
History of O.C.I. 1843-1903

The second Head-Master of the Ottawa Grammar School was the Reverend John Robb, M.A., who had been a clergyman in Scotland. During his five years tenure at the school he always wore his clerical garb. In a cupboard he kept the bell, the cane and the linen duster he wore to protect his gown during school hours. When his boys wanted a half-holiday to see the St. Patrick's Day parade, he refused permission. In retaliation pepper was sprinkled all over the wood-stove. The coughing and sneezing began throughout the school but Mr. Robb kept everyone in until four and flogged several students. A further incident led to Robb's "retirement." He was hearing Charles McKay's Latin lesson and when he struck McKay in anger, McKay kicked back. A real struggle ensued. A Board meeting was held immediately and within a few days Robb was gone.

O. Timothy Millar, M.A. was the fourth Head-Master of the Ottawa Grammar School from 1856-58. A ruddy-complexioned red-haired native of Ireland, Millar was "a scholarly man and a graduate of Trinity College, Dublin." During his regime and a part of that of principal Ross', the Grammar Schools were gradually placed under the direct control of the Education Department of the province.

Top Left: Another Scot, William Aird Ross, later Judge Ross, became third Head-Master. He taught in Glengarry before coming to the Grammar School in 1850. In 1856 he resigned to enter the study of law. During his term at Dalhousie as principal and teacher he achieved his B.A. from Queen's University. His colleagues described him as "always a student" and a man of "strong and decided character." He was a law partner with Hon. R.W. Scott, K.C., then Secretary of State for Canada and became judge of the County Court of Carleton and the City of Ottawa in 1874.

Bottom Left: Fifth Head-Master Reverend H.J. Borthwick, M.A., was born and raised in Scotland. At Edinburgh University he took extensive courses in Latin, Greek, Moral Philosophy, Mathematics and Hebrew. After his arrival in Canada in 1845 he took a Theological course at Queen's. He then became Master of English and French at Longueuil, Quebec, private tutor for the family of D. Thompson, M.P. of Haldimand, Ontario; assistant principal in Hamilton; first principal at

Newmarket; Head-Master of Queen's College Preparatory School, Kingston; Head-Master of Frontenac Academy, Kingston. In 1859 he was appointed principal of the Senior Grammar School of the County of Carleton at a salary of one thousand dollars per annum. He remained until 1862 when he moved to Manitoba where he became pioneer missionary, teacher and Inspector of Public Schools. During his regime the Brough gold medals were introduced. For a brief time, under the aegis of former student and later teacher Master George Kennedy, the Meteorological Observatory was connected with the school. In 1890 the Dominion Government transferred it to the Marine Department and placed the instruments at the Experimental Farm.

Top Left: Sixth Head-Master Dr. John Thorburn, like so many of his predecessors, was born and educated in Scotland. Prior to taking his appointment in Ottawa in 1862, he taught at Yarmouth, Nova Scotia and St. Francis College, Richmond, Lower Canada. During Thorburn's tenure of almost two decades, the school made steady strides, the staff increasing from a two-master to a five-master school and establishing its reputation for academic excellence. In classics and mathematics his students always stood high and it was under his regime that two out of the five scholarships offered for competition in Canada were won by S.W. Hunton and Fred W. Jarvis in 1877, thus pushing the Collegiate to the forefront of Canadian secondary schools.

Bottom Left: The seventh Head-Master of the Ottawa Collegiate Institute was John Macmillan, B.A. Born in Scotland Macmillan took some teacher-training there before he moved with his parents to Chatham, Ontario. It is reported that Macmillan chose his career in early manhood and decided on Toronto Normal School as the best possible place to equip himself for his life-work. When he graduated with a First-class certificate he was one of the three teachers chosen to go to Ottawa to introduce the new Normal School methods. But Macmillan had long coveted a university education and, while teaching in the Ottawa Public Schools, prepared himself for entrance to the University of Toronto. He graduated in 1864 with the silver medal in Metaphysics and Ethics, and the Prince of Wales Prize. The following September he became assistant master in the Ottawa Grammar School and principal in 1881 when Dr. Thorburn resigned. He completed forty years of continuous service in the Ottawa Collegiate Institute.

Reverend Dr. S.S. Strong, first chairman of the Board of the Ottawa Grammar School came to Canada in the 1830s, highly recommended to Sir John Colborne who at that time administered the Government of Upper Canada. For a time Strong was acting chaplain to the forces stationed in Quebec. He then served as Assistant Minister in St. George's Church, Kingston, and in 1837 was appointed to the newly built Christ Church, Bytown. The first Board meeting was held in his study.

TRUSTEES 1843-1903

The provisions of the law in the early part of the last century were very indefinite respecting High Schools or Grammar Schools, as they were then called. By the Act of 1807 the Grammar Schools (more properly District Grammar Schools) were managed by Boards of Trustees appointed by the Lieutenant-Governor in Council. It was provided that the number of such trustees should not be less than five. Usually the Boards were made up of local clergymen, and other persons who might be interested in secondary education, and who were recommended by the patrons of the Institutions concerned. This mode of appointing trustees continued with very little change until 1853 when the Grammar Schools were first brought under the direct control of the Education Department. In 1853 it

was enacted that the several Grammar School trustees of each county should meet and select from amongst themselves three trustees (one to retire annually) for each of the Grammar Schools. It was further provided that three other trustees for each school should be appointed by the County Council. All subsequent appointments were to be made by the same body.

Dr. Ryerson, Chief Superintendent of Education, became responsible for our Secondary Schools about 1853, and from that time he made an effort to improve the Classical or Grammar School, which occupied the field. He could not, however, modify them so as to remove the prejudices of our people against them, and he could not for the time, abolish them, since they met, as they existed, the wants of the more wealthy of our citizens who were wedded to the classics. These citizens appreciated culture; they had the time and the wealth, which made it possible. They were generally members of our Legislature and could readily legislate on education so as to meet their own ends.

Ryerson endeavoured to modify these schools and re-organize them much in the way he had been able to do, and do successfully, the public schools. He introduced the study of new subjects, and he changed the condition on which the Government grants were divided so as to place the study of Latin on the same basis as that of mathematics. Hitherto, Latin was the only subject that counted in the distribution of the grant. The effect of this change was immediately felt and it had its place in the development of our modern Secondary School. From that day to the present there has gone on a constant struggle between the subjects that might be classed as "Culture" subjects and those that are of practical value.

These changes led gradually to a keener appreciation of the Grammar School it is true, but still among the masses of our people indifference remained. The period from 1853 to 1871 was largely barren of results, commensurate with the expense and the efforts put forth. The majority of our legislators were indifferent too, and few changes were made in the Act other than those necessary to facilitate local control. As a whole, however, they seemed to have been lifeless schools.

Professor George Paxton Young, a prominent educationist, was appointed Inspector of these schools in the sixties. He prepared in 1866 what has proven to be, and what may not inappropriately be termed, "The Lord Durham Report on Secondary Education in Upper Canada." The old oracle has said, "All things have two handles; beware of the wrong one." Professor Young had the instinct to seize the right one, and through his efforts a complete revolution in Secondary Schools followed five years later. Since 1871 therefore, we have had a system, perhaps imperfect, yet on the whole creditable.

The winners of the Gilchrist Scholarship, 1877 (left) S.W. Hunton, B.A., (London) and Fred W. Jarvis. Hunton went on to McGill and the University of London and became Professor of Mathematics, Sackville University. Jarvis chose Edinburgh University but his career was cut short by an early tragic death in 1881. During Thorburn and Macmillan's terms in the 1870s to 1890s Ottawa Collegiate Institute was endowed with many prizes and scholarships; the Brough gold medals, the Edward McGillivray prizes, the J.P. Featherstone gold medals, the Governor-General's medals, the Allan Gilmour gold and silver medals, the Senator Clemow medals, the Denis Murphy Medals. Many other outstanding citizens donated medals, prizes and money to O.C.I. including Sheriff Sweetland, McLeod Stewart, George Hay, Robert Blackburn, Charles Magee, J. Lorn McDougall, A.M. Burgess, J.S. Durie, R.L. Blackburn, James Hope, C.T. Bate and T.C. Bate.

The Act of 1871 removed many of the defects of the old Grammar Schools and introduced the new names of High School and Collegiate Institute. Shortly after this, seven of the older and larger Grammar Schools were raised to the status of Collegiate Institutes. These were Cobourg, Galt, Hamilton, Kingston, Ottawa, Peterborough, St. Catharines. According to Dr. Ryerson's Report in 1872 the objects and duties of the High Schools were two-fold: "commencing with pupils who have completed the work for the first four classes in the Public Schools, or that equivalent, the High Schools were intended to complete a good English education by educating pupils not only for commercial, manufacturing and agricultural pursuits, but for fulfilling with efficiency, honor and usefulness, the duties of municipal councillors, legislators, and various public offices in the service of the country; also to teach the languages of Greece and Rome, of Germany and France, the mathematics, etc., so far as to prepare the youth for certain professions, and especially for the Universities, where will be completed the education of men for the learned professions and for Professorships in the Colleges, and Masterships in the Collegiate Institutes and High Schools."

— *History of Ottawa Collegiate Institute, 1843-1903*

When Lisgar was damaged by fire in 1873 a former principal of Lisgar enlisted the aid of an ex-Lisgarite to restore records of early Honour Rolls and Scholarships. This is one of the earliest lists of medals awarded in the Sixties provided by J.S. Brough from a remarkable memory no doubt flexed and well-used from the memorization of long passages of literature—particularly Shakespeare—for his English teachers.

On April 22, 1904, the writer received a letter from Dr. John Thorburn, of the Geological Survey of Canada, formerly principal of the Collegiate Institute, asking the writer's services as an old student, to assist in obtaining a list of the gold medals awarded to the Dux of the highest form up to the time when in 1875, Lord Dufferin and others donated medals. The motive was to complete records partially destroyed in a fire which happened several years previously.

Happily the writer at the time was in correspondence with the Rev. H.J. Borthwick, M.A., principal of the Institute, while the former was a student, during an interval of some two years of absence from the family home in Edinburgh, Scotland. The appended list of awarded gold medals mainly made up from the diaries of Rev. Mr. Borthwick, the fifth principal, replaced the portion of the Institute's roll of honor injured in the fire. The fire which destroyed the Collegiate building happened on January 30, 1893, but some time before the mishap the writer, while passing through the main hall, read the roll of honor set up there, and can vouch for the correctness of the appended list which gives the year, name and donor respectively: 1861—A.J. Christie, Jas. Brough; 1861—R.S. Hudson, A. Friend; 1861—E.D. Cox, Jas. Brough; 1862—H.P. Hill, Jas. Brough; 1863—McL. Stewart, Jas. Brough; 1864—C. Jones, Jas. Brough; 1865—H. Allan, Jas. Brough; 1866—W.G. Brown, J. Thorburn; 1867—D. Robertson, Jas Brough; 1868—J.I. MacCracken, The Trustees; 1870—J. Hodgins, The Trustees; 1872—A.J. Bell; The Trustees; 1874—G.M. Greene, The Trustees; 1875—S.W. Hunton; Lord Dufferin.

A PRINCIPAL'S RETROSPECT

At the end of Lisgar's first fifty years of establishing traditions, precedents and standards of excellence in Ottawa, Principal John Macmillan was well qualified to make a summation of Lisgar's past. Already teachers' salaries were emerging as a major concern and he accurately foresaw the growth of science in the curriculum of schools and everyday life in the twentieth century.

This retrospective, written in 1899, is excerpted from *History of the Ottawa Collegiate Institute, 1843-1903.*

One very striking method of showing the progress of the school during the sixty years of its existence is to give a series of contrasts in regard to the building, the personnel of the teaching staff, the salaries paid to the teachers, the equipment, the library, and the number of students. Perhaps a fairer and more adequate estimate of the progress made can in this way be obtained, than by almost any other method that might be adopted.

The present large and handsome structure owned by the Board and valued at ninety thousand dollars, contains seventeen class-rooms, two spare rooms for study, the Principal's private room, a room for the Masters, and another for the library—in all, twenty-two rooms, excluding of the waiting rooms downstairs for the accommodation of the students. The extension to the main building erected in 1901 contains eight class-rooms and cost thirty thousand dollars.

In 1864 the teaching staff consisted of two members, the Principal taking all the work in the senior classes, and the assistant all the subjects in the junior classes. There could in these circumstances be no adequate specialization, as this can be secured only when the staff is larger and when a more advantageous distribution of subjects among the members of the staff becomes possible. This distribution of subjects is amply provided for in the present staff of fifteen, among whom, exclusive of the Principal, is a specialist in Classics, one in Mathematics, one in English, one in Science, one in Modern Languages, and one in the Commercial Department. In addition to these, four other members of the staff have specialist qualifications, one in Mathematics, two in Modern Languages and one in Science.

One of the crying evils connected with the subject of education has always been the utter inadequacy of the remuneration received by the teachers from whom so much is imperatively demanded. Public opinion has not yet reached the point of insisting that Boards of Trustees shall pay salaries in some degree commensurate with the qualifications and training demanded from the teacher, the difficulty and responsibility involved in teaching, and the national importance of the results of that teaching. The Trustees of the Institute, believing that in the last analysis the teacher makes the school, have always stood for efficient teaching and have striven to attract and retain the services of the best available men by offering reasonably adequate salaries. During the early years of the school's life very inadequate salaries were no doubt paid and even the early Principals gave their best and highest to the welfare of the school for a salary which would neither be offered to nor accepted by many assistant teachers. But the salaries were not only small, they were also irregularly paid, while at present the one-tenth of the annual salary is invariably paid at the end of each of the ten teaching months of the year. Teachers can therefore meet monthly their financial obligations. The total sum paid in 1903 was $18,205. The following schedule of salaries, furnished by the Secretary, is now in force. Male assistants other than specialists begin at $900, and have an annual increase of $50 until the maximum of $1400 is reached. The initial salary for specialists is $1200 and increases annually by $75 until the maximum of $1800 is reached. The Principal's salary is for the first year $1800 and increases by $100 a year until the maximum of $2600 is reached.

The time may soon come when secondary education shall be as free as that obtained in the Public Schools. Until that time arrives a very considerable revenue will be received annually from school fees. In 1903 the total sum received from this source amounted to $10,109.50.

Whatever changes may in the near or more remote future be introduced into the curriculum of studies for High Schools and Collegiate Institutes an increasingly large amount of attention will assuredly be devoted to science. Practically no provision was made in the early history of the school for the teaching of science as now demanded by the Department of Education. The present Principal began the teaching of chemistry in an ordinary class-room, with absolutely no apparatus, the only appliances available being a piece of chalk, a text book, and a blackboard. Now three large class-rooms, one for chemistry, one for physics, and one for biology are wholly devoted to science. Each room is amply furnished with all the appliances now deemed necessary for proper experimental work, so that all the benefits from the only true method of teaching science are enjoyed by the students who in larger numbers every year are taking courses in science. The value of the apparatus now at the disposal of the Science Master is $1,518.22.

That a reference library whose shelves are filled with standard books on each department of study is indispensable for master and pupil alike will now be universally admitted. Yet for a long period after the organization of the school no books other than those supplied by the masters themselves were available for the use of the pupils. This defect was partially remedied after the removal of the seat of Government to Ottawa, when the books in the parliamentary library could under certain conditions be consulted by masters and pupils. The only true and permanent remedy, however, is the school library. The Trustees have for some time voted an annual grant of $100 for the school library, the present worth of which is $1,260.40.

For some years a preparatory class was maintained to keep up the supply of those seeking to enter the Institute; but this class has long been abolished, for candidates in increasingly large numbers come up from the Public Schools for the annual Entrance Examinations. At first,

one class-room held all who attended from the Public Schools, now the supply is so large that four class-rooms are needed to hold all who are admitted after passing the Entrance Examination. The total number entered on the roll in 1903 was 610, of whom 349 were boys and 261 were girls.

* * * * *

In the early days of the Dalhousie Grammar School young ladies were not included in the regular classes. At most, they might aspire only to participation in a much-circumscribed special course. Few, indeed, offered themselves for even this limited instruction. However, in 1943 there still lived on Flora Street in Ottawa, Mrs. Susannah Rivington, one of the Collegiate's early prizewinners.

Mrs. Rivington loaned to the Centenary Committee a prize that she had won the year before Confederation, an anthology entitled *The Harp of Canaan*, being selections from the poets compiled by Reverend J. Douglas Borthwick and containing a poem written by Thomas D'Arcy McGee especially for the occasion. The flyleaf bears the inscription, perfectly preserved, and in excellent script:

> *Presented to*
> *Miss Susannah Kidd*
> *as best in Arithmetic at an examination*
> *held June 26th, 1866.*
> *H.S. Borthwick*
> *Principal,*
> *Ottawa Collegiate School*

Susannah Kidd married Thomas Rivington on the day that McGee, one of the illustrious Fathers of Confederation, was assassinated.

Mary Masson was the first girl graduate and lived long enough to be an active member of the Collegiate Centenary Committee. No only was she the first young lady to be graduated from Lisgar but she won the only two medals awarded for competition in her graduating class.

ILUSTRIOUS GRADUATES; 1843-1893

Honourable W.C. Edwards: is one of the most prominent and better-known Senators of Canada; he is also one of the most successful lumber merchants and manufacturers of our country, carrying on extensive operations in both the provinces of Ontario and Quebec. He is one of the "old boys" of the old Grammar School and has succeeded in climbing to one of the highest positions his country offers.

Born at Clarence, 1844, he was educated at the Ottawa Grammar School and, when quite young, entered the lumber business at Thurso, Quebec. In 1868 he started business and established the firm of W.C. Edwards & Co., whose sawmills at Rockland and New Edinburgh on the Ottawa River are now among the most extensive and prosperous in the whole Dominion. He is a director in many companies and takes a practical interest in agriculture and stock farming.

Ryan, Percy Carroll, B.C.L., 1892 (McGill)

Ryan, Percy C., Barrister, was born in Ottawa, 1871, educated at the Ottawa Collegiate Institute, where he was gold medallist in Classics and Mathematics, and silver medallist in Modern Languages; he continued his studies at McGill University, where he took the Jane Redpath scholarship in Arts, and graduated B.C.L., and Elizabeth Torrance gold medal 1892. Called to the bar the same year; he has since practised in Montreal. He was as appointed Eng. Sec. to the Commission for revising and amending the Code of Civil Procedure, 1892, and became lecturer on Roman Law and Civil Procedure in McGill University not long afterwards.

Honourable Erskine Henry Bronson: manufacturer and legislator, is the son of the late Henry Franklin Bronson. Born at Bolton, Warren, New York in 1844, he was educated at the Ottawa Grammar School and Sandy Hill, and, joining the Bronsons and Weston Lumber Company, succeeded to the presidency of the company on the death of his father in 1889. He was for some years on the Ottawa School Board, and was a member of the City Council, 1871-1877, being also chairman of the Finance Committee. He represented the City of Ottawa in the Ontario Legislature for a number of years, being first elected in 1886, and later became a member without portfolio in Sir Oliver Mowat's Cabinet.

William Brymner, R.C.A. Among those ex-pupils of the old Grammar School who have distinguished themselves in the field of art, William Brymner ranks high. He is the eldest son of the late Dominion Archivist, Douglas Brymner, F.R.S.C., LL.D. &c. William attended the classes of the old school on Union Square, and was a quiet though very diligent scholar. He studied art under the best masters in Paris, and has exhibited both at the Paris Salon and the Academy in London. For many years he has had charge of the Art classes of the Art Association of Montreal, the largest and most flourishing school of Art in the Dominion. In 1892 William Brymner was commissioned by the authorities of the Canadian Pacific Railway to paint four series of pictures illustrating the magnificent scenery of the Canadian Rocky Mountains along the line of the C.P.R.

Dr. James Stewart was born in the County of Russell, Ontario, 1847. He was educated at the Ottawa Grammar School. He pursued his medical studies at McGill University (M.D., 1869); continuing them at Edinburgh, Vienna and Berlin. He was admitted a L.R.C.P. and L.R.C.S., Edinburgh 1883. He practised at Brucefield and Montreal where he made a speciality of nervous diseases. From 1883 to 1891 he was Prof. of Matera Medicine and Therapy in McGill University, and then held the chair of Med. and Clinical Med.

REMINISCENCES OF LISGAR

GEORGE KENNEDY 1843-1853

George Kennedy, writing in 1900, looked back on his years as a student at Lisgar during two separate periods from 1843-1853. He returned in 1860 as Second-Master.

> *"There are no times like the old times,*
> *They should never be forgot;*
> *There is no home like the old home.*
> *Keep green the dear old spot;*
> *There are no friends like the old friends,*
> *May heaven prolong their lives!"*

"'Tis Sixty years Since" was the alternative title Sir Walter Scott gave to his first novel, *Waverley*, published in 1805, because it was a tale of the Jacobite rebellion of 1745, just sixty years before. "'Tis sixty years since" the Dalhousie District Grammar School was opened and I am asked to write some reminiscences of that early period. It is sixty years since, a little white-haired laddie, I was first taken to the school by my elder brother Donald, who was one of the big boys as I was one of the little boys.

Things were very different then from what they are now. The Capital was then only a little town, or rather two little towns, of perhaps five thousand people, Upper and Lower Towns, separated by Government Hill, which was fenced in all round. The road between the two towns wound from where the corner of Bank and Wellington streets now is, in a south-easterly direction past the site of the present Dominion Methodist Church and then easterly along the southerly boundary of the two graveyards, Catholic and Protestant, which occupied the space a little to the west of what is

The Ottawa Collegiate Institute as first erected in 1874 with stone from lumberman Skead's quarry. Judging by the activity on the road, the sidewalk and the school steps this photograph was taken on the occasion of a special event like the official opening or graduation.

now City Hall Square, and then northerly to Sappers Bridge. But foot passengers had the privilege of entering the sacred precincts of Government Hill by turnstile gates and crossing the hill by numerous foot paths. These gates were at the east end of Wellington Street on the one side and not far from the west end of Sappers Bridge on the other side. There were also two large gates, but these were seldom opened except for the passage out or in of the soldiers, whose barracks occupied the top of the hill, for Bytown was a garrison town, and its little society was made gay by the presence of the red-coats. There were very few houses south of Sparks Street. Le Breton's Flat was covered with small cedars and pines; Centre Town did not exist, and Lower Town scarcely reached to Sandy Hill, and New Edinburgh was considered a long way off.

The streets were not paved; there were no sidewalks; no gaslights. People going out in dark nights used to carry lanterns with tallow candles in them. In fact, timid people would rather not go out at all at night, for the memory of the Shiners had not died out.

The only mills at the Chaudière were Daniel McLachlin's grist mill and sawmill, to which were added a year or two after John Perkins's grist mill and Philip Thompson's sawmill, a little further down the stream. There was no railway, nor for several years after. But there were very many steamboats. Before the construction of the St. Lawrence canals, all the traffic between Montreal and the West was sent up the Ottawa to Bytown and thence by the Rideau Canal to Kingston, so in summer the place was very lively. Little steamers, just big enough to pass through the locks were constantly coming and going with long tows of barges behind them. And there was one big passenger steamer running between Bytown and Grenville, the *Shannon*, which had two walking-beams, and which carried a small cannon, the firing of which announced her arrival as she made a big sweep round Nepean Point to reach her landing place at the foot of the locks. She was probably not a very fast boat, for I remember some years after when a new steamer, the *Speed*, was put on the route, what a great achievement it was looked upon that the owners could advertise in large type "Through to Montreal by daylight."

I was not one of the first pupils of the Grammar School, but I attended it very soon after its establishment. We occupied the lower storey only, the upper being vacant. We sat on backless forms before long desks of uniform height for big and little boys alike. We had no steel pens then; all our writing of strokes and pot hooks was done with quills, which the master mended for us every day with his penknife— the origin of the term is easily seen. As for books I have recollections of *Carpenter's Spelling Book, Lindley Murray's English Reader, McCullough's Third and Fourth Reading Books* and *Lennie's Grammar*. As for arithmetic I did not get far enough to need a textbook before I left, but the

James Mather, architect for 1874 building.

recognized authority was Walkinghame's, which disguised itself under the specious title of *The Tutor's Assistant*.

There was a sandpit near by, which was a source of perennial delight to us little fellows, for besides the pleasure of jumping into it, we built or rather dug wonderful troglodytic mansions in its sides. The bigger boys had their games of pallet (since evolved into baseball) and shinny (now developed into hockey).

It is indeed a melancholy reflection to me that so many of my comrades of those days have died or disappeared from my view if perchance still living. Rather I might say so few are left. There were the McKays, Aleck, John, Charles, and Tom, all gone; the Ritchies, Robert, James, George, and Thomas, all gone except Thomas; John and Willlie McInnis; the Aumonds, Alfred, Charles, and Billy (I prefer to speak of them in the familiar terms of our boyhood); John and Andrew Rogerson; Thomas Burgess; Charley and Andrew Barreille; Joe L'Esperance; Charley Pinhey; Jimmy McTaggart; William Stirling; Jack Nicholson; Nathaniel Graham; William Ring; the Porters, Aleck, Tom, and Davy; Stephen Kenny; Samuel and Brown Roberts; William Blyth; Francis Oriel; Eb. Playter; Sidney and Massey Baker; Duncan and Donald McArthur; George and Joey Stevenson; Jim McDonnell; Wilbrod and Theodore Besserer; Clinton King; John

Top Left: Lisgar Street, 1903, going through to the Driveway, with Lisgar Collegiate. Note the bell tower moved to the south side, the recent addition to the south side of the original building, and the rear of the Drill Hall. Cartier Square, Lisgar's playing field was leased from the Department of National Defence. The student entrance is from the west side.

Top Right: One of the halls and classroom doors in Ottawa Collegiate Institute, 1903. Note thick double swinging doors and narrow halls. Probably looking west.

Middle Left: View of Lisgar Collegiate east and south sides from the Driveway, 1903. Note the newly constructed east wing (1902) and the Drill Hall. The Military Stores building has not yet been constructed.

Bottom Left: The main hall, photographed in 1903, with entrance to the principal's office flanked by two academic Honour Rolls. Now the library.

Malloch; and many others, now since, alas! mere "*voces et praeterea nihil.*"

I might relate some incidents, trivial in themselves perhaps, but which affected my young mind not lightly, as when one morning while all standing during the recital by Mr. Wardrope of the Lord's Prayer, Charley Pinhey suddenly fell back in a faint, or when in a game Massey Baker split open James Ritchie's forehead by a misdirected blow of his shinny. The most impressive incident, however, was the explosion in the schoolyard of a can of powder in the hand of Tom Porter. I remember as if it were but yesterday his agonizing cry when brought into school, "Oh! it's sore," and Mr. Wardrope's gentle words, as he bandaged up the poor mutilated hand, "Don't cry, Thomas, don't cry." And what a shock it was to us all when we were told next morning that he was dead of lockjaw!

In 1852 I returned to the school, which had become the Carleton County Grammar School and was then under the management of Mr. William Aird Ross, now the respected ex-County Judge, and was located in a wooden building on the north-west corner of Elgin and Maria streets. I know not how adequately to express my obligations to Mr. Ross for the great benefits bestowed on me by him during the year and a half I was under his tuition. Along with a vigorous and energetic nature and an unconquerable will he had the faculty of instilling into some at least of his pupils a part of his own ambition to excel and of fostering a desire for knowledge which but for his inspiration might have been left in unconscious slumber.

ANDREW HOLLAND 1855-1858

Former pupil Andrew Holland was obviously a school "cut-up" and has rather different memories of Principal Ross from those of his predecessor, George Kennedy.

If my memory serves me right, my first experience of the Grammar School was when it was located at the north-west corner of Elgin and Albert streets, somewhere about the year 1854. The building was an old frame, clapboard affair on Elgin Street. We had Mr. W. A. Ross as Principal, and a rare specimen of the strict pedagogue he was. He inclined very much to the birch, until, one day, he ran a splinter through Fred Harvey's finger. Fred fainted at the sight of his own blood, and the result was reform, the abolition of the rod and the substitution of leather as an instrument of punishment.

Some of the pupils he used to lick every day on general principles. I got my share, and, after years of reflection I have come to the conclusion that I deserved all I got, and probably more. Especially was it the case after emptying my neighbor's bottle of ink into Mr. Ross's coat pocket while he was inspecting the writing lesson of the boy on the other

R.W. Nolan, caretaker, 1885-1903. If we can possibly judge from the Diary of Sydney Woodburn, the chief tasks of the caretaker were to try to keep the school heated and the cafeteria liveable. Teacher "Fuzzy" Irwin described Nolan as "a white-haired, white-whiskered Irishman" who had command of the basement. "Summoned from above, he rarely had time to remove the soot, oil and ashes from his hair, whiskers and clothing, and would appear above ground a fiery, sooty, gum-chewing Vulcan to fill inkwells or make minor repairs."

side who, at this date, I think was Jim Sutton or Jasper Lockwood. He licked the whole form without finding out who did it and I held my peace, inasmuch as they would have done it unto me.

A few days later we had our revenge. A big boy from Aylmer, one of the Aylens, had forgotten his books, and next morning came to school without having his exercises prepared. The class was called. Aylen did not rise. The Principal demanded explanations. Aylen said he had forgotten his books and had not prepared his lessons, consequently he declined to stand up with the class. It was a distinct repudiation of authority and the school held its breath in awful but suppressed expectancy. Then a thing happened that was not on the programme. Mr. Ross advanced between the benches to use the strap. Aylen swung his foot out from under the desk, caught the teacher a sort of drop kick just below the belt and Mr. Ross went out of business. Aylen gathered up his books and retired. He was too big for that school.

There were a number of us at the school who were hard propositions for any master to run up against. Alex Christie was a fairly tractable boy; so were Bob Donaldson and the Hicks. Jasper Lockwood was not, nor was Albert Macdonald, nor his brother Charlie. Jim Sutton and Jack Durie could always be depended on when a fight was on between our school and the Lower Town boys, but they were usually shy about getting their eyes blackened or their clothes torn as explanations would not be accepted at home.

J.K. Stewart was a student full of mischief. Tommy Thompson, son of the City Treasurer, was always a philosopher. He and my brother George were souls with but a single thought— and that was to get away from the turmoil of the playground and search for bugs, snails, shells, and things that would add to their natural history collection. Neither was worth a button in a fight; they were Doukhobors without knowing it.

At the time there was a strong sectional feeling between the boys of Lower Town and those of Upper Town, and it mattered not if a fellow could take honours in his class, if he could not hit straight from the shoulder when a scrap was on. Bob Hick and his brother Fred were of the studious kind. They were not robust boys and were not really in it in shinny or any of the rougher games in which we delighted. Alex Christie was a student but he was also a fighter. Fred Bradley and his brother Richard were big and strong— Fred in the field and Dick in his class. Dick seemed to see nothing but the serious side of life. Big, good-natured Fred was too fond of fun to be a student, and I doubt if he would have graduated with honours in a twenty years' course, except in athletics. Sherwood Cox was just beginning to loom up as an intellectual champion when he died. Ned Cluff had the elements of a dead game sport and a stayer from the time he first made his appearance in school in short pants. How he afterwards graduated on the field of sports and became an authority on insurance is known not only in Ottawa but over a large section of the continent.

Alex McCormick, Nat Hay, Jim Leslie, Will Scott, and others were too small to be counted on in a game of shinny or rounders, and were a source of anxiety to the more thoughtful ones of us when we went in swimming. Have any of our boys ever experienced a more delightful swim than they used to have in the luke-warm muddy water of the canal in the long June days of the fifties? Have they ever caught or missed such big fish as we used to hook at the foot of the locks, or did they ever have such fun in skating as we had between Sappers Bridge and Hartwell's in the cold days of November? I think not, as far as I am personally concerned. All joys seem tame and all sorrows commonplace now compared with the joys and sorrows of the old Grammar School days of 1855 to 1860.

Later on came William Ogilvie, steady as a clock but full of quiet humor; Alex Lumsden, an earnest student but always ready for the playground; John McLatchie, Tom Birkett, sturdy, independent, and masterful; George Sutton (Jim's younger brother); Dave Kenly, George Blyth, Godbee Brown, Tom McDermott. By the way, Tom lived then in the little cottage over on Cooper Street. It was a clearance on the edge of a swamp, and between it and Elgin Street was an Irish settlement known as Corkstown. Tom's residence seemed to be away in the bush at that time. The old roller rink was located in later years just about at the mouth of the creek that used to drain the swamp extending from Elgin Street away back to Bank Street, and at its mouth the boys gathered to swim and fish, settle personal differences with the fists, and incidentally have some fun with old Tom Hodgins and his wife, Belle, well-known residents of the Corktown settlement.

As I write, incidents come back to my memory that I had almost forgotten, many of which, though interesting to some of the survivors, could not well find a place in these memoirs. Deb Chitty, in those days, was a lank-bodied boy. He used to scrap when the boys would ask: "Is it cold up there?" His brother Harry was a dapper-looking young chap, alert, always neat, and gave promise of the histrionic talent that he subsequently developed. Erskine Bronson was good in Latin and classics generally. He was almost too reserved in manner from boyhood to be counted on as a safe comrade in any mischief that would afterwards require explanation. I cannot remember much about Dick Langrell, son of the then Chief of Police.

How many of us can remember when we used to have daguerreotypes taken at Lockwood's gallery, near Sappers Bridge? It meant an exposure then from three to five minutes, and the results were sometimes awful. I have some of those horrors yet. In another generation they will be worth their weight in Buffalo robes, to a photographer's society.

We had the Bytown & Prescott Railway then, telegraph connection with Prescott, and a daily paper. The Crimean War, and the Mutiny in India, panoramas of the trek of Joe Smith and his Mormons to the Great Salt Lake, and of the Gold Rush to California were the big excitements of the period.

Boys did not read so many novels at that time as they do now. A copy of *Sixteen String Jack, Jack Shepperd, Pawnee Bill, Sweeny Todd the Ruffian Barber*, or any other good yellow book worth reading cost a shilling. By the time it was read by the owner and his friends, there would hardly be enough left to light a cigar with.

At that time only a select few in Ottawa knew what tomatoes were; bananas were a curiosity; it was generally supposed that cultivated grapes would not ripen here. We lighted our homes with candles and conned our lessons by their feeble light. Coal-oil lamps were then coming in, but they were used only by experts in lighting, who knew how to avoid creating an explosion. The oil at that time (called "Rock Oil") had the maximum of smell and the minimum of light, but it was an improvement on the wax or tallow candle.

In those days the Indians played lacrosse on Barrack Hill; Grammar School boys looked on with admiration and envy, little dreaming that in their day and generation they would beat the Indians at their own game. We had no clubs then; no baseball club, no lacrosse club, no football club. Godfrey Baker (at that time postmaster), Major Galway, "Bill" Cluff (now city auditor) and a few others made up a cricket team, and that was about the extent of the organized sport of the day—outside of horse-racing, which was, of course, beyond the means of Grammar School boys. How Collegiate boys of the present day would pity our ignorance of electric motive power, electric railways, steamships, phonographs, telephones, elevators, "conigrams," moving pictures, fast presses, illustrated daily newspapers and the thousand-and-one other conveniences of everyday life of the twentieth century. The marvels that we have seen since then are only an indication of what the present generation will see long before the year 2000.

My final experience as a pupil of the Grammar School was in the building now part of the Windsor Hotel, about where Mr. George Cox subsequently carried on his engraving business for some years. For a time Mr. Millar was Principal, and was succeeded by Reverend H.J. Borthwick I think, with George Kennedy as assistant. It's a long time ago.

The wonder to me, when I come to think of it, is that a disaster did not occur at the school on Metcalfe Street. There were three flats. The upper one was just an open attic with a small portion near the stairs so arranged that when the Principal came up the stairs any boy who was doing mischief up there could slip down without being perceived when the teacher in charge reached the landing. The mechanics who finished the building had left a few two-inch planks behind. These we inserted between the wall-plate and the rafters. They made powerful levers with two or three boys on the end of each plank and the roof would rise from four to six inches. Why it did not slide off into the street has always been a mystery to me.

I often wonder how so many of the boys of that period in the history of the Grammar School escaped being hanged, and grew up to be respectable, staid old citizens, pillars of the church and successful professional and business men. I think we were more thoroughly grounded at that time in the three R's than boys are now, and hadn't to worry so much over the trimmings which occupy so much of the time of those who came after us. The "trimmings" we got from the teachers then were of a different character, and I think productive of more real benefit to the school than the modern methods.

GEORGE C. HOLLAND 1857-60

My recollection of the Grammar School begins about the year 1857. The teacher was Mr. W.A. Ross, now Judge Ross, a pedagogue of the old school, with unbounded faith in the virtue of the rod as a means of developing the intellectual powers of his pupils. To do him justice, he was one of the best teachers I have ever known, despite his love for the birch. If he kept constantly before him Solomon's remark about the use of the rod, he had a high sense of duty to those committed to his care, and in his desire to appear as impartial as he really meant to be, was, if possible, more severe in punishing his own nephews than in castigating other boys in the school.

As many of us know Judge Ross personally, I need not describe his appearance, further than to remind some, who may have forgotten the past, that little men sometimes possess muscles of iron and sinews of steel. I have seen him tackle and thrash boys that stood head and shoulders above him. Sometimes he caught a Tartar, but on the whole he could be counted upon to come out on top in a scrimmage, and he maintained discipline in the school and advanced his pupils in a manner that merited the commendation of the whole community.

My recollections of the school on Queen street are very dim. I was one of the small boys and sat in the very front row. Beside me sat Dick Harvey, a lad about my own age. On the whole we were fairly good boys, but occasionally we sought diversion from the monotony of our studies in ways not allowed by the rules of the Institution. One day we had caught a big blue-bottle fly. There had been a sensational hanging somewhere about the time and it occurred to us that we would execute the blue-bottle to see how such a show would look. We got a hair, made a noose of it, slipped it over the fly's head and were about carrying out the sentence of death, when a few sharp raps of a rule over our knuckles reminded us that there was a higher law which we had infringed. We got further reminded the same day, and our ardor in executing the death sentence on the blue-bottle during school hours was promptly and permanently cooled.

It was while attending the Queen street school that I played truant for the first and only time in my life. My brother was absent from home for a week and I did not care to go to school without him. My companion was Tom Swalwell, a son of the late Anthony Swalwell. We were not chums, but the morning that my brother left home, I met Tom and readily fell in with his suggestion that we should take a vacation. We spent that day in the fields. Next day was rainy, but we were afraid to go to school and face Mr. Ross. Tom and I spent the day under cover of a pile of slabs. I think it rained the greater part of that week, and Tom and I put in a miserable time. I was glad when Saturday came, and with it my brother. The following Monday we went to school

Bicycling pals J.E. Wallace and W.A. Graham. Although they look young enough to be students, these two travellers are teachers at Lisgar, Wallace a teacher of Junior Mathematics, 1883-1898, described as "an excellent disciplinarian and teacher" and Graham, B.A., 1895-1903, as a teacher of Junior English and Mathematics.

together. My brother could account for his absence; I could only account for mine by a frank and full confession. I expected, of course, to be flayed alive, but for once justice was tempered with mercy. My case was referred to the home authorities, and the culprit was cautioned and allowed to go under suspended sentence.

Among my schoolmates I had few intimate friends. I can recall, however, three—Tommy Thompson, son of the city chamberlain, "Addie" Carroll, son of the resident Methodist clergyman, and Sherwood Cox, a half brother of ex-Mayor Cox. Sherwood was bright and ambitious, and subsequently was gold medallist of the Collegiate Institute. He was my chum, and his untimely death was my first vivid realization of the inevitable separations which come to all of us sooner or later.

Our playground after school hours was in the region now comprised between Sparks and Albert and Bank and O'Connor streets. It was low and marshy, but there were dry places suitable for our purposes. West of what is now Bank street and south of Queen street were fields of grain

and I can remember the interest we took in the first mowing machine we ever saw. It was used to cut a field of oats which extended from the south side of Queen street out to where Charlie (now Doctor) Graham's people used to live— away out of town as far south as Maria street. On the east side of O'Connor street between Sparks and Queen streets, and covering all the ground up to the British Lion hotel (now the Brunswick) my uncle cultivated a fine vegetable garden, as an adjunct to his hotel "The International" then situated on the opposite corner west of what is now Bryson & Graham's departmental store, and was a very popular man with the small boys of the neighborhood from the time the first cucumber came in until the last melon was killed by the autumn frost.

There were few public amusements in Bytown, but fires always furnished an agreeable change from the monotony of school life. A conflagration in those days was something to stir the blood. There was no paid fire brigade, no cordon of policemen—nothing to interfere with the picturesque and exciting incidents attending a fire. In the absence of waterworks or deep inexhaustible wells, the water supply was hauled in barrels from the river. To stimulate the water vendors to their greatest activity, the first man to arrive with a barrel of water for the hand-engines was paid a bonus, and the result was a mad race of water carts to the scene of the fire, and a scrap among their drivers over the bonus. When the volunteer fire brigade happened to be short of hands to work the pumps, bystanders were impressed into the service, and we boys occasionally were allowed to help the pumping brigade.

The street lighting was in keeping with the water supply. The lamps were few and far between, and were fed with oil— whale oil, I think. Afterwards came the gas lamps, marking a distinct advance in civilization. I can well remember the lamplighter, with his ladder over his shoulder, going his rounds in the twilight—this is, when the moon was in its first or last quarter. Under the contract between the city and the gas company, there was to be no competition between the company and the man in the moon. Each had its appointed time for lighting the streets, and consequently, in cloudy and stormy weather, the streets were at times shrouded in Egyptian darkness.

In the absence of more practical issues, there was a good deal of sectional and sectarian bitterness in the city. The boys west of the canal looked down, literally and metaphorically, upon the boys who dwelt in lower town. The latter were mainly Irish and French and attended the separate schools. There was a good deal of border warfare, and sometimes, despite the vigilance of constable Langrell, a raid in force from one territory into the other. My brother and I took part in one such crusade. The upper town boys collected their forces on the hill back of where the post office now stands, and marched across Sappers Bridge to give the enemy battle in his stronghold, somewhere in Letter O. Our parents got wind of the expedition, so did the constable, and while the latter lay in wait for the raiders behind one of the kopjes of Major's Hill, the former made a rear-guard attack. I can remember my brother and myself being ignominiously captured and taken home, by an unsympathetic parent, who could not appreciate our desire for glory and our zeal for the cause of upper town. What he did for us the constable accomplished for the expedition as a whole.

An election in the fifties was something worth taking part in, and my memory of one in particular remains vivid to this day. The contest was between Mr. Scott (now Hon. Mr. Scott, Secretary of State) and the late Mr. Bell. I had no idea what the issue was, but I recollect that lower town was for Scott, while upper town was for Bell. That was long before the ballot was introduced, and I think the polling extended over three or four days. There was wild excitement, and we upper town boys shouted ourselves hoarse crying through the streets "Hurrah for Bell." I do not remember the slogan of the lower town boys.

From Queen street the school was removed to a frame building, at the very outskirts of centre town—in fact, the

very last building on Elgin street, at the corner of what is now called Albert street. South of the school house the land sloped abruptly into a swamp where in play hours, at the right season of the year, boys could always depend on finding plenty of frogs. In front of the school, situated in the middle of the square, was the old town hall and market place. South and east of it, a common stretched to the canal basin, and on the south side of the basin, hugging the shore all the way over to the Deep Cut, lay Corktown, a community which has long since disappeared, but of which those who were Bytown boys have very distinct and interesting memories.

There was no playground connected with the school. "No pent-up Utica confined our powers"—we played where we pleased and as we pleased. At one time—I think when the siege of Lucknow was a subject of all-absorbing interest— we constructed a fort of sods on an eminence back of the town hall, a little south of where the police court now stands. It was quite a structure, in shape like a Martello tower, but, of course, without a covering of any kind. When it was completed, we divided our forces, a few of the big boys undertaking to hold the fort against the combined assault of all the others. Being one of the small boys, I was attached to one of the assailing parties. The ammunition was sods taken from sandy ground, and when a combatant was struck in the face with one, he retired from the conflict, temporarily blinded. The battle raged furiously for two days all through the noon hour, and score of boys had to be led to the canal basin to have their eyes washed; breaches had been made in the fort, more by the defenders, who were running short of ammunition, than by the assailants; there was every prospect that in a few minutes the garrison would either have to capitulate or the fort would be taken by storm, when the teacher, or the town constable, or perhaps both, appeared on the scene and stopped hostilities. It was exasperating to be cheated of a hard won victory, but the warriors had to bow to *force majeure* and blow about what they could and would have done if—

Boys who had any ambition to learn under Mr. Ross found him helpful, if harsh; boys who had no desire to learn found him stern, I might almost say merciless.

I was the innocent cause, on once occasion, of getting a big boy, for whom I had a very warm friendship, severely punished. His name was Fred Bradley, a brother of our respected fellow-citizen, Mr. R.A. Bradley. I always liked to be near Fred, and we sat side by side on a long bench. One day, I rose to get a drink, and in my absence Fred deposited a crooked pin on my seat. I sat down, but immediately rose to a point of exclamation. In an instant the teacher had me by the collar and demanded why I had raised such an outcry. I explained that something sharp on the seat had hurt me. There on the seat was the crooked pin, and it was evident that it had been placed there by either one of my neighbors. Fred owned up to it at once and took his "licking"

The caption in the first history of Lisgar says "Group of 'Old Boys', 1877." Since this group of "Old Boys" is composed of young men, we can easily assume they were seniors at Lisgar then and leaders in school activities. Such a group would likely include the leaders of the Lyceum, the debaters in the Mock Parliament, the editors and writers of the *Vox Lycei*, the president of the Athletic Association.

like a man. He shed never a tear; I did the weeping for him, and would not be comforted because I had brought punishment on my friend. Many years afterwards I met Fred on a train and recalled the circumstance; he had forgotten all about it.

When Mr. Ross dropped school-teaching and became a lawyer the school was moved to Metcalfe street, opposite the old Methodist church, and, if my memory serves me, the next teacher was Mr. Millar. I have no very distinct recollection of him, but my impression is that his stay in the Grammar School was short. He was succeeded by the Rev. H.J. Borthwick, who brought to the institution new and improved methods, and contrived to maintain excellent discipline without resorting to undue severity. Of all the teachers I have known, I should place Mr. Borthwick in the front rank. Under him the school thrived and the attendance increased. Then, too, if I recollect right, young ladies appeared in the classes to the great advantage of the institute. Their

presence had a wholesome effect on the boys, while their industry and diligence had a stimulating effect on the whole school.

I can recall one memorable incident that occurred while I was a pupil under Mr. Borthwick—the unroofing of the Methodist church. It happened one stormy night, if I remember correctly, in 1859. The church—not the present structure but a smaller and less pretentious building—was directly opposite our school, at the north-west angle of the street. It was metal-roofed and apparently very substantial, but a fierce gale from the north-west lifted the roof from the walls and dropped it on the intersection of Metcalfe and Queen streets, completely blocking both thoroughfares. When we arrived at the school house in the morning the highway looked as though it had been paved with tin during the night. We found a novel playground on which to spin tops and indulge in such sports as the smooth surface seemed best adapted for.

It was, I think, in Mr. Borthwick's time that Rufus Hudson first appeared in the Grammar School. He was a short, thick-set boy, with a round smiling face and ruddy cheeks. He came from Chelsea, and I am under the impression that he walked to and from school, taking such chances for a ride as the farmer's rigs afforded. From the first he made his mark in the school yard and in the classes. He passed with honors, and subsequently at Toronto University had a brilliant career. He is at present one of the trusted head officials of a large loan company in Toronto.

Sawtell Thompson was a boy who was always getting into scrapes. He was a stout, full-blooded lad, with a loud voice and rough manner, and with a decidedly florid complexion. After leaving school he was in the grocery business on Rideau street until his death some years later. Charley Perry, son of the city engineer of that day, was left-handed, and enjoyed the distinction of being the best shot with a snowball in the whole school. In the frequent snowballing contests he was a tower of strength to the side which secured him.

During my last year in school—the winter of 1860—at Mr. Borthwick's suggestion, we entered upon a journalistic venture. *The Grammar School Weekly* was not exactly an up-to-date newspaper; it did not appear in print, and its circulation, though select, did not warrant us in soliciting advertisements. An editor was appointed and contributions from the pupils in all the classes were invited. Every Friday afternoon the collection of papers was read to the contributors, the rule being—no contribution, no admission to the entertainment. After the reading of the papers there was a free criticism of them, each contributor pointing out defects in any of them but his own. The journal was still flourishing when my school career ended, and probably was the first step towards the establishment of the admirable Lyceum of to-day.

In the spring of 1860 when I bade farewell to the Collegiate Institute the school was in a flourishing condition. Its progress from then is familiar to most of us, and we can judge, from its usefulness in the past, how valuable it is to-day and must in the future be to the whole community. The change and development of the city has not been greater than the progress of the school. The Grammar School of Bytown could no more be compared to the splendid school of to-day, than the scattered straggling villages of Upper and Lower Town could be compared to the stately capital of the Dominion of Canada. Nevertheless, I cannot help thinking that in some respects the old school under Mr. Ross and Mr. Borthwick could stand comparison with the Institute under its present excellent staff.

CASEY A. WOOD 1865-70

There was an active and flourishing company of school cadets about 1866, of which I think (Colonel) Tom Evans was a member. I remember that we used to march to the ranges on the banks of the Rideau and practice with the muzzle loading carbines.

When the school building was opposite the City Hall it was the amiable custom every winter, of those first out of school, to station themselves opposite the front door and force the boys who made a later exit, including the "kept ins," to run a snowball gauntlet. The luckless ones who were thus exposed to the fusilade were afterwards free to join the blockaders and inflict similar punishment on the still later ones. This form of discipline became at one time so popular that the best shots, including those who were ambitious to improve their social standing in the school republic, used to congregate before study hours in the morning and fire at marks while waiting for human victims. It thus happened that a school pastime stimulated punctuality; it was better to come early and avoid the rush. I presume one remembers the tricks played by one's fellow-students and the horse-play *quorum pars magna fuit* longer and more vividly than the more important incidents of school life.

A very effective punishment, mostly administered by our always beloved Head-Master John Thorburn, was the writing of "pages." This clerical work was done either while we tarried "weak and weary" after a day's real or pretended work or was carried on at our homes. When first instituted it took many long months to decide what is meant by the word "page." Some imaginative Fourth Form boys ventured the opinion that *any* page would do, irrespective of the *length* of the lines in it. No, said the teacher, we shall mingle instruction with your punishment; you shall write your pages from that compendium of all historic truth—Collier's History of England. Good, said we, the history exhibits numerous "sawed off" pages that can be copied in an instant. New wrangles thereupon arose as to the minimum number of *lines* that constitute a "page." Finally a compromise was effected by the choice of the same page. A fine of six pages meant six copies of the same page. And now, after the lapse of thirty years I believe I could still tell how "the riotous Prince Hal became transformed into the brave and wise King Henry the Sixth" and "went back on" his boon companions. To a good many of us (and there were so many of us that were not good!) this form of retribution seemed so certain that we began to anticipate it by the accumulation of pages. At odd hours the "riotous Prince Hal" was again and again reduced to paper against the day of need. For a time pages were also written (for a consideration) by sisters, small brothers and even—also for *considerations*—by other boy's sisters, until that source of supply was cut off by an edict prohibiting pages written in a female hand. Finally it was decided that, in cases of doubt, the burden of proof would lie with the individual presenting a page, that it was written by his own hand. This restriction imposed on a legitimate trade, was not an unmixed good because it increased those difficulties that come to the front when, for instance, one whose penmanship generally resembled

Reverend T.D. Phillips, M.A., Mathematical Master, 1878-1880, desribed as "a popular teacher and a good player of cricket".

the progress of a fly dipped in ink over a piece of white paper, attempted to show that a "page" written in schoolboy's copper-plate was an every-day example of his own handwriting.

When a boy was fined a certain number of pages it was a great satisfaction to rise in his place, advance to the teacher's desk and pay something on account; perhaps, in flush times, to wipe out the whole debt. Soon pages became articles of trade and barter, their market value rising and falling in accordance with the well known laws of supply and demand. Every morning a ledger was produced and a call made for pages; the boy who had none was fined an additional page and if his line of credit had unduly expanded it was curtailed by an invitation to remain for an hour and do more "Prince Hal's."

About this time an epidemic of stamp collecting prevailed in the school and my friend W.J. Christie, the best penman in our form, wrote, with a fine 303 Gillott's, six microscopical pages on a sheet of white foolscap. These were ornamented with marginal scrolls and perforated with a pin to resemble part of a sheet of postage stamps, and thus exhibited to admiring school-fellows. When the inevitable fine was imposed William advanced to the desk and, in the Presence, slowly

and ostentatiously detached one "stamp" and presented it in payment. The teacher was too wise to discuss the matter before the class but he was detected in making a careful study of that page to see that no lines were omitted.

It was the proud boast of one boy, whose present high official position prevents a mention of his name, that although fined pages, whose number equalled that of the leaves in Vallambrosa, he never wrote but six. As his account generally showed that number, or multiples of it, he constructed a convenient packet of the six pages aforesaid which, being paid in were readily abstracted and not missed from the accumulated pile in front of the teacher while that much abused man was straightening out the accounts of other delinquents. Anyway, the teacher himself was to blame; his constant approval of Greek institutions and his unlimited praise of Greek ideals finally infected us and that is the reason we generally adopted the Spartan code, that the crime consists not in the commission of an error but in allowing it to be found out.

As will be remembered by most of the "old boys," about five minutes at the end of each hour were allowed for the interchange of teachers; it thus often happened that the master in classics, for example, who, the previous hour, gave his attention to pupils on the first floor was obliged to reach the top floor for the next recitation. On going up he often met on the way another master from some other room. It frequently transpired, owing to conferences between teachers meeting in this way and outside the class-rooms, that, from ten or fifteen minutes at a time, the pupils were left alone. Doubtless in these days that time would be occupied by the boys in discussing the next lesson or in study. We, however, filled it in by working out ingenious problems in strategy. As soon as the teacher left the room a sentinel was placed at the door and then the fun began. Among the plots carried on to our satisfaction was the practice of bowling during these precious intervals. An abandoned orrery—part of our incipient physical science laboratory—was seized and the sun, moon, and earth, not to mention a few lusty planets made out of hardwood, were divided among the revellers. Nine-pins were constructed out of the small firewood that fed the big "Three Rivers" stove. When all was ready the game was played in the back of the long school-room. If there are any Marquis of Queensbury rules governing "nine-pins" we followed them. As soon as the sentinel notified us that the representative of law and order was approaching all was quiet; the heavenly bodies were restored to their orbits in an old desk and the firewood was distributed among various hiding places. As far as I can remember, this was the only elaborate piece of horse-play that went on for months without discovery by the authorities. It escaped detection partly because it took place on the first floor disturbing only the warehouse men below us, and partly because it was well understood that some considerable noise was always to be expected of Fifth Form boys when left alone.

During the hot summer days there was a daily pilgrimage of boys to the Rideau Canal for a cool plunge generally at the "ram-pike," the stump of a large tree that at that time projected and, I trust, still projects above the limpid waters of the canal. "Swims," you may know, were generally prearranged expeditions. They followed a sentence of that sign-language, uttered by the opening and closing of the fore and middle fingers of the right hand, that I doubt not were also made by small boys to one another on the streets of Nineveh, Damascus and Troy, a thousand years before Horace told us how good a thing it is to take a bath after exposing ourselves to the heat and burden of the day. Of course it was against the law (most of our fun in those days was illegal) "to bathe within sight of inhabited houses" but what were we water-loving youngsters to do? One of our natural enemies, a stern, relentless constable named Silcox, watching an opportunity "to do his duty" espied four of us, with our heads above and our bodies beneath the water. He invited us to come out and be arrested but with our clothing safely hidden in the bushes we defied and even reviled him. One boy, less fortunate than the rest, had gone ashore and begun to dress. Him the vigilant minion of the law threatened with dungeon, manacles and bodily torture, unless he revealed the names of the wretches in the water. Yielding to force all our names were given up; we were hailed before a Justice of the Peace and fined (how well I recollect it) one dollar and costs per boy. Good grew out of our troubles, however, because there followed an agitation for the setting aside of parts of the Ottawa water front, for school bathers which resulted in our being allowed to indulge ourselves where the sight of naked small boys would not bring "a blush to the face of any young person."

THE SIDNEY WOODBURN DIARY 1878-1880

Sidney Woodburn was the son of A.S. Woodburn, publisher of the *Ottawa Journal* and owner of the Ottawa Steam Printing Press, which published the *Ottawa City Directory* and *Hansard*. The *Journal* offices were located on Elgin Street not far from Lisgar.

Sidney wrote extensively in his diary, recounting his daily activities, school, holidays, and life in Ottawa. The new Drill Hall had just opened near Lisgar and he spent many hours watching the militia and participating in their events. Lantern slide shows at church were popular entertainment and an opportunity to meet girls whom he describes in great detail in Pitman shorthand. Walking a young lady home from one such evening, he speaks of the liberties he would like to have taken and how far he actually got—not far at all by today's standards. It shows a typical teenager's infatuations. In his scrapbooks are newspaper articles, reviews and etchings (no photographs yet in the papers) of actresses like Lily Langtry, the Jersey Lily, some of whom performed at the Russell House located, before it burned, where Confederation Square is located.

From his diary entries he did not consider himself a top student; he frequently comments on the nagging of his mother when he habitually slept late, failed again to do his homework, or skipped classes. His marks also got him into trouble with his mother; Father does not seem to have been the disciplinarian in the family and father and son often took refuge in the *Journal* offices.

Sidney writes often of the time spent in the slate room in Lisgar's basement, smoking cigars. Slates were used for everyday schoolwork as paper is today.

After school Sidney worked in the *Journal* office doing odd jobs. One entry describes a new form of communications. Situated at Lansdowne Park, Sidney could actually talk through wires to his father at the *Journal* office on Elgin Street; he said the new sensation was called "phonography."

Sidney was a member of the Ottawa Bicycle Club, still in existence today. He raced the old-style bicycle, the "penny-farthing." He and his teammates won cups and medals and were proudly photographed with their bicycles. In his last diary entry, Sidney writes that he was entering an important race; with the strain of pedaling the heavy iron penny-farthing bicycle on the dirt and sand of an unpaved Elgin Street, he burst his appendix and shortly after, died. He was twenty-one.

The County of Russell Agricultural Society's medal struck for Sidney Woodburn, 1883, for first prize in bicycling races.

To Sydney Woodburn for winning the one mile bicycle race, a medal of exquisite craftsmanship given by the Independent Order of Oddfellows, August 8, 1883.

Woodburn also won a large silver cup at the Caledonian (Highland) Games that same year at either Perth or Maxville. The Games were imported from Scotland in 1819 and gradually moved westward across Canada in the nineteenth century.

Letters of condolence were typically ponderous with the heavy language of the day. As the death occurred in the summer, many of Ottawa's more influential families were at their homes at Blue Sea Lake. Mrs. Lizzie Parnell, a cousin of Mrs. Woodburn, wrote of the sad hour and the family's affliction and then plunged on for five pages with the latest gossip from that summer community: whose husband was a drunkard and whose wife was enjoying her seasonal freedoms. Even the "Witch of Plum Hollow," Mrs. Barnes, mentioned Sidney's death when she wrote after being consulted by Mrs. Woodburn about the possible location of a stolen lamp and safe taken in a break-in at the *Journal* office.

A younger brother, Fisher, had died a few years earlier. Older sisters had moved away studying art and music. A sister, Naida, was born the year after his death. With no male heirs to whom he could leave the *Journal*, A.S. Woodburn sold the business to P.D. Ross one of the most active and influential citizens of Ottawa in his time, an all-round athlete, coach, and manager of many teams, member of all kinds of civic committees and Boards, and publisher-owner of the Ottawa *Journal*.

DIARY OF SYDNEY A. WOODBURN

Tuesday Jan 1, 1878. New Year's Resolutions. Duties to perform; Music, School studies, Collect papers, Save Money, Cleanliness, Sunday School Verses, Exercise, shorthand. No more stories to read. To wind my watch. To write in my journal, account of weather, and how much money I get. To look to see how many marks I miss and to look to see these many things. Attend to drawings. When I hear a lecture I should imitate it.

Monday Jan. 7. School opened today and so I went. It was cold so we got hardly any schooling. The promotions were made but I was unfortunate enough not to be promoted. I intend to have my name on the reports at the end of the month. It was very cold today but it wasn't windy. I did not come home for dinner today. I stayed down in the basement with the boys. After tea went up to Uncle Robert's for medicine. I came home and went to bed.

Tuesday Jan. 8. Got a ride up to the school with Andy. Went in but there was no school on account of the cold. Went up to the office and from there went to Stephen's for a pair of moccasins. Tried out two pair and brought them to the office. Decided to take square toes and return the others. Then went back to school but there being no fire there was none. Came home, took dinner. After tea went up to the office to help Mr. Bennett with the book-keeping. Got letter for Albie and gave it to him. Exchanged 7 ct for $1.10.

Wednesday Jan. 9. Took breakfast and went to school. Was a little late. We had not any lessons this morning but just got in order. First we drew for numbers and I got on my paper 5. Then we arranged slates. Mr. Parlow asked me to help picking the good slates. Then took the broken pieces down in the cellar. Recess was wrestling. I did not get any slate so I had to do without one. Down in the cellar there was a lot of things of years past away as old maps, desks, etc. They keep the ink down in the cellar and there is any amount of empty bottles. There are also a couple of furnaces.

Wed. Sept. 25. Today we had Latin. Managed to get through it. No matter whether you know the lesson well or not, you feel so nervous that it is hard to say it. In the afternoon I went to the gymnasium. After six o'clock Emmett Rice and myself were alone and I learned the "swinging drop" off the bar. After tea I went upstairs and studied my lessons. Mother sent me up to the office with rosettes but it was shut so I returned. I then brought in a scuttle of coal. Acted a little on my bar with Willie Driscoll.

Thursday, Sept. 26. At dinner time I went up to the office. I seen the boiler. It is in running order now. I got the *Illustrated News*. I then walked home with Mr. Bennett. After school this afternoon I went to the gymnasium. It was pretty cold. Today our teacher, Mr. Agnew, touched on politics. He said that coal was got cheaper from the States than from Nova Scotia. He said that was one of the benefits of Reform. I shouts out that the people would have work and be able to pay for it. Willie [Driscoll] asked to me to go to Aylmer [to his home].

Friday, Sept. 27. This morning I decided I would go to Aylmer with Willie. I was pretty near being kept in school today but I got off and prepared to start for Aylmer. I went up to Windsor House and met Willie who had went before. I saw his mother after a time. We then drove to Aylmer, with a very lazy horse or perhaps I should say a poor horse. It was pretty cold going. I seen Willie's brothers and sisters. Acted a little on the bar they had. Mr. Driscoll proposed that we should go up the river [Ottawa] in the yacht tomorrow.

Sat. Sept. 28. This morning Fred Driscoll and I went into the garden and got grapes. We then went out for a row with Willie. Then we got on the yacht and steamed to Horse Shoe Bay. There was some friends of the Driscoll's there named Street. They have a camp there and Mr. Driscoll went away in the evening. We had a great duck stew for tea. We found we could not get home that night so we went to bed. We three of us slept in one end of the bunk.

Mon. Sept. 30. Yesterday there was no shooting as it is against the law. Amused myself by rowing. Today we got up very early to hunt deer. We all separated. A boy named Wilson from Ottawa was my companion. We waited for a long time but no deer came. We heard shots and the barking of the hounds. Some time later we returned to camp——. Street came back saying that he had shot a deer in the bush. We returned to Aylmer this evening. Before we returned we went up the creek for deer.

Tues. Oct 1. This morning found me at Aylmer. Got up and took breakfast and away to Ottawa. Mr. Driscoll gave me a quarter of the deer to take home and Mrs. D. gave me a few grapes. We were in time for school. Their man drove us into town. We had the venison for dinner this afternoon. I did not feel very well on account of my——[shorthand]. I went to the gymnasium this evening. Mother received a knitting machine this evening.

Wed. Oct. 2. After school when I was upstairs Mother told me to harness the horse and go up for Mrs. Heath. I harnessed and went. I then went back to the office. Andrew was bricking the floor of the boiler house. I addressed and stamped some books. I went to Kirby's for my watch. He said it would be done by Saturday. Today in school a fellow named Richards put something down my back that made it itch very much. I gave him a touch on his cheek. Called for Mrs. Heath.

Thurs. Oct. 3. After school I went to the gymnasium I exercised a little. While there, an extra came saying that [Ned] Hanlan had won the boat race. This makes him Champion of America. Just after school I did the examples in arithmetic for tomorrow. Studied my Latin in the evening. It rained very hard for a while this afternoon. Willie is studying very hard just now. I says at dinner or in the morning I will try and waste no time. I have often thought so but never carried it out.

Friday Oct. 4. Yesterday afternoon I went to the gymnasium. Took tea and read the paper [*Citizen*]. I found Knox here when I came home to tea. He was to Lachine and seen the Boat Race [Hanlan's championship]. When he was leaving I asked him to get his flute for me. Miss Parnell came as we were at tea. Miss S. Higginson came after. I went to the gym after tea. But did not exercise myself. I seen Willie Story and Ab Heney there. After this I went with Miss P. to corner to catch the street car.

Tues. Nov. 26. In the afternoon we had a Latin examination. It came like a thunderbolt on us or anyway me as it was in no way expected. I did not make a good examination. I fear that my chances of promotion are small. Oh, I hope that I may pass into the Upper First but this world does not regard thoughts. I would be unhappy until I was in the Upper First. After the holidays I will know whether I passed or not. In the evening I was up at the office. Got coal oil.

Wed. Nov. 27. Went up to the office after school. We were told that we would have a half an hour only for dinner tomorrow. It was very slippery in the evening and it was queer to see people walking. I stayed up very late studying my Geography and Geometry. I am sure we will have Geography and I think we will have Geometry. They are getting pretty well fixed up at the office now.

Fri. Nov. 29. This after we were told by Mr. Agnew that we would have a half holiday tomorrow. Just before school was dismissed Mr. Thorburn told us that we would have a whole holiday.

Sat. Nov. 30. I washed the clothes this morning. I went to office in the afternoon. They had some lithographed pictures of the Marquis [of Lorne] and Princess [Louise]. After tea I went and we put oil on the pictures and made them transparent. We then hung them up to dry till show day. I then went home.

Mon. Dec. 2. This morning turned out very wet to the great disappointment of the general public who wished to see the reception of the Governor and Princess. I was at the office and went out and distributed some bills saying that the Reception was postponed. Seen the cavalry on Parliament Hill. I intended to go to Mrs. Letts but did not. Was at the office after tea.

Tues. Dec. 3. Today had to go to school again. There is a great want of knowledge about the Reception of His Excellency and Princess Louise. Mr. Agnew said that he noticed some of the school boys pushing at the reading of the Address [presumably the Govenor General's]. We got our Geometry papers back. I got very low marks.

Wed. Dec. 4. There was a holiday today on account of it having been a public holiday. I was at the office and helped to put (up) the big flag with which we were decorating the office on top of the office. I [also] fixed a decoration on the window. We sold all of the transparencies which Father got from Montreal. There was a grand procession this evening in honor of the Marquis and Princess.

Thurs. Dec. 5. The papers of course had a great deal about the procession. One incident told in the paper was a lady from the country, anxious to show her devoted loyalty to the Royal Party, threw a bouquet which struck the Marquis on the cheek. I was at the office this evening.

Fri. Dec. 6. I washed the clothes this afternoon instead of tomorrow. There was not much for me to wash as I think mother washed before I came from school. I rung [sic] the clothes through. I intended to go to May Fiske's Blondes [a play] tonight but I could not find Willie Story. I was at the office and asked Knox to come but he said he was going to a tea-meeting. He said if I waited till tomorrow he would go. I decided to wait till tomorrow.

Sat. Dec. 7. Slept very late this morning. Then at the office I asked Knox would he come to the Opera, for sure, tonight. He said yes. After tea I called for him at Uncle Thomases. We went direct to the play. When we got in I saw Sam Williams, J. Nicholson and M. Greyburn. Seen the play and went home. Father was not home when I arrived, so I went up to the office and seen Smith. I came home with Father.

Fri. Dec. 13. This is the last day of school for some time. We were told that we would have until Tuesday, the 9th of January. Willie went home after school [presumably to Aylmer]. I went up Elgin Street with him where we met his grandmother's carriage, so he got in and drove away. He

took his books home with him. I read "proof" with Mr. Bennett before tea. After tea I seen Sam Williams. I showed him the office. I walked home with him and had a talk. Will Story passed so I went into the house.

Mon. Dec. 23. Yesterday Father and Mother invited Mr. and Mrs. Lett and Mr. and Mrs. Grant, the former for dinner and both the former and the latter for tea. I went to Sunday School and then Willie Story and I went to the Dominion Methodist Church in the evening. The snow was pretty deep this morning so I shovelled the snow away from the door. Mr. S. was doing likewise. he lent me a book in the evening. Today I was at the office.

Wed. Dec. 25. This morning when I awoke I heard Lillie, Mabel and C running around. I seen one of my stockings laying on the floor. When I examined it I found an apple, orange, some raisins, a knife and a silk handkerchief. In the morning I went up to the office to see about the steam but I found Hudrow there. All the folks but me took a drive out. I started out to Grandmother's with a pair of shoes as a Christmas present for her.

Tues. Dec. 31. 1878 New Year's Eve. This evening I went into Willie Story's house and we talked for some time. We thought we would go to Watch Night Service. We went and stayed past 12 o'clock. The church that we went to was the Dominion Methodist. I did not go in to Will Story's after Service but went into the house. The door was locked but I soon got in and went to bed.

Mon. Jan. 13, 1879. Allie did not go away today as he expected. I did not come home [from school] for dinner today. I was going to the rink after school but Allie did not like to go so I stopped and went with Allie to his Uncle Kingston's for a parcel. We went to Howell's grocery store to see Mr. Selwyn about Allie's snowshoes but he was not there. We went down to his house and got them from a woman. Allie, Will Story and I harnessed Tom in the "train" and proceeded to take a drive. We called for Annie Story and Annie W., and took them. Had a long drive.

Tues. Jan. 14. I got up a little earlier than usual on account of Allie's going home. Andrew drove he and I down to the Hull station. I then went back to the road where Andrew had the horse. We drove to the office and I waited until dinnertime. While there I went on several messages. After dinner I "rung" the clothes for mother. I then studied my lessons until the evening and then I went with Willie Story to the rink. I brought an article over to Mrs. Miles when going. I did not go to school today.

Wed. Jan. 15. I went to school today. It is very cold. I took no dinner with me today. It was very cold in school this morning but in the afternoon the sun shone and was tolerably comfortable. I did not go to the rink this evening but stayed at home. Mother went down to Mrs. Letts this afternoon. She did not get back until near eleven. I was going to go down for her but on looking over my "time-table" I found I had not time enough so I did not go. I got a letter at the door for Father. I gave it to him.

Sat. Jan. 18. This morning I went to get my photograph at Topley's. They said to come at 12:30. Which I did. I got my photos taken after waiting some time. I went with Knox at tea time to Stewarton. After tea Knox and I adjourned to his workhouse. We fiddled away at the clock for a good while. I went home before ten, Knox coming with me to the corner of Stewarton. I bought a pie. Knox was at the house before we went up. I got my Scrap Book today. I gave Willie Story his Bill that I got for him in school.

Mon. Jan. 20. At school today I bargained with a couple of fellows to take a couple of histories from me. I got them at Henderson's at 25 cents a piece. I went with Mother to Topley's. I went for my proofs which I got. There were four of them. In the evening Knox called for me to go and skate. We went and skated for a while. After that I went home and studied my lessons some as there are some lessons not to

be prepared very quickly. Knox I think went to a party after that. Willie Story was at the rink.

Tues. Jan. 21. I gave the two books that I bought to the fellows who ordered them. Mr. Thorburn taught us Geometry today. I got the music from London which I sent for per order in the *Illustrated News*. Annie got her autograph Album from Allie this evening. He put in a very nice piece. I went with Willie Story and Wm. to the rink this evening but did not stay very long as I had to study. I got the Algebra and Grammar from Willie Story. I studied until the big hours.

Wed. Jan. 22. I tried to get a couple more of the *Brief Annals of History* at Durie's and Hope's but they had none. I brought my photograph proofs to Topleys. Mrs. Lett was here this afternoon. I had hard work trying to study my lessons. I went over to Mrs. Miles to tell Mother Miss May was here. I afterwards went home with Miss May. I asked Mother and Father could I stay home [from school]. They said no. I stayed up pretty late in the hopes of getting a reprieve but no—.

Some members of the Ottawa Bicycle Club, 1882, posed proudly with their pennyfarthings. To the left, bearing his medals, is Sidney Woodburn. Perhaps one of the others is Willie Lett, Sidney's best school friend who often rode and raced with him.

Thurs. Jan. 23. When I got home from school today you may depend I studied my Latin. Yesterday I asked to be excused from French and Latin. I was excused. I studied a good part of the evening and then went to bed. I was at the office after school. I got the *Illustrated News* and about 50 rulers to distribute in school. I also got a few pens and pencils. I went home somewhere about half past six o'clock. I hear that we are going to have a party tomorrow evening.

Fri. Jan. 24. I distributed the rulers in school today. I got through Latin pretty well. Shortly after I came home the ladies began to arrive. Mrs. Patterson, Lett, Barber, Flannigan, Grant, Shaw and Story. Misses Lett and Parnell and Messrs. Duffy, Grant, Hinton and Shaw were here. Willie did not go home this Friday as Mother asked him to stay. I tried one dance and as it was about the first time I guess I made a poor hand at it. I drove Birdie Barber and little Miss Flannigan home. After I drove the Letts home.

Tues. Feb. 4. I did not study my French for today expecting that Father would write a note saying that I was not to take French any more to Mr. Ami. But I was surprised to hear him answer "No" as I thought he had decided to let it stop. Mother had a good deal to say to Father about my stupidness etc. I resolved that I would go through French to please them and not be called a blockhead and so on. I got through in a kind of a way my French today.

Wed. Feb. 5. This afternoon, shortly after coming from school, I began at the first of the French Book and got over the lessons which the class had gone over this term. Willie told me how to pronounce the words. Willie and I studied very late. I think it must have been one o'clock when we got in to bed. After I came home from school I got some bread and cheese and took it easy for an hour or so and then proceeded to study.

Wed. Feb. 12. The Carnival is this evening, I thought I would not go unless Albert Hinton came. I thought he would not come but when I was in the kitchen after tea I heard his voice upstairs, so I came up and found that it was him. I asked him to do some factors for me. He did some of them. We went over to the rink, I paying ten cents for both of us. The Governor and Princess Louise were there. The Carnival was very good. William Story was a clown.

Thurs. Feb. 13. This evening I asked Willie Story would he come to the Opera House tonight as the play was "Uncle Tom's Cabin." He said that he had not the necessary clink but I quieted that by lending 25 cents to him to go. We went, the place was crowded but we managed to see pretty well. The little girl personating Eva acted very well. I liked her part the best. She was so natural. We returned home at once, of course. Today was the opening of Parliament but tomorrow will be the Grand Opening.

Students at Ottawa Collegiate Institute, 1890.

Sat. Feb. 15. I was up at the office today. This is the Great day up there, that is "pay-day." I helped a little up there. Isaac paid me my 1.50 which I lent him to pay his doctor's bill. After tea I went up street and went into Farr's Bookstore where I seen Mr. and Mrs. Bennett. I bought about 40 cents worth of valentines and pictures. Directly after tea I went to Bennet's and got some butter. I snowshoed it across the square [Cartier?] for to try how the "shoes" went.

Wed. Feb. 26. As usual I came home for dinner [from school] and escaped being late by a close shave. We got out pretty late—twenty minutes to one o'clock. It only gave us about 18 or 19 minutes to run across the "Square," eat my dinner and run back again. Mother was telling us that Mrs. Haney that used to live near by had got a fortune of $12,000,000 and she said also that the heiress had promised to pay off the debt of the Baptist Church.

* * * * *

Mon. Sept. 22. This morning I went up to the office and did not go to school. I stayed up there most of the day. This day begins Exhibition Week. The people who are entering their things for Exhibition are in a flurry to get their things out there. Father has a telephone connected with the grounds and his office. It is a "Bell Telephone" with the "Blake Transmitter." It is wonderful how clear sounds can be heard through it.

Mon. Sept. 29. This evening at near six o'clock Andrew and I went down to the boat for the purpose of meeting All. After waiting for some time the boat arrived and I got All. We had a hard work carrying his heavy trunk which is full of school books, etc., up the long stairs from the boat. Mr. Anderson of the Provincial Show was here tonight for tea and at the table there was quite an interesting chat on several scientific subjects such as the End of the World. I had a chat with Willie Story after tea.

Tues. Sept. 30. This is All's last day here for some time. We drove him down to the station shortly before 10 o'clock. Alexis Helmes came down, too, to see him off. When we got there we found Horace Pratt about to start off for the same place so that All will have company. While waiting in the train All showed me how to do a short and easy deduction. Alexis and I waited until the train started and then a farewell to All and turned our backs sorrowful that we would not meet again, at least for some time. There will be a good many changes before we meet again. I hope for the best. Time will tell.

HARRIETTE M.H. SMIRLE 1895-1898

Sometimes a line from an old song, a peculiar odor, or a distinctive taste will bring up in a flash the whole panorama of a phase of past life, and so by a sudden revelation, rather than by any defined process of thought, we are led back to some bygone experience. So it was that to-night at dinner as I broke a bun,—a plain, curranted, baker's bun,—when the first morsel touched my lips, some chain of memory suddenly awoke, and the laughing, chatting crowd of College girls faded away as by a magician's spell, and I found myself sitting on the top rung of a ladder at the head of the basement steps of the "Ottawa Collegiate," eating what we girls called a "broughten lunch." A sordid boarding-house bun was the medium which brought back my old Collegiate days, and vitalized and made real to me a past which was growing more or less vague.

It is not always wise to stir the placid pools of school memories of an enthusiastic O.C.I. girl—there is so much that demands attention, so many things always were happening at that famous "Collegiate?" It is a platitude to speak of our school-days as the happiest time of our life—everyone knows it except the supposedly happy school-boy. He chafes at his bonds and looks on the future when he will be out in the great world, his own master. Then when this ideal is realized he longs for his bonds. Years have a way of lending a glory and glamor, we know, and yet the pleasant memories which are the heritage of every O.C.I. graduate whether of the "sixties" or the "nineties," are not fictitious. Life really was rich then, pulsing with wild thrills and joys and sorrows to me, a Collegiate girl in the early teens.

In looking back I find, strangely enough, that it is only the pleasant things that seem to remain. Things that I, in my youthful sorrow, or indignation, always thought would rankle and come up between me and my future happiness, seem somehow to have disappeared, or have to be dragged out from very dusty corners of memory, and then (oh fickle human emotions!) not mourned over or railed at, but simply smiled at kindly, as though one said, "Poor little girl." Writing extra lines, and getting no marks because you left out a minus sign, were however, very real sorrows then.

In the first weeks of our Collegiate life our horizon suddenly widens. How learned one feels when a new teacher comes in for every class, and how we go home and talk patronizingly to our chums, who are public-school girls, and regale them soon with spicy scraps of class-gossip. A large part of the glory lies in referring to our new teachers familiarly by their first names, or nick-names.

The years in the Lower Forms were always full of interest,—it was the transition period, when the new scholars were being adjusted to the new life. There were some very funny individual instances of adjustment; many times the conflict waged hot between specially obstreperous youths and specially young or excitable masters. Lower C every year gave a famous picnic to Kingsmere, generally on an impossibly cold day. It was a glorious occasion calculated to thrill the most blasé Third Former. I seem to see us yet, an eager, expectant group, standing amid our baskets at the rendezvous in the chill of the morning awaiting a full muster of the crowd, each anxious to sit near the teachers in the bus, to see what they were like when they were *men*, not *teachers*, and later marvelling that they ate such solid things as sandwiches, that they could spread table cloths, and climb mountains like ordinary human beings. And then in the purple of the evening coming home while the sun was sinking behind Kingsmere, quiet but happy; perhaps joining in the snatches of picnic choruses, or sitting apart wondering how life would be supportable when there would be no more Kingsmere picnics! Time adjusts even such serious problems as that.

I shall never forget the day that Lord Aberdeen visited the Collegiate for the first time. Lower C was warned to "show up well," which meant, to the girls, to have their smooth braids transformed into kinky masses of tangle. A school-girl's way of expressing herself is always through her back hair. Her attitude towards life may there be read as in a book. Whether it was because of the external or internal fittings of my head I don't know, but I thought equal to the strain of sustaining the Form's honor on the fifth proposition in Euclid, which was the one selected for exhibition purposes. I had three or four carefully chosen relays, who were to expect occasional questions to show their familiarity with the work, and to enhance my position. Of course all of this was impromptu—the proposition was to fall on us, the next day, in the nature of a surprise. We were well armed for that "surprise." When His Excellency came he smiled reassuringly at our tense, though apparently indifferent, faces. "How many know the *Pons Assinorum*?" was his first question. Things were coming right our way; Mr. Wallace smilingly brushed off the board,—anticipating, with labored carelessness our hands went up—mine and the relays with more vigor and determination as befitting our position. This was my supreme moment. Then the blow fell. "Oh indeed, all of you I see, you find it easy. I did too when I was at Eton. 'Ass's Bridge' is a misnomer!" and he proceeded to ask a few elementary questions, and left for the higher Forms. The memory rankled long after the kink was out of my hair.

All the teachers hold their own peculiar places in our hearts, even those whom we systematically plagued. The general idea was that new teachers were meant to be harassed, and it was the place of the Lower Forms to do this. It was a duty they seldom shirked. I could shake my little old self when I think how unmanageable and capricious we were, and how we thought it a grand "score" when we got a teacher angry and off his dignity. This, however, did not often occur.

Of all the happy hours spent in the Lyceum I shall not pause to speak. The society besides being a rare intellectual stimulus, gave us a bright shining hour at the fag end of the week. My experiences as an impromptu speaker and debater are as real to me as though it were yesterday. How unnatural, how foreign seemed to me my arms and feet,

how strange the sound of my voice! How far, far off was my sheltering seat—the ceiling was as the vault of heaven. The faces of my listening friends seemed like phantoms in a dream, relentless, diabolical as judges of the Inquisition; one is seldom called upon to face a more trying audience than a crowd of school-chums. Some day I hope to forget it all—but the time is not yet. However, I learned a self-discipline on those Friday afternoons that stood me in good stead throughout my college course, and will help even more in the world outside.

The last day came,—it takes a girl, a school-girl, to realize the significance of a "last day." I and my three good chums, who had "wrought, and thought, and toiled" together for five years, were well armed for the occasion. All week we would remind each other, in tragic tones, "Girls think of it! A week from today—!" Imagination failed. In the solemnities of a deduction it would dawn on us—"This is the last time I'll ever have to bother with the triangle A B C." We felt sorry for the triangle A B C. At lunch on the old ladder we'd wonder who would sit there next year, we'd run after the much-enduring, ever-obliging janitor to tell him he wouldn't have long to be kind to us. (His fortitude under the blow was truly marvellous.) We even made a business of carving our names surreptitiously on forbidden surfaces, so that the generations to come would look at them, and wonder and say things, we could afford to indulge this sentiment for we would soon be beyond Collegiate jurisdiction, and someone else would have to sandpaper those scratches. We arranged affecting farewell scenes with our particular desks and cloak-room pages; and if a teacher reproved us we looked at him sorrowfully, forgivingly,—he would be sorry when he wouldn't have us to scold. We felt badly for the old O.C.I.—it was suffering an irreparable loss. Things would never be the same again. But when the actual day did come, amidst all the hustle and prosiness of commencement exercises we quiet forgot our part. The teachers wished us good-bye and hoped we'd be back—which was well meant but unfortunate, considering that only failure at the departmentals would restore us to our old haunts. I did indeed allow myself one lingering look at the Fourth Form room, the arena of so many triumphs and defeats, one last glance at the all too familiar round face of the Form clock,—then forth from the shelter of academic halls into the great outside world. I rejoiced in my new freedom, but even then with a strange premonition that "unchartered freedom tires," a feeling that I should sometime wish for the old O.C.I. days again. In a dim way I realized that I had learned from the character and training of my teachers, something more fundamental, more abiding than the knowledge of cube roots and words. Since then I know that he is a wise scholar, and will be an important force for good in this world-struggle, who takes to heart *all* the lessons taught at the O.C.I.

Long after we got forth, we graduates look to our master and friend, Mr. Macmillan, with the old childish awe and respect

A group of "Old Boys" at Reunion, 1903. Again the names are not documented but we can make a good guess that this is a distinguished group of Lisgar Alumni returning to early fields of glory. We do know that of the twenty-nine speakers on the platform for that occasion a number of "old boys" were called upon including; Dr. George Kennedy, Andrew Holland, City Auditor Cluff, J. Bishop, School Inspector Robert H. Cowley, Alderman Chas. Hopewell, Percy C. Ryan, Sam McDougall, Sir James Grant, the renowned physician, J. Lorn McDougall, Jr., Hamnet Hill, Carden Cousens, paleontologist Henry M. Ami.

for a character in which we saw no weakness, mingled with a maturer admiration for one whom we know to have been always in the cause of right, "zealous, beneficent, firm." The standard he held before his students was high; he implanted ideals which must always remain with us, whether or not they blossom forth in achievement. Even yet we think of him as one whose "well done!" we would like to have. Influence has a beginning but no end,—

> "And yet the old schooling sticks, the old grave eyes
> Are peeping o'er my shoulder as I work.
> The head shakes still."

And so we pass, and new faces come to the halls to feel the old thrills and heart-throbs which are the heritage of every undergraduate,—and they, too, pass. And sometimes we grow retrospective, and look back and see the long years of student-life aglow with all the glory memory lends, and we say, "Happy school days!" They gleam behind,—those shining hours, and we long for the time when we wore our hair in a meek braid behind, when life's only problems were to be found between the covers of an algebra.

J. LORN McDOUGALL, JR. 1885-1890

In our day the front of the school stood back from Lisgar street and a long flight of wooden steps started in the middle of a small shrubbery of lilacs and other bushes, all growing according to their own sweet will. This of course was the entrance for the teachers. We ducked through a little gate in the close board fence which surrounded the boys' play-ground. Inside the building a fine air of antiquity prevailed, although in reality it was then only about ten years old. Though very different from to-day we did not quarrel with our lot. The stairs to the basement might be as dark as the entrance to Avernus, but to us also the descent was easy as we flung ourselves boldly down on our way to the open air.

During the first two or three years of this period and for several years previous, the basement had its season of excitement recurring at the beginning of the half-year, when the old boys initiated or "bounced," as it was humorously miscalled, the new boys. While it lasted, every noon hour a reception committee waited there for the new-comers,

J.E. Wallace, teacher of junior mathematics, was obviously a man for extra-curricular activities. This photograph of a happy group of O.C.I. students was taken at his annual picnic, 1897.

and as they came in, one by one, received them with open arms and escorted them across to what was known as the bell-room, where they were introduced to the bell-rope in a manner more striking than pleasant. As may readily be imagined these initiations did not take place without vigorous objections on the part of the victims. Many a gallant fight was put up by stout-hearted freshies with their backs against the wall and their fists pounding every face within reach; nevertheless the new boy who escaped was a rarity.

One year an unusually strong and numerous lot of new boys appeared. After a week of great excitement and hard work they had all been "bounced" strictly according to custom. But by this time the new boys had become well acquainted with one another and heartily fell in with the delights of bouncing the other fellow. They determined to reverse matters and started in one morning to bounce the old boys. The previous excitement was nothing to that which now arose. The old students were up to all the tricks. They realized full well, that the bell-rope wielded by a strong and revengeful new boy, was to be respected and even dreaded. They all fought desperately. Struggle after struggle took place in the old basement but, one after another the old boys were forced into the bell-room and put through the initiatory process once again. There is, of course, no doubt that the new boys would have hardly been successful had it not been that each old boy, as he was bounced, no matter how hard his struggles before, immediately joined in with the bouncers and assisted them in securing their next victim. Finally it came about that every one in the school was bounced except three. Two of these were noted for their strength, the third for his dignity. One of the strong men,

now a minister and resident of Pincher Creek, Northwest Territories, then a foot-ball scrimmager, was overcome by guile. He had been asked to assist at a bouncing accomplished with apparently extreme difficulty, when to his amazement, once over the threshold of the fatal chamber, the crowd dropped the supposed victim and fell on him. Having surprised him into entering the room there was no great difficulty in putting him through the required procedure. The man of dignity was the next proposition. He was in the old Fourth Form and as an Upper School boy had the right of going up to the rooms without waiting for the opening bell. He never lingered a moment in the basement and held no conversation with any Lower School boy. To even approach him was to take a liberty, but the school determined to intrude upon him in a body after they were dismissed. At half-past three there was a full attendance in the basement. The man of dignity came, he was bounced. Asked for a speech he got as far as "Who was the instigator of this dastardly outrage?" Whereupon the crowd collapsed and disappeared as one man. The third of the trio, now a physician in the city, has still a bouncing—and a good one—coming to him. How it was that he escaped, I have forgotten.

During this period there existed a marked distinction between the Upper and Lower School. The former possessed certain privileges, insignificant in themselves, but creating a decided feeling of dignity and responsibility. The latter, on the contrary, with its crowded forms afforded to an enterprising boy a field of amusement unequalled in the city. Every year one or other unfortunate new master spent most of his time trying to preserve order amongst the bandits who held down the back seats in the Upper and Lower First. There, in the modest retirement of the back rows, dime novels were read, marbles stolen from despised Model School kids, rolled mysteriously frontward, lines were written for presentation to masters kind enough to request fifty autograph copies of "The curfew tolls the knell of parting day," pens tastefully adorned with paper wings came sailing up, to land in the wall over the master's head, or, better luck still, in the heads of the studious good boys in the front seats.

The grand triumph, however, of the Lower School of those days came about thus. One of its most energetic and popular members upon his return, after an unexpected absence of a couple of days to attend the funeral of his great-grandmother's cousin (so his excuse read), and, incidentally, the interesting seances of a visiting ventriloquist, announced that he had become initiated into the magician's secrets and was prepared to demonstrate to the whole Form that he could throw his own voice anywhere. It required only a little persuasion to induce him to promise to make an experiment that afternoon. He was to occupy a back seat and wail like

a cat, sending the sound under the master's desk. When school opened in the afternoon the class was crowded, although the seats immediately surrounding the talented ventriloquist had been vacated by weak-hearted persons of little faith, who feared to become involved in subsequent events. The master was busy at the board when a noise started from the back of the room, the like of which was never heard in the Collegiate before or since. The wail of all the cats on earth seemed concentrated in that sound. It went circling around the room and might, if it had been left alone, have eventually located under the master's desk, but, unfortunately for our fellow-scholar, before that could happen he was up before the desk being publicly rewarded for his effort—three on each hand—with a promise of more to follow if it should occur again. Ventriloquism dropped suddenly out of favor.

But the O.C.I. boys did at times some things seriously enough. We, who attended the old school last century, were ardent politicians. Back in 1886 we were discussing "Unrestricted Reciprocity," the "Ross Bible," and other questions which the expectant world waited open-mouthed for us to settle.

A Gay Nineties photograph of the girls of O.C.I. posed in front of the school with the accoutrements of tennis and croquet. Their teacher is impressive in tailored suit and feathered hat, and it would appear that the junior girls wore a kind of uniform—middies and skirts—but that the older girls were free to choose their school dress.

These topics, strange as it may be, evoked more enthusiastic discussion than the time-honored question—"Resolved, that the orator owes more to his talents than to his training;" whose discussion runneth to the time when the Collegiate boy knoweth not to the contrary. Finally, after all our discussion, the edict went forth from the Head-Master's private room that we might have an election. P.C. Ryan, now a leading lawyer of Montreal, was the Liberal candidate; F.A. Magee, an ornament to the Ottawa bar, was the Conservative candidate. John McNichol, now a clergyman in Toronto, was the returning officer. All the struggle of an election took place during the fateful week. Red badges and blue badges were as plentiful as in the borough of Eatsanwill; and although we did not find it necessary to lock up voters in coach-houses, or place them under pumps, the interest was none the less keen. I remember one day, when, in an atmosphere surcharged with political electricity, the rival candidates addressed the discriminating electorate. The meeting was in the "Third Form" room.

I remember that to my youthful, and possibly biased mind,—does all the bias vanish with the earlier days of youth—the Liberal candidate seemed to have the best of the argument. It was in the lower forms that the canvassing was especially active; and every student appeared as a prospective political worker. But the long, active, speech-making week passed and the votes were cast; and we of the defeated party solaced ourselves with the thought that while it might appear to be

> "Right forever on the scaffold,
> Wrong forever on the throne;"

yet if we had another election the tide would turn. But our worthy Head-Master decided that we had had *foison* plenty of politics—and he wouldn't let the tide turn.

FIFTEEN MEMBERS OF THE LADIES' REUNION RECEPTION COMMITTEE, 1903.

Miss Helena de C. Topley, Mrs. Ide,

Miss M. A. Northwood, B.A., Miss B. M. Scott, Mrs. F. R. Latchford, Mrs. D. A. Campbell, (B.L.,)

Mrs. Fred Graves, Miss B. Barber,

Miss K. Waddell, Miss Mary Masson,

Miss I. Macmillan,

Miss. B. M. Thompson, Mrs. Doney

Mrs. Shotwell, (B.A.,)

Mrs. S. E. O'Brien.

(All are ex-Pupils of O. C. I.)

For what is readable in this sketch I am indebted to S.J. McLean, Professor of Political Economy in Leland Stanford University, California, and J.G. Gibson, of this city, barrister. The rest I wrote myself.

MORRIS MCDOUGALL 1894-1899

Morris McDougall was one of a clan of five McDougalls who attended Lisgar about the turn of the century and went on to university. He received his B.A. at University of Toronto, 1903.

When one tries to light up the picture of the O.C.I. in the Nineties with the pale and ineffectual candle of memory, one finds how deep and impenetrable are the shadows. Still, some figures, events, and impressions take form in the flickering light. These were the days, just following the death of Sir John A. Macdonald, when a number of premiers passed across the stage on Parliament Hill; when Laurier first became Premier; when a Canadian contingent, including militiamen from Ottawa, went to England to take part in the Diamond Jubilee of Queen Victoria; when a young Lancer by the name of Winston Churchill joined in a charge against the forces of the Mahdi at Omdurman in the Soudan; and when Americans began a war with the Spanish with the slogan "Remember the Maine." It was before the first roll of drums was heard from South Africa, and before the first horseless carriage made its appearance on the dusty, semi-macadamized roads of the Capital. I am speaking of a period from the fall of '94 to the spring of '99.

Do not imagine that the students of the O.C.I. about fifty years ago did not take a lively interest in politics and at least a passable interest in world events. I well remember the heated arguments in the classroom over the election of '96 when Laurier gained power. As for world events, I can still hear the exhortation of that sage, benign pedagogue "Colonel" Stothers: "What's the use of my teaching you history when you won't even study the history of your own day? Read the papers." Someone had looked blankly at him—not myself, I believe, although I am not sure—when he posed a question on something that had just taken place. Contemporary history may not have been on the formal curriculum, but Mr. Stothers did his best to keep us abreast of the times, and I think he succeeded to some degree. We looked on Queen Victoria, of course, as an imperishable institution. The empire would not be the empire, or indeed the world, without that august figure on the throne in London. I am afraid that when the battle of Omdurman took place, none of us knew of the existence of Winston Churchill. But don't hold that against us. This defect in our education has since been rectified.

We occupied the old small stone school, less than half the size of the present building. There was no driveway fronting the canal. Between the canal and the school was a fair-sized yard where we kicked around the football. One of my classmates could punt the ball over the school, quite a feat when you consider how much bigger and heavier the regulation ball was in those days when there was no forward passing. We drilled twice a week on Cartier Square, and also practised football team play there, with the hope that we might beat the Montreal High School, and perhaps might individually get a chance later on of playing with the Ottawa city team [afterwards the Rough Riders]. Our heroes were the stalwarts of the Ottawa and the Ottawa College football teams, of the Capital lacrosse and the Ottawa hockey teams.

As a school the "collegiate" did not shine in sports, although a number of the students became well known on the ice and gridiron after they graduated. There was plenty of skating after school hours at the rinks, as long as the ice lasted—this was before artificial ice—and for a time in the fall on the canal, although this was a dangerous pastime. I recollect seeing the final stage of a tragedy as we came out of the school door one afternoon. One of the students who had got out earlier had seen a commotion on the canal bank and, rushing over, had dived through a hole in the ice to attempt to rescue two little boys who had fallen in. He had brought them out but efforts to resuscitate them were unavailing. If there had been boy scout training in those days, it might have been different.

There was no skiing among the students. There were probably not more than twenty pairs of skis in Ottawa, and as far as I know, no student had a pair. One or two boys from the country came to the school on snowshoes. They were a hardy breed, those farm lads, and there were many of them who tramped the highways for five, six or more miles to the O.C.I., getting lifts of farmers' sleighs if they came along and if the farmers didn't use their whips to keep them off. By the end of the five years at the school, those boys were champion Marathon walkers.

And speaking still of the winter months, I recollect clearly that the lunch you brought in your schoolbag or overcoat pocket was frozen stiff as a board in the basement at noontime, for good old Mr. Nolan, excellent caretaker and full of Irish witticisms, never mastered the mystery of keeping the cellar warm. His energies were centred on keeping the schoolrooms habitable. Earmuffs were never worn by the student. They were considered a mark of effeminacy. It was much more manly to have red, pulpy ears which you had thawed out with snow in the schoolyard.

CHRISTINA J. MCEWEN 1898-1900

The course of study at the Collegiate Institute is necessarily severe. In order to compass the desideratum of passing the departmental examinations, the students must give themselves to their work. There are times when even brilliant students are afflicted with deepest melancholy regarding the outcome of their strenuous work. The basement is the usual place for bursts of grief and despair. Cheering words and the hearty (sometimes too hearty) clap on the shoulder are grand restoratives. Under the influence of these the despairing ones are pretty sure to experience a wave of courage, that makes them go on steadily again. Horace makes mention of minds being "purified by terror;" if that be so, then the scorpion whip of the exams, must prove a fine purifying agent.

In the Fourth Form, during the period of which I write, the pupils were from widely different strata. Some were from aristocratic homes surrounded by all the amenities that wealth and culture can bring; others were from humble abodes that knew somewhat of the pinchings of poverty. The O.C.I. is democratic and owns only the aristocracy of worth. All met here on a common footing. A bright agreeable lot they were, wise, fun-loving, charming girls and spirited manly boys.

Notification from McGill University of entrance to the 1860-61 session in Zoology and Botany for Lisgar graduate, Peter A. McDougall, one of the earliest of generations of his clan at the collegiate.

The atmosphere in our Form was varied as that of out-doors. There was the steady trade-wind of work, the gust of hilarity, the breeze of humor, the whirlwind of mischief. This last was followed usually by cyclonic denunciation from the master who happened to be in charge. If any irregularity in deportment occurred during a spare hour, *i.e.*, when the class or part of it was not occupied with any of the masters, the Principal dealt personally with the erring ones. On occasions a mistake in the identity of the mischief-makers occurred. Once, during a spare hour in the Fourth Form room, some one pushed a stem of a Union Jack into one of the girl's coil of hair. The Jack itself waved bravely above her head but far enough back not to be seen by her. She went on studying and forgot about it. Presently there was an explosion of laughter among the boys. The Principal came into the room, glanced quickly over the now suddenly silent, studious group, and bent a reproving frown upon the wearer of the flag. She returned his look so steadily and with such an expression of

injured innocence that he grasped the situation and went off with a smile of amusement in place of the frown.

On the second floor above the basement is the chemical laboratory, where we covered ourselves with pinafores, sulphuretted hydrogen, and glory. This last was when by many experiments we discovered the particular brand of *salt* that had been given us for investigation. We often failed in this and were as much at fault as the lady who asked to be set down at Epsom street when Rochelle was the one she wanted. So our salts were sometimes so mixed that we were in despair of ever being able to find them out. For this department of our work, the fine optimism of our Science Master created an atmosphere that kept us alive in spite of the obnoxious fumes from our test tubes.

The library is a room which the Fourth Form girls are not likely to forget. Clustered in groups about the table and in the window alcove, they spent the spare hours mostly at hard work. They indulged, however, in frequent brief digressions which were often more profitable than work. At these times they discussed problems of life and being. Hard thinking was done here, in fact much of our best work. Here, too, we had some of our best fun. Very rarely there was an excess of mischief. This last usually ended disastrously. One incident will doubtless be stamped on the memories of those who were present during the spare hour on which it occurred. It happened in this wise. One of the girls in madcap humor arrayed herself fantastically in the red, white and blue bunting that had been carefully folded away in one of the library drawers. She mounted the long library table and to the delight of the rest pirouetted from end to end in an improvised skirt dance. The fun was at its height, when the door was thrown open and there stood Mr. Macmillan. The scene was changed instantly to one in still life. Everybody "froze" for a space that seemed an age. Then somebody offered a hand to the danseuse. She dismounted from the table and with the aid of the others began to doff her draperies. Not a word was spoken. The situation was too awful for words. Later the culprit was summoned to an interview with the Principal, but what occurred never became generally known. However the skirt dance did not became a popular form of relaxation.

Toward the close of 1899 the Fourth Forms conceived the idea of having an "At Home" for the senior classes and for the students of the two previous years. The latter were attending the universities at Montreal, Kingston, and Toronto, or had gone to take charge of country schools. The idea was, that the students and the teachers should have a re-union and social good time. The Principal was consulted. He favored the plan and the committees went to work with a will to prepare for the entertainment of their expected guests. A topic promenade, refreshments and music were provided. The invitations were sent out and the first of the "At Homes," that have now become a feature of school life at the Collegiate, was held.

As to the recreations at the O.C.I., there was the Lyceum on Friday evenings during the winter term. Then there were the athletics for the boys. The girls were left for the most part to their own devices. They walked and talked together a great deal, often went for rambles after school. They visited churches and studied their architecture. Sometimes when the House of Commons was in session they went in a body to listen for an hour to debates. Occasionally they visited the Experimental Farm. They went to the National Art Gallery and discussed the pictures. They made excursions to Rideau and Chaudiere Falls and other points of interest within reasonable walking distance. Thus they laid up a store of delightful memories and gained the blessing of communion with the great "Outdoors" at the same time.

A pleasing device of the Fourth Formers, that helped to enliven the routine of studies was the celebration of the girls' birthdays. At the beginning of the term a register was made of all the birthdays that were to come on school days during the term. On these days the celebrant found her desk covered with boxes of candy, made by the donors, and with other gifts. The boys of the class participated in the celebration by helping to dispose of the candy, but they usually rose to the occasion and arranged that a box of cut flowers would be among the gifts. The flowers were arranged as a bouquet placed on the master's desk and enjoyed by the class for the rest of the day. Then they were placed in their box to be taken home by the recipient and treasured with the other gifts as evidences of the thoughtful kindness of her school-fellows.

Little mention has been made in this series of sketches, of the scholastic learning gained by the pupils, for after all what is the greatest thing that students here experience? Not what they cull painfully from books but whey they gain involuntarily from what their teachers and their school-fellows *are*.

PRESIDENTS OF THE LYCEUM

W. Walker	1884	C.C. Chitty	1890
J.F. Orde	1885	J.G. Gibson	1890
W.A. Graham	1885-86	H.H. Hurdman	1890
W. Hardie	1885-87	O.E. Culber	1890
J. May	1885	W.A. Scott	1890-91
H. Wilson	885	J.H. Lamonth	1891
W.A. Stewart	1885	F.B. Proctor	1891
Percy Ryan	1886-87	S.R. Tarr	1891
N. Ballantyne	1886	George Gilmore	1891
J. McNichol	1886	W.J. Macdonald	1891-92
F.A. Magee	1887-88	A.J. Kerr	1892
J.F. Johnson	1887	F. Scott	1892-93
W.J. Simpson	1887	W.F. Fitzgerald	1892
J.F. McGillivray	1887	W.H. Alexander	1892-94
C.N. Sparks	1887	A.W. Tanner	1892
R.J. Chisholm	1888	S. McDougall	1892
N.F. Connor	1888	A. McDougall	1895
W. Macoun	1888	E.W. Richards	1895
H.A. Howell	1888	C.F. Ballentyne	1895
J.F. Blyth	1888-89	R. Turley	1895
J.J. McLean	1888-90	G. McKinnon	1895
H.H. Horsey	1888	R.M. Stewart	1896
E.F.H. Cross	1889	C.K.P. Henry	1896
Geo. A. Lindsay	1889	A.F. Chamberlain	1896
G.L. Lamb	1889	Richard Kenny	1896
O.K. Gibson	1897	R. Timberlake	1900
G.K. Askwith	1897	M.O. Ardley	1900
T.A. Watterson	1897	Flossie M. Allan	1901
E.J. Carson	1897	R.J. Hand	1901
H.M.H. Smirle	1898	L. Tompkins	1901
W.D. Lowe	1898	A.H. Taylor	1901
C.I. Chubbuck	1898	Marion I. Whyte	1901
T.S. McMorran	1898	Geo. Fenton	1902
Morris McDougall	1899	L.B. Kingston	1902-03
A.G. Scott	1899	M.G. Odell	1903
Mac.B. Davidson	1899	J.R. Mills	1903
R.G. Pushman	1899	E.O. Jackson	1903
B.H. Thompson	1900		

THE "PHI, CHI, PSI"

Ottawa Collegiate, Rah! Rah! Rah!

"My, that sounds familiar," someone remarks; "Oh! I know now; that's our old school yell. Didn't we enjoy giving that yell ourselves when we were young!"

How often people are heard to say this, but how few know just when, how and why this familiar "yell" originated. In the *Vox Lycei* of January 18th, 1895, is found an editorial entitled—"The Why, How and What of an O.C.I. Yell," by W.H. Alexander, now professor of Classics in the university of Alberta. It seems there had been some dissatisfaction regarding school spirit in the O.C.I. and as there had been no improvement in spite of sundry hints and suggestions, the *Vox* Editor wrote an editorial in his paper to try to help matters.

As a foundation to work on, he advanced reasons why an O.C.I. yell should exist. First, he said, all organizations, large and small, had a distinctive shout. An institution as large as the O.C.I. might surely do as well as any "little razzle-dazzle, hobble-gobble hockey team." He quoted a celebrated English athlete to prove that a good yell, well given, aided the team as well as amusing the spectators. He then considered "how" an O.C.I. yell should be given. He showed how the call must be given in unison and with the greatest possible force. Also, that it must not be given on any trivial occasion, but must be kept for times of special rejoicing or need.

Having dispensed with two-thirds of his explanation, he attacked the "what of an O.C.I. yell." He suggested that contributions be received from the pupils, and as a start, submitted four samples. The fourth yell, was our well known "Phi, Chi, Psi," which is to be heard, lustily shouted, all the way from Ottawa to Montreal, whenever our teams go to contend in their many games.

This yell was accepted by the Athletic Association and the O.C.I. boys have taken the greatest of pleasure ever since from both shouting and hearing those stirring lines. In a letter received recently from Mr. Alexander, he accounts for the Greek words by the fact that he was making a special study of classics, but for those who know nothing of the great language, he adds that the words "Aeï Protos" can be translated by the expression "Always on the Top of the Heap." The O.C.I. is still able to honestly claim that elevated position and may she never see the day when she will be unable or unfit to claim that distinction.

The Collegiate takes this opportunity to thank Mr. Alexander for the yell that has helped so many foot-ball and basket-ball teams to success. Every ex-pupil of the O.C.I. in France, England or Canada, wherever he may be, is proud to be able to say he once yelled:

Phi, Chi, Psi,
Kappa, Lambda, Pi,
Aeï Protos,
Protos, Aeï.
O.C.I.
Hulla Balloo, Hulla Balloo,
Hulla Balloo, Bala.
Ottawa Collegiate,
Rah! Rah! Rah!

— *Vox Lycei*, Spring 1918

THE DIAMOND JUBILEE REUNION

On September 10 and 11, 1903, the first Reunion in connection with the Ottawa Collegiate Institute was held to commemorate the Diamond Jubilee of the founding of the school. The following account is reprinted from the *Ottawa Journal*:

Collegiate old boys representing almost every profession came from various Provinces of Canada, and from many States of the American Republic to attend the Re-union. Over sixty years ago the school was founded, and if there are any boys now left, who attended the first classes, they must be white-haired old men, whose ages are well nigh the Psalmist's utmost limit. The younger generation of scholars—those who attended the school before the fire—the boys of 1890 and of the eighties—were in evidence. Then there were the old girls, too.

The building was very prettily decorated. Flags were hung effectively in all the corridors, and festooned over the arches. Flowers, peculiar to the fall, were everywhere in abundance- - -Overhead, on the pillars and arches, more flags were draped. Down the halls on small stands were large vases of cut flowers, roses, asters, etc., and everywhere were palms gracefully spreading their stately branches. The Convocation Hall was likewise profusely decorated with flowers, bunting and Chinese lanterns. At the rear of the speaker's platform and hanging on the wall was a motto bearing the words "1843-1903."

About two o'clock in the afternoon the ex-pupils and old boys began to arrive in considerable numbers to register. Four books were available, but notwithstanding this fact many had to wait quite a while until their turn came. After registering they (each) were presented with a badge and invited to inspect the building. To many of them the present Collegiate Institute was entirely new and only by conjecture could they recall what the school was like when they had been pupils and what part of the building it formed now. Little groups of old boys, and lady ex-pupils, could be seen in various part of the building - - - some were telling amusing stories of youthful pranks, and others were speaking in voices low and respectful of some of their old class-mates who had already passed away. Not a few were endeavoring to place the old school and trying to locate the old rooms, the old stairs and where they used to be situated. Again all were casting watchful eyes over the newcomers in the hope of recalling the familiar face of an old class-mate, although not seldom names had been forgotten.

At 2.45 all present went out on the lawn and a group photograph was taken by Mr. S. J. Jarvis, himself an

Ottawa Collegiate Institute Reunion — Diamond Jubilee Group. — (by S. J. Jarvis.)

ex-pupil. At 3 o'clock an adjournment was made to the Convocation Hall, where the speeches were made. Fully 300 were present and it certainly was an inspiring audience, composed as it was principally of ladies. Judge MacTavish, the chairman, led to the platform an imposing array of speakers, some 29 in all, and he proceeded to warn them to not speak too long- - -

The conversazione held at the Collegiate Institute at 8 o'clock attracted a very large crowd and the building was crowded from top to bottom. Many more also registered last night, some having only come to the city on the evening trains while others because of work could not come in the afternoon. The ladies of the Reception Committee met the visitors at the door and gave them a charming welcome- - - Later in the evening in the Convocation Hall refreshments were served and a short hop later indulged in by those so inclined. The Guards Band was present for most of the evening and furnished music.

An interesting event of the evening was the presentation of a purse of some $30 to Mr. R.W. Nolan, the popular caretaker of the Institute for more than fifteen years and the friend of every Collegiate pupil during that time- - -

The following morning many of the visitors were given a trip around the city on the electric cars and in the evening tendered a banquet at the Russell House.

These three ladies were on the collegiate staff in 1903 when the Diamond Jubilee was celebrated.

Top; Elizabeth A. "Sis" Tomkins who taught Junior Mathematics and English 1902-1933. Far beyond her day in the reminiscences of ex-pupils, she remains one of the most memorable characters of the teaching staff.

Middle; Jessie M. Scott, a teacher of Junior English from 1892-1906. As was the custom in those days, Miss Scott resigned to be married but returned to Lisgar as Mrs. Lewis in 1924 to act as librarian until her retirement in 1939.

Bottom; Aletta E. Marty , M.A., Senior Modern Languages 1903-1919. In 1919 Miss Marty resigned to become Inspector of Secondary Schools for Ontario, a field then very rarely invaded by a woman. She died shortly afterwards on board ship returning from South Africa where she had been on an exchange of High School Inspectors. At Queen's University her brilliant career is commemorated in the Aletta E. Marty scholarship in English.

LISGAR *1893 to 1943*

Previous page:

Inset - Ottawa Valley lumber rafts below Parliament Hill,
Ottawa, at the turn of the century.

Background - Lisgar circa 1930s.

INTRODUCTION
THE SECOND FIFTY YEARS

By the time Lisgar Collegiate celebrated its fiftieth anniversary in 1893 momentous changes had occurred in the country as well as in the city that surrounded the old school and to which it was so closely linked.

Upper and Lower Canada had been united into the Province of Canada in 1841, two years before Dalhousie Grammar School was established. By 1848 some form of responsible government had been brought into effect but without representation by population. In 1855 Bytown with a citizenry of ten thousand became a city; two years later Queen Victoria chose it as the capital of what then constituted Canada: the provinces of Ontario and Quebec. Continued bitter opposition from Kingston, Montreal, and Quebec City—rival cities for the status of capital—delayed the construction of the Parliament buildings, but work finally was begun in December 1859 and finished in 1866.

Albert Edward, Prince of Wales, later King Edward Vll of England, had arrived in Canada in 1860 to lay the cornerstone for the nation's new Parliament buildings. On August 30, with the Prince on board, the newly renovated steamer *Phoenix* came opposite the Gatineau River where it was met by a fleet of river steamers "all gaily decorated and crowded with passengers who cheered wildly." Then, according to one historian, "One of the grandest sights ever witnessed appeared in view; one thousand two hundred rivermen and Indians in costume met the steamers and escorted the prince into the capital of Canada."

In 1867, by the British North America Act, the Province of Canada united with Nova Scotia and New Brunswick to become the Dominion, this nucleus expanding with the entry of Manitoba in 1870, British Columbia in 1871, and Prince Edward Island in 1873. By the time Alberta and Saskatchewan had joined the Dominion in 1905 one of the most transforming and cataclysmic centuries in the history of mankind was beginning to unfold, and faintly and far off in the distance was heard the atavistic rumblings of world wars destined to metastasize the flow of life on two continents.

Sir John A. Macdonald, Canada's legendary first Prime Minister, had died in Ottawa in 1891; forty years later civil servant Gordon Rogers—then shorthand assistant and private secretary to the Honourable Mr. John Carling—remembered attending the funeral from his residence to Cataraqui Cemetery in Kingston:

. . . I recalled the eleventh of June, 1891, when in Honourable John Carling's private car I had been one of a small company to attend the late Prime Minister's funeral. I remembered, too, that Fred Desjardins was in charge of that car. . .

I saw Sir John A. Macdonald in his private car in London [Ontario]—the Forest city—less than two months before his passing. . . . I remember how every loyal Conservative was to wear, every sixth of June to come—"Macdonald Day"—in his lapel a rose upon a maple leaf. That inspired idea lasted for a year or so. Perhaps some loyal Conservative of today may start up the short-lived practice.

In 1893, by the time Lisgar Collegiate celebrated the beginning of its second fifty-year period of pedagogical influence on Ottawa, the settlement at the junction of three rivers had changed from "a subarctic lumbering village" to a bustling parliamentary and civil service centre, the capital of a new country.

BRIEF ARCHITECTURAL HISTORY OF LISGAR COLLEGIATE INSTITUTE 1893-1908

1893

Destroyed by fire, January 1893.

Re-occupied December 1893.

1902

East wing added on.

1908

West wing added. Fourth floor added.

The great railway era had been ushered in, with many little privately owned rail lines competing furiously for the civil service travellers and the growing numbers of Canadian entrepreneurs. There was ambitious rivalry, for instance, between the St. Lawrence and Ottawa Railway (via Prescott) and the Brockville and Ottawa Railway (via Smith Falls), the advertisements of the St. Lawrence and Ottawa Railway guaranteeing passengers "Four Trains each way daily. Comfortable sofa cars at night and palace cars by day." In 1873 the Grand Trunk Railway promised an "acceleration of speed on all its trains" and that "from January 1873 onwards all its express trains would run from Montreal to Toronto in 13 hours."

As early as 1859 Pakenham's illustrious citizen, Andrew Dickson, had shocked a railway meeting by presenting his vision of a cross-Canada rail line from the east to the west coast. Judge Malloch, chairman, rushed from the meeting and implored Mrs. Dickson to "come and get your man. He has gone clean crazy and is talking of running a railway from the Atlantic to the Pacific. If you don't come and get him he will be talking about a railway to the moon."

On November 7, 1885, some seventeen years after Andrew Dickson's death, Sir Donald Smith, at Craigellachie in the Eagle Pass, drove the last spike in the transcontinental Canadian Pacific line, carrying in its timetable the stations at Carleton Place, Almonte, Arnprior, and, as Andrew Dickson had hoped, Pakenham.

Throughout Canada the latter half of the nineteenth century was infused with an enthrallment of royalty, nobility, prominent citizens, a deference to the upper classes à la English mode. But Ottawa especially was injected with high-society excitement as succeeding prime ministers and governors general, along with their socially conscious ladies and hostesses in residence at Earnscliffe and Rideau Hall, were filling social calendars with carnivals, skating parties, costume dances, soirées, fêtes musicales, curling bonspiels, and official receptions for visitors from around the world.

This semi-subservience in the presence of semi-royalty was expressed by Dean E.A. Howes of the University of Alberta, a former student at Ottawa Normal School, recalling in the *Citizen* his childhood in the Gay Nineties and some of the cultural events during his schooldays:

"How would you like to listen again to the cantata of Queen Esther? Of course I know that the present Mrs. F.A. Jones [wife of the principal] was one of the stars of that performance but I am speaking apart from that. Personally, I can never forget my feeling of importance when I, as head usher, escorted Their

Excellencies, Lord and Lady Aberdeen, to their seats. I remember wishing that my parents could see how their eldest son had come along."

And again, not without its air of subordination, William Hardy in a reminiscence of his days at the Ottawa Collegiate Institute (1890-95) relates a near-tragic incident involving a vice-regal visit from the Earl of Aberdeen, then Governor General:

His advent was warmly welcomed for we felt pretty sure, and we were not disappointed, that it meant a holiday. I shall never forget his inspection of the top class of the school in Latin. The members of that class were Thornton Bowles, W.B.H. Teakles, George Northwood and myself. First of all when the party, consisting of the earl and the countess and an aide-de-camp, arrived, there was some difficulty about seating them.

The room afforded three chairs, one a nice leather-seated affair, another a very passable creation, and a third which was "claudus altero pede," as the Latin grammar hath it, which being interpreted is, lame in one leg. The aide-de-camp refused any seat whatever, evidently not intending to stay long, and that helped matters out a little bit, but in the excitement which followed the arrival of the guests, the wrong shuffle was made, and when the cards were dealt, lo! Mr. Jolliffe [the teacher] had the leather-seated one, the countess the medium, while the unhappy governor was balanced precariously in the "siege parlous."

That aroused our humorous sense to begin with and when Mr. Jolliffe handed the governor a Virgil open at the fourth book, and said, "We begin, sir, at such and such a line— nox erat," and the earl replied in what we considered a very English accent, "Oh, yes, nox erat." It was too much for Northwood, who broke loose with a regular snort in which we all joined in varying degrees.

Then when the aide-de-camp was offered a Virgil, he, though a gallant soldier, turned visibly pale and cried, "Oh, bless me, no! I never could stand a Latin book." But notwithstanding all these incidents the recitation passed off very well indeed. I might add as I have already hinted, that we got our expected holiday and enjoyed it immensely as the skating was good.

For the working masses there were fairs, exhibitions, travelling circuses, winter carnivals, political gatherings— events in which, if they could not participate, they certainly could play a spectator part, as in the O'Connell Centennial in Major's Hill Park on August 6, 1875, when the Irish of Ottawa—all 8,021 of them, the largest racial segment of Ottawa's population at that time—celebrated the hundredth anniversary of the birth of Daniel O'Connell, the great Irish "Liberator" in the long struggle for Catholic emancipation.

A public holiday had been proclaimed by Major W.H. Waller, president of St. Patrick's Literary Society. The St. Lawrence and Ottawa Railway, the Canada Central, and the palatial river steamers all ran crowded excursions to the city. Three Irish societies, including the Irish Catholic Temperance Society, organized the event. A great Irish scholar, Reverend Dr. O'Reilly of Dublin, and Reverend Father Stenson, parish priest of Almonte, preached at nine o'clock in St. Patrick's Church. But the orator of the day was that outstanding Irish Canadian Parliamentarian, Nicholas Flood Davin, who swayed a packed audience in Gowan's Theatre on Albert Street. The big event was in the afternoon at Major's Hill Park, which was crowded with marquees and "democrat" wagons and two-wheeled carts. After the concert at Gowan's Theatre, the leading Irish of Canada held a banquet in the Rideau Club.

* * * * *

The nineteenth century was a time when, in a forthright manner, one "knew one's place" in the order of things. But by the turn of the century a new air was blowing through the land and one might climb the social ladder through individual achievements; for example, Thomas Ahearn, J.R. Booth, Daniel McLachlin, and David Gillies all had humble beginnings, indeed, but their entrepreneurial successes and subsequent wealth made a place for their descendants in the upper echelons of Ottawa society.

As well, urban sophistication had come to the city with the formation of two exclusive men's clubs, the Rideau and its contemporary, the Ottawa Club which was organized for the city's elite who could not afford the expensive membership of the Rideau. Nevertheless the charter membership list was impressive and included names that since then have echoed down through Ottawa society in the civil service, the military, the professions, and the business life of the city: Armstrong, Billings, Burritt, Blanchet, Code, Colson, Cross, Devlin, Edwards, Egan, Fisher, French, Fripp, Germain, Guy, Henderson, Hurdman, Jarvis, Kidd, Lindsay, McConnell, McKay, Nettle, Panet, Poupore, Powell, Ross, Russell, Smith, St. Jacques, Tachereau, Todd, Tyrell.

Amongst the rules for the Ottawa Club were: no dogs, no smoking in the Reading or Dining rooms, no tipping, "no talking amongst the servants while on duty." It lasted for only a few years, while the Rideau Club continues its elitist stance to this day.

The Gay Nineties—and the decade before and after— were characterized by a hectic flurry of social events, dramatic, operatic, musical, terpsichorean, athletic.

The society columns of both the *Citizen* and the *Journal* described these events cursorily for the less fortunate layers of Ottawa society. On March 20, 1893, the *Citizen* recorded a cross-sectional list of events:

Thursday evening the great attraction at the Opera House was "Grossmith." The house was packed, and with the exception of the galleries, evening dress was the rule all over. The curtain fell a little after ten o'clock, and the guests who were invited to the reception at Government House went right down there for a few hours more of pleasure, which His Excellency so thoughtfully provides for them every week. Grossmith also proceeded to Rideau Hall after his performance, to tread the social stage for a while.

The most exciting event on Friday of this week was the hockey match, between Quebec and Ottawa, in the Rideau rink, the home boys scoring 14 goals to nothing. The excitement was intense amongst the large gathering of spectators, among whom were noticed: Mr. and Mrs. Fred White, Mr. and Mrs. Palmer, Miss Burrows, Miss Taylor, Mr. and Mrs. Lemoine, Miss Mackey, Mr. and Mrs. S.H. Fleming, Mr. W.A. Allan, Mrs. Crombie, Mr. and Mrs. L.K. Jones, Mr. and Mrs. Sydney Smith, Mr. Newby and others.

On Monday, March 13th, Mrs. Clayton, Daly Avenue, gave an afternoon tea to about thirty people. The same evening, Mr. and Mrs. Wilson, of the Montreal Road, gave a dance at their residence to a large number of guests. On that evening, too, the Literary and Scientific Club met at Miss Gwynne's, Metcalfe Street, and a very enjoyable evening was spent. Recitations were part of the program as usual, and music and song contributed their quota to the entertainment.

The final match for the silver medal presented by Mr. William Hutchison for competition by the members of the Governor General's Curling Club, took place in the presence of a large number of spectators, including Lord Stanley. It resulted in a victory for Mr. H.F. Sims who defeated his opponent, Lieutenant Colonel Irwin, by one point. The match throughout was keenly contested and brought out some excellent play by both parties. The ice was in very good condition, considering the lateness of the season.

Resident Gordon Rogers, writing in the *Citizen* in 1938, recalled some of the shows he had seen in the Gay Nineties:

Back in '89 Big Bill Nye and little James Whitcomb Riley made a first appearance in Ottawa in the old Albert Hall on Albert Street, next to the Grand Opera House. Roberts wrote: "At ten o'clock Nye pulled out a watch in his slow way, and said something about his mother not letting him stay out late—which was not funny as the seats were fancy prices."

Riley was easily the favorite—the best—and an evangelist who meant business, with a dash of the "drummer." He wore glasses, had large blazing blue eyes (like Hon. Andrew. G. Blair's) and a quite large Romanesque nose. I had the honour of a twenty-minute walk and talk with him; asked him how he liked Colonol [sic] John Hay's "Pike Country Ballads." He said he liked 'em alright but didn't like swear words in poetry. . .

Mr. Rogers described another theatrical event of his times:

I recall the time when Ab Heney pulled a funny one in histrionics. It was at the old Russell Theatre. The piece was a tragic one, of about thirty minutes, called "Rosalie," played as a finisher of the evening. Miss Edna Thomas, Ab Heney and Harry Sproule comprised the cast.

Just before the final curtain rolled down, Ab had to lift his chapeau and say "bonjour" or words to that effect. In lifting his chapeau, he also lifted a wig, good and clear, and all unconscious of the good measure he was handing the house. He got what he hadn't expected—a whale of a laugh; particularly from the gods; who from their Olympian elevation had a better view of the "tragedy" of Ab's misadventure. . . Having a bald head myself, I failed to join in the Gargantuan laughter. . .

At a time when live entertainment of all kinds was the rage, the Rogers seem to have been avid theatre-goers, for Mrs. Rogers, also reminiscing in the *Citizen*, recalled some highlights of her experiences, including the recitation by Miss Gertrude MacIntosh (daughter of the late Honourable Charles H. MacIntosh) of "The Curfew Shall Not Ring Tonight": "Standing near the footlights (which were candles behind tin) she would swing out gracefully toward the audience in the business of ringing a bell. Later I heard Pauline Johnson recite 'The Song My Paddle Sings' with the graceful rhythmic movement of a single-blading stroke." Mrs. Rogers remembered when De Wolf Hopper in *Wang* looked as though he were "in the flies" when, atop what looked like a good-sized real elephant (and maybe was), he rode onto the stage at Ferguson's Grand Opera House on Albert Street.

* * * * *

By the time Lisgar had reached the second fifty-year period of its history (1893-1943), Ottawa had become the Sporting Town, sustaining a fierce rivalry with Toronto, which had engendered the unflattering epithet "Hogtown." Citizens of the Capital City were enriched not only by a lively and diversified theatre but also by a multiplicity of leagues and athletic clubs and a phenomenally extensive variety of sporting competitions and activities, including snowshoeing, lacrosse, skating and speed skating, skiing, bicycling, soccer, football, polo, cricket, baseball, basketball, roller skating, roller polo, track and field, fish and game, riding to the hounds at the Hunt Club, boxing and wrestling, ski-jumping at Rockcliffe Park, horse racing at Connaught Park in Aylmer, golf played on early Aylmer golf courses.

In the nineteenth century, baseball had been an almost universally participatory sport, but by the turn of the century it began to be replaced by sports like skiing, football, and golf, which required more expensive equipment, thus excluding the masses. Often the new sports also necessitated expensive club memberships. For a number of reasons, including a great increase in population, sporting activities became less participatory and amateur, more spectator and professional. Obviously, Lisgar was to be influenced by these shifts as different games and sports lost and gained in popularity.

In February 1886 Ottawa City Council records showed that "The Frontenac Snowshoe Club of Ottawa asked the city for $150 to aid them in entertaining one thousand snowshoers from Quebec City." They got the money and the *Citizen* reported that "the meet was a great success." But by 1900 Lisgar's Snowshoe Club, one of its first clubs, had disappeared from the roster of extra-curricular activities listed in the *Vox Lycei*.

By 1904-05 the Ottawa Silver Seven Hockey Club had put Ottawa on the map by winning three Stanley Cups, a trophy originated by Lord Stanley of Preston, Governor General of Canada from 1889 to 1893.

In 1909 the *Citizen* reported that "Ottawa's sporting cup was full to the brim." It listed the championships of that peak year: *Rugby*—Interprovincial League Championship, Ottawa Rough Riders. *Hockey*—Stanley Cup, World's Championship, Ottawa Hockey Club; Interprovincial League Championship, Cliffside Hockey Club. *Paddling*—Mile war canoe, senior singles, intermediate singles, all held by the New Edinburgh Canoe Club. *Trap-shooting*—Eight-man team championship of Canada and amateur singles championship of Canada held by St. Hubert's Gun Club. *Rowing*—Senior four championship of America, senior four championship of Canada, intermediate 140-lb four championship of Canada all held by Ottawa Rowing Club. *Swimming*—50-yard championship of Canada and 100-yard championship of Canada held by Gordon Johnstone, Ottawa Canoe Club. *Tennis*—Singles championship of Canada, doubles championship of Canada: Captain J.F. Foulkes held the former and Captain Foulkes and Mr. R.S. Raby the latter. *Soccer*—Soccer championship of Ontario and Quebec held by Ottawa Soccer Team. *Lawn Bowling*—Toronto Trophy at Niagara-on-the-Lake won by R.R. Farrow's team of Civil Service League. *Putting the Shot*—Dominion

C.A.A.U. championship held by Detective Mortimer Culver. *Rifle Shooting*—Dominion Rifle Association, Grand and Bisley Aggregates won by Sergeant G.W. Russell, G.G.F.G., with record scores. Daily Graphic Cup won at Bisley by Sergeant W.A. Smith, G.G.F.G. Duke of Cornwall's Cup won by Private A. Wilson, 43rd D.C.O.R., at O.R.A. meeting, Toronto. Cadet championship of Canada won at D.R.A. meeting by Sergeant Norman Retallack, Ottawa Collegiate Institute Cadets.

Compared to baseball, which is supposed to have originated in Cooperstown, New York, in 1839, basketball was a relatively new sport in North America at the turn of the century. It was invented by a Canadian, a Lisgar graduate, Dr. James A. Naismith of Almonte, Ontario, in 1891 while he was physical director of the International YMCA Training School in Springfield, Massachusetts. A medical graduate of McGill University, Dr. Naismith was asked to design a competitive game that could be played indoors, have simple rules, be beneficial to people of all ages, not require expensive equipment, and avoid rough play. Games were first played with peach baskets hung overhead. Millions of participants all over the world play basketball today. As football faded out at high schools like Lisgar, basketball became the game of choice.

* * * * *

An inhibited period of history despite its name, the Gay Nineties were marked by inhibitory clothing: women were restricted by laced corsets, big bustles, layers of skirts and petticoats, huge hats, high-button boots; men wore celluloid collars, starched shirts and cufflinks, skin-tight trousers, formal jackets, Derby hats.

Just as the old-timers would have us believe, the climate appears to have been indubitably colder in winter in nineteenth-century Ottawa than it is now. When in the winter of 1892 the Ottawa River froze right up to the foot of Chaudière Falls, Captain W.T. Lawless, one of Ottawa's great renaissance or decathalon sportsmen, snowshoed right up to the foot of the falls.

Only the wealthier were swathed in fur coats, but most people could afford to keep their heads warm with fur hats—Persian lamb, mink, otter, seal, astrakhan, plucked beaver—ranging in price from eight to fifteen dollars. There were all kinds of imitation furs for those of lower income. Wool wristbands, knitted by one's mother, sister, or sweetheart, were almost universal and were worn in accordance with the theory that "if your wrists were warm you kept your whole body warm."

One of the most talked-about and unorthodox businessmen in Ottawa, furrier R.J. Devlin, predicted a great storm for November 27, 1882, and exhorted the good buyers of the city to get ready for it with some of his winter apparel, particularly his fur coats and fur hats. He advertised this storm in several editions of the *Citizen*, reminding the public of his prediction.

The morning of November 27 broke warm, even sultry. But then about eleven-thirty in the morning there was a sharp change in the wind out of the northwest. It began to snow. It snowed for three days. When it was all over, eastern Canada had lived through the greatest snowstorm in its history and R.J. Devlin had set records in his business.

Before the days of the Better Business Bureau and other watchdogs of business practices, in true Sam Slick style, Yankees were playing some queer tricks on the gullible and slow-moving Canucks of Ontario and Quebec, shipping "wooden nutmegs" and "Basswood cheese" to less canny buyers across the border.

In the *Citizen* of 1930 Albert Moore told how his uncle, lumberman David Moore, in the 1860s bought a "smart-looking United States manufactured buggy" in Ottawa. During the first trip from the Moore homestead in Tetreauville to Aylmer, the buggy fell apart. On examination, it was discovered that the ends of the spokes on the buggy wheels had not been cut into either the hub or the rims; they had merely been pressed and glued into place. The tires, instead of being made of iron, were made of leather, pressed on wood and ingeniously painted to look like rubber.

In the '80s and Gay Nineties before the turn of the century, Ottawa was inundated with a profusion of head-spinning new inventions: horse-drawn street railway cars, arc lighting, gas pipelines, electric lights, electric streetcars, telegraphy offices, telephones, new snow-cleaning equipment of amazing efficiency and manoeuvrability, flushing toilets, head-phone radios.

One of the men most responsible for all these modern changes in the city of Ottawa was Thomas Ahearn. Born in 1855 on Lebreton Flats, Ahearn began his career as a messenger boy for the Montreal Telegraph Company. In his spare time he learned telegraphy and became one of the fastest operators on the continent. He had risen to the position of local manager of Bell Telephone when he joined forces with W.Y. Soper to start an electrical business. One of their first installations was electric call bells in the Hull office of the giant E.B. Eddy Company in Hull.

The Ahearn and Soper Company branched out into taking contracts for Bell Telephone electrical work, forging the new lines between Pembroke, Ottawa, and Montreal, setting a record of thirty-three days from start to finish of the Ottawa-to-Montreal line. Ahearn's passion for inventiveness in electricity brought the first electric streetcars to the Capital City.

In addition to Thomas Ahearn and his genius for creating electrical devices and promoting the use of electricity, the Ottawa area seemed to have an impressive group of "minor mad inventors." A farmer named Beckett near L'Orignal invented a precursor of the snowmobile and hydroplane. The Ottawa *Citizen* of March 1939 gives a detailed account of how Beckett built his amazing boat, which "ran on land, water or ice." The *Citizen* commented further: "as a whole, the boat was a very clever contrivance, but it was not very practical as it had no speed and was not suited to carrying passengers. . . It certainly got a lot of advertising for him for miles up and down the [Ottawa] river."

Beckett had his big day in 1860 when the steamer *Phoenix*, carrying the Prince of Wales passed upriver to Ottawa and stopped for a few minutes at L'Orignal. Beckett paddled around the *Phoenix* in his amazing multi-use craft all freshly painted for royal eyes.

In the 1870s John Clancy of Ottawa was busily creating his flying machine, pre-dating the Wright Brothers in conception if not in reality. With the help of carpenter and cabinetmaker George Russell, and with funds from his own pockets, he built the lower part of the Clancy flying machine described "as the hydro-plane type." Clancy, however, failed to entice the people of Ottawa to invest in his invention. He left his flying machine lying in the Russell Boat House at the Canal Basin where it was found by Andrew Jones some years later when he bought the boathouse.

Looking at the uncompleted airplane one day, Mr. Jones got the idea of transforming it into a water bicycle. In due time and after some major alteration, he launched his water bike in the Canal Basin where it attracted considerable interest for a short while. Then it, too, disappeared from the scene and a few years later even Mr. Jones' boathouse was gone.

Out in Chesterville, one of the many satellite service centres for the huge rich farming community surrounding the capital, a new-fangled musical contraption called a Gramophone was hailed as "an evil thing" that would "demoralize the district."

At first the dangerous talking machine was available only in the United States, so Taddy Coyne of the Connaught Settlement a few miles out of Chesterville ordered one from Sears-Roebuck in Chicago. Mrs. Mary McDiarmid in a 1933 *Citizen* described the community reaction in the Gay Nineties when the amazing American machine arrived at the Coyne homestead:

When Thomas R. Coyne [her father-in-law] heard about it he was horrified to say the least. He wouldn't allow it near the house, because, he insisted, it was an evil thing, bound to bring bad luck to anybody who went within hearing distance of it. He cautioned me to stay away from it, saying: "Mary, do you know that Satan has horns?" Somebody had informed him that the talking machine had a long horn.

The very thought that a Coyne would bring such an "evil spirit" into the settlement—to demoralize the inhabitants—was really more than the old gentleman could stand. He told "Taddy" the reason he had to send to the United States for it was that no sane Canadian would handle such a dangerous instrument.

Nevertheless, the inhabitants got a great kick out of the machine. People came from miles around to "Taddy's" place to hear it, and he was constantly besieged with requests to exhibit it at entertainments in the schoolhouse and other places—which he did on innumerable occasions.

And some very fundamental and important new inventions had been imported into Ottawa as early as the 1850s, when it was still Bytown. James Brough, one of Ottawa's first dry-goods merchants, had "brought sanitary appliances from Scotland" which he had installed in his new building on Wellington near Kent. It had always been touted that the first "sanitary appliances" of a "more or less modern type" had been installed in the old Russell House Hotel in the 1860s. But in a *Citizen* article of April 1929 James Brough's son verified the earlier installation in the Brough residence and described the sanitary system: "In the cellar there was a large cistern from which water was collected from the roof. From the cistern, water was pumped by a force pump to a large tank in the attic. From the attic, the conveniences were fed by gravity. The bathroom had marble tiling and the wash basin and bath were of marble. From the house, the sewage was carried in a box-drain down Kent Street or 'somewhere.'"

* * * * *

In the last twenty-five years of the nineteenth century Lisgar Street between Elgin and The Driveway had become resplendent with major institutions of learning: the Ottawa Normal School, the Model School, and the new triple-storey Lisgar Collegiate, three durable stone and architecturally impressive buildings.

For a number of years prior to 1875 Dr. Egerton Ryerson, chief superintendent for education for Ontario, had urged upon the government the necessity to provide additional institutions for the training of public school teachers, and the desirability of having the educational system guided and controlled by a cabinet minister.

Ryerson had his way and, in 1875, on a site that was part of the By estate and then occupied by a squatter, the first unit of the Ottawa Normal School was erected at a cost of eighty thousand dollars. Candidates for First Class Certificates and for Second Class A and Second Class B Certificates were required to study reading, spelling, writing, etymology, grammar, composition, geography, arithmetic, mensuration, algebra, natural philosophy, physiology, Euclid, education, drawing, music, botany, school law, bookkeeping, and chemistry.

John A. MacCabe was the first principal of the Normal School. Dean E.A. Howes was a student under MacCabe in the 1890s, and in a 1935 article in the *Citizen* he recalled MacCabe and the code of conduct of his time:

I can still hear his stately platitudes, proverbs and prohibitions. I can hear him say, "There is a regulation, ladies and gentlemen, to the effect that you must be in your boarding-houses by 10 p.m. I trust you will honour this regulation."

In this connection [Howes continued], you will recall that we chalked up a nine on one side of the door at 125 Slater Street and a ten on the other side in order that we might truthfully say that we had come in "somewhere between nine and ten."

The Model School, which was part of the Normal School, was erected during the autumn of 1879 and occupied the following spring. One of the most appealing features of these private schools was the addition of special subjects not included in the curriculum of the public schools of the time: physical training or military drill (Sergeant E.B. Cope), drawing and writing (Martin Sparrow), music (W.G. Workman), conversational French (J.A. Guignard).

The first principal of the Model School, E.D. Parlow, developed and fostered a code of honour among the boys under him that became a tradition of the school. Firmly fixed and handed down from class to class during his twenty-two-year term, it was not difficult for his successors—Dr. J.H. Putman (later school inspector), Dr. F.A. Jones (later principal of the Normal School), Dr. C.E. Mark, H.L. Leppart, W.J. Neale, and E. Oakes—to maintain the code and possibly improve upon the high ideals that marked the first years of the Model School.

John C. Macpherson, once chief of the Industrial Statistics Branch of the Dominion Bureau of Statistics, was among the early students of the Ottawa Normal School. He attended the class of 1879 and, years later, recalled some of the amusing incidents of his student days there, incidents that illustrate how different from today were the attitudes, code of conduct, rules, and regulations of his time.

In contravention of one of Principal MacCabe's edicts, Macpherson and another young man called on two of their lady classmates at their boardinghouse. No sooner had they settled down for an evening's visit when a loud rap came at the door. Peeking out the window through the curtains, one of the young ladies saw Principal MacCabe at the door:

There followed the wildest scramble. My companion took a header out the nearest window, landed on a sloping roof, rolled to the hard ground ten or twelve feet below. I dived under the sofa and lay there without breathing. Meanwhile, the two young ladies spread out their dresses on the sofa, took up their knitting and called "come in." Principal MacCabe stayed an hour but never appeared "to tumble to" what was going on. My hour under the sofa without breathing seemed like an eternity.

Macpherson was not easily frustrated by the Victorian rules of his era. On another occasion with a friend and in company of a couple of the young women from the school, he was strolling along "lovers' walk"—again in contravention of MacCabe's rules—when who should chance upon them all but E.B. Cope, drill sergeant at the Normal School!

Macpherson recounted the ending to his adventure: "Cope told us he intended to squeal on us. But I fixed that. While my friend ran the girls home, I took Cope over to the Russell House Grill and bought him the finest oyster supper he had ever packed into him. That seemed to silence him and we all got off."

In contrast to the gentlemanly codes of conduct being instilled in the Model School boys, at St. Patrick's School on Nepean Street the old Ottawa Valley tradition of "recreational violence" was being maintained. From 1885 to 1888 James Walsh attended the school run by the Christian Brothers for both day students and boarders from the city and the Valley. He described some of the stirring events of his career at St. Pat's in the '80s:

St. Patrick's School was attended by boys who hailed from two sections of the city particularly noted for their pugilistic tendencies—Ashburnham Hill and Corktown. There certainly was no love lost between the two factions—and one of the rules in force at that time was that all the pupils at dismissal time in the afternoon were accompanied by guardians until they reached the corner of Kent and Nepean streets or the corner of Lyon and Nepean. This was supposed to guard against any after-school fisticuffs between the lads from Corktown and Ashburnham Hill.

But the boys easily found a way to outwit the guardians. As soon as they had left their charges at the corner of Kent and Nepean, the lads from Corktown would circle around the block where they would find the lads from Ashburnham Hill eagerly waiting for them right in front of Dunn's Plastering Works which had a huge yard—a great place for battle which would rage hammer and tongs until Ned or Jim Dunn came out and chased them home.

I well recall some of the boys who attended old St. Patrick's in those far-away days: Alf, Harry and Billy Smith [of the Seven Smith Brothers of hockey fame], Tom Mooney, Henry and George Higgerty, Walter Carney, Barney Mullen, Billy Binks, Jimmy Egan, Jimmy Enright, Charlie Neville, Jack Shea, Jack and Billy Codd, Patrick Murphy, Tom O'Meara,

Henry Dooley, Patrick and Peter McCabe, Frank Reddington, Jack Kenna, Charlie Watson, Jack White, the Mahoney boys from the Lebreton Flats and many others.

Ottawa Ladies College opened in 1872 on Albert Street. Evidently one of the gentler forms of amusement for the citizenry of Centretown and presumably young men in droves was to watch the "March of the Petticoat Soldiers" along Albert, Sparks, and Rideau streets as the girls were taken out by their teachers for daily exercise. Many years later Mrs. Robert Brown, daughter of Ottawa architect L.M. Mather, found in her scrapbook a poem composed by two Ladies College students and patterned after the "Charge of the Light Brigade."

"THE MARCH OF THE PETTICOAT SOLDIERS"

Half a year—half a year,
Half a year onward,
All in the O.L.C.
Lodged the Half Hundred;
"Forward the Bright Brigade,"
Our Guardian Angel Said,
Down to old Sparks street
Marched the Half Hundred.

Flourished their scarves so white,
Flashed all their eyes so bright;
Oh, how the fellows stared,
Each gent waits a while,
Hoping to catch a smile,
Then through the line they broke,
Oh, that's a killing joke!
And then they marched back,
Yes, all the Half Hundred!
Teachers to right of them,
Teachers to left of them,
Fellows in front of them,
Whistled and blundered.
Glanced at by beau and swell,
Boldly they marched and well,
Down by the Russell House,
Down by the First Hotel,
Marched the Half Hundred!
When can their glory fade,
After the show they made?
All the city wondered.
Honour the Bright Brigade,
Flirt with each pretty maid,
Jolly Half Hundred!

Ottawa, 1872

* * * * *

Up to 1897 the Public Works Department of the federal government had limited its scope to the buildings on Parliament Hill, the Governor General's Residence in New Edinburgh, the Post Office, the Supreme Court Building, the Geological Museum on Sussex, the Langevin

Block on Wellington, a few insignificant buildings at the Central Experimental Farm, and the Art Gallery (replaced in 1918 by the Hunter Building).

At the turn of the century Lisgar Collegiate was surrounded by the district of Centretown, an area filled with imposing and sometimes beautiful Victorian residences, with gardens and estate grounds, lived in by the hoi-polloi of Ottawa: judges, professionals, industrialists, businessmen, contractors, senior civil servants, embassy people, and yes—even a poet named Duncan Campbell Scott.

American writer Anson Gard in his book on Ottawa and the Valley, *The Hub and the Spokes*, gives detailed accounts, street by street, of the people of prominence and achievement who crowded into Centretown and sent their children to Lisgar. On Metcalfe Street, for instance, he lists many of national prominence:

Hon. Clifford Sifton, Minister of the Interior, and Superintendent-General of Indian Affairs; Hon. Wm.S. Fielding, Minister of Finance; R.L. Bordon, M.P., Leader of the Opposition; the Hon. Joseph I. Tarte, M.P.; Thomas Birkett, M.P.; D. Murphy, M.P.P.; C. Berkeley Powell, M.P.P.; Lady Richie and others. There are here the beautiful residences of many lumbermen, which is Ottawa's term for "millionaire." They don't speak of wealth as we do; they simply say: "He is a lumberman," and I know what they mean.

And again from *The Hub and the Spokes*:

Cartier Street from Lisgar—it starts at Lisgar—to Minto Park is one of the finest residential streets in Ottawa. Here we find Charles Magee, ex-President of the Bank of Ottawa and Vice-President of the new Crown Bank of Canada; John Coates, civil engineer; Edward Seybold whose castle of red sandstone is possibly the finest house in Ottawa; Dr. J. Sweetland, the Sheriff of Carleton County; Edward Moore, lumberman; Fred Avery, the Treasurer of Hull Lumber Company; Newell Bate of Bate & Co.; H.K. Egan, capitalist; J.R. Booth, several times "lumberman," railway and steamship magnate; Walter C. Mackay; Fred. W. Powell, manager of the Rideau Lumber Co.; Dr. Frederick Montizambert.

Gard gives us further historical data:

O'Connor Street on which once lived one of Canada's greatest statesmen—Sir John A. Macdonald—has some beautiful homes and many men of national prominence. Sir John's home is occupied by the Wheeler sisters, relatives of one of our vice-presidents, Wheeler, and also of our well-known poet and popular writer, Mrs. Ella Wheeler Wilcox, whose works we all so delight in. Sir John's later home was "Earnscliffe" on McKay Street at the foot of Dalhousie Street which overlooks the Ottawa, not far from one branch of the Rideau River where it enters the Ottawa. It may be seen from the steamer "Empress" shortly before the landing at Queen's Wharf.

Frederick Cook, Ottawa's popular ex-Mayor, has his residence on O'Connor. Here is the home of the Honorable Andrew G. Blair, late Minister of Railways and Canals; Honourable Sir Richard J. Cartwright, K.C.M.G., Minister of Trade and Commerce lives on O'Connor. Here we find "the gentlemen from Vancouver," R.G. Macpherson, M.P., Richard Blain, M.P., and A.T. Thompson, M.P.

But government buildings were already putting pressure on beautiful old Centretown and its architectural heritage. In *Ottawa Past and Present*, A.H.D. Ross chronicled some of these changes:

As the Dominion advanced in prosperity and the volume of government business increased, pressing demands were made for increased office accommodation; so the following new buildings were erected: In 1900 and 1914, additions were made to Rideau Hall; in 1902 the Dominion Astronomical Observatory was erected on the grounds of the Central Experimental Farm; in 1904 the Victoria Memorial Museum to house the Geological Survey of Canada, in 1905 the Archives Building and the Royal Mint, in 1913 the Connaught Building, and in 1918 the Hunter Building. Some idea of the enormous expansion that has become necessary since 1897 may be gathered from the fact that in 1897 the total cost of construction, repairs, furniture, rentals, staff and maintenance was $333,911; for 1907, $1,128,750; for 1917, $3,154,713; for 1919, $4,994,045; for 1921, $5,117,100; for 1923, $3,111,761; and for 1925, $3,516,605.

In 1878, before the Chaudière Division of the Sons of Temperance, Miss Jennie E. Cross of Hull had read a paper in which she predicted modern air traffic, the completion of the great ship canal up the Ottawa, making Chaudière Falls into a harbour, corsetless women with bobbed or shingled hair, and the Ottawa of the future spread twenty miles in each direction, a city of "terraced gardens, gay bazaars, and palatial homes." Miss Cross also predicted that in the twentieth century Ottawa would still be the capital of "our proud Dominion" but would then include "the entire continent, we having compassionately annexed the United States to our Dominion to protect them from 'Sitting Bull' and 'John Chinaman.'"

By the time Lisgar was one hundred years old in 1943, some of Jennie Cross's predictions would have come true.

During the period 1893-1943, the second fifty years of Lisgar history in Ottawa, the school was to celebrate its Diamond Jubilee and its centenary with appropriate festivities and the return of hundreds of grateful alumni to its hallowed halls. Additions were to be made to the building, the east wing in 1902 and the west wing and fourth floor in 1908. Dress was to be gradually less formal, the code of conduct more open and free, school punishments to evolve from corporal to detentions and more astringent expulsions. The Students' Council was to be established and new clubs and sports were to be added to extra-curricular activities: a History Club, Audio-Visual Club, Red Cross Club, Lisgar ski team, Lisgar swimming team, Girls' rifle team, fencing team.

The grammar-school-turned-collegiate had established an "Old Boys' Club" as Lisgar names like Holland, Wright, Billings, Perley, Panet, Hill, Edwards, Pratt, McDougal, Bronson, repeated themselves generationally at Lisgar graduations. Many of these graduates, returning to Ottawa after university, became the solid citizens who volunteered their expertise and time on church boards, theatre boards, school boards. Conflict of interest had never been heard of; "pulling strings" was a way of life. The Head-Master or Principal of Lisgar was a leading civic figure and the Lisgar annual concert one of the main events of the social season in the Capital. The learned and illustrious addressed Lisgar assemblies; Canada's Governors General made annual inspections of the school and gave inspirational addresses to the awestruck student body.

Two world wars and a world-wide depression were to be compressed into this brief span, tragic events that were to have an impact on the student body and to be mirrored in the *Vox Lycei*, its writers reporting on casualty lists, prominent Ottawans addressing the School Assembly on the necessity to buy war bonds, results of Mackenzie King's infamous plebescite on conscription, the need for girls to become "farmerettes" to replace the young men gone to war. The call to arms was sounded in both the prose and the poetry of the school magazine.

"AUX ARMES"

Come from the mountain, the stream, and the forest,
Come from the hill and the plain and the shore,
Come like the torrent in spring when it roareth,
Come that the Teuton may threat us no more.
Come all ye loyal hearts stout and courageous,
Come all ye British men, true to the core,
Smite, as the sea smites in wrath when it rages,
Fight for your land as your fathers before.
When shall Canadians bow to the tyrant?
When shall we follow in chains at his heel?
When shall the voice of our loved ones be silent,
And our manhood laid low by usurper's steel?
Never while breath in our bodies is left us,
Never while blood in our veins courses free,
Until grim Death in our life has bereft us,
Our Northland, our Homeland, we'll battle for thee.
Answer the summons then, great-hearted Britons,
Remember brave Belgium, so trampled and seared,
Show this proud Vandal, who boastfully threatens,
That Canada's sons are a foe to be feared.

— Henry Bleakney *Vox Lycei*, 1917

Premonitions of the Second World War were to be accurately reflected by *Vox* contributors who were writing serious and thought-provoking essays such as Henry Bleakney's 1917 "Co-operation of the States of the British Empire and her Allies in the Prosecution of the War," and Kenny Brounlee's 1937-38 "European Summary." Both young men laid the causes of the wars to Germany's economic aims.

From Henry Bleakney:

In discussing this question, it is of great importance properly to appreciate the aims and ambitions of Germany. In the past it has been the common opinion of the allied peoples, that Germany's object in this war was political world-domination. However, great statesmen of the day are realizing more and more, that it is an *economic supremacy* which Germany sought, and is seeking. The Honourable Mr. Hewitt, member of the British House of Commons for Hereford, summed up the matter in these words, "There is one great key to the whole German movement, extending over many generations, and that is the economic aims she had in view." Thus in a word, lust of gold, rather than lust of glory, is responsible for plunging the world into this horrible war. But this is not an entirely original case, because in almost all wars, whatever may have been the causes attributed to them, blind avarice has had a great share.

Throughout all these destructive, life-changing and power-shifting upheavals Lisgar maintained its academic standards of excellence, a standard set in another century by first principal Thomas Wardrope and exemplified into the twentieth century by a growing list of Rhodes Scholars, Ontario scholarships, individual scholarships established within the school, and entrance scholarships to Canadian universities.

The Great Depression of the 1930s had at least one positive effect: many great teachers like Walter Mann of the English Department at Lisgar remained at the high school level because they had not the funds to continue on at university and obtain their Ph.Ds, thereby qualifying for university professorships. Lisgar was to be the richer for having many of these people of excellence.

Beloved Sis Tompkins of the Mathematics Department was to be the last teacher on Lisgar staff without any pedagogical qualifications, and the formidable Jessie Muir was to lead the battle with the School Board for equal pay for equal work.

There were some lighter moments, however. In a 1932 *Vox Lycei* Valentine Barrow looked forward to a glorified city of Ottawa, predicting a City Debating Society, a city-management form of government, a greatly enlarged Ottawa Ski Club, a National Theatre, a National Capital Orchestra, the establishment of a gymnasium and shooting gallery for businesswomen.

THE LYCEUM
1893-1903

The Lyceum, one of Lisgar's earliest and most unique organizations, was to remain active for only ten years into the school's second fifty years. By 1903 the *Vox Lycei* had replaced the Lyceum as "the voice of the people." In this excerpt Alf Sykes winds down the history of the Lyceum.

Owing to the fire which caused the pupils to be scattered for some months, there were no meetings of the Lyceum from January 27th, 1893 to November 16th, 1894. The year 1894-95 proved, however, to be one of the most stirring in the society's annals.

During the winter of 1895, there was a memorable clash (dare I say row?) between the editor of *Vox* and the executive. For some reason the executive committee passed a motion that the editor of *Vox* should, every Thursday, submit that paper to them for inspection. This the editor naturally refused to do, and threatened to resign if the motion were not withdrawn. The motion was not withdrawn, nor did the editor resign; consequently the executive appointed three of its members to prepare the next *Vox*. At the next meeting there was a very heated discussion and finally a number of the boys resigned from the society. The letters of resignation are interesting: pointed, emphatic, some almost vituperative. [. . .ex-pupil, the Reverend Robert Turley, in a letter to the school, recorded the not so savory and certainly not parliamentarian-like ending to this executive conflict:] "Morgan distinguished himself by a slashing attack on the executive after which a vote of censure was passed on the unfortunate committee. Then when their opponents, in triumph, pounded down the stairs, the executive grasped their opportunity and, in the absence of their foes (no motion to adjourn having been made), the motion of censure was rescinded and all account of it ordered to be omitted from the minutes."

At the open meeting in April [1895], there was a novel feature on the programme. In the words of the records, "a number of the boys took possession of the platform and in grand style gave the school 'yell' to the great surprise and delight (?) of the audience." Mention must also be made of the excellent work done by the Glee Club, under the leadership of Mr. L.H. Alexander, M.A.

The year 1896 was a quiet but profitable year. There were, however, a few special features. On February 14th the meeting took the form of a Mock Parliament of which Mr. R. Kenny was Speaker, Mr. C. Ballantyne, Leader of the Government, and Mr. Funnell, Leader of the Opposition. The question under discussion was "That the Government give a grant of one million dollars for militia."

Two weeks later, for the first time, I believe, in the history of the society, ladies took part in a debate. The speakers were Misses Maybee, Downing, S. Bowles, and E. Young, and at the conclusion of the debate "a beautiful bouquet was presented to each by Mr. Macmillan, on behalf of the lady members of the society." Some weeks later there was a three-sided debate, a very unusual thing, on the respective merits of Annexation, Independence, and Imperial Federation as aims for Canadian statesmen.

* * * * *

The winter of 1897 saw a remarkable innovation in the conduct of affairs in the Lyceum. In January of this year, for the first time in its history, the office of president was filled by a lady, Miss Hattie Smirle. The innovation proved a success, and since that time, as the list of officers shows, ladies have had their fair share of the honor and responsibility of presiding.

During this term two meetings were of special interest. On March 4th in the YMCA Hall there was a debate between representatives of the Lyceum and of the Ottawa East Debating Society. The subject sounds familiar this year ('94),—"Resolved that the British Colonies should be united under a scheme of Imperial Federation including Commercial Union as advocated by Hon. Joseph Chamberlain." Though our representatives, Messrs. J. Watterson and A. Armstrong, ably upheld the affirmative, they failed to win. Some weeks later the principal feature of the programme was a "Mock Trial." The editor of Vox was charged with publishing defamatory libel against Mr. A.H. Askwith. Mr. A.H. McDougall, B.A., acted as judge, Mr. R.M. Stewart as counsel for plaintiff, and Mr. Edwards as counsel for the defendant.

One of the features of this school year was the publication of a souvenir edition of Vox and a dramatized version of the Mock Trial held a month or two before.

These somewhat bare outlines of the Lyceum work for the years 1895-1898 may be supplemented by extracts from letters by old members. Miss Harriet Smirle [later Mrs. Wilson], one of the most active members of the nineties, writes:

. . . The winters of 1895 and 1896 were seasons of unusual life and development, culminating in a regular renaissance in the fall of 1897.

Debates of no inconsiderable merit were indulged in by members of the top forms, while the lower forms listened in awe-struck admiration as their seniors held forth on such learned subjects as "Corporal Punishment," "The Abolition of the Senate," and "Canada's Place in the Defence of the Empire." There was nothing giddy about these debates—debaters, students, and teachers took them as seriously as if they emanated from the floor of the House of Commons.

For the first time, the society had a girl president. Girls debated, gave speeches, ran committees, even composed and read the Vox. At first, the boys looked on indulgently—they were not in the least jealous, just a little hopeless for the prosperity of the society, that was all. However, the Lyceum prospered strangely. The meetings that winter were full of interest, and the attendance and enthusiasm of the students never flagged. There were many humorous incidents in connection with impromptu speaking. One day Miss B. consented to make her maiden speech if she were given the subject "My favorite author." The president had supreme power in this—he it was who handed out the ominous little slips of paper on which was written the subject for discussion. He was "primed" and agreed to give Miss B. the coveted subject.

But fourth formers are never above a little joke—and besides Miss B. had scored on a deduction that day when Mr. L. had failed at the board. She trod up lightly, thinking of how easily she would convince everybody that Kipling was the great genius of the ages. The little paper rustled pleasantly as she opened it, and there was written on it in large type: "Look out! Your back hair is coming down." With one horrified clutch at the back of her head, she retreated precipitately, ingloriously, without having broken the peace, and spent the rest of the day in planning an elaborate revenge. It didn't transpire—school revenges seldom do. . .

Another remarkable speech of that session was on "Boys and their frailties." The subject was inspiring, and the eloquence of the fair speaker so telling, the treatment so exhaustive that the president, being a man, rang her down, to save unpleasant disclosures.

One of the most memorable debates was a so-called "impromptu" between four of the fourth-form girls. Heretofore girls had seldom debated and then only when supported by a manly form on each side. On this occasion, the four had to be warned a week ahead, so as to get their nerve up to the strain—and their "points" incidentally. They took their places at the front, the light of a noble resolve shining on each face. Each had one great dread that "words might fail her and she wouldn't be able to think of a thing to say." It was a most unnecessary worry as the next half hour of excited discussion proved. There seemed to be an inexhaustible fund of verbiage; *words* never failed them, but *patience* threatened to do so more than once. The subject was "Resolved, that a northern climate is more desirable for residence than a southern." . . .

* * * * *

[Mr. Sykes incorporates the reminiscences of two more former pupils of Lisgar:]

Miss Margaret Young contributed the following account of an amusing incident:

Once there was an instrumental trio that gave the meeting a good laugh. The school boasted of but one piano seat and, as it was clearly impossible for three girls to sit on it at one time, it was necessary to use three chairs. But the chairs were too low. So, after some planning and practising beforehand, it ended in the three marching in, one after the other, to the piano, each carrying one of the big lexicons to be put on her chair and quite unmindful of the sacrilege that was committed. The procession wound up with the roll of music which, on account of its extreme old age and dilapidation, was entrusted to one of the other girls so that its leaves might be turned with more care than the nerves of the performers would permit. At the end, each picked up her lexicon and departed amid cheers.

Mr. E.J. Carson, a former president now in Winnipeg, writes as follows:-

About the only debate I recollect distinctly is the one in which Ostrom distinguished himself by proving conclusively that "Life is Not Worth Living.". . . R.H. Armstrong, I remember, too, on several occasions in debate or discussion gave early promise of that earnest, yearning, self-forgetting and attention-arresting style that today gives him such a strong hold on his audience in his pulpit declamations.

As to the general value of the society's work, one cannot speak too highly of its benefit. Of course there is always the usual value of such organizations in aiding the timid speaker, reciter, singer, or musician to gain confidence and in training its members gradually in methods of public procedure. But it seems to me that the Lyceum at the Ottawa Collegiate Institute has, by bringing both sexes and all grades together on a common basis, had a special mission which athletic sports, too, have always fostered— that of creating and maintaining among the students an *esprit de corps* which makes the graduates look back with fond recollections to the days spent within and about the old familiar walls, and always gives them a peculiar fellow-feeling for one another if ever they chance to meet later out in the cold world of reality.

[Mr. Sykes extends his text:]

The pages that follow are chiefly from the pen of Mr. L.B. Kingston who was, during the years he writes of, one of the most enthusiastic and valuable members of the society.

In the next year, 1899-1900, the society had perhaps its most successful year of this period. The debates held were numerous and good; a very amusing one, an impromptu, on the subject "Resolved, that women should not wear feathers" will, I have no doubt, recur to all who attended the meetings of the society that year. The affirmative was taken by Misses McEwen and Ardley, the negative by Messrs. Musgrove and Wood. The arguments of the speakers and the manner in which they were put forward provoked a great deal of laughter. The judges gave the decision for the affirmative, but whether the ladies followed up the principles they had been advocating so strongly I do not know.

In this same year, a Mock Trial and a Mock Parliament were held. . . . The subject discussed by the Mock Parliament was "Preferential Trade," the government being represented by Messrs. Pushman, Wood, Ross and Bray; the opposition by Messrs. Rose, Nobles, Musgrove, and White. . .

[Mr. Sykes again:]

It is chiefly to this year that the following letter from Miss Mary Ardley, B.A., refers. Miss Ardley's success in intercollegiate debating in Toronto while she was an undergraduate at MacMaster, may, to some extent, be due to her training at the Lyceum.

. . . There were those who learned to make good impromptu speeches but the best test of a pupil's ability was in debate in which many gave promise of great things in the future. Of these, I can mention but a few. There was Morris Macdougall, a deep thinker who spoke with much ease and without any apparent nervousness; Gordon Fleck, logical and clever, with a bright, attractive manner of speaking; R. George Pushman, clear-headed, quick to see weak points in his opponent's arguments, and always ready to answer, logical and interesting. There was also Ralph Timberlake, thoughtful, very much in earnest, and full of his subject; Arthur McGregor and Harry Nobles, both able and attractive debaters, earnest and argumentative; and others.

Nor was public speaking confined to the boys alone; several of the girls were also well able to uphold the honors in speech-making and debate. Those who heard them have not forgotten Eileen Clemow, the bright, eager speaker who brought forward such clever arguments; nor Bessie Thompson, so calm and deliberative and yet so convincing; nor Grace Scott with her bright speeches and good arguments. Nor should we omit Miss McEwen with her slow, deliberate utterance, her pleasant, natural manner, and her touches of humor; nor Mary Blackadar, bright and pleasant, with an easy flow of speech. . .

Of the good the society accomplished I cannot begin to tell. It gave us such a training in parliamentary rules and proceedings that, if no other good came of it, it has earned the right to exist. It cultivated our literary taste by its programmes of choice readings and addresses, to say nothing of the educational value of the *Vox Lycei*, which profited both its readers and its editor. The Lyceum was of incalculable value in training its members in debate and public speaking; we learned, too, how the business part of a meeting should be conducted, as well as some of the trials that fall to the lot of those responsible for good weekly programmes. The critic, too, gave us wise and timely suggestions which were usually followed out in the same good spirit in which they were given. The Lyceum brought out the capable but sometimes diffident pupils, and showed those who had executive ability and could lead, as well as others who worked well in less conspicuous places. . .

[Mr. Sykes incorporates another former pupil:]

From the contributions of Mr. L.B. Kingston the following paragraphs are taken:

In the following year, 1900-1901, the executive found it difficult to maintain the high standard which the literary part of the programmes had reached the preceding year. . . but one afternoon two former members of the Lyceum, Lieut. Gordon Stewart and Corp. Douglas Lyon, who had both seen service with the first contingent in South Africa, were prevailed upon to attend the meeting of the society and relate some of their experiences. . .

In the year 1901-1902 . . . a debate between the third form represented by Messrs. Dunlevie, Payne, and Gerard and the fourth represented by Messrs Kingston, Anderson, and Brennan took place on the subject: "Resolved, that the Government should prohibit the proposed sale of the

Canada Atlantic Railway to American capitalists." The debate was won by the representatives of the fourth form who had argued the negative side. . .

During this year the Glee Club was revived and choruses, two-part songs, and rounds again were heard in the Lyceum meetings.

[Mr. Sykes resumes:]

And now I come to the last season of the Lyceum. The outlook for a good year for the society was gloomy enough and nothing was done till the beginning of January. Then the society was started on a term which proved fully as successful as that of 1899-1900. The number of debates held was large and the quality very good. An innovation was made one afternoon by having, in place of the customary debate, a mock banquet, if so it may be called, for there was no banquet, only after dinner speeches. Mr. A.H. McDougall acted as toast-master, and thirteen or fourteen members of the third and fourth forms proposed and responded to the toasts. A great deal of interest was taken in this and the affair proved a great success.

At the end of the term, an evening meeting of the society was held and the trial scene from *The Merchant of Venice* presented. Those taking part were: Miss M. Masson, Portia; Miss C.C. Henry, Nerissa; Mr. O. Workman, Shylock; Mr. F. Dunlevie, Duke of Venice; Mr. L.B. Kingston, Antonio; Mr. R.M. Graham, Bassanio; Mr. H. Meldrum, Gratiano; Mr. H.B. White, Salerio; Messrs. J.R. Mills, N.H. Hay, C.M. Ross, and V. Dawson, magnificoes. Footlights and other electrical connections were installed by Mr. B. Brown and this made the hall look quite theatre-like and contributed in a great measure to the success of the meeting.

During these five years, the Lyceum has been successful in its mission to give the students a chance to learn a little of the art of public-speaking. Without a doubt, there will be many a businessman, lawyer, judge, or member of parliament in the years to come who, as he closes a telling address before the directors of a company, before a law court, or in the House of Parliament, will think of the time when he made his first halting attempt at public speaking before the Lyceum in the Ottawa Collegiate Institute.

W.J. Sykes, pupil, teacher at Lisgar, Ottawa Librarian

Although Sykes would not record it in the O.C.I. History, the Lyceum resurfaced several times later, particularly in the 1920s, but never with the same vigour and participation.

LISGAR CADETS
"ARMA VIRUMQUE CANO"
1893-1947

**94th Cadet Corps
Service Medal of
Herb Beall,
1927.**

According to H.W. Beall, Battalion Commander of
the 94th Cadet Corps in 1927, the Corps was
organized at the Ottawa Collegiate Institute in
1903 by Lieutenant R.S. Simpson (a Commercial
teacher). The Corps was affiliated with the 43rd Duke
of Cornwall's Own Rifles and their successor—
the Cameron Highlanders of Ottawa. Not much is
recorded about life in the Corps from 1903 through
1911. But Beall's chronology of the corps indicates
that 1911 marks the first mention of any social
activities.

The *Vox Lycei*, Spring, 1915, describes the Cadet
Corps Sleigh Drive, probably setting a precedent for
a winter social event that was to remain popular with
Lisgar students well into the 1940s.

At the beginning of the year, the general Committee
of the Cadet Corps decided that something should
be done for those in the corps who do not shoot. In the
past years all the fun has been enjoyed by the shooters—
the trip to Toronto, and the prizes at the Spring and Fall
Matches. Accordingly, a sleigh drive was decided upon,
the eventful date being Friday, January 29th.

The drive was supposed to start at eight o'clock sharp,
and although it may seem hard to believe, we actually
drove off at 8:15. The night was clear and cold—
somewhere about 20 degrees F—but as everyone
was warmly wrapped up, the cold was not keenly felt.
There were two buses. The chaperones, three in number,
occupied the first bus, which contained the solitary males
and a few fussers. The second bus held the fussers,
who were most disappointed (?) at being chaperone-
less. Order was strictly maintained in the first bus, and
in the second, the cadets had something better to do
than shout.

Sgt. Chesley had brought along his little mouth-organ, and in spite of the cold, he regaled us with many melodies. He has a splendid repertoire of tunes—what matters it if they are some ten years old?

We drove out the Driveway to the Exhibition Grounds and home by Bank Street. To the surprise of all, we passed Lisgar Street, and continued to Sparks. The reason for this was evident when we drew up in front of the justly famous "Boston Lunch."

A large cargo of pork and beans was shipped on board, and we sailed for the Collegiate at about thirty knots an hour. Here we disembarked and all hands were fed. After supper, tables and chairs were speedily put out of sight, and dancing commenced. Our old stand-by, Hughie Huggins once more rose to the occasion, and with that air of superiority, which he alone possesses, he condescended to operate upon the piano. There were ten dances, which were greatly enjoyed by the participants.

BRIEF CHRONOLOGY

1903: 94th Cadet Corps organized at Ottawa Collegiate Institute.

1912: 94th consisted of one company, about 100 cadets, equipped with Ross rifles. Rifle range constructed on fourth floor.

1914: Shooting "a main concern." Girls' Rifle Club "steadily progressing."

1915: Stress laid on instruction in flag signalling—semaphore and Morse.

1917: Corps had 130 members under Lt. A.A. Burridge, its "well-liked instructor."

1918: 94th consisted of one company of seven platoons. Rifle team won the Imperial Challenge Trophy.

1919: Commercial and Technical Cadet Corps (No. 775) organized as separate unit from 94th; latter thus reduced to four regular and one signal platoon.

1920: Every boy in Lisgar enrolled in 94th.

1922: 94th strength reduced to 522 because of organization of 1070th Cadet Corps at Glebe. Bugle Band flourishing under Bugle Major Clifford Meagher.

1923: Lt. W. "Van" Riddell (Ottawa Highlanders) appointed full-time Cadet Instructor for Lisgar, Glebe and Tech. 94th and 1070th each a battalion of three companies. Brass Band organized in addition to Bugle Band.

1924: New uniforms issued. Officers' Mess dinner and Military Ball (joint Lisgar and Glebe functions). Cadet camp at Barryfield. 94th, 775th and 1070th inspected as a brigade on Parliament Hill.

1926: 94th and 1070th provided Guard of Honour for Field Marshal Viscount Allenby when giving public address at Glebe—first such honour for Canadian Cadets. Stretcher-bearer squad added to Corps

1927: Lt. "Van" Riddell Brigade Commander at Inspection. Medals presented to Cadet Battalion Commanders (this practice later extended to Adjutants and senior Company Commanders.)

1928: Lt. Riddell resigned as Cadet Instructor. Teacher appointed in each school as Cadet Administrator (W.D.T. Atkinson at Lisgar). Inspections at Cartier Square.

1929: Interest in Cadets declining. Inspections at Lansdowne Park. Capt. L.H. Meng succeeded Mr. Atkinson as Cadet Administrator.

1931: Cadet uniform allowance cancelled. Reduced grants threatened existence of 94th. Saved through efforts of Capt. Meng and Principal F.A. Stuart. "A" Company won the McGuire Cup at the Inspection—first time for the 94th.

1933: 94th again won cup for best company on inspection, also First Aid District Trophy. Shooting transferred to range at Drill Hall. Change in pattern of uniforms.

1934: Grants for Junior Cadets (ages 12-14) abolished. 94th again in jeopardy, but survived, thanks to efforts of Louis Meng. Glebe and Tech did not have cadets at Annual Inspection.

1935: 94th reduced to one company. Entire Corps present at Jubilee Service on Parliament Hill—the only Cadet unit still existing under O.C.I. Board's jurisdiction.

1937: 50th Anniversary Number of *Vox Lycei*. For the first time in many years, no article on the Cadet Corps.

This was the second low point in Lisgar Cadet history.

Too much credit cannot be given to Captains Menzies and Cross, and to the chaperones, Miss McManus, Mr. and Mrs. Howie, Mr. Gilchrist and Mr. Ellis. At 11:50 the Dance broke up, and with cheers for the Cadets—so ended the 1915 Cadet Drive.

Interest in the Corps, and specifically in target shooting, increased dramatically in 1912 with the construction of the rifle range on the fourth floor of the Collegiate. The *Vox Lycei*, April, 1914, reported on Lisgar's success at the United Empire Trophy Match:

During the past summer the O.C.I. Cadet Corps certainly brought credit to itself in the shooting line. In the early part of the summer, it succeeded in winning the senior section of the C.R.L. matches in competition with other schools throughout Canada, and later, at the beginning of July, the championship of Barriefield Camp. During August the ten or twelve practised daily, and the result was shown in the O.R.A. meet at Toronto. There, besides winning numerous individual prizes and money amounting to about $200, the team carried home the City of Hamilton Centennial Trophy, and the Cadets' Trophy. A week later the team again kept up its pace in the D.R.A. and won its greatest competition, the United Empire Trophy Match.

Phone Queen 498

W. J. CARSON
Painter & Decorator

WALLPAPER
PAINTS
GLASS

291-293 Laurier Ave. West
OTTAWA

Geo. E. Preston & Sons
Civil and Military
Tailors
217 & 219 RIDEAU STREET
OTTAWA
CANADA
Established 1870

Professor Laing

Wishes to thank all patrons for their attendance at the Collegiate Dancing Class, and hopes to see all his former and future students for the coming Fall Season in the near future.

Private Lessons will be given daily during the Summer months at St. Patrick's Hall or Jardin de Danse, Britannia.

For particulars please Phone

Studio: Queen 1323; or
Residence: Rideau 1418

THIS SPACE TO LET

For particulars see
BUSINESS MANAGER "VOX LYCEI,"
Ottawa Collegiate Institute

While girls were excluded from membership in the corps themselves, they did form their own rifle teams in the years following construction of the range.

GIRLS' RIFLE CLUB: Hon. President—Miss Locklin; President—Laura McDougall; Vice-President—Helen Miller; Secretary—Francis Heron The Girls' Rifle Club, 1914-1918, owing to its limited facilities was forced to confine its membership to members of the fourth and fifth forms. It aimed to promote straight shooting and, for this purpose, each year held a competition among its members and entered the Ontario Rifle Competitions.

In 1916 Miss Mary Reeve and Miss Coral Moorhead were first and second in the school competitions and Miss Francis Heron was successful in the Provincial Competition.

* * * * *

A further report on the O.C.I. Cadets from the *Vox Lycei*:

Early last spring [1921], as soon as fine weather permitted the use of the ranges, our boys knuckled down to serious practice, so that when the big event of the year—the Dominion of Canada Rifle Association meet was held here during the latter part of August, our team was in A1 condition.

This meet was held at the new Connaught ranges which are situated about twelve miles up the Ottawa River and directly opposite the town of Aylmer. These are the most up-to-date ranges on the continent and have the most modern equipment. The team representing Lisgar at this meet were as follows:—Lea Shearer, Vic George, Stewart Bruce, Kenneth Fosbery and Bob Burns. At this meet Lisgar won the Cadet Match and was awarded the White Memorial Trophy, a handsome clock, presented by the 43rd Regiment, D.C.O.R., as well as a large cash prize.

* * * * *

Cadet Major J.L. Shearer reported on cadet activities in the *Vox Lycei*, 1922-23:

For the Cadet Meet of the O.R.A. in 1922 Lea Shearer, Edwin Charleson, Stewart Bruce, Kenneth Fosbery, Bob Stephen and Vic George represented Lisgar.

The team met with great success on this occasion. The following is from the *Citizen*:—"Shooting under extremely adverse conditions, the Ottawa Collegiate Institute rifle team at Long Branch today, won the Pellatt cup for the third time in decisive style. The trophy which now becomes the property of the O.C.I. carries with it five miniature cups and $25 cash."

There were 23 teams competing consisting of 216 boys from all Ontario. Capt. Vic George, with a score of 62 out of 70, headed the individual list, taking the gold medal, a spoon and $20. Second and closely following the winner came Maj. L. Shearer, winning the silver medal, a spoon and $15. Bronze medals were won by Lieuts. Bruce and Charleson. In winning one out of two trophies, five miniatures, the gold and silver medals, two bronze medals, two out of three spoons and $74 cash, the O.C.I. team made quite a dent in the prize list.

In addition to these two major events, our boys entered the Canadian Rifle League outdoor series held here last spring and succeeded in winning the following trophies:—Silver cup engraved with C.R.L. monogram—to Cadet Lt.-Col. Minter; two silver spoons to winners of first class standing— Lt.-Col. Minter and Cadet Maj. J.L. Shearer; two second class spoons to Cadet Capt. E. McKinley and Sgt. S. Webster.

* * * * *

One of the Cadet corps' pivotal figures, teacher L.N. Meng, in the second history of Lisgar, 1843-1943, wrote of his protégés:

Since 1903 the Cadet Corps has been in continuous operation. During the decades 1920-1940, sniping at cadet training became a popular pastime, with the result that interest waned in some Ottawa schools to such an extent that their corps were disbanded and their equipment turned in. At Lisgar, however, each year saw a sufficiently large number

of senior boys turning out for the training to form at least one company. In February 1943 one hundred cadets of the Lisgar Corps wore, for the approval of the Minister of National Defence, the first one hundred uniforms of the newly designated Royal Canadian Army Cadets.

Rifle shooting always has been a favourite part of the training of the Corps. In 1912 a rifle range was constructed in the east attic of the school where, despite the lack of heating facilities, practices were held and competitions fired through the months of October to March. Major Desmond Burke, winner of the King's Prize at Bisley, spent much of his spare time on the range while he was a student at Lisgar.

According to the records, the following were the Officers Commanding the Corps from 1910-1943:—R.H. Uglow, P. Conroy, J.A. Loy, E.A. Devitt, N.E. Sharpe, Captain Menzies, H. Brookins, E.A. Davis, P.M. Currie, M. McFarland, H. Winter, W. O'Connor, L. Shearer, F. Taylor, L.A. Robertson, H.W. Beall, L.C. Williams, H. Hunter —.Ogilvie, R. Tilley, R. Salmon, C. Lochnan, K. Wilson, H. Cairns, W. Lynch, C. Robson, L. Poitevan, D. Chance S. Bateman, A. Kniewasser.

The following extract taken from the 1918 *Vox Lycei* reveals the spirit of the Corps:—"Of the four Corps of the four respective years preceding hostilities, every member but ten answered the call, and these were either physically unfit or disqualified in other ways. Forty decorations were pinned on the breasts of ex-members of the 94th."

* * * * *

In the 1920s Marjorie Mowat was one of the members of those early Girls' Rifle Teams. She reminisces:

I have often wondered about the fate of that shooting gallery (on the fourth floor) and I tried to get to see it at a reunion celebration and was told it was now off bounds to the public and filled with heating pipes etc.

In 1919-1923, I attended O.C.I. (as it was then called) when I started the only High School in Ottawa. Glebe Collegiate was built later—with a swimming pool which I considered a big addition.

In 1920, a friend persuaded me to join a group of girls to take shooting lessons. She was three years older than I and now deceased so I cannot ask her, but as I remember we paid 50 cents each. We went up to the scary dark attic. Our teacher was a young boy named Desmond Burke.

Now at this late date I have so many questions. Why were girls included in shooting lessons? In 1920 women were something less than active in other more important areas.

When I attended Teacher's College in 1923-24, I was appointed to interview Agnes Macphail—our *first* woman M.P. She invited us all to tea in the Parliamentary Restaurant— after that every year all girls from Normal School were invited to have tea with her.

The Field of Honour.

Heu pietas, heu prisca fides, invictaque bello
Dextera! non illi se quisquam impune tulisset
Obvius armato, seu cum pedes iret in hostem,
Seu spumantis equi foderet calcaribus armos.
Heu miserande puer! si qua fata aspera rumpas
Tu Marcellus eris. VIRGIL.

ALFRED WHEELER ARMSTRONG
1914—1915
Private, 156th Battalion
Killed in Action, September 27th, 1918

JOHN DOUGLAS ARMSTRONG
1902—1905
Lieutenant, Canadian Engineers
Killed in Action, April 9th, 1917.

PAUL LYDON ARMSTRONG
1903—1908
Lieutenant, 73rd Battalion, R. H. of C.
Killed in Action, October 29th, 1916.

HAROLD B. AULT
1910-1914
Sergeant, 3rd Battalion
Killed in Action, August 30th, 1918.

FREDERICK GRAEME AVERY
1909—1913
Lieutenant, Royal British Engineers.
Killed in Action, April 13th, 1918.

EDWARD CARLETON BAKER
1895—1896
Captain, 228th Royal Engineers.
Died of Wounds, September 18th, 1916.

MAURICE BAUSET
1903—1906
Temp. Captain, 22nd French Canadian Battalion
Killed in Action, Battle of Somme, September 16th, 1916.

FREDERICK CHARLES BENNET
1901.
Private, 1st Pioneer Battalion, C.E.F.,
Killed in Action, June 13th, 1916.

HUGH BRADDISH BILLINGS
1914—1915.
Flight Lieut. Royal Flying Corps.
Died, a Prisoner in Germany, 1917.

EDWARD ERROL BOUCHETTE
1906-1908
Lieutenant, Killed in Action, October, 1918.

GORDON HARPER BOWIE
1909-1914
Accidentally Killed, 1918.

JOHN BERNARD (DON) BROPHY
1907—1913
Flight-Lieutenant, Royal Flying Corps.
Accidentally Killed on Service in England,
December 24th, 1916.

The O.C.I. rifle team, Champions of Canada, 1911, holding cups, shields and guns. Some of these young men no doubt would use their expertise in the Flanders Fields of World War I, 1914-1918. Back row, L to R; Pte. Hector, Sgt. Devitt, Sgt. Donaldson, Pte. Taylor. Middle; Col. Sgt. Sanders, Cpl. Conroy, Lieut. Holder. Front; Pte. Wright.

The five famous women from Alberta spent years promoting women's rights. In regards to women becoming Senators, the question was finally settled in England. Here at No.1 Downing St, five great judges finally decided that the B.N.A. Act saying persons could be appointed to the Senate meant women too. This was in 1929 but it wasn't until 1931 that Mrs. Cairine Wilson was appointed our *first* woman Senator.

I always remembered that 1929 ruling when women were declared to be persons and therefore eligible to become Senators, because I was married in 1928—a year before I was officially a person and yet have happily survived sixty-two years of marriage.

I started this by wondering about why girls were taught shooting so long ago. . ."

Jim Beall, student (1957-1962) and teacher (1968-1977), son of cadet historian Herb Beall and one of generations of Bealls at Lisgar, also recalled in considerable detail the famous "Fourth Floor":

At Lisgar in the 1960s, the Fourth Floor was always referred to in capital letters. Unlike the third floor (Science), the second floor (Math and French), the first floor (English and History), or the basement (Geography and Food), the

Form 4B, Ottawa Collegiate Institute, March, 1917, posed in the civvies some of them would soon be exchanging for military uniforms. Standing, L to R; Thurlow MacCallum, Carman Shaver, Howard Terrance, George Grout, Fergus Lothian, Charles Ahearn, Harold Bush, Roland Larrabee, Cyrus Jandrew, Sheldon Shoemaker, Lawrence (Bob) Brown, Bill Howe, Caldwell Scobie, Maynard Spratt, James O'Halloran, Lorne Carr-Harris, Oliver Adams, Edward Winter, Keith Todd, Beverley Sturgeon. Kneeling; George Salton, Gerald Connell, Peter Webster. Absent; Lawson Gillespie, Thomas Eadie, Cyril Watson, John Macoun, Edward P. Taylor. The photo was taken by Lawson Gillespie and carefully preserved by Fergus Lothian.

Fourth Floor harboured no mundane reminders of the tedium of school life—classes, exams, teachers. In fact, few of us knew just what the Fourth Floor did harbour, though there was much speculation. I recall sitting in physics class on dreamy afternoons, while Louie Meng refought the battle of Vimy Ridge, my friend George Rogers and I drawing pictures of the Fourth Floor, complete with skeletons of students detained and forgotten, cells for teachers, instruments of torture, and other delights.

The Fourth Floor was separated from the rest of the school by a mesh screen of the sort used in schoolyard fencing, which ran along the second half of the stairway. If you were brave enough, or foolhardy enough, and if you didn't look down the 100 or so feet of open stairwell, you could climb this screen; indeed, a number of senior boys, members of the Hi-Y, I think, actually did so. But their reports were deliberately and irritatingly vague.

One day during Christmas exams George sought me out in the cafeteria with exciting news—somebody, a custodian probably, had left the gate in the screen unlocked. Filled with the delicious trepidation which always attends illegal activity, and equipped only with a camera, we slipped up the stairs, through the gate, and opened the heavy counter-weighted metal door.

It was everything we had hoped for. The whole Floor was in semi-darkness, illuminated only by some small and very dirty windows. Various rooms and passageways disappeared in total blackness: the camera's electronic flash provided our sole reliable means of navigation. There were no skeletons or engines of torture, but we did discover dozens of old theatre sets: a ship's cabin, a 19th century parlour, a tropical island, complete with distinctly Canadian pine trees, and fantastic ragged costumes.

To our left, down a long corridor, was the shooting gallery, used by cadets in the 1920s and '30s. A few targets were still tacked to the wooden hoardings, impressively drilled through the centre with clusters of shots.

In another room, we discovered a veritable museum of old science equipment: various antediluvian biological specimens, elaborate glass apparati, some electric gizmo which Edison himself might well have constructed. George, a collector by nature, stuffed his pockets with bits and pieces of whatever he could find. I made off with a wooden instrument box, inscribed "LS Kingston, IVB, 1902", which I still have.

One of the more interesting features of the Fourth Floor landscape was a skylight which looked directly into the girls' washroom, two floors below. While we were pruriently examining this startling phenomenon, we heard the distant voice of Lorne Rentner berating some poor miscreant in the second floor hallway. Mr. Rentner's voice had a strange compelling quality—even though we were protected by two floors, it instilled in us that mixture of fear and guilt which was one of his hallmarks. With casual deliberation, we made our way back to the metal doorway and down into the light of common day.

In 1976, during the renovations, the Fourth Floor was stripped. Its treasures were either discarded or packed off to the Board Office, fluorescent lights were installed, and it became the home of the new heating and air-circulation equipment—very practical and much needed, I'm sure. It is now, quite simply, the fourth floor.

And from the *Vox Lycei*, 1924-1925:

By 1920, every boy in Lisgar enrolled in 94th, now organized as a battalion 650 strong with military instructors for signalling, boxing and wrestling. Drills and musketry training were held in class hours.

Interest in shooting reached its zenith in 1924 when Desmond Burke, a former student and cadet at Lisgar, succeeded in winning "the greatest honour in marksmanship that the world has to offer, the King's prize." Burke's win, at Bisley, of "this singular honour for which the leading marksmen of the British Empire for over half a century have competed," ensured continued diligence on the range. Shooters, of both sexes, were inspired by the exploits of Burke who, at the time of his win, was a member of the Governor General's Foot Guards. The training Burke received as a cadet at Lisgar laid the foundation for future success. In fact, in *Canadian Bisley Shooting*, Beall indicates, Desmond Burke acknowledges the "help and encouragement early in his shooting career" provided by Lt. A.A. Burridge—instructor of the Corps. Burke returned to the range at Lisgar as an instructor and again contributed to the success of the marksmen and women of the Collegiate.

THE BISLEY WINNER

*"The tumult and the shouting died,
The captains and the Kings depart-"*

-Kipling

Long in our memory will remain the scenes of the triumphant return of our former school fellow, Desmond Burke, bringing with him the greatest honour in marksmanship, that the world has to offer, the King's prize. It is not necessary to recount the details of the great achievement of our ex-cadet musketry officer in bringing to himself, to his city, and to the 94th Lisgar Collegiate Institute Cadet Corps, this singular honour for which the leading marksmen of the British Empire for over half a century have competed.

While Musketry Officer, Desmond did much in the way of promoting rifle shooting among his fellow cadets, and it may truly be said that the early training and foundation of his remarkable ability that stood by him on that memorable day on the Bisley Rifle Ranges, was attained while a cadet of the 94th Cadet Corps.

G.H. HATCH
(Publicity Agent, 94th O.C.I.C.C.)

The Bisley Winner

"The tumult and the shouting dies,
The captains and the Kings depart—"

(Kipling).

Long in our memory will remain the scenes of the triumphant return of our former school fellow, Desmond Burke, bringing with him the greatest honour in markmanship that the world has to offer, the King's prize. It is not necessary to reclunt the details of the great achievement of our ex-cadet musketry officer in bringing to himself, to his city, and to the 94th Lisgar Collegiate Institute Cadet Corps, this singular honour for which the leading marksman of the British Empire for over half a century have competed.

While Musketry Officer, Desmond did much in the way of promoting rifle shooting among his fellow cadets, and it may truly be said that the early training and foundation of his remarkable ability that stood by him on that memorable day on the Bisley Rifle Ranges, was attained while a cadet of the 94th Cadet Corps.

G. H. HATCH,
(Publicity Agent, 94th O.C.I.C.C.)

LIEUT. DESMOND BURKE

Salute to Desmond Burke, the Bisley winner, from the *Vox Lycei*, 1924-1925.

Officers of the 94th Cadet Corps, 1918-1919. Back row, L to R; G. Bleakney, D. Martin, A.A. Burridge Cameron, J. Puddicombe. Sitting; M. MacFarland, P.N. Currie, D. Baxter.

Throughout Lisgar's 150-year history thousands of former pupils and former members of the Lisgar Cadet Corps have donned uniforms to fight for their country where danger threatened. One of them won the Victoria Cross.

Edward Holland, a mounted rifleman in South Africa and a machine-gunner in World War I, is the one who merits an individual plaque at the school entrance beside the Rideau Canal. The *London Gazette* citation for his Victoria Cross tells us that on November 7, 1899, Sergeant Holland "Did splendid work with his Colt gun and kept the Boers off the two 12-pounders..."

A school history notes that Holland was scarcely old enough to be considered an old boy. It adds: "Among those who have done good work in keeping up the reputation of Ottawa in military affairs and in whom the Collegiate Institute claims the right to feel the pride of Alma Mater the following names are found: Major Basil Bell, who served in the North-West Rebellion of 1885; Lt.Col. A.P. Sherwood, commanding officer of the 43rd Rifles, Major Bertichinger of the Field Battery; Major Brown of the Dragoon Guards. . ."

The Cadets continued to remain an integral part of life at Lisgar throughout the 1920s; however, by 1929 the Corps had begun to lose its allure. Historian Beall makes the following entry for the year 1929: "Interest

Officers of the 775th Cadet Corps, 1920-1921. Back row, L to R; Lieut. H. MacCormack, Mr. Howie (instructor), Lieut. A. Simpson. Front row; Lieut. A. Duchemin, Capt. V. George, Lieut. H. Graham. The *Vox Lycei* of that year reported that "the band, under the able leadership of Band-Master Mayotte, has grown to twelve pieces." The 775th had developed into "a regular Corps, complete with band, Signallers, Shooting Gallery, and a real Company of four man-sized platoons." Their shooting range was in Rockcliffe Park.

in the cadets declining, non-cadets spend the half-holiday for inspection by lining the route of march and hurling hoots and jeers of derision at the cadets." He goes on to chronicle the events that indicated a decline in fortunes of the Corps over the course of the 1930s.

This marks the end of the second phase of the Corps. According to ex-Lisgarite A.E.L. Caulfield:

Herb Beall's memories of the old shooting gallery are different from mine. We used old, inaccurate Ross rifles, firing from the prone position, under Des Burke's instruction. Des and I were given the job of closing and opening the lower Assembly Hall doors every morning, on signal from the Principal: I think we were called monitors: it was a great way to get to know everybody.

* * * * *

Beall's cadet chronology continues:

1938: *Vox* again has picture of Cadet Officers, and notes that shooting competitions are well advanced.

1939: 94th (along with contingents from Glebe and Tech to whom they loaned equipment) took part in Guard of Honour for Royal Visit in May. Small arms drill intensified. 775th and 1070th reactivated.

1940: Old Ross rifles finally recalled by government.

1941: 94th won Sherwood Trophy for best Corps in Ottawa Area. In order of seniority these now included Lisgar, Ashbury, La Salle, Tech, Glebe, and St. Pat's.

1942: Big Army Cadet Camp at Connaught Ranges, with 94th among units in advance party. Training in common infantry weapons, poison gas protection, and map reading. Tanks displayed "in action." Prefix "Royal" conferred on Canadian Army Cadets (R.C.A.C.) by His Majesty King George VI.

1943: 94th 300 strong. Squad of 94th "modelled" first of new uniforms issued to R.C.A.C. Mass church parade on Parliament Hill for all Cadet Corps in Ottawa. Training extended to Bren gun drill and aircraft recognition.

1944: 94th represented R.C.A.C. at Victory Loan ceremonies. Artillery platoon formed. Rifle team for D.C.R.A. matches coached by L. Meng.

1945: Sherwood Trophy won by the 94th for the last time.

1946: Apparently the last full year of operation for the 94th, although details regarding actual disbanding remain obscure. In the Annual Report ledger, now held by the Army Cadet League of Canada, the last entry for the 94th is for the year ending March 31, 1947. It included the following information:

Corps strength—senior 277, junior 88, total 365. No. of Instructors—3, including 2 civilians. No. of teams entered in D.C.R.A.—1 (130 cadets fired annual test). Uniform and Band grants—paid. Instructor—Captain L.H. Meng.

Beall made his summation: "It is fitting that the last known official report of the 94th Cadet Corps should close with the name of the Officer whose dedication above all others, kept the Corps in being during the lean years, and guided it through the final period of achievement."

A few years later when the trend towards replacing "School" Cadet Corps by "Open" Corps, mostly under militia sponsorship, was well established, the 2360th R.C.A.C. Corps was formed by, and attached to, the Cameron Highlanders of Ottawa. Although the impetus for its establishment came from a group of Lisgar students, there is unfortunately no evidence that it perpetuates or carries on the traditions of the old 94th, whose association with the Camerons had endured over so many years.

* * * * *

The years 1938-1946 have been identified as "Phase III" by Beall. Again, he chronicles the highlights of these years in the Corps. Obviously, "Phase III" was a busy time for the Corps in light of the hostilities in Europe during this period. Indeed, during this period in the life of the Corps, training took on a very practical nature.

The parade drill was still of importance; however, the Cadets of "Phase III" found themselves training in common infantry weapons, poison gas protection, map reading, Bren gun drill, and aircraft recognition. There was an urgency and a sense of purpose to the training that had not been seen since that initial group of Cadets was mustered late in the nineteenth century to defend against marauding Irish nationalists from south of the 49th parallel.

L.H. Meng writing in the second history of Lisgar, noted that:

One of the first Lisgar boys to be listed as missing (in World War II) was Flying Officer Clarence Robson who commanded the 94th in 1938. Squadron Leader Mervyn Fleming, D.F.C., now leading the famous "Moose" Bomber Squadron of the R.C.A.F., Pilot Officer Raoul Jenner, winner of the George Medal, Flight Sergeant John Haime, B.E.M., and Major George Browne, D.S.O., (won at Dieppe) were all cadets while at our School. Hundreds of others are on active service, carrying on their duties in a similar manner.

This year, two hundred senior boys will voluntarily spend many hours, after classes, in the Rifle Range or at the Drill Hall going through a rigorous course of instruction. If and when they are called upon, the 1943-44 personnel of the 94th Lisgar Collegiate Institute, Royal Canadian Army Cadets, will carry on as those who have gone before have done.

The casualty lists, alas, already contain the names of many who received their first military training with the Lisgar cadets. Undoubtedly others will follow. It is, however, a source of legitimate pride to know that in academic and extra curricular activity so also in the Cadet Corps, the lesson of good citizenship, with the appreciation alike of its privileges and its responsibilities, has been well taught and well learned at Lisgar Collegiate Institute.

This period, for all its activity and real war experience marked the final stage of the Lisgar Cadet Corps. Beall makes note of the contribution made to the Corps by Captain L.H. Meng "whose dedication, above all others, kept the Corps in being during the lean years, and guided it through the final period of achievement."

* * * * *

Former Cadet David Godwin Chance writes of the Second World War period:

I thought I might recall some of the events during my time with the Lisgar cadets from 1938 to 1942. Memory is a fickle thing and I am not sure of all the events that took place, but there were two that are fixed in my memory; the visit of the King and Queen in 1939, and my year as Battalion Commander in 1942. The first, of course, was the highlight. It will be recalled that in 1939 Canada's armed forces were at a very low ebb and the powers that be had to call in all sorts of groups in addition to the permanent and militia units to line the streets that the royal couple were to travel.

Lisgar, Glebe, Tech, Lasalle and I believe Ashbury cadets were called to the cause. Lisgar and Glebe had corps in existence, Lisgar being the older of the two, but Tech formed the corps for the event. As they were not supposed to have experienced officers some Lisgar boys, including my brother Peter, were "seconded" to lead the Tech boys.

Award spoon of G.E. Rickwood 1930.

Ottawa Collegaite Bugle Band, 1924.

I am not sure how the Tech boys felt about this lead. I know Peter was a little apprehensive the first day he was to assume command.

We were equipped with uniforms that probably were first issued in the late Twenties. Khaki summer drill tunics and britches with puttee leggings. Puttees were difficult to put on at any time but were even more difficult to keep up on the thin legs of first and second form boys. I was made a sergeant because a friend of my brother, Keith Kearney, was my platoon commander. We were also equipped with the famous W.W.I. Ross rifle—without breeches. The weight of the rifle was a little burdensome for the younger boys. Hugh Douglas and Peter Burke, not wishing to carry rifles elected to become the stretcher-bearer party. Their military bearing was noted when they gave a smart "eyes right" to the war memorial when it happened to be on their left.

Our Bugle Band could play one march—"Cailing"—quite well and of course the general salute. I believe the King and Queen heard that salute nine times during their visit to Ottawa. Tommy Davies was the lead bugler who, with the crook attachment, could play a sort of descant which livened up the salute and "Cailing."

Memory also recalls that King Edward Avenue which we lined one day, had a central boulevard planted with large elm trees; a little different from the avenue we see today.

I can't recall too much of what happened during the following years except we did our route marches, fired target rifles in the firing range on the top floor and at the drill hall.

In April and May of 1924 the 94th was completely outfitted with new uniforms. The "old issue serge" was replaced with "an air force pattern forage cap worn on the right side of the head, an open-necked tunic after the Norfolk cut, with khaki shirts and royal blue ties. Detachable shoulder-straps also of royal blue. Trousers were cut as breeches, with dark blue hose taking the place of the old binding puttees." Posed in their new military garb for the *Vox Lycei*, 1924 are; Top row, L to R; Lt. W. Cox, Capt. L. Robertson, Lt. L. Williams, Lt. J. Johnston, Lt. K. West, Capt. C. Gamble, Maj. G. Hatch (OM); Second row, Lt. H. Putnam, R.S.M. B. Doran, Lt. E. Howard, Lt. J. Lyon, Lt. E. Burke, Lt. W. Blackburn, Lt. W. Bradley, Lt. H. McGuire; Front row, Maj. J. Anderson, Maj. C. Taylor, Lt.Col. F. Taylor, Lieut. W.V.B. Riddell (instructor), Maj. D. Grant (Adj.), Maj. C. Clark, Capt. H. Munro. On floor, Maj. P. Foran, Lt. J. Blair, Lt. J. Chapleau, Lt. E. Haines, Lt. F. Donahue.

Wartime officers of Lisgar Cadet Corps, 1943-1944. This was a very active 94th, drilling and practising under the sharp eye of L.H. Meng, but also attending church parade, taking Governor General Athlone's salute, having numerous inspections and attending cadet camp in the summer at Welling, Ontario. Many of these young men were to leave school to join the forces. Lined up between Lisgar and a military store are; R.S.M., F. Lathey, Lt. B. Whittle, Lt.Col. (Reserve) S. Bateman, Lt. D. Coupland, Maj. G. Croil, Lt. G. Thompson, Lt.Col. A. Kniewasser, O.C. Lt. D. Kirby, Maj. M. Trewin, Lt. S. Truman, Capt. G. Wilson, Lt. J. Kirby, Lt. R. Armstrong, Capt. R. Code, (Adj.).

Cartier Square, 1920, houses of old Centretown in background with Lisgar cadets being drilled by officer. Herb Beall, cadet historian, notes that the cadets are wearing the old uniforms.

In the fall of 1941, Mr Louis Meng, a great teacher, storyteller and enthusiastic supporter of the Cadet Corps promoted me to Battalion Commander with Ron Rankin second-in-command and Ben Shapiro as adjutant. Our rifles had been returned to the government and some of our uniforms over the years seemed to have disappeared so that not all of us could be outfitted for the inspection in the spring of '42. As it turned out, I could muster my father's First World War officer's cap, the tunic of the cadet uniform with Father's Sam Browne and grey flannels. Other cadets had full or partial uniforms. We were a brave but motley crew as we paraded to Varsity Oval for our inspection.

Later that summer I was outfitted with a complete uniform but not as Colonel of the Corps but as Aircraftsman Second Class (AC2). A major drop in rank but not in pay. Some of the other officers in the 1942 corps were my twin, John, who was head boy, Peter Wright, Bill Patrick, Bob Hill, Colin Shaw, Andee Lauzon and G. Cook.

My last connection with the Cadet Corps was when I had returned from overseas in 1945. I was asked by Louis Meng to join the inspection party again at the Varsity Oval. Needless to say the corps looked much smarter in the new

105

Entrance to the mysterious fourth floor, once the site of shooting range, later storage for leftovers and obsolescences, now partially filled with heating ducts.

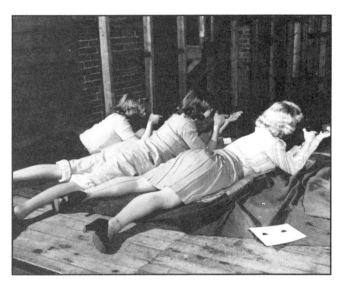

The girls rifle club practises rifle drill on the Fourth Floor. Gold and silver ankle bracelets were very popular during the 1940s and sometimes bore the name of and perhaps a message from a "steady." L to R.: Irene Woolford, Barbara (Fenton) Fisher, and Nancy (Lewis) Robson.

uniforms than the 1942 corps but, with or without uniforms we all have happy memories of our time in the cadet corps.

I don't know if the cadets prepared us for service in the regular forces but many of the boys who served in the cadet corps also served in the forces as is evident by the plaques in the main hall listing the names of all who served.

SALUTE TO LISGAR C.I. 94TH CADET CORPS

There's something about a soldier
There's something about a soldier
There's something about a soldier
That is fine, fine, fine.
He may be a fifth form student
Who's witty, wise and prudent
He may be a single fellow of
Grade nine, nine, nine.
But there's something about his bearing
That's due to the crest he's wearing
There's something about his spirit
All ashine, shine, shine
So we'll be there with the rest
And place them with the best
And cheer the 94th
Because it's yours and mine!

The Cadet Corps at Lisgar remains an integral part of the early history of the school. Many of the young men ("Old Boys") went on to distinguish themselves on the battlefields of the Empire. Following the Second World War there was a dramatic decrease in support for matters military. The horrors of this period had finally destroyed any vestiges of innocence regarding the absolute atrocity of armed conflict. Because of this fatigue with war the Cadet Corps has never resurfaced at Lisgar and, from the late Forties until renovations of the entire physical plant, 1976-79, the rifle range was used as a storage area for theatre sets and other miscellaneous items.

Remembrance Day for many years at Lisgar was commemorated inside the school. But when the last war veteran teacher retired in 1991, it was decided students would attend the November 11th Memorial Ceremony. A thousand Lisgarites marched the half-mile to the National War Memorial in Confederation Square to see the ceremonies honouring the men who gave their lives in two Wars, a number of them ex-Lisgarites trained in the 94th.

* * * * *

Austin Lawrence, in a 1992 paper prepared for Dr. Janet Marchain, further illuminated the mystery of the "Fourth Floor," this time from a present-day student's point of view.

The fourth floor of Lisgar Collegiate Institute is the attic of one of the most venerable scholastic institutions in the city. Every time one walks up the east staircase to the third floor and passes those steep steps that lead to the locked steel door at the top of the landing one wonders what secrets the highest level of the school hides. The mind may leap to visions of arcane Victorian science experiments, an arsenal of weapons, or perhaps straps and canes left over from the last century's days of physical punishments.

In September 1942, on instruction from the Ontario Department of Education, a scheme of defence training was included in the school curriculum. All Lisgar students were given training in communications, aircraft identification, fire-fighting and other roles in civilian protection. Here student Cadet Art Bray shows civilian Ann Thompson how to correctly don the gas mask.

The most interesting fact about the fourth floor is that is was used as a training area for the Lisgar cadet corps. They often trained at the Drill Hall just beside Lisgar but the shooting team needed their own range and the military related courses also needed facilities for rifle practice. They decided to construct a rifle range because of the rising popularity of shooting competitions in Canada at the time and also because the government wanted an increase of military instruction in the curriculum.

In 1912 a rifle range was constructed in the east attic of the school. The fourth floor shooting gallery was born. Practices and competitions were held at the attic rifle range from October to March. The range was not the most pleasant place to be in the school as it lacked heating facilities. Herbert Beall, an LCI student between the years 1922-27, commented, "The rifle range was an intimidating place for us students. It was dark and dusty."

The rifle range was only opened for valid reasons. "A padlocked door of wire mesh kept away unchaperoned students," recalled Beall. It was 22 meters long and four targets were used at a time. The target consisted of a large steel plate that was covered by wooden planks. Originally the targets were lifted by makeshift pullies, but then in the 1930s they were merely tacked on to the wooden planks. The planks were not replaced very often. "I remember it was always difficult finding a spot on the wood that was

not filled with holes," remembered Walter Mann, teacher at LCI from 1933-68.

The practices were held after school for the men's and women's teams as well as all interested cadets. Therefore no science classes were disturbed by loud gunfire going off above their heads.

Between the two World Wars it was compulsory for the male student body at LCI to become members of the cadet corps. "When I was at Lisgar we all had to shoot a few rounds and be in the Lisgar cadet corps," remarked Beall. In the 1933 Vox Lycei it was stated that all cadets must make use of the rifle range. Before 1933 it was only used by those who were interested. This system was changed because it had become new education policy that all LCI cadets (which was all male Lisgar students at that time) must shoot and have in-house competitions.

Records are unclear as to when the range was put out of commission because after 1946 the *Vox Lycei* made no mention of it and neither Beall nor Mann are certain as to the date of the gallery's demise. "Shortly after World War II the cadet corps was dropped" because "a lot of the boys refused to turn out for cadets after World War II. They became disillusioned and wanted peace," recalled Beall. The attitudes of the government and the educational system towards the military instruction of youth in school had also changed after the World Wars.

In 1954 the martial equipment was turned over to the military and the attic was used for the ignominious role of storage, mainly of drama props. "When I first arrived at Lisgar Collegiate Institute in 1952 only six rifles and six old cadet uniforms were left in the attic," related Robert McMichael, Principal of Lisgar between 1972-76.

In 1976 Lisgar Collegiate Institute was renovated at a cost of about $4.8 million. During the course of the renovations the rifle range was eradicated. "During the renovations the fourth floor was stripped. Its treasures were either discarded or packed off, fluorescent lights were installed, and it became the home of the new heating and air-circulation equipment," bemoaned Jim Beall, teacher at Lisgar from 1968-77.

Today the fourth floor is reached by climbing the east staircase up past the third floor then opening a heavy fire door and climbing a marble and iron staircase. The fourth floor rooms are divided by walls of, variously, old brick, lumber and also naked gypsum board. In some places the ceiling are quite low and the only windows are the round ones that can be seen from the front of the building. The floors are of rough, unfinished wood that is very old. The cracks between the floorboards contain numerous .22 calibre shell casings which are the only leftovers from the rifle range.

A few things are stored in the various empty rooms of the fourth floor. They include, broken auditorium seats, old air filters, sewing machines, art stands, modern tables and chairs, framed paintings, and old-fashioned desks, the turn-of-the-century variety that are usually bolted to the floor.

However the attic is mainly filled with air circulation equipment; many of the rooms contain some part of the air flow system.

There is much graffiti on the walls. Most of it is on the brick walls and is from various time periods. Some of the graffiti is from the 1930s and 1940s, most is from the 1970s and a fair amount is from the late 1980s and early 1990s. Pretty well all of the graffiti consists of the name of the perpetrator and the date. The marble staircase even continues past the fourth floor up to a tiny landing (a fifth floor!) and a four and a half foot door which leads out onto the roof.

The attic of Lisgar Collegiate Institute has a past that is longer and maybe even more interesting than the whole histories of some high schools in Canada.

* * * * *

Colonel James Ralston, Federal Minister of Defence in Mackenzie King's Cabinet during World War II, congratulates head boy and cadet leader Sydney Bateman after review of the Cadet Corps.

On November 11, 1992, ex-Lisgarite Joel Slone returned to his old school and was very disappointed to find nobody in. When guidance counsellor Doug Arrand informed Mr. Slone that the principal and the students were up at the Cenotaph for a Remembrance Day Ceremony Mr. Slone told this story;

"Fifty years ago to this very day I was on my way to Lisgar from my home on Goulburn Avenue. I was walking down Laurier and as I was crossing the Laurier Street bridge I noticed the troops, the Cameron Highlanders and others, marching under the bridge on their way up to the Cenotaph for the Remembrance Day Ceremony, 1942. It was an instantaneous decision—it struck me out of the blue—and rather than turn down towards Lisgar, I carried on down Laurier to Metcalfe, up Metcalfe to Queen to the recruiting office where I signed up immediately as a member of the air force. After doing all the paper signing, I marched back to Lisgar, walked into Johnny Dunlop's office and announced 'I quit'. I have never been back to this day. I brought my daughter with me to see my old Alma Mater which I left fifty years ago to the hour."

THE GLEE CLUB, THE ORCHESTRA, THE SCHOOL ASSEMBLY, THE ANNUAL CONCERT

During the first fifty years of Lisgar's history student extra-curricular activities were limited to involvement in the *Vox Lycei* and the Lyceum, the first an outlet for literary, creative, reportorial talents and the second for oratorial, intellectual and political talents. But shortly after the turn of the century these student talents were given further outlets in the Glee Club, the Orchestra, the School Assembly, and the Annual Concert. The emergence and history of all these is recorded in *The History of the O.C.I. 1843-1943* and is reprinted here.

At the turn of the century there were no organized musical activities in the O.C.I. Then, as now, there were talented pupils in the school who might contribute a solo or a chorus on a Lyceum program, but with no morning assembly (and indeed with no convenient place of assembly until after the building of the west wing in 1908) there was little incentive and scant opportunity for concerted musical effort.

Just as in the history of mankind voices were created before trombones, so in the history of the O.C.I. the Glee Club came into being before the Orchestra. In the early years, the Glee Club would become active for special occasions only, but it was an important organization by 1912, and the first few annual concerts given by the school were presented under its aegis, since the Student Council had not yet come into existence. The first concert was produced in the new Assembly Hall, with properties rented from the Dominion Theatre, and had on its program, inter alia, Haydn's Toy Symphony, in which the few musicians in the school did the skilled labour while the athletes and belles of the day rent the welkin with toy trumpets, rattles and vocal accompaniment. In these earlier efforts, musicians well-known throughout the city were engaged to rehearse and conduct the performance, although much assistance was given by regular members of the staff, notably Mr. H.C. Mann, who sang in the bass section, and Mr. W.E. Donaldson, who did a tremendous amount of work with both the singing and the speaking parts of operettas and was president of the club for many years. Mr. James A. Smith, later Musical Director of the Public Schools, conducted the Glee Club in one year, and the late J. Edgar Birch, then organist at St. Andrew's Church, in another. In fact, in the 1914 concert Mr. Birch conducted the Glee Club, while Mr. (later Dr.) J.W. Bearder conducted the orchestra in the operetta "Spanish Gypsies," the orchestra of the evening being strongly reinforced by musicians who had long since passed school age.

Although by this time the Glee Club had become well-established in the school, the Orchestra did not become a permanent organization until a little later. Even so, it was the first regular school orchestra in Ontario and possibly in the Dominion, and its beginnings are therefore interesting. Immediately after the new Assembly Hall was built in 1908, Dr. McDougall had transferred the opening morning exercises from the class rooms, where they had been conducted by the Form Masters, to the Hall where the whole school could come together as a unit. This in itself was another first for the old School,—it was the first to hold regular morning assemblies, a practice now followed (a long way behind in some cases) by most large schools in the province. These assemblies were without music of any kind until the second year of the war; but when the first big casualty lists began to come back and spread gloom throughout the community, the students wished to sing patriotic songs at their morning exercises. To accompany this singing, a few musically inclined boys of the school, among whom was Hugh Huggins (now organist at All Saints' Church), asked Dr. Bearder to form them into an orchestra. With the blessing of Dr. McDougall this was done, and the first orchestra came into being. It was small, and for the special occasions continued to be augmented by outsiders, as the photographs of the 1916 concert reveal.

It was not until 1917, that the orchestra blossomed forth into full flower. Meanwhile the young musicians who had formed the first orchestra had graduated and others had come in. There was still no permanent equipment, but Dr. Bearder, who was by now the regular director of the Glee Club, conducted the music of the assembly on a voluntary basis. Some time in that school year a few of the bolder spirits among the student musicians of the school conceived what appeared to be the revolutionary idea of appealing to the Board to spend some money on them. Dr. McDougall sponsored their deputation, which was led by Dave Adamson, No. 1 student violinist of the time. The Board was very interested indeed, and bought traps, bells and stands, much of which equipment—somewhat battle-scarred it is true—still does service in the Hall. With this encouragement, the orchestra never faltered. In 1919,

Dr. Bearder was appointed Director of Music. He was present at all morning assemblies, and capably directed the Orchestra and the Glee Club in all its activities. Later he gave part time to the Glebe, and still later, part time to the High School of Commerce, and before he retired in 1938, he had conducted and arranged musically a total of forty-seven annual concerts, twenty-five of which were at Lisgar.

The annual concert, which has had a continuous existence since 1913, featured operettas for the first ten or twelve years of its life, "The Yokohama Maid," "H.M.S. Pinafore," "Captain Crossbones," "The Lass of Limerick Town." They were colourful and ambitious productions. Not the least intriguing part of the performance was the preview which the audience had of the singers as they paraded up the side aisles before they sang—a situation which arose from the lack of an entrance backstage.

In this long line of operettas a historian might be pardoned for picking out two outstanding occasions. The first was in the performance of "The Magic Key" sometime in the late 'teens. For this operetta it became necessary to procure a huge key to be carried about the stage by the hero. Some helpful pupil, who had a relative in authority in one of the neighbouring houses of correction, borrowed or "lifted" one which might have been used to lock a dungeon. Gilded and bedizened by the students, it was a feature of the show, but alas, it vanished mysteriously and magically after the last performance.

The second incident occurred in the concert of 1924, on the night when the tower on the Museum was riven asunder, more or less, by an earthquake. In the middle of the performance the good old O.C.I. shook as it had never shaken before. The piano floated away from the accompanist, and the stage props did a rhumba all their own. The audience and some of the performers began thinking of hasty exits; but Miss Roxie Carrier, who was singing a solo at the time, paused long enough in her performance to say, "Sit still please. It's just an earthquake." Everybody gasped, sat still, and let it quake.

With the change in the school curriculum in 1937, music became a class-room subject as well as an extra-curricular activity. In 1938, Dr. Bearder retired after twenty-five years of service and Mr. Albert Procter, a High School teacher and specialist in music, assumed the combined duties of teacher of music, leader of the Orchestra, and director of the Glee Club.

* * * * *

The social reporter of the *Vox Lycei* 1918-19 described the Annual Concert at Lisgar, an event that attracted a city-wide audience:

Another milestone in the history of the O.C.I was passed when, on the 14th and 15th of March, the Annual Concert was held. Undoubtedly this year's concert was the best for many years. The whole-hearted interest of a number of

Early in the fall of 1918 Prof. J.W. Bearder organized the first orchestra in high school history. The orchestra put joy into morning assemblies, played at the monthly dances during the winters and played an enormous part in the success of the annual concerts. During its first winter the orchestra appealed to the school for $100 to purchase instruments. Total collections reached $105. This is a photo of Lisgar's first orchestra, 1918-1919. Standing, L. to R.; M. Lathey, J. Baxter, R. Code, R. Anderson, O. Cameron, E. Gorman, L. Goodall, H. Vagan, C. Lathey, C. Summers, H. Gray, A. Bruce. Sitting; C. Menzies, D. Adamson, J.W. Bearder (conductor), Misses T. Sauvé, G. Read, M. Wallace.

O.C.I. orchestra, 1920-1921. Standing, L. to R.; A. Devenney, R. MacIntosh, S. Bruce, R. Charles, H. Segaolowitz, J. Baxter, G. Gowling (librarian), T. Graham, C. Summers, Mr. Lathey, E. McKeever, ? Minter. Sitting; Misses J. Watt, M. Cameron, J. Clarke, C. Gamble, C.L. Code, J. Fisher, O. Graham, C. Moorehead, M. Ogilvie, M. Kendall. On floor; McKeever, B. Shenkman, B. McCarthy, J. Johnson, R. Binks.

The Glee Club cast for the operetta "Captain Cross Bones" performed for the ninth annual concert, April, 1921. The Lisgar concerts were a major social event of the season, involved months of work in practice, figuratively speaking "a cast of thousands," and hours of work on extravagant sets and behind-the-scenes lighting. Unfortunately, the over one hundred players in this photograph were not identified by the *Vox Lycei* reporters. But we do know that Grace Ely, Royal Williamson, Ernie Perkin, Miss Grant, Art Bartram, Miss Wyne Wallace, Miss Peggy Nichol, Carmen Summers, Bob MacIntosh played major roles. Mr. Bearder and Miss Gilhooly directed. The two previous years had also seen major productions, "The Yokohama Maid" and "Pearl the Fishermaid" in which Grace Ely again starred with Maynard Booth, Syd Harris, Marion Moffatt, Arthur Pennington and Gurth Donaldson.

pupils of the school, and the hearty co-operation of certain members of the staff made possible the almost unparalleled success of this great factor in the life of the school.

The Operetta, "Pearl the Fishermaid," excelled, if anything, last year's production. Its plot entailed more decisive action, brought forth more dramatic situations than "The Magic Key." The setting is in a little Welsh fishing village. Pearl, the Fishermaiden, is a "waif of the ocean," having been cast up by the sea sixteen years previous to the opening of the story, and who has since dwelt with her foster parents, Mistress and Daddy Whelk. Lorenzo, a renowned brigand chief and his companions come to shore to repair their vessel. Lorenzo falls in love with Pearl, renounces his old life, and discloses his identity to the Fishermaiden who, as she reciprocates the love, fears for his safety, knowing a price to be set upon his head. How Pearl goes to Court and pleads for her lover, how amusing complications ensue, and how Pearl eventually saves her lover's life, are all well worked out in the second and third acts of the Operetta. Lorenzo "turns out" to be the King's long-lost son, and Pearl is discovered to be the princess who was betrothed in infancy to Lorenzo. The court jester remarks quaintly on the new turn of affairs and all ends happily to the sound of bridal bells.

The different characters were exceptionally well portrayed by the actors. Miss Grace Ely was "Pearl," and Mr. Maynard Booth, "Lorenzo." The parts of "Daddy" and "Mistress Whelk" were played by Mr. Syd Harris and Miss Marion

Moffatt respectively. Mr. Arthur Pennington personated the King, while Mr. Gurth Donaldson, resplendent in costume of red and yellow, acted well the role of court jester.

* * * * *

The *Vox Lycei* of April 1914 reported on a variety of speakers who addressed Lisgar's Morning Assemblies during that year. From that *Vox:*

During the year many prominent men have visited the school and have delivered very instructive and interesting talks, which we have all enjoyed.

In January, Hon. T.W. Crothers, visited the school. In his talk on "Work and Play," he pictured to us the view which we should take of our school work. He said that unless we regarded it as play we would never succeed.

Rev. Mr. Bowie, of London, England, visited us in January and gave us a very interesting account of the schools of London and the divisions into which that city is divided.

On February the fourth, Prof. Shortt explained to us the value of education for the Civil Service. He said the value of education was to train the mind and hence make it capable of grasping new work quickly.

On February, twenty-third, Rev. Prof. Boyle, of Trinity College, Toronto, pointed out to us the many advantages for students entering college, which were to be found in Trinity College. He also encouraged young men to enter the ministry.

Dr. W.A. Scott of Toronto, who was once a pupil of the O.C.I., explained to us the value of the short time we spend here, and advised us to make the most of it. He also spoke of his own days spent at the O.C.I.

A course of instructive lectures have been given to the commercial forms. Mr. Cambie lectured on "Banking." Mr. Stewart McClenaghan delivered an address on "Retail Business Methods," and Mr. Cecil Bethune has given two lectures on Fire Insurance,—one on February 25th, and the other on March 25th.

* * * * *

THE ANNUAL CONCERT
LAWRENCE RENTON
1935-1939

I can't recall the exact year or day, perhaps 1935 and maybe late in the month of March, but I know for sure it was the annual Lisgar concert. This gala stage show, complete with the sale of homemade fudge at intermission, was like a command performance for parents, sisters, brothers, relatives, friends, and neighbours—and anyone else you could badger into buying a ticket. That wasn't an easy task, considering the poor economic climate of that period, as most of the world was locked into a devastating depression. Finding a spare quarter (or whatever the price was) to blow on such a questionable piece of entertainment could play the devil with most household budgets.

Nevertheless, in spite of a deep recession, ticket sales must have been brisk, as that Friday night, about fifty-seven years ago—give or take a year—there was a full house.

For me this is where the fun that night began. Miss Persie Meadows was my English teacher (Lit. and Comp.) that year. "Persie," as she was affectionately known by the students, was a striking-looking, straight-backed, ample-bosomed, good-sized lady, with a perfectly polished English accent who could put the fear of God into her students.

Shakespeare and the like were required reading and study, and Miss Meadows could make the students memorize passages of *As You Like It*, etc., etc., then require that they reel them off in class flawlessly. Of course, in the process you were stopped frequently to have your pronunciation and enunciation haughtily corrected as you shook nervously.

Persie always required her students to play a strong part in the annual concert program, and this particular year was no exception. We weren't asked what we would like to do, we were told emphatically that our class would present the story of *St. George and the Dragon*.

I know I wasn't very good, or very interested for that matter, in English Lit. and Comp. My father repeatedly told me so, and Miss Meadows essentially said the same thing by giving me terrible marks—though I think I did squeak by with a pass. However, I was not daunted as I knew I was good with my hands; a few basic tools, a few bits and pieces,

and I could make or fix just about anything. When our overpowering Persie requested volunteers to design and fabricate St. George's armour, shield, and sword, the dragon's head, body covering, and tail, I jumped joyously to the challenge and immediately offered to make all the props. My spontaneous offer must have quickly endeared me to Miss Meadows as she abruptly announced (in spite of my poor marks in English) that Lawrence would play the part of St. George.

Making St. George's armour, shield, and sword was easily done with cardboard, scraps of wood, glue, and nails, and a little paint; but making a realistic dragon head, a body-covering (for two guys), leg coverings for the same guys and a five-foot-long tail taxed my ingenuity and my material supply to the limit. And please keep in mind that neither school nor parents had any money for supplies.

Presto! Without boring you with how it all was made and with what, it all was made. I delivered the props to Miss Persie in good time for rehearsals—and guess what? She heaped praises upon me for such a wonderful job. With Miss Meadows's skilful coaching and directing, rehearsals went extremely well as the big night came closer and closer.

Dwaine Merkley was the front half of the dragon and Doug McLean the rear half. Dwaine, bent over at ninety degrees and with his head inside the dragon's, could see where the dragon could or should go, while Doug, also bent over at right angles with his hands locked onto Dwaine's hips, followed wherever the front half led him. Since Doug could not see, the delay effect gave the dragon a realistic snakelike motion.

The night of nights finally arrived, along with nervousness everywhere; the big brown curtains parted or lifted (my memory fails me here) and there we were, *St. George and the Dragon*. And did we do our stuff! Nervousness disappeared, the fight was on. I can't remember if there was any dialogue or if someone recited the story. But I do vividly recall slashing my silver-painted wooden sword at the charging, snarling, growling, and hissing horrible dragon, while being at the same time very careful not to bruise my hidden classmates or knock the gruesome fangs out of the marvellous dragon head that I had so laboriously made. As St. George I defended myself ably from attacks by the angry roaring monster by using my white-painted cardboard shield, which sported a crimson cross from the top to bottom and from side to side.

Lots of action on stage and a great lighting effect from the deeply recessed row of footlights along the front of the stage, added even more excitement to the production. But it was difficult for the dragon to see where it was going. The audience cheered wildly as it became obvious that St. George was winning and the dragon was about to be slain. Sensing the audience, St. George and the two parts of the dragon put hearts and soul into the final action. The dragon wheeled about in a mad rage, charging at St. George,

Cast of the operetta "If I were a King" performed for Lisgar's twenty-fourth annual concert, 1937. Back row, L to R; P. Box, R. Campbell, N. Ackland, C. O'Malley, R. Maloney, S. Allen, M. Turner, J. Atherton, H. Jost. Front row, D. Trentadue, W. Steadman, C. LeRoyer, G. Gennis, J. Bray, P. Howlett, A. Harris.

The chorus for the operetta "If I were a King." Back row, L to R; L. Jarvis, I. Sparks, E. Carter, R. Maloney. Middle row; B. Teevens, A. Hemmington, L. Coupal, C. LeRoyer, K. Kincarney. Front row; C. Munro, G. Bodovsky, D. Glasgow, S. Freedman, P. Simpson, M. Loper.

tossing its huge head up and down and from side to side, emanating terrifying noises not only from its mouth but from its belly as well.

And those wonderful footlights, which were creating such a dramatic effect, were about to assist in the dragon's death. This row of lights, deeply recessed in a metal trough the full length of the stage, consisted of unprotected hundred-watt bulbs spaced about every six or twelve inches apart. Then the front half of the dragon in its final charge came perilously close to walking into the footlights. As the front half abruptly changed direction ninety degrees to get away from the lights, the back half, not seeing at any time where the front half was headed, spun around in an arc that brought Doug's feet into the slippery metal trough. Try as he might he could not get enough traction to get out of the trough and his feet kept smashing electric lights as he skidded along the trough. Still hanging onto Dwaine (who now was changing his course to reduce the angle the two of them made with each other), Doug was unable to get enough foothold to extricate himself. The crashing and banging of exploding light bulbs, the white fumes and sparks rising with the shattering glass, coupled with the dragon's desperate efforts to right itself, broke up the entire audience—a decibel metre could have probably hit ninety or more that night.

St. George could not tolerate this destruction any longer as the dragon continued to attack foot after foot of lights, and the audience continued to roar with laughter. Enough was enough. He sent his trusty wooden sword crashing down on the head of the dragon (Dwaine's head was well protected by the wooden frame inside the head covering.) The dragon got the message and died there and then with his back feet and long limp tail resting in the footlights' trough. A few grunts and groans from the expiring dragon was all to be heard from the prostrate reptile as the laughter in the assembly hall slowly subsided.

Strangely enough—and probably a good thing—I have no recollection of Miss Meadows's reaction to the ignominious end of her play, nor do I recall who paid for all the broken light bulbs.

* * * * *

Charles Atlas, the Thirties and Forties equivalent of Arnold Schwarzenegger, used to make some wonderfully outlandish claims in magazines like *Popular Mechanics* and *Mechanics Illustrated*, obviously aimed at young men. For example, in a full page advertisement of the March 1940 issue of *Mechanics Illustrated*, there's a full-length photo of gorgeous Charles himself with the claimer, "Twice winner of the title, 'The World's Most Perfectly Developed Man.' " Further ballyhoo in the ad indicated Atlas could, through his secret "Dynamic Tension" in only fifteen minutes a day (he doesn't say in how many days) give your skinny, flabby, pep-less body a new suit of muscles that would be the envy of everyone. Elsewhere in the ad he confesses "I MYSELF was once a

97 pound weakling. I was too frail for sports, ashamed to strip for a swim or gym, pushed around by everyone in my neighbourhood."

Believe me there were plenty of Charles Atlas physiques around Lisgar in my day, but I don't recall any one of them ever parting with a dime to Charles Atlas to build themselves from scrawny adolescents to prize-winning muscle men.

One of these natural physiques belonged to outstanding gymnast Alex Fawcett, a shorter version of Charles Atlas with thick sinewed hands covered with callouses created by his many hours of vise-like gripping of the high bar, his specialty. Alex didn't laugh or even smile very often and he certainly was a young man I would never have trifled with— he'd have broken me in two like matchwood.

Now, in order to tell my second story of the Lisgar concerts, I must diverge a little.

Lisgar's annual concerts were probably no different from any other high school concerts in two respects at least. Things that went wonderfully well and those that went wonderfully wrong. I use the word "wonderfully" because in both of my concert stories it was the things that went wonderfully wrong which added an unplanned dimension of humour that seemed to tickle the audience—if the amount of laughter was any indication at all.

Considerably more than half a century has expired since I attended or took part in a Lisgar concert, so please bear with me when I say I'm not absolutely certain that all the details of the following hilarious episodes are exactly correct. But I certainly can convey the essence.

As I remember, it was customary to hold numbers like recitations, solos, plays, skits, in the first half of the concert. During intermission sickly sweet home-made fudge both chocolate and vanilla, tooth-breaking peanut brittle and questionable quality cinder sponge toffee were all sold by Lisgar girls to anyone in the audience who could wrestle up fifteen cents or maybe it was only a dime. No doubt all of this candy was probably made in the Domestic Science classroom by the same gals who sold it. While the candy sale was going on, the stage was being hastily, but hopefully, safely, prepared for the gymnastic part of the program of which I think I may accurately say the high-bar solo always stole the show.

A squad of muscular young men clad in natty, short-sleeved grey jerseys and white side-striped blue pants, flitted around the stage area pushing and pulling the gear and unrolling numerous well-worn once white tumbling mats. To me, these mats were so thin and so hard that when you landed on them, they felt like third-grade palliasses stuffed with crushed stone. No blue, vinyl-covered thick impact-absorbing foam slabs in those austere days! For that matter I don't think foam rubber was yet invented.

OTTAWA COLLEGIATE INSTITUTE
PRESENTATION of the OPERETTA "THE YOKOHAMA MAID" by the STUDENTS - APRIL 17-1920

SEVENTH ANNUAL CONCERT
PRESENTATION of "PEARL the FISHERMAID" - O.C.I. MAR-15-1918

As I remember, there were flush-mounted steel plates set in the stage floor to which the stabilizing cables of the high bar were fastened or hooked. These steel plates dictated the position of the high bar and all other equipment was placed accordingly around the rest of the stage area.

Let me repeat:

There was no question that the high bar performers stole the show on concert nights and never failed to thrill the audience, particularly when giant swings were executed. It was then that the gymnast seemed to disappear into the raised stage curtains as he went over the top and thankfully re-appeared a split second later on the down-side. The thin steel cross bar would bend frighteningly through the effect of centrifugal force created by the speed of the gymnast swinging in these giant circles. Before the eyes of the entire mesmerized audience, the vibrating stabilizing cables would

draw as taut as a violin string on one side and then slacken off on the other. The reverse of this would occur as the same centrifugal force pulled hard on the cross bar. Many in the stilled audience would whisper to each other their concerns about the safety of the bar and its fastenings to the stage floor. Many asked themselves was the cross bar itself about to fracture in two? During high bar performances there was always an eerie silence throughout the whole concert hall partly because of the safety concerns and partly because of the thrill of watching the performer.

In the concert I so well remember one of the performers that night was Alex Fawcett who was in my class that year. As you might expect a high bar specialist possessed, as well as strong arms and legs, a great set of stomach muscles so necessary to achieve giant swings. After jumping up to reach the bar, Alex slowly began swinging back and forth

THE ORCHESTRA

Lisgar Orchestra

Officers for the year 1924-25:—

Musical Director—J. W. Bearder, F.R.C.O.
Honorary President—Mr. I. T. Norris.
President—Sol Kavalsky.
Vice-President—Stewart Lintell.
Secretary-Treasurer—L. Freiman.
Librarian—N. W. McKeever.
Assistant Librarian—J. Bell.
Committee—Miss H. Ogilvie (Chairman), and K. Reed,
   J. Meagher, L. Coplan.

like a well-oiled clock pendulum, gaining speed and height with each arc—reaching for the exact momentum which eventually would carry him over the top.

The audience was absolutely hushed; one could now easily hear the faintest of sounds floating around the ancient assembly hall. As the solo performer strained his solar plexus to its maximum to go over the top for the first giant swing, I heard familiar easily identifiable noises emit from the gymnast. There was no doubt in my mind the sounds I heard were what I thought they were.

Remember now, in the thirties one did not laugh at such bodily embarrassments. One was to turn away and ignore the event, hoping it would not be repeated.

On the downward part of the swing all was totally quiet, but when Alex flexed his solar plexus to go over the top for

the second giant swing, his gastro-intestinal system gave a repeat performance. This time, though, one muted chuckle was heard in the audience and then another, and another.

I remember being seated next to my mother that night. My mother was a gentle, well-mannered lady, not prone to laughing when someone was in an embarrassing situation. After the first few giggles from the audience, she turned her head and looked at me with raised eyebrows. A faint smile came over her face and I knew then that it was in order for me to return the smile without being guilty of bad manners.

Alex a true performer, continued his giant swings, each time emitting the now undeniable sounds. As he made his valiant arcs, the giggles increased, crescendoed into laughter. My mother and I, no longer able to contain ourselves, joined into the audience participation. The full house rolled in the aisles—so much for Victorian manners—as Alex arc-ed on stage, a young professional adhering to the age-old dictum of the theatre—the show must go on.

The next day Alex verified all our suspicions. In order to get home from school for a bite to eat and back early to Lisgar for his performance, he had bolted a can of beans!

* * * * *

I have some more stories of Lisgar in my time. In those days the lockers were double, that is, they had an upper and lower section each for a different student. The seniors got the top section and the juniors the bottom. Fifth Former Lionel Dent (later the dentist) was above me and he always left his locker door open. Every time I rose from my lower section locker I cracked my head on his steel locker door—I always had wounds on my head and have some scars to this day. Finally, one time I got the courage to complain to him. His reply was, "Never mind, my boy, your turn will come in the upper section. And then you can get even."

Bicycles were very popular in my time. Virtually nobody had a car. We bicycled everywhere including to and from school. There were no bicycle stands and the bicycles were strewn everywhere in the school yard. When you came out, you had to find yours and then disentangle it. I particularly remember an ingenious lad named Keith who fixed his bike so that he could jump off it when he arrived at school, push it away, and it would remain standing up. To do this he had bent his front wheel slightly in one direction and the back one in the other direction so that they made a three-point balanced upright. But boy! it must have been something to drive!

I also well remember a lad named Borthwick who used to bicycle in from Ramsayville to Lisgar—we were all impressed by that feat and sometimes raised a cheer when he arrived, especially in bad weather. "Here comes Borthwick again!"

Eric Nichols, the renowned math teacher, the infamous math teacher also coached the senior football team at Lisgar in my time. For years we had been unable to beat Glebe. Finally Mr. Nichols devised a plan. He had his entire senior football team grow beards, and then he taught them how to growl, fiercesome, frightening, neanderthal growls. When this transformation was complete he turned his team loose on the Glebe team. They capitulated completely.

THE SCHOOL SONG

Here's to dear old Lisgar school!
Shout till the grey walls ring
Phi Chi Psi for thy dear sake;
Let every loyal Lisgarite sing.
Here's to all the happy days,
Here's to the memories dear;
And to thee we pledge our ways
When we leave for our career.

To the girls, to the boys,
To all the old pals when we meet again,
To the rooms, to the halls,
To the staff who helped to make us men,
To the teams, to the games,
To the school that helped us make our names,
To the grey, to the blue,
To the glorious colours we knew -

Fenstad-Colcord-Vallée

Oh! Raise your voice and cheer again,
Sing as the years roll by,
Stand and shout aloud once again
The glory of O.C.I

Then here's to all the knowledge gained,
Here's to the friendships dear;
For thy memories we'll retain
When we leave for our career

—Written in 1934 by Cecil Heeney.

ATHLETICS
1893-1943

The second history of Lisgar, 1843-1943, was written by a committee and published for Lisgar's centenary celebrations. The Editorial and Publication Committee comprised W.P.J. O'Meara, K.C., Chairman, J.J. Dunlop, W.D.T. Atkinson, J.L. Shearer, W.I. Garvock, A.L. Stevenson, Sidney Bateman. For this edition, W.I. Garvock, contributed a comprehensive history of boys' athletics; Dorothy Bishop and Jessie Smith, both girls' gym teachers at Lisgar, compiled the history of girls' athletics during their time.

This first section is excerpted from Garvock's writing:

The motto, "Alere Flamen," has ever been before every class of Lisgar students. Down through the years not only has Lisgar's aim been to keep the lamp of knowledge burning brightly but it has also been a school tradition to maintain a high standard of athletics and sportsmanship and that esprit de corps so intimately associated with the Blue and Grey.

In spite of the lack of a football campus of their own with running track, tennis courts and hockey rink, and in spite of a gymnasium with pillars obstructing the playing floor, Lisgar athletes have overcome these handicaps and won many interscholastic and other championships.

The 1922 Lisgar Collegiate Senior Rugby team. Standing; D. Williams, Don Young, T. Thompson, F. Fortune, Mr. A. A. Burridge, F. Taylor (Director of Athletics), H. Yelland, C. Ackland, G. Rock, W. Skuce. Sitting; Mr. I. T. Norris, R. Slemon, R. St. Germain (Capt.), H. Chevrier, B. Buist. Front Row; G. Yelland, G. Rooney, T. Rooney.

DOMINION CHAMPIONS 1922

ALF. GOULLET
CHAMPION
SIX DAY
BICYCLE RIDER

FRANK BROWN
1/2 and 1 Mile Champion

W. COLES, London
10 Mile Champion

NORMAN WEBSTER
5 Mile Champion

ELSON MacKAY
1/4 Mile Champion

WILLIE SPENCER
UNITED STATES
PROFESSIONAL
CHAMPION

The Choice of Champions

THE 1922 Dominion Championship Races for all distances were won on C.C.M. Bicycles.

Willie Spencer speeded his way to the American Professional Championship on a C.C.M. Flyer Track Racer.

He says "It is the best racing bike."

Alfred Goullet, the greatest of all six-day racers and one of the best all-round riders in the world, won the International Six-Day Race at New York on a C.C.M. Flyer.

THE C.C.M. Flyer is the choice of the Champions because it most perfectly meets their exacting requirements.

Whether for racing, for pleasure, or for riding to school or wherever you want to go, there are C.C.M. Models to meet all needs. Prices today are $15 to $20 lower than "peak" prices.

We will gladly give you the time records of any of the champion riders if you'll drop us a line to our head office at Weston, Ontario.

C.C.M. Bicycles

MASSEY — CLEVELAND — COLUMBIA
RED BIRD — PERFECT
CANADA CYCLE & MOTOR COMPANY, Limited
Weston, Ontario

Montreal   Toronto   Winnipeg   Vancouver

As was to be expected, a large number of the school's pupils and ex-pupils enlisted in the First Great War and won distinction for themselves and their old school. On the Honour Roll are the names of many who had courageously played for Lisgar in hard-fought tussles on the football field or on the ice and afterwards fought bravely and laid down their lives in the great cause of liberty and freedom. In this global war more than 90 percent of the athletes from Lisgar are flying with the R.C.A.F. and the R.A.F., sailing the seven seas with the Royal Navy and the Canadian Navy, or fighting with the Canadian and Imperial land forces.

With the school yell in their ears on a crisp, autumn day, Lisgar has battled many an opposing team in the great game of rugby. Blue and Grey players have always been well enough versed in Greek to know that this rousing yell carried a challenge, "Keep on top of the heap." Lisgar could always be depended upon to supply promising players for Intercollegiate teams at McGill, Queen's and Toronto, as well as for those doughty fighters, Ottawa Roughriders, who won many championships with Lisgar ex-pupils on the team.

Rugby has been played at Lisgar since the '70s. C. Jackson Booth, a great drop kicker and fleet runner, and his brother, the late Fred Booth, played the game in 1877, and C.J. Booth, in 1882, introduced the game he learned at Lisgar to Queen's University, where soccer had previously held sway, starting the Tri-colour on its triumphant journey through Intercollegiate rugby history.

Lisgar's rugby teams from 1903 to 1912 were not in any organized league but played with teams from Ashbury College, Ottawa College, Loyola, Montreal, Kingston, Renfrew and Pembroke high schools, Brockville, Rideaus, the Civil Service, Sandy Hill, and New Edinburgh. Ottawa College Small Yard players were generally heavier and older than the Lisgar students in this period, and many a stout battle was fought on Cartier Square and Varsity Oval between these old rivals.

In 1906 the players were: E. Paisley, B. Frith, S. Metcalfe, E. Erwin, C. Gorman, G. Roberts, V. Bishop, H.S. Smith, C. Parr, F. Baker, A. Johnston, Walter Blue (Capt.), L. Roberts, R. Young, A. Dowling, C. Steele. C. Campbell, L. Brown, J.W. Hedley, coach.

Rugby players who also played about this time were L. Cassells, C. Chipman, S. Christie, H. Conley, J. Boyce, E. Pope, B. Aylmer, J. Harold Ramsey, Gordon Johnstone, who was also a champion swimmer, paddler and hockey player, and Jack Lewis, who afterwards starred at McGill. Smirle Lawson, who afterwards was a star halfback with the University of Toronto, champions from 1909-12, learned the game at Lisgar.

The 1909 rugby team, which won all its matches, defeating Kingston C.I. twice, comprised R. Acheson, G. Dalton, R. Young, E. Lowrey, G. Valentine, J. Fournier, C. Venning, J. Sully, Carson Kendall (Capt.), W. Pennock, G. Monk,

G. Smith, A. Coburn, B. Ami, T.G. Lowrey, W. Megloughlin, B. Claffy, W. Fitzpatrick, W. Stroud, J.W. Hedley, coach.

John A. Sully, who played on the rugby and baseball teams and took a leading part in all school activities, was a pilot in the First Great War. He became Air Vice-Marshal, R.C.A.F. In the 1944 King's New Year Honours List he was made a Companion, Order of the Bath (Military Division).

Lisgar's 1911 team, which beat Loyola 6 to 4, when Don Brophy kicked two field goals, and played Montreal H.S. to a 10-10 draw, consisted of E.P. Wilson, J.S. Goddard, Don Brophy (Capt), A.D. Pope, W.G. Treadwell, L. Lamplough, J.H. Odell, D.P. Kirby, V.S. McClenaghan, F.N. Falls, E.L Rainboth, E. Smith, K. Fleck, A. McLachlan, R. Drake, and B. Dalglish.

SPORTING AND ATHLETIC GOODS

Hockey Sticks
Hockey Skates
Hockey Pucks
Hockey Boots
Shin Guards
Snowshoes
Toboggans

Hockey Sweaters
Coat Sweaters
Jerseys
Pants
Skies
Sleighs
Scout Outfits

Bicycle Sundries and Repair Shop. Cleveland and Brantford Cycles. Canoes, Guns and Ammunition and Indian Motor Cycles. Boxing Gloves. Punching Bags.

KETCHUM & COMPANY, LIMITED
Cor. BANK and SPARKS STS., OTTAWA   PHONE Q. 499

Don Brophy excelled in all branches of athletics. He won the all-round championship for three years, was a star rugby, hockey, basketball, and baseball player. At sixteen he played for Ottawa City and later for McGill. He was killed flying with the Royal Air Force in the First Great War.

The successful 1913 team which defeated Renfrew, Loyola, and the Y.M.C.A. City League team: R. Smith, L. Watson, A. Urquhart, D. Talbot, C. Bishop, P. Barnett, K. Urquhart, C. Forsythe, C. Pratt, L. Hemphill, F. Rogers, E. Devitt, H.C. McCarthy, J. McFadden, T. Quaile, W. McLean, Fred Cowan, O. LaFleur, A. Kendall.

With the appointment of Mr. A.A. Burridge as Physical Culture Head in 1916, the school had the advantage of a coach who had specialized in several departments of athletics. Inter-form rugby was organized with 16 teams and 270 boys taking part. All branches of athletics received a fillip. The programme was arranged to attract the largest number of players and not merely those who were naturally adept at games. In track and field events classes were arranged according to weight from 85 pounds to 135 pounds.

Rugby felt a new lease on life from the new programme. The team was undefeated in 1915 and 1916. In 1917 Lisgar vanquished both Loyola and Ottawa College, a unique achievement. Nothing daunted, the team of 1917 played two games in Montreal the same day. They defeated Westmount in the morning but lost to Loyola in the afternoon.

Players on these teams were: 1916—D.B. Code, C. Pratt, D. Rock, E. Hanna, L. Brown, B. Puddicombe, G. Gillespie, Don Kirby, R. Hutchison, C. Dagg, A. Strachan, S. Gamble, H. Bleakney, R. Smith, Jack Lynch, C. Scobie (Capt.), E. Caldwell, L. (Bones) Little, E. Thomas, and G. Heasman.

The 1917 team: E. Boyle, L. Leahy, G. Gillespie, R. Hutchinson, Don Kirby, A. Strachan, J. Armstrong, E. Dion, R. Cherry, R. Walker, B. Kidd, L. Little (Capt.), E. Davis, L. Fraser, J. Lynch, D. Hill, and M. McDougall.

The 1918 team, which captured the City of Ottawa championship by defeating New Edinburgh and winning and losing a game with Ottawa City, follows: R. Walker, E. Harshaw, A. Stewart, E. Boyle, S. Gamble, Don Kirby, R. Hutchison, A. Strachan, Ellis Thomas, L. Fraser, L. Little (Capt.), L. Rochester, E. (Bud) Thomas, E. Dion, G. Kavanagh, W. Parmalee, C. Lynch, and W. Inglis.

* * * * *

The *Vox Lycei*, 1919, reprinted an article on the THE WAR'S ATHLETIC LESSON by W.M. Gladish, Sporting Editor of the *Ottawa Journal*.

One of the direct results of the terrific European conflict was the elevation of sporting activities to their proper plane of recognition among practically all classes of the community. The value of athletic diversion was vividly demonstrated in the theatres of war and, at the same time, it became recognized that healthful exercise among civilians is invaluable—particularly in instances of mental stress. It has often been told that the soldiers of the Canadian army received their first training on the fields of sport many years before anyone dreamed of a war that would wipe out 15,000,000 souls. Then, when our sportsmen became Crusaders against the despotic Hun-Lord, it was soon found that the athletics would play no small part in maintaining the morale of the fighters.

"Make every soldier an athlete," was the word which came to Canadian training camps from overseas in the fall of 1915, and, forthwith, the officers in charge of training operations proceeded to make play out of military routine as much as possible. Every recruit was urged to play his favored sports during all his spare moments. Equipment of all kinds was provided for the purpose. Men donned boxing gloves, played baseball, soccer and lacrosse or appeared in the role of track athletes. Platoons, companies, battalions and brigades played regular schedules. Bayonet Fighting and Physical Training became a sport competition. It was sport to train in Trench Warfare Schools. It was almost sport to get up in the morning.

Whenever there was any danger of a unit or a corps becoming stale while engaged in the actual business of warfare along those bloody lines in France, what happened? There was more sport. As soon as the troops were sent back to rest billets, there was athletic diversion. The word "rest" was much abused during the years of the war. As soon as a man laid down his rifle, he picked up his baseball bat, his lacrosse or his boxing gloves. In other words, a change was a good as a rest—in fact it was a decided improvement under existing conditions.

How many of us follow the same idea in our civilian lives? When the mind becomes sluggish, the legs weary and the eyes heavy, the best plan, I find, is to go out and get tired. This may sound funny but it is true nevertheless. Sometimes we hear somebody say that "there is no rest for the weary," but in nine cases out of ten there should be no inactivity— need for sleep excepted—provided a distinct change in activity can be secured. When the brain cracks, the "crack" of the baseball bat should be sweet music to the ears. I mean by this that athletic diversion should be the cure.

A man or a woman is as old as he or she feels. If he or she would only get out into the open air and get mussed up in some game or other, he or she would feel years younger before the afternoon or evening is over. Show me the man who is waiting at the plate for the pitcher's delivery or is crouched on the gridiron waiting for a pass and I will point to the man who has forgotten all about office or lesson worries. If you cannot participate in rough-and-tumble sports and if you cannot give and take in hockey, football, soccer, lacrosse, and other games, you can still seek your athletic diversion. Your bicycle gives you healthful exercise and you can walk. You should always keep in mind the thought that a perfectly healthy person can make an invalid of himself by lying in bed—if he lies there long enough.

The athletic lesson of the recent war is that every person should be an athlete of some kind. When you think you are tired, think of your sport and go to it. You'll forget that tired feeling unless you have both feet in a grave.

* * * * *

[Garvock continues;]

Lisgar triumphed in 1920-21-22. The Interprovincial, Interscholastic champions of 1922 were: D. Williams, Don Young, T. Thompson, F. Fortune, F. Taylor, H. Yelland, C. Ackland, G. Rock, W. Skuce, R. Slemon, R. St. Germain (Capt.), H. Chevrier, B. Buist, G. Yelland, G. Rooney, and T. Rooney. This team won from Ottawa College 14 to 9 and outclassed Renfrew 42 to 10 to capture the Dolan Cup.

Ralph St. Germain, who excelled in rugby, baseball, hockey, basketball, and other sports, was given the Ardeil Medal, emblematic of the best all-round rugby player in the O.C.I. by D.H.T. Ardeil, a well-known Toronto sportsman.

The Interprovincial Interscholastic Lisgar Rugby Champions, 1923. Back row, L to R; Ky Taggart, Lou White, Lyle Laishley, George Rock, Jake Jamieson. Front row; H.E. Minnes, Don Young, Jack Fortune, Goggy Monk, Fred Taylor.

Don Young was later captain of McGill's Senior rugby team and one of the best flying wings in Canada. He was also a brilliant basketball player at Lisgar and McGill.

Following up the success of 1922 the Blue and Grey won the Interscholastic championship of Eastern Canada in 1923, with the following team: G. Monk, G. Rock (Capt.), J. Fortune, F. Taylor, F. Tighe, Don Young, E. Minnes, W. Warp, L. Reynolds, L. Laishley, M. Taggart, L. White, J. Jamieson, L. Lamplough, D. Ellis, F. Echlin, V. Grimes, W. Fowler, and D. Morrell.

By defeating its rivals Glebe and Renfrew C.I., Lisgar won the Interprovincial, Interscholastic championship in 1924, and was awarded the Dominion championship when Hamilton C.I. defaulted. The members of this team were: L. Driscoll, D. Masson, D. Legate, W. Telfer, E. Burke, W. Cox, E. Borthwick, F. Taylor, J. Fortune, G. Coburn, H. Munro, E. Halliday, J. Jamieson (Capt.), G. O'Connor, L. Robertson, and H. Putman.

Lisgar won the Eastern Canada Interscholastic Junior championship in 1928 without losing a single scheduled game. Practices before breakfast, signal drills at noon, and hard formation plays after school were part of the Spartan training schedule that produced this success.

The 1928 team follows: J. Edwards, N. Murray (Capt.), L. Blouin, C. Keefer, R. Maley, R. Sheppard, E. Benoit, T. Kettles, L. Levison, M. Lawrence, E. Thomson, G. Pallister, G. Fenton, D. Ahern, M. Fagan, H. Howard, H. Grundy, K. Cawdron, D. Davidson, G. Henderson, B. Clauson, G. Herman, E. Drulard, head coach; M. Appel, assistant coach.

Between 1930 and 1943 many excellent rugby players were developed, although the school teams were not as successful as in other periods. Most of these pupils, who were proficient in sport, are now in the armed forces. In this period some of the outstanding players were: T. Hughes, V. Knowles, Ted Edwards, R. Packman, H. Bickerton, I. Brown, O. Legault, R. Wright, G. Preston, Phil Rioux, E. Smith, K. Marriot, "Jock" Murphy, K. Hall, C. Dagg, L. Potvin, C. Heeney, Digby Cosh, J. Cummings, T. Bishop, E. Villeneuve, A. Charbonneau, H. Avery, J. Varette, B. Trainer, Bert White, O. English, V. Carroll, "Dip" McLaurin, Bill Austin, D. Taylor, W. Warwick, D. Parker, W. Hardy, T. Fraser, E. Martin, J. Lambert, A. Marion, E. Taylor, I. Sparks, D. Segmour, "Red" McMahon, J. Stuart, R. Corbeil, D. Barber, "Rock" Robillard, J. Dehler, Russ Scharfe, E. McCullough, Gladu Fleming, K. Moore, R. Henderson. W. Webster, E. Faulkner, L. Jarvis, P. Tripe, W. Armstrong, Bernard O'Meara, Guy Hamel, K. Lussier, Bill Murray, F. MacCaffrey, D. Fairweather, H. Wood.

* * * * *

HOCKEY

In 1920 at the peak of the Capital City professional hockey mania, Ottawa Collegiate Institute, the only one in the city at the time, through its hockey athletic executive realizing the futility of operating a senior team without some definite objective, decided to organize, fund, and enter a team in the Intermediate City Hockey League.

The goals were not only to create interest among the hockey players in the senior team and give them a challenge but also to bring the name of Ottawa Collegiate Institute into prominence in athletic circles in Ottawa. At O.C.I. at that time there was an adherence to the belief that "a school which neglects sports will inevitably decline in spirit and attendance."

Sixteen hopeful hockey candidates turned out for the first practice in December. Three Lisgar stars had already moved on to teams in the senior Senior City League, Boorne, Dewar and Harold Darragh; therefore the new Senior Lisgar team was composed of W. Richards, R. Gavin, A. Blair, L. Lamplough, W. Pinhey, C.M. Berigan, A. Duchemin, D. Lough, C. McGuire, R. St. Germain, R. Reid, with H. Simpson as manager and C. Kearns as business manager.

At the time there were six teams in the Intermediate City League; St. Pat's, Victorias, Queen's, LaSalle, Parkdale, and O.C.I. The league was operated in two halves, LaSalle winning the first half and Queen's the second. In the playoffs for the championship, LaSalle emerged victorious by defeating Queen's. Owing to unfavorable weather, a few of the league games had to be cancelled at the end of the season, when spring arrived too early and all ice melted.

In addition to their regular league games, Lisgar played six exhibition games: at Parc Royal, Hull, against the Bank of Commerce; at the Lisgar rink against Gowling's Business College; at the Lisgar rink against the ex-pupils, and two exhibition games in Pembroke.

The *Vox Lycei*, the yearbook of O.C.I., in its sports section editorialized that "Games with the school teams of the upper Ottawa Valley towns are greatly to be encouraged for they are all-star aggregations and most hospitable in their treatment of visitors."

The heavy hockey schedule of the Lisgar Senior Team in the 1922-23 season is hard to credit in terms of both student energy and funding for travel. The team played several exhibition games out of town and was successful in them all, defeating Queen's University at Kingston, Kingston Collegiate at Kingston, and Carleton Place at their rink. Home exhibition games were played against the Department of Railways and Canals, St. Brigid's, Gunners, New Edinburghs, LaSalle, E.B. Eddy's, and Ashbury College.

The team line-up was as follows; goal, B. Carley; defence, G. Monk and R. St. Germain; centre, Alex Smith; wings, L. Lamplough and V. Grimes; subs, D. Ackland, T. Thompson, E. Percival and Tommy Westwick.

"Roy" Reid who started the season in nets for O.C.I. was put out of the game by an attack of scarlet fever, raging almost as an epidemic in the city at the time. However, his replacement, Bert Carley, was said to "play in sensational form all season."

Over the years prior to the 1920s, other future hockey stars learned at Lisgar not only their Latin and Greek but also their stick-handling and skating, young men like the four Roberts Brothers, Jack, Eddie, Laurie and Gordie (Gordie afterwards played for McGill and for the Montreal Wanderers while at McGill). Harold Darragh and Harry "Punch" Broadbent of the Ottawa Senators, Jack Fournier, Letham Graham, Jerry Davidson, Norman Scott, Stewart Christie, Eddie Cuzer, Carson Kendall, Grey Masson, Gordon Johnston, Howard Raphael, Paul Armstrong, Basil Frith.

The Cliffside team of 1904-05, which won the Junior City League Championship that year, was composed of the following Lisgar ex-pupils: J.W. Maynard, L. Cassells, H. Raphael, N. White (Captain), D. Blair, G.O. Scott, C.P. Harris, H.H. Bate, J.A.O. Gemmill.

Paul Armstrong, T.L. Cory, C.B. Parr, Basil Frith (Capt.), A.N. Scott, B. White, A. Johnston, R. Thackray, G. Scryer, H.C. Graves, C. Gorman, and D.H. Masson made up the 1906-07 Lisgar hockey Senior Team. Of these, Basil Frith was the outstanding most versatile athlete, excelling in baseball, football, basketball as well as hockey. He later starred for Toronto University in rugby and hockey. Paul Armstrong was an exceptional tennis and hockey player and later played with Eddie Cuzner and Basil Frith for Varsity. Eddie Roberts, Eddie Cuzner, C.B. Parr, Paul Armstrong, Don Masson and Gordon Johnstone were all killed in the First World War.

The 1909 team was composed of G. Valentine, B. Claffy, J. Fournier, W. Stroud, R. Acheson, E, Lowrey, and Tom Lowrey who went on to influence the *Ottawa Journal* for many years as city editor.

* * * * *

The *Vox Lycei* of 1914 described in enthusiastic detail an "away" game:

On Friday, February 27th, the Ottawa Collegiate Hockey Team travelled to Renfrew to play their old rivals, the Renfrew Collegiate team. It was originally intended that ten players should make up the party, but, owing to more important engagements elsewhere, or perhaps to pure indifference, two of these ten failed to put in an appearance, and the train pulled out of the Union Station with the following

In 1932-1933 Lisgar won the Junior E.O.S.S.A. hockey title by defeating Commerce in what was described by the *Vox Lycei* sports writer as one of the "hardest fought play-offs in High School history." They were photographed in their civvies; Back row, L to R; D. McLaurin, B. Loeb, O. Legault, O. Dufour, D. Utman, D. Hall. Middle row; W. Shaver, K. Bartram, J. McDonald, R. Baker, F. (Frank) Boucher. Sitting; B. White, G. Day (captain), Eric Nichols (coach), P. Monk, A. Blouin.

Collegiate players aboard: T. Kavanagh, A. Proudfoot, E. Proudfoot, A. McGuirl, W. Powell, W. McLean, A. Urquhart, and S. Wilson.

After an uneventful trip we arrived in Renfrew at about a quarter to eight and went immediately to the rink. There was a crowd of three or four hundred out to see the game, and, when we stepped on the ice, a number of Renfrew Collegiate girls arose and gave their school yell with great vigour.

The game was played in three twenty-minute periods and the wet and slushy ice had the players tired out before the first twenty minutes were over. Renfrew scored a goal in the first period and O.C.I. evened up in the second. The third period was bitterly fought and body-checking was the only means used in stopping a rush. Once or twice the Ottawa Collegiate forwards had no one to pass but the goal tender, and threw away their chances by wretched shooting. About a minute before full time Renfrew scored and, although the O.C.I. team fought right to the last with that gameness

characteristic of all teams wearing the Blue and Grey, it was unable to score and the game ended with the score 2 to 1 in Renfrew's favour.

After the game the O.C.I. players were the guests of honour at a dance given by the Renfrew boys who, by the way, certainly know how to treat their visitors. We enjoyed ourselves immensely and, as our train left at 2 o'clock, the dance was brought to a close at 1.30.

It was a very sleepy bunch of hockeyists who arrived in Ottawa at 4.30 Saturday morning, but every one was satisfied with his trip, and there was not one but was ready to declare that a finer bunch of sports than the Renfrew Collegiate pupils, would be difficult to find.

Renfrew players came "down the line" for a return game.

The excitement over the Renfrew and O.C.I. home game began the morning one of the boys announced from the platform that the tickets were to be put on sale. Shortly after, Form 11 B distributed their song sheets, and thereafter the sole subject of conversation can well be imagined.

On Friday evening at 6.45 the crowd assembled at Dey's Arena. The fussers and their friends chose one side of the rink, and the bachelors, and Sam McVeigh's [crowd] chose the other. Then for the next few minutes the boys entertained themselves with the school yells, "Mr. John the Baptist" and many other tuneful melodies.

The referee appeared and the noise subsided, while the players took up their positions. A blast of the whistle and they were off. The play was fast from the start, and the teams appeared to be evenly matched. However, Poulin caught the Renfrew goal-keeper when he wasn't looking, and slipped one in, and great was the joy of the rooters. Shortly after the fussers had the audacity to give a "Phi Chi" for Renfrew, which immediately brought forth a volley of jeers from Mr. McVeigh's side of the rink.

Throughout the game the Collegiate players showed good form, and played a very consistent game. The scorers for O.C.I. were: E. Proudfoot, 2; Watson, 2; Poulin, 1; Oliver, 1; McGuirl, 1, making a total of 7, as compared with 1 for Renfrew.

A great deal of praise is due to Wilson the Collegiate goal-keeper, from some of the splendid stops he made, which, had they been let in, would have made the score much closer than it was.

This game gave O.C.I. the championship of the series by 5 points, they having previously been beaten in Renfrew by a 2 to 1 score. The players who had the honour of helping to defend the Blue and Grey were: G. Wilson, E. Proudfoot, A. Proudfoot, W. Powell, C. Poulin, S. Davis, S. Wilson, L. Watson, J. Oliver, A. McGuirl, W. McLean, A. Urquhart, and K. Urquhart.

* * * * *

The Senior hockey team of 1922 was one of the best Lisgar ever produced, led by such players as Dean Ingram, Ralph St. Germain, Alex Smith, and R. Gavin, captain of the 1920 Lisgar rugby team.

Harold Darragh played for Lisgar. He and Alex Smith, of course, went on to play for the Ottawa Senators on championship teams. On this 1922 team were also E. Barclay, R. Reid, L. Lamplough, M. Bergin, D. Lough, W. Richards, T. Thompson.

In 1923 the Lisgar line up, still playing in the Senior City League was; B. Corley, R. Reid, G. Monk, R. St. Germain, Alex Smith, L. Lamplough, V. Grimes, C. Ackland, T. Thompson, E. Percival and Tommy Westwick. In 1924 when Lisgar won all of its exhibition games, Ted Rooney, M. Bergin, and Andy Blair had joined the team.

For three years in a row, 1932, 1933, and 1934, Lisgar won the city Junior Hockey Championships, the school being represented by such players as "Dip" McLaurin, "Toots" Day. Frank Boucher (also of Ottawa Senator line up later), J. Cummings, B. White, Cooney LeFebre,

O. Dufour, O. Legault, B. Loeb. A. Blouin, C. McDonald, D. Utman, C. Bartram, D. Hall, M. Shaver, R. Baker, P. Monk, Bill Bangs, R. Peters, A. Jamieson, J. Lafoley, D. Packman, A. Brady, D. Thomson, J. Wilman, B. Pozitsky; P. Freidman, and Philip Tripe, Managers. Later players were John Chance, David Chance, Rocky Robillard, D. Taylor, V. Neville, and "Jock" Murphy.

Peter Chance in 1937 won the Dominion Junior Figure Skating Championship and the Canadian Amateur Figure Championship gold medal. Nigel Stephens won the Junior Figure Skating Championship of Canada in 1943.

The absence of a school rink for many years discouraged competition between forms and interest among the student body. Rinks were started from time to time but the efforts to cope with some of the storms of winter provided more exercise in shovelling snow than in skating or in playing hockey.

* * * * *

In 1992 ex-student J.D. Dunfield of Ottawa looked back on his childhood near the auditorium where the championship Ottawa Senators were practising and playing in the 1920s:

I lived on the corner of Metcalfe Street and Waverly Avenue, which was about four short blocks from the old auditorium. I believe the Old Ottawa Senators must have often played on Saturday nights because I was not allowed out on the weeknights while going to school.

With my small weekly allowance and the profits from the sale of the *Saturday Evening Post*, I was able to purchase the 25 cent "rush-end" standing-room tickets. If you arrived about an hour before a game you could usually find room to stand up against a steel handrail about halfway up the end zone.

This was the best position to secure the odd hockey puck that ricocheted up into the stands. Thank goodness the players did not use the "slap" shot in the 1930s as there was not any protective glass around the boards. Of course, the goalie did not wear any face mask and the forwards and defence might have had Eaton's catalogues under their stockings for shin pads.

The care of the ice was labour-intensive. After each period three men would come out with long-handled brooms, which had faggots or twigs tied around the end of each pole. With a wide sweeping motion the three men would work their way from one end of the ice to the other end, after which the small ridges of snow would be pushed down to one end with hand ploughs and shovelled into a trapdoor behind the goalposts and just off the ice surface.

There were only six teams in the NHL in those days and Ottawa was in the Big League. At one time Montreal and New York City had two teams but it was generally a six-team league. Player trades were not common and you could remember the names of most of the players on each team. Ottawa was probably the cradle of hockey talent with the Finnigans, Kilreas, Cowley, Beveridge O'Connell, etc., filling the rosters of many teams.

* * * * *

[Garvock continues:]

BASKETBALL

Basketball, perhaps, has flourished more than any other sport at Lisgar in the last fifty years. A large number of students have taken part in this sport, and, due to the interest aroused in interform or interclass games, the standard of play of the teams representing the school was higher.

Before the present boys' gymnasium was put in the basement of the west wing in 1908, basketball was played in the former assembly hall in the old section of the school. P.D. (Wickey) Wilson, Newton Kendall, S. Cormack, Basil Frith, H. Burrows, Howard Raphael, and Townley Douglas

(Capt.), were on the 1906 team which played in the newly formed City League.

The team of 1907-08, captained by A.J. Fraser, with G.L.D. Kennedy, F. Cormack, C. Kinsella, H.S. Smith, and B. Frith, captured the City League championship.

Victory again perched on the Blue and Grey colours when the 1908-09 team of Alexis Helmer (Capt.), Earl Johnston, W. Megloughlin, C. Claffy, and Art Knox won the Intermediate City League championship.

The new west wing as noted provided a gymnasium under the assembly hall. In the *Vox Lycei* of 1913 there is a vigorous demand "that the colossal posts of the gymnasium floor be protected from assaults of the basketball players." A fear was expressed that "the continual jar from the violent contact of the skull and other parts of the anatomy might bring down the posts supporting the floor of the assembly hall and the seats." Some terrible catastrophe like that which followed the strong-arm act of Samson, when he brought down the house at Gaza, may have been in the mind

In 1930 the Lisgar Girls' Senior Basketball team won the Ottawa Interscholastic championships. From their *Vox Lycei* photo: Standing, L to R; K. Wayling, B. George, E. Cherry, H. Lockhart, E. Skuffham. Sitting; C. Waddell, M. Little (captain), I. Christie.

The 1924-1925 City Basketball Girls' Championship team. They defeated Glebe for the cup and went on to defeat Queen's University in an exhibition game, score 28-40. Back row, L to R; S. Hopkins, H. Lambert, I. Graham. F. Robb, I. Corry, G. Parr, I. Brittain. Middle row; M. Minter, E. Smith, W. Grant, Miss Kilpatrick (coach), H. Ogilvie, R. Robertson, G. Ferguson. Front row; L. Meighen, A. McIntosh, G. Stanyer (captain), G. Fairbairn, E. Seaton.

Bloomers and bobbed cuts of the mad-cap Twenties. This is not a championship basketball team, although some of its members went on to win the Lisgar 1924-1925 City Championship. But this photograph is important as illustrative of the sporting garb of Lisgar girl athletes as well as of what the well-dressed teacher wore in that period of history. L to R; teacher Kilpatrick, E. Seaton, H. Ogilvie, G. Parr, M. Minter, R. Robertson, E. Esdale, D. Esdale, L. Corry, F. Robb (captain).

of the *Vox* writer of the time who also observed, "It never seems to have occurred either to the Board or the Athletic Executive that the players might be injured."

Lisgar won the City Intermediate basketball championship in 1913-14 with these players: H. Salter, C. Fraser, K. Cassells, D. Talbot, C. Poulin, Milks, K. Vogan, and in 1916 defeated Westmount and Montreal High School. The next year they won the senior City championship by beating the strong Y.M.C.A. team 37 to 34 and 19 to 17. Players on the team in 1916 and 1917 were: L. Little, E. Anderson, W. George, L. Brown, E. Hanna, B. Kidd, C. Scobie, D. Code, C. Fraser, S. Danby, H. Henderson, S. Davis, A. Menzies, H. Salter, L. Poulin. E. Crain.

The new rule about "personal fouls" put into play about this time gave the lighter teams a better chance to show their skill. Lisgar was able to overcome the handicap of inexperience and could compete on more even terms with heavier senior teams like the Y.M.C.A. In 1917 and 1918 Lisgar won the City championship. By defeating Montreal High in Montreal and Shamrocks in 1918 they captured the eastern Canadian championship. The teams these years: C. Scobie, D. Code, B. Kidd, E. Anderson, L. Little, E. Hanna, W. George, L. Brown, H. Robertson, E. Cooper, C. Goodeve, C. Gillespie, S. Gamble.

In the *Vox Lycei* of 1918, the sporting editor described in detail one of the highlights of Lisgar's basketball history:

Basketball was nearly over for the season here when the Shamrock Club, of Montreal, arranged the series for the Championship of Eastern Canada. Collegiate, in the draw, were to play Friday night, and if winners, Saturday also. The team and a few loyal supporters left Friday morning. After a quiet rest in a vaudeville show they hied them to the scene of battle. The Rosebuds, a strong team from Montreal High, were our opponents. Under another name they were known as the Champions of Montreal. To describe the contest between the two teams would tax the ingenuity of Mr. Standard, who wrote the Dictionary—fast, vite, celer and a few issimuses. To sit still in watching was impossible. Rosebuds were wonderful shots, and given a chance, they would score from any angle. But thanks to our boy giant, Kirby, and crafty "Chas." Goodeve, chances were few. Bones, Gillie, and The Red did the rest. It was close until near the end when a few quick baskets broke their hearts. Score 35-19. Finals—O.C.I., vs. Shamrocks. Here was a team with wonderful combination and a star named Rubins. Lightning is slow compared to the play of this game. We were primed to smother the mighty Rubins. And smothered he was. While he was gasping around our stone-wall defence and his teammates were displaying their combination to no effect, Little was showing how a real basketball player can outwit a defence or drop baskets from any given point. Gillespie shot, batted, and twisted the ball

The Lisgar Collegiate Senior Basketball team, Champions of Ontario 1941. Most of these young men were destined for the services during World War II and two of them, Dwaine Merkley and Allan Hague were to lose their lives overseas. Back row, L to R; J. Seed (manager), B. Shapiro, G. Mackey, S. Barr, A. Hague, J.T.H. "Butch" Rothwell (coach). Front row; R. MacDonald, A. Mackey, D. MacLean (captain), J. Leggett, D. Merkley.

into the net under trying conditions and displayed wonderful ability. The final score was 38-28 for Collegiate and Rubins scored only four baskets. . . Sleep that night was 0 "x." The ten knights in the spare room rested not. Who blames them? The school never had a team bring home such honours or trophies. "Hail to the Champs," as Deacon Cleary has said.

* * * * *

[Again from Garvock:]

In the early '20s basketball was still the most popular sport at school. More boys and girls were playing than ever before. More than 100 teams and more than 500 players were taking part in 29 inter-mural leagues.

In 1921-22 Lisgar was once more Intermediate City champion with R. Rivington, H. Darragh, D. Lough, R. Slemon, W. O'Connor, J. Law, G. Hutchison and D. Mix.

Lisgar was represented by Wayne Cleary, Don Young, Louis White, Harry Yelland, H. Jamieson, D'Alt Mix, G. Barnet, and Rex Slemon in 1923 when they won the Eastern Canadian championship.

In 1924 Lisgar won the Eastern Canadian interscholastic championship for the second year in succession and for the fourth time in five years with the following team: E. Nichol, L. White, R. Boyce, J. Russell, Don Young (Capt.), E. Burke, L. Laishley, Anderson, J. Jamieson.

In 1925 Lisgar captured the Ontario Interscholastic championship with such stalwarts as E. Nichol, Don Young, E. Burke, F. Ambridge, J. Jamieson, L. Laishley and H. Munro.

Lisgar Midgets were Eastern Canadian champions in 1926 and the Juniors were awarded the crown in their league in 1929, when they defeated Renfrew with the following team: Maley, Edwards, Benoit, Henderson, Davidson, Brodie, Shipman, Kettles.

The Bantams in 1937 were champions with the following: A. Greenberg, K. Checkland, A. Mackey, G. Mackey, D. McLean, "Duke" Abelson, R. Robillard, M. Shore, R. Stamos, W. Stock, A. Walsh, D. MacEachern. Most of these players along with Alan Hague and John Thompson made up the team of 1939 which won the Junior E.O.S.S.A. championship. The Midgets also were interscholastic champions in 1939 with the following team: M. Ginsberg, W. Armitage, S. Barr, W. Howlett, P. Pollock, F. Leppard, M. Cohen, R. MacDonald, J. Bodnoff, B. Shapiro, G. Greenberg, W. Morden.

The senior basketball team won second place in 1939 when three teams under the splendid coaching of J.T.H. Rothwell and Mr. E.A. Nicholls reached the finals of their respective league and the Junior and Midgets each won a championship.

Success crowned the seniors' efforts in 1940 when they defeated Glebe after 14 years of keen rivalry for the E.O.S.S.A. crown. In the Ontario championship they lost to Windsor Vocational School 33 to 30 but the next year after a brilliant season won the E.O.S.S.A. laurels and then defeated London and Hamilton to capture the blue ribbon, emblematic of the Ontario S.S.A. championship at Toronto—the only time this high honour has been won by an Ottawa team.

The Lisgar Girls' Track Team of 1932-1933 won the E.O.S.S.A. championship of Eastern Ontario by one point, Muriel Droeske winning the Junior 100-yard dash and the running broad jump. They also won the Capital Theatre Trophy (shown here) for the third consecutive year. Back row, L to R; H. Stuart, I. Smiles, D. Taggart, M. Droeske, E. Westwick. Front row; T. Oleson, M. Renwick, G. Olicoeur, I. Morris, E. McPhail.

The players on these two senior teams for these two years which brought high honours to Lisgar and Ottawa City were: G. Mackey, A. Mackey, D. McLean (Capt 1941), K. Checkland, D. Merkley, L. Fee, R. Avery (Capt. 1940), J. Leggett, R. Canning, A. Hague, R. McDonald, S. Barr, B. Shapiro and J. Seed, Manager. A. Mackey held the individual scoring championship in 1942 and J. Foulds in 1943.

$$* * * * *$$

Lisgar's gymnastic team in recent years won five senior and four junior championships. Their representatives made an excellent showing in the Ontario competition in Toronto when M. Tkachuk, H. Chaput, F. Dixon, V. Franklin, N. Stinson and A. Hague brought home individual championships.

Alan Hague, president of the Students' Council in 1939, was a leader among his fellow students. He was proficient at basketball, gymnastics, rugby, track and hockey. He was one of the first of the many Lisgar students to enlist in the War and made the supreme sacrifice while flying with the R.C.A.F. in 1943 in England.

$$* * * * *$$

TRACK AND FIELD SPORTS

Track and field sports dormant for many years were revived in 1906 with a Field Day at Lansdowne Park. C.P. Kinsella, Gus Mott, W. Megloughlin, W.I. Garvock, George Schryer, R. Forsythe, L. Tubman, R. Connors, A. Fraser, G.H. Rochester, G. Monk, and Gavin MacFarlane were among the senior winners of these popular sports. Megloughlin and Kinsella were all-round champions. J.J. McKinley, Leith Graham and Don Brophy were junior champions.

Seven records were broken at the successful Field Day of 1910. Don Brophy was the senior champion in 1911 and H. Salter junior champion. Others on the athletic team that year were L. Rainboth, V. McClenaghan, G. Rochester, R. Tubman, G. Caldwell, D. Talbot and D. Beach.

Jean Bryce, Ada McCormick and Marion Williams were winners in the girls' [track and field].

To stimulate interest in the Field Day sports an ornamental clock had been put up for competition among the forms by the Athletic Association in 1894. This timepiece, a fine specimen of the craftsmanship of some artistic Tubal-cain, stands on a metal base and weighs more than 50 pounds avoirdupois. On either side of the case an iron figure of a dashing cavalier in coat of mail brandishes a sword. Third Form won it first. Upper A captured it in 1895. Like the dove from Noah's Ark which had no place to rest the soles of its feet, the old clock has been shifted around a lot. From 1895 to 1906 there is no trace of its movements.

At the Field Day in 1912, when Don Brophy again won the senior all-round championship and Kit Leggo the junior championship, there were more girls' events. Throwing the ball aroused much interest. Quoth the Vox: "Though the spectators were endangering their lives, for you were not sure where the ball would land, they crowded around the throwers not only to see the throwing but to see the way in which the ball was thrown."

The Athletic Association, like great political bodies or church organizations, was most often in need of funds. In 1919 the fees were 50¢ for boys and 25¢ for girls. "Only the poor, either in purse or in spirit, failed to join," was the considered verdict of the *Vox* Editor. Cliff Cottee was senior boys' champion in 1919 and Miss M. Grant senior girls' champion. Other champions were A. Quackenbush, J. Gordon. R. Gavin, R. McWhinney, C. Devenny; and Margaret Robertson in junior girls' events.

By 1920 the Athletic Association controlled all branches of sport with 500 boy and 350 girl members out of a school enrolment of 1100. "The financial condition of the Association was a little better this year," was the expert diagnosis of the Editor of the *Vox*. But there was still room for improvement in the matter of equipment for the rugby team. Apparently the team collective looked like Joseph's coat of many colours for, according to the critical, observant *Vox*, "No two members of our team had sweaters of the same pattern." This sartorial deficiency evidently could be remedied, "If everyone joined the Athletic Association and boosted it."

Lisgar won second place in the first Dominion Track and Field Interscholastic meet held in Montreal in 1923 when C. House captured the Intermediate championship and won most of the points for his team. The team consisted of Fred Taylor (Capt.), C. House, M. Keddie. G. Waugh, A. Kenney, G. Grant, J. Lawler, B. Baker, W. Easdale. This team was

coached by Mr. R.D. Campbell, then teaching at Glebe, who has since trained and coached a host of great athletes and a long list of winning teams at Glebe.

Lisgar's track team in 1936 won the Intermediate interscholastic relay race with Rus Scharfe, J. Grant, J. Ellis, Bob Conley, and G. Prodrick. Next year the juniors won the Horovitz Trophy at Cornwall with a team composed of Morden, Mackey, Boutin, Robillard, Hughson, Taggart, Checkland, Webster, A. Hague, and Purdy.

Under the coaching of Mr. E.A. Nicholls and Mr. J.H.T. Rothwell, Lisgar produced a number of track and field stars, several of whom broke Interscholastic records at the E.O.S.S.A. meets, when Lisgar was second in most of these competitions. Among these were: A. Weston, who broke the record in the discus throw; V. Knowles, who broke the district record in the 100 and 220 yard dashes; G. Prodrick, a record holder in the sprints and broad jumping, who still holds the record for the 75 yard dash; A. Purdy, intermediate high-jump record holder, who cleared the bar at 6 feet 1/4 inches in the senior class; A. Hague, who broke the record for the hop, step, and jump; and a pole vaulter and broad jumper of note; Bud Morden, holder of the junior Ottawa crown; E. Carey, junior high-jump winner; L. Smith, victor in Intermediate high-jump, Ward Hughson, Art Mackey, Bert Edmunds, Doug Jones, "Rock" Robillard, S. Kydd, W. McRae, A. Weston, A. Pozitsky, P. Jones, E. Wiseman, E. Checkland, R. Scharfe, W. Chipman, N. Moore, M. Berlin, and K. Stamos.

* * * * *

THE STORMING OF GLEBE

Storming the citadel of their "parvenue" rival in learning at Glebe Collegiate, the entire male student body of one hundred year old Lisgar Collegiate marched yesterday afternoon through the "tents," or rather, corridors in the camp of the Philistines who had beaten them so often on the playing fields.

Executed with perfect timing that caught the blue and gold cohorts by surprise, the first warning of the "commando raid" was a cacophony of sound that surged up the street, bringing the Glebe principal, W.D.T. Atkinson, to the window. Rising above the crescendo of blaring bugles and throbbing drums sounded the "rebel" yell of triumph, and then Principal Atkinson realized that the "invaders" were from Lisgar and that the occasion required a strategic capitulation.

As he let down the drawbridge, and retreated to the postern gate, the Lisgar phalanx surged in and swirled through the corridors, giving a yell that in spite of the bewhiskered age of Lisgar sounded impressively modern. It was the same "Rah, Rah, Rah" call to battle that had carried Lisgar to heights of achievement in the period of its pristine glory in

those days of the old O.C.I., when "the dear old blue and grey" were unbeaten in intercollegiate sport.

The Lisgar "army" leaders carried a banner that proclaimed: "We may be old but we don't creak." Around it the battle waged, for by this time the Glebe warriors were getting organized, and the order went forth to "man the exits." Seeing their retreat threatened, the Lisgar Timoshenkos called for a withdrawal in depth.

It was executed in the face of fierce resistance, but the Lisgar raiders gained the street intact and with light casualties.

Then they marched back to the noble grey pile that constitutes their bailiwick near The Driveway.

Here they were met on the steps by their own master strategist Principal J.J. Dunlop, who lauded the success of their raid on Festung Glebe. In due course, the assemblies of both schools will doubtless witness the handing out of decorations.

From the *Ottawa Journal*, 1943.

BASEBALL

Baseball, like hockey and rugby, had its season but it was a short one before final exams loomed menacingly on the horizon. Lisgar played in the Intermediate City League.

After an absence of several years Lisgar was again represented in the Intermediate City League in 1921 with the following team: R. Gavin, J. Gower, R. Taylor, L. Lamplough, Thompson, Dean Ingram, R. St. Germain, A. Quackenbush, M. Neale, H. Simpson, N. Kidd.

* * * * *

In *The History of O.C.I. 1843-1943*, ex-student Nichol, B.A., reminisced about a famous baseball game of his youth between Lisgar staff and students. Nichol had played catcher in professional baseball in his youth:

As I write I am looking at a postcard snapshot of the O.C.I. Senior Baseball team of 1910. In this group were Mr. D.A. Campbell (Pres.), J.A. Sully (Sec.), now Air Vice-Marshal, W.W. Nichol (Mgr.), Commercial Master McNabb, playing member on the team; student players and others were the Valentines, Gus and Joe, Jack Goddard, Hugo Morris, Bunny Stroud, Eldon Wilson, and Ross Acheson. O.C.I. boys who also played were Gordie Rochester, Art Brown, A. McMillan, Don Stapleton, Len Rombough, Don Brophy, Jack McCullough, and others whom I cannot recall. This club had a fine record up and down the Ottawa Valley both for skilled performance and gentlemanly demeanour on and off the field. The capture of the Ottawa City League Intermediate Championship was a crowning achievement.

Ottawa Collegiate Institute Baseball Club, proud champions of the Upper Ottawa and City League, 1906. This would mean that the high school team played "away" games up the Valley at perhaps Arnprior, Renfrew, Pembroke as well as against city league teams. Back row, L to R; G. Mott, 1st base; W. White, left field; H.S. Gemmill, Sec. Treas., short stop; S. McDougall, right field; H.T. Douglas, 2nd base. Centre row; C. Parr, centre field; E.P. Murphy, manager; D.A. Campbell, president; G. Rice, coach; R. Smith, pitcher. Front row; B.M. Frith (captain), catcher; D. McCann, 3rd base; G. Smith, pitcher.

During the following years the growth of interest in the game, fostered by the success of the senior team, led to the formation of many rival playing groups challenging its supremacy. Sides were taken and clamour was rife. An unexpected event created a happy diversion. In fun the school faculty members posted a challenge to the reputedly strongest of the contending groups. The challenge was promptly accepted. On the following Friday afternoon, the opposing nines lined up on Cartier Square for "the battle of the Century." Gus Valentine was umpire and Mr. Smeaton scorer. The teachers' team comprised Messrs. Kaiser, Paterson, Halbert, Hood, Hutchison, Stevenson and McNabb. Mr. D.A. Campbell and W.W. Nichol constituted the battery. All were old college players, experienced in the ways of the game, as learnt on the university campus when they were in their prime.

The game ended in favour of the staff, score 15-3, amid the whole-hearted cheering of the multitude in recognition of the sportsmanship exhibited by both victors and vanquished with a tribute to the latter who put up so gallant a struggle against great odds.

Unfortunately, the names of the latter are not readily accessible but many will be found on the school's Remembrance Roll of the Great War. The living are now holding posts of responsibility and honour in the life of the nation, worthily upholding the traditions of the Lisgar Collegiate Institute.

[Garvock continues:]

After the war of 1914-18 boxing and wrestling attracted the attention of young commandos in the embryo. Honore Chevrier, who afterwards represented Canada at the Olympic sports at Amsterdam, was an all-round boxing and wrestling champion in the early '20s. Herb Hanna, Vernon Snow, Frank and Bob Echlin, R. Malot, M. Brodie, Herb Ide, Bill Westwick, Fred Taylor, and Don Masson were proficient in these sports. Lisgar defeated Glebe in the Assault-at-Arms in 1925 and 1926. These manly sports have been stopped of late at Lisgar.

Golf became a school sport in 1932 when Lisgar won the Brown trophy with a team consisting of F. Corrigan, N. Campbell, Lorne Cox and Edward Bothwell, and fencing was started in 1933 under the direction of Mr. R.S. Whittle.

Tennis has been played at Lisgar but not as consistently as some other sports. Space was provided on Lisgar Street but the courts were not always in shape.

The *Vox* of 1921 tells of the many enthusiastic tennis players in the school but "the so-called courts across the way are not fit to play on, and a large number of tournament games were played on other courts in various parts of the city."

Lisgar's boys' team of G. Mineau, C. Donaldson, H. Chaput and C. McNairn won the interscholastic shield in 1931

I was a classmate of the great Rocky Robilliard. He played everything and he did it all well. And I guess he was always on the rink or the football field or the baseball diamond or at track and field, because one time I remember his father came to Lisgar and said to him, "Rocky, come home. We never see you."

I met Rocky on the street one day after we graduated and I said to him, "I hear you are going into dentistry, Rocky." And he said, "No, Bill, no. You have to be too polite to be a dentist." And he went into Phys. Ed.

William Bloom, 1937-1941.

and again in 1938 with the following team: Colin Smith, Ted Heaps, Andy Fogarty, and Dennis Ross.

* * * * *

Lisgar's record in Intercollegiate competition, it will be seen, is a proud one, but at Lisgar intramural competition is considered more important. It is the aim of Mr. Rothwell, the Physical Director, and Miss Jessie M. Smith, Directress of girls' athletics, to have every boy and girl reap the advantages of competition and to develop the physique of every student.

Intramural competition has grown from a small beginning with little interest to the present successful state of affairs with a lot of interest shown. Last year more than 200 games of interform basketball were played. Everybody was on a basketball team which played during health classes.

Lisgar's girls under the expert coaching and guidance of Miss Jessie Smith and Miss Dorothy Bishop have established an impressive record in interscholastic sports, but more important intramural competition is the most important part of the athletic programme. They succeeded Miss Jessie Kilpatrick, who before leaving Lisgar for Brockville Collegiate had been a successful directress of girls' athletics.

Lack of a playing field has seriously handicapped outdoor games like rugby and track and field sports. The nearest rink is more than a mile away. It is to be hoped that long before another centenary rolls around Lisgar will have a playing field of her own.

* * * * *

SKIING

Formed in 1920 at the suggestion of Eddie Condon, who wrote to the *Vox* of that year that skiing was not new but was mentioned by Xenophon in 400 BC, a ski club has flourished ever since. Lisgar students have shown their skill, endurance, and courage in this great winter sport by capturing at various times the Southam,

The Lisgar Ski Team of 1928, Interscholastic Champions. Note "state of the art" equipment. The fittings could be adjusted for either downhill or cross-country. Left to right; B. Clarke (captain), P. O'Keefe, L. Williams, P. Cawdron, J. Currie.

Although the world was entering a deep economic depression by the time 1930 rolled around, it was a banner year for Lisgar Collegiate in many areas of school life and particularly athletics. Here is the Lisgar ski team with three championship trophies. Standing, L to R; C. Darch, G. Ogilvie, H. Worden. Sitting; J. Currie (captain), J. Edwards.

Gray, Kirby and Baird trophies in competitions with other schools. Eddie Condon, while at Lisgar, won the International Intercollegiate championship among university students at a ski meet at McGill. John F. Taylor later was Canadian champion. Other outstanding skiers were Phil Wright, Don Cruikshanks, Fred Taylor, Ted Reid, Dick Skuce, George MacCormack, K. West, L. Grimes, George Jost, and Bud Clarke, a Dominion champion who represented Canada at the last Olympic games in Germany, P. O'Keefe, J. Blair, L. Williams, P. Cawdron, J. Currie, R. Lewis, Tom Dubroy, John Fripp, Dick Barber, and Bill Lewis.

The Vox Lycei, 1922-23, recorded the election of officers and the winter's activities of the first ski club at Lisgar. From the 1920s on the sport was to grow by leaps and bounds.

The organization meeting of the O.C.I. Ski Club was held early in December when the snow was conspicuous by its absence, but it was enthusiastically attended by a larger number of pupils than usually attend meetings of this sort of other athletic clubs. Great things were prophesied and planned and it can be said without any doubt that it turned out to be a great year and weather conditions were as nearly perfect as possible throughout. There were nearly as many people skiing in Ottawa this year as there were skating, and in two years there will be more skiing than skating. As an example of how popular skiing has become the Senior Lyceum dance had to be cancelled for no one could or would spare an evening's skiing to attend a mere dance.

"Hikes" were held mid-weekly every Wednesday after school to Rockcliffe and Fairy Lake, and were well attended by the boys, the girls evidently finding it inconvenient to come to school dressed for skiing. The "hikes" usually took the form of practice in jumping and turning, the short period of daylight remaining after school making it difficult to arrange a cross-country trip or a hike. Skiers were handicapped this year, in that there was no teahouse at Rockcliffe in the early part of the winter and only a store at Fairy Lake open on week days.

The two all-day hikes to Ironsides and Camp Fortune were voted a huge success and we intend to have many more similar to these next year. Also, many pupils took advantage of the kind invitations of Ottawa's two major clubs, to go on moonlight and all-day Sunday hikes up the Gatineau.

The Gray Cup was, as usual, the centre of interest among boys of the club, the small entry lists for its events being accounted for by the prevalence of so much sickness at the time of the competitions. (However despite this, the competitions were a great success, and keen rivalry was evidenced amongst the competitors). The "Gray" Trophy stands for annual competition in all-round skiing amongst the members of the Cliffside Ski Club attending the O.C.I. and this year was won by "Ted" Reid, who came second in the running event, first in the turning, and second in the jumping. "Gus" Hurdman being sixth in the race, second in the turning, and first in the jumping, came second in the competition beating Fred Taylor who was third, by one point. The latter was first in the race and third in both the turning and jumping. Charlie Blair, Dave Ellis, and Frank Echlin followed respectively in that order.

* * * * *

Despite the posts and corner obstructions in their third-floor gymnasium, once the girls' cafeteria, intramural competition in volleyball and basketball has always been the most important, if the least spectacular, part of the girls' athletic program.

The *Vox Lycei* of 1924-25 announced the formation of the Girls' Athletic Association.

For the first time in the history of the school, the girls have an Athletic Society, independent of that of the boys. At the beginning of the school year in September, the various clubs were formed, and from them the officers of the association were elected. It was thought that if "we women" of the O.C.I. became independent, a greater interest would be shown in the athletic activities. Last year when the girls were asked to become members of the school athletic association, a great many did not respond, but when a membership campaign was started this year, each girl felt that it was her own organization, and if she was a "good

sport," she joined at once. The result was that every girl in the school became a member of our first Association.

Honorary President, Dr. A.H. McDougall; Honorary Vice-President, Miss J. Muir; President, P. Baldwin; Vice-President, Marion Forward; Secretary, Inez Graham; Treasurer, Miss Kilpatrick: Committee; K. Knight, M. Blanchfield, Helen Ogilvie, Phyllis Forde, Violet Smith.

As all recognized associations of the school must have a member in the Student Council, it was necessary that an amendment be made in the Constitution, whereby the Girls' Athletic Association should be allowed one member in the body of the Council.

* * * * *

From the Lisgar history, 1843-1943:

From 1928 to 1942 awards were made for general proficiency in intramural athletics. The following were school champions in that period: Isabel Lockhart, Norah Donnelly, Muriel Droeske, (2 years), Kay Wayling, Mary Renwick, Nora Mosley, Clemie MacDonald, Winnie McClury (2 years), Elizabeth Fenton, Val Brampton (2 years), Lois Pratt and Barbara Fenton.

In addition to the major sports of track and basketball dealt with later, Lisgar girls have been active at different periods in tennis, skiing, swimming, rifle shooting, and tumbling.

In the early years of girls' athletics at Lisgar, intramural track meets were held each fall at Lansdowne Park. On the 1919 meet the *Vox* reports: "The clashes of the boys and girls provided the onlookers with dazzling excitement and swiftness in every race."

That year the senior champion was Miss M. Grant and the junior Miss M. Robertson. Such meets were held almost every year until the formation of E.O.S.S.A. and the establishment of girls' track competition in 1929.

Lisgar launched herself into the new venture with immediate success; Elsie Proctor won the 100 yard dash in 11 and 4/5 seconds, a record she surpassed the following year in a time of 11 and 3/5 seconds. The junior team of Elsie Proctor, Gloria Jenkinson, Mabel Standing and E. Westwick, set up a record of 54 and 2/5 seconds in the 440-yard relay, which has not been surpassed in E.O.S.S.A. competition since.

In the intervening years, until the war forced suspension of the track meet in 1941, Lisgar teams won the Capital Trophy, emblematic of highest total points, in 1930, 1931, 1932, 1939 and 1941. Relay teams won almost without a break and records were equalled or broken by Muriel Droeske in 1931 in junior broad jump (16 feet, 2 inches), in 1931 also Gloria Jenkinson in senior 100 yard dash, (11 and 4/5 seconds), Evelyn Watt in 1934 in senior high jump (4 feet, 6 inches) and in 1935 in the dash, Elizabeth Fenton in junior high jump (4 feet, 9 inches) in 1936. In recent meets Val Brampton, Muriel Shea, Lois Pratt, Barbara Fenton, and Erla Holmes have been outstanding.

The famous pillars of the old gym, now the cafeteria. Losers sometimes blamed the padded posts for their losses, but Lisgar's teams learned how to use them to their advantage. They were the bane of the referee's life and occasionally the cause of injury. Photo taken prior to 1951.

Since the introduction of basketball at Lisgar, it has always been a keenly contested intramural sport. In the early years the game was played, bloomers and all, on a three-divisional court. Later, when intercollegiate rules were adopted, players covered two-thirds of the floor. At first pennants were awarded the winning classes each year, but in recent years the teams have competed for cups and crests.

Outside games were played at one time against the Y.W.C.A. and the Normal School, but the establishment of Glebe Collegiate permitted the formation of a regular city league in 1924 that has functioned ever since. Lisgar won in the senior competition that year with a team composed of: W. Grant, F. Robb, G. Graham, M. Minter, G. Fairbairn, G. Stanyar, L. Brittain, A. MacIntosh, E. Smith. In 1926-27 the junior team won first place in the intercollegiate league with this team: D. Anderson L. Jeans, J. Louis, I. MacDonald, M. McGovern, A. Dufour. Both seniors and juniors won in 1929-30, the seniors reaching the E.O.S.S.A. play-offs. The team that year consisted of K. Wayling, B. George, E. Cherry. I. Lockhart, E. Southam, K. Waddell, M. Little, I. Christie.

In recent years the junior school teams have won the city league in 1941, '42, '43. In 1941 the teams were runners-up in E.O.S.S.A. competition; in 1942 they were E.O.S.S.A. champions. In 1943 E.O.S.S.A. discontinued its basketball tournaments for the duration of the Second World War. The 1942 team consisted of: B. Fenton, H. Hulse, M. Pratt, M. Duguid, L. Hall, J. Nash, C. Witty, L. Laakso, N. Lesonsky.

* * * * *

Hockey mania in the 1920s, when Ottawa was a network of leagues and the Ottawa Senators were playing in the National Hockey League, led to the formation of the first known Lisgar girls' hockey club.

The *Vox Lycei* of 1928-29 reported:

A new organization was introduced into the school this year by the Girls' Athletic Association, namely, a girls' hockey club. A meeting was called in the early part of the season for the purpose of organizing teams. It was found that there was a sufficient number of hockey enthusiasts among the girls to form three teams. The boys very kindly allowed us to have the use of the rink two nights a week.

The club has been very successful this year, and it is to be hoped that next year the girls will turn out as well as they have this season. If that be the case and an interest in hockey can be aroused among the girls at the Glebe school, it may be possible to arrange for interschool games.

List of officers: Hon. Pres. Mr. Strader; Pres. C. Hague; Vice-Pres. M. Reid; Coach, Louis Meng.

* * * * *

Up until the advent of television for the masses in the 1950s, sports writers were very important people in the community, as well as on the staff of the *Citizen* and *Journal*. They often described a game graphically almost blow by blow for readers who had no way of either hearing or seeing an important confrontation between, let us say, the Ottawa Senators and the

A long tradition of championship girls' tennis teams was begun at Lisgar in 1930 when the tennis team became Ottawa Interscholastic Champions and carried off the Ottawa District Lawn Tennis Association's silver shield. Back row, L to R; G. Logan, Miss J. Smith, R.O. Halloran. Front row; M. Little, B. Hart (captain).

Coach R.S. Whittle with his 1933-34 E.O.S.S.A. Championship Gym team. L to R; H. Chaput, F. Dickson, M. Tkachuk, J. Trafford, G. Kerr with coach Whittle standing behind.

Montreal Canadiens, or Lisgar Collegiate and Ottawa Tech. When Lisgar won the E.O.S.S.A. hockey championship two years in a row, 1932-33 and 1933-34, a *Citizen* sports writer was inspired to create for his readers biographical sketches of the champions, now excerpted here. This memorabilia was contributed by a descendant of the Boucher Lisgar hockey dynasty.

Frank Boucher—Captain and left wing; age 15; weight, 148; son of George Boucher, Ottawa Senator's coach. Frankie has played an important role in leading Lisgar juniors to their second straight E.O.S.S.A. hockey title. He was the Student League's leading marksman, and played good hockey as a member of the Ottawa Boys' Club Junior City League aggregation. Besides being a promising hockey prospect, Frankie performs creditably on the gridiron.

James Cummings—Goal; age 16; cool and collected in his position. Jimmy has turned in an excellent brand of goal-tending for the Blue and Grey. His work in the finals against Tech was unusually good.

Gordon "Toots" Day—Centre; age 16; weight, 100; a slender, smooth-skating pivot man. Day's play-making would be a credit to a far more experienced player. The Lisgar center-ice star was a prominent Junior City League performer in the colors of the Burghs, and was a backfield member on Lisgar's junior football squad.

Omar Legault—Right wing; age 16; weight, 144; this is Omar's second year with the twice-crowned championship team, and his goal-getting tactics helped his team considerably. He was captain of last year's junior gridiron team.

Dave Hall—Defence; age 16; weight, 150; a forward with last year's juniors, Dave was shifted back to the rearguard this season and has handled the new assignment in fine style.

Pete Peters—Defence; age 16; weight, 150; this is Pete's first year with the junior hockey team, but his consistent work has worked havoc with incoming puck-carriers.

Frank Lefebvre—Centre; age 16; weight, 142; although this is his first year with the team, Frank has shown enough talent to warrant a position with the champions.

Donald Thomson—Right wing; age 16; weight, 134; "Ching" is another who is serving his first season with the champions, but his fine stick-handling and tireless back-checking has helped immensely.

* * * * *

The *Citizen* in a 1940s article headed "Gym Classes of Today are Far Cry from Old 'Jerks,'" with Lisgar gym teacher Dorothy Bishop looked back fifteen years in Ottawa school athletics to describe some of the changes:

The old timer, of even fifteen years ago, would hardly recognize the modern gym class. Physical jerks, clubs, dumbbells, bloomers and middies, all are gone. In their place are modern exercises, apparatus work, folk and modern dancing, and much trimmer shorts and rompers. Even the vocabulary is different. We call it "health" or "physical education" now!

The new health course in high school is designed to give the student fun and relaxation, to improve the co-ordination of mind and body, to help her develop certain sports interests that may become hobbies later, and to encourage co-operation and sportsmanship. That's a big order. Naturally it is accomplished in varying degrees and with varying students.

The most recent addition to the physical education program takes place outside the gym itself. In addition to practising it the student now studies health. One period a week in Grades IX and X is spent in class room study, where the student works on charts and drawings and posters, and engages in elementary research in the history of health discoveries, and in contemporary community health agencies.

In Grade IX the student studies elementary anatomy and physiology to discover the necessity of certain health habits. She learns why the body needs sleep and sunshine, well-balanced meals and good posture, why both under-exercise and over-exercise are dangerous.

In Grade X the student concentrates on the more social aspects of health. She studies how the knowledge of the body has increased since the days of primitive man's superstitions; learns of the great discoveries of Harvey and Pasteur, of the Curies and Banting; explores the modern community health agencies; sanitary inspections, clinics, social service organizations; discovers what is being done and what yet remains to be done in the international war on our most dangerous diseases—tuberculosis, heart disease, cancer.

Every high school student, unless exempted by a doctor, spends two periods in the gymnasium. That is not nearly enough by itself to keep her physically fit. She is encouraged to practise good health habits at all times and to participate in out-of-school sports. Most students need little encouragement. They swim, play tennis and badminton, skate, ski. All this is the natural supplement to their physical activities in school; without it the hour or so a week in class would mean very little.

THE VOX LYCEI
1893-1943

From the first editor of the *Vox Lycei* to the last, many editors of the *Vox Lycei* went on to continue writing in some form —as a hobby, an avocation, or, in some instances, professionally. The first editor, Mark G. McElhinney, appeared in 1935 when the *Citizen* reprinted a 1909 article that he wrote. A veteran auto and motorboat enthusiast, he had been asked to tell the story of the introduction of automobiles in Ottawa. The following is excerpted from that article:

The early machines which came to Ottawa were of the single cylinder type, called "one-lungers." They were serviceable, but noisy, and some of them are still (1909) doing good work daily.

Their chief disadvantage was the liability to stall except under expert handling. Their engine power was too small in proportion to their weight. A 1,000 pound car carried a seven-horse-power engine; today the same car carries usually twenty-horse-power and the great advantage is obvious.

Three years ago (1906) a number of Ottawa motorists met and formed the Ottawa Valley Motor Car Association, their object being mutual protection and the encouragement of a better feeling between themselves and the other users of the roads. This association has grown and become strong and has accomplished in a great measure the objects which called it into being. The opposition, the prejudice, unjust legislation, both attempted and obtained, which had to be combatted, only those who were in the struggle can appreciate.

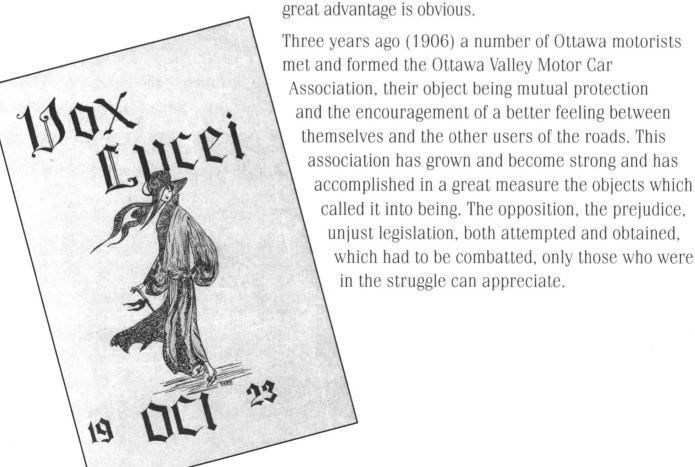

139

Made to Sell Cheap
— OR —
Sold To Make Good
Which Do You Prefer?

Overland Cars
are Sold To Make Good

Overland Model 80

AN "OVERLAND" FOR EVERY NEED

Model 81 T.—$1160
"   80 T.—$1450
" (6) 82 T.—$2000
F. O. B. Ottawa

Investigate Before Buying.

International Motor Co.
294-6 LAURIER AVE., WEST
OTTAWA

Advertisement in *Vox Lycei*, March, 1915.

The writer would like to hazard the prediction that in five years (1914) there will be 1,000 motor cars in Ottawa; the aggregate value of these will be easily one million dollars, and the city will be entering the snowless and dustless age. Not only this but By Ward market each morning will show dozens of farmers bringing in their produce in "utility" cars.

I cannot tell with accuracy who was the first Ottawa owner of a motor car, but it seems to me that Mr. E.C. Grant's De Dion Voiturette was the first, although the Ottawa Car Company imported an electric car pretty early in the game. Mr. H.G. Ketchum brought in a Rambler Runabout and Mr. Harry Brouse a Century Tourist. Mr. Wilson of Bank Street, also was early in the field with the Pierce Motorette, a narrow-gauge car, which was alright in the city but did not work on the ruts of country roads.

The Millens of Hull were pioneers in the steam car and some of their experiences in the wilds of Quebec province would make good reading.

Amongst the first who brought in what we call big cars were: Messrs. Ketchum, J. de St. Denis Lemoine, Lt-Col. Hurdman, G.P. Harris, A. Fleck, Dr. Graham, C. Jackson Booth,

J.A. Seybold, G.H. Millen, E.A. LeSueur, W.Y. Soper, H. Brouse, W.H.A. Fraser, and P.H. Shaver. Some may be here omitted as I have to trust to memory and the club list.

* * * * *

In the last year of the First World War, Joseph Leahy, editor of the *Vox Lycei*, 1918, wrote an editorial announcing the formation of Lisgar's Students' Council:

The year 1918-19 has witnessed the inception in the life of the school, of the institution now known to us all as the Students' Council. The existence of such a body has long been deemed desirable by those who have given the matter the slightest thought. Now the idea has materialized, and for the past year, regular monthly meetings have been held, at which all matters in any way connected with student activities are propounded, fully discussed and finally dealt with.

"To co-relate and supervise all student activities outside of school hours." This is, as stated in the constitution, the function of the council. It should be obvious to all that the powers of the council are of a legislative rather than of an administrative nature. It is not intended that it should represent an arbitrary authority in its own sphere, entering the councils of the various school societies and informing them of what they shall and shall not do. This is, of course, not the purpose of the council—but to try to see that none of our revered and tested institutions lapse or cease to exist; to oppose all unnecessary friction between institutions; to see, as far as is possible, that all energies are guided in one channel and concentrated to one end—and that end not the particular preference or individual desire of one society, the mere unit, but the ultimate benefit of the school. However, as it is stated in the constitution, all student activities fall within the jurisdiction of the council.

And of whom and by whom is the Students' Council constituted? There are eleven members in all, including [Principal] Dr. McDougall who is an ex-officio member, three members of the staff and seven students. The chairman of the council is the President of the Fifth Form, elected by the Fifth Form upon the annual re-opening of school in September. Then, we have the Captain of the Cadet Corps, representing all military affairs connected with the school; the President of the Glee Club; the President of the Athletic Association; the President of the Senior Lyceum; the President of the Junior Lyceum; and these together with the Publicity Agent, who is selected by the council, compose the student representatives. Dr. McDougall and the three teachers, also selected by the council, complete the list.

In the context of the formation of the Students' Council, to be dedicated to leadership and composed of leaders, this editorial by Joseph Leahy is one of the most passionate and important ever published in the *Vox Lycei* in its ninety-year history. In essence it is not only a plea for leadership but an exhortation on the crucial

"THE SCHOOL"

Nigh half a hundred years have haste and fled,
Since this great school its small beginning knew
Made for the future by an earnest few
Who saw the need: much more might
  well be said
Of that event. And when its way was led,
Up through the years which bless'd it as it grew
It made those great who wore the gray and blue,
Who left for us the torch to bear ahead.
So help the good old school! Get in the game!
And make her greatness greater yet, and show
In doing so the old-time spirit lives.
O, help her nourish thus the age-old flame
To win new laurels, yea to make her grow
The finest, whate'er fate or fortune gives.

C.A. Nicholson, *Vox Lycei*, 1919

need for balance between every individual's recognition of his rights and responsibilities in society and his acceptance of them. This balance is also essential for the stable and healthy functioning of institutions such as Lisgar, municipalities such as Ottawa, and democratic countries such as Canada. It is as applicable to today's society as to that of 1918, when it was published:

Every branch of activity in this school is formally headed by officers, responsible officers, officers drawn from [among] the pupils themselves;—class officers, officers of the various clubs and organizations, representatives of every phase of the School Life all on a democratic basis. But is it not true that the vast majority of these [individuals] *forget* that, by the fundamental principles of democracy, he who assumes public office is not absolute, is not unfettered, is not free to do his will; *he is a privileged, responsible servant to society.* He is bound in honour to serve that society, which by electing him to office, has shown in him its confidence, its faith. If he does not realize, that, first and last, his duty is service, then, as a citizen of this age he is found *wanting*.

This year a Collegiate Club was organized. That club held *one* meeting, then—it vanished; vanished utterly. And why, why should an organization so admirably fitted, in its very nature, to be a moving, vital influence in the School, why was it so abruptly withdrawn from the life of that School? The answer—its elected officers refused to realize the responsibility of their position; their duty, to serve.

One of the earliest photographs taken of the *Vox Lycei* staff, 1911. Front row, L to R: M. MacCormac, W.J. Sykes, F. Sanders, H. Plaskett, Miss E. Oliver. Back row: G. Rochester, J. Odell, Miss J. Campbell, A. Ross, Miss L. Joynt, Mr. G. Caldwell.

First Students' Council, from the *Vox Lycei*, spring, 1919. A.A. Burridge would be captain of the Cadet Corps. Dr. A.H. McDougall was then principal and A.E. Marty, H. Clark Mann, teachers.

Another concrete illustration:—some time before Christmas, a certain Fourth Form passed a *unanimous resolution* to erect a Roll of Honour to all the ex-pupils of that Class who had enlisted for Active Service. A truly laudable purpose, and one which, if carried out, would surely have been a fitting tribute to our gallant boys, battling for us and for Humanity! But what was done? A committee was appointed, and directed to see that the project was carried through. A certain number of pupils were given lists of the names of ex-members of that Class, and were asked to ascertain which ones had enlisted. *But there all responsibility ended!* That Committee, pledged to carry out the wishes of those whom it represented, then *slacked off*, and *betrayed the trust of the Class*! Since the appointment of that committee, not one meeting was called, absolutely nothing was done! As a result, and as a result of similar breaches of trust, that Class has dropped from a position of recognized superiority, to one of *contempt*.

When the *Vox Lycei* was well under way, a meeting of the Class Officers was called to discuss important matters in connection with this Paper. Whereas there should have been an attendance of seventy-five, in reality less than *twenty-five* pupils appeared. At a later date another meeting was called, and a special invitation was extended to all Class officers. Did they respond? They did not! Less than one-third of those invited, came to that meeting, and the meeting was a failure. And those pupils are the ones in whom is invested for safe-guarding, the fair name of our Collegiate!

Why are some classes remembered with pride and admiration, whilst others are utterly forgotten? Is it because of any intrinsic difference in the worth of those classes? No, absolutely no; every class in this Collegiate is as good as any other class; every class in this School possesses potentialities which if realized would produce results simply astounding in their nature. But we declare it rests with these Class officers, these Class leaders, to transform these mighty potentialities, by their example and inspiration and enthusiasm, into an intelligent moving force. This force if properly manifested, will accomplish—miracles.

This School could be made the most successful, the finest, the greatest in the World. It could be done, if only its leaders would grasp the principles of responsibility; of responsibility and service. And the School itself would respond. With heart and soul it would respond; its dormant possibilities would flash out, and with might and will would it join with its leaders in adding name and fame to our Collegiate.

Shall it be done? What about it, you officers, you leaders, you pupils of this great School? Is not "Our School—the Best," a goal worth striving for? Will you do it?—Officers and pupils of the O.C.I.—Accept the challenge of the world! Resolve to work, work for the School, and so work for Canada! Resolve to put your all into that work, and so be worthy to be called—Canadians! And surely as you do, you will make this School a School of Men, and men you will be, yourselves.

* * * * *

The discontinuance of Lisgar's very influential Lyceum did not entirely mean the cessation of all debates. The Vox Lycei of April 1914 reported on two very interesting subjects for debate, both premonitory of things to come:

During the winter term a series of two debates was held between representatives of our Collegiate Institute and those from Kingston. The first of the two was held in Kingston, when Messrs. Jeffrey and Moran from Ottawa were pitted against Messrs. Rayson and Germain from Kingston. The subject was: "Resolved, that military training should be compulsory in Canada," our boys speaking for the affirmative. Our representatives carried off the honours with flying colours.

PRESIDENTS OF THE STUDENT COUNCIL 1918-1944			
J.R. White	1918-19	Frank Corrigan	1931-32
Miss Marjory Pritchard	1919-20	Ed. A. Eligh	1932-33
Byron Howard	1920-21	Ken Wilson	1933-34
Miss Jean Clark	1921-22	Victor Knowles	1934-35
J.N. Anderson	1922-23	Stan Kozlowski	1935-36
Louis C. White	1923-24	Hector Chaput	1936-37
James R. Johnston	1924-25	Gerry Prodrick	1937-38
Douglas N. Argue	1925-26	Alan Hague	1938-39
Arthur Pettapiece	1926-27	Arthur Fee	1939-40
Pat Howard	1927-28	Wilson Morden	1940-41
Clifford S. Perry	1928-29	John Chance	1941-42
Robert Sheppard	1929-30	Douglas Dale	1942-43
A. Reid Tilley	1930-31	Sid Bateman	1943-44

Collegiate Board of 1936-1937. Back row, L to R; W.D.T. "Chubby" Atkinson, M.A., Dr. Campbell Laidlaw, J.J. Slattery, Cecil Bethune. F.A. Stuart, M.A., C. Phelan, J. Albert Ewart. Front row, L to R; A.E. Provost, P.D. Wilson, K.C., Hamnet Hill, K.C., (chairman), Mrs. C.H. Thorburn, O.B.E., James Warren York, K.C.

Three weeks afterwards a return contest was held in our Assembly Hall, when Messrs. May and MacDougall argued with Messrs. Rayson and Taylor on the subject: "Resolved, that women in Canada shall vote on equal terms with men.

The final year of the First World War had stirred O.C.I. to a flurry of new activities and a succession of changes, all reflected in the *Vox Lycei* of 1918;

An old ex-pupil, in the person of Miss Winifred Harvey, spoke to the girls alone. Miss Harvey is a graduate of Trinity College, Toronto University, and has been appointed by the Ontario Government to direct farm-work amongst women. She had a most important message for the young ladies of the School, and we hope that many will take it to heart, and serve their King and Country by engaging in some kind of farming work this summer.

Mayor Fisher, whom all of us now feel to be a bona-fide member of the School, was again with us on the occasion of the awarding of the prizes of the Fisher Competition.

Dr. Oswald J. Withrow, captain and returned man, who is now a member of the Council of the YMCA, gave a most instructive and timely talk on "Sex Education." His remarks were much appreciated by the whole School, as revealing in its true light a subject both pure and noble, and yet so often misinterpreted and misunderstood.

Another returned man, and also an ex-pupil of the O.C.I., Major Menzies, delivered an important message of hope and optimism from the Front. The major, who, as a Canadian Chaplain, has rendered great service to his country, was enthusiastically received by his Alma Mater. He is indeed a true example of the kind of manhood the old O.C.I. turns out.

Mr. H.P. Hill, the prominent Ottawa lawyer, one morning urged the School to buy Victory Bonds, and Mr. H.I. Thomas spoke at a most enthusiastic meeting held in the interests of the Patriotic Campaign. Both pressed the great need of generosity and giving upon us, and judging from the response, their words struck home. . .

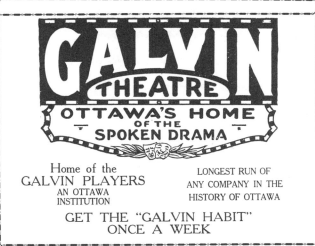

Ads from the 1928 *Vox*, Turrets cigarettes and Calvin Theatre.

Dr. [Wilfred] Grenfell, the hero of service, while in Ottawa honoured the School as never before, by consenting, in spite of extreme ill-health, to address the O.C.I. He gave a vivid and lasting picture of the heroic work amongst the fishermen of our North-Eastern waters, and left in the minds of many new vistas of life and service.

* * * * *

In his time, as well as being Associate Editor and Editor of the prestigious but now defunct *Ottawa Journal*, Grattan O'Leary was renowned as a writer, a silver-tongued orator in the Irish tradition, an influential member of the Conservative Party. On December 19, 1929, at the special Christmas Assembly he addressed the students of Lisgar on *Books and Education*. Erudite, philosophical, humble and honest, his message delivered in the Twenties is entirely applicable to today when English must still be considered as the fundamental underlying discipline to all others. Reprinted in the *Vox Lycei*, 1929.

I speak to you as one who, compelled to leave school at the age of thirteen, has had reason all through life to know and to appreciate the value of education. And the education I have in mind is not that which merely teaches men to remember, but rather that which teaches them to think; the sort of education which helps men to debate a thing through to the truth; the quality of learning which Lord Morley had in mind when he said that an educated man was a man who knew when a thing was proved. There are several ways, I suppose, by which one might secure an education of that kind. But I suggest to you young people today that there are few better ways of doing it than by cultivating now and maintaining throughout your lives a knowledge of the great writers of the present and the past.

Literature alone will not make a good citizen; it will not make a good man. History, indeed, affords all too many proofs that scholarship and learning by no means purge men of rancor, of vanity, of arrogance, of what somebody has called "a murderous tenacity about trifles." But what I do hold is that books help us to distinguish the false from the true; assist us in interpreting virtue and justice; awaken within us the diviner mind and rouse us to a consciousness of what is best. That, after all, is education.

I am far from supposing that everybody is born with the ability for using books, for reading and studying literature. On the contrary, I frankly admit that the habit and power of reading with reflection, comprehension, and memory all alert and awake, does not come at once to the natural man any more than many other sovereign virtues. What I do venture to press upon you is that it requires no superhuman force of will in any young man or woman to get at least half an hour out of every day for disinterested reading. Some will say that this is too much to expect, and the first persons to say it will be those who waste their time most. Now, in half an hour you can read fifteen or twenty pages of Burke; or you can read some of the greatest masterpieces of prose or poetry. I ask you to multiply that half-hour by 365, and consider what treasures you will have laid up by the end of the year; and what happiness, fortitude and wisdom they might give you during all the days of your life.

Not that you should try to read everything. The object of reading is not to dip into everything that wise men have ever written. In the words of one of the most winning writers of English that ever existed—Cardinal Newman—the object of literature in education is to open the mind, to correct it, to refine it, to enable it to comprehend and digest its knowledge, to give it power over its own faculties, application, flexibility, method, critical exactness, address and expression.

May I stress, for just a moment, the word "expression"? As a journalist, I am often asked by young men how they may learn to write. Frankly, I am not sure just what should be done. I have very little faith in rules of style, though I have an unbounded faith in the virtue of cultivating direct and precise expression. It is not everybody who can command the mighty rhythm of the great masters of human speech,

Sixth Vox Lycei of Eugene Forsey, Mar. 4, 1921.

Editorial.

The Value of Living in Canada's Capital.

If, *it is true,* as a great Englishman has said, that "To talk with great men is a liberal education"; it surely follows that even to hear great men speak is an education in itself. Perhaps we students of the Ottawa Collegiate Institute too often fail to realize the priceless advantage which we have over our fellows in other cities in the presence here of Canada's legislators, the greatest among her sons from coast to coast; perhaps, too, our loving teachers, in mistaken zeal, inflict upon us too much homework for us to go to the galleries of Parliament and improve our minds. For very real mental culture, and much valuable information in regard to our coming responsibilities as citizens, can be gained from listening to the eloquence of such men as Meighen, that prince of debaters, and of Sir George Foster and Dr. Michael Clark, two of the foremost orators in the Empire. Those desirous of improving their knowledge of French may hear that language spoken on the floor of the House in its purest and most fluent manner; and _above_ all, those who are fortunate enough to possess a keen sense of the ludicrous may cultivate their tastes in this direction by listening to the flowery exuberance of Mr. Mackenzie King. (Any Liberals present will kindly forgive the Editor, who is a lifelong, dyed-in-the-wool Tory.) It is thus readily seen how great and how varied are the advantages we enjoy in living in the capital of the Dominion. Now that Parliament has re-opened is an opportune time for both teachers and pupils to think this over. It is an even more opportune time for the Lyceum Executive to consider staging a mock

Student editor Eugene Forsey's editorial from the handwritten *Vox Lycei*, March 4, 1921.

One of the best *Vox Lycei*'s in the history of publishing at Lisgar was that of editor W.F. Ade, 1930. Here he is with his staff. Top row, L to R; E. Beahen, L. Marks, G. Ogilvie, A. Laidlaw. Middle row; D. Cromarty, Mr. Blake, M. Stevenson, G. Logan, Jessie Muir, Miss Fillion, D. Ryan, J. Barber, E. Blackburn. Sitting; G. White, H. Bedford-Jones, W.F. Ade, G. Rickwood, R. Tilley. Although it was a Depression *Vox* it had a great collection of ads.

who can equal a Macaulay or a Gibbon. But everyone can make reasonably sure that he knows what he means, and whether he has found the right word. These are things that cannot be gained by writing for writing's sake. They can be found only in thought, in a true love for the glories of our English speech.

It is something we should all try to cultivate. For we Canadians are notoriously deficient in our use of English. We are prone to sneer at oratory and eloquence, to ignore the value of correct expression, to extol the virtues of the "strong silent man." It is all a profound mistake. Words, after all, are what distinguish man from the animal, and they have been the great agency through which liberty and civilization and all mighty human causes have progressed down through the centuries. Whenever I dwell upon these things, I think of what was once said by Mr. Rudyard Kipling at a Royal Academy banquet in London in 1906. It was tthen that Kipling used his immortal phrase describing the beginning of human speech, how a "masterless man" arose and discovered words that "became alive and walked up and down in the hearts of all his hearers." And continuing, this great English phrase maker said:

"The magic of literature lies in words, and not in any man. Witness, a thousand excellent strenuous words can leave us quite cold or put us to sleep, while a bare half hundreds words breathed by some man in his agony, in his exultation, or in his idleness, generations ago, can still lead whole nations into captivity, can still open to us the doors of three worlds, can stir us so intolerably that we can scarcely bear the look of our souls."

And so my advice to you young men and women this morning is to cultivate and sustain a love for good books. They will teach you more of life and truth and beauty. They will give to you a deeper appreciation and understanding of the majesty and the glory of the heritage of our English speech. They will encourage you in victory, be your consolation in defeat; be your truest friends and companions when you yield to the conquering years.

* * * * *

A page of student-teacher activities, some definitely extra-curricular and some academic, *Vox Lycei* 1936.

OUR SCHOOL SONG

I

We'll sing you a song of a school we know
Sing of the glories of the O.C.I
It dates from the time of long ago
Sing the traditions of the O.C.I.
Since first the old school had its birth
Its halls were trod by men of worth
Who've spread its fame o'er all the earth
And added glory to the O.C.I

II

And we today within its halls
Must keep the banner waving proud on high
And do our bit whate're befalls
To bring fresh honour to the O.C.I.
And when in some far distant day
From out its halls we take our way
We one and all shall cherish ay
Fond recollections of the O.C.I

CHORUS
Shout, work and battle for the O.C.I.
Phi, Chi, Psi, Kappa, Lambda, Pi
Come and hear us while we cry
"Up with the colours of the O.C.I."

W.D.T.A. (Chubby) Atkinson, *Vox Lycei*, 1930

The remarkable "Chubby" Atkinson was a teacher and Lisgar principal before he became principal of Glebe Collegiate, Ottawa. The editors of the *Vox Lycei* some years after the end of the First World War asked him to do a retrospective explanation of the origins of Lisgar's school song. In doing so he also composed a fascinating memoir of a First World War soldier. This is excerpted from the *Vox Lycei*, 1930:

A request has come to me to give some account of the origin of the song, "The Colours of the O.C.I." Naturally it divides itself into two parts, the words and the music: but if you have the time and the *Vox* in space, just smother your yawns, and, as Aeneas said to Dido, "Incipiam—I shall begin."

First, the music.

January, 1919, found me at Edinburgh University in company with about seventy other "beastly Colonials" as our English friends sometimes called us when they thought we couldn't hear them. We were still in khaki, and on full pay augmented by a liberal allowance to buy haggis in lieu of the ancient codfish and Australian veal, known to the vulgar as rabbit, with which the government had fed us at camp. After a couple of months' lectures, we were unexpectedly told that we would have a month's holidays for Easter. I don't know whether the Army authorities knew about this or not; but we certainly didn't enlighten them, and we accepted the days of rest with gratitude.

After loafing for about three of the weeks in Edinburgh, two of us found ourselves slightly wearied of our diet of oatmeal porridge, and decided to try the potatoes in Ireland. Each of us had—mirabile dictu—about fifteen pounds of good old British currency—so we planned a trip, in typical Yankee tourist fashion,—six days to "do" the country. As you shall see, we "did."

Roy, my companion, (I call him Roy chiefly because that was his real name) was a breezy Western lad from the Railway Corps. After vainly trying to coax a few other of the boys to come with us, we set off alone, took the night boat from Glasgow, and landed in Belfast long before breakfast the next morning. We must have stayed in Belfast all of two hours, and then decided to "do" Dublin in the afternoon. We "did." We spent the afternoon and such part of the night as we foolishly did not give over to sleep in that delightful spot, and then went to Cork early next morning. The town we "did" in the record time of three-quarters of an hour, kissed the Blarney stone two hours later, and went on to Killarney that evening in order to "do" the lakes the next day.

We got in about dusk. Finding the dining-room at the hotel closed, we hied up town to find the wherewithal to replenish the inner man. Going past one humble spot—they all looked humble enough—we espied a red-headed girl apparently in charge. Roy's great weakness, among others too numerous to mention, was (or is it "were" Mr. Mann?) lasses with Titian locks. So we forthwith entered.

Pause now, à la Henty, for some contemporary history. We were in the heart of the Sinn Fein country. The Easter rebellion was but three years back, and the country was seething with the discontent that afterwards broke out into open hostilities. There had been no conscription in the country. It was filled with young men who, we had noticed with sad regret, paid scant respect to two august Canadian officers of the sublime rank of Lieutenant; in fact they were inclined to scoff at us. Some of the later bickering with the police had already begun, and there was at that very time martial law in Limerick, which was, I suppose, about fifty or seventy-five miles away.

But back to our muttons! Enticed by the appearance of the auburn-tressed damsel, we entered the tea-room, or whatever it was. But immediately we had wished we hadn't; for it seemed to us that the entire male population of Killarney was in the background, and they seemed to have forgotten to put out the mat with "Welcome" on it. I don't suppose there were more than ten of them altogether, but even that seemed about eleven too many. However, Roy had a Military Cross, and I am not built for speed, so we kept our dignity,— and our seats. It didn't increase our feelings of ease to any noticeable extent to hear numerous mutterings behind our backs, particularly after we had made gestures of friendship, which were turned down cold. And then, all but two went out. That didn't help either. We wished they had stayed

The 1936 Students' Council. Back row, L to R; Bill Boss, Norman Moore, Jerry Fee, Ira Brown, Hector Chaput. Middle row; Bert Sculthorpe, Tom Shipman, W.B. Mann, M.A., Alice Meabry, Doris Packman, Lois Tomkins, Anne Anderson, Frances Dent, Bill Hanley, Mr. W. Showman, M.A. Front row; Miss L. Smith, B.A., Miss R. Hills, B.A., Stanley Kozlowski, Mr. E. Lapensee, B.A.

where we could keep our eye on them. However, we finished our refreshments, and finally engaged the younger of the two remaining Irishmen in conversation. By this time we had taken off our overcoats; and the "Canada" badges on our tunics—there were none on our top-coats—lent an entirely different aspect to the affair. Before, we were merely British Officers, loathed and hated; now we were brothers in arms, sufferers under the cruel heel of Britain.

It transpired that Mick, the younger Irishman, was the "swateheart" of the fair Judy whose amber locks had brought us in. The other chap, who possessed a walrus moustache and whose name I forget, had some similar interest in the proprietress, a rather angular lady of uncertain age. Then there was a dark-haired little flapper of possibly sixteen and apparently unattached, whom we for obvious reasons christened "The Map of Ireland.".

Tempus fugitted. There was some sort of curfew law in the town and the shop windows had to be closed; but by this time we had established an entente cordiale all round, and we were invited to a rather dingy back room, where more eatables and drinkables were produced. Somehow or other we got to singing, softly, lest the police get inquisitive; and after we had got rid of a few Canadian airs, Mick took up the

burden. He had a fine untrained tenor voice, and he crooned away at some of the old mournful Irish folk songs. Then he went on to a few songs of the rebellion and of these later times, the first of which is the tune you know so well in your school song. The title is "Whack fol la diddle," which means absolutely nothing at all; it is just like the "fol de rol rol" of some of our own songs. There were about five verses, all containing the most exaggerated sentiments of loyalty toward England; but one was supposed to see that the singer meant the exact opposite of what he said. The first verse and the chorus ran:—

We'll sing you a song of a land we love,
Whack fol la diddle lol la di do day.
A land that rules all lands above;
Whack fol la diddle lol la di do day.
Let peace and plenty be her share,
Who kept our homes from want and care
Oh, God bless England! is our prayer
Whack fol la diddle lol la di do day.
Whack fol la diddle lol la di do day.
So we say. Hip hooray!
Come and hear us while we pray
Whack fol la diddle lol la di do day.

Of course Mick sang several other songs of a similar nature; but this, both words and music, particularly struck my fancy, and I asked where I could get a copy of it. So the next day before we went to see the lakes, Judy met me and escorted me down to a store where with a great deal of "Hush Hush," I was able to secure a copy of this and a couple of other songs, along with a few Sinn Fein souvenirs, all of which were very much forbidden at that time. . .

As to the words of the song, as they are known to the students of the O.C.I., I plead guilty to perpetrating them. But I also plead as excuse that they were written in a big hurry, for reasons which shall appear.

In the spring of 1927, the Lyceum was at a loss to know how to conclude its season; so some of the staff suggested a teachers' program. At that time we had on the staff four or five who could (and would) put on a number each, besides a body of whole-souled choristers who agreed to form a chorus. We had to have music right smartly, and I put the words you know to the old tune in a big hurry for fear the chorus would back out.

Incidentally this meeting of the Lyceum was a startling success. Some of us rather feared the outcome. It was just possible that we might be the recipients of some unwanted coppers tossed at us by the unsatisfied cash customers— a thing not entirely unknown in the annals of the O.C.I. However, we seemed to capture the hearts of the audience right away by taking a high F in the chorus of the first song. We intended this as a serious effort but the audience took it as a joke, which is perhaps just as well. Anyhow, everything else that we did that afternoon was regarded as high humor. Four or five of the staff contributed stunts, all the way from playing the piano handcuffed to delivering foolish monologues; and the program was brought to a conclusion by the initial singing of "Up with the Colours of the O.C.I.," after Miss Jessie Muir had explained and fervently blessed it.

Some time later, Mr. Bearder provided an orchestration and put it in your morning repertoire beside "Mother Machree" and "A Song of Canada."

* * * * *

The editorial staff of the Vox Lycei 1927-28 decided it was time to boast about its success in the advertising department, a success that led to the enlargement of the annual yearbook:

In 1926, under the leadership of Gerald Cameron, the Advertising Staff set a record by bringing in some $800 worth of ads; in 1927, under Moe Appel, it established a new record of over $900; again in 1928, under the worthy Mr. Appel, the staff set a practically unbeatable record of over $1000. To the Advertising Staff, then consisting of

The Ottawa Normal-Model School

Will re-open Tuesday, Sept. 4th, at 9 a.m. Pupils enrolled last year are expected to be in their places on opening date.

Course extends from the Kindergarten to the First Form High School, and French is begun in the Primer class.

There is room for a limited number of new pupils in several forms. The Principal will be in his office at the School on Elgin St. from 3.30 p.m. until 6 p.m. each day, beginning Aug. 29th, to interview parents regarding the registration of new pupils.

W. J. NEALE, Principal.

ASHBURY ..COLLEGE
(Rockcliffe Park, Ottawa)
Resident School for Boys

New Memorial wing, containing large gymnasium, lavatories, shooting gallery, etc., will be opened this fall .

Special preparations for Universities and R. M. C. Staff of English University men.

Successes 1922, 2nd place McGill Arts Matric. All candidates for R. M. C. successful; 1st class honors Toronto Matric.

A few day boys are taken.

School re-opens September 14th.

For Calendar, apply Secretary.

Ottawa Collegiate Institute

Re-opens Tuesday, September 4th.

At nine o'clock the returning pupils of last year will meet in the Assembly Halls of the Lisgar Street and the Glebe Schools.

At two o'clock on the opening day, in the Assembly Hall of the Lisgar Street Building, all pupils who have passed the Entrance, either by recommendation or by examination, and who propose to attend the Collegiate Institute, will meet and be formed into classes, some of which will be for the Lisgar Street building and others for the Glebe building.

There are no fees for resident pupils, but under the provisions of the Adolescent School Attendance Act of Ontario, attendance is obligatory on all under sixteen years of age, who are not specially exempt.

From August 27th to September 3rd the Principal of the Collegiate Institute will be in his office, Lisgar Street, each afternoon from two o'clock to five, to consult with parents or pupils.

CECIL BETHUNE,   A. H. McDOUGALL, B.A., LL.D.,
Secretary-Treasurer.   Principal.

OTTAWA LADIES' COLLEGE
(1869—1923)
RESIDENTIAL AND DAY SCHOOL

Matriculation Course, Music, Art, Household Art, Elocution Commercial.

For Prospectus and Further Information Apply to the Principal Miss I. J. Gallaher.

School Re-opens Tuesday, Sept. 11th.

The CARLETON SCHOOL for Girls
———— 152 ARGYLE AVE., OTTAWA ————

WILL RE-OPEN FRIDAY, SEJTEMBER 14

For the enrolment of new pupils and consultation with parents.

CLASS WORK WILL BEGIN MONDAY, SEPTEMBER 17

when every pupil should be in her place. Thorough teaching and personal care are offered. Special advantages are available for a limited number of resident pupils. A carefully chosen staff has been engaged.

INTERVIEWS DURING VACATION BY APPOINTMENT ONLY TELEPHONE C. 748

Opening announcements of Ottawa schools, 1930s.

Mr. Appel, C. McGuire, J. McKay, and R. Dick, went the major part of the credit for the extension of the school magazine to 128 pages.

* * * * *

Virginia Preston, a Lisgar student writing in 1992, compellingly re-creates Lisgar during the war years of her ancestors' generations, 1914-18 and 1939-45:

High upon the wall of the main entrance and lobby to Lisgar Collegiate Institute, four wooden and brass plaques give silent testimonial to the horror and tragedy of the two Great Wars of the twentieth century. Hundreds of names line the corridors, demonstrating the ravages of modern warfare upon two generations of young men. More than two thousand Lisgar students and graduates enlisted for active service between the periods 1914-1918 and 1938-1945; of these, nearly three hundred were killed, most of whom never saw their twenty-fifth birthday. Each of these young men had once known the community of Lisgar Collegiate and surrounding Capital City. And when they fell in foreign lands their friends, colleagues, parents, and teachers were united through a common pride and grief.

The *Vox Lycei* has always been a barometer of school feeling, for it is designed to preserve for the future the ideas, feelings, and doubts of the times. The volumes published during the war years are, as a result, fairly accurate reflections of the nature of student concerns and priorities of those periods; inevitably, information and discussion about the wars permeate these volumes.

There are observable and similar trends in student feeling with respect to the First and Second World Wars. At the start of the confrontations, the student body seemed exuberant, excited, and confident about the prospects of the nation and her allies. An example of this carnival-like atmosphere is a young Lisgar Cadet Corps (the 94th Highlanders) captain who loudly claims that "rumour has it that Hitler is scared to death of the 94th." This type of comment did not appear in 1941 after two years of "total war," the battle for Dunkerque, and the arrival of long list of fallen sons, friends, boyfriends, and older brothers. Lists of men in active service, and remembrances for the dead moved to a more prominent spot at the front of the volume. That year, the editorial staff of the *Vox Lycei* solemnly described the document as being "more in the nature of a

Miss Tomkins with roses. This photograph of some distinguished Lisgar old boys in an old classroom, seated at the old-style desks was taken at the Centenary celebrations in 1943. Included are: Percy Harris, president, Harris Coal Co.; Brigadier-General Charles MacLaren, director and president, MacLaren Paper Co.; Allan Ross, president, Ross Building Construction Co.; Clarence Steele; Lawrence Freiman, president, A.J. Freiman Department Store, Ottawa; Kenneth Greene, Canadian Ambassador to Australia. Miss "Sis" Tomkins was an all-time favourite teacher at Lisgar.

wartime record" than the publications of previous years. A heavy pall of sobriety and shock seems to have hung over the student body. The result is a strange and unnatural maturity born of war-weariness, sorrow and horror:

"Can we expect that because we have fought for our very lives and the form of government that we believe in, suddenly once the fighting is done things will take on a rosy hue such as they have never had before? ... I do not think so. We shall have to work even harder than ever to achieve these things. They are not a reward for fighting, the fighting has given us again the right to attempt to obtain them."

— John Gray, *Vox Lycei* 1945

Much of the young people's enthusiasm stemmed from the propaganda of the day and the fact that they were too young to take part actively in the cataclysms that rocked the world. With the exception of a few young men and women in the fourth and fifth forms, they were not old enough to enlist as soldiers or nurses; the rest of the student population was eager to help but unable to participate. As a result, there was an overwhelming fascination with the war. Manifestations of their curiosity are abundant in the *Vox Lycei*; particularly in the "Literary" section which is replete with tales of gallantry, valour, and courage like J.R. Nicholson's "How He Won the V.C." (*Vox Lycei*, 1919). Other examples include a proliferation of war poetry. Another phenomenon was the appearance of academic-style essays analyzing everything from the coming of peace to the position of China in the Second World War.

The students were deeply fascinated by personal experiences of the war. Despite the fact that pupils continued with their schooling and social lives with an air of relative normalcy,

Finlay Hood's art classroom. In his earlier days at Lisgar he taught almost every subject on the curriculum but during the greater part of his forty-year career at Lisgar he presided over the L-shaped art room on the top floor of the east wing. Another contribution to the school was the diary which he kept of daily events from 1920-1939.

it seems that the war was never far from their thoughts. Soldiers returning from the front were invited to the school and eagerly questioned. Letters from ex-pupils on active service were read aloud in daily assemblies and, in the latter half of the Second World War, were published in the *Vox*. Similarly, immigrant students were questioned about their experiences; such was the case with a grade eleven student, Colin Shaw, who retold his experiences during the London Blitz in the 1941 *Vox Lycei*: "During the night a shell from one of the guns came down without exploding in the air and it exploded on hitting the ground in the road outside. The concussion blew twenty-five percent of the hotel windows out, and shrapnel, nearly red hot, came flying in through the windows." The students seemed to thrive on the first-hand recounting of the events that they would only otherwise encounter over the crackling wireless, in the newspaper, or in paperback novels.

Inevitably, some of this fervour was directed towards the war effort. The Red Cross was one of the first charity organizations to receive support from the Collegiate. In 1916, the Montenegrin Red Cross and Relief Fund received a hundred and fifty dollars from Ottawa Collegiate students and staff. At the time, this was an astonishing sum. Throughout both wars there were a number of Red Cross dances and socials, and, during the Second World War, students set up Lisgar Red Cross Societies. Unfortunately, the club received fluctuating amounts of support from the student body. Another charity programme in which students played an active part was the sale of war stamps. Homerooms were pitted in competition against one another to see which could raise the largest sum of money.

Other students took on part-time or summer work to replace the part of the workforce fighting overseas. Some found employment in the Civil Service while many others turned to factories to give their support and to earn extra money. Another programme was designed to alleviate the Canadian Farming Industry which had lost many of its younger employees. Young men and women became "Soldiers of the Soil" and "Farmerettes" (depending upon their sex) and would leave school early each year to spend their summers working, not fighting, in the fields. In addition, many of the young women sewed and knitted for men in active service, for refugees, and for the Red Cross.

In the early part of the twentieth century, the role of women in society was changing at a rapid pace. A primary reason for this was the loss of the predominately male workforce to the two world wars. Women had to step forward to keep the machinery of the nation working. Many young women of school age graduated to take government or Civil Service jobs while other "girls [were]... leaving school too soon, lured by quick money in temporary war-time jobs." This trend can be seen in a business advertisement for the Gowling Business College of Ottawa in the 1918 volume of the *Vox Lycei*: "During the month of April, 1918, we had to refuse

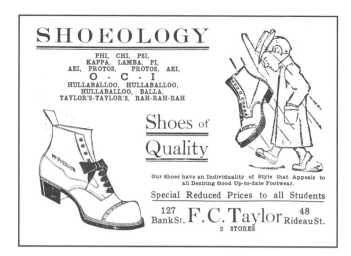

SHOEOLOGY

PHI, CHI, PSI,
KAPPA, LAMBA, PI,
AEI, PROTOS, PROTOS, AEI,
O - C - I
HULLABALLOO, HULLABALLOO,
HULLABALLOO, BALLA,
TAYLOR'S-TAYLOR'S, RAH-RAH-RAH

Shoes of
Quality

Our Shoes have an Individuality of Style that Appeals to
all Desiring Good Up-to-date Footwear.

Special Reduced Prices to all Students

127
Bank St. F.C. Taylor 48 Rideau St.
2 STORES

37 calls for help from business men because we had no one ready to send. . . Young Women you must take the places of the Boys overseas."

This change in the Canadian social structure can also be seen by comparing the number of women enlisting as WRENS in the Second World War with the number doing the same or similar hospital service in the First; this number increased several fold and their work was given greater credit than ever before by their country and peers as women nurses were listed as members of the active service. Significantly, at the same time

(in 1945), Q. Sachs of the twelfth form published an article in the 1945 *Vox Lycei* entitled "The Battle of the Hem Line" which argues that despite the shorter hemline, women would never begin wearing trousers in public.

* * * * *

Student Joan Finnigan entered Lisgar in the fall of 1939 a few days after war was declared. In 1944, in her final year, as editor of the *Vox Lycei*, she was in a good position to summarize "The World War Two Years" to which she had been witness at Lisgar.

YOUTH STYLED IN 1944

Yet all experience is an arch wherethro'
Gleams that untravelled world whose margin fades
Forever and forever when I move.
—Tennyson's "Ulysses"

Last night I went down to the station to say good-bye to the boys, to the gang I had swapped answers with, and copied notes from, since way back in first form, since the memorable September of 1939.

Since then every year, just about this time "The Hand" has come into our school and beckoned—and they have gone, blindly, eagerly, with the longing of youth to be tested by the unknown, and the confidence of youth in ultimate success.

The lads for the war in a 1942-1943 photograph from Joel Slone who signed up on Nov. 11, 1942. Standing, L to R; Ken Lussier, - -, Jim O'Leary, Raymond Willis-O'Connor, Charlie Miller, B. Bate, Marsh Wright, Don McGregor, Joel Slone, Bob Olson, Howard Pridham, Bill Patrick, Frank Farrell, Guy Hamel, Alan Potter, Allan Egan. Front row; David Edelson, - -, Weldon Forsyth, Johnny Powers, Don Grills, Mac Foulds, Ken McCuaig, Cam Smith.

Lakeside Gardens, Ottawa's favourite summer dancing spot during the 1930s and '40s. Originally located at Victoria Park on Holland Avenue, Lakeside gardens opened as a vaudeville theatre, became a motion picture house, was dismantled in 1905 and moved to Britannia Park where it became a dance hall. Many famous musicians and bands played there including Norma Locke, Eddie Hall, Woody Hill, Berkley Kidd's Orchestra.

An unidentified shooting instructor gives pointers to Lisgarites who attended the school during wartime. L to R; Barbara McCallum, Rita Pranzke, Mary Moxley, - -, Maxine Waldron, - -, - -, Nancy Lewis.

A number of Lisgar girls joined the forces during the war, 1939-1945. Here the W.A.C.s swing down from Parliament Hill.

The Union Station was a roar and a turmoil, a stage set for a thousand dramas. The noise was the noise of a thousand actors speaking their lines simultaneously. There was laughing and singing and secret crying. Not for the first time, nor the last has the station rung with "good-bye" "good-luck," "all men must be free." There were school yells, "Phi Chi Psi" and "St. Pats! St. Pats! Rah! Rah!" louder, I think, than I ever heard them before. There were handshakes and proud eyes and short swift kisses. Then a Man drew back the Gate and they passed through.

Last night the actors were deeply engrossed in their lines but I was on the outside looking in and I couldn't help wondering if—these boys, going away—these girls, staying behind—felt that their youth was being robbed, that it was the wrong time to be young. All the way home I found myself comparing these days with pre-war high school days.

Those were big brother's "old glory" days. We saw them with awe-stricken eyes through the living-room doors after Bill had pleaded a strong case and Dad was forking over two dollars for the "gas-eater." Or we saw them in the kitchen when Bill came to Mum in desperation asking her to "do something" about the bow-tie on the rented tux.

Those (according to rumour, fact and snapshot albums) were the days of madly-painted jalopies and couponless gas. Those were the days of stalwart football heroes and championship high standard teams. Those were the days when every guy took his gal to the games in a car, when you could have the gang in after school without going butterless for two weeks, when there were (believe it or not!) five men for every girl. Those were the never-a-care days—after high school you shifted to university to become college bred, which, as one bankrupt father expressed it, was a four-year loaf on the old man's dough. Those were the days of irresponsible adolescence, when a youth's only political conviction was the "girls' skirts should be definitely shorter" or "what this country needs is a good five-cent cigar." He lived safely in his Ivory Tower and no ten-ton blockbuster ever knocked him out of it.

Today the O.E.R. has triumphed—after that you walk. The football team ain't what it used to be—the senior boys have gone. If you have the gang in, you padlock the refrigerator and feed them arrowroot. We manage to survive without tennis balls, bobby pins and canned pineapple. We don't have formal dances and we don't buy new evening dresses. The "stock" at the summer cottage is rather poor (the oldest is twelve) and we apply for a job in the Civil Service. In the city, youth,—adolescence— keyed to a wartime pitch, with what little recreation there is cut to a minimum, or inaccessible because of gasoline rationing, complains of a state of "no-where to go," "nothing for kids our age," and attempts to invent a new form of amusement. Sometimes in technical or legal terms this is called juvenile delinquency. Girls are leaving school too soon, lured by quick money in temporary wartime jobs. Boys are laying down books for

WIT AND HUMOUR

A doting young female stopped a young R.C.A.F. flier in front of the Red Triangle the other night. "I think it's perfectly wonderful" she gushed, "to think that you go into the air to die for your country." "The heck I do Madam," said Richards. "I go to make some other fellow die for his."

*****

I am going to show you," said the Flying Instructor in mid-air, "that I have got complete confidence in your flying ability." He threw the stick out of the plane. "Oh, that's how you do it," remarked Al Potter (former L.C.I. student), and threw his stick out, too.

*****

George Thompson was writing a letter home to his mother from camp. "The food in this camp is absolutely poison," he complained. And then he added "and such small portions."

*****

The Cameron Highlander Sergeant Major strode into the Drill Hall. "All right, you lazy apes, Fall In," he exclaimed. The Cadets grabbed their hats and swarmed out; all but one, who continued to loll around in a corner. "Well," roared the Sergeant. "Well," remarked Cadet Croil, "there were a lot of them, weren't there?"

*****

Instructor (just after tailspin): "I'll bet 50% of the people down there thought we were going to be killed that time." George Neal: "Yes sir, and 50% of the people up here thought so too."

*****

Mr. Irwin: "I thought of sending some of this tobacco to the front."
Mr. Nichol: "How can you be sure the Nazis will get it?"

*****

Mr. Lalonde: "What is the difference between a submarine and a blonde." Laddie King was stumped for a reply. Mr. L.: "Oh come, come, think." "I can't," said King, "after all, I have never been out with a submarine."

*****

McDougall: "But sir, I'm from Lisgar Collegiate."
Recruiting Officer: "Ignorance is no excuse."

*****

Lisgar draft dodger: "They can't make me fight."
Selective Service Officer: "Maybe not, but they can take you where the fighting is, and you can use your own judgment."

guns too soon, forgetting that the post-war world will require scholars as well as sailors. Yesterday eighteen was a pathetic broad-jump from childhood. Today at eighteen we are men and women. We are forced to become men and women when we are confronted with big issues, big responsibilities. We learn young that we must make our big decisions—alone. Thus—we are an independent, serious, realistic generation—young for a day.

If I were to say to you, "Are you sorry you are young today?" and you said "Yes" I should say, "See to it then that your children don't have to grow up in wartime. If you put as much effort and determination and money into building a peace as you have into breaking the enemy there will be no more wars for your children or your next-door neighbour's children."

And if you said "No," I should answer, "Then you are a person after my own heart. The experiences I have had, the people I have met and, more than all that, the tomorrow of promise that lies before me, the future of a new world that this—my generation—holds in the palm of its hand is surely recompense for a madly-painted jalopy I never owned."

What a time to be young!

* * * * *

Obviously, there was something about a sailor.

Lisgar cadets on school roof practising aircraft recognition in the days when the temporary wartime buildings were alongside and the view was unobstructed to the Parliament Buildings.

Several letter excerpts from men on active service were published in the 1944 and 1945 issues of the *Vox*. Once again, the letters arrived from points all around the world and spoke of completely different experiences. One letter from Flight Lieutenant Eli Barker was sent from a German Prison Camp while another wrote from the Philippines after the Philippine Invasion. Some of these young men described a certain sense of horror and loss. Others wrote that they were having the time of their lives. Together, these letters helped to form the opinions and images of war held by the Collegiate students back home.

LETTER EXCERPTS FROM THE BOYS

. . .Well we're a long way from the old college room at 482 Johnson (never could spell that) aren't we, Gord? Old Queen's will soon be opening its gates for another term, and let's hope it is the last one we miss. I look forward to sitting down with the gang around one of Mrs. Billing's apple pies, and—

Eng[land]?—oh, it's swell. Beautiful is hardly superlative enough. It's quite different from Canada, its beauty being small and dainty as a mother, while Canada is wild, rough, untamed as the son. England seems so toy—toy trees, toy cars, toy trains, toy houses, toy road—like a model country. —I am with two fellows I trained with in Canada—

L.A.C. Bud Morden, R.C.A.F., England

. . .I am permitted to say that we took part in the Allied landing at Naples (which was really a very good do) and that we were in on the Italian Fleet surrender. I have seen quite a few of their ships in Malta and they don't look too bad— it must be shameful to have to surrender the way they did. In the Naples area we had quite a bit of fun. I was flying a great deal and saw more than those who didn't. We were up flying on my birthday, and it would have been a happier one if the Germans had come up to fight us. I flew low over the Isle of Capri and I have never seen such a beautiful place in the air. I suppose it smells from the ground though. We all enjoyed our invasion. . .

Lt. Commander Dig Cosh, R.C.N.V.R.—Fleet Air Arm
(Killed in action)

. . .I stayed at the English-speaking Officers Club, which is a lovely old home in the centre of London. They look after twenty officers at a time and the atmosphere is very pleasant—not the usually crowded feeling present at other places. We had supper there in a homey dining-room and then went out to the Covent Garden, which is a huge ballroom of circular construction, with two bands playing in the centre. There were all kinds of music—a lot of this crazy English stuff. The place looks like a barn dance when they start it. They all know the dances and sing at the same time. We left for home about one. The town was alive with people, over half of them lost the same as we were. After yelling for a taxi till we were hoarse, we decided to walk.

Lt. Pete Daubney, R.C.A.C.—Overseas

. . .I am all crewed up now and what a League of Nations it is! A New Zealand pilot, an English navigator, an Australian bomb-aimer, an English gunner and yours truly. We get along splendidly even though we come from such widely separated corners of the earth.

So far I have met two ex-Lisgar men—a chap named McEvoy, he was a couple of forms behind me at the school but we recognized each other and fell all over each other. The other chap was Purvis.

Sgt. Mel. Duncan, R.C.A.F.—Overseas

. . .We went to Detroit the other day on a 24 hours pass. We were at the U.S.O. for a while. You don't pay for a thing here, consequently we had dinner and supper among the pretty girls. The streetcars and buses are free and the shows half-price! At the U.S.O. they wouldn't even let us pay for a stamp! While waiting for a street-car on Sunday a fellow picked us up and drove us around Detroit! . . . The hotel was full so the manager took us to his home for the night and drove us back into town the next day! They certainly treat the boys well in the U.S.A.

Don Johnson, R.C.A.F.

. . .In that town in South Africa there was a Canadian-American Club. One day I was leafing through the visitor's book when I noticed the name of Al Hague. Beside each name there was a column for remarks and Al had written Phi Chi Psi. . .

The best part of Calcutta is the American Kitchen. This is a restaurant owned by a South American where you can get apple pie à la mode and Maxwell House coffee. It's the first place I've visited where you can get either of these.

Al. Wilcox, R.C.A.F.—Overseas

I am still in this blasted Libyan Desert which I think I've been up and down more times than the British ever chased Rommel back and forth. I take my hat off to the "Tommies." It's bad enough to live in the place, let alone fight in it. Although when they did push through they didn't leave us much to live in. Anything that looked like a building was destroyed by Gerry or us. Anyway, out here you are better to sleep in the open or in tents, because in most of the Italian buildings you will have lots of little companions work their way into your blankets and give you a good many nights of restless sleep until you have killed the last one.

I have had a few trips to Cairo and Alexandria since I have been here. They are the only places we can go when we get leave. Parts of them are quite modern with stores and buildings like we have at home. But I guess the biggest part of them is the native quarter where all the bazaars, etc. are. It is very expensive down there; you can spend money faster there than any place I've been so far.

Warrant Officer Doug. McLean, R.C.A.F.
in North Africa

. . .In all it stands as an expression of that wonderful spirit which exists in this Air Force of ours. It brings out that strong bond of comradeship which exists between every boy in the blue uniform and his buddy. There are seven boys up in a bomber tonight over enemy territory. Each one has that never-say-die spirit. They had it long before they took off. They had it long before they arrived in England, or Africa. They inherit it from their training schools and stations in Canada. . . .In two or three hours I will be leaving No. 5 I.T.S. for good. . .

Sgt. Pilot Gord MacKay, R.C.A.F.,—Overseas

. . .Last Monday night (Nov. 22/43) I attained one of my ambitions I have held ever since I became an Air Bombadier—that was to be right in there when we paid a visit to the big city [Berlin].

Things are really looking good over here now, the headlines this morning say "Less Than Six Months for Victory."

(This next part was written from a German Prisoner-of-War Camp).

. . .Here I am in a place I never expected to be. I am well, safe, uninjured so there is no need to worry. Please send parcels. Have seen quite a bit of Germany en route. Red Cross feeding us O.K. I do hope that you have heard I am safe before this.

Ted Capreol, R.C.A.F.

. . .I have kept in touch with some of the Lisgarites and while in England spent several days with Joe Leggett, Alan Hague, Duke Abelson and Doug McLean. I arrived in London very early one morning and as I was registering at the Leave Club I noticed Al's name. I rushed up to his room and gave him a hearty shake. I wish you could have seen the expressions come over Al's face. While we were in London together we went out to see John Hicks and Bob Heeney. I ran into Doug in an Adjutant's office in England—I was just walking towards the door when a knock sounded and in walked Doug MacLean. Needless to say the Adjutant's office was a bit disrupted. I met Digby Cosh at Gibraltar when I was on my way to Africa. He certainly does Lisgar justice in his naval uniform. . . In Italy now and quite near Joe. . .

Dwaine Merkley, R.C.A.F.—Overseas

(Two days after Mr. Dunlop received this letter Dwaine's death was reported.)

. . .We walked into the nearest town after supper to-night. I don't think I should like to settle in Malta—too many goats! One little thing shocked us a bit. A woman opened the front door of her house and drove out about a dozen goats.

. . .I have quite a collection of money now English, French, Italian, Maltese and B.M.A. (British Military Authority) money which is used on the desert. The French is the best. You get wads and wads of bills in exchange for one little pound.

. . .Harry and I hitch-hiked into Valetta. It is much the same as Algiers and Tripoli—narrow alleys, dirty streets and hundreds of kids. We saw two of the smallest dogs I ever saw—smooth-haired black like Maggie's "Fifi," scarcely six inches high, with spindly legs and pointed faces. Harry claims they were just big spiders. . .

L.A.C. Ralph Witty
Attached at R.C.A.F., written at Malta

. . .Speaking of fruit, the lads to-day were picking large ripe juicy oranges off trees not many yards from their gun positions! The more confirmed sun worshippers were stripped to the waist.

. . .The last movie was about a month ago—Astaire and Rogers in "Shall We Dance." In the middle of the show half the audience was called away to smarten up some of Hitler's Youth. The boys got back in time to see the end. . .

The Auxiliary Service Supervisor, Canadian Legion who had a portable projector and power supply put on the show. There were some tanks harbouring on our position. It was a novel tableau—gunners caped in great-coats and blankets and tank crews sitting on turrets silhouetted in dim starlight all watching Hollywood!

Maj. "Bud" Browne, Central Mediterranean Forces

* * * * *

THE ANSWER

Back and forth through the shadows a young man walked aimlessly, his head bowed except for the occasional glance that he flung towards the West where the last feeble rays of the dying sun wandered in and out of the pines. Twilight slowly merged with night and a bright moon rose through

---

TO LISGAR'S GLORIOUS DEAD

Shall we forget the sacrifice of these
Who in the hey-day of their live's best years
Forgetting all the love they left behind,
Rose to the call and left us to our fears;
Who went to guard us as our men of yore,
And died, alone, unsung, on foreign shore?
Shall we forget those who gave their youth away?

We evermore shall guard the mem'ry fresh
And evergreen in the annals of the free, of these,
The brave who fought on land and sea and
  in the air.
They counted not the cost, though dear it seems
To us who knew these lads, who proudly joined
  the fray.
May we hear the call as clear as they
Who now have passed; may we, like them, obey.

—Gordon C. Wilson *Vox Lycei*, 1944

161

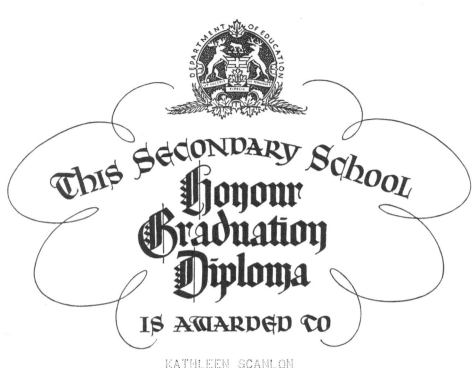

This **SECONDARY SCHOOL**

Honour Graduation Diploma

IS AWARDED TO

KATHLEEN SCANLON

a pupil of

LISGAR COLLEGIATE INSTITUTE

...mpleted satisfactorily a five-year Secondary

...urse in accordance with the requirements of the

...t of Education for Ontario and who has obtained

...in the following optional subjects of Grade 13

ALGEBRA, TRIGONOMETRY, GEOMETRY,
LATIN, CHEMISTRY, FRENCH,
ENGLISH, GERMAN, GREEK.

never had a chemistry class in my life! KOS.

OTTAWA

...y of ___ AUGUST ___ 194 3

George C. Drew
Minister of Education

Principal of School

W.C. Macartney
Chairman of School Board

This is what a high school graduation diploma
looked like in the 1930s and '40s. Inset
photo taken April 28, 1940, shows Kathleen
Scanlon Pedersen, class of '43 in Lisgar
"uniform," and friend Hilda Rowley Shaw.

the trees casting its ghostly shadows over the earth. And still the young man walked. And he thought—the answer; if I only knew theanswer—. Suddenly he turned and strode towards the house. His step was confident. His mind was made up. The future was before him and he was ready for it. On the doorstep he paused, turned, and looked once again at the moon. The door closed silently and he was gone. . . . and the answer. . . . ?

* * * * *

"Name?"

"Michael Fromant."

"Age?"

"Eighteen."

"Education?"

"Senior Matric."

"Fine. Now just fill out these forms. You'll find ink and. . . . "

* * * * *

"Aift Ight Aift Ight Aift—keep your distrance in those files—Quiet in the ranks—Flight—Halt! Well, well, well—you lads are perking up—about twenty more days of this and. . . ."

* * * * *

". . . .and you must realize that Aircraft Recognition is one of the most important of your subjects, not only here in I.T.S. but throughout all your life in the R.C.A.F. as a member of Aircrew. Now the first aircraft that we take in I.T.S. is the. . . "

* * * * *

"Now remember Fromant what I've told you. Hold her steady and take your time. We've all got to solo the first time you know. . . ."

* * * * *

". . . . so that you may always fly a straight, true course, not only in battle but also in the life that faces you. May these wings be a milestone in your career and see you through thick and thin, good and . . . . "

* * * * *

". . . . it will be fighter sweeps today fellows. Fromant, you'll have Porcupine one with MacChagarty and Jones as two and three. Your course will be . . . ."

* * * * *

"The R.C.A.F. issued its 801 casualty list of the war yesterday, containing 48 names and including four men killed on Active Service Overseas, 21 men missing on Active Service after Air Operation Overseas, and seven men missing on Active Service in Canada.

OVERSEAS

Killed On Active Service:

Ericeson, T.L., W.O., Montreal P.Q.

Ensigne, H.G. Flt/Lt., Long Island. N.Y.

Dunning, L.W., Flt/Sgt., Espanola, Ont.

FROMANT, Michael Sean, Sqd/L., D.F.M.,1773 Warnclife Heights Drive. . . ."

* * * * *

This was the answer.

John R. Gray, *Vox Lycei*, 1944

* * * * *

Compulsory war service became such a political hot potato that Lisgar's *Vox Lycei* editorial staff 1941-42 took a Gallup poll from which the following is excerpted:

Recently a number of Lisgarites were questioned concerning their opinion of the forthcoming plebiscite. Many different views were expressed but perhaps the concensus [sic] of opinion was expressed by a senior student who said, "I think conditions have changed so much since Mr. King made his promise that the government should disregard the pledge and should go ahead and conscript men and wealth immediately."

One prominent fifth former answered as follows, "I think there is absolutely no reason for the plebiscite and that the government should act right away and conscript whomever it wants—as long as it doesn't take me."

"I think the government is justified in presenting the plebiscite, and although there are many good reasons for voting otherwise, I would vote to free the government from its pledge," said one boy. . .

One of the more radical members of our senior hockey team said, "I think that the plebiscite is a waste of time and money and I think the government is deliberately bringing this matter up to delay our war effort."

Of those questioned, 27% thought that the government was justified in presenting the plebiscite and only 9% said they would refuse to release the government from its pledge. . .

* * * * *

Lisgar student Virginia Preston continues her 1992 observations:

Students lived with the new realities but a different, carefree, and more prosperous age was within living memory (even for youths of fifteen years). In fact, they were confronted with the realities of the world at war every moment of every day. Even something as simple as having friends over after school involved previously stockpiling butter for two weeks.

For Men Only—*VOX* 1943-1944

Boys! You have been criticized and flattered behind your backs but in a recent survey the girls came out in the open and expressed their opinions about dates and mates.

Do wear brown brogues, tweeds, diamond socks, wool ties and V-neck sweaters like Cedric Archibald's.

Remember to hold open the doors, and help her off with her coat in the movies. You have no idea how much girls stress the little things.

Buy raglan coats with a split up the back. We don't like fitted or belted-at-the-back jobs.

Sports jackets and school sweaters are tops.

Make a good impression on the parents when you meet them. Mother and Dad are usually good judges of character and types.

We like masculine, ambitious, athletic boys.

A pipe makes a man seem a man. Any one can smoke cigarette.

We hate flashy ties, braces, armbands, bow ties and orange, pointed shoes.

Don't wear trousers that bag at the knees. To be typically high-school you don't have to be untidy, sloppy.

We know boys like to talk most of the time, but please let us get a word in once in a while.

We're not looking for Clark Gables or Frank Sinatras. We're looking for personality, character and a sense of humour.

We like a boy other boys like.

We tab as childish (1) boys who have lewd minds; (2) boys who boast of their drinking parties; (3) boys who swear to impress us.

We like a boy who will suggest places to go, things to do.

We dislike spectacular dancers. All we ask is someone who stays off our suede shoes, keeps time to the music and, travels smoothly.

Wear your cadet uniforms. It's true that there's something about a soldier.

We dislike boys who take you to a dance and give every other girl in the place a good time, or boys who whistle at other girls when they're with you. Labelled as wolves.

We like to talk to boys who recognize us as an intelligent equal. We resent boys saying "a woman's place is in the kitchen."

We don't like inferiority complexes in boys. On the other hand we don't like swaggering conceit. Just be self-confident.

We loath brilliantine.

Don't wear fedoras to school, least of all zoot fedoras.

One girl in a thousand likes a zoot suit!

It is bad taste to ask a girl if you can kiss her good-night—just kiss her.

For Women Only—*VOX* 1943-1944

It was easy enough to draw the boys into a conversation when the topic was girls! Here is what they think about femininity. Take it or leave it, girls!

We like plaid skirts and sloppy sweaters—on some girls.

Blue is still our favourite colour.

We like healthy, shiny, clean-looking hair that looks or is naturally curly.

We hate chunky, junky jewelry. Wear pearls and identification bracelets.

We can't bear to hear a girl swearing. (As much as we swear ourselves.)

There's hardly anything we like more than girls in full-skirted evening dresses.

We prefer the athletic type—a girl who can swim or play tennis.

1% of us like a girl merely for her looks.

The other 99% of us (with an eye to the future) look for personality, and at least a few brains. We like vivacious, fun-loving decent girls.

Hair drooling over one eye usually gives us a wrong impression (or the right one!).

High giggles make us grate our teeth.

We hate the sight of bitten nails. Some of us like bright polish. More of us don't.

We like girls who smile often.

Don't wear slacks unless you're the one girl in a thousand who has a tall, slender figure. (If you only knew what men think of girls in slacks!)

Please go easy on the paint. It's an awful shock and disillusioning when it rains.

We like fragile jewelry on black dresses.

Thumbs down on runs in stockings, crooked seams and hanging slips.

Cheap perfume or even too much of Chanel No. 5 is nauseating.

We refuse to date a girl who talks about the other boys she knows or who flaunts a frat. pin and quizzes "Guess who gave this to me?"

We detest a gossip.

We like tans, spectators and broom-stick skirts.

We hate girls who swoon over Sinatra. (Too bad we can't hide our jealousy.)

The cheapest thing we ever see is a girl smoking in the street.

We like a maiden who sometimes gives a thought to how much (or how little) we have in our pocket. Our allowance is only 25c a week.

Standish Hall, Hull, for years and years part of the social history of Lisgar students.

High school-age students during the First and Second World Wars had a rough coming-of-age; young men and women who had grown up to expect a gradual improvement in the quality of life learned that they would have to fight for what they already had, and youths, as robust as that of any other generation, were daily confronted with death. Some of such encounters with mortality came with the death of brothers and fathers; others among the fallen were schoolmates.

Other incidents abound in the *Vox*. In 1918 the yearbook recorded the deaths of several of Lisgar's alumni: "When in June of last year so many of the fourth and fifth form boys enlisted, Reston Smith, one of the fifth's most popular members, joined the Royal Flying Corps . . . after but fifteen days service [he] was accidentally killed at an aerodrome on January 25th, just one week after his nineteenth birthday."

Another very young Lisgar student died accidentally in England during that same year. Eighteen-year-old Arthur Leroy Dean would normally have been completing his studies at the Collegiate; instead, the *Vox* lamented that "news of his untimely death came as a severe blow to his many friends" (*Vox Lycei*, 1918). The *Vox* of 1918 records an incomplete Roll of Honour listing the names of seventy-two Lisgarites during the war under that age-old slogan "dulce et decorum est pro patria mori." In 1919 the *Vox* ran an essay in memory of three former pupils, Eric May, Rutherford Dunlop, and Murray MacFarland "who are remembered as fellow-students by many who are still in the school." The

three classmates died within a month of each other: Eric May was fatally wounded at Rouen, Murray MacFarland was shot down over the German lines, and Rutherford Dunlop was killed near Inchy en Artois in the fighting around Cambrai. Each of these tragedies was felt deeply by those who knew them back home.

The experiences of Lisgar Collegiate students at home and overseas fighting in the wars were, in many ways, representative of the experiences of many Canadians during those tumultuous years. They were among the most exciting and horrifying periods of these individuals' lives and certainly bred memories and values that remained with them for many decades to come. To a certain degree, these youths had inherited problems from preceding generations and were made to pay dearly, sometimes with their lives, for the errors of their parents, grandparents, great grandparents, and all the other generations who had implemented the policies and held the beliefs that eventually led to the most massive and bloody wars the world has ever seen.

Nevertheless, at the end of the day, many students were proud to have grown up in those violent and turbulent years. For they believed that, as a result, they held the key to the future: "We are the youth of today, but tomorrow it will be our job to shoulder the great problems of the world, and particularly of Canada. We must prepare ourselves for this greatest of all human tasks—maintaining the peace."

EDITORS OF *VOX LYCEI*: 1904-1944

Miss A. Gorman, G. Pitts	1904	P.N. Currie	1920
Newton Kendall	1904-05	Byron W. Howard	1921
Hector Benoit, Sidney Payne, Geo. Smith	1905	E. Gardner	1922
T. Cassels, Miss Marion McDougall Jack Clarke		Miss M. McDougall	1923
Miss Lucy Robinson	1906	D.M. Morrow	1924
Miss Baskerville, Oscar Y. Brown,		C.T. Daly	1925
Miss Mary Leggo, Herb S. Smith	1907	H.W Beal	1926
T. Sidney Kirby, Norman M. Halkett,		H.H. McCallum	1927
Thos. Kirby, A. Ogilvy	1908	L.C. Williams	1928
R.B. Genest	1908-09	Carter Storr	1929
Harold Hudson, Addison Bukman,		W.F. Ade	1930
Norman Retallack, Hubert L. Uglow	1909	A.R. Tilley	1931
W.P.J. O'Meara	1909-10	Carl Lochman	1932
Miss Gladys Dillon, Harry Sifton,		Miss Valentine Barrow	1933
Thos. Ogilvy, J.A. Sully, S.B. Macpherson	1910	S.C. Checkland	1934
Geo. Shortt, Frank Sanders,		Jack Storr	1935
H. Gibson Caldwell, Wendell McL. Clarke	1911	Gerald Fee	1936
E.T. Chesley, G.W. Guiou	1912	John Fraser and Dick Barber	1937
C.L. Jeffrey, D.P. Kirby	1913	Miss Lillian Helps	1938
Paul Sykes	1914	Alan Purdy	1939
Eric Horsey May	1915	Malcolm Barrett	1940
(Not Published)	1916	John Chance	1941
John C. Armstrong	1917	Ellis Perrin	1942
Joseph Leahy	1918	Arthur Fee	1943
Leslie Stevenson	1919	Joan Finnigan	1944

FIFTH FORM REVIEW 1939-1944

. . . . Pen and copy of *Senior Latin Prose and Composition* lying face down in defeat. News of Tarawa and Sicily and Ortona . . . Girls knitting busily and badly on Red Cross sweaters. Bicycles piled near the girls' door and blue and gray ribbons in a cold fall rain. Last minute reviews, frantic scribbling and Christmas exams nearly finished.

Dim streets in the evening and tired people jamming into buses and clutching their newspapers with the screaming headlines and the trim expensive ads. Men making speeches about the promise of the New Year and the fuel shortage.

New work. . . new notes in classes . . . History tests.

Glorious week-ends of skiing on powder snow in sharp clear air.

Return, short periods in the library, long periods of maths, skating at the rink after four. Long talks to and from school. . . what we believe in. . . what we shall do. . . dates, careers, the war.

Ski clothes in the class rooms and numb hands awkwardly scribbling biology notes.

. . . Rehearsals for the concert. . . recruiting for ushers and stage-hands. . . nervous, hopeful rehearsals, teachers at their wits' end wondering who is skipping and who really

IS "painting scenery." Then the tenseness as the curtain rises on Lisgar's thirty-second concert, the smiles and congratulations as the curtain falls for the last time on another well-earned success.

Again exams roll around (do they never stop?) We dazedly endure them and manage to recuperate. . . .

. . . The excitement of seeing the boys leave —from the first big splurge (THE Dance) to the last hurried farewell at the station.

. . . Analyzing the style of Joseph Conrad and the chemical composition of oxalic acid.

. . . White blouses appearing in the halls. . . new leaves and green grass.

Final exams drawing near. Another chapter in Chemistry. Shakespearean and Italian Sonnets. Time out for the Spring Dance. Pages of scribbled notes, questions and answers, frantic dashes to the library.

First formers lying lazily in the warm grass by the canal, laughing happily through their noon meal.

Alice Bawden, *Vox Lycei*, 1944.

REMINISCENCES OF LISGAR
1893-1943

THE STUDENT'S TEN COMMANDMENTS

1. Thou shalt be neat in person, and at all times cleanly. The back of thy neck and thine ears shall be scrupulously scrubbed, and the conditions of thy nails shall not be such as to give the impression that thou art in mourning.

2. Thy demeanour shall be dignified and cheerful. When thou are reproved by the teacher thou shalt smile, yea, verily, when thou art given a detention or detentions, thou shalt smile and they shall love thee for thy high spirits. For verily I say unto you, happy is he that basketh in the sunshine of the teacher's favour.

3. In the Hall of Assembly thou shalt sing the Old Sweet Songs with gusto, and thou shalt find favour in the eyes of the Director of Music.

4. In the hallway thou shalt not roll thine eyes and show thy teeth at some fair damsel, lest her "beau" see thee and swift retribution overtake thee.

5. By the same tokens, thou shalt not make love upon the premises or in any wise permit the Arrows of Cupid or the Attractions of the Fair to disturb thy studies.

6. In the classroom thou shalt conduct thyself like a gentleman. Thou shalt not spit on the floor, nor chew gum, nor let thy voice be raised in tumultuous song, nor drum upon thy desk, nor throw chalk at the blackboard, nor upon the floor, nor at the roof that is above the floor. For in so doing thou angerest thy loving instructors.

7. If thou art in a mixed form thou shalt write no notes. For, verily I say unto you, it is a distracting and exceeding dangerous pastime.

8. Thy meals shall be taken at the proper and appointed time. During class thou shalt not regale thyself with popcorn, peanuts, lollypops nor charms, nor any other manner of stomach-destroyers and teacher-enragers. Truly, three meals a day shouldst be sufficient unto any man.

9. If thou hast not thy homework done thou shalt say:- Our house caught fire and I had to quench the flames, or give some other equally good excuse, and, if thou canst not do so, drown thyself, for the bottom of the canal is preferable to the wrath of the teachers.

10. Observe all these rules and the years of thy captivity in this stone edifice shall be as a pathway of flowers, and thou shalt find favour in the eyes of all.

—*Vox Lycei*, 1922

MRS. MARGARET WINTERS McDOUGALL, 1911-1915

I attended Lisgar from 1911 to 1915. In looking back now all I can say is that it was a difficult world we lived in— no radio, no TV and very few people owned motor cars— certainly not any students I knew. We had the silent movies. There was a movie theatre on Sparks Street called the "Nickel" where admission was 5¢.

In the winter of 1910-11 the City of Ottawa suffered a severe epidemic of typhoid fever—several girls had their hair cut off and rather than attend school with cropped hair they wore mob caps to school; a sort of dust cap with a frill. I had typhoid fever and lost several weeks of school. I was nervous about passing my entrance in June. In those days everyone had to pass an exam to enter high school.

The major event of my time at Lisgar was the outbreak of World War I, 1914-1918. Being so young at the time, I am sure we had no idea how serious it was—it seemed to us more or less of a show with soldiers marching, bands playing and flags waving. The boys were all so excited and could not wait to get into uniform.

I think on the whole I liked school, it was a more formal age. The teachers addressed the girls as "Miss" and the boys were called by their surname. I remember, very well, some of the teachers and I like to think they were dedicated to their profession. Miss Marty taught languages and was generally popular. I think my favorite was Mr. Hardy who taught Latin; a most gentlemanly figure—I could not imagine anyone acting up in his class.

GENERAL STANLEY TODD (RET'D), 1913-1915

When in the Model School, up to the year 1910, we used to look at "the big boys and girls" coming along Lisgar Street and wonder what terrific subjects they would be taking and how terribly difficult their homework must be. It was a great inspiration to enjoy the present [at Model] and let the future take care of itself.

It also taught me self-preservation. We used to hide in the lunchroom after school to avoid the odd big boy who delighted in roughing us up, removing anything like lapel buttons, watches if attractive to him though precious to us.

It all added up to the impression that the Collegiate was a great place of learning, but also taught us—for the first time—that when we attained this great place in the world we would also have to take care of ourselves.

Father was sent to London [England] on business in 1910, and it was thought that it would do no harm to take myself and my younger brother along with them. This potential holiday didn't last very long. At Christmas Father met the headmaster of one of England's great boarding schools and off we went—in theory for six months, in reality for nearly three years. At school we arrived dressed as we did in Canada with short pants and long stockings and a flat Canadian accent. We were teased unmercifully as "Colonial"— "Indians from the Colonies." When we returned to Canada dressed as English kids with bow tie, knickerbocker trousers with coloured golf stockings and English accent, we were again teased as "Blokes."

As a youngster I wanted to join the Royal Navy. At the first chance, I was twelve years old, but unfortunately got sick at the time of entry. Next year I passed the exams and I went to Portsmouth for a personal interview to see if I was suitable to enter Osborne for training as a midshipman. The commander who interviewed me asked me, "How old are you, my boy?" I drew myself up to my full height and said, "Thirteen, sir." His reply: "Thirteen? My boy, you are far too old for the navy." Later that year I thought if I couldn't go into the navy I would try for a commission in the British army, as a profession.

It was then decided that we should come home, and I would eventually go to the Royal Military College in Kingston, if I could make it. We came home in August 1931, and after a testing exam I entered the Lisgar Collegiate Institute in September 1913 in the 3rd Form. In those days we had Forms 1, 2, 3, and 4 instead of Grades 9, 10, 11, and 12. We wrote Matric. from the 12th Form, but there was a 5th Form or Grade 13 for those who didn't wish to go to university. It was a sort of Junior BA Class.

In those days Lisgar had about eight hundred students, as I recall it. Dr. McDougall was the principal. He was a big man—tall, about two hundred and ten pounds, with grey or white hair. We called him "Punch"—I never knew why. I only saw him, thank God, at the morning assembly in the big auditorium, which I believe is just the same today as it was then, with certain stage improvements. As I remember, other staff members—some more than others:

Mr. Norris: Our 4th Form teacher. We called him "Ikey" for no known reason. I will always remember him as a friendly man with almost a permanent, kindly smile. Taught us mathematics and geometry, algebra, trigonometry—

the whole business. No one was ever scared to go to Ikey after school and tell him you didn't understand: he would patiently do the whole lesson over again on the blackboard and stay with you until *he* was satisfied you understood.

He was a great personal friend of each student who was really trying, and only interested in getting you through your Matric. I wish I could thank him. With latter-year knowledge, we possibly took him for granted. He even telephoned us at home during the week we wrote our papers, asking how we were getting on and telling us not to worry because we were well trained.

Others that I can recall: *Mr. Mann*, who taught us English. "*Marty*," who taught us French. I can't remember her name. She was good—strict and severe. Always wore a plain black skirt with a white blouse. We called her "Marty."

Jessie Muir I always liked but don't remember what she taught. As indeed I also remember *"Sis" Tomkins* and *Mr. Gilchrist*, who taught Literature. We had no sports

instructors nor really any facilities for sports except what we did on our own on Cartier Square. There was, however, a drill instructor. We had a good Cadet Corps.

I will always remember my classroom for the 4th Form. It was at the back facing the Ordinance Stores. The Drill Hall and Cartier Square were important to me as my father was one of the officers of the Governor General's Foot Guards who marched out of that Drill Hall to the Northwest Rebellion in 1885. After the First War, in 1921, I also was an officer and drilled with G.G.F.G. twice a week. So that whole area of Lisgar Collegiate—the Ordinance Stores, Cartier Square, Laurier Avenue Bridge, the Drill Hall, and The Driveway— all became part of myself.

In May 1915 we wrote the Entrance Exams for RMC in the Drill Hall, with candidates from the whole area, eighteen papers in all. Six three-hour papers, nine to twelve noon, in six days, Monday through Saturday. Two two-hour papers in the six afternoons, one-thirty to three-thirty, and three forty-five to five forty-five. Entrants to RMC were admitted on

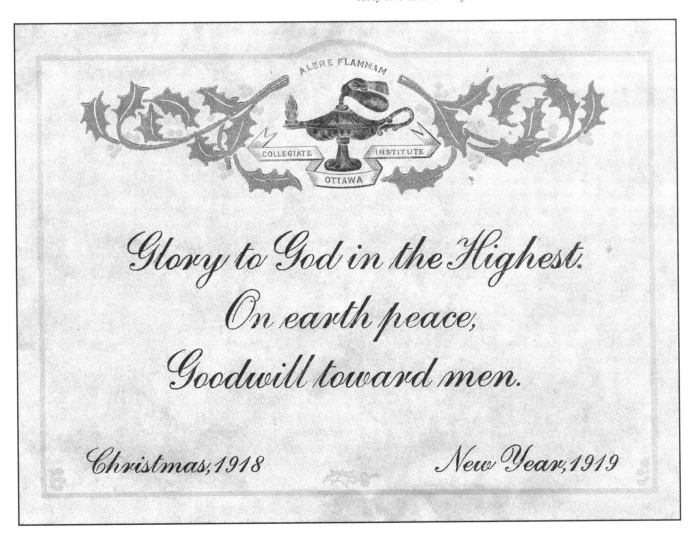

Principal A. H. McDougall attempted to send Christmas greetings to all the Lisgarites serving at the in World War I. With an accompanying letter expressing "thankfulness and pride in the noble part you have taken in the great fight for justice and for all that is great and good in civilization", this card was sent to # 343149, Sig. W.S. Caldwell, Signals, Wireless Station, France.

the basis of total marks. Supposing there were one hundred and fifty candidates in Canada, all writing for a chance to go to the college, and there were only sixty-five vacancies. Number 65 got in, whereas Number 66 failed, maybe by only one mark in eighteen papers! It was a terrible strain for those like myself who had set their hearts on going to RMC. Youngsters of today are no longer subject to the same stress.

I've mentioned this because life at Lisgar was very much embedded not only in my memories but as part of my character. Later in the spring of 1940 I was with my regiment in Petawawa and the time came to go overseas. We were loaded onto a CPR troop train and despatched to the east coast via Ottawa, Montreal, and Moncton. The train crawled through Hull, over the bridge, passed the Chateau, and then along the canal and passed slowly by Lisgar. I left behind my wife, my family, my home, and all the familiar surroundings around which my whole life had centred. Between me and all that meant everything to me were the glass windows of that crawling train that was taking me to the battlefields of war for the second time at age forty-two. It tore the heart out of me.

Lisgar cadets Mordy Hughes and Dick Gavin "horse around" in front of the school with civilian O'Connor, circa 1920s.

And Lisgar Collegiate lives on in my current memories of all the foundations of my love and happiness of my life in Ottawa to which I was not privileged to return. While much of that has now passed on, Lisgar Collegiate lives on. It was a great emotional honour for me to address the school in the great hall on Armistice Day in 1978, and a large picture of the school hangs in my bedroom, to ever recall what the school did for me. May it long continue to do so for those who are privileged to study within its halls!

Some classmates whom I remember:

Danby: Went through for medicine and finally practised on Rideau Street.

Yates: Harry was the son of M. Yates, who was private secretary to Sir Robert Borden. Harry joined the British air force and became the private pilot of Lawrence of Arabia. He subsequently became one of the first successful chiropractors of Ottawa.

Margaret Winters: Was the daughter of Charlie Winters, who was with my father in the Northwest Rebellion in '85 and eventually a Major General Military Secretary to Tom Hughes.

Harry Wood: Also RAF, became an instructor in the air force and a classmate of mine at RMC.

Bev Thorburn: Son of the bookstore Thorburns. Also a classmate at RMC.

Mr. Lewis: Owned an electric store. Was mayor of Ottawa at that time.

LENORE A. PRATT, 1914-1919

Lenore A. Pratt was a well-known poet who had many poems published in Canadian magazines and newspapers and in several anthologies of Canadian poets. She also had two Ryerson Chap Books of her poems published. She was the daughter of James Tucker, who was leader of the student revolt at the University of Toronto in 1895. The following is reprinted from the Ottawa *Journal*, November 8, 1958:

I am attending a concert in the Glebe Collegiate Auditorium. Perhaps the string quartet is deep in ponderous slow movement; my attention wanders. To the right of the stage hangs a portrait of the late Dr. A.H. McDougall, a remarkably life-like portrait, so much so that I quail before the keen glance of the eyes.

Once again I am 14 years old, I have been summoned to the principal's office of the Ottawa Collegiate to pay a 50-cent fine for defacing my desk with elaborate initials in red ink. Trembling, I await a stern reproof; instead there is a twinkle in Dr. McDougall's eyes as he orders the offending initials removed. Other episodes of student days come to mind, and before I am returned to the present by a gust of hand-clapping, I have strayed into the distant years 1914-18.

Outwardly the old stone building on Lisgar Street has not changed greatly since the September day in 1914 when we entered Form I by the gloomy little Gothic door at the east. A vacant lot and tennis courts across the road have disappeared. There, on fine Spring and Autumn days, we sometimes took a half hour of physical training under Miss Emily McManus. It was called calisthenics in those days. Out of doors we had lady-like "drills." In the girls' gymnasium we had Indian clubs, wands and dumbbells, or we played basketball, in baggy serge bloomers and middies. Miss McManus ("Biddy," as she had been nicknamed long before my time), correct in ankle length grey worsted skirt and white shirtwaist, led us through intricate numbers. Everyone found calisthenics a bore.

One term during the preliminary line-up there was the diversion of a squeaking floor board. Its exact position was the secret of the class hoyden whose heel, applied ever so lightly, produced the most distracting squeak. In vain Miss McManus appealed to the culprit's sense of honor. I suppose that squeaky board may still be there. Sometimes we were allowed an interlude of dancing to "Smiles," or "Too Much Mustard," played on the gym piano.

Lower School years were carefree. As yet the war made little impression our 14- and 15-year-old minds. Morning after morning in assembly we sang lustily "Land of Hope and Glory," "Rule Britannia," "The Maple Leaf Forever," "Recessional," and both "O Canada" and "The Marseillaise" in French. To this day I have never been able to sing the last two in English.

But as Dr. McDougall began reading letters from ex-pupils overseas, from the front and from hospitals, there was a growing sense of the glory and tragedy of the time. There were days when with deep regret he would inform the school of yet another casualty. As we advanced to the Upper School, many of these brief announcements carried shock and sadness. With these boys we had perhaps worked on the editorial board of the *Vox*, or chatted during recess, or debated at Lyceum meetings. Death was unbelievable.

Yet looking back, they were sunny years. The course of study was not difficult; algebra in those first years held no numbing terrors; geometry was in the elementary stage, and needed only a good memory.

We had wildflower expeditions under Mr. F.A. Stuart, class sleigh rides to the wilds of Hogs Back. The excitement of an annual operetta and play, and once, an all-day trip to distant Ironside with Mr. Donaldson in charge. That was the day I found a fascinating creature, a millipede with a bright wavy fringe of legs. Unhappily, on its death a few days later it proved unsuitable as a specimen for my insect collection. As the date for handing in collections drew near, we prowled the Driveway, we turned over stones, we lurked in gardens with our jam jars reeking of cyanide.

Our irrepressible classmate, she of the squeaky board, handed in a display of one sulphur butterfly surrounded by a dozen bumblebees. Mr. Donaldson was not amused. Dorothy's mischief drew increasingly severe impositions, and long hours after school.

Anything in the way of youthful exuberance met with displeasure, it seemed. I recall the incident of my blackboard illustrations. In Winter, I sometimes took my lunch to school, joining the group of girls from Westboro, Britannia and Rockcliffe who were obliged to take their lunches the year round. We quickly ate our sandwiches in the classroom, chattered with friends by the drinking fountain, strolled arm in arm through the silent corridors, and caught up on homework.

We scribbled sums and exercises on the blackboard. This gave me the idea of drawing scenes from "Ivanhoe" one noon hour. Spurred on and encouraged by my small enthusiastic group of classmates, I covered large areas of blackboard with episodes from the book, and with caricatures of the Lady Rowena, of Brian de Boisquilbert, of Gurth, the swineherd of the beautiful Rebecca. There was an ominous silence when our English teacher, Mr. Oscar Ellis, entered the room in the first period after lunch. He clearly did not appreciate my efforts. The guilty person was asked to stand. I stood: I cleaned the blackboard: I remained long after school copying pages of Sir Walter Scott.

We had crushes, likes and dislikes, even violent antipathies! We were free with pet names amongst ourselves, with nicknames for our teachers. Young people can be cruel and insensitive. The staff was tagged "Nosey," "Porky," "Sis," "Hopping Harry," "Hank," "Ikey," "Biddy," "Cozy." Some we simply called by Christian name, Bill, George, Jessie. Even Dr. McDougall was not spared; he was "Punch" from the day I entered Form I until my last day in Form V. Mr. Stothers was "The Colonel;" tall, dignified, quiet-spoken, he was, of all the staff, the teacher I truly loved and respected. History, ancient, medieval and modern, was a pleasure; with what dry humor we were told "Achilles sulked in his tent."

My crush—everyone had a crush—was the slim and lovely young Beatrice Gilhooly, newly appointed to the staff. With her masses of burnished gold hair she was like a heroine from Tennyson. Miss Tomkins, a brilliant mathematician herself, had no patience with the stupid, and filled me with sheer panic. As my grasp of algebra weakened, I sank lower and lower in her estimation. Terrified of her snapping black eyes and caustic comment I would fumble helplessly at the blackboard, my mind a blank. Surely in the history of the O.C.I. no one ever descended to the depths as I did, with an 11 percent on one examination, and a red-pencilled "disgraceful." For years I kept that sheet of foolscap as a mortification of the flesh.

During the period 1990-92 while this history was being compiled some students in Janet Fader's senior classes, as a contribution to Lisgar's story, undertook to do taped interviews with Lisgar alumni. As with the papers of Janet Morchain's classes, the acknowledgements in the back of the book will list credits. Copies of the papers submitted by both the Fader and Morchain classes will be deposited in the Lisgar archives for use in further research projects. This memoir is excerpted from Jeff Hsu's interview.

Caption on photo says, "O.C.I. gym team, 1920's." Here they perform on old Cartier Square in front of the army stores building, long gone from the square. Army stores was between Lisgar and the Drill Hall.

JEAN MCLEAN, 1925-1926

When I was sixteen my father, a judge, was moved from Halifax to Ottawa where I enrolled at Lisgar. School was a way of life then; there weren't many things one could do outside of school. I took English Literature, History, Geometry, and was part of many school activities. I played the violin in the school orchestra although I couldn't "play for beans." Sports-wise I participated in tennis, volleyball, basketball, and took part in the Girls' Rifle Club. We practised shooting at targets with rifles while lying down on dirty sandbags. Target practice took place on the, later forbidden, and then cryptic, fourth floor.

Classes started at eight-thirty in the morning and included an hour's break for lunch. There wasn't much to be found in the school's small cafeteria. There was no milk available and you couldn't get a full meal. Tables were not provided so many students ate outside by the Rideau Canal. The south building had not been built, of course, and looking at it today one might wish it hadn't been. In place of it there was an empty lot which extended to Cooper Street. There was a shed there and someone—out of boredom perhaps—dared me to jump off it. Perhaps out of boredom as well, I did— and sprained both ankles while executing the foolish stunt.

Although it was the Roaring Twenties there were no flapper fashions at Lisgar in my day. Students wore sweaters, skirts— nice girls didn't wear slacks then—and flat-heeled shoes. Nobody tried to outdo each other—how times have changed! And there was no snobbery—how times have changed!

There was no smoking allowed by students, no gum-chewing, no lateness, and respect towards teachers was part of

school policy. For those who broke any of these rules— especially being disrespectful towards teachers—there was detention after school! One could be made to write lines, do extra work or even solve math problems, the latter being a great asset to me as I greatly improved my geometry during a month's detention. Teachers could implement their own unique punishments; one time I had to pull my over boots on and off one hundred times because I put them on one minute before the lunch bell rang.

On the eccentric side, my Ancient History teacher who was eighty years old made students recite long passages from a textbook. Most students just kept their books open and read it out of the corner of their eye. But sometimes a student from behind would close the book and leave the poor student stranded. It took me two years to pass Ancient History.

My best friend was Lillian Meighen, daughter of former Prime Minister Arthur Meighen. I used to get into trouble because of Lillian. Yes, it was she who dared me to jump off the shed! Another classmate, George Jost who became a well-known American doctor, was a chronic nose-bleeder and was usually excused from class when his nose began to pour forth. Once, while he was out in the hall with his nosebleed, he slouched over and wrote his name in blood on the wooden floor with the help of a friend. The stain lasted three years.

H.W. BEALL, 1890-1927

My own time at Lisgar covers the mid-1920s. However, both my mother and her brother, my uncle Percy Wilson— better known as "Wickey" at Lisgar and throughout his subsequent life—went to Lisgar and between them covered the period from about 1890 to 1905.

The first anecdote that I can recall about Lisgar was my mother saying—this would be about one hundred years ago—that she and the girls were terrified when a big muscular teacher got into a fight with a big muscular boy. They had quite a battle, and the young ladies were scared stiff. However, it apparently ended happily, at least for the teacher, because that same teacher was the principal of Lisgar by the time I got there. He was Dr. A.H. McDougall, known both affectionately and respectfully as "Punch" McDougall by the school, and he of course was a great administrator, a great principal, and a good disciplinarian. Dr. McDougall was principal not only of the Ottawa Collegiate Institute but eventually of both Lisgar and Glebe for a short period.

My uncle, "Wickey" Wilson, was first a pupil at Lisgar and later a member of what was called the Ottawa Collegiate Institute Board, now part of the Ottawa Board of Education, at the time that I was a pupil at Lisgar. He used to regale my chums and me with stories of the shocking behaviour of the boys at Lisgar in his day. Now old Unk was quite a raconteur and quite a leg puller, and I'm quite sure that some of the stories that he told us were apocryphal, to say the least. But one I'm quite sure is substantially correct, and this concerned a young and quite naive teacher the boys apparently gave quite a hard time to. One day after a particularly bad session, these boys had the teacher in his home room and they trooped out and left him there and locked the door and took the key with them, indeed, they said they wouldn't let him out until he promised he wouldn't tell on them. The promise was given and the teacher came out. The promise was kept and everything must have worked out because that same teacher was teaching at Lisgar by the time I got there. I think it was Latin that he taught and his name was Graham. I only know him as "Shorty" Graham— every teacher was known by a nickname in those days. Mr. Graham was certainly an excellent teacher and, by the time I was there, also a very good disciplinarian. So this is perhaps one occasion when a little contretemps between the teacher and the students turned out to everybody's benefit.

My own time at Lisgar was between 1922 and 1927. I think among quite a few extra-curricular activities that I can recall perhaps the one that I enjoyed most was being an editor of a class periodical—a monthly publication, a newspaper we put out called The 4D Oracle, 4D being the number of the class, the way the forms were lettered in those days. And I think The Oracle came out every month during the academic year. Its distribution greatly exceeded the number of people in the class because others were very interested in it and wanted to see what The Oracle had to say in the way of jokes about them, or their friends, or their teachers. In fact, imitation, I guess, is the sincerest form of flattery—at least one other class paper started up during that time, but it didn't last as long as The Oracle did.

Besides myself, the late Archdeacon Wilfred Bradley was another editor of the paper. He was a well-known cleric in Ottawa for many years and died just a few years ago. Delmar Rosborough, who was in the post office for the balance of his career, was another editor. We had columnists and sports writers and so on. One of the columnists, I think, was Sauly Kabalski, better known later in Ottawa as Sol Max, who headed up a big ladies' apparel shop. And then Moe Lackavitch was our business manager, and I think Ruth Robertson was the editor of a girls' sports column and so on. At any rate, The Oracle was quite a success and I think that they are somewhere in the archives. We turned over a few years ago to Doug Arrand a number of surviving copies of the thing, so they may be somewhere in storage in the school.

Wilf Bradley and I were very good friends right through from our first year in Lisgar until the time of his death. During our classes we'd try to get seats close to each other. One year—I think this may have been when we were in Fourth Form and Fourth E—I had the seat in front of Wilf and, at this particular time, we both had a bug about playing chess. I guess we thought we were going to be chess champions or something. And Wilfred had a little chessboard and a miniature set of chessmen which he could put on his desk. When I was sitting in front of it, the teacher couldn't see the game that was going on. I would wait until the teacher was writing something on the board, then I would turn around and move my piece to whatever position I wanted, and then I would face front and Wilf would make his move, and so on.

I don't think we did this very often, but one particular day we were playing chess in a French class taught by Mr. C.A. Latour, affectionately known as "Nap" because of his startling resemblance to Napoleon the Emperor. At any rate, Wilf and I were both reasonably good in French and we didn't think we'd lose very much if we devoted a bit of attention to this game. So we were playing in this fashion, and suddenly I guess I took too long to try to make up my mind because I looked up and here was a shadow over me and there was "Nap" frowning down, and he looked at the board and he put his finger on one square and said to me, "Move da horse there."

Then he turned around and strode back up the aisle. Of course everybody roared and Wilf and I were both pretty sheepish and put the board away hastily, and that was the end of chess in class. I thought this was a very good example of how a teacher would handle a situation that could have got quite unpleasant. He did it extremely well and everybody thought it was great.

Another teacher who was very accommodating with the students was a young J.J. Dunlop who taught Literature at that time. On one occasion I recall he went out of his way to let the class put on a little bit of a play that we were studying in English Literature. The play was Shakespeare's As You Like It and the bit that was taken out was the wrestling scene. Apparently there was a professional wrestler in class

A *Vox Lycei* artist's version of affluent alumni of 1921. The caption reads: It will be particularly interesting to collegiate students to hear of the popularity of certain of our ex-pupils at McGill. "When we say that the McGill life and that McGill is one of the best schools on the continent, we need make no further comment. At the recent university elections Sid Davis was honoured with the presidency while J. Gordon Quakenbush was elected secretary. At the same elections Allan J. Macmillan was elected president of the Dental Undergraduate Society and I.H. Laishley secretary."

called Charles Stapleton and the hero—much to everybody's surprise—apparently knocked Charles out. I played the Duke and one of the courtiers was played by Joe Belanger. Charles is lying prostrate on the ground and the Duke said, "How dost thou, Charles?" The courtier then looks up and says, "He cannot speak, my lord." But Joe Belanger translated this as "My lord, he can't speak." So, of course, this went over well with the class. Big uproar. There was much applause and laughing until suddenly the door flew violently open and in strode the vice-principal, "Ikey" Norris, who had been teaching analytical geometry in the classroom below. The noise of our wrestling scene and class amusement, apparently, had got too much for him and his class. So he came up to see what was going on. I suspect old John Dunlop might have had his knuckles vilely rapped over that, but otherwise it was a great success.

I guess the most important stage production that I had any part in at Lisgar was putting on the trial scene from *The Merchant of Venice* at the Lisgar concert. I played the part of Shylock, which was my supreme effort, I guess, in acting. But the interesting part to me here was that I had to get a wig that showed a bald forehead and straggling grey locks at the back, and a gabardine. And we didn't have these in our property room and had to rent them from a shop across

the river in Hull. It was just across the Alexander Bridge, the interprovincial bridge. So after school, the day of the concert, I had to go across the bridge and into this shop. The lady who ran it wasn't there; her husband was a barber and I waited in the barbershop and waited and waited, getting more and more fidgety, and finally the lady came and I got my wig and gabardine. I ran all the way across the Ottawa River, down Elgin Street, down Lisgar Street, into the Collegiate where I guess the concert was already under way. They were wondering what had happened to old Shylock. Had he got cold feet and run away?

I think I ate a chocolate bar while the makeup people were putting my things on, and I got on to the stage just in time to say my beginning lines, "I have possessed your grace of what I purpose," and so on. All that worked out all right, especially for me because I didn't have time to get nervous— which I otherwise would have been.

Then there was another incident. This occurred at the time where Portia stays Shylock just as he is about to plunge the knife into Antonio's breast. I thought I'd done a remarkably good job in expressing exasperation and in letting the knife go, dropping it to the floor *point down*. The floor, however, was covered by an expensive rug that our property manager, Eddie Howard, had borrowed from Freiman's department store for the occasion. Eddie didn't think it was funny at all. In fact, Eddie nearly jumped out of his skin. But I guess the damage wasn't too bad, so we didn't hear anything more from Mr. Freiman.

I think that was the same year of the concert in which the great earthquake occurred. In those days the Lisgar concerts were given on two nights and the performance was the same on each night except that one night had an operetta and the other night had a play. So it was the alternate night to *The Merchant of Venice* when there was the great earthquake, and Roxie Carrier in the operetta earned great undying fame when she kept right on singing through her piece while the stage was rocking and reeling.

The 1920s were great days for cadets and for target rifle shooting at Lisgar. Interest in the 94th Cadet Corps was particularly high for two reasons; first of all, World War I was just over and military affairs were still very much in the forefront in everybody's mind. Also, to crown it all, Desmond Burke in his final year at Lisgar won the King's prize at Bisley in 1924. This Bisley competition in England is considered to be the top—now Queen's prize, then King's prize at Bisley— is the top award in high-power rifle shooting throughout the world—then, as it is now. Des Burke was nineteen years old at the time. His achievement, of course, spurred tremendous interest in shooting at Lisgar on this account.

In a book that Burke wrote many years later—the definitive book on target shooting called *Canadian Bisley Shooting*— he gives great credit to the then-cadet instructor and PT head, Arthur Burridge, for encouraging him and allowing him and other members of the team to use the rifle range, which at

Dear to the hearts of Lisgarites of its period, the old Assembly Hall where morning assembly was held from the 1920s to the 1950s at first on a daily basis, then on a weekly basis, now occasionally. Morning exercises in the Assembly Hall in the early days included the reading of a passage from the Bible, school announcements, music from the orchestra, singing of favourite songs and O Canada, taking of attendance.

that time was on the fourth floor of the old Lisgar building. There were also other top-notch shooters at the same time as Des Burke, people like Ken McGregor, who is now living in Kitchener and who is a retired insurance executive, and Leslie Best, who was a very good friend of mine and died a few years ago. Doug Pooler, Eddie Charlston, a good many others, were on a team that for the 94th Cadet Corps cleaned up just about every available trophy for cadet shooting at that time. And also did very well, most of them, as members of the Governor General's Foot Guards Rifle Team. There were also later shooters who continued this tradition; people like Brian Meredith and Philip Foran and Leslie Williams. In my day someone put up a pedestal in the assembly hall right in front of the center of the stage, a pedestal made specifically to hold the top cadet team rifle-shooting trophy in Canada because Lisgar had won it so often. This of course was fine, but a couple of years after that Lisgar lost that particular trophy and I don't know when it came back. It was perhaps a case of pride going before a fall.

HOWARD HARRIS, 1926-1928

When I went to Lisgar Collegiate in Ottawa, I walked to school for years and hundreds of miles. And the wind was always in your face. No matter what way you went, it was always in your face. Every day I walked direct from Gatineau Point to Lisgar, between seven and eight miles twice a day. I took the ferry across from Rockcliffe—it cost five cents to cross the river. I didn't row; the guy rowed. Everybody wanted to go on the river. He'd have about seven or eight people in the boat. Then up the hill at Rockcliffe and right down Nicholas Street, right through to Lisgar Street. In the wintertime I'd just run across the ice, so I saved the five cents and spent it at school. I used to go every day to Bowles Lunch. I'd walk every day to Nicholas Street, then up Rideau to Bank, down Bank to Lisgar. Back to school. For twenty-five cents I used to have a fried egg sandwich and a piece of lemon or custard pie, usually custard, two doughnuts, and a glass of milk. And when I came in, the cook would say, "Here he comes, drop one on." They knew me. I had the same thing every day.

Some of my teachers at Lisgar were Lorne Rentner and Johnny Dunlop and Miss Jessie Muir and Blake and Sis (E.A.) Tompkins. When Sis Tompkins was in the room, she was very much the commander of the room. Nosey Stewart was the principal and nobody liked him. He had a great big nose so we called him Nosey, and we were reprimanded for it more than once. Anyway, he'd come into the room and he'd say, "Oh, Miss Tompkins, your room is much too stuffy!" And he'd go to the back, and there were four windows and he'd open up the four. And when he was opening up this one, she was slamming the other one down. And when he got to the fourth one, she was right behind him and slammed it down. Then she just stood looking at him. She didn't care what she did because they were just pleading with her to stay. She was about five years over her retirement age at that time. He was livid but he couldn't say anything to her. She'd quit, you see. On the spot. So he went out the door and closed the door after him. And then she'd say to her students, "With that interruption over, we'll continue with our lesson!" I loved that lady.

One time Sis Tompkins went to a meeting. It wasn't in the school at all, it was out in one of the churches. You know how well men like meetings, and these two guys right in front of her were bored to death and talking. They were businessmen from the city. So finally she grabbed both their ears from behind and she pulled their faces together and she said, "I'm Sis Tompkins from Lisgar Collegiate, and if any brats in my school interrupted like you two imbeciles, I'd have them expelled!" She nearly pulled the ears out of their heads.

After travelling eight miles to get to school I was sometimes a little bit late. So I had that freedom of the "late slip," but this day Miss Tompkins came into our classroom as a relief teacher and I happened to be late that day. I don't know why she had glasses—she did more reading above them than below—and she's looking down over them and she says, "Is there a Harris here?" I said, "Yes, Miss Tompkins." She says, "You're late." I said, "I've got a late slip. I can be ten minutes late without being classed as being late." She says, "It says here you're late." I said, "I know I *was* late, but I have a late slip." "You'll have a detention," she said. "But I've got a late slip. I don't have to have a detention," I argued. She said, "You will have a detention." So I said, "Well, if I'm going to have a detention I'm going to have one. What's the big deal?" And she said, "Harris, I'm glad you've accepted the inevitable!"

Rentner was cross, but I liked Rentner; he was a good teacher. He'd say, "I'm not going to bother you kids. If you want to know something about algebra, I'll try my best to tell you. But if you're not interested, I'm not a bit interested either. So you can just sit there." He said that to all the students. It was Blake I had the problems with. There was rows of seats, but on the outside row there was two together. And there was another class used to come in, and this little Jewish girl, I know her yet—she was a Rivers—Irvine

River's sister—she used to come and sit there beside me. So I kind of liked her. But Blake, he wouldn't let me talk to her, so I got mad and said something nasty to him. And he was going to catch me and give me a licking, or take me to the principal so that the principal could give me a licking. But when Blake went to catch me, I snapped, and I hit him.

When I went to school here in Lisgar, their book of the year was *Vox Lycei*. Well, Pat Ryan was the editor this particular year. I had a picture taken of me with a girl out here—she wasn't a girlfriend, she was a friend of my cousin, and they used to come out here at the weekend. And they had taken a picture of her sitting on my knee and her arms around me and her face up against mine, sitting on the side of a sleigh. Well! I made the bad mistake of letting them see that picture and Pat Ryan wanted it. I said, "I know what you're going to do with it. You're going to put it in *Vox Lycei* and I don't want it in there." "No," she said, "I promise on a stock of Bibles I won't do that." I'm always trusting, so I gave it to her.

She said, "Thanks," and she put it down her dress front and she said, "That's going to be in the *Vox Lycei*." I got her down on the floor and I'm sitting on her stomach and I had my hand down there trying to get the picture back and Mr. Galbraith came in. He was an old English teacher. "Harris! Unhand that girl!" I said, "I'm after something down here and I'm going to get it." And he took one of the books like that and he was hitting me over the head. Yes, this was in the classroom. She was on her back, helpless, and I had my hand down there and I finally got the picture out. "Okay," I said, "I'll quit now." Oh, Galbraith was livid. He said, "You go to the principal."

I was in Lionel Lapensée's French class, and, of course, when you had nothing to do, you get into mischief all the time. And somebody said something smart and I started to smile. Lapensée looked at me and he said, "What are *you* grinning at?" (Oh, was he bad-tempered!) I said, "It's a free country. A person can grin or smile if he wants to." He said, "Get out into the hall!" It would have ended there if the kids had just let it go. But they all gave me a clap as soon as I went out the door. So out the door Lapensée came. "I'll show you if it's a free country or not." And he grabbed me by the ear, and we're on the third floor, and he was a short guy, and he pulled me all the way down three flights to the principal's office. I thought he was going to pull my ear out.

Nosey Stewart was in the office. "Harris, what's the trouble now?" he said. "No trouble," I said. Lapensée said, "He was impertinent to me." So Nosey asked for details and I told him that Lapensée had asked me, "What are you grinning at?" and I had told him: "It's a free country and a person can grin or smile if he wants to." And Nosey roars out, "That's not a case of freedom! That's a case of impertinence!"

The Harrises weren't particularly sports-minded. They did not go into Ottawa for hockey games or anything like that.

I played rugby—it was rugby then—and I played football at Lisgar and I held the championship for boxing amongst the high schools. While I was there, they stopped the boxing and they haven't had it since either. The last bout that I had was with a fellow by the name of Wright, and the school principal and the instructor got into a word fight over the thing. There was no more boxing after that.

I boxed Ed Lennie from Glebe. He was two hundred and ten pounds; I was a hundred and eighty. There was Percy Codron. He was a good athlete in our own high school. And that fellow, Wright, that was a sad tale. Nobody ever told me what the rules were, you know. I hit Wright one time and he was kind of groggy, and I hit him again, and he went down. I wasn't supposed to hit him again, you see. That was in the rules, but I didn't know that. So they carried him out and he didn't come to for about ten minutes, but I still lost that fight—I lost by a foul.

We had fifteen boxing classes between Lisgar and Glebe. I fought in two classes. I fought in the hundred-and-fifty-eight-pound class because I was a hundred and sixty—they allowed two pounds. And I fought in the open league. I won both my fights. Another little guy, Ed Zoomer, was in the Bantam-weight and he won his and we lost everything else. We used to meet every morning in the assembly hall, and the next day after the fights we went up to get our prizes. I got two silver cups and Zoomer got one. We got, "Rah! Rah! Rah! for Titanic Harris and Zoomer" and all the rest of it. Big Day!

The first football game I ever played was just between classes at Lisgar. I'd never seen a football before. Didn't know any of the rules, but I scored all the points: a hundred and twenty-five to zero! I carried the whole blasted team all the way up from the centre line to the goal. And every time we got a goal, we had to go back to the centre field. I was always in the buck formation when we came out with the ball, so after that they called me Bucky Harris.

One day in school, Sis Tompkins tried to open the windows, but they were all stuck. One of the guys said, "Get Bucky in. He'll open it." Miss Tompkins sent him into the next room to fetch me. So he comes in and says, "Miss Tompkins wants you." I couldn't think what on earth she would want me for.

Cartier Square adjacent to the Model School Grounds, used for skating and hockey during the winter, football practice and baseball in autumn and spring. In the foreground are the changing huts with Lisgar, the long drive sheds for the cavalry, Military Stores and Drill Hall in the background.

THEY ARE REGISTERED AS	TO US THEY ARE	THEIR WEAKNESS IS
Everett McGuire	Mickey	B.N.A Act
Rita McComb	Tiny Tot	Miss McDermott
Desmond Carty	Des	His Cerebellum
Betty Kettles	Goonus	McGill
Inez Smith	Inie	Camp Borden
Gerald Prodrick	Jerry	Sally?
Elizabeth Bryan	Beth	Voice
Kenneth Ross	Kenny	Singing
Lyle Jarvis		
Ruthilda Callaghan	Inseparables	Each other
George Spear	Georgie	Chelonia or turtles
Victoria Brown	Vicky	Spiders and Harry
Harry Bell	Dudley	Girls
Tom Davies		
Bill Lewis	Lisgar's Ski Team	Money
Dick Barber		
John Fripp		
Vincent Young	Vinny	Blushing
Margaret Sage		
Lilian Helps	Marg and Lil	Hitler and Mussolini
Byron Matatall	Barney	"Stardust"
Malcolm Welch	Mal	Zoology
Kenneth Brownlee	Ken	Lil' Audrey
Carolyn O'Malley		
Patricia Gill	Janet and Connie	Do-Nuts and coffee
Gerald Fenton	"Bear"	Bea and capitalism
Frederick Sims	Freddy	French
Eleanor Snelgrove	"Ma"	Byron
Bea Kemp	"B"	The Big Apple

Vox Lycei, 1937-38.

But I went, and she says, "I want you to open those windows, Harris. Do you think you can?" I said, "Well, I can always try." So I hit this one and it opened. Pow! and the next one opened. I hit all four the same way and they all opened. The guy says to her, "I told you he'd open them!" My stock with Miss Tompkins went up about a hundred percent that day.

Anyway, I graduated from Lisgar in 1929. I was going to Queen's for engineering. I didn't know what to do, you know? In those days there was no student direction at all. Anyway, my father died, so I never did get to go to Queen's. I worked for a few years to make a few dollars and then I came home and took over the farm.

GORDON F. HENDERSON, 1926-1930

The stately old grey stone building overlooking Colonel By Drive and the Rideau Canal has been the focal point in the lives of a large number of Canadian and Ottawa citizens. It is fitting that some of us who had the privilege of being among that number record some of our recollections of the stories and people that it could relate or describe would it give tongue. These recollections are limited to the period between 1926 and 1930.

It is a wise institution that records its history. Such a history is a tribute paid by the present to the past. However, the frailties of these reminiscences reflect the frailties of memories in an attempt to trace people and events of so many years ago. I trust I will be forgiven for errors and omissions in a personal attempt to look into the mists of time in relation to those past years.

The period 1926-1930 encompasses good times and bad times. We attended Lisgar during the boom days, the bust of 1929 and the ensuing depression. Because of the stability and security incident to a civil servant base we, in Ottawa, were to a considerable extent insulated from the misery that followed in 1929. The period was essentially a happy period. I personally look back upon that period as the glory years. I started Lisgar in the second year having taken my first year of high school at the Ottawa Model School where we obtained a superb grounding for what was to follow.

ExaminationReprints

"The Best and the Cheapest"

MIDDLE SCHOOL
(1915-1929)

Algebra	15c.
Ancient History (with two maps)	15c.
Canadian History	15c.
Chemistry	15c.
French Composition	15c.
Latin Composition	15c.
Geometry	15c.
Physics	15c.
German Comp. (1921-29)	15c.

UPPER SCHOOL
(1915-1929)

Algebra	15c.
Chemistry	15c.
French Composition	15c.
Geometry	15c.
Latin Composition	15c.
Modern History	15c.
Physics	15c.
Trigonometry	15c.
German Comp. (1920-29)	15c.

Free Catalogue for complete list of other subjects, Model Answers.

The James Texts

BELLEVILLE, ONT.

In the 1930s and 40s students could buy examination reprints and with careful study of previous exams "call the questions" on their own exams.

My first lasting impression relates to the daily opening assembly. All classes met in the Assembly Hall where we sang a lusty "O Canada" in French and English to the renditions of a full orchestra led by the late Dr. Harris Crowson on the piano and Mitchell Franklin on the violin. Often we were addressed by prominent Ottawa citizens. One of those addresses that has long lingered in my memory was delivered by a Dr. Ami, a distinguished biologist, whose message was that every type of living being attempts at each generation to be better than the previous generation. He taught us to distinguish progress from mere change. More importantly, from a student standpoint, the assembly provided each of us with the opportunity to address the school membership in any matter of our interest, whether it was to support an educational, cultural or sporting activity. It gave me my first forum to speak to an audience in public.

Our teachers in those days manifested an excellence that would be hard to match in any community and at any time.

Our first principal was A.H. McDougall followed by Messrs. Stewart and Dunlop. The ultimate sanction was to be reported to one of them.

My first home-room teacher as C. "Chubby" Atkinson, who later became the revered principal at Glebe Collegiate. He was not only a significant force as a Latin scholar and teacher and later as an administrator, but his knowledge of limericks, with which he regaled the class, brought him national exposure. Mr. Maybee and Miss M. Standing were the other Latin teachers who gave us the basics in languages.

Those who taught us French were formidable. "Jessie" Muir and Messrs. Latour and Lapensée taught us French grammar with enthusiasm, but regrettably the curriculum was not directed to teaching us to converse in the French language. An opportunity was missed.

English was taught by Messrs. Gilchrist and "Hank" Mann. They were at the twilight of their careers but their experience as teachers was reflected in their students.

Mr. Kaiser taught us history. In those days, the class stayed put, and the teacher came to the class. Mr. Kaiser was somewhat forgetful. I recall that he asked the class where we were in the course. I don't know how long Napoleon spent on the Isle of Elba, but we had him there for three weeks. I cannot remember the name of my teacher in ancient history in the fourth form, but I would like to record my appreciation for his encouragement in those years to the members of his form.

In the field of science, Mr. Smeaton with the brogue of his native Scotland taught us chemistry. A talkative student would likely find the blackboard erasure on his lap. "Fuzzy" Irwin taught us physics. He was an accurate shot with a piece of chalk. A student who went to sleep in the class would find some of that chalk whizzing past his or her ear. His lecture on acceleration always puzzled me until I learned that when he said "per second per second." he was not stuttering. Mr. McKay in physical geography taught us the mysteries of the world around us. At an early age we were impressed with the importance of the environment. Finlay Hood taught "Art."

I have left to last on the academic side, the mathematics side because I thought they excelled amongst their peers. They were Miss Tompkins, Miss Hills, Mr. Rentner and Mr. Strader. They were among the leaders in their field and influenced favourably the lives of the many students whom they taught.

I have sought to personalize my record of our teachers. It is as I remember them. I acknowledge that each student may well have a different impression.

On the athletic side of our life at Lisgar, we were first taught by Arthur Burridge in the year of his retirement. Elmer "Butch" Drulard then came to us from Windsor. Until his arrival, Lisgar had languished in boys' competitive sports. He took over a group of untrained students whom he motivated into winners. In his first year, the Junior football team won the Eastern Ontario Secondary School Association championship without losing a game. With the help of the posts in the old gym, the junior basketball team again won in its league beating its traditional rival Glebe. Glebe, under the direction of the late Bob Campbell, had had an unmatched history of victories. On the boxing front, an ex-Olympic champion and former Lisgar student, Honore Chevrier, taught us the manly art of self-defence. Boxing ceased to be a sport at Lisgar when it was cancelled by Mr. Stewart. On the baseball front, Clare Forster who learned to play at Lisgar during the period with which we are concerned, became a "big leaguer."

There were many cultural and other sporting activities at Lisgar. We enjoyed a balanced education. Although extracurricular activities were encouraged, excellence in education was never sacrificed.

The history of the institution is reflected in the eyes of the community and indeed the nation.

In 1926, two former pupils of Lisgar were held up to us as role models. Eugene Forsey and LeRoy Kindle were granted Rhodes scholarships. In both cases, their careers fulfilled the promise of brilliant students. The one as a senator, a constitutional expert who was rewarded as a Companion of the Order of Canada (the highest level of that Order). The other as an eccentric but distinguished geologist who is reputed to have discovered the Denison Mine.

G.E. (Ted) Beament, O.B.E., C.M., E.D., C.D., Q.C., L.S.M., LL.D., left Lisgar in 1925. He still carries on his legal profession in Ottawa after a most distinguished career in the military, as an educator and as a lawyer. He was appointed a Member of the Order of Canada.

I embark into an exercise of mentioning some of the students of 1926-1930 with trepidation as I have not had a continuing relationship with so many of them. It is with apologies to those who are omitted that I commence that exercise.

Henry F. Davis became Chief of Protocol in the Canadian government and was honoured with an appointment as a Member of the Order of Canada. His appetite for learning continued into 1992 when he received a further degree at Carleton University.

Mitchell Franklin is a successful entrepreneur in his adopted province of New Brunswick. He too was rewarded by his country, for his contribution to it and his philanthropy, by an appointment as Member of the Order of Canada.

David Cromarty has just retired as a Judge of the Supreme Court of Ontario after serving that Court with distinction.

In my years, the brilliant students included Howard Hunter, who became an official at the Department of National Revenue, Robert Sheppard who became a senior engineer at Bell Canada and Stanley Williams who became head of Research and Development at Dominion Engineering, Pulp and Paper Division. Dr. Lionel Perlman has recently retired after practising his profession in the city as a paediatrician. Harry Sigler, Q.C., still practises his profession in Ottawa. Archie Laidlaw, Q.C., who also practised law in this city became Commissioner of Patents and the architect of many reforms in that government department.

The armed services included many of our students, during the war years. Charles Dillon has retired in Victoria, B.C., having attained the rank of Admiral in the Senior Service. The late Bob Laughton (the happy warrior) served as Lieutenant Colonel in the army and in senior positions in several government departments. He was the father of Barry Laughton, currently a teacher at Lisgar and the father of my esteemed partner, Robert Laughton, Q.C. Philip Hurcombe, Q.C., became Judge Advocate General, Navy. Percy Cawdron is another who rose rapidly in Her Majesty's Service as did many others whose names have now escaped me.

Duncan Davidson joined the Metropolitan Life at Ottawa where he rose to a high official position as Vice President before retirement. "Dunc" was one of those who was a member of those winning teams motivated by Mr. Drulard.

Dr. Otto Klotz enjoyed an enviable Canadian reputation as a biochemist. He is the father of Trevor Klotz who practises law in Ottawa.

Others of that winning team included Bob Sheppard, "Benny" Benoit, who became Principal at the High School of Commerce and John Edwards, who continued his football career at Queen's University and the Toronto Argonauts. He became a valued member of the athletic staff at Queen's.

MOVING PICTURES

An interesting departure from the usual trend of school life was offered one morning in February when the Board, ever on the look-out for something to improve the student mind, introduced moving pictures as a means of teaching. The first film traced the progress of wheat from the fields to its exit from the flour mill. The second illustrated logging in British Columbia. Here the logs were followed from the forests to the finished lumber. These were both interesting and instructive and were without doubt enjoyed by all. By way of entertainment, a film of animated cartoons was shown which provided amusement for everyone. No more pictures have been brought to the school since, but it is hoped that we will soon again be given an opportunity of seeing some.

— *Vox Lycei*, 1922

Juvenile basketball team, 1930. L to R; J. Edwards, R. Jack, G. Henderson (captain), H. Bertrand, D. Davidson, L. Brown.

Hugh Way, after graduation, became a senior engineer with Dominion Rubber. It was at Queen's University where he became the intercollegiate running champion at 100 and 200 yards. His records stood for many years. Bill Westwick gained many honours as Sports Editor for the late lamented *Ottawa Journal.* Alf Gratton, after a hockey scholarship, joined the engineering staff of General Electric in the United States. The Wiseman brothers became noted athletes in the realm of basketball in Ottawa. The late Carl Durant became the city boxing champion in his weight class. Ralph Jack, an all-round athlete, was a champion swimmer and later a member of the Ottawa Rough Riders. Moe Appel was the manager of the Junior Football team that I have mentioned above. He became the Senior fund-raiser for the Jewish Community in North America. His younger brother, Toby, owned and operated a successful women's dress establishment on Rideau Street.

Many local establishments bear the name of those who attended Lisgar in this period. Lawrence Freiman continued the tradition of A.J. Freiman Ltd., on Rideau Street in Ottawa. A group of pharmacies operated in Ottawa under the Molot name for years. They were run by Abe, Rueben and David. Rueben was a basketball star at the University of Toronto. Dave was nicknamed by us as "Giant" not because of height but because of his "heart." Norman Campbell, father of the well-known Kanata realtor of the same name, continued the family pharmacy on Sparks Street for many years. Stein's dress shop still exists on Bank Street. Schaffer's

store graced Rideau Street for several years. Lionel and Edgar Marks owned Dominion House Furnishing on Bank Street. The Zelakovitz family, Zobe and Joe, carried on the tradition in the food business with Joe being a star with the Ottawa Roughriders. Gerald Brown became a member of the Canada Relations Board and is the father of Henry Brown, Q.C., another of my partners. Dr. James Hilton added lustre to his name as a leading physician. Syd Hobart became a senior member of the Department of National Revenue. Oscar Juneau looked resplendent in the scarlet coat of the R.C.M.P.

On the distaff side, Enid Palmer married Stuart Wotherspoon, a prominent lawyer who practised his profession with distinction in Ottawa. Kay Bray married Reid Wilson, an official at Metropolitan Life. They are the parents of Rich Wilson, a prominent lawyer in Ottawa known to some as the "Laird of Manotick."

I know that when I put this pen down, there will be others who will come to mind. In the meantime, I may say that the students of 1926-1930 contributed to the fabric of life in both this community and the larger community of this country because of their experiences at Lisgar Collegiate.

Lisgar Collegiate as an institution cannot be divorced from the people who were an integral part of it. In recording my recollections, I would be remiss if I did not acknowledge my debt to those individuals who had a lasting influence on my life.

Miss Tompkins, my form teacher in Grade Three as we then knew it, gave me confidence in myself. She, above all others, taught me to think for myself.

Messrs. Atkinson and Druland taught me the importance of perseverance. I learned that effort can often outmatch raw ability. Make the most out of what you have even if it means overachievement.

To my classmates and my companions in athletics, I learned how to get along with others. Whether consciously or not, I learned about the integrity of the individual and the importance of human rights.

DR. JAMES HILTON, 1927-1932

Mr. Strader who taught trigonometry was "one of the best teachers" I ever had. He was a very fussy man, always neat and meticulous, and he sharpened his chalk to make sure he had the neatest possible diagrams.

Mr. Rentner was just the opposite. He, too, taught maths, in this case algebra, but he was a messy, sloppy man who never cleaned the chalkboard, often just smearing it a little. Part way through Fifth form, I discovered that I needed an extra math class to qualify for McGill. I was forced to drop modern history in favour of algebra, and was coached by

Mr. Rentner at his own home until I had caught up with math class.

Mr. Gilcrist, or "Gilly" as he was known, was an English teacher close to retirement. He had a hard time keeping order in class, and so the class was often noisy and boisterous, but he either couldn't see it or simply ignored the noise.

The principal at Lisgar at the time was "Nosey" Stewart. "Chubby" Atkinson taught Latin while I attended Lisgar, but later went on to be the principal at Glebe. Mr. Atkinson was an excellent teacher when he felt like it, but when he didn't he would often assign some exercises to the class and spend the period playing with a file spike, raising and lowering it up and down the side of the desk on a piece of string.

Clubs and student activities were not substantially different from today. The Lyceum (drama club) would put on plays several times a year. I was president of the tennis club for a year. Dances were held two or three times a year in the gym, and featured live bands. At one dance some friends convinced me to play the piano during intermission so that they could continue dancing. When the band returned, I was offered a job. Unfortunately, I could only play by ear, and had to turn the position down. And so our lives go in other directions!

The Driveway and the Rideau Canal have always been an integral part of Lisgar student life, for lolling on the grass, for picnic lunches, for forbidden crap games, for cadet parades like this one.

I was also in the Cadet Corps every year I was at Lisgar. We were given uniforms and guns (without the bolt) for practices, which were held weekly. In the spring, the Corps would march to Parliament Hill for a competition against other schools, going through formations and a march-past. A local commanding officer would judge, and the winning corps would get a shield. These competitions were later banned from the Hill at the insistence of Agnes MacPhail.

SIDNEY KATZ, 1930-1934

As I turn my thoughts back to Lisgar in the 1930s, fond memories come flooding in filtered through the golden light of years remotely past. For me, it was both the best of times and the worst of times. The best of times because, as a kid from a small elementary school in Sandy Hill, Lisgar offered me new, exciting opportunities—cultural, social, and athletic. I was able to play on the basketball, football, and track team. For a time, Bob Corry and I—a fellow classmate in second year—wrote and published a clandestine newspaper which we cleverly named The *Weakly Onion*. It abruptly ceased publication when a copy fell into the hands of our Principal, Nosey Stuart.

As an aspiring journalist, I was thrilled by my involvement with a real magazine, *Vox Lycei*. I recall that one year we shopped around to find a photographer who would take our pictures at a bargain rate. Finally, we discovered an eager young man, new to Canada, anxious to establish himself as a photographer. He agreed to take all our pictures at a flat rate of five dollars each. The photographer, I recall, had a rather unusual name: Yousef Karsh.

And how can I ever forget my eventful adventures as a member of the Historical Society? I was approached by Mr. Blake, the society's advisor and also our history teacher, who asked me to write an historical play for presentation at our final meeting. The fact that I had never written a play before seemed a poor excuse to turn Mr. Blake down. I somehow managed to produce a three-act epic, which among other things, included a reenactment of the assault on the Plains of Abraham, culminating in General Wolfe's conquest of General Montcalm. In a way, it was a low-budget precursor of such current mammoth epics as *The Phantom of the Opera* and *Les Misérables*, featuring a cast of thousands.

I would be remiss if I failed to mention that the star role in my masterpiece was played by my friend and classmate, the late Lorne Greene. Lorne easily won the part because he was the only Lisgar student who had all the skills demanded— he could sing, play the violin, dance, deliver lines in a stentorian voice and cleverly improvise in spots where the script was obscure or flimsy. Lorne gave a magnificent performance, the harbinger of his future distinguished career in theatre.

I'm grateful to Lisgar because it provided me with the opportunity to fulfil one of my childhood fantasies. For some obscure reason, perhaps deeply hidden in the labyrinth of

After an evening of dancing and jiving at Lakeside Gardens or the Ranch House you might take your girl to Teskey's to eat. There you could dance to a local band or for a nickel in the juke box hear the Big bands play songs like, "Moonlight Becomes You," "Deep Purple," "Moonlight Serenade," "Tangerine," "I Don't Want to Set the World on Fire."

my unconscious, I always wanted to belong to a real, live marching military band. In the Lisgar of the '30s, participation in the school Cadet Corps was obligatory. I can recall my excitement upon learning that there was an opening in the Bugle and Drum Corps. Naturally, I jumped at it. In September, I was presented with a shiny brass and copper bugle, and henceforth, every Thursday after school, the band held a rehearsal in an upstairs room of the armoury on Cartier Square. The Big Day arrived in May—Inspection Day, when all the high school Cadet Corps in Ottawa met in the Exhibition Grounds to vie for a trophy for excellence. I have not forgotten a single delicious minute of the experience.

We assembled on Cartier Square, buttons, shoes and bugles shined to a dazzling sparkle. Playing at full blast, we led the Cadet Corps down the Driveway, to the deafening plaudits of the admiring throngs! It was a day of pride and utter fulfillment.

Although many decades now intervene, I still recall my teachers during the Lisgar years. I still feel indebted to my generous and understanding second year English teacher, Audrey Brown. She banished my lack of self-confidence by lavishly praising my essay assignments and assuring me that I had the makings of a fine journalist. Wherever you are, Audrey, thank you and bless you. There was "Chubby" Atkinson, who nurtured our taste for good literature by devoting generous portions of his class time to reading choice passages to us. How can I forget Mike Strader who actually made algebra and trigonometry enjoyable!

And there was Bill Smeaton, who courageously attempted to interest science-idiots, like myself, in chemistry. I must confess, not without considerable shame, that the only thing I clearly remember about chemistry class was an incident involving Irene Crawford, a rather stunning fellow student. As usual, I misunderstood the written instructions for

The war depleted the athletic teams at Lisgar. This is Bill Mitchell's Senior Football Team 1943 with Bill Pratt as water boy. Many of these young men were to very soon exchange football gear for the uniforms of the navy, army and air force. Back row, L to R; Bill Mitchell (coach), Morley Smith, G. Thompson, A. Kniewasser, J. McKinley, T. Extence, R. Sharpe (captain), D. McGilligott, D. Kirby, G. Toller. Second row; R. Armstrong (manager), A. Stevens, P. Birkett, J. Tapp, D. Gray, A. McDougal, L. King, B. Richard, J. Kirby, G. Croil. Front row; J. Mellish, H. Harold, D. Armstrong, Bill Pratt, B. Wilson, K. Clark, K. Campbell, D. Lindsay.

carrying out an experiment involving several lethal chemical solutions and it led to a catastrophe. My test tube exploded showering Miss Crawford with a corrosive substance. She was rushed to hospital for treatment and, fortunately, her injuries were minor. Being a budding journalist (and definitely not a future chemist) I made the best of the bad situation by exploiting the incident to promote my writing career. I phoned the story in to the Ottawa *Citizen* where it duly appeared the next day. Naturally, I omitted the name of the nincompoop who caused the accident.

Viewed from this distance, it is only now that I fully appreciate the stark contrast between our idyllic life within the halls of Lisgar and the dark events unfolding in the outside world. We had slipped into a severe economic depression and with political dictatorships firmly entrenched in Spain, Germany, and Italy, we were being propelled towards war.

Because of the Great Depression our prospects of finding a decent job or being able to afford university were remote. For a brief time we had a Prime Minister named R.B. Bennett

who solemnly vowed, "I will end unemployment or perish in the attempt." Being a politician, and a disobliging one to boot, he kept neither promise. There was no unemployment insurance, no health plan, no Canada Pension. Many of the songs we danced to at our school socials were silly songs, escapist in nature, designed to take our minds off our troubles. Songs like, "Three Little Fishies," "The Music Goes Round and Round," and "Goody, Goody." But the occasional one did have lyrics which were realistic, like "Brother, Can You Spare a Dime?" and "I Can't Give You Anything But Love, Baby."

After a decade of mounting international tensions, in September 1939 the world was at war. Although pacifist sentiment was popular among our generation, we realized that our very survival was at stake and we laid aside our anti-war convictions.

We recent Lisgar graduates enlisted in large numbers, in the army, navy and air force. We were frightened by what lay ahead but we tried not to show it. Some of us—including some of the brightest and the best among us—never

POETRY

The Indians eat it with their shoes;
The Eskimos drink it in their booze;
The Russians keep it locked in banks;
The Germans use it in their tanks;
They say it comes from some queer bear;
That's the stuff on Kniewasser's hair.

Doug Coupland.

returned from overseas. Those of us who were fortunate enough to make it back home, were irrevocable changed by our extraordinary experiences during our years of service. We would never be the same again. But one thing that endured, unchanged: our memories of our golden days at Lisgar, a fleeting period of security, discovery, growth and contentment. It brings to mind the words of William Cowper, one of the poets we studied in Gilly Gilchrist's English class:

"How peaceful were the hours we once enjoyed. How sweet their memory still."

BILL PRATT, 1942-1947

My Grandfather Pratt was a blacksmith—ran a four-man blacksmith shop in the town of North Gower. Died very young of tuberculosis along with his daughter and his first wife, my grandmother was his second wife—it damn near wiped out the bunch of them. And my father Ford Pratt always devoted his time to helping the tuberculosis foundation, but he did that in the city of Ottawa. He was educated in North Gower.

My dad was an athlete. Everybody wants to talk about Walter Pratt who's a cousin of my dad's, but in fact Bill Westwick the sports editor of the *Ottawa Journal*—was doing a fifty-year wrap-up of hockey in the capital and called my dad the "finest hockey player the capital has ever produced." There was no money in hockey in those days, as you know. He played rover. I was told by his friends when I was a kid that he was a tremendous skater. You know the rover was usually the guy who could skate the fastest because he played both attack and defence. And he played sixty minutes.

He went into the Civil Service when he was seventeen. He retired when he was fifty-two after thirty-five years' service. He was a Deputy Minister of the Interior. He spent most of his time as Private Secretary to the Liberal Ministers, the Honourable Charles Stewart, James Alison Glenn, a few people like that. He worked with Charles Stewart a long, long time. And when 1932 to '35 came along and R.B. Bennett came into power, he got knocked down to the National Parks Department and worked on publicity and promotion of national parks—hence all the archival correspondence between him and Grey Owl.

I grew up in an atmosphere of politics, senators, judges and so on. My dad's curling team—he skipped—the third was a guy called Lester Pearson, the second was Justice Abbott and the lead was Dave Simm who was head of the Customs. . . And Dad in his later years ran all the ladies curling here in the city of Ottawa, you know, he was kind of the inspiration behind that.

I grew up in Sandy Hill, 63 Blackburn Avenue. We lived there the whole time.

In those days the boys had gangs, "The Sandy Hill Gang." We were called "The Rinky Dinks." "The Sandy Hill Rinky Dinks." I think I played nine different sports, and it was no big deal. You played this and you did that, you played football, and you played baseball, and you played soft ball, you played soccer, you swam, you boxed, you did everything.

Fun. Fun. We'd get one of the French kids. Two of us would grab him by the shoulder and the ass of the pants and put him into Dr. Chartrand's hedge high enough that he couldn't get out again without help, you know. So somebody would have to come along and help him out, you see. We always had a little recreations like that. Now that I'm back in Ottawa for this year, I find Ottawa to be a French city almost as opposed to the English city it was when I left and yet, you know, French kids were French and English kids were English and there was no big deal made about it when I was young.

We used to go to the Auditorium to watch the Ottawa Senators play in the Quebec Senior Hockey League, and after the game was over if Ottawa was playing Quebec or Montreal, the French kids would maybe try to gang up on us. But we were tough enough to look after ourselves. We used to wait for a bus to come along, and we'd come out of the back door of the auditorium on the street behind the auditorium and we'd grab the bumper of the bus and just slide along on our feet, you know, and get out of the area very quickly.

I went to Osgoode Street Public School, York Street Secondary School, and Lisgar. I got accelerated in Grade Four and Five. And so when I came to Lisgar I was very young and very small and Wright Neil, who later became the principal here, flunked me in Grade Nine. And he probably did me a real favour because I hadn't had a setback to that point at all. I was just flying along. It wasn't that I was a brilliant student, I never was. But I could get by. I think the school system failed me a little bit in that probably I got accelerated and shouldn't have been accelerated.

Ottawa was a small village then. It really was. The connections were incredible. When I came to Lisgar it was just like "old home week." I was Lois and Marg Pratt's kid brother. That had pluses and minuses. But that athletic gene came down in all of us. My older sister was probably the least active of all of us, but the rest of us were all good. But I really wasn't good at any sport. A dilettante. I played for Butch Rothwell on the basketball team you know, and he used to tell me, "You know you're not really good enough, but you're not good enough to throw off." That was the way with Butch.

Bob Masson and I remember the march up Lisgar to Elgin to Queen (where we picked up a motorcycle escort—Art Pelletier rode in the sidecar), down Queen to O'Connor, down O'Connor to Catherine, to Bank, and south to Carling. Going west on Carling, we marched in utter silence (no music, no yelling) and then boom into side door of Glebe and then back to Lisgar. There were no more than four or five who didn't return.

I remember going up to Johnny Dunlop, our beloved principal, and saying, "It was a great surprise, and we have all come back." He looked at me very seriously and said, "I don't condone what you have done, I should expel you, but, because you have all come back, I won't." Then, with the greatest twinkle in his eyes and a broad grin, he went on to say, "Chubby called me and said it was a complete surprise and a great effort."

— John S. Kirby, 1939-1943.

Growing up in Sandy Hill was different. We were all lazy. So we'd come up Osgoode or Somerset Street and we'd cross over the Rideau Canal, and crossing over the canal meant crossing over all the railways tracks, and crossing over all the railway tracks was crossing on trains that were moving. So sometimes we'd get on a train and we'd come through between a couple of cars and then drop off. The canal wasn't used for skating in those days so it was getting down the one side and back up the other side which was tricky. It probably took us longer to go across the railways tracks, but it was fun.

And we used to make great big snowballs and wait till a steam engine would go by and try and drop it right down the funnel, and the funnel, of course, would throw it right up at us again. We had a lot of fun. To me life was so easy. Although it was the Depression, and we had no sports equipment and we couldn't afford anything, we had no extra money for anything like that. We still had a ball, we really did. For example, we couldn't afford a baseball bat or a baseball or gloves some days, so we'd go over to the Rideau Tennis Club and wait till somebody hit a tennis ball out over the court and we'd grab it and run, you see. And then we had a tennis ball and we played Danish rounders. What's Danish rounders? Well, you would stand there, and I'd be right opposite you, and you're the pitcher and you'd just loop the ball to me in an arc and I would hit it with my fist. When I hit it with my fist the outfielders would either catch it or miss it and I would run the bases just like baseball but with smaller bases. But we all had a fist and we could always steal tennis balls and so we always had a game we could play. Sometimes we'd maybe have an old worn-out football

playing a pick up game on the street and the lady across the street—her name was Vicky Usborne—the lumbering Usbornes—she would call the cops on us. So down would come the cops and they would say, "Okay, boys, give me the ball," and they would take the ball. "We told you last week and we told you the week before, keep the hell off the streets." Now, one of the kids we played with was a Gleason boy and his father was the desk sergeant at police headquarters, so we'd go up to Mr. Gleason's door and rap on it, "Mr. Gleason, the cops were down and stole our ball." And he'd say, "Okay, boys, describe it to me." And we'd say, "Well, it was an old football and it had little taddy on the end and the rubber was sticking out one place." "Okay, leave it with me," he'd say, I'll see what I can do." So next day he'd come back and say, "Here's your ball, boys," and he'd throw it to us. It would be a brand-new ball! And he'd say, "Is that it?" And we'd say, "Oh, yes, Mr. Gleason. That's it. That's it."

You know the old expression, "I'll take my ball and go home," it was very valid in my days. Somebody would have a ball, and we'd be playing with it and we wouldn't play the game the way he or she wanted to play it, so they'd take their ball and go home and we were out of luck.

My first hockey uniform was a pair of old Toronto Maple Leaf socks—I don't know where I got them from—a pair of *Chatelaine* magazines, an old pair of my dad's gloves—hockey gloves that basically had the hands out of them—we had to make extra loops in them so they'd stay on, you know.

My dad did a lot of work for the Ottawa Senators Hockey Team because of his hockey connections. He used to get them jobs in the Civil Service. Clerks in the off-season. So we had two seats right behind the players' box—I think that was compliment to Dad for the work he did for the hockey team. My brother and I got all the broken sticks from the hockey games. We'd take the broken sticks and repair them, so that's where we got all our hockey sticks for our hockey team. We'd take a good bottom and a good top and splice them together and make our own hockey sticks. People laugh at us now—"Couldn't be that way," they say. But that's the way it was. No helmets, no shoulder pads, no nothing. And nobody really got killed. We weren't skating as fast in those days.

Movies. The only time I ever got expelled from Lisgar Collegiate was for playing hookey to go to a movie. Jane Russell in *The Outlaw*. The first of the risqué movies. She was a well-built lady. And she got into bed with this guy—he'd suffered a gunshot wound or something—and she was going to comfort him. And did comfort him. Anyway, the next morning Mr. Dunlop got up on the stage and he said, "I'd like the following people to come up here," and I was one of them. Up I went. There was a whole gang of us. And we were expelled from school for just a day. But movies weren't big deals.

Let's go back to Sergeant Gleason again. Eddie Gleason's father, manager of the great Ottawa Senators. Sergeant Gleason used to give us passes to the Français Theatre,

The wartime teaching staff from the *Vox Lycei*, 1942-1943. Back row, L to R; J.W. Neil, A.B. Fallis, W.H. Showman, R.S. Whittle, W.F. Ade, C.P. McArthur, B.J. Flynn, H.C. Mann, A.H. Irwin, E.J. Lapensee. Middle row; A. Procter, W.F. Mitchell, Miss D. Bishop, Miss J. Rogers, Miss P. Meadows, Miss I. Brown, Miss J. Smith, Miss M. Hills, Miss L. Smith, Miss R. Hills, S.R. Felker. Front row; T.J.H. Rothwell, E.F. Legon, W.B. Mann, Miss E.S. Thompson, L.H. Meng, J.J. Dunlop (principal), J.W. Strader (vice-principal), H.M. Tennant, L.W. Rentner, E.A. Nicholls, L.L. Lalonde.

the one in the market, and we used to go at nine o'clock in the morning and we could stay all day And we'd see Lon Chaney, Boris Karloff. He'd scare the living daylights out of you. And we'd hide under the seats at the movie.

We had a cabin at Camp Fortune. I used to ski with Wally Mann. He was a hell of a skier. A hell of an athlete. People don't realize how good an athlete he was. We damned near got killed the two of us. He only had a little sports car. . . It would be, let's see, '42, wartime. He and I were good friends, although he was a CCFer you know. And my dad was WOW! Wally Mann! CCF, you know. And Wally ran on a ticket one time, ran as a politician, tried to get elected, you know. I just liked the guy. I still like him. Anyhow, we were coming down from the Gatineau one time, from Fortune, and there's a railway track in there—at Wakefield? Somewhere there, and it was snowing badly and I would say that maybe the train missed us by a dozen feet. We went across in front of it. Whew!

And a Dorothy Bishop story. As a matter of fact I was talking to her the other night, visiting at a mutual friend's place and I said to her, "Would it be fair to say that you had a temper?" She said, "Oh yes, I guess you could say that."

And she came out of the gym, the girls' gym on the third floor and her classroom was on the second floor right in front of what they called the boys' stairs, and she came down there and she stormed into the room and I can even remember she had on something red and I thought it matched her temperament, which I told her, and we had been making a hell of a noise in the classroom. When she walked through the door there was absolute, dead, utter silence, and somebody had the window open so she walked over to the window and she took the window and she slammed it down—I thought she was going to break the glass—and she slammed it down and she turned around and she said, "Now that I am here don't any of you have any courage to make noise?" I picked my books up off the desk and threw them on the floor. And she said, "Well, Bill, at least you have courage. Doesn't anybody else have courage?" Again absolute, utter, dead quiet.

She wasn't the worst chalk flinger. Mick Nichols was the one. Or a ball if you were in the gym. Nothing serious. Cy [L.W.] Rentnor would come down and he'd lift some guy right out of his seat by the ear and boy! all of us had a great respect for that teacher. That was one of the best courses

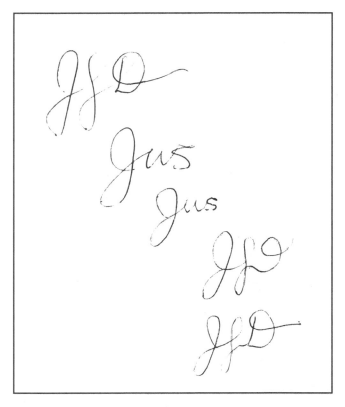

While at Lisgar Bill Pratt could forge principal Johnny Dunlop's signature for the use of himself and friends. Forty years later in the Lisgar Alumni office, he made two or three tries before he got it right again.

I had—trigonometry. He taught trigonometry—it was the best marks I ever had because I knew I couldn't screw around in his class. Boy! you'd better get busy or he's coming after you.

Pop McArthur who was the exact opposite. That's where Rich Little got his start you know, by imitating Pop McArthur. Pop left the room one day—this is the story I'm told by Bob McArthur, his son—Pop left the room one day and Rich got up and imitated him and the class just broke up.

Mike Strader's favourite saying, "I'll bet you a cookie to a doughnut." I don't know why, it was just the expression he had. Mike Strader used to play games with me. He'd be reading out the marks eighties, seventies, and we'd be getting down into the forties, you know, and I'm starting to sweat here because I'm in trouble. I don't know what I'm going to tell my mother or my father tonight. And he'd get down into the twenties and who's on the bottom of the list but Bill Pratt. He's got twenty-seven. And then Strader said, "Oh my god! I'm sorry I've got it upside down. It's really seventy-two." And I had sat there the whole time sweating. It was his devilment, you know. He just loved to pick on me. Curly Proctor too, you know. . .

I was the head of the bugle band. The military bugle band. I played bugle, a B-flat bugle. When they sent us a new piece of music, I'd give it to somebody who could read music and say, "Here play this damn thing." So they'd play it and then I could repeat it. And Curly said one day, "Bill, we're going to teach you how to read music." So I said, "That would be nice," you know, and so he spent about two weeks trying to teach me how to read music and then he gave up in total disgust. But, oh, one day I led the orchestra in place of him in the auditorium at assembly. As the leader of the bugle band I was the guest conductor but I couldn't read a damned note of music.

We did a whole bunch of things at Lisgar that we would have got expelled for, if we'd ever have got caught.

It was the 24th of May. There was a fire extinguisher right outside Wally Mann's door. His door was right at the far end down next The Driveway, and outside was a fire extinguisher. We put a Roman candle hooked into the top of the fire extinguisher and we lit it just as we changed classes and we were all the way up to the science room on the third floor, and it was still firing right down past the principal's office, almost to the library. Every time it would go off we could hear the screaming "Look out!" "Here it comes again." We could hear it all the way upstairs.

Up in the science room on the third floor, our teacher— he taught us aircraft recognition, too—I can't think of his name. A big tall guy. Yes, Flynn. Anyhow, we'd be waiting to go in to his class and the girls used to come out of their gym and there was a fire hose right at hand there. So we used to take the fire hose off the rack, turn on the water and drive the girls back into the gym, soaked. One time—and I don't remember who it was—but we drove her right clean across the room and against the wall—there was a bench there and, even when she sat down on the bench, we were still soaking her. And then, of course, we always shut the hose off, abandoned ship, and were long gone by the time anybody came up to ask, "Who did this?" Nobody knew by then.

Phosphorous has to be kept in oil. In Fuzzy Irwin's chemistry class we took some phosphorous out of the bottle that was being passed around for experimentation purposes, and we wrapped it in a paper which we'd soaked in oil. And we brought it down to the basement, and we put it on top of the locker next to where the air intake was. As the oil dried the phosphorous started to smoke and the acrid smoke went into the system, and all through the school, and they had to shut the school down for the rest of the afternoon because they couldn't determine where this acrid smell was coming from. So we had the afternoon off. We never really got punished for anything we did. We used to go up to the shooting gallery on the fourth floor. As cadets we were required to turn in so many targets of such and such an accuracy. We had a rack that held the .22 rifles, and it allowed you to adjust your sights with a screwdriver, you know, to get it exactly correct. Well, we put the gun in that

Principal Dr. A.H. McDougall, 1904-1928, who also served as principal of Glebe Collegiate Institute, 1922-1928. Born in North York County in 1859, he attended Toronto Collegiate Institute and went on to the University of Toronto, graduating with a B.A., in 1882. Coming to Lisgar in 1889, he quickly revealed himself as an outstanding mathematics teacher. He instigated morning exercises in the assembly hall, a project which had great success and is held dear in the memories of hundreds of ex-Lisgarites.

Principal F.A. Stuart, 1928-1939.

Like teacher and vice-principal I.T. Norris, F.A. Stuart attended high school in Mitchell, Ontario. He was an honours graduate from Toronto University and a medallist in science. He joined the Lisgar teaching staff in 1915. Many changes in the structure of education were brought about during his years in office, some through a revision of the curriculum and others through his untiring efforts in keeping abreast of the changing time.

Principal John J. "Johnny" Dunlop, 1939-1951.

Yet another in the long line of Scottish headmasters and principals at Lisgar, John J. "Johnny" Dunlop was born and educated in Williamstown, Glengarry County. His initials are still very apparent on the wall of his old schoolhouse there, now the Norwestern Museum. World War I interrupted his studies at Queen's. He served overseas with the Princess Pat Canadian Light Infantry, returned to Queen's for his degree and was hired on in 1921 by the Ottawa Board of Education. He served at Lisgar as English teacher, head of the department, vice-principal and as principal from 1939 until his death in 1951.

rack and we could fire five bullets into the target and we could put them within the head of a pin of each other, because we were firing right off of this rack. And we turned those targets in as our real score. Oh, I was a super marksman—courtesy of that rack. Then there was a little bit of a light bulb used to show below the protective barrier, and we used to spend hours, literally hours, trying to shoot that light bulb out, and periodically we'd get it.

Up there on the fourth floor in the shooting gallery there was a hatch that was locked. Well, .22 bullets dispatch locks pretty quickly, so Boom! Boom! and we had the lock open. And then when we undid the lock and pulled up the hatch, lo and behold, we're looking down at the girls' dressing and shower area! We should have sold keys to that lock! As it was, when we left Lisgar we willed the keys.

My real pals were a mixture of guys—as in life I never got close to a lot of people, which is rather interesting, although I prided myself on knowing everybody in the school—I knew everybody in the school, but I never really got close to anybody.

The big thing that was happening during the time I was at Lisgar was the fact that the war was on. Absolutely awful thing. You know, you'd see a guy like—Let me use two examples, Duke Abelson, Alan Abelson's older brother, and Alan Hague. Alan Hague and Duke Abelson, good basketball players. Butch Rothwell's stars, you know. And we kind of looked up to them and then, all of a sudden, one day they enlisted and away they went to war. And both of them got killed.

I was never old enough to get into the army or the air force or whatever, but my brother-in-law, Ken Lussier, he was a decorated hero, and he went over at seventeen and a half, and came back having been in France for a month, got knocked down by a German airplane, parachuted into France, got taken out through the underground; came across in a submarine to England. And when he came back he was only eighteen and a half. He'd been a sergeant, he was now an officer, he had a Distinguished Flying Cross, he had another decoration. And standing up on the Lisgar assembly stage, it was hard for us to imagine him just the year before on the football field.

We used to go to the movies on Saturday morning and we'd get the Warner-Pathé News, and we'd watch the guys landing at Dunkirk or wherever, but it was all from afar. We really had a good life at home. And I felt that my years at Lisgar were fantastic, too. I used to forge notes—I can still sign JJD [John J.Dunlop] as well as he could and JWS as well as Strader could. And it fooled Nick Nichols. Nick used to collect the late passes, and I had a pad of empties and I could sign one for myself anytime I was a little late and hand it in and he'd say, "I don't know where you keep coming up with these late passes all the time, Bill," and I said, "The principal's a friend of mine, you know." I finished Thirteen. Yes, I'm the only guy that ever graduated in '46, '47 and '48. I was talking about going to Queen's University. But then I worked for Red Dutton in the summer of last year— I worked for Red Dutton in the summer of '48. Doing what? Construction out in the West. Radium Hot Springs, British Columbia. Got the job through hockey connections, Dad, friends. Red Dutton who was at our place for supper, said, "What are you going to do?" I said, "I'd like to drive a truck." And he said, "Well, I've got lots of trucks. Come on out to Calgary." So I took the train out to Calgary. Then he paid me all winter to go to school. Lisgar. I got a hundred and twenty-five dollars a month to go to school at Lisgar and Mother had a friend who needed a chauffeur for her Buick Convertible and I drove for her as chauffeur. So I drove a Buick Convertible to school and I had a hundred and twenty-five dollars a month. That was a good year at Lisgar, 1948-49. I got a lot of new friends that I didn't really need. I went back again in '49 to work for Red Dutton and I never came back again.

All my life has been learning. You never quit learning. I learned something in Lisgar that stood me in line my whole life and I shortened it down a little bit, "To thine own self be true, thou canst not then be false to any man." I think in the middle there's "Shall follow as the night to day, Thou can not then be false to any man." And I've used that as my personal motto my whole life.

My whole life has been self-education, moving from challenge to challenge. I often have said to my engineering friends—and I'm often mistaken for an engineer—but I've often said to my engineering friends, "I'm not handicapped with education." And they look at me crooked. They just don't like me to say that, but the fact is that I had a crew of two Ph.Ds, a whole bunch of engineers, a whole bunch of architects, a whole bunch of everything, and I was the boss because I was co-ordinating them all—I don't have to think of the problems of one discipline. I can visualize the whole thing. They said that the Olympic Saddledome could not be built. "It cannot be built, Bill. You can't build the goddam thing." Now, every time I sit in it I have a beautiful feeling, I have a beautiful feeling because there it is. And what did I know about the Olympic Games? Nothing. There's a book about that thick—it's called *The Olympic Charter*—and it tells you how to run the Olympic Games. Now I suppose an educated man would take it home and read it word for word and operate on it word for word. One of these days I'm going to read it. Why haven't I read it? Because it would inhibit me.

So what was I doing in Kuwait fighting fires? Broadening an education, taking a post-graduate course in oil well firefighting, looking at the philosophy of another nation, looking at the Arab philosophy, which is very shallow. . .

LISGAR'S CENTENNIAL

Lisgar's next anniversary celebrations took place November 26th, 27th, 1943. Despite the fact that the 100th birthday occurred during the middle of the Second World War, 1939-45, hundreds of ex-Lisgarites and graduates came from all over the world to attend the festivities and walk down memory lane through its hallowed halls and classrooms. Many of the celebrants were in army, navy and air force uniforms. Under the auspices of Lisgar's very active and highly-organized Alumni Association scores of volunteers worked on committees for many months beforehand.

Student Eileen Mahoney, on staff of the *Vox Lycei*, 1943-44, reported on Saturday's events:

Saturday, in contrast to the previous day, was marred by wet snow and a blustery wind; but failed to keep the crowds away or dampen their spirits. Friends who hadn't seen each other since their school days were reunited and lived again in happy reminiscence, the good old days at Lisgar.

Stripped of its decorations the boys' gymnasium returned to normal. Basketball games were played which interested the onlookers and certainly were fun for those taking part. In the girls' gym a basketball game between the Lisgar "old" girls and more recent graduates took place—something you would only see every hundred years.

As a climax to the two days of celebration, a banquet was held in the ball-room of the Chateau Laurier, where gathered hundreds of former teachers and pupils. An impressive moment in festivities occurred when Helen Hulse presented Miss E.A. Tompkins a beloved member of the teaching staff for many years, with a corsage of red roses. Then the entire assembly rose to its feet and sang "For She's a Jolly Good Fellow," followed by three hearty cheers. Miss Bessie Scott Lewis and Mrs. J.J. Dunlop were also presented with corsages.

Following this, the toast to the school was proposed by J. Warren York, K.C., and was responded to by Mr. Dunlop, who recalled marching and fighting alongside Lisgar boys in the last war and the fine spirit and courage possessed by each. In conclusion he paid tribute to those Lisgar graduates who are playing their part in this war and said, "Please God, most of them will return and in due time they and their sons and daughters will play the traditionally fine part in the community and Canada, that their predecessors have in the past."

The old Masters were toasted by Lieut. Col. E.A. Devitt and the reply to the toast was made by Mr. H. Clark Mann, a former teacher of English at the Collegiate.

Sidney Bateman, president of the present students council, toasted the old boys—singling out a few of Lisgar's distinguished graduates, Air Marshall Bishop, Air Vice-Marshall Sully, Major General Kennedy and others as examples of the calibre of Lisgar graduates. He expressed the hope that their successors—today's students—will take a prominent place in the peace that is to come. In answering the toast Hon. W.D. Herridge said, "the mighty cavalcade of men and women who have graduated from Lisgar have turned their manifold good works to the history of Ottawa and Canada."

In toasting the sister schools Miss Helen Hulse said that underlying all the rivalry there is a sincere liking for one another and that graduates and pupils from each school will work together for peace. Mr. W.D.T. Atkinson, principal of Glebe Collegiate replied to the toast.

A former member of the Lisgar teaching staff and now of Glebe Collegiate, Miss Beatrice Gilhooly, toasted and compared Ottawa to a "Grand Lady," with all her lovely assets. Her toast was replied to by Mayor Stanley Lewis.

The toast to Canada was proposed by a Lisgar graduate, Bernard B. O'Meara, now in the R.C.A.F., and was responded to by Capt. J.R. Connolly, R.C.N.V.R., Director of Special Services.

And so Lisgar's Centenary Celebrations came to a close. We cannot give too much praise to the teachers and various committees who so untiringly gave their time and effort to make the occasion one to be long remembered. Our sincere thanks are also due the cadets who spent long hours directing guests, supplying information and being "Johnny on the spot."

On Friday and Saturday afternoons Vox Lycei staff members Mavis MacArthur and Don Felker interviewed many ex-Lisgarites who attended the 100th. The results of a questionnaire were as follows:

The average time the interviewed grads had been out of school was 44 years. In reply to the question, "Do you think the school is doing a better job today than in your day?" 53% thought the school was doing a better job today, 17% disagreed and 30% were undecided. When asked "Have you fulfilled your school-time ambition for a career?" 36% said they had, 64% (some due to war-time conditions) had not fulfilled their school-time ambition.

MacArthur and Felker compiled opinions of ex-Lisgarites going back as far as 1870 who were present at the Centenary.

1870. Mr. Grant went to old Grammar School and won the gold medal for the Victoria Cadets in his final year and later was on the school board as trustee. Mr. Grant believes Lisgar is doing a much better job today than in his day. He was especially interested in the new uniforms of our cadets.

1881. Miss Mary Masson was the first girl to graduate from the Collegiate. She was alone for two years with twelve boys. While at the O.C.I. she won two medals. Didn't think the school had improved since 1881.

1882-1886. Mr. N.F. Ballyntyne attended Lisgar reunion in 1903. He thinks the school is altogether different.

1884-1886. Mrs. Eddy still resides in Ottawa and liked the school better in the olden days.

1884-1888. Adam Ballyntyne thinks Lisgar is a fine institution. Liked the display of new pictures.

1884-1888. Mr. Frank O.C. Hutchison thinks the education is much more varied than in his day. He has fulfilled his school-time ambition for a career.

1885-1886. Mr. I.E. Cross thinks the school is doing a much better job now and enjoyed the celebration immensely.

1893-1898. Mr. W. Crowe stated that the teachers of today cannot compare with the former teachers.

1894-1899. Mr. Corlis Keyes thought the school was doing a much better job now. Liked the manual training display and has fulfilled his school-time ambition for a career.

1900-1904. C.M.B. Chapman thinks the school is doing a much better job today and especially enjoyed the display of the more recent graduates. He didn't fulfill his school-time ambition for a career as he wanted to be a doctor and is now a stenographer.

1900-1905. Judge A.C. McDougall son of the former principal thinks the school is not doing a better job now than in his day and he has fulfilled his school-time ambition for a · career.

1911. Major General Kennedy resides in the city, doesn't think the school is doing a better job today. He enjoyed the old pictures and stated that his career is exactly opposite to his plans.

1914-1919. W.E. Haughton resides in Ottawa, believes the school is carrying on well and he liked the *Vox* pictures.

1924. Miss Margaret Dorris resides in the city, thinks the school is doing a much better job now. Liked the display in the album room. She has not fulfilled her school-time ambition for a career.

1929. Flight Lieutenant W.A. Fuller travelled 3000 miles to attend the centenary. Liked the display in the album room. Has not fulfilled his school-time ambition because of war-time conditions.

1936. Flying Officer R.C. Bennet travelled 120 miles to attend the centenary, thinks the school is doing a much better job now than in his day. Liked the old *Vox* pictures. Hasn't fulfilled his school-time ambition because he hasn't burned the school down.

Lisgar Collegiate Institute Centenary Celebration November 26-27, 1943

LISGAR *1943 to 1993*

Previous Page:

Background Photo: A 1983 aerial view of Lisgar taken at the 140th celebrations. Scores of returning Lisgarites grouped on the playing field beside the new gynasium to form the number "140."

Foreground Photo: A 1972 view of Lisgar taken by Malak to honour retiring Principal J. W. Neil. The view to the Gatineau Hills and the Parliament Buildings is still considerably unobstructed but the high rises are in process. Taken prior to renovations, the Drill Hall peeks out behind the school and Cartier Square is covered with wartime temporary buildings. Lisgar was still a thruway.

INTRODUCTION
1943-1993

"Plus ça change, plus c'est pareil."

If Ottawa's image as a Civil Service town was only half sketched by the 1930s and the early 1940s, the course of the Second World War completed the portrait. Like puffballs, government "temporary" buildings erected for war workers, part-time and full-time, sprang up all over the city's centre core, including on Cartier Square, Lisgar's playing ground. These so-called "temporary" buildings were to remain for ten, twenty, thirty, even forty years after war's end in 1945.

Daily, as the federal government grew bigger and fatter, more and more civil servants ascended and descended Ottawa's public transport system, setting the rigid rhythms of the city while, parallel to this mundane movement of commuters, the limousines of the international ambassadors to Canada rolled to and fro from close to one hundred elegant embassies, also transporting a growing number of government workers, albeit foreign.

A Parisian town planner named Jacques Greber had been hired to make "Ottawa on the Ottawa" like "Washington on the Potomac" or, as it has been dubbed more recently, "The Washington of the North." Greber's master plan tried to rationalize the inevitable problems of jurisdiction between municipalities, the federal government, and the governments of Ontario and Quebec. The two provinces were already linked by five bridges across the Ottawa River but the gulf was to be widened by the Quiet Revolution in Quebec.

PHILOSOPHY OF THE OTTAWA BOARD OF EDUCATION

"The Ottawa Board of Education will ensure that each student has the opportunity to develop to his or her full potential as an individual and as a member of society."

STUDENT RIGHTS

1. All students have the right to an education.

2. All students have the right to security of person and property.

3. All students have the right to basic freedom of speech and peaceful assembly.

4. All students have the right to learn in a drug-free and alcohol-free environment.

5. Students have the right to form a students' council.

6. All students have the right to receive awards.

7. All students have the right to an Ontario Student Record.

8. All students' organizations have the right to the use of school facilities.

9. Students have the right to representation on individual school advisory committees.

10. Students have the right to appeal procedures.

11. Students have the right to earn an exemption from June examinations.

STUDENT RESPONSIBILITIES

1. All students have the responsibility to attend school daily.

2. All students have the responsibility to be on time for all classes.

3. All students have the responsibility to ensure the rights of others to study and learn.

4. All students have the responsibility to take part in the learning process and to be active learners.

5. All students have the responsibility to come to class with necessary books and materials.

6. All students have the responsibility to complete all assignments and meet deadlines.

7. All students have the responsibility to communicate with the school in the case of absence.

8. All students have the responsibility to respect school property and learning materials.

9. All students have the responsibility to secure proper authorization for circulation or distribution of material on school premises.

Despite a failure to untie this Gordian knot, for almost fifty years Greber's plan was to be unremittingly instituted at the price of whole areas of heritage buildings in both Ottawa and Hull. Fulfilling the Canadian penchant for self-destruction and lack of pride in history, the Rideau Street Convent, the Capital Theatre, parts of Byward Market, the historic mansions of Centretown (including the Lisgar Street house of poet Duncan Campbell Scott), the uniquely Quebecois municipal buildings of Hull all were demolished.

The name of the Federal District Commission was changed to the National Capital Commission. Funding was greatly extended, as well as powers, and land acquisitions began for individual parks, parkways and parklands like the Gatineau. Greber's recommendations for height restrictions on buildings in downtown Ottawa were subverted by developers who soon had a pallisade of glass and plastic high-rise buildings obscuring the core of the nation. These slums of the future were counterbalanced in part by a new greenbelt which ringed the city, and parklands which bordered the Ottawa River, rimmed the Rideau Canal and ribboned the banks of the Rideau River. At the same time, the

post-war population exploded and new suburbs began to engorge the adjacent rich and fertile farmlands of the Ottawa Valley.

Unlike their counterparts in World War I who had given their limbs and their lives in the name of freedom and "everlasting peace" for their country, Canada's World War II veterans were to be rewarded by their government, these rewards taking the form of land grants or gratuities which might be used to further education at any level. This government policy jump-started the Canadian post-war economy. Returning veterans took up farming, started new businesses, returned to school and university, married and spawned a generation to be known later as the "baby boomers."

Some of the ex-servicemen reached as far back as intermediate and high school for accelerated courses to enable them to catch up with their lives and enter university. Later, many of them would gratefully acknowledge that, without the government gratuities, they would never have seen the inside of a university, let alone graduate in law, medicine, engineering, science, business administration. This post-war generation was also to become the widespread "nouveau riche" of the Fat Sixties and early Seventies, creating a breed of Hippie boys and Flower girls dedicated to protesting their parents' materialism, while at the same time, compliantly living high on the handouts as they chorused "Make love, not war," smoked the hash and shot the drugs.

Post-war and into the Fifties Marshall McLuhan, Canada's foremost pundit and one of its few philosophers, living or dead, was expounding on "The World as a Global Village." His theories influenced the entire English-speaking world. That same world, already shrunk to a global village, was being held in the vice of the Cold War between Russia and the United States. This brazenly manipulated psychological phenomenon engendered a generation which was to grow up in fear of death by nuclear war and the world-wide annihilation that would inevitably follow. It also fostered the construction of atomic bomb shelters (some of which remain underground today, like the one at Carp, Ontario, built for high-level government escapees), and to peace movements such as the Canadian Peace Research Institute. Parents at the cocktail hours and over the dinner tables argued the pros and cons of maxims "Better dead than Red" against "Better Red than dead." The fundamental premises of these two diametrically opposed stances, one based on principles and one on expediency, were to infiltrate the underlying philosophy of political parties, governments and educational systems.

In the Western World the economic boom of the "Hippie" Sixties and Seventies occurred in tandem to an explosion in technology. Man was not only to walk on the moon but also to give his memory over to a machine. The ensuing "Industrial Revolution" with all its resultant displacements and unemployment was to make the Industrial Revolution following Hargreaves' invention of the spinning jenny in the seventeenth century, by comparison, look like a small plant closure in the boondocks.

Paradoxically as Western World workers were caught in the dehumanizing maelstrom of this technological revolution, there emerged a resounding new emphasis on the RIGHTS of the individual, particularly if he belonged to a minority cultural group, was disabled, politically incorrect or socially on the fringe. The necessary counterbalancing of the RESPONSIBILITIES of the individual in society seemed to become lost in the shuffle as Canada struggled to maintain its differentiating multicultural image. To many observers it seemed as if majority rights had become passé.

The latter part of the twentieth century in Canada was also to be characterized by highly organized professionally run interest groups, advocacy groups, lobby groups, pressure groups, ecology groups, social issue groups, multiplying not numerically but geometrically. In this pother of articulate voices, from a period of dormancy the Feminist Movement resurfaced as one of the most powerful, influential and well-funded on the social scene.

In this phase of Lisgar's history, 1943-1993, politics began to influence, distort and subvert all education in Canada. As the money multiplied in the educational coffers, and as the Educational Minister grew to be one of the most important portfolios in the provincial governments, so the critics were created, came forward and spoke their pieces. Nobody was as surprised as Saskatchewan teacher and educator Hilda Neatby when in 1953 her critique of Canadian education, *So Little for the Mind*, became a best-seller. But, as it turned out, there were a lot of listeners out there ready for somebody to sound out the call for "a return to the basics" in primary school and to traditional education for the high school.

In a 1959 Cambridge lecture, *The Two Cultures and the Scientific Revolution*—destined to become a world classic—writer and scientist C.P. Snow was to enunciate an erudite warning about the widening gap, the total lack of communication and comprehension between the literary intellectual and the scientific communities, a gap he rigorously contended as dangerous to the entire well-being of the post atomic-bomb world. "When these two senses have grown apart," he stated, "then no society is going to be able to think with wisdom." A large part of his very receptive audience was listening well and hard. They were acutely aware from their own life experience that Hiroshima was not an isolated incident designed to save Allied lives and end a war, but a Pandora's box with a far more horrendous content than any previously opened by mankind. The plague it released was amorality.

Before Lloyd Dennis and Emmett Hall ever appeared on the Ontario educational scene in 1968, people of foresight in the field were already contemplating possibilities such as Enrichment, Acceleration, and "Special Ed." As early as the 1940s Mrs. H. Barber, for many years the only woman on the Ottawa Board of Education (in those days all Board members being volunteers with busy crowded "other" lives) researched and presented to the Board a paper on the Gifted Child. "There is nothing so unequal as the equal treatment of unequals," she wrote.

The Hall-Dennis Inquiry into Education in Ontario probably changed education in the province forever by advocating a switch from traditional teaching methods to the child-centred system, a system which was to attempt to provide every single child with full development of his own unique potential, whether the child was a

J.W. Strader succeeded
"Johnny" Dunlop upon his
death in 1951. A Mathematics
specialist, Mr. Strader had joined
the Lisgar staff in 1923 and was
named assistant to the principal
in 1938. Sharing Emerson's belief
that "the secret of education lies
in respecting the pupil," for the
seven years of his principalship
he maintained a close association
with the student body and is
remembered for that. He died
in 1957.

V.N. Bruce, vice-principal of
Glebe Collegiate filled the
vacancy created by Mr. Strader's
death. A noted scholar in his own
field, science, and an educator
with international experience,
Mr. Bruce's career was cut short
by his sudden death in 1960.

slow learner, handicapped, globally gifted, or a member of a minority group.

The impact of Trudeau's 1982 Charter of Rights and Freedoms was felt everywhere in Canadian society, including high schools where it changed student-teacher relationships and altered disciplinary methods. Members of minority groups, if vociferous enough, could sometimes call the shots. The school code of behaviour had to become more liberal and, in this context, whether a female student had a right to dress innappropriately at school, or a responsibility to dress appropriately, could become a "cause célèbre." It might have helped the solution of multitudinous subsequent "rights" cases in the courts if Trudeau had had the foresight to draft a Bill of Responsibilites at the same time as his Bill of Rights.

In 1988 the Supreme Court of Canada ruled to give full separate funding to Roman Catholic schools in Ontario. Ottawa found itself with not one, not two, but five School Boards—the Carleton Board of Education, the Ottawa Board of Education, the Ottawa Roman Catholic Separate School Board, the Carleton Roman Catholic School Board, the Conseil scolaire de langue française

d'Ottawa-Carleton—all conflicting, overlapping, and bureaucratically burdensome. As anyone with a cricket's brain could have predicted, other minority groups immediately began to form lobby groups to demand the same separate funding for their own parochial schools. Meanwhile Egerton Ryerson who had devoted his whole life to the establishment of free, non-denominational schooling for every child in the province of Ontario was spinning in his grave in a Protestant cemetery near Toronto.

* * * * *

In this fifty year span of its history, 1943-1993, the relatively higher standard of living amongst Canadians, the inflationary spiral, the strong evidence of "the rich getting richer," all was reflected in Lisgar, perhaps more than in any other Ottawa high school, because of its demographic base. A student allowance in 1943 might have ranged from twenty-five cents to a dollar a week. By contrast in 1993 Lisgar students had money for breakfast, lunch, and snacks at the cafeteria, trendy clothes, cars, summer travels, ski weekends, Easter on Florida beaches, special teacher-supervised trips to Europe, Great Britain, Russia, and the United States,

Appointed vice-principal in 1951, J.W. Neil succeeded V.N. Bruce. Mr. Neil came to Lisgar in 1939 as an English teacher and in the early 1940s was closely associated with the development of the Guidance program. He led the school through the turbulent Sixties and Seventies. The calibre of his leadership remains a legacy at Lisgar today.

Principal Robert G. McMichael was born in Port Arthur and finished high school there. After RCAF service, 1941-45, he returned to Queen's for his BA in Mathematics and Physics, followed by one year at the University of Toronto in Meteorology. He taught Mathematics at Lisgar 1952-58, went on to Ridgemont High 1958-72, when he returned to Lisgar as principal, retiring after four years.

Born and raised in Toronto, Stephen J. Glavin went on from Oakwood Collegiate to the University of Toronto for his Honours B.A. in Latin and French, with a Greek minor. He was head of Classics at Nepean High School, Vice-Principal and principal at Laurentian High School before coming to Lisgar as principal, 1977-87.

all expenses paid for by Lisgar parents. There were new labs and equipment for the Science classes, full-time librarians and computers in the library, synthesizers for the orchestra, rugs on the floors.

While the *Vox Lycei* became more a literary and photographic magazine the *Lisgarwrite*, the monthly tabloid founded in 1988, functioned not only to inform students about school, city, and world politics and news, but also as watchdog and mouthpiece for equality throughout school life. Girls' sporting activities were to assume an equal importance with those of boys, and, as girls became more aggressive, girls' athletics ranged to include field hockey, downhill skiing, ski jumping, soccer. *Lisgarwrite* leadership was manifest in new courses on sexual awareness, drug abuse, AIDS awareness, and condom use.

The emphasis in curriculum—to the grave detriment of spelling and grammar—was to shift from the Classics and English to Science and Mathematics. Educational philosophers like Piaget in cognitive thinking and Chomsky in language development, influenced changes in teaching methods and deeper understanding of the learning process in all its ages and stages.

Extensive new studies on the physiology of the human brain would also make an impact upon the educational system and particularly in reference to the intensively documented evidence of the differences between the male and female brain, these differences manifesting themselves in different abilities, different viewpoints, different career preferences.

Almost daily schools and teachers in this era were required insidiously to take on more supervision of students, to involve themselves in more extra-curricular activities, indeed, often to have to assume in the students' lives the responsibilities of absent, abdicated, and sometimes irresponsible parents. The Guidance department had to extend itself beyond mere advice about courses, careers, and university entrance requirements to dealing with the emotional problems of separation and divorce, "melding" and deaths in the nuclear families.

One of the most unifying forces in Lisgar life, the morning assembly was phased out while, at the same time, schools boards evolved into top-heavy, alienated, expensive power structures. The teaching profession was no longer male-dominated and Jessie Muir's battle of the 1920s for equal pay for equal work had been won. But two teachers' strikes, one in 1975 and one in 1992, were to add an ugly dimension to alienation by eroding student-teacher relationships.

Despite continuous dedicated lobbying by Canadian writers and writers' groups such as the Writers' Union of Canada for use of more Canadian textbooks in all school disciplines and more Canadian writers' works on the school curriculum—particularly in English and History—the changeover to more Canadian content was minimal, much to the detriment of Canadian identity. War continued to be an unpopular subject and high school curriculum devisers, using the old bury-your-head-in-the-sand ploy, kept the history of World War I and World War II, "out of sight, out of mind" of the history teachers. To accommodate Canada's increasingly multi-cultural image, the language department at Lisgar expanded to include German, Spanish, Japanese, and Mandarin.

Throughout this period the school system was constantly being bombarded by angry critics, new theories of learning, complicated administrations, new rules for codes of conduct, demanding minority groups, and major changes in diploma requirements. Researchers and thinkers were unremittingly presenting (a presentation accelerated by the miracles of technology) revolutionary data and evidence not to be ignored, yet sometimes necessitating their incorporation into the system. Many of these researchers and thinkers were impressive authors, psychologists like Professor Howard Gardner who, in his 1991 book *The Unschooled Mind*, asked "How can we help our students move beyond rote learning to achieve genuine understanding?"

Indeed, Gardner, in *The Unschooled Mind*, broke new ground and set new goals for the educational system when he postulated what we all have suspected for so long—that there are different kinds of intelligences and different ways of "knowing" the world. In his research and writing Gardner separated seven intelligences—linguistic, logical-mathematical, spatial, musical, bodily kinesthetic, interpersonal, intrapersonal—and went on to say; "Where individuals differ is in the strength of these intelligences—the so-called profile of intelligences—and the ways in which such intelligences are invoked

and combined to carry out different tasks, solve diverse problems and progress in various domains." It is predictable that his theory of not one but multiple intelligences will reverberate through and influence the twenty-first century schools of educational philosophers.

From the 1940s onward all around Lisgar in old Centretown, developer's "progress," the federal government's aggrandizements and the Greber Plan combined to eat away at the priceless heritage buildings that in any part of Europe or Britain would have been preserved with pride in the name of national identity. In old Centretown they often fell without a fight—and in the middle of the night. This conniving and amoral process was to destroy the original unique character of Ottawa and shake the very foundations of Lisgar itself—except that, in its case, there was to be a battle.

As school boards became more politicized, high schools were encouraged to form Parents' Advisory Committees and Lisgar's has had a record of achievement. When the Ottawa Board announced that one of its high schools must create a Gifted Centre, the Lisgar Parents' Advisory Committee lobbied for and got it. When bilingualism and French immersion became issues, again because of the Lisgar parents' lobby, Lisgar was declared an extended French Centre while Glebe was designated a Bilingual Centre. The controversial decision to install condom machines in Lisgar began with students' initiative. Their case was presented to the Parents' Advisory Committee which endorsed the idea and lobbied the Board for its approval. This was given on condition that a sexual awareness program be instituted at the same time, and this was done through the *Lisgarwrite*.

But nothing changed academic excellence at Lisgar. If anything the standards had been raised. Parents lined up at four in the morning to gain entry to Lisgar for their children, some to pay $3,300 a year in fees if out of district, and $7,000 if out of province and out of country. However, somehow, surreptitiously over the years, the underlying philosophy had changed from "an education for life" to "an education for earning a living."

ATHLETICS
1943-1993

Born and raised in Ottawa, Joe Leggett attended Lisgar from 1935-1941. When he graduated from the Ontario Agricultural College with his B.S.A. he returned to Lisgar in 1960 as teacher in the Physical Education Department and coach of many teams. He retired in 1981. During his twenty years at Lisgar, he saw many changes. He talks of some of them in the introduction to his record of athletics at Lisgar during his time, 1960-1981.

Over the years the basic changes in the philosophy of physical education at Lisgar have been considerable. Two underlying tenets have led to a more than one hundred percent increase in the class time now allotted to physical education in the curriculum. a). Recognition that exercise is important to the physical and mental health of the students and b). that learning ability is enhanced by regular physical activity. Where once two periods a week were considered all that could be spared from the academic schedule now it is normal to have P.E. scheduled for one period per day.

Around the time of World War I, physical training (P.T.) as it was known meant calisthenics (physical jerks), gymnastics, and some sports skills. In the Thirties calisthenics were replaced by Swedish rhythmic exercises. More emphasis was placed on games and sports skills. Today the variety of skills and activities incorporated in the boys' and girls' programmes is more varied and challenging. To the activities once considered essential have been added tennis, golf, badminton, soccer, lacrosse, wrestling, cross-country skiing, fitness training, weight training, outdoor education, many co-educational, especially in the senior years. Exposure to such a variety of activities helps students choose those games and individual sports and fitness activities which they can pursue after leaving school and continue for a lifetime.

Girls first hockey team at Lisgar was formed in 1947: president, Norma Finnigan; vice-president, Phil Duncan; secretary, Nonie Melville. Glebe challenged Lisgar and was roundly routed 9-3. This is a photo of the Girls' Athletic Association of that year, including some members of that original hockey team. Back row, left to right: Norma Finnigan, Ruth Stewart, Phyllis Duncan. Front row, l to r; Pat Lowe, Margo Winters, Jane Thurston.

In the early 1930s the dress code for girls' gym classes required that the much-hated gym bloomers be worn. Somewhat later these were replaced by a one piece blue outfit which was a big improvement but still not really very popular with the girls. Today they wear shorts and an appropriate top.

A gym dress code was not always in place on the boys' side. In the early days all that was necessary was a pair of rubber-soled "running shoes"—if you didn't have them you were sent directly to the Principal's office! In those days the students would rush to the gym, rip off their shirts and get into the activities as soon as possible. Today the boys buy their Lisgar-crested shorts and T-shirts and must wear appropriate rubber-soled shoes before they can participate.

Some time before the new gym building was constructed it was decided that showers would be an asset for the Physical Training Department. A new shower room was therefore constructed in the basement of the main building beside the boys' gymnasium. It is said that henceforth classrooms after gym periods smelled sweeter.

Pressure for a new gym, finally, in 1950 resulted in action. The only land available was the girls' play yard, baseball diamond, and tennis courts directly across Lisgar street. The new building contained a modern double gymnasium with spectator seating and moveable dividing doors between boys' or girls' gym classes. Each duplicate facility had its own office for the teachers, dressing-rooms, and showers for the students. As the school population increased a new addition was added to the West side of the building to give space for shop, music, and regular classrooms.

The wonderful new structure left no outdoor playing space whatsoever. The only grounds available for football teams and other sports practices was the empty lot at the corner of Nicholas Street and Laurier Avenue on which D.N.D. later built their National Defence Headquarters. The teams and coaches did their best trying to conduct normal practices; but they had to contend with pedestrians crossing the lot or the odd alcoholic transient from under the bridge attempting to join their huddles. This was also the area where the school discus throwers practised their speciality and where sometime an errant throw might go over the embankment in amongst the cars parked beside the railroad tracks (all since removed).

This was not an enviable situation for Lisgar teams. The School Board gradually began expropriating and knocking down the houses east of the gym building and thus enlarging a playing area. It was not ideal. Even although an athlete making his run for the take-off into the long jump pit seemed to disappear in a depression that was once the basement of a torn-down house, nevertheless it was our own. There was no room for a hockey rink. Intramural hockey was ended.

Eventually all the houses east to the Driveway and between Lisgar and Cooper streets were expropriated. When completed the field gave Lisgar an adequate area. However an outdoor rink was ruled out because it would ruin the grassed surface of the field. This continued Lisgar's "rink" problems going back one hundred years.

The area proved to be inadequate for two football teams to practise simultaneously with the soccer team; therefore, it was decided to have only one team—an intermediate team—to compete in the newly formed intermediate league for players under eighteen years of age. This suited Lisgar which, because of its academic nature, was having a difficult time getting enough eligible senior players.

For many years football was a major factor in creating Lisgar school spirit. Most of the student body and a good many teachers went to all the games played at "Varsity Oval" (just across the Rideau Canal) or at Lansdowne Park. "Football Fridays" were introduced around 1939 by shortening the periods and having school close at one thirty to allow for "double header" (junior and senior) football games to start at two o'clock and finish before it became dark.

But after World War II more students found part-time jobs on their afternoons off and the crowds grew smaller. With the loss of "Varsity Oval" and Lansdowne Park for use by the high schools, fewer people found their way to the games which were played at the suburban schools, Laurentian, Rideau, Brookfield.

The high cost of equipment necessary for the modern game brought about the demise of Lisgar football. Originally, the school provided the helmets and the padded football pants. The school also bought the sweaters but each player paid for his own when—and if—he made the team. Players were

The glory and the ecstasy, the mud and the cold of a Lisgar "Football Friday" of the Fifties. Classes were condensed for school closure at 1:30. After one of these games the Students' Council sponsored its annual Football Dance. From the *Vox Lycei* 1958-59.

told that the necessary cleated boots were sold by Byshe's Sports Store on Bank Street and that the manager Bill Roe would give them a discount. Each player had to bring his own shoulder pads, but it was not uncommon for juniors and seniors to reduce the cost by sharing the same pads and exchanging them between games. Unlike the hard plastic cantilevered "state of the art" pads of today, early pads were mere slabs of leather backed by felt padding. Today everything is provided by the school except for shoes and plastic mouth pieces which are personal items.

Finally, the growing lack of support from the student body, the high cost of equipment and transportation and the less than adequate practice area all conspire against continuing football. However the end of football at Lisgar did not mean the end of good competitive team sport. Basketball became the popular team sport and Lisgar went on to win city and Ontario championships.

As more and more sports have been added to the P.T. curriculum the number of individuals playing, competing, enjoying, keeping fit, establishing fitness habits has increased ten-fold.

The 1940s. Coaches of boys' sporting activities: Mr. H. Rothwell, Track and Field, senior basketball; E. Nicholls, bantam and midget basketball, junior football, Track and Field, gymnastics; Bill Mitchell, senior football, junior basketball; Arn Fallis, junior hockey; Ernie Legon, senior hockey. Coaches of girls' sporting activities; Jessie Smith and Dorothy Bishop.
1941-42. Ron Rankin, Ben Shapiro, Ken Lussier, Bill Blue outstanding senior football players. Art Mackey starred on the basketball team winning top scoring honours in City League play.
1942-43. Mac Foulds starred for the senior basketball team winning "King of Courts" scoring title as top scorer in league play. Lisgar bantam wins championship. For the duration of the war EOSSA track meets were cancelled and EOSSA basketball awards cancelled. Girls' interschool athletic activities were greatly curbed because of transportation difficulties—rationing of gas, volunteers to drive, expenses.
1943-44. Lisgar bantam basketball team won the City championship for the second year in a row. Gerry Conger won the league scoring title. Mr. Bill Mitchell left the staff to join the Royal Canadian Navy.
1944-45. Bantam basketball dropped leaving midget, junior and senior divisions. The midget basketball team, winning ten games in a row, won the championship trophy. In one game alone Gerry Conger scored forty-eight points. Lisgar players dominated the three sections of interscholastic basketball league. Ralph Saslov led the seniors with seventy-eight points, Ed Cashman the juniors with sixty-eight and Gerry Conger the midget with one hundred and fifty-five. Ralph Saslov was crowned "King of the Courts," the fourth straight year that a Lisgar player had won the senior basketball scoring honours.

In the 1950s Lisgar girls began establishing a reputation as champion tennis players. This is the O.H.S.S.A. championship team of 1956. Left to right; Elaine Calkoen, Ann Harris, Gail Irwin, Ann Irwin, Elaine Frick.

1945-46. Bill Mitchell returned from overseas and resumed coaching the senior football and junior basketball teams.
1946-47. Johnny "Snowball" Bourada, goalie, was the star of the senior hockey team which reached the semi-finals. Coached by Eric Nicholls, Lisgar juniors, starring Gilbert Hill, Bill Drummond and Ernie Wormington ended atop of the league, but lost out to St. Pat's in the finals. Bill Mitchell left to become Director of Athletics at the Ontario Agriculture and Veterinary College in Guelph. John Carruthers joined the staff as a history teacher and took over as coach of the senior football and junior basketball teams. The first recorded girls' hockey team was formed at Lisgar in hopes that other Ottawa high schools would field teams and accept challenges. President; Norma Finnigan; Vice-President, Phil Duncan; Secretary-Treasurer, Nonie Melville.
1947-48. With John Carruthers coaching for the first time the senior football team reached the semi-finals against Tech, Glebe, Ottawa University and St. Pat's. Bob "Masher" McMonagle starred. In Track and Field Lisgar won the senior interscholastic division in a meet at Britannia Park and came second in the combined divisions. Outstanding were; John Calvert and Al Rankin in the mile relay; John Calvert and John Kilrea (descendant of Ottawa Senators famed Hec Kilrea) breaking records in the 440 yard dash and shot-put events. In girls' hockey Lisgar defeated Glebe 9-3. Girls sports were beginning to recover from the limitations of the war. Intramural basketball and volleyball leagues were reinstated. The Annual Lisgar Sports Day was resumed. The junior track team of 1948 won almost every event at the Kingston track meet and came home with the trophy.
1948-49. For the first time in ten years the junior football team coached by Eric Nicholls made the finals. Interscholastic hockey was discontinued this year due to the high cost of equipment. Intramural hockey on the school's own outdoor rink took its place. In girls' badminton, Sheila Leggatt retained her senior girls interscholastic championship,

winning for the third time. Lisgar was fortunate this year in having three of the top Canadian junior tennis stars on the girls' tennis team: Pat Lowe (Captain), Miriam Rainbotti and Diane Lowe. Joined by Simone Tachereau and Joan Matthews they formed the strongest tennis team Lisgar had ever produced which they proved by winning the Interscholastic Tennis Championship for the second straight year against Elmwood, Glebe, Ottawa Ladies' College. The Lisgar Ski Team was one of the strongest ever to represent Lisgar with the president of the club, Andy Tommy winning the Junior Tachereau Trophy, the Junior Journal Trophy, the O.S.C. Preliminary Meet and the Southam Cross-Country Race. Frances Lee, straight from the Ontario College of Education and a recent graduate of Toronto University with a Bachelor of Physical and Health Education degree, joined the Phys. Ed. Department.

1949-50. Lisgar girls won the Ottawa Interscholastic tennis title for the third year in a row. The girls' hockey team performed in exhibition games under new head coach Bruno Rouleau. Lisgar's most prominent skier Andy Tommy represented Canada in the World Championship meet at Aspen, Colorado and also in the North American Championships at Banff, where he won the Canadian Junior Title for the second year in a row. The boys' tennis team won the title for the first time since 1936. The players were: Ned Rainboth, Wes Nichol, John Milliken, Pierre Robichaud, Hewitt Bostock. Mr. Kal Hokkinen joined the Phys. Ed. staff. A recent grad in Physical Education from McGill University, he took over coaching duties for senior football and junior basketball. Intramural hockey continued to play a big role in the sports activities with Mr. B. Rouleau coaching seniors and Arn Fallis juniors and bantams.

1950-51. The interform leagues in basketball and hockey which gave every student a chance to play were a popular feature again this year. Teachers McArthur and Nicholls arranged these games. The boys' Athletic Association act in the "Lisgar Review" was one of the hits of the show and included a well-drilled gymnastic team directed by Hokkinen and show-stopping "ballet" starring John Clarke, Allan Richens, John Freeth and Al Carter. Track and Field gained in participation during these years with Lisgar placing second to Glebe in both the big spring meets in 1950. Paul Streeter starred by winning both the 100 and 220 yard dashes in the intermediate division and running the anchor leg for the winning Lisgar relay team in the 880 yard relay. Burt Kellog and Peter Redfern deserve honourable mention for the juniors. Fisher Park High joined the city interscholastic circuit.

1951-52. The junior football team coached by Harold Rothwell and Don Loney captured the Junior "B" Football Championship. It was the first time a Lisgar team had captured a football title since 1928. The senior boys basketball team was in the final series for the third year in a row after defeating Glebe in the semi-finals. However they bowed out to Tech in the finals by 109-82. The junior basketball team led their league in season play but lost out to Glebe

in the semi-finals. Although bantam basketball had been discontinued as an inter-school league, it was decided to hold a round robin tournament for the Beamish Trophy signifying Bantam Basketball supremacy. Lisgar won the trophy by defeating St. Pat's, Tech and Glebe and also had two individual players in the top two places in individual scoring, Bob McAskin 33 points and Ernie Zoppa 31.

1952-53. October 24, 1952. The new Lisgar Memorial Gymnasium was officially opened by C.F. Cannon, Deputy Minister of Education for Ontario. Stanley Higman, Chairman of the Collegiate Institute Board was chairman for the occasion. Mr. Proctor was in charge of music and guest speakers included: G.T. Green, chairman of the building committee, who performed introductions, Wilhelmina Dowler who brought greetings from Lisgar's recent grads, and Judge A. Gordon MacDougall who spoke for the "less recent grads." Charlotte Whitton carried greetings from the City Council. Since the discontinuance of interscholastic hockey five years before, Lisgar had struggled to uphold Canada's national game even through it was through interform contests. Under Bruno Rouleau's guidance the league thrived in two sections, junior and senior. A unique method of naming the teams added to the fun. The senior teams were Protractors, Erasers and Test-tubes, the juniors Poets, Historians, and Chemists. Before the season started there was some question as to whether Lisgar would be able to field a football team because of an insufficient number of boys turning out for the team and a general lack of interest. However the game was continued. The Lisgar Bantam Basketball team again prevailed and won the Beamish Trophy for the second straight year at the annual bantam basketball round robin tournament. No doubt inspired by the new gymnasium, girls' junior and senior volleyball teams were organized for the first time to play against Fisher Park High School, Glebe Collegiate and Commerce High School. At the end of the season a tournament for both juniors and seniors was held at Lisgar with Lisgar placing third in junior and first in senior competition.

1953-54. Coached by Bernie Black the junior football team won the Junior "B" Championship. The seniors coached by Hokkinen reached the semi-finals only to be defeated by St. Pat's. The senior basketball team was the winner of the Consolation Trophy at the annual Carleton College Invitational Tournament. Under the guidance of Bruno Rouleau interform hockey had another good year. Harold Rothwell organized the interform basketball for another outstanding season with over three quarters of the boys of the school participating. The bantam basketball team under Hokkinen was the winner of the Beamish Trophy for the third consecutive year.

1954-55. The junior football team coached by Bernie Black won the Peter Sinclair Memorial Trophy symbolic of the Junior "A" Championship. Arn Fallis organized a smooth-running interform volleyball league which resulted in great participation. This year a number of Lisgar girls took over Champagne Bath Monday evenings for about six weeks in training for their Bronze Instructor's Badges. The cheerleaders this year were: Rich Little, G. Perry, H. Cross, D. Schwartz, P. Savage, G. Haye, J. Blair, and J. Stevenson.

1960-61. In 1960 Tom Cooney left Lisgar to take up the post of Head of Physical and Health Education at Oakville Collegiate. He was replaced by Joe Leggett who came from Laurentian High School in Ottawa, having also taught and coached at Ottawa Tech. Basketball continued to be a prominent sport at Lisgar with Lisgar teams providing good keen competition against the other schools. Unfortunately no Lisgar team won a championship in 1960-61. However, the girls won the Senior Interscholastic Volleyball Championship for the first time. Lisgar girls also won the Track and Field Championship for the first time.

1962-63. This year marked the return of Lisgar to the interscholastic hockey league. By this time Laurentian, Brookfield and Rideau High Schools had joined the interscholastic league.Early in the fall term the boys' tennis

team won the Interscholastic Tennis Championships of the city. In first and second singles Mike Hammon and David Ryan won; in doubles, Paul Henry and Clarke Slemon paired to win. The team consisted of Mike Hammon, David Ryan, Paul Henry, Clarke Slemon, Stuart Langford and Mike Belcourt. The girls' tennis team of Shirley Grant and Elspeth Fordyce, doubles, and Joanne Schneider, first singles, and Suzanne Langford, second singles, reached the finals, but were defeated by Glebe 2-1. Lisgar girls won the Track and Field Event for the second year in a row. Coached by Fran Lee, Lisgar girls' senior basketball team won the Ottawa High School Interscholastic Championship. Under the guidance of John Carruthers the Lisgar Curling Club boasted a large number of enthusiastic members who enjoyed the regular activities and acquitted themselves well in competition. A team of Alan Davey, Gord Cunningham, John Lane and Erik Nilsson finished in second place in the Ottawa Schoolboy Bonspiel held at Christmastime. Rideau

In 1971 Lisgar's volleyball team not only won the City Championship against Brookfield but went on to the Ontario championships in Belleville. Eleven games later Lisgar and Parkdale from Toronto faced off in the finals. But Parkdale's six foot, ten inch spiker proved too much in the end. Front row, left to right; Eric Whist, Dale Trottier, Reynold Hu, David Robinson. Richard Krzanowski, Ron Kelly. Back row, left to right; Bob McNeil (waterboy), Doug Sally, Paul Armstrong, Jon Love, Kim MacKenzie (captain), Rob Pitfield, Terry Stoqua, Barrie Laughton (coach).

Coach Barrie Laughton's 1969 City of Ottawa Boys' Volleyball Champions. Back row, left to right; coach Laughton, Philip Strong, Jack Vee, Drew Love, Lorne Bowles, Jon Love, Phil Lanouette, Frank Desipio. Front row, left to right; Denis Racine, Benjy Sadavoy, Ian Donnell, Phil Lis, Boroslav Gruber.

Curling Club was the venue. This was not only the entry of curling into the roster of Lisgar sports but it was also the beginning of the Davey family curling tradition.

1963-64. The Lisgar girls' tennis team was again runner-up in the annual Scholastic Tennis Tournament, losing out to Glebe in the finals. The members of the team were Suzanne Langford—first singles, Marion Sherwood—second singles, Simonne Dion and Susan Fraser—doubles, Shillington coached the team. Early in September the boys' tennis team successfully defended its title as Ottawa Interscholastic Tennis Champions. The team consisted of: Mike Hamman—first singles; David Ryan—second singles; and a doubles team of Nick Stowell and Stuart Langford, with Doug Hart as a substitute. The team was managed and coached by Paul Henry. In boys' cross-country skiing, Stephen Kendall was the winner of the junior event in which he was up against the stiffest competition that Ottawa high schools could muster. Lisgar girls, entered the annual Track and Field event as defending champions but slipped to sixth place. In girls' basketball the senior team under Miss Lee finished second in their league, but were defeated in the quarter finals by a powerful Ridgemont team. The junior basketball team this year under the coaching of

O.F.S.A.A. "AAA" Basketball champions, 1973-74. Back row, left to right; Larry Hale (Coach), John Horwitz, Peter Metuzals, K.C. Keller, Bob Sebera, Joe Didoli, H. Reid. Front row; Ron Hughes, Larry Kane, Matt King, Pat Stoqua, Ray Dyck, Dan Kelly, Don Kilchrist.

**The 1980 City of Ottawa Junior Girls' Volleyball champions.
Back row, left to right; Alex Gill, Jane Lister, Bryn Lister,
Charlotte Wang, Diane Smallridge, Jennifer Hicks,
Patricia Seymour, Barrie Laughton (coach). Front row;
Vale Bachelor, Jennifer Ball, Sarah Hill, Sandy Scott,
Lynn Hustwit, Sheila Scott, Lana Stoll.**

Miss Shillington succeeded in winning all their regular
league games, although losing in the finals to Ridgemont.
At the interscholastic badminton tournament Lisgar placed
second to the championship Laurentian team. Paul Henry
came first in boys' singles and Bill Scott and Bill Mills won
the boys' doubles. Other members of the team were Barbara
Bloor, Naomi Fudemoto, Hatto Fischer, Sheila Gardiner and
Sue Keddy. For the second year in a row coached by Fran
Lee the senior girls' volleyball team won the Ottawa High
School Interscholastic Championship. They went on to
become All Ontario Volleyball Champions.

1964-65. The year 1964 marked the entrance of the Lisgar
soccer team into the newly formed high school league. Guided
by Mr. Forster and sprinkled with many nationalities, the
team showed great strength. Hungary, Poland, Germany,
Thailand, Brazil, Argentina, England and Canada were
represented. The team qualified for the semi-finals but they
unfortunately lost to the eventual championship Tech team.
One player of note was Ricardo, the "Argentinean Flash,"
whose ball control and scoring ability made him the most
outstanding player on the team and perhaps in the league.

**Posed in front of the Lisgar trophy cases is the 1973
championship volleyball team which defeated Fisher Park
for the City Championship, Confederation for the Ottawa-
Carleton championship, Deep River for the Ottawa Valley
championship. They missed the provincial semi-finals
by one game. Back row, left to right; Gregg Buchanan
(manager), Chris Brown, Sandy Castonguay, Gwilym
Evans, Doug Sally (co-captain), K.C. Keller (co-captain),
Jim McLaughlin, Weislav Wojtal, Mark Zelinski, Peter
Rukiewicz, Dan Kelly (manager), Barrie Laughton
(coach). Front row; Kevin Goudie, Ed Kryzanowski, Geoff
Robinson, Ian Dunlop, Mario Gianuzzi, Basel Abouarrage.**

Fifth consecutive City of Ottawa Volleyball champions, 1974. Back row, left to right; Coach Barrie Laughton, Gwilym Evans, Tim Hadwen, K.C. Keller, Miodrag Babic, Mark Zielinski, Peter Rukiewicz. Front row; Don McMullen, Matt Hadwen, Ed Kryzanowski, Kevin Goudie. Absent; Dan Kelly, Ian Dunlop, Geoff Robinson.

The boys' tennis team brought home the City Championship for the third consecutive year. The members were: Mike Hamman, first singles; Paul Henry, second singles; David Ryan and Stuart Langford, doubles; Hatto Fischer, substitute. In bantam basketball Lisgar finished first and Henry Green won the individual scoring crown. In the senior scoring race two Lisgar players, Allan Munroe and Bob Rouleau, took first and second. In Track and Field at the Ottawa Valley Meet the combined points total of the boys and girls placed Lisgar first. Outstanding for the girls Joan Fisher (later to compete for Canada at the Olympics) was first in the high and long jump events, second in the 100 yard dash. Record-breakers on the boys' team were: Richard Powell, high jump; Ian McKie, discus; Steve Kendall, 440 yard dash; and the senior relay team of David Bean, Joe Zwickl, Jim Thompson and Hatto Fischer. In the 1964-65 year the curling club had an extra large co-ed membership participating at the Rideau Curling Club after school two days a week under the guidance of Arn Fallis. Members of this club to go on in organized curling after they left the school were: Bruce Davey who competed for B.C. in the National Briar, later chairman of the annual Ottawa and District Bonspiel; and Ross Davey who became president of the Rideau Curling Club. Larry Hale joined the Physical Education Department. **1965-66.** During the 1965-66 curling season Lisgar's intermural league was expanded to six teams, with skips Dave Van Dine, John Froley, Ross Davey, Ian Worthington, Bruce Davey, and George Wright. At Christmas Alan Davey

The 1992 Junior City Lisgar Lords basketball champions with coach Bill Fraser. Back row, left to right; Alex Hutton, Amy Rutherford, Claire Reilly-Roe, Jennifer Kingsley, Cara Waterfall. Back row; Irene Vandoros, Victoria Horton, Darren Sutherland, Laura Tugwell, Breagha Carr-Harris, Lila Fraser, Sass McCarthy, Sandra Dejesus, Courtney White.

with Ross and Bruce Davey and David Van Dine won the Consolation Prize of the Ottawa Schoolboy Bonspiel, Ottawa Division. In the girl's bonspiel the Lisgar team of Revia Fischer, Shirley Wilson, Dorothy Scott, and Florence Fridgen were second to Brookfield in the finals. In mid-February Lisgar curlers won the Cole Trophy. Mr. Bob Behan was the coach and staff advisor for the club.

Once again in Track and Field this year, it was the Lisgar girls who placed first in the City finals. Outstanding performances for the girls' track team were: Joan Fischer, 1st in 220 yds, long jump and high jump, 1st in hurdles; Noreen Slack, 1st shot-put Jr. Relay Team (B. Muhleg, J. Fisher, P. Pick, B. Mallon) 1st Sr. Relay Team (Sue Labreque, S, Keene, Lynn Howard, A. Rowley). The 1965 Lisgar swim team got off to a great start with the girls' team winning back the trophy they had won two years previously at the annual Girls' Meet. The combined boy-girl team led by Zibor Szcranya with three wins and a second place brought honour to Lisgar at the Age Group Swim Meet held at Glebe in April. The girls' ski team won the Heggtveit Trophy at Vorlage proving themselves to be the best girls' team in Ottawa. The team members were Linda Swan, Christine Batchelor, Rosie Lang, Nancy McDougall, and Alison Murdoch. Bill Fraser joined the English Department in 1965. Since then he has been actively involved in coaching boys' and girls' basketball, Track and Field, and football. Terry Prichett "Prichett's Pirates" joined the staff in 1966. He has been an active coach of both boys' and girls' soccer from the fall of 1966 through to 1992.

1966-67. This year the Lisgar girls' tennis team came out on top in the Interscholastic Tournament held at the Ottawa Lawn Tennis Club. Their victories in the finals against Rideau High School won them the Ottawa District Tennis Association Trophy, symbolic of the City Interscholastic Tennis Championship. Members of the team were: Lilian Wagner, first singles; Barb Muhlig, second singles; Alison Murdoch and Anda Sysolins, doubles; Calla Fireman, substitute. The girls' senior basketball team had an exceptional season placing first in the central league with a record of nine wins and one loss and eventually winning the City Championship for the first time in six years. In Track and Field the girls had another good season with several outstanding performances by individual athletes. In several meets Joan Fisher came first in the 100 yd. and 200 yd. dashes and the long jump. Barbara Muhlig dominated the triple jump at several meets and Tania Muslika came first in the shot-put at the Eastern Meet. Boys' Track and Field Team enjoyed one of its finest seasons ever. Lisgar athletes distinguished themselves as City champions and came very close to claiming bragging rights for all of the Ottawa Valley. The Lisgar contingent was narrowly defeated by Arnprior by a score of 112-1/2 to 112. The Junior Team, led by Chris Ouimet, the day's most outstanding junior athlete, won the trophy as the best team in their division. Henry Green and Richard Bordeleau were double winners in the intermediate and senior divisions respectively. At Christmas, Lisgar

entered the Ontario Schoolboy Curling Bonspiel. A team of Lyle Whately, Campbell Edwards, Chris Whately, and George Wright won the Ottawa Championship by defeating Hillcrest High School 9-4 in the finals. They went on to defeat Renfrew and Cornwall before reaching the Provincial finals and losing to Uxbridge, the eventual winners. A second curling team of Rich Van Dine, Ross Davey, Bruce Davey, and Alan Davey won the consolation of the Ottawa Valley Schoolboy Bonspiel. In skiing, Lisgar was represented in the Dalton Wood Event by Chris Frank, Dave Dyer, Mark Talbot, Bob Donnelly, Norman Ducharme, and Joe Patenaude. Competing against fourteen high schools in the Junior Varsity Meet, Lisgar took top honours. The tournament consisted of four disciplines; slalom, giant slalom, cross-country and jumping. Also, in another competition, Kent Omhalt-Jensen, a member of the second team, was winner of the Nordic Combined Trophy. The Lisgar girls' ski team victory marked the sixth win in eight years. Frances Lee retired in June of 1967 after twenty years at Lisgar, the *Frances Lee Award* presented in her honour. The winner of this trophy is the senior girl "who has participated actively and contributed the most to the athletic programme at Lisgar."

1968-69. Senior Boys' Soccer—City Champions. The senior boys' soccer team was crowned City Champion after what may be remembered as one of the most peculiar sporting events of the Collegiate's history. Capping an unbeaten season, Pritchett's Pirates, as they were known, found themselves faced with a play-off final against a very tough Sir Wilfred Laurier team. After regulation time, two overtime periods, and more than half an hour of sudden-death, the teams remained deadlocked in a 2-2 tie. The game was called on account of darkness and resumed the following day. Within five minutes the offence managed to score against a tough defensive squad from Laurier and thus claim, for the first time in history, the City championship in Senior Boys' Soccer for L.C.I. Junior Boys' Basketball captured the Junior Cage Trophy for the first time since 1939, after an exemplary season in which they suffered only one loss by a mere two points, and finished in first place overall. The team won the championship in two consecutive games to claim the title. Boys' Tennis—champions in 1962-63-64-67-68. Bad weather forced cancellation of tournament in 1969. Winner of Ottawa and District Lawn Tennis trophy in 1967-68. Girls' Tennis—champions in 1966 and again in 1969. Barrie Laughton joined the staff in 1969 and has been coaching volleyball ever since. The Fallis-Laughton Trophy, awarded annually to the person who contributes the most to volleyball at Lisgar, was donated by the players to honour coach Laughton and former coach Arnold Fallis. Hugh Fraser, outstanding sprinter, graduated in 1970 and went on to represent Canada in international competitions, including the Olympics. Blake Dunlop, outstanding tennis player for Lisgar and hockey player with the Ottawa '67s, went on to a lengthy career in the N.H.L. With his brothers Scott and Craig he competed on championship tennis teams in the late 1960s. Under the leadership of Bill Hollingworth, a wrestling team was formed in 1968. Mike Toumanoff, Howard Hunter, and Jerome St. Marie were early stars of the wrestling team.

The 1970s. Senior Boys' Basketball had an exemplary record over the course of this decade; as City Champions from 1970-71 through 1976-77 inclusive. As Provincial Champions in 1973-74, a year in which they finished the season with a phenomenal 44 wins and 0 losses. They were winners of the provincial consolation award in 1972-73 and again in 1977-78. The Senior Boys' Volleyball squad also enjoyed remarkable success in the 1970s. They, too, were City Champions for the years 1970-71 through 1977-78; as well as Provincial Champions in 1970-71 and 1977-78, and the runners-up at the provincial level in 1971-72. Boys' and Girls' Varsity Tennis Team won every City Championship in the 1970s. Junior Boys' Basketball, champions in 1971-72 and 1977-78. Girls' Ski Team, champions in 1975-76. Junior Girls' Volleyball, champions in 1979-80. Pat O'Brien left Lisgar in 1963, after coaching Senior Boys' Basketball for four years. The Pat O'Brien Trophy, was donated by players and former players to honour their coach. It is awarded annually to the person (not necessarily a player) who contributes the most to volleyball at Lisgar during the season. Eric Nicholls retired in 1972 after many years at Lisgar. He was active as a coach and a teacher in the Physical Education Department in the late 1930s, 1940s, and early 1950s. Steve Glavin became principal of Lisgar in 1977 and took over as the coach of the tennis team in September 1977. He coached the team to consecutive championships through to his retirement in June 1987. Marilyn (Shillington) Sloan retired in 1974 after teaching in the Physical Education Department at Lisgar since the early 1960s. There have been many "family affairs" over the course of Lisgar's athletic history. The following distinguished themselves during their time at Lisgar: The Davey Brothers, Terry and Pat Stoqua, Drew and Jon Love, Paul and Dave Armstrong, Lorne and George Bowles, Matthew, Peter, and Anthony Hadwen, Kim and Dave MacKenzie. Marge Blackwood was a key member of the tennis team in the early 1970s. She joined the Pro Tour and went on to compete at Wimbledon. Pat Stoqua graduated in 1976, and went on to star in football and basketball at Carleton University. He also played professional football for the Ottawa Rough Riders in the 1980s. Jon Love, a graduate in 1972, was an all-round athlete (basketball, volleyball, badminton, gymnastics) while at Lisgar and went on to become one of the all-time leading scorers in basketball at Carleton University. Paul Armstrong also graduated in 1972 and found success as a basketball player at Carleton University. He became coach of the team at Carleton in the late 1980s. K.C. Keller graduated in 1975. He arrived at Lisgar from California and was a valued member of both the basketball and volleyball teams prior to accepting a volleyball scholarship at U.C.L.A. upon graduating. The major renovations in the summers of 1975 and 1976 meant a late start to the school year and resulted in the cancellation of the football season. In fact, football was never again offered at Lisgar and many schools in the Ottawa area followed suit over the next ten years. Hockey resurfaced (briefly) in 1976-77. By the mid-1970s, interest in cheerleading was diminishing. There was continued sporadic interest over the course of the 1970s but the activity did not survive into the 1980s. In some sports where both boys and girls competed simultaneously (tennis, skiing, track and field, cross-country running, badminton) co-ed meets and some combined championships appeared. By the end of the 1970s there existed competition in Junior Boys' soccer as well as a varsity league for girls. Water polo began very early in the 1970s and by the end of the decade it and competitive swimming were very popular interscholastic sports.

1980s. This period marks a few significant changes from the preceding decade. The move to accelerated programmes on the academic front led to large numbers of students graduating by the time they were sixteen and seventeen years old. As a result, while junior teams continued to do well, we lacked the bodies necessary to field competitive senior teams. June 1981 marked the retirement of Joe Leggett who had been head of the Physical Education Department for twenty years. The Joe Leggett Trophy is awarded annually to the boy who has made the most valuable contribution to the intramural programme. Joan Sobieniak also retired in June of 1981. She had been with the Physical Education Department since 1972, and was Assistant Head of the Department from 1974 until the time of her retirement. In 1981, under the leadership of new Department Head Jim Woods, several new activities appeared including boys' rugby and girls' touch football. A much greater emphasis on recreational activity under the leadership of the Lisgar Athletic Association took place. The new association was an amalgamation of the former Girls' and Boys' Athletic Associations and was part of the move toward co-ed activities in class, in recreation, and in competition. Under the guidance of Jessie Smith, a member of the Lisgar Physical education staff since 1976, a very popular part of the L.A.A. has been the annual leadership camp held every fall to motivate and inform the student leaders of the L.A.A. Junior Boys' Basketball: champions in 1980-81, 81-82, and 83-84. Junior Boys' Soccer: champions 1982-83. Junior Girls' Basketball: champions in 1984. Alpine Ski Team: combined champions in 1985-86. Tennis Team: won every year! Senior Girls' Soccer: champions 1986. Cross-Country Skiing Relay Team: won the Ontario championship in the winter of 1984.

Geoff Wells graduated from Lisgar in 1981 and went on to become an outstanding basketball player at Carleton University and later to play professionally in Europe. He "put something back into the programme" when he helped coach our junior team in 1985-86 and our senior team during the 1988-89 seasons. Sean Holmes graduated in 1983 and went on to star as a soccer player at Carleton University.

In the fall of 1990, the tennis team was finally defeated after an astounding twenty consecutive interscholastic victories. Girls' touch football continued with successive championships in the falls of 1986 and 1987. A talented group of female basketball players led by Shannon Fraser and Jennifer Laughton (daughters of Lisgar teachers/coaches) won a junior championship in 1986-87 and a senior championship in 1988-89. Jennifer Laughton went on to play basketball for Queen's University.The Alpine Skiing team continued to do well with championships in the 1986-87 season and again in the 1991-92 season. Under the dynamic leadership of Cathi Chambers, we were finally able to win a Track and Field championship in 1990-91. The win marked the first championship for the track and field team since 1966-67.

Robert MacMillan passed away during the 1987-88 season after coaching the swim team for many years. The Robert N. MacMillan Award is a tribute to his memory. It is awarded annually to the boy or girl in grades nine to eleven who makes a significant contribution to the swimming program while maintaining a high level of proficiency in science. Jim Woods left Lisgar in 1991 after ten years as Head of the Physical Education Department. Larry Hale, who hads been teaching at Lisgar for twenty-seven years, took over as Department Head.

During the 1991-92 school year the city and the schools within were ravaged by a meningitis outbreak. Lisgar lost a very talented young athlete by the name of Mohammed Zamiruddin. In his memory, the award given to the top junior male athlete of the year was renamed The Mohammed Zamiruddin Memorial Award.

—Joe Leggett and Larry Hale.

STUDENT PRESS AT LISGAR

1883-1992

There seems to be a gap in student newspaper production between the 1920s and the appearance of the *Bull Sheet* in 1973.

Doug Arrand, a Lisgar guidance counsellor who attended the school in the late 1950s, recalled that there were no newspapers throughout his school years. Later, when he began teaching at Lisgar in 1967, the first newspaper he encountered was *The Flounder*. He had no recollection of the *Bull Sheet*. Thus, the *Bull Sheet* may have been a peripheral effort, probably not read by many outside of 11D, the class which published it.

Arrand suggested several reasons for this gap in Lisgar's press history. The long school day which, he said, lasted until 4:10 in the afternoon left little time for outside activities. He also suggested that the work load was heavier during these years and that students were involved in different activities. Yearbooks, rather than newspapers, were popular at the time.

"In fact," he explained, "most of us were surprised to get to university and find that such sophisticated newspapers were being published by students."

The first issue of the **Lisgarwrite** was published in April of 1988, and revolutionized student newspaper production at Lisgar. The paper was laid out on the only Macintosh SE computer the school owned at that time, using *Ready Set Go* software.

The basic layout designed for the first issue by Layout Editor Imran Haq set the standard for future editions and defined the "*Lisgarwrite* look" which persists to this day. The layout consisted of professional-looking graphics and laser printing.

The first *Lisgarwrite*s were printed on 8 1/2 by 11 inch paper and sold for 25 cents. Their content was dedicated exclusively to covering school events and did an exceptionally thorough job, writing about more school organizations than any previous newspaper.

As the number of high school yearbooks increased in Ottawa, the competition made it impossible for the Lisgar Press advertisement solicitors to garner sufficient advertising money to meet the needs. Advertisers like Jarvis' and Hope's book stores, Murphy-Gambles, Byshe Sporting Goods who had supported Lisgar for decade upon decade, dropped out. As an alternative each Lisgar class undertook to raise their own funds for Lisgar publications and were given advertising space in the Vox Lycei for innovative artwork. This one reprinted from the Vox Lycei, 1974-75, is from class 11F of that year.

Owing to its good writing and attractive layout, the *Lisgarwrite* was awarded the top prize at the *Ottawa Citizen*'s high school newspaper competition in June of 1989.

In 1988-89, the *Lisgarwrite* made yet another format change, this time from white, letter-size paper to tabloid-size newsprint. The basic elements of layout remained the same, but by this time the photograph problems had been brought under control.

The third issue of the year began a trend that would grow throughout the following two years: analysis of world events. The front page story covers the inauguration of American president George Bush, and other stories discuss current events such as Quebec's Bill 101.

During 1989-1990 the *Lisgarwrite* was plagued by over-coverage of current events. Opinion articles were written about the environment, the GST, Columbian drug lords, VIA Rail, federal budget leak, Chinese dissidents, a two-page spread about Eastern Europe, Earth Day, South Africa, the Intifada, Meech Lake, Temagami, Solidarnosc, and the passing of Harold Ballard.

Writing about current events is not in itself bad, and certainly shows a concern on the part of students for social justice and political change. However, during the 1989-90 school year, the *Lisgarwrite* suffered a loss of readership among students because few were interested in reading about events that by the time of printing were out of date and had already been covered by the mainstream media. Readers demanded more coverage of school events and organization, but there were few writers interested in covering these topics.

The 1988-89 *Lisgarwrite* was awarded third place at the *Ottawa Citizen*'s high school newspaper competition.

The 1990-91 year was a new beginning for the *Lisgarwrite*. Almost the entire staff of the previous year had graduated,

In 1964 the *Ottawa Citizen* established high school newspaper and yearbook awards. Since then Lisgar has been consistently in the winners' lists. This is a 1988 photo of *Citizen* competition winners; left to right, Anne Leblanc, Merivale High School; Bettina McCulloch, Hawkesbury District High School; Jacqueline McGregor, Arnprior High School; Theresa Chung, Lisgar. Chung also won an award as one of the most valuable staffers on a school newspaper.

and few of the new executive members knew much about producing a newspaper. As editors, Anna Kisielewska and I were sent to a four-day long newspaper camp at Brock University to learn about the process, and further workshops sponsored by the *Ottawa Citizen* followed during the year for other member of the staff.

Imran Haq was replaced by his younger brother Rizwan as Layout Editor, thus establishing what would become to be known as "The Haq Dynasty."

In the 1990-91 year the staff decided to avoid covering world events altogether, but somehow an article about the Dalai Lama snuck into the first issue. The first issue of the year also pioneered the "centre-spread" layout which contained a description of every club in the school, all sixty-five.

The *Lisgarwrite* staff also began to broaden their personal interests in journalism. Entertainment Editor, Naomi Lazar, received a position as a radio disc-jockey for Carleton University's radio station CKCU, and wrote music reviews for their monthly magazine *Trans FM*. This allowed the *Lisgarwrite* to obtain concert photographs from *Trans FM* photographer Shawn Scallen as well as interviews with music personalities such as Elorious Cain, disco king.

The final issue of the year was yet another "layout revolution." Lisgar purchased several new typefaces including Liberty which was used to create a new Masthead. The printing was done on a linotronic machine at a commercial printing shop which gave the newspaper the highest resolution ever. Adding to the polished look was top-quality art work by Quy Luong who later went on to pursue graphic design as a profession.

The main editorial concerning censorship had been faxed in from Reims, France, at a cost of ten dollars per page. The feature article on page three was later quoted by the *Ottawa Citizen* in a front page article about teenage crime and "swarming."

By this time, the price of one copy had increased to fifty cents. The *Lisgarwrite* had also conducted its first ever survey which interrogated students of all grades on their feelings about the administrative decision to hold exams in January rather than in April. The decision was reversed the following year, and the newspaper's staff likes to think that the change was in part their doing.

This issue regained the title of "Top Overall High School Newspaper" in the *Ottawa Citizen*'s competition. Rizwan Haq represented the organization at the annual awards banquet as the "most valuable member" and the Haq Dynasty continued its reign as his younger brother Salman joined the layout team the following September.

The 1991-92 school year was a year of growth for the *Lisgarwrite*. The first general meeting of the year was attended by a record number of over 40 people and this number remained steady through most of the year.

The actual size of the publication nearly doubled with the year's first issue from twelve pages to twenty and was followed by a spring issue of sixteen pages. And the staff felt justified in doubling the price to one dollar. The cost of producing this year's first issue came to nine hundred dollars for the one thousand copies which were printed.

Advertising content and revenue rose as ads were continuously solicited from area businesses. A plan to publish four issues was interrupted by a month long teachers' strike and a final issue was scheduled to appear in early June.

Yet another format change was introduced by way of a full-page front page photograph. The first issue commemorated Mr. Larry Wade's thirty years at Lisgar with a distorted photograph taken of him through a convex mirror. The

---

BRIEF CHRONOLOGY OF STUDENT PRESS AT LISGAR 1883-1992

Philomath (Handwritten)
Vox Lycei (Handwritten) 1883-1921
Bull Sheet 1973
The Flounder 1974-1978
Alere Flammam 1981-1982
The Flounder 1982-1983
Lisgar Free Press 1983-1984
29 Lisgar 1986-1987
The Lisgarwrite (Letter size) 1988
The Lisgarwrite (Tabloid format) 1989-1992

second issue used a large photograph of Lisgar co-president David Applebaum's head which had the initials LCI shaved into it as a result of a fund-raising slave auction.

Editorials became rather lengthy in this issue, but they were balanced by a large number of articles covering most school events and sports. The newspaper also attempted to become more involved in student life by organizing a Black and White and Read All Over Day during Grade Nine Initiation Week. The "minor niners" raced through bowls of red Jello, flour, and black licorice, all the while answering the timeless question, "What is black and white and read all over?!?" with agonized screams of *"The Lisgarwrite!! The Lisgarwrite!!"*

Lisgar students have been publishing newspapers for the past 109 years. Their formats and styles have varied throughout the years, but certain characteristics have endured. Editorials have constantly demanded and encouraged school spirit and involvement in student activities. Reporters have tracked the trials and tribulations of successive generations of Lisgarites periodically living in an environment of renovation and construction. The modern computer-designed newspapers of today share with their handwritten predecessors a strong concern for patriotism, as well as for social, political and environmental issues.

Throughout the years there has been an underlying foundation of humour to everything that has been published, and an ongoing battle of the sexes has periodically surfaced. A survey of Lisgar student newspapers reveals a student body which has always been fashion conscious and has maintained fascination with "alternative" culture, unconventional music and films (for example, most films reviewed in recent decades had been playing at the Mayfair and the Bytowne, Ottawa's repertory cinemas). A rivalry with Glebe Collegiate permeates the publications. Over a century of writing also gives testimony to the endurance of such Lisgar institutions as the Students' Council, the LAA, the *Vox* and continuing customs such as grade nine initiation week. The staff of all past newspapers display an impressive level of writing in most cases, and a high level of imagination in all. Without fail, they show themselves to be willing and enthusiastic to adapt to new publishing technologies.

But above all, after analyzing Lisgar's newspapers from their beginning, one cannot help but conclude that Lisgar students have always had something to say, be it proselytizing, controversial, enlightening or just plain reportorial.[1]

---

[1]Luiga Chwialkowka, editor, *The Lisgarwrite* 1990-1992, excerpted from her paper for Dr. Janet Morchain.

VOX LYCEI EDITORS 1945-1993

Editor	Year	Editor	Year
Jack Gray	1945	Rose Kohr, Ross Pennie	1970
Debbie Pierce	1946	Jane Harkness, Kathleen Benidickson	1971
Virginia Nairn	1947	Tim Stowell, Helen Pitt	1972
David Ellis	1948	Victoria Freeman, Steven Samson	1973
Mary Hill	1950	Sam Krane, Alan Gaffen	1974
Jim Philips	1950	Louise Van Winkle, Peter Firestone	1975
Tilya Gallay	1951	Christina Cole, Alison Colvin	1976
Garry Fraser	1952	Ros Blaiklok, Cardine Rushforth	1977
Dick Foran	1953	Marysia Bucholc, Robin Leckie	1978
Pauline Gallay	1954	Janet Pond, Susie Viets	1979
Catherine Prime	1956	Allison Pond, Inez Alvarez	1980
Robin Kotze	1957	Elizabeth Sampson	1981
Gothan Clements, Janet O'Brien	1958	Dan Lyons, Min Ku	1982
Mary-Ann Quick	1959	Min Ku	1983
Barry Kelly	1960	Chui-Ling Tam, Patrick Hill	1984
Larry McDonald	1961	Joyce Taylor, Shyan Ku	1985
Karl Theil	1962	Kally Murphy, Monica Song	1986
Sylvia Lam	1963	Monica Song, Annalisa Baird	1987
Ian Sadinsky	1964	Annalisa Baird, Pablo J.R. Navarro	1988
David Donahue, Wendy Lane	1965	Pablo J.R. Navarro	1989
Toby Fyte	1966	Stephanie Tsao, Elizabeth Pang	1990
Daphne Read	1967	Elizabeth Caskey	1991
Daphne Read, Sheila Wright	1968	Deborah Coward, Andrew Anderson	1992
Susan Smith	1969	Sharon Duff, Marlisa Tiedeman	1993

LISGAR
1950s-1970s

THE 1950S

The 1950s at Lisgar were happy times. The Girls' and Boys' Hi-Ys were at their peak of activities and success, and so were many other Lisgar clubs. Happy as the times were, however, the Canadian Forces were intent on recruiting men for the Korean War in 1953. The *Vox* conducted a poll in which 50% of the students believed that nuclear energy and weapons would preserve mankind, and an equal percentage believed that there could not be a Third World War. The poll also revealed that only 60% of Lisgarites intended to go to University. Lisgar Collegiate Institute underwent a number of physical changes: the library was remodelled; World War I and II memorial plaques were hung in the main entrance hallway, and more trophy cases were installed where we could display our many awards.

—Vox Lycei, 1983-84

ELEANOR BATES DUNN, 1951-1955

September 1951. Lisgar Collegiate—where I'm about to enter Grade 10. It's the fourth school for me in as many years. York, Rockcliffe, Elmwood and now Lisgar. I am apprehensive. Will I know anybody? Will it be easy to make friends? High school friendships are cemented in Grade 9. It's not easy for newcomers to break into established cliques.

Canada is at war. Some place near China called Korea. We don't call it a war, however. It is an "action"—but no one seems to be able to explain what the difference is between a war and an action. We are afraid of the Communist menace. Russia and China are the big enemies. We take two newspapers at home, the *Evening Citizen* and the *Evening Journal*, plus *Life* and *Time*, so I'm well up on the subject of the Red Peril and Korea. Earlier in the year, General Douglas MacArthur did

In a *Time* magazine issue, June, 1955, prize-winning writer and graduate of Lisgar, Paul Quarrington posed for Karsh for a Canadair ad springing from the anxious years of the Cold War between East and West.

This is the first school I've been to where we change classrooms for each class. Going down the stairs, we are told to keep right. Same for going up stairs. We are extremely orderly. Nobody steps out of line.

In the winter, I get to school by streetcar. In the summer, I ride a bicycle. I carry a lunch and sometimes I eat in the cafeteria, but most days I eat in one of the classrooms which has been set aside for students who brown bag.

The gym at Lisgar is neat. There are pillars in the middle of the floor. Those in the know say this is what gives Lisgar its advantage in basketball. The Coach builds the pillars into the defense. Whatever, it works. Our senior and junior teams are constant winners. We are not so hot at football, but we loyally support our teams on Football Fridays—when they play in such locations as the University of Ottawa stadium—almost directly opposite Lisgar, across the canal, or over at the St. Pat's field. The big event is the season final—games are played at Lansdowne Park.

Lisgar is not a big school in terms of number of students. There are five Grade 10 classes, an equal number of Grade 11 and 12 classes but the number drops off for Grade 13. A lot of the girl students leave at the end of Grade 12, to go to Normal School or into nursing. Some go to work in the government or the Met Life.

There are four public high schools in the city—Lisgar, Glebe, Commerce and Tech. Nepean would join the group in 1951 when the city annexed Westboro. Catholic girls go to Immaculata, the Rideau Street or Gloucester Street convents. Catholic boys go to St. Pat's, the University of Ottawa High School or LaSalle Academy on Sussex. We keep pretty much to ourselves, although St. Pat's boys would frequently turn up at Lisgar dances.

There are a lot of Jewish students at Lisgar. I don't find this strange. There were a lot of Jewish students at York, not surprising as the Jewish community in the city was pretty much located in parts of Lowertown and Sandy Hill. I meet an old friend from York, Marsha Katzman.

I have made some other friends. Sheena McGibbon, like me, is another transplant. Daphne Berlin is interesting. She lives north of Hull on the Mine Road and has horses. I sometimes ride to her place on Saturday on my bicycle.

his old soldier thing and faded away. I am an admirer of President Truman. He seems to be much more a man of action than our grandfatherly prime minister, Louis St. Laurent. I enjoyed reading in *Time* about how President Truman wrote a music critic who hadn't liked his daughter's singing—I understood about the beefsteak for the eye, but I wasn't sure what the president meant when he said the critic would need a supporter for down below when the president got through with him.

Lisgar is certainly an interesting school. The top floor is locked off with iron gates. Nobody goes up there—although there are all sorts of rumour about the place. Somebody tells me the top floor was used as a rifle range to train Lisgar boys in the cadets during the war.

Scholastically, Lisgar is reputed to be tops. I do well in Latin but I have an advantage—I had Latin in Grade 9 at Elmwood. Latin is one of the courses we all have to take—English, French, Maths, Science, History are the others. Options are limited to Shops (boys only), Home Economics (for the girls), Art and Geography. I choose Geography and do well, thanks to *Life* magazine. We all have to take Gym—the girls dislike it, mainly because of the hideous gym suits—blue bloomers—which we have to wear.

Mr. Showman teaches Latin. Mr. Meng teaches Science. He regales us with tales of his experiences in the First War. Mr. McArthur is the History teacher. Without fail, every day Rich Little entertains us prior to class with his imitations of Mr. McArthur. Mr. McArthur is not amused.

We do not have a music program at Lisgar. The school orchestra is made up of people who own their own instruments. Evelyn Feldman plays the piano. Sol Gunner plays violin as does Anne Tolmie. The orchestra performs at assemblies, the Lord's Prayer is recited, the principal, Mr. Strader, reads announcements. Sometimes the school choir sings.

There are a lot of clubs at Lisgar—something for everyone, depending upon your interest. Some clubs, such as the Audio-Visual Club, are restricted to boys only. Girls aren't supposed to be interested in learning how to operate sophisticated equipment such as slide and movie projectors.

Our entertainment consists of going to football and basketball games, or participating in sports ourselves. Skating is popular in winter. I am lucky in that my parents can afford to give me skis. We also go to movies—every Saturday a gang of us go to the show at the Capitol, the Centre, the Regent or the Linden where they always have a double feature matinee. We read movie magazines and we have photos of our favourites stuck to the inside of our locker doors with sticky tape.

There is not too much socializing between boys and girls in Grade 10. We go to sock hops, but the girls all stand on one side of the gym and the boys on the other. Older students are more daring. They actually dance. A lot of girls get tired of waiting for boys to ask them to dance and they dance together. We do not go to the more formal dances such as the Spring Prom. You need a date for those affairs. Besides, our parents aren't too keen on us growing up too fast and don't encourage dating. Platonic friendships between boys and girls aren't encouraged much either. These could lead to trouble.

Skirts and blouses, or a jumper and blouse are normal school attire. Nobody— not even the boys—wears jeans. We like Football Fridays because in addition to getting out of school early, we can wear slacks. The boys wear leather oxfords or loafers, the girls wear saddle shoes, oxfords or penny loafers—all leather and always well polished. Some of the richer girls have twin sets—a matching cardigan and pullover. We learn to sleep at night with our hair in pin

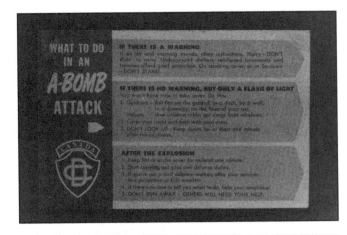

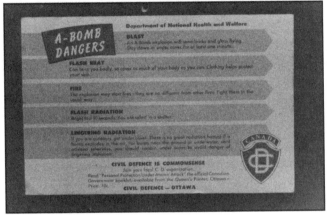

During the Cold War as the East and West built arsenals of atomic bombs and children lived in this life-threatening environment, signs like these were posted in schools.

curls. The boys sport crewcuts but there are a few who adopt the DA or "Duck's Ass" greaser style.

We are well-behaved. We respect our parents and do what we are told. We respect our teachers too, and do what we are told. Most of us come from homes where "spare the rod and spoil the child" is more than just a platitude. If you get into trouble at school and your parents are called, you will likely get ten times worse at home. No rebels in this group! Most of us come from two-parent homes. Those who have only one parent most likely lost their dads in the war. Kids from divorced homes are few and far between. It is pretty rare for somebody's Mom to go out to work—unless she is a war widow.

By year end, my circle has expanded to include Marvel Miller and Joyce Harwood. We are starting to notice boys and all of us have developed "crushes." Boys become the main topic of conversation over cherry cokes at the Connaught, and the subject of endless phone conversations. Maybe our social lives will improve in Grade 11. Meanwhile, there are yearbooks to sign and plans to be made for how we're going to spend the summer of 1952. September seems a long time away. . .

* * * * *

> One morning at an assembly a "streaker" ran across the stage. Mr. McMichael, the principal, asked people, "Who was that?" "We don't know, sir," everybody replied, "we didn't recognize his face."

September 1952. How did you spend your summer vacation? Camp Davern for two weeks. Riding bike to Rockcliffe Air Base to visit Sheena and swim in the base pool. Trip with parents to U.S. New blue jeans. Go to movies. See *High Noon* with Gary Cooper, the year's Oscar winner for Best Actor. No swimming at Britannia or day at the EX. Parents too afraid of polio scare. From the lofty perspective of Grade 11, the Grade Nines look small. And there are more of them than there were last year. There is a major hole across Lisgar Street. They are working on the long-awaited new gymnasium. It will be connected to the school by— wonder of wonders—a tunnel under the street! Lisgar never had much of a schoolyard anyway. Football practice is now confined to a small piece of greensward closer to the canal.

I am struggling with Geometry and Physics. I can get by in Geometry by memorizing the theorems and hopefully picking up a mark or two on the problems. I cannot grasp this subject. Physics is equally as bad. Mr. Fitzsimmons teaches Physics. He has reddish hair and a military moustache with waxed ends. He wears tweed jackets and a scarf called an ascot. Very dapper — the British aviator look when the aviators weren't flying.

Latin is going well. As is English and History. French is not a favourite subject. All those tenses and all those verbs. But the tortures of Geometry and Physics are worse than anything. My friends seems to do well in math—especially Sheena and Joyce.

Marvel Miller has introduced us to the wonders of *Seventeen* magazine. Oh, if we could only get to the U.S. Dreams of Jonathan Logan dresses, Ship n' Shore shirts and Capezio shoes! I am following the U.S. elections in *Life* and *Time*. My parents speak in admiration of Adlai Stevenson. But he goes down to defeat at the hands of General Eisenhower. Richard Nixon, the vice-presidential candidate is also in the news. He goes on television and tells the country about his wife's cloth coat and his little dog Checkers.

Square-dancing is all the rage. Princess Elizabeth and her husband, Prince Philip (Boy, is he handsome) visit Ottawa and are entertained by Governor General Vincent Massey—the first Canadian to hold the office. One of their entertainments is square-dancing. The royal cachet has made it fashionable. We learn later that the Princess wasn't too sure she should participate in such strenuous activity— what with being preggers with Prince Charles.

There is more talk of communists in the civil service. That's about the only exciting thing going on in the city.

Mr. St. Laurent still sits on Parliament Hill and Leslie Frost is secure at Queen's Park. It is a conservative time and we are conservative too. There are no political clubs at school and no thoughts of protesting anything ever enter our heads. We are consumed with schoolwork and dream of what our answer might be if someone asked us for a date.

A new girl joins the gang in the lunch room. Her name is Maija and she is from Latvia. She has a number tattooed on her left arm—a souvenir of Hitler's camps. She is a "DP" or Displaced Person.

Sad news. A former Lisgarite has been killed in Korea. Alex Grey. His sister, Marjorie, is a fellow student. One of the McNabb twins, Don, also dies—of pleurisy of all things. He played Junior hockey, which sort of set him apart from the crowd.

The basketball team does well. Ernie Zoppa and Dick Charron and John Justinich and Bob McAskin are big stars.

We are mad about Johnnie Ray. His hits "Cry" and "The Little White Cloud That Cried" are our favourites. Parents can't stand Johnnie Ray. They much prefer Perry Como. We go to the Rideau Theatre and are given funny glasses to watch the 3-D movie *Bwana Devil*. We are mad for William Holden in *Stalag 17*.

In March 1953, Stalin dies. Little do we know it, but 1953 is going to be a big year for world events.

Grade 11 is really a "nothing" year. I am glad I have passed all my courses. We talk about what Grade 12 will be like. For some of us, it will be their last year as they move on to Normal School, nursing school or the working world. I am thinking about university—but what will I study? What will I be? Anything having to do with science or maths is out— I'm a dunce on both counts. Miss Lashley suggests I might consider something involving English. I'll think about it over the summer. . .

* * * * *

September 1953. I have spent the summer working as a counsellor at Camp Davern. We are paid the grand sum of $100 for the entire summer—more money than I've ever had to call my own. I buy a Brownie camera and start a new hobby.

The Korean War has ended but there is a new place-name in the news we are starting to become familiar with—a place called Dienbienphu where the French are fighting— somewhere in Indochina.

Princess Elizabeth is now Queen Elizabeth.

A couple of other exciting things happened during the summer. I got a driver's licence and Sheena's father bought a TV set. Little do we know what an effect this will have on our lives. Little do I know, as I sit comfortably in the McGibbon living-room watching Jackie Gleason, that I will regularly appear on TV someday as will Adrienne Poy.

Lois Leadley Bourne, class of '52 kept this photograph, a great collection of the would-be musicians amongst her classmates, Jim Dunlop and Cecil "Bucky" Brown on guitar, the others alas, forgotten. In this submission to the Lisgar Archives she writes, "—my brother Allen Bourne was a cheerleader—remember those pre-game rousing yells in the Auditorium?—Allen was part of the 'Spike Jones' imitation band at showtimes—I wish I could send 'memory pictures' of the 'Romberg' concert, first dance in the new gym, bats in Mr. Proctor's class, slabs of marble falling off the walls with a crash, Mr. Mann taking us through 'Hamlet'—"

Principal J.W. Strader presented the first "L's" ever awarded by the Students' Council to eight members of the graduating class for outstanding service to the school over a period of four or five years. Front row, left to right; Janet Swerdfager, Marjorie Nicholson, Sally MacDonald, Norma Nicolaiff. Front row, left to right; guest speaker, R.G. Robertson, then Deputy Minister of Northern Affairs and National Resources, Fergus Oliver, Neville Poy, Morton Low, Donald MacNabb.

Grade 12. The Grade Nines are even smaller this year. And there are more of them still. This is the year of decision. Make sure I have the credits to carry on into Grade 13 and the credits to get into university.

Mr. Felker teaches chemistry. Unfortunately I am not one of his prize pupils. I am pretty good at memorizing stuff, but somehow all those formulas seem to escape me. I am having trouble with algebra too. Better concentrate on Latin. University entrance requires Latin or two maths. It's doubtful that I'll make entrance through one math course in Grade 13, let alone two.

Some of us are taking Grade 13 subjects as options. I am taking history. Sheena and some of the other math whizzes are taking trigonometry.

Our social lives are improving. Yes, we are being asked out on dates—funny, isn't it, how the guys you really think are neat haven't any time for you—but we are having a good time. There are dances at school and our crowd organizes house parties, always carefully chaperoned by parents. The guys in the gang include Norman May, Tim Murray, Sol Gunner, Dave Alexandor, George Wall and my friend Fred from St. Pat's. We organize costume parties and on other occasions we get out our best party duds. I record every event for posterity with my camera.

The big event of the year is the opening of the new gym. Now that's a party! Parents and students throng the place for the official opening which includes a dance. I am playing basketball on the senior girls' team. The new gym is great—there are seats for spectators, decent change rooms and even showers, although few of the girls use them. The only thing that hasn't changed are the blue bloomers. How come we can't have more modern gym attire—like shorts—we ask? The reason we hate the bloomers so much is that the guys make fun of us when they see us wearing them.

We are still going to movies—but with male companions. Marilyn Monroe is in all the fan mags. There are rumours that she's having a romance with Joe Dimaggio.

The polio scare has subsided. An American doctor has discovered that gamma globulin injections are effective in preventing the dread disease. The Communist menace is still around. Russian tanks are sent to quell an uprising in East Berlin. *The Old Man and The Sea* by Ernest Hemingway is reprinted in *Life*. We are reading *MacBeth* in English class. I enjoy reading and spend a lot of time at the public library where I try and get the latest bestsellers. A silly song, "Doggie in the Window" is a big hit for Patti Page.

I drive the family car a lot. With wheels, we go to Lakeside Gardens, the Ranch House and Teskey's at Hog's Back. Sheena's father gets her a little car—it is an ancient Austin. Most of the guys in the crowd have access to cars also. We like to go to the stock car races at Lansdowne Park.

Sharon Wilson is leaving at the end of the year to go to Normal School. Anne Tighe is going too—to take a secretarial

You are cordially invited to attend the
Graduation Ball
presented by the Central Students' Council
at the Lisgar Gymnasium
on Friday evening, May thirteenth
nineteen hundred and fifty-five
at nine o'clock

$4.00 per couple
Please present at door

Bill MacCauley's Orchestra
Dress Semi-Formal—Free Corsage

Eleanor Bates Dunn and her escort George Wall entering the gym for the Graduation Ball, 1955.

course. Sheena has decided to follow in her mom's footsteps and become a nurse—but she's going to take a BSc. Her father says that if she's going to spend five years in school she might as well become a doctor. Joyce is going into nursing too as is Marsha Katzman, but they're coming back for Grade 12. Marvel won't be back. She's heading for nursing, but will do Grade 13 at Alma College. I am still not sure what I want to do. I send off for some pamphlets from some nursing schools. I explore the idea of becoming a teacher.

I have to write the chemistry and algebra final exams and the provincial exam in Grade 13 history. I barely squeeze through in algebra and I fail chemistry. I will have to repeat it—thank goodness Grade 13 history is out of the way. It's too bad they don't have summer school for people who fail subjects. . .

* * * * *

September 1954. Another summer spent as a counsellor at Camp Davern. Frances Meredith was a counsellor too. I have been following the Army-McCarthy hearings in *Time* and everybody is talking about the amazing Roger Bannister and his feat—breaking the four-minute mile.

Grade 13. The Grade Nines really look like little kids this year. This is the year when I really have to buckle down. I have dropped maths in favour of Latin. I am having another go at Grade 12 Chemistry and not finding it any easier the second time around. I enjoy Botany and Zoology, including the dissections—first the worm, then the frog, finally the cat. Miss Bishop, my English teacher, is helping me focus on what I want to do after this year. She thinks I have a talent for writing. I am looking into the Journalism Program at Carleton College, but I go off on the Thanksgiving trip to Queen's anyway—just to see the place and what it has to offer. (We visit the medical school where some students are working on cadavers. I guess you eventually get used to the formaldehyde stink. The cadavers are quite pickled and leathery in appearance).

I am playing basketball again this year on the seniors and we are doing pretty well in the league. I am also refereeing intramural girls' basketball. Gives me something to do over the noon hour. There is a new school in the league this year—Fisher Park. First new high school opened in Ottawa in eons, so they say.

Christmas exams go pretty well, except for that dratted Chemistry. It has become the albatross around my neck like in the *Rhyme of the Ancient Mariner*. We are gearing up for the school concert. It will be a major undertaking and I have been put on the Publicity Committee. I get written up in Austin Cross's column in the *Evening Citizen* and I get to appear on Gord Atkinson's radio program on CFRA. Austin Cross compliments me on my handwriting.

Rich Little, of course, is one of the headliners with his impressions of Ed Sullivan. I am familiar with Ed Sullivan and "Toast of the Town" thanks to the fact my father has finally relented and purchased a TV set. We have our own quartet—The Blue Tones—Bill Altow, Ken Mirsky, Jim Dempsey and Mike Rasminsky. Everyone is into male quartets as a result of the great success of the Crew Cuts, with "Sh-Boom" and the Four Aces with "Three Coins in the Fountain" "Standing on the Corner" and other hits. The Boys Hi-Y Shakespearean Guild puts on a performance of *Julius Caesar* which would make poor old Shakespeare roll over in the grave. Players include Bob De Pencier, Hugh Hiscox, Norm May, Dave Alexandor, Tim Murray, A.J. Quarrington and Bob Maudsley. Pat Presland demonstrates her tap dancing skills and the Girls Hi-Y production number features Eleanor Biggar, Pat Blackwell, Alison Burns, Diane Davidson, Judy Delaute, Carol McMehan, Fran Meredith, Nancy Pritchard and Helen McKnight. The concert is sort of a "last hurrah" for many of us. There's an air of finality about it.

Lisgar has a music program this year, instruments and all. Sheena, Joyce and I are taking music as an option. Joyce is concentrating on her French horn. I have been assigned to the clarinet and Sheena gets the bass fiddle. Trying to squeeze that fiddle into her little Austin to take it home to practice is an almost impossible task.

In April, we realize a dream, and during the Easter vacation Sheena, Joyce, Barb Smith and I head off for Syracuse, N.Y. with me behind the wheel. A generation of cross-border shoppers has been born. We have saved our pennies and we splurge on all sorts of things we have only read about in *Seventeen* magazine.

The senior boys win the city championship, proving once again that basketball supremacy is Lisgar's. We write the final exams. Every Grade 13 student in the province writes exactly the same exam in each subject. Then we anxiously await the results. Sheena will be going to Queen's, Joyce is heading for nursing school at the Hotel Dieu Hospital in Pembroke. Marsha is enrolling in nursing at the Civic. For me, J-school and my date with Elvis lie ahead. . .

* * * * *

There was something bittersweet about the summer of '55. I worked at the Met Life as a clerk to earn money for college. We held a series of house parties—looking at the photos of the last one, in August 1955 at Joyce's, I see a group of young people—girls in semi-formals and guys in suits—all looking forward to what the future would bring. We knew that come Labour Day, the gang would be breaking up. Some of us kept in touch, but time and other interests took their toll. Lisgar was a memorable experience for me, and two teachers had a great deal of influence on me—Dorothy Lashley and Dorothy Bishop. They set me on the road to a sometimes weird and sometimes wonderful career that has lasted some thirty-four years.

THE 1960s

School life in the '60s continued on in similar style; however, transitions were in occurence. The suits and bouffant hairdos worn by Lisgarites were replaced by mini skirts and long hair. Nevertheless, the students were the same thinking and feeling people concerned with life and living. One head boy stressed the importance of completing Grade 13; he himself had returned to complete his education after six years away from school. He had a wife and daughter by this time. There were the common complaints of seniors being disinterested with school and its activities. However, the Vietnam war affected them very much. One contribution to the *Vox* was a letter from Saigon: "It is a war that turns the Vietnamese against each other and has Americans fighting for something they don't even have themselves, if that is not wrong."

—*Vox Lycei*, 1983-84

MRS. ELEANOR TODD, 1956-1972

The first highlight for me regarding Lisgar was the day I met Mr. F.G. Patton when he was Director for Ottawa Board of Education. I was chairperson of "Home and School" for Carleton Heights and he came to our school to give us a most interesting talk on Education in Ethiopia (now Eritrea). After that he asked me if I was a teacher and wanted my credentials. "Just what we need at Lisgar" said he, and told me about the plan of Accelerated Classes. I was really interested in that. However I had two more years to carry on my Nursery School at our home, when by then, our last child would be ready for Grade 1. The Ottawa Board of Education did not forget and I was at Lisgar the Fall of '56. I was happy to be there and working with Mathematics again.

In the 1966 Junior Math Contest Randolph Franklin was third out of 7500. Randolph's first year at Lisgar. 1967 Junior Math Contest, Randolph Franklin, Robert Fedosejevs and Gayle Benson were the champions of the province, and Randolph was the top student in the province. I remember when I picked out the three to go into the contest. Gayle said she could not make it. But, with the boys and me urging her, we won! Soon after that Dr. Kenneth D. Fryer came to Lisgar to present the University of Waterloo Provincial Shield to our winning team. Also, at the ceremony, the University of Ottawa awarded a shield to Lisgar Collegiate in recognition of the fact that its students achieved together the best record among Ottawa Secondary Schools in the Math Contest.

In 1967 we stood third in the province in the Senior Contest with Erik Lockeberg, Alex Lightstone and Randolph. Randolph and Erik were the only two Ottawa high school students to place at the top of the International Math Contest. A total of thirty-five winners in Canada and the United States were named for a list of thousands of students competing.

Cheerleaders continued a tradition at Lisgar football games. Left to right; Stephany Laird, Chris West, Diane Peachy, Arta Zoldners, Pat Peacock, Naomi Fudemoto.

Skirts went up, and up.

Lisgar voted to have both a Head Girl and Head Boy. Elizabeth Baird and Bruce Laffin led for the 1969-70 term. In a word to the student body in the *Vox Lycei* they observed, "It is often said that at the high school and university age we tend to think that we know it all. At the beginning of our executive term, we too, thought that we had all the answers. As this year passed, though, we came to realize we didn't know it all then, and would probably never come close to achieving all the answers."

The 1960s was not only a time of rebel students but also, it would appear, a time of rebel teachers. The lad on the kiddy bike is teacher Peter Kerslake, then head of the English Department.

Randolph, 14, was in Grade 11; Erik, 16, was a Grade 13 student. In 1968 Randolph stood 2nd in the Senior Contest; in 1968 he stood 26th in the Math Problems Paper; in 1969 he stood 2nd in the Senior Contest; 1969 he stood 1st in the Math Problems Paper out of 806. Also Robert Fedosejevs stood 9th in the Math Problems Paper.

Joyce Lu in 1971 was the 4th in the Ontario Senior Math Problems Paper—the best after Randolph. Sheila Embleton, with Joyce, was 15th. Joyce achieved a 98% scholastic average in Grade 13 at Lisgar—the highest in the Ottawa area. At Commencement in 1971 she was given all the Awards and Scholarships for Mathematics.

The last time I saw Joyce was when she came home from Radcliffe College for the February Break. She asked my husband and me for dinner with her parents. She seemed to be happy at the College except, she said, she was not challenged enough. That made me think of the times she would come into my room and I would give her a problem to work out on her own. Soon after she went back to the College, we were told of her sudden death. Dr. and Mrs. Benjamin Lu decided to establish the Joyce Lu

Scholarship Memorial Fund, a Mathematics prize in her memory.

* * * * *

From student Elizabeth Legg's 1992 interview with William (Bill) Fraser, Lisgar student 1956-61, later English teacher and Head of English Department:

William (Bill) Fraser at Lisgar was a very athletic young man who belonged to several teams, including football, track and field, and the high-jumping team. Although he persisted in trying out for the basketball team every year, he never succeeded in making it. Perhaps this is one of the reasons that he eventually went on to become one of the outstanding and dedicated coaches of the senior boys' basketball team at Lisgar. As well as his athletic involvement he was also a member of the Hi-Y Club, a service club associated with the YMCA. He did not join this club because of its visits to old age homes though, but for the simple reason that it was a status club.

Mr. Fraser said he particularly remembers that in his time there were still separate entrances at the school for the boys and girls and staff. As a teacher, he said the loud clanking of the heating pipes at times made hearing the teacher impossible. The classrooms were always either too hot or too cold.

On the social side Mr. Fraser remembers fondly the Grade 13 boys, the "cool ones" anyway, going out with Ridgemont girls. He explained that every lunch hour one of the guys who had a car would drive all his friends over to Ridgemont to see their girlfriends.

Although he said there were never any "food fights," Mr. Fraser does remember one event which he will never forget. He described how one teacher and one of the vice-principals marched into the cafeteria, grabbed a student and hauled him out—presumably to the main office—as the whole student body watched in stricken silence. But being a "Minor Niner," Mr. Fraser never even thought to ask what happened.

As to crime and punishment in Mr. Fraser's days, students got expelled for cheating. Detentions were given to the whole class if it was too rowdy. If a student was sent to the vice-principal's office, that meant big trouble. No smoking was allowed for a radius of one block around the school. Students were not allowed to go to their lockers between classes. Everyone had to stand up to answer questions.

Two friends remembered best by Mr. Fraser are "Moose Stanley," a football friend, and the son of an archbishop, who was caught by the vice-principal playing crap by the canal. A regular activity every lunch hour by the Rideau Canal were the crap games: one was the "big game" which involved big bills and which always had an audience; the other was a smaller game involving only nickels and dimes. Mr. Fraser particularly recalls one noon hour when he and

Old stairs at boys' entrance from basement to first floor. The steel gates were closed every night and for dances in the gym.

The old stairs from the second to the third floor. Note the old windows, the old marble wainscotting, the old oak floors and the exposed radiators.

his friends were playing a friendly game of crap down the canal. Someone happened to glance upward and there was the vice-principal peering down at them with a pad and pencil in his hand, writing down all the students' names! Including Bill Fraser's.

Another canal incident that sticks out in Mr. Fraser's mind is the time that he and his brother discovered an elderly woman's dead body in the canal. Fraser's father had driven them to school at 7:30 a.m. as usual and they had wandered over to the canal to pass the time. Since it was autumn and the water had been drained from the canal, it was hard to miss the woman's body lying before them. They returned to Lisgar and the authorities were notified. But it was not a murder mystery.

A few teachers that Mr. Fraser remembered well were Mr. Carruthers who had been a wrestler in university, Mr. Mann who was an inspiring English teacher, and Miss Bishop, an English teacher as well who could "rip you apart" with her powerful smile. "If her smile was directed at you," Mr. Fraser said, "you knew you were in trouble."

According to Mr. Fraser, there were two types of guys: the hard rocks who slicked back their hair into a duck's tail, wore dark jackets with the collar up, and were said to be "the tough guys;" and then there were the "clean" ones who wore button-down shirts and cotton slacks. No jeans or shorts were allowed. White athletic socks were thought to be "cool." Many people wore desert boots, Hush Puppies and white bucks.

During Mr. Fraser's time at Lisgar as a student, another memorable incident occurred one day in Math class between a student named Mike Heenan and teacher Carruthers, the ex-wrestler. The students were being rowdy—talking excessively and throwing chalk—and Mr. Carruthers was about to punish the whole class when Mike Heenan stood up to take the blame, not out of consideration or selflessness, Mr. Fraser observed, but just to be a smart-ass. Of course, Mr. Carruthers was not about to let this opportunity slip through his fingers so he invited Mike Heenan to the front of the class and told him to face the blackboard. After Mike did this, Mr. Carruthers delivered a hard cuff to the back of Heenan's head, causing him to hit the chalkboard face first, and stagger back to his seat.

* * * * *

For Janet Fader's 1992 oral history project, student Catrione Sturton interviewed Lisgar alumni David Jeanes, 1961-65.

David Jeanes went to school in Ottawa because Gloucester, where he lived, didn't have a high school. His neighbours attended Rideau, Hillcrest, and Lisgar before Gloucester built a high school. Throughout his years at Lisgar Mr. Jeanes was in the Accelerated programme. This meant that you graduated in four instead of five years, by skipping Grade 11 and fitting its courses into the other years. As a result there

In October, 1968, hundreds of ex-Lisgarites returned to their old high school for the one hundred and twenty-fifth reunion, a three-day conglomerate of archival displays, parades, feasting, dancing, sports nights and play-offs, speeches, special assemblies, photographic opportunities, discoveries of long-lost friends and classmates, meetings with favourite teachers, and tours of the school—including the old shooting gallery and bats on the Fourth Floor.

were very few electives. In Grade 9 there was a choice between Latin and typing. At the time no one thought that typing was important unless you wanted to be a secretary, so everyone took Latin.

Mr. Jeanes felt that the teachers who taught at the school were very old and had been there for a long time. Mr. Neil was the principal and Mr. McMichael was the V.P. One teacher that Mr. Jeanes remembers particularly is Mr. Lou Meng. Mr. Meng was the oldest teacher at Lisgar, and was a veteran of Vimy Ridge in World War I. He would spend at least half of every class telling them war stories. He never actually taught them anything about science. He would just point them to their textbooks to read for themselves.

Another teacher, Mr. Rentner, was the math teacher. He was remembered for his love of palindromes (note the spelling of his name). Many of the teachers still referred to the Grades as "Forms."

Mr. Jeanes' Grade 9 homeroom and Geography teacher, Mr. Wadell, encouraged his students to join the AVA—the Audio Visual Aids Club. Students had to pass a series of tests such as carrying a heavy tape-recorder from the basement to the third floor, threading film on to a projecter in sixty seconds, loading a projector in the darkness. This was made more difficult by the fact that the equipment

was more cumbersome that it is today. In Grade 12 David Jeanes was the president of the AVA.

The AVA did the sound and lighting for dances, skits and plays. Assemblies were held every few weeks. Lisgar was overcrowded so, during assemblies half the students went to the auditorium and the other half would listen over the P.A. System. At assemblies a passage from the Bible was read by a student—which Mr. Jeanes did several times. They always sang the school song.

One very exciting thing that happened was the chocolate bar sale. A sort of mania gripped the school. Someone even composed a sales pitch song to encourage motivation to sell. The whole school sold chocolate bars and, in the end, raised $700 which went towards buying a trampoline for the school.

Mr. Jeanes had a friend who went to England and came back with the record of a brand new group, still unheard of in Canada. Shortly after, the Beatles released their first song, "Please Please Me," and soon everyone was talking about them. The students decided to do a "concert" (air band) to promote an upcoming event. They used the records of the new group and everyone was extremely excited.

Frank Collier, one of Mr. Jeanes' friends appeared in the concert with the "Beatles." He enjoyed it so much that it led him to become a musician. Currently he is reporting on the elections in the Philipines for the CBC.

Even the famous came back for the 125th anniversary at Lisgar, Adrienne Clarkson, Betty Kennedy, Eugene Forsey, Peter Jennings.

Mr. Jeanes remembered that in his time the staircases were for going in one direction only—one for going up and the other for going down. Boys weren't allowed to wear long hair. In fact, one of Mr. Jeanes' friends got suspended for long hair and his hair didn't even touch his collar!

When he graduated, Mr. Jeanes got a Lisgar L. He also got Lisgar silver pins for: having a high average, being head of AVA, being head of the Library Club and having a perfect attendance record for four years.

* * * * *

Wendy Hagglund wrote this piece as an assignment in English, 1992. A second generation Lisgarite, her father, Rod Hagglund, along with Herb Beall and John Boehmer, was a member of one of Wright Neil's first gifted classes at Lisgar. Mr. Hagglund is now a part of a government "think tank."

I was only eleven the day I decided that I wanted to attend Lisgar Collegiate. My older sister Andrea had finally given in to my incessant pleading and agreed to take me with her to a Lords basketball game. As I sat in the gym watching my cousin Jenny and the rest of the Lisgar team trounce Glebe, I knew I wanted to be a Lisgarite. But it wasn't the enthusiasm of the L.C.I. crowd, nor the blue and grey paint drying on my cheeks that made up my mind. It was my father's anecdotes of his Lisgar days as he reminisced on the way to the game.

For most students, choosing a high school is an individual decision based on programs and a geographical area. In my household it is definitely a family affair. My father attended Lisgar during the mid-sixties, in the days when the two buildings were still separated by a busy city street. He recalls that "The tunnel was dank and had rats," so most students opted to play a lively game of Dodge the Cars between classes. The entire area to the west of Lisgar was dominated by an expanse of the "temporary buildings" constructed during the Second World War, and Regional Headquarters hadn't even been thought of. Lisgar's interior landscape was just as different from today's as her outward surroundings. A spiral staircase wound its way from his homeroom, the Geography room in the corner of the basement to backstage in the Auditorium. His desk, and almost all others in the school, were scarred survivors from the turn of the century, with flip-up seats and inkwells, reminiscent of Anne of Green Gables. One of my father's most vivid memories, though, is of Lisgar's staircases. One was designated the "up" staircase and the other the "down," with Vice-Principal McMichael patrolling the stairs to ensure no student dared take the wrong set of steps. Dad once committed the cardinal sin of going up the down staircase and can still recall getting, as he puts it, "Royally yelled at."

Fashionwise, kids today probably wouldn't survive more than a week at Lisgar in 1962. Jeans were strictly forbidden except for two days out of the year. In preparation for the Prom or School Concert, workers were permitted to wear jeans. Of course, there was always an excess of volunteers. Tight black pants called stovepipes and long-sleeved shirts were "in" for the boys. Girls wore skirts or dresses as slacks were not allowed, and there was a constant heated debate over whether culottes (divided skirts) should be permitted.

Teachers in my father's time were an entirely different breed, particularly the Lisgar faculty. Many of them had 30 to 40 years of teaching experience and were veterans of the First World War. They were strict and commanded respect. One of my father's favourite physics teachers, Mr. Meng, seemed more like a history teacher who had missed his calling. After about five minutes of physics equations, he would switch over to lecturing on Canada's involvement in WWI. My father fondly recalls fighting up one side of Vimy

Ridge and down the other in Physics class, and can recount almost every Canadian battle of the "Great War."

My dad was never really into sports: at six and a half feet and only 15, he was too awkward for the basketball team and too tall for most other games. He does remember football as being "the" sport at Lisgar when he attended. Football Fridays were a popular event amongst the students. The administration would shorten classes every Friday when there was a game so that a large delegation of students could go and cheer on the players. The truth was that all but the diehards just went home!

My father's favourite activities were mostly academic. He was a member of Lisgar's Champion "High Time" team (comparable with Reach for the Top) and he loved to play Chess and Bridge. Unlike now, when it is one of the staple entertainments during spares, card-playing was frowned upon unless it was done in a specified room at a fixed time with appropriate supervision. So my father was forced to resort to sneaking in games before regular hours with two friends and a teacher, whose name he still will not reveal. The secret Bridge games continued merrily until one morning, while the teacher was out of the room for a moment, my father and his friends were caught "red handed" by the ever-vigilant Vice-Principal McMichael. My father's biggest surprise, though, came not when he was apprehended, but a moment later when the teacher returned to the room. Instead of springing to the boys' defence, he assumed a suitably shocked expression and nodded soberly as they were read the Riot Act. My dad recalls this as one of his prime lessons in the Realities of Life.

Interviewing my Dad about Lisgar made me realize a lot about my school and my father. I was surprised by his insistence that High School is in many ways harder today, and that his classes of rote memorization and "all-or-nothing" final exams were nothing compared to those we have now, where the emphasis is on year-round learning.

My father couldn't remember what colour the walls of the (now horribly pink) cafeteria were in his day, but he could describe in detail his locker-mate Grant's favourite

lunch of lettuce and vinegar, and the resultant smell that permeated their books. He remembers the running contest in Mr. Showman's Latin class to be able to count to ten in the largest number of languages, and Mr. Rentner the Math teacher who collected palindromes (his name was one) and could tell students what their father had scored in Algebra a quarter-century previous. Above all he let us know that Lisgar meant a tradition of learning that you could never forget.

* * * * *

VICTORIA FREEMAN, 1969-1972

Lisgar was the place where I first encountered Communists. Real Communists. Tall silent young men in dark clothing who, when they did speak, spoke with heavy accents and without definite articles. Diplomats' brats: Poles, Czechs, Bulgarians. They impressed me because they excelled at math and physics, having studied it years before in kindergarten behind the Iron Curtain.

I suppose I was first attracted to them because to my middle-class WASP sensibilities they seemed exotic. Perhaps also because I too was an outsider, not a member of the social set from Manor Park or Rockcliffe, or the tougher neighborhoods of Lower Town or Sandy Hill, but someone flown in to be a 9F suck (I was Minister of War for the McBoingBoings in the 9F war between the McBoingBoings and the Shadboltists). There was something very mysterious about these young men, especially Rysiek and Mirek, Polish twin brothers: for weeks I watched them walk by the canal at lunch hour, swaying gracefully like two tall black trees.

They sneered at things Canadian. Their father was a member of the Polish Communist Party. Rysiek, whom I fell in love with, challenged every belief I had inherited from my parents and my culture, even if he was only parroting what he had learned from his parents and his culture. On every political question our opinions were diametrically opposed, and we would argue and argue and argue—a lot of it was flirtation.

And so there were parties with vodka, Polish sausage, and tinny AM music. I learned to say "You look like a caveman" in Polish and give the Polish response to someone who sticks out his tongue: *Cows have longer ones, but they don't boast about it.* I watched countless, endless soccer games.

From the Wojtals I had my first real encounter with the heavy weight of European history, for Rysiek's mother had been forced to walk from Siberia to Berlin as part of a Soviet labour camp, and Warsaw had been virtually razed during the war. I learned about the brutal suppression of the Warsaw Uprising, about the destruction of the Warsaw Ghetto. Later, after my first year of university, I spent a month with Rysiek travelling around Poland, and ended up on my own, at the age of 18, in Moscow, the heart of the Evil Empire.

* * * * *

Hey Kids

"The Hottest Thing on Wheels"

MUSTANG '66

Zero to 90 mph in 14.7 seconds
(¼ mile drag)

Choice of High Performance Engines
289 cu. in.   200 hp   4400 rpm
289 cu. in.   271 hp   6000 rpm

*Come in anytime to Ottawa Motor Sales
and see this "Bomb"*

Also on display Ford Galaxie-Fairlane-Falcon available in convertibles, hardtops, Station Wagons, coaches and sedans.

Always a choice selection of guaranteed used cars at

1850 Bank St. (at Walkley Rd.)
733-6931

FORD
Jim Brown's
OTTAWA MOTOR SALES

THE 1970s

The start of the seventies was not without turmoil and both teachers and students expressed discontent with the school system. The teachers held back voluntary service, coaching teams, giving advice outside of their official capacity. In 1973 and again in 1975 the teachers went on strike. Students began challenging the curriculum and teaching methods of the staff. A grievance committee was established to act as an intermediary for the voicing of suggestions between faculty and students. Several experiments were undertaken, including 80-minute classes and shortened lunch hours.

Concerns for LCI did not dwindle—in fact, the future of Cartier Square was questioned as was that of the school. Over 13,000 concerned people were present at a meeting to "Save Lisgar" and in 1974 plans for renovations were under way. The final result was a combination of modern, (carpets in the hallway), and traditional, (the architecture), when renovations were completed for the start of the 1977 school year. The newly remodeled school was ceremoniously opened and many proud Lisgarites celebrated the changes.

—*Vox Lycei*, 1983-84

* * * * *

MARY KETTLES, 1933-38 AND 1968-88

When I graduated from Lisgar in 1938, it never occurred to me that 30 years later I would be back at Lisgar as a teacher and Head of a Department at that. I wonder what my First

---

ANECDOTE—CIRCA 1970
(GLEBE'S 50TH ANNIVERSARY)

A carload of Glebe Collegiate Senior Boys arrived "en masse" to attack the hallowed halls of Lisgar!

While they were inside playing their pranks— and I don't clearly recall what those pranks were—our boys, led by Ian MacKenzie, carried out their tasks at hand.

Those Glebe guys thought they had been so smart— little did they know they had been outwitted! When they made for the "getaway car" with the Lisgar lads hot on their heels, they were astonished to find that their trusty vehicle would not start.

Only after they had gone slinking down the street with their tails between their legs did we discover the reason for this technical difficulty. The distributor cap had mysteriously disappeared.

—Catherine (Hart) Rayment, 1967-72

Form Geography teacher, Mr. Fair, would have thought. His comment on my October interim report had been "strict attention necessary." Maybe his admonition had its effect.

One of Lisgar's strongest points was, and still is, its great mix of people. With their broad background of races, traditions, economic status, and interest, they develop a school which is a real mosaic. On my first day back as a teacher, I had just finished the usual routines with my Grade 9 class when two girls arrived at the door. One was newly arrived from Poland with very few words of English, the other, a Grade 13 girl of Polish background. The older girl translated, and helped the newcomer, Stasia, through the routines of the day. For the first few weeks she came around occasionally to make sure Stasia was becoming adjusted. Such wonderful support! In the same class was a Korean girl who'd been in Canada just a few months. Her English was very limited too. By Friday, those two girls were walking around the halls together. . .sisters in that, though they couldn't communicate much with each other, they couldn't communicate with the rest of the class at all. Remember the year we had something like eleven different nationalities on the soccer team? We won the championship that year.

Well do I remember that out-of-school Education program in the spring of 1971. Many students were involved in activities far removed from the classroom. Rene Charron took some students to Quebec City to experience the French milieu. Ian Waddell took his Accelerated Class to Toronto and Niagara. The History Department took busloads to Kingston. Miss Forward took Home Economic girls to Upper Canada Village. Craig Stratton took two groups of students to his farm. Some of my students were greatly impressed by the reminiscences of his uncle, well into his eighties. He told them things even Stratton had never heard before. Barrie Laughton, Stephen Cheung and I took 69 students by train to Moosonee, the "end of steel." The first night we catnapped on the train en route to Cochrane. Some got up to see the sunrise. At Cochrane they got out of the train to work off steam, and some of them began throwing Frisbees. Up to that point, Mr. Cheung had seemed to be wondering what he'd got himself into. But he suddenly hopped off the train and said, "Do you mind if I join you?" He was the star Frisbee tosser. His reticence simply evaporated. A few minutes after our arrival at Moosonee, a couple of students from the high school were shooting for the basket in the gym. One tossed a basketball to one of our students, and, as spontaneously as that, an unusual informal basketball game was going on. We spent the night in Moosonee, crossed to Moose Factory on an island in the river, and watched the ebb and flow of the tide.

I particularly remember field trips. On one, Grade 13 students went via Hawkesbury, Vankleek Hill and Beauharnois to Montreal. I remember the gasp when the students suddenly saw the generating station and the falls in front of them. After visiting the ALCAN plant we had lunch and saw a

The first Pollution Action Committee at Lisgar, 1973-74. Lisgar was to set a precedent and become a model for other city, regional and national schools. Left to right; Liz Hamilton, Roy Williams, Ann Trevithick, Morna McLeod (Pres.), Anthony Burton, Janice Munro, Philip Hanna, Francisco Alvarez, Cathy Bystram, Cathy Alexander. Absent; Paul Sibbeth.

Of all the fly-by-night mutinous activities and clubs to arise at Lisgar during this decade, perhaps the most expressive of pure rebellion was SNURD described by its organizers as "a national organization dedicated to prolong, indeed create and maintain a form of sanity in everyday existence. It sneers at intrepid hypocrisy. It questions what is taken for granted. It is one branch of the tree of life." Back row, left to right; Gazim Snurd, Metratroid Snurd, Bilbo Snurd, Alfonsatekc Snurd, Braxa Snurd. Front row, left to right; Ams Snurd, Ooklidd Snurd (R. Bos.), Magellan Snurd (Head writer and Philosopher), Grunion Snurd (Head Broad), Cranston Snurd (Mastermind). Founded by Doug Brierley and Craig Fordney, SNURD stood for Student National Union for Recreational Development. Callidak, an off-shoot, was the brainstorm of Alan Taylor.

boat go through the locks. As we turned from the locks, one of the boys grinned at me. "It's been a great day, and we haven't even got to Montreal yet." Those are the things that make teaching worthwhile.

What did I appreciate most about teaching at Lisgar? Associating with staff and students. There were a lot of rugged individuals in both. I learned a lot from other staff members and from students. I think they learned some things from me. My aim was always to get them into situations where they had to open their eyes, see things for themselves. That's what education is all about.

Many thanks to all the students who kept me alert. I'll never forget the reaction of a Grade 9 class the last day I ever taught. They wanted to know why I was retiring. Nothing I said seemed to satisfy them. On the spur of the moment, I asked them if they liked doing homework. They wondered what I was driving at. Then I told them I started doing homework in Grade 1. "I've been doing homework for fifty years and I'm tired of it." That satisfied them.

* * * * *

Head of Social Sciences, Janet Morchain in 1992 described her observations and sensations on coming to Lisgar in 1973:

My experience had been totally at suburban schools, new, squeaky clean, indifferent. Three different suburban schools, all similar. I came to the old Lisgar before renovations. I cherish that experience. I noticed the iron-wrought staircases, the marble on the stairs and in the washrooms. The stained glass windows. The castle-like exterior. I had never seen anything like that elsewhere. I noticed the students studying in the old window seats, in various nooks and crannies. Never seen before at other schools. I noticed the orchestra in the pit—quite unique.

I noticed the bookroom at the back of my classroom, the spiral staircase going up to the auditorium. Students escaped up this staircase when the lights went out for a film. One of the many old books in this bookroom was coverless, and entitled *Our Kings and Queens*. On the last page, I found that "Our Present King" was Edward VII, still living. I could not believe how traditional the texts and the approach to teaching. In my own department, no one had taught outside of Lisgar Collegiate. Not a woman in sight. Teachers on the

Students' Council, 1977-78. Back row, l to r; David Littlejohn, (Head Boy), Tom Hughes, Borden Hum, Peter Hadwen, Laurie MacDonald, Monica Mueller, James Forester, Manof Bhatia, Chris Parsons, Martin Smith, Kate Nelles. Third row; Marina Schein, Susan Li, Lisa Clarke, May Zayed, (Head Girl), Pat Whitridge, Sylvia Uhthoff, Peter Uhthoff, Simon Tooke, Jonathan Tsao, Alan Riddell, J.C. Declerck, Tom Waddell, David Mount. Second row; Kathryn Seymour, Eva Bild, Naomi Thomson, Bradley Adshead, Brant Mossop, Carmen Scaffidi, Philip Fleming, Magda Kwilecki, Sandy Salmins. Front row; Conrad Fernandez (Chairman), Debbie McKinnon, Kim Knox, Marysia Bucholc, Robin Leckie. Absent; Althea Brown, Chris Christensen, Lisa Christensen, Tanya Duff, Alex Graham, Masoom Haider, Kim Hannaford, Mike Harrison, Calleta Johnson, Tom Kovesi, Sindy Norton, Solda Rosas, Joanna Sinclair, Przemek Tomowski, Geoff Wells.

staff who had gone to the school. I could not believe how well the Grade 12 history class did on their Christmas examinations. The median was nearly 90%.

I could not believe the sense of tradition, the sense of a school identity, the loyalty to the school, things considered "for the school," the suspicion of outsiders, the parents who had also gone to the school, the grandparents, the poor state of the building, the dust.

I had first heard of this school as an undergraduate at the University of Toronto years earlier. It was famous. Its name was known outside of Ottawa, like Jarvis Collegiate. When I first learned of my appointment to Lisgar's History Department, I gasped. Such was the reputation of Lisgar to an outsider. On coming to Lisgar in September 1973, I gradually sorted out what was fact and fiction, myth and truth. It has been my good fortune, by the luck of the draw, to experience the uniqueness of the old school.

* * * * *

Paul Bennett attended Lisgar in the 1970s and sat on the board of the alumni association of his old alma mater until 1993. In remembering Lisgar he chose to discuss fellow student Wayne Lennon's protesting candidacy for a seat on the Ottawa Board of Education. Wayne's election campaign symbolized the increasing "bed-fellowing" between politics and education in the 1970s and 1980s.

One of the first questions I asked Wayne Lennon ten years after his unsuccessful candidacy for the Ottawa Board of Education, was whether his long, curly pony tail would have put the average Ottawa voter off. After all, the voters were parents, not their children. Lennon immediately answered that he had never given his "image" a second thought. As soon as he announced his candidacy, he found out he needed some photographs, so the first place he headed was a $1 photo booth on Rideau Street. There was no time for a hair cut or manicure.

The 1972-73 term was only Lennon's second year at Lisgar, but he had already made his mark. He had been active as the senior Central Students' Council (CSC) representative, a member of the Dance Committee and a drummer in various bands.

According to Lennon, it was as a result of his participation as a student representative on the Lisgar Advisory Committee that he decided to run for the Board of Education. He felt that students' views were not adequately considered when it came to matters of their own education. This view was also shared by Kevin Murphy, the junior CSC Representative. At a CSC meeting, Murphy suggested that students encourage their parents to run for the Board of Education. Lennon took this one step further and decided to present himself as a candidate.

In the November, 1972, municipal elections, Wayne Lennon, a nineteen-year-old student set another Lisgar precedent by seeking a seat on the Ottawa Board of Education. He was his school's rep to the central Students' Council of Ottawa and a member of the Ottawa Board of Education's Student-Trustee Sub-Committee. Lennon said he ran because "the Ottawa Board of Education doesn't listen to the student's point of view."

Campaigning would not be easy. There were a total of 45 candidates and voting for the Board had not been divided by Wards at this point. Incumbents such as Jane Dobell and Eva Berry had an enormous advantage over unknowns like Lennon. Where would a student find campaign funds? Indeed, as the Ottawa *Citizen* pointed out, it was probably "more difficult for students to succeed as candidates because they do not have the money to launch extensive campaigns."

Lennon managed to raise $200 in campaign funds, primarily from students and their parents. One parent donated $10 because he thought it wonderful that a student should be part of the campaign. Eighty dollars of this went to his distinctive yellow signs.

Lennon chose fellow students, Rob McBride, another recent Lisgar arrival, as his campaign manager, and asked Bill Gorham, the Audio Visual Aids (A.V.A) club technician, to be his driver. Both were political neophytes, but keen. Lennon readily admits that they had no strategy and that the whole campaign was run "off the seat of their pants." Neither did he have any expectations of winning or having any major impact.

Lennon recalls the first "all candidates" meeting at which no one ventured to speak first until he broke the ice, for which he believes he probably got some credit. He also recollects that at another meeting, one voter asked whether the three student candidates had good academic marks, which would at least be some standard of measurement, in light of the fact that they had no other "track record." Lennon was able to advise that his most recent report card had entirely A's and B's!

There were several amusing or noteworthy incidents in Lennon's campaign. In order to convince the Ottawa electorate that teachers were taking the race seriously, the Ontario Secondary Schools Teachers' Federation (OSSTF) decided to back a slate based on interviews with each candidate. Lennon went into his interview well-prepared, as a congenial member of the OSSTF had provided him with the entire list of questions! Despite this tremendous advantage, Lennon was not able to secure the teachers' endorsement, as he was allegedly found "inexperienced."

The 1979 candidates for the Student Leadership Programme at Kallalla outdoor centre on Lake Notre-Dame, Quebec. The camp was established for the purpose of teaching leadership skills. Each club in the school was invited to send candidates. Back row, left to right; Chris Provencher, Kate Nelles, —Cuddington, Joyce Eagleson, Janet MacLaren, Doug Watt, Lana Stoll. Third row, l to r; —, Phil Fleming, Troy Beach, Chris Wood, Danny Lacroix, Jamie Easterwood. Second row, l to r; teacher Cathy Smith, Heather MacDonald, Rebecca Shaig, Jane Gill, Sheryl Smith, Penel Woods, Heather Watt, Alex Gill, Patricia Seymour, Elizabeth Walker, Kevin McCabe. Front row, l to r; Jane Lister, Janice Wells, Laura Hutchins, Ceilia Nelles, Kathryn Seymour, Vicki Binavince, Erika Klee, Derek Wylie, Shawn Clarke. Lying in front; teacher Heather Cobourg, Elizabeth Rennie.

Lennon did manage to secure the endorsement of the Ottawa *Citizen*, for reasons of which Lennon is not entirely certain. He recollects that while the first fifteen minutes of the interview were dedicated to educational issues, the remaining time was spent discussing the merits of the then immensely popular rock group, "Deep Purple!" Lennon was subsequently described in a *Citizen* editorial as "a wise and sensitive 19-year-old, who deserves support not as a student representative but on his own merit."

Lennon also received the endorsement of a rather multifarious group of 49 individuals known as the "Committee for a Better Board of Education." Membership on the Committee was based primarily on putting up $5 each and assessing the candidates in a rather divergent manner. A close look at the Committee names will reveal those of Robert McBride (Lennon's campaign manager) and Ross Morrison, another Lisgar student who supported Lennon's candidacy and was active in the *Lisgar Free Press*. These two ensured that Lennon's name was put forward.

Lennon recalled with a chuckle how a Glebe resident running for City Council mistakenly perceived Wayne as a

"frontrunner" and tried to ride on Lennon's coattails! The City Council candidate hired a bright double-decker bus and drove around the Glebe, storming into supermarkets distributing campaign material. While Lennon did not really approve of or participate in these tactics, he did appreciate the exposure.

As luck would have it, Lennon finished "out of the money," but in a respectable 27th place out of 45 candidates, with 4,897 votes, considerably ahead of the two other student candidates. Lennon recalls the election night campaign party, at which the results were so slow in coming in that everyone fell asleep before the tally was known. Lennon was woken up the next day by the mother of a school friend who advised him: "You lost, Wayne. Go back to sleep."

What was left after the election? Little, except "taking back the empties." While events at Lisgar resumed more or less as before (we were in the middle of a teachers' work-to-rule), there was no question that Lennon's campaign had involved Lisgar students in civic politics as they never had been before.

The Architecture of Lisgar Collegiate Institute

From its inception in 1863, until the erection of its permanent home in 1874—the precursors of the Lisgar Collegiate Institute, the Dalhousie District, the Carleton County, and the Ottawa Grammar School—occupied five different sites around the city. Repeatedly, the young institution outgrew available space and had to relocate, time and again, to accommodate an ever-increasing student body. Robert O'Brien, a long-time history teacher at Lisgar, outlines the history of these moves in his essay, "Sites and Buildings," with quotations from *A History of the O.C.I. 1843-1903*:

Prior to the erection of the Collegiate Institute building in 1874, the Grammar School had been located in five consecutive buildings. Each of the buildings had been erected for a different purpose, and not one of these purposes had anything to do with education. The first was intended for a dwelling house. The second, from its location and the way in which it was laid out, was supposed to have been intended for a wholesale store. The third was built and used as a carpenter's shop for some time. The fourth had evidently been intended for a retail store and when it ceased to be a schoolroom it became an insurance office. The fifth was said to have been intended for a boarding house. It was once rented by the trustees, and the school was removed there as soon as it was ready for occupation, in the fall of 1861.

In 1872—following passage of the 1871 Ontario Schools Act which authorized the construction of seven Collegiate Institutes across the province, one of which was to be located in Ottawa—the Board of Trustees of the Ottawa Collegiate School Board began to search for a permanent home for the school.

> **BRIEF ARCHITECTURAL HISTORY OF LISGAR COLLEGIATE INSTITUTE 1951-82**
>
> **1951**
>
> New gym building built. Tunnel built.
>
> **1976-79**
>
> Renovations to both buildings.
>
> **1982**
>
> Mall built between two buildings on Lisgar Street.

On June 17, 1872, the board of trustees acquired the land upon which the Collegiate now sits for $3,200. A squatter who was working the land at the time of purchase was persuaded to relinquish all claims to the property for the sum of one-hundred dollars. Architects W.T. Thomas and W. Chesterton and contractor George Crain, began work on construction of the Ottawa Collegiate Institute. The corner stone marking completion of the project, was laid by His Excellency Lord Dufferin on June 4th, 1874; the total cost of the building, exclusive of the heating, was $25,594. The heating system for the building "four hot air furnaces," was provided by Messrs. Blyth and Kerr; however, it became apparent that this system was inadequate:

> Thus new hot-water heating apparatus was introduced taking the place of the hot-air furnaces. This, too, was found unsatisfactory, and the Smead-Dowd system was introduced in 1888. In making this change the architect erected a huge chimney right in the centre of the main hall, near the entrance door. The new system made for some years a great improvement in the heating, but the big chimney marred terribly the main hall of the school, and darkened it considerably. [Stothers: OCI p.14]

Over the years 1874 through 1892 repairs were undertaken to compensate for usual wear on the physical plant of this school. In 1892—again due to an increase in the student population—it became necessary to expand the size of Lisgar.

Four rooms were added to South end, bringing the building out to Lisgar Street. The front of the building was faced on Lisgar Street. The "1874" stone was placed over the doorway and principal's office moved.

> On January 30, 1893, the Ottawa Collegiate Institute was ravaged by fire and classes were held at other schools in the area pending the completion of renovations following the fire. The building, somewhat modified internally, was ready for occupation on the 1st December, 1893, and the classes again assembled under one roof. There was one very marked change after the fire, and that was in the

> floors, desks and blackboards. Previously the floors were pine, the desks were all whitled and disfigured, and of the old type, with two at a desk; the blackboards were of plaster. In the new building hard-wood floors, unfortunately yet unpolished, save by spatters of ink, were put down throughout the entire school, and the new, modern, single desk was introduced into all the class-rooms. Single desks had been in a few of the rooms before the fire, but the great majority of the rooms had still the old form. Blackboards of slate, from Pennsylvania, had been put in the four new rooms, but after the fire they were introduced throughout all the class-rooms. The paint in the old building had been a two-shade French grey; now in the rooms it became terra-cotta, while the wainscotting of the hall was grained and varnished. Painted glass windows were placed over the main entrance in 1892,— at the same time that the stone steps were built—on the completion of the first addition to the original 1874 building, just as they are to be seen today. The old Library room was adapted for a Principal's room in 1892, and has been used as such ever since. [Stothers: OCI p.15-16]

Over the next fifteen years the OCI was expanded two more times. Both enlargements reflected the growing need for classroom space and facilities required by a modern educational institution. In 1903 an east wing was built which provided eight new classrooms plus improved facilities for boys in the basement. James Mather was again the architect, with the firm of Holbrook and Sutherland doing the construction work. At this time the furnaces in the school were changed from wood burning to coal, which was much cheaper. The second addition was the construction of the west wing in 1908. This new section contained classrooms, laboratories, a gymnasium, and a 1200 seat assembly hall. A city guide book reported in 1910 that "Ottawa has lately erected an addition to the collegiate institute of splendid proportions which has cost $200,000, so the school equipment will be exceptionally complete in every respect."

By 1908, "the building as we see it today was substantially completed;" however, over the years several alterations were made to the inside of the school. In 1912 the attic over the east wing was transformed into an indoor rifle range. In 1915 fire once again struck the school, but this time it was in the west wing and damage done to the boy's gym and the science rooms. The year 1923 saw the opening of the cafeteria, something which was considered an important facility in a modern school. During the 1930s the lecture theatre on the third floor was replaced by a Home Economics room while the auditorium received a projection booth for screening films and lighting school plays. In 1940 the girls' gym was removed from the third floor to make space for more science classrooms. After that the girls had to share the gym in the basement with the boys.

By the late 1940s when it was apparent that the population was again too big for the school, a new building was

Lisgar, 1902, with a belled bell tower, a missing third floor and three chimneys for fireplace heat.

Lisgar pre-renovations, 1968-69, with almost a hundred years of city dirt collected on lumberman Skead's stone exterior. Girls' entrance on Lisgar Street still used.

Somewhere in the period 1940 to 1970s fire escapes were ordered like this one, an escape hatch out of the French room and the art room windows.

Lisgar prior to 1940 and probably dated about 1935. The small wooden building peeping out on the west side of the building predates the beginning of the temporary buildings on Cartier Square. No fire escapes.

constructed across Lisgar Street to help alleviate the pressure on the school's space. In 1951 the new south building was opened, housing a new gymnasium for both the boys and the girls, in addition to increased locker and change facilities. It was linked to the old school by way of a tunnel which ran underneath Lisgar Street.

This time the building was designed by J. Albert and A.J. Haxelgrove, the Collegiate Institute Board's official architects, with Ross-Meagher Limited as contractors. Rather than mimicking the stone facade of the old school the architects chose to construct the new building out of concrete blocks faced with limestone and glass brick, giving it a much more modern look. This building was again enlarged in 1962 when a music room, an industrial arts shop, two classrooms, and two commercial rooms were added.

The one-hundredth anniversary of the completion of the Collegiate Institute building on Lisgar Street was marred by a threat to the very existence of the school. As the centennial of the gothic edifice on Lisgar Street approached, the viability of this venerable institution was called into question. Faced with declines in student populations in the core of the city, and disproportionate costs of running antiquated physical plants, and an Ontario Fire Marshall's report questioning the basic safety of the school, the Ottawa Board of Education had some hard choices to make. Some trustees advocated closing Lisgar in an attempt to save money. The situation was further exacerbated by a ministry of education guideline concerning repairs. Should repairs exceed fifty per cent of replacement cost, the ministry indicated, the building in question should be abandoned. To determine the cost of repairs, the board retained the firm of Schoeler & Heaton to study the structural integrity of the school's buildings and estimate the cost of repairs. Completed early in 1975, the Schoeler & Heaton study concluded that relatively minor changes were needed in the south building; however, renovations to the north building were projected to cost in excess of four million dollars. Subsequently, the board sought an independent estimate from the firm of W.S. Burnside Ltd., construction managers. The initial projected cost was found to be accurate and the board now had a reasonable estimate of the cost of refitting Lisgar Collegiate Institute.

The record of Canadians in preserving their history and heritage has at times been found wanting, but it is encouraging to observe that more and more often, a stay of execution is now granted before the wrecker's hammer falls. In the case of Lisgar Collegiate, from the debates emerged a program to save the building. The National Capital Commission, the City of Ottawa, the Ontario Heritage Foundation and various local citizen groups each pledged funds to complement the generous grants supplied by the Ontario Ministry of Education for this unique project.

In response to this very real threat to the survival of the school—parents, staff, students, and alumni—mobilized and formed the "Future of Lisgar Committee."

The briefs which were presented to the trustees of the Ottawa Board of Education from the Committee for the Future of Lisgar were compelling, impassioned documents indeed, not only intending to sway voters towards preserving the architectural heritage of Lisgar but, on a much more profound level, to describe the values, goals, traditions which would be lost to the community if Lisgar were to be replaced by another modern monolithic high-rise institution—as some wished to see.

From student to principal, from historian to sociologist, the people rose to the defence of the preservation of an ancient collegiate which had become "part of the living tradition of the world's great schools."

These briefs and this public discussion in committee, in newspapers, in home and classrooms served not only to rally support for the preservation of Lisgar but also to bring to the forefront and sharply into the public awareness the standard of educational excellence established by Lisgar over such a long period of time, its athletic records, its achievements in scholarship, and, underlying all of this, a subtle communication of its indescribable and mysterious uniqueness.

From the *Ottawa Citizen*, Saturday, March 24, 1973:

When Principal, J.W. Neil retired in June 1972, he left on file a number of documents dealing with efforts to improve the school's outdoor physical education facilities and to provide one additional teaching station inside the school. For many years Lisgar students had used Cartier Square, but, since World War II, Cartier Square had been occupied by the "temporary buildings" housing the National Defence Headquarters.

The Lisgar Collegiate School Advisory Committee, under the able leadership of Mrs. Marion Perry, organized a meeting on "The Future of Cartier Square" to be held on March 29, 1973. The *Ottawa Citizen* headline and full-page story of March 24 ensured a capacity audience. On the platform panel were the Mayor of Ottawa, Pierre Benoit; the Chairman of the National Capital Commission, D.H. Fullerton; the Chairman of the Ottawa Board of Education, Mrs. Jane Dobell.

The meeting on the future of Cartier Square became in a sense the first meeting in recent years on the future of Lisgar. The Mayor expressed interest in Centretown housing and keeping a school to serve the needs of the people involved. The N.C.C. chairman stated that the N.C.C. was very much interested in retaining the building because of its heritage value. When it was suggested by someone that Lisgar should be scrapped, the site sold by the O.B.E., and the money obtained used to enlarge or modernize one of the other schools, or to provide a housing site, the N.C.C. chairman made it clear that it was unlikely that the N.C.C. would allow any part

of Cartier Square to fall into the hands of a private developer. The N.C.C. would try to ensure retention of the building, but whether it remained as a school was up to the O.B.E.

Two other related events were taking place during the same period. The Centretown Community Association was undertaking a Centretown study in an attempt to prevent the destruction of a residential core in their part of the city and its replacement by high-rise commercial or apartment buildings. The O.B.E. was also conducting a Centretown study (as part of a study of the whole city) in order to project future school population, and it became evident that all of the students presently attending the four Centretown schools could be accommodated in three, and possibly even two, of the four schools. Of four possible plans under consideration for "The Re-organization of Secondary Schools in Central Ottawa," two suggested that Lisgar be "discontinued."

On April 2, 1974, when things looked more uncertain, the committee for the "Future of Lisgar" held another meeting which brought 1,300 people to the school, filling the auditorium and a number of classrooms. Speakers included the committee chairman, J. W. Lawson; Vice-Principal Michael Weeks; Head Girl, Christie Laidlaw; Head Boy, Peter Blaiklock; R.A.J. Phillips, a representative from Heritage Canada. O.B.E. trustees who attended were impressed by their concern.

Dr. Bruce A. McFarlane, then Professor of Sociology and Anthropology at Carleton presented a compelling societal case for the preservation of Lisgar in the Centretown core.

I plan to speak first as a resident of Centretown (for the past 13 years), second as a parent of elementary school-age children who hopes his two sons will be able to attend Lisgar, and third as a Sociologist who has specialized for some twenty years in the fields of the Sociology of Occupations and the Sociology of Education.

Centretown and the central core as we all know, has seen some rather startling changes in the past fifteen years: the replacement of family residential quarters—including many fine old Ottawa residences—by high-rise office blocks and apartment blocks; a shift in the population characteristics from families with children to singles and married couples, old and young; a drop in the absolute number of school-age children; and a dramatic increase in open parking lots. To forestall further moves in this land developer and land speculator inspired process and to attempt to refurbish the area in keeping with its status as the central residential area of Canada's capital city, various citizen's groups have joined forces with the City of Ottawa's planning Department. Through their Concept Plan they are now trying to create a central city residential area such that it once again will become an attractive place for family living.

A very important ingredient in a family's decision-making process regarding the district wherein they will live is the presence of "good" schools, particularly, a "good" high school. There are people who choose to live outside cities and send their children to country schools, and those who choose to live in the centre of a city. Each group has, no doubt, important reasons for choosing to live where it does. One of the important reasons for many of us choosing Centretown as a place to live is the preference for living in a heterogeneous community—a community mixed as to social, economic, religious and ethnic origins—and this is one of the things we in Centretown value in our schools. *Lisgar Collegiate is such a school.* (The foregoing sentiment, by the way, in the 1970s is not out-of-keeping with the general and wider orientation of Canadians at large).

Of singular importance in Lisgar's case now that the Ottawa Board of Education has introduced the free choice system at the secondary school level, is the fact that Lisgar Collegiate, which has long been the choice of many who did not reside in the immediate vicinity, is situated only a few minutes walk from the central hub of OC Transpo's extensive public transport system—a sizeable proportion of all its bus routes going north, south, east or west pass through the Elgin-Slater-Wellington-Confederation Square section of the city. Hence, Lisgar is an easy point of access for high school pupils who do not live in the immediate vicinity but are desirous of the quality education offered there. All-in-all, given the above it is unlikely that there will be any surplus of school places at Lisgar in the immediate future. *Hence, to recommend the destruction of Lisgar Collegiate at this time is to fly in the face of all the evidence that suggests its present location is ideal for a high school facing the future.*

It has been pointed out by some critics that Lisgar is an "old" school and should be replaced. This has been said not only by those who would like to see a new building for its own sake but also by certain school authorities whose building regulations are such, I believe, that if the costs of rehabilitation of a school exceed 50% of the costs of replacement then the school "has to go." It is indeed fortunate for Western Civilization that no such general rule governed the activities of the ecclesiastics responsible for the care of Europe's and Great Britain's churches and cathedrals in the numerous immediate post-war periods of the past century. Otherwise we would all have been deprived of an important ingredient in our heritage, that is, numerous Norman, Gothic and other style church buildings, many of which represent the apogee of western architecture, would have been demolished, because of a rule-of-thumb guide, governed by economics rather than cultural and social considerations. (On this point, it is not without interest that many of Western Europe's and Britain's finest secondary schools are housed in quarters some centuries older than the building in which we are at present).

There has also been some concern expressed by sections of the public that Lisgar has gained its reputation for excellence

Gutted to the original stone and down to discovery of the old fireplaces.

Scaffolded exterior with students' art work.

New windows, dropped ceilings, beginnings of sub-flooring and insulation.

During renovations, while gutting the building, workers discovered the exterior front wall of the original 1874 building with three distinct window frames. The contractor, realizing the heritage value of the discovery, tried to reach to Board of Education to see if they wanted to save the wall. Unable to reach the Board on a Friday afternoon, the contractor got to Principal Glavin who made the decision to save the wall. When the Board failed to back him, the staff and students of Lisgar raised $8,000 to save the wall. In 1984 the Lisgar Alumni raised another $14,000 for the stained glass windows, designed and constructed by Northern Art Glass of Ottawa.

at the expense of other schools in the wider Centretown area. I think that it should be noted that the reputation and goals of academic excellence and technical competence in secondary schools are hard won and are achieved only in the long run. *Instant reputation*, while perhaps possible in the "Pop Star" world, is not obtainable in the educational world. It takes a long time and considerable devotion and experience before a school's reputation for excellence in its various activities can act as an attractive force for both pupils and teachers alike. In education the second rate is not improved *ipso facto* by the destruction of the first rate. Rather, the other in its desire for improvement can only be encouraged towards excellence by the presence in its midst of a first rate school and the goodwill, assistance and encouragement of the school authorities in a school's search for melioration.

There are many who point out that the present school lacks certain physical and other amenities which, it is believed, one has come to expect of a modern high school. I would like to point out that the presence in the city's centre of most of Ottawa-Carleton's and indeed, Canada's prime cultural centres—National Gallery, the National Arts Centre, the Victoria Museum, the War Museum, the National Library and National Archives, the Mint, the Houses of Parliament, the Supreme Court, and so on—all within easy walking distance for Lisgar's pupils means that some of the physical and cultural facilities deemed necessary for suburban and consolidated rural high schools are not necessary here. The same holds true, of course, for sports and arts and crafts facilities when the public and quasi-private facilities— McNabb Community Centre, the soon-to-be-completed St. Luke's Community Centre, the YM-YWCA—are taken into consideration. That is to say, a high school in Ottawa's centre town need not be built in the 1960s image of those high schools in the new suburbs and rural areas where provision had to be made to ameliorate the cultural privations of the residents.

Perhaps the most moving brief of all came from writer and historian R.A.J. Phillips, then Executive Director of Heritage Canada.

In a small Newfoundland outport, the statistics were dancing to the music of the planners. In a generation, per capita income had soared, the store was stocked with unaccustomed goods, medical services were on call, and children were receiving education once undreamed of, in consolidated schools and in the exploding university of St. Johns.

Still there was melancholy in the voice, and in the talk of that old fisherman and his wife. What more could they want from this horn of plenty which, the planners said, was spilling in their little peninsula?

"Well, I'll tell you," he said slowly, with the voice of a man who had thought long on what is meant by quality of life. "We no longer hear the sound of young voices."

Lisgar after renovations (and before the mall) with cleaned stonework, new tinted windows, girls' entrance removed, all fire escapes gone.

"The sound of young voices." They are not found on the walls of planners' offices, or in statistics of enrolment, or in the schemes of developers. They are our living heritage.

That mighty pile of limestone, Lisgar Collegiate, is also part of the heritage of the National Capital. Young voices have been heard there nearly a century now. They have brought a dimension to the life of the capital's downtown for which the most lucrative—and no doubt—hideous high-rises proposed by downtown merchants will never substitute.

We have built wisely and foolishly downtown. We have built a National Arts Centre which was wise, though the press made its $44 million price tag into a cheap household joke. No one blinked at this month's announcement of a $50 million palace for bureaucrats nearby. We have built commercial towers which have become visually offensive slums in the first decade of their life.

But, wise or foolish, we can build only still, concrete and glass. We have not built anywhere the sound of young voices.

Lisgar Collegiate does not deserve immortality because a great act of history was unfolded there. Nor would anyone claim it is a unique and compelling example of our architecture. But Lisgar Collegiate is a product of its age, a different age than ours, a product that gives variety to our city, a survival that evokes the sound of young voices then and now.

Every stone of Lisgar is a testament to that solid sense of solid Victorians who planned their priorities well. Its like will never be seen again. When the wall-to-wall education of our tinselled suburbs is giving unregretted way to the fickle bulldozer a few years hence, Lisgar will still remain as a monument to the place earlier Canadians gave to the education of the young.

Despite all the vandalism recently committed against our

243

The new Memorial Hall looking towards Wally Mann's old room and the new archival display cabinet. The old bench-warmers' bench has been retained.

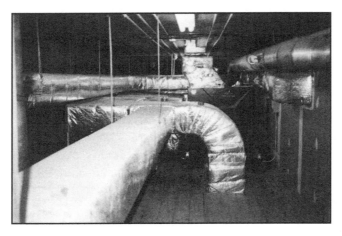

The rifle range today.

A unique view of the new gym building taken through a round window on the fourth floor by student Austin Lawrence.

city's heritage in the name of private profit, I am confident the Lisgar building will stay. I would expect someone to suggest the compromise that its occupants be removed and that the building be put to other use. At least that much enlightenment is now possible. But if that were all which was suggested for Lisgar Collegiate, this monument to education would become a hollow sepulchre.

"Modern adaptive use" for the buildings of our heritage is a phrase I do not attack. But modern adaptive use for Lisgar Collegiate means using rooms for teaching computer programming where once Greek and Latin were the subjects. It does not mean silencing those young voices.

To me it seems inconceivable that Lisgar the school should be lost. It is part of our irreplaceable history, like the Canal it looks down upon, like the Hill which it looks up to. It enshrines the intellectual merits and achievements of generations of Canadians who made this capital and this country. But much more: it enshrines the ideals of academic excellence which will be the foundation of future achievement. Is it teachers and students who create these standards? Hundreds and hundreds of ordinary teachers, tens of thousands of ordinary pupils have passed through here; teachers and students like those in any school. They had no physical advantage in their class-rooms or their playing fields. Indeed the very opposite was true. Yet they maintained standards of excellence which no one surpassed. Perhaps the reason can be no more exactly defined than a certain heritage, a heritage which incredibly now is threatened.

There are, then, many reasons why I defend the life of Lisgar. Because of its own heritage of living excellence which no engineers can manufacture elsewhere. Because it gives a dimension and quality to the downtown of our capital. Because we must temper the sterility of concrete and glass with people of every age. Because young people should live and work and play in the centre of any city which truly lives.

Because, finally, we understand that Newfoundlander who grasped the quality of life better than the planners did. Because, that is, we must hear the sound of young voices.

They are our living heritage.

Robert G. McMichael, principal during the years of momentous change, 1972-76, describes some of the events leading up to the preservation of Lisgar and preceding the opening of restored Lisgar, November 4-5, 1977.

April 19, 1974. Deadline for submission of entries in the Essay Competition, "Why Lisgar must be Saved."

June 4, 1974. Students, staff, members of the "Save Lisgar" campaign, and invited guests held a noon-hour picnic on the playing field to celebrate the 100th anniversary of the first Lisgar building on the present site.

July, 1974. O.B.E. authorized a two-phase feasibility study. Tearing apart of walls, probing, tracing of early construction

The new trophy case with photos of Lisgar Head Girls and Boys above.

patterns, etc., occurred. Then all areas had to be restored for the opening of school.

September, 1974. The Ontario Fire Marshall inspected the building and presented a report. Some immediate remedial work had to be done. A new fire alarm system was installed.

October, 1974. The architects presented a report on the Phase I study. On the basis of the preliminary estimates, the O.B.E. authorized the more detailed Phase II study. There followed more extensive probing and a more careful costing process.

November, 1974. Report of the Educational Specifications Committee presented to the Director of Education, A. Cummins, and to the Architect. (Committee composed of three Lisgar staff members, Area Superintendent, O.B.E., Assistant Superintendent for Property).

Lisgar Department Heads had been asked to submit suggestions for needed facilities that would improve the teaching and learning situation. These had been incorporated in a thirty-five page document along with a statement of the philosophy of the school and its curriculum opportunities. This document was then presented to the Area Superintendent.

January 13, 1975. Architects presented Phase II Report to the O.B.E. Subsequent publicity.

January 22, 1975. O.B.E. Property Committee toured the building and met in special session. Motions passed: "Approval *in principle* that Lisgar Collegiate be continued on its present site. The Board to explore methods of financing such renovations."

June 13, 1975. Proposed Renovations. Call for tenders for Construction Manager.

Summer 1975. "Pre-Design Exploration." To avoid unexpected discoveries during later construction, and in the absence of accurate plans from the original construction and subsequent upgradings, the O.B.E. authorized a Pre-Design Exploration which involved more extensive probing, tearing apart and restoration by September 1975.

October 6, 1975. O.B.E. Property Committee re-affirmed its earlier decision to proceed with refurbishing Lisgar at a cost of approximately $4.8 million. Subsequent meetings of the Finance Committee and of the full Board confirmed that the project would proceed using the three-phase approach.

October 31, 1975. A Grade 12 Graduating Class Special Assembly held. The Principal announced "plans must now be made for allowing the builders three and a half months' access to the building."

November, 1975. The "School Year" committee formulated

proposals for the balance of 1975-76, then submitted them for approval to the Area Superintendent. (a) Shorten the school year to allow the contractor into the building by June 4, 1978. (b) Extend the length of the school day from March 22 to May 27, with examinations from May 28 to June 4. (c) Teaching staff to be out of the school by June 18. (d) The Fall term to begin September 20, 1976. Ministry of Education approval.

June 5, 1976. Hard hats became the order of the day. The site foreman made it quite clear. "Wear them or we'll shut down the operation immediately."

June 18, 1976. Teachers finished their duties and cleared belongings from the building.

June 26,1976. The *Ottawa Citizen* continued its interest with the article "Revealing its true face" and some pictures of the demolition process. The gutting of the third floor was an amazing scene; a twenty-foot length of interior stone wall, several feet thick, had to be removed to allow for enlarging and improving the science department facilities; the demolition crew said that it would take several days; two weeks later the "several days" job was completed—just one example of innumerable similar problems. The Fire Marshall had insisted that the magnificent west stairway from basement to fourth floor had to be moved about fifty feet further west so that it would be immediately outside the auditorium entrances on the second and third floors. That accomplishment was in itself an engineering feat worthy of several chapters.

The architectural firm of Schoeler and Heaton and the construction consultant, W.S. Burnside Ltd., which had carried out the Feasibility Studies and the Pre-Design Exploration and had made the cost estimates, were chosen to carry out the three-phase renovation project. In one of the Lisgar Advisory Committee meetings, the hope had been expressed that the architect selected would have some appreciation of Lisgar's heritage and that he would take an imaginative approach to the renovation design. Certainly Architect Michael Lundholm fulfilled all expectations and was most receptive to suggestions. William Burnside assembled a wonderful team of mechanical, electrical and structural engineering associates. Dalton Minty, Vice-President of BFH, the Project Mechanical Engineers, gave an excellent description of "Lisgar's Second Century" in the June 1976 issue of *SECOSCOPE*, the staff magazine of the Shawinigan Engineering Company Limited.

August 30, 1976. Registration of new students and discussion with returning students needing time-table changes began. Director A. Cummins had attended a Spring staff meeting to answer questions about the altered school year and to assure teachers that they would not be expected to return until the students did on September 20. Nevertheless, Principal and Vice-Principals, members of the Guidance Department, and a number of Department Heads came in to help with the registration.

September 3, 1976. As our concerns about a realistic school opening date began to show, William Burnside and the O.B.E. Superintendent of Operations did their utmost to ensure that certain areas were cleared on a progressive basis.

September 13, 1976. Vice-Principal Robert D. Green, himself a former teacher and a former student and Head Boy at Lisgar, and who was a tremendous asset during the project, made an unexpected trip to Belleville—his mission (with the authorization of the Project Manager) to pick up from the hardware supplier keys for all the doors so that teachers and students could have access to the classrooms.

September 20, 1976. Students assembled in the gymnasium, and the new school year began. Even more flexibility was needed now as the contractors were still in the building, and daily shuffling of classes occurred to allow for completion of certain areas.

November 5-6, 1976. Graduation Exercises for the 1975-76 class were held, and again the Contractor and Care Staff had the auditorium ready. The platform floor had been finished the previous evening, and the drapes hung "between performances."

December 1976. Phase I ended and along with it came the retirement of Principal McMichael. Earlier in the month, the Renovation Project Team had reported to the O.B.E. that it now appeared that Phases II and III of the plan could be combined in the Summer of 1977 with a possible saving of $200,000.

January 26, 1977. The call for tenders went out and the new Principal, S.J. Glavin, prepared for another revised school year, a summer of demolition and restoration, and a fall opening.

November 4-5, 1977. A Special Assembly and Open House were held to dedicate the rejuvenated Lisgar Collegiate Institute.

—Chris O'Brien, Bob McMichael.

LISGAR, IN THE 1980s

In the 1990s it was more difficult to find good memoirs of Lisgar in the 1980s than in the 1940s. Recently graduated students are too busy looking forward to look backwards. But the *Vox Lycei*'s staff *Chronicle* of 1981-82 compensates for this logical lack by its lively insightful description of a year's events at Lisgar from initiation of the "Minor Niners" to the dispatch of the last section of the *Vox Lycei* to the printer in Whitby.

* * * * *

During the first two weeks, Student Council opened up the Stationery Shoppe. Everything from looseleaf paper, pens and pencils, rulers, to graph paper and different coloured duotangs were sold there. On September 17, representatives from each homeform were elected to Student Council. We then had a pizza day to alleviate bagged-lunch boredom and peanut-butter-and-jam depression.

On September 25, the grade 9s, having made ". . . a very wise choice," were formally welcomed to ". . . the best school in Ottawa, if not in the entire country." A few days later, the "minor niners" were again subjected to the rigours of academic life on Ribbon Day. The grades 10 to 13 students were given ribbons and the grade 9 students were given identifying old Lisgar buttons. They had to collect the most ribbons from the senior students by making them speak (yes, actually speak!) to a grade 9 student. Tactics ranged from "Do you know what time it is?" to "I love your pink socks! Where did you get them?" (The puzzled student immediately vehemently denies wearing pink socks, and is promptly stripped of his ribbon.) The winning homeform, 1D, won free admission to the first dance of the year. William Murray of 1D got away with the most ribbons, collecting over 50 of them.

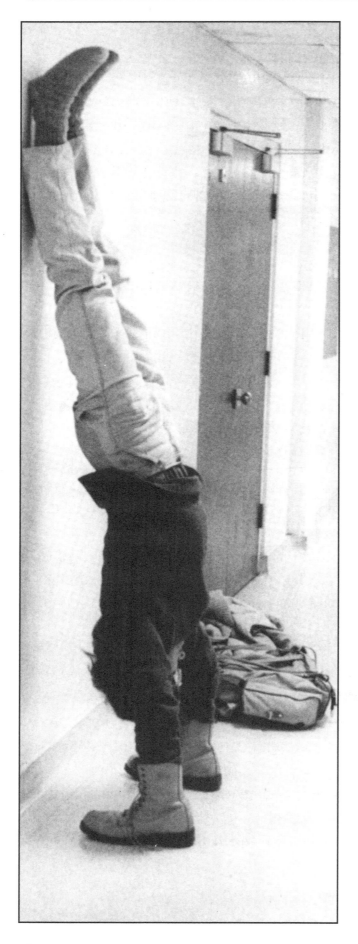

The Wheelathon was held on a rainy afternoon, the first day of October, to raise money for local charities. The participants had to manoeuvre their way through an obstacle course, on wheelchairs. Everyone could picture more clearly the difficulties faced by people in wheelchairs in gaining access to buildings accessible only by stairs or by too-steep ramps.

On Friday, October 2, enthusiastic contestants paraded in the main hall with their gaudiest, tackiest, and most colourful ties, as they vied for the first ever "Golden Lamperd" trophy. Mr. Lamperd, founder of another great Lisgar tradition judged among the many tie-rrific(!) and tie-rrible(!!) ties.

That night, in the gym, the first back-to-school/TGIF/raise-money-for-the-destitute-*Vox* dance was held. It was a tremendous success, even though a fuse was blown in the middle of a disco song. There were no more disco songs that evening.

The Flounder, our school newspaper, is now known as the *Alere Flammam*. It is apparently floundering less this year, and under the editorial expertise of Sander Cohen, the first issue was sold on October 2.

The Drama Club is one of the oldest and consistently popular extra-curricular activities in the school. Over the years the Drama Club has played a major part in annual concerts, school assemblies, improvisations on the mall, and dramatic productions for school and public at large. Lisgar has had many prize-winning entries in the Dominion Drama Festivals. This is the Drama Club 1983-84. On the ladder; Peter Cureton, Marie Fraser. Second row, left to right; Paige Kemball, Tracy Dunn, Cynthia Galland, Anna Matynia, Jennifer Gravel, Tracey Rossignol, Margaret Iveson, Karla Weys, Brad Redekopp. Front row, l to r; Scott Taylor, Danny Darin-Zanco, Nick McKinney, Frances Goodwin, Vanessa Thomas, Melanie Carker. Front; Patricia Bukta.

During the 1980s under the leadership of Sam Saunders Lisgar students created prize-winning ice sculptures on the canal for Ottawa's Winterfest. Here are the creators of Jazzy Paws, 1981-82. Rachel Mah, Gaye Ansell, Dave Leggett, Barbara Appleton, Cynthia Bail, Sarah Withey, Mary Ballentyne, Hugh Neilson, Eva Riccius, Anne Fielder, Victoria Welsh, Melanie Lum, Jim Hamer, Winnie Lee, Marie McFaul, Satish Chumber, Chris Willette, Ron Miller, Pam Church, Susan Liver, Joanna Bellamy, Esther Goros, Jennifer Bayne.

The week of October 13 to 16 was Club Week, in which many of the clubs got a chance to show the school what they did. There were displays in the main hall organized by Lynne Kamibayashi and various club activities at lunchtime. The Club Week assembly was highlighted by Mr. Kerslake's stage debut to a full house as the debonair Captain Kirk in the Star Trek skit.

Only four days later, eight delicious flavours ranging from lemon to chocolate coconut made their cafeteria debut as the stars of our first ever "Donut Day."

Metalically clothed creatures, with some semblance of human form, mingled in the halls with conventional Earth beings: jostling one another, staring strangely and emitting stifled squeals of surprise and wonder. An invasion from Planet Anizev? Mais non! 'Twas the dawning of a new day, October 23, 1981, Space Day!

Star Trek, the Motion Picture, was shown in the auditorium—the first film in three years on which Student

Council has made money! The Computer Club provided video space games in the main hall and the Debating Club tried to resolve whether or not Earth was the only planet, the others being figments of our collective imagination.

Lollipops were ordered at the end of October to raise money for our Foster Child. Messages from secret admirers, good friends and vengeful enemies could be sent with the candy to sweeten, or sour, that special someone's day!

The Reach for the Top team played their first game of the year, defeating Ridgemont High School by a score of 300 to 260, on October 24.

On Friday night October 30th, the eerie Lisgar gym was the focus of a very weird gathering. Covens of witches, gaggles of goblins and hordes of other peculiar creatures of the night were seen streaming through the doors and inside where they gyrated and contorted their bodies to flashing lights and loud rock music. It was the scene of one of the year's most ghoulish events—the Hallowe'en Dance!

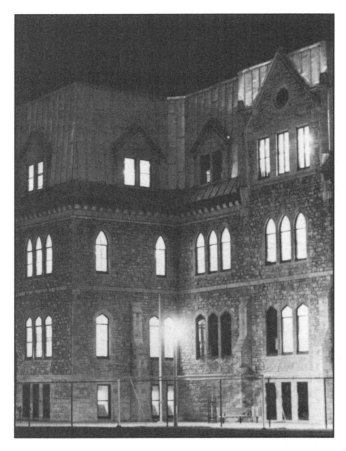

Approximately nine thousand visitors signed the registry and passed through Lisgar on May 3, 4, 5, 1984, when for the fourth time, Lisgar Alumni Association staged a Lisgar reunion, this time the 140th. Newly renovated Lisgar was an architectural glory when lit at night to welcome its graduates and friends.

As these creatures twined in and out of circular formations, shrieking and yelling like the most heathen of banshees, a subtle change came upon the group. They moved in closer, gathering in a semi-circle around the disc jockey, careful never to pass beyond an invisible boundary. The Time had Come.

Slowly, slowly, a select few, the most eccentrically dressed of the group, drifted slowly into the middle of the semi-circle, dancing, as the crowd watched, fascinated. The strain was evident on the dancers' faces as they slithered, jerked and twisted to the rhythmic music. The air grew tense. Finally! A Decision! The Judges have Decided! They summon Peter Barszczewski to the front, to the position of honour. He has been Chosen—Best Hallowe'en Costume 1981.

The first week of November was Careers Week. There were vocational surveys and interest tests for grades 9 to 13 that revealed to budding bartenders or prospective physicists their interests and aptitudes.

On the night of November 7, many members of the class of '81 came back to haunt the Lisgar halls. Commencement, a well-established fall ritual, saw the return of many students and their proud parents and relatives for the graduation

ceremony. After the formal handing out of awards and congratulations, the now legitimate high school graduates headed out to friends' houses to renew old acquaintances and to celebrate.

After only a remarkable two days of publicity, Casino Night was held with Lisgar's very own Cabaret in the gym on Friday, November 13. Besides the usual gambling tables, one half of the gym was used for a dance. Later on in the night, Ottawa magician, John Milkes, performed his amazing magic tricks to a captivated audience. A floor show followed, featuring singing, dancing and even Johnny Askwith doing a strip tease to the tune of "Patricia the Stripper." Oh! how they called for an encore! At the end of the evening, all the big spenders and the big winners at the tables were invited to spend a little more at an auction for anyone with money to burn.

The Talent Show, a showcase for Lisgar talent of the highest (?) calibre, was hosted by Johnny of the strip tease fame on November 18.

November 20 was Mystery Day, and a festival of Alfred Hitchcock films was shown to eager audiences. Three of Hitchcock's chilling classics, *The Birds*, *The Man Who Knew Too Much*, and *The 39 Steps*, rattled the nervous systems of the hardiest souls.

The Lisgar Scavenger Hunt, a test to try even the wisest, started out with eight avid teams, later narrowed down to four staunch survivors. The teams had to answer questions of devious ingenuity and they also had to bring in assorted "Lisgar" articles such as items of Lisgar clothing, a rule from the September Stationery Shoppe and a tag from one of the lollipops sold in October. By dint of great exertion and unflagging perseverance in this most strenuous exercise, the team composed of Nick Davies and Heather Bruce finally succeeded in coming out the winner.

GWND (Great White North Day for the uninitiated), got off to a sizzling start as hot pancakes were served at the unholy hour of 8 a.m. on a Tuesday morning. Bleary-eyed students trudged in to a steaming hot feast for sore eyes.

Our co-presidents Brian Mitchell and Mitchell Anderson dressed down in their best lumberjack jackets, hats and scarves, and strolled the halls saying, "Eh? You're such a hoser, you hoser!" It was their own contribution towards the preservation and promotion of Canadian culture in the Golden Age of Bob and Doug Mackenzie. Right, eh?

Almost 200 people jammed into the auditorium to see that irreverent satire of King Arthur and his cohorts, *Monty Python and the Holy Grail*. The most successful film that Lisgar has had in a decade, it was shown after school to a hysterical crowd on December 4.

Big, striped candy canes were sold and sent to the homerooms of beloved friends and others, again with the appropriate season's greetings.

The leaves that had long ago turned red, orange and yellow, had long ago fallen off, and now lay under a cover of fresh white snow. In the last week before exams, troubadours from the Carol Club decked the halls with the sounds of their music. The last day of carolling in the halls, a small band of wandering minstrels accompanied a large band of singers in totally destroying the former calm and reserve of the front hall. Rousing verses of "Jingle Bells," "Deck the Halls," and "O Come All Ye Faithful" set the very floors shaking and got us all into the mood for Christmas.

Even the *Alere Flammam* got it all together for Christmas, as they put out their second issue in the same school year, although under the direction of a different editor. The editor for this issue was Mike Smart.

On December 11th, we were all entertained by the Christmas assembly, and especially by the teachers' skit, *'Twas the Night Before Christmas*, in which Mama (Mr. Reid) and Papa (Mr. Laughton) frolicked gaily on stage in anticipation of jolly old St. Nick! Dainty and delicate, bedecked and bejewelled with tinsel and stars, the sugarplum fairy (Mr. Monsour) pirouetted onto the stage. And with a wave of her wand—Poof! the children (Mrs. Smith, Johnny Askwith), nestled snugly in their bed, saw visions of sugarplums dance in their heads.

But Hark! 'Tis not Herald Angels that sing, but 'tis the sound of reindeer roofs, pawing gently on the roof. Then down the chimney, whom should appear, but the jolliest, merriest, liveliest of all men, Santa (Mr. Boehmer) himself. He filled all the stockings, left the presents under the tree and was off in a flash, carried through the crisp night sky by his devoted reindeer (Mr. Fraser, Mr. Kerslake, Mr. MacDonald).

For the 140th reunion two of Lisgar's most famous graduates, Lorne Greene and Rich Little, reminisced and entertained the standing-room-only crowd in the Lisgar gymnasium.

Merry Christmas to All

and

Good Luck on Exams!

As everyone scurried frantically about, cramming for exams and wishing for the holidays, a Christmas tree was set up on the first floor. Underneath, there were boxes of canned foods brought in by students to support the canned food drive.

The last day of the exams was joyously celebrated that night by carolling at Cartier House, a sleigh ride and snowball fights at City Hall. This was followed by a party, hot chocolate, and popcorn at the home of Janet Green!

Only three days after New Year's Day, we were cordially invited back to school by teachers just bursting with the desire to see our studious young faces again! To get back into the spirit of things, a "Design a Lisgar Button" contest was held. Michael Kidd was the winner of the winning button design.

The first *Vox* dance of the new year was on Friday, January 15. The next morning, the Reach for the Top team played their second game, this time against Nepean High School. Lisgar soundly routed Nepean by a score of 440 to 115.

That weekend was also spent, by campaign organizers, in gearing up for the Head Thing election on January 22. The eventual winner, and successor to the renowned Rubber Duckie, was the beautifully shellacked, elegantly adorned, and exquisitely refined, Lisgar Cafeteria Oatmeal Muffin! Where else but at Lisgar could one have a varnished muffin with plastic legs as a mascot! Close behind the muffin was Mr. Qadri's wardrobe (represented by a tie), as first runner-up, and second runner-up was that royally Canadian fellow—Miltie the Mountie.

On January 29, after four days of hectic betting to win, place, or show, the teachers' team and various student teams got together on the canal for the Sled Race. The course ran from Lisgar Street to Somerset Street. Winners of the race were David Mount, Alison Murray, Dan Lyons and Min Ku of the *Vox* team. They were closely pursued by "Woodie's Machine" and the "101st Transport Battalion." Most creative of all the sleds was "The Royal Flush." Designed by Karen Kung, Rick Sodhi, Serge Platonow and Annie Ng, it cruised leisurely down the canal, complete with Handel's Water Music and a plunger. The winner of the greatest number of tokens was Dan Lyons, who received a dinner for two at Houlihan's.

January 29 was also the day that the Snow Sculpture team started work (at Dow's Lake) on their sculpture of a band of swinging jazz musicians (of the furry type).

The fourth annual Lisgar Invitational Debating Tournament on January 30 was again a success. Eleven teams from all over Ottawa came, to debate "Be it resolved that there is a distinct Canadian identity." The day's intellectual endeavours also included impromptu topics such as "Resolved that the sane are really the insane." After the final model debate on "Be it resolved that good debaters are not nice people," the winners were declared: J.S. Woodsworth proved the best team, and Trish Kell from Gloucester and Alex Graham from Ashbury both received the top speaker awards. Special thanks to Jennifer Jolly who organized the tournament and took care of all the last minute details.

Starting on February 2nd, careers speakers from many different fields came every Tuesday, to speak about, and to discuss their careers. On February 4th, the opening night of Winterlude, Lisgar's snow sculpture "Jazzy Paws" won second prize. The $500 prize money will go to the art department.

Roses, and dark, milk, or white chocolates were sent to the homerooms on February 12. That night, the A.V.A. co-ordinated the music for the Valentine's Day Dance. The A.V.A. will also be working on the school play when it is performed in mid-April.

On the bright, early morning of February 13, the Reach for the Top team played a very close and exciting game that was tied many times until the closing snappers when St. Pius surged ahead to defeat Lisgar, 385 to 310.

February 15 to 19 was Spirit Week—a week of zany activities to relieve the monotony of perpetual tests and assignments.

The Spirit Week assembly, in first period Monday morning, gave us previews of the events to come. Our co-president Brian Mitchell, who sometimes bears a remarkable resemblance to Mr. Glavin, read the morning's announcements, and news from the realm of athletics! Tuesday's game show at noon set the tone of the week as zealous contestants battled ferociously to be first in such earth-shattering events as the ripping apart of a Rubik's cube. A P.D. day on Wednesday was a welcome relief after the exhausting activities of the previous day. By Thursday, everyone was ready for the slave auction. Willing students displayed themselves on stage in the hopes of being purchased by a kind master. Little did they know! The very next morning, these lowly slaves indulged their masters' every whim as they walked the halls in fantastic costumes and did deeds of which no grade 9 should be a witness. . .

Orders were taken for Lisgar jackets—the first time in over five years that they have been available.

Busy bankers and players won and lost hundreds of dollars in the Monopoly Tournament of the first week of March. And on March 5, the last section of the *Vox* was sent off to our publisher in Whitby.

The Care Staff and L.E.A.F.

The Care Staff

Since the early days of the "one-man wonder" caretakers, many changes have occurred at Lisgar in relation to its cleaning and maintenance. I talked with Mike Schingh, Supervisor of Buildings, in his computerized office near the cafeteria from where he manages the care staffs of Elgin Street, York Street, Viscount Alexander, and Lady Evelyn schools, as well as Lisgar Collegiate. His staff of thirty to thirty-five trained personnel cleans continuously and daily, as well as carrying on maintenance of the buildings. At Lisgar there is an engineer on duty as well as a full-time carpenter.

Well, fifty years ago you wouldn't have the machinery like we have nowadays commercial vacuums, floor scrubbers, waxers, polishers, and the cleaning techniques we have today compared to back then.

Fifty years ago I imagine all they did was put a hard floor wax paste on and polish it whereas, today, we apply liquid floor finish and then we would buff it with what we call a 244-wax emulsion spray which basically puts a protective coating over the wax, and then all we have to do is go in and just buff it to get the dirt off instead of having to scrub it with the water and everything. Now it is just a simple process once a week in the classroom.

There's no way of keeping the lockers clean or anything like that. We go through them once a year—and the rest of the year the things are rotting in there. Again back fifty years ago of course the ventilation systems weren't what they are today either. Back then they probably heated with coal whereas now we heat with natural gas. Much cleaner, much better for the environment, and cheaper.

Under the leadership of Mike Schingh, this is Lisgar's 1993 hard-working, friendly, helpful Care Staff. Front row, left to right: Miachel Larabie, Jacqualine Nabon, Susan Sparling, Danny Fournier, Jim Pratt, Mike Schingh. Back row, l to r; Danny Lapointe, Leo Deslauriers, Tim Munro, Mike Hodgins, Walter McCallum.

With care and concern, Lisgar's cafeteria staff works daily to prepare nutritious and attractively presented meals and fast foods for staff and students. Left to right: Benita Cefaloni, Anna DiMagno, Sandra Wyman.

There's been a lot of changes in lighting. Basically, we got away from incandescent bulbs and into fluorescent, energy-saving bulbs, and we've even upgraded those over the years. In the past six months at Lisgar we've upgraded all the lighting in the hallways. It used to be indirect lighting. Now it's direct lighting which will save a lot of energy. We've gone to a high-efficiency type fixture in the hallways. It is better for students' eyes. With indirect lighting your eyes are always straining because when you have indirect you're going to have shadows.

Another change here. Basically we're upgrading all of our electrical pumps to a more efficient-type motor that uses less energy. We're putting special sensors in the rooms that turn the lights on and off automatically so they save energy. We've replaced all the weather stripping on all the exterior doors in the building to help save on energy—really trying to cut the costs involved with the building. The computers, the word processors, the Xerox machine and so on, those still have to be turned on and off manually. But our fan units are all on computer now. And the rest will be. A PUC box will control what times they come on and off. I can monitor through my main computer here, all my buildings and I can alter them. So eventually I won't have to have a person go round and do that.

The air conditioner has got sensors and it will automatically adjust itself to what it needs. The same with the heat. So long as the boilers are on. It depends on the time of the season. The newer buildings that we're building now are all going to be controlled with computer. Lights will come on and off depending on the light coming into the room.

Lisgar is a real challenge as far as the exterior maintenance because it is stone. We're continually having to work on it, repointing it, making sure that the stone isn't flaking away, constant, constant work. Acid rain is definitely having an effect on the stone. You can see it actually on the stone. It just flakes it away. Basically you have to hire a stone mason but it's expensive. If you don't keep up with it, it will be more expensive.

We take care of the interior wood on a weekly basis, or daily basis. Some brass is shined but not the big plaques in the main hall. We don't touch those because, as soon as you start shining the brass, it's going to get onto the wood and then you're going to have a real maintenance problem. So it's better just to leave it alone. And, again, it's time consuming. We've been reduced in manpower here because of reorganization or whatever that most companies are going through, so I don't have the time to do all that now. But the wood is looked after.

Lisgar's recycling program hasn't added to our work. The student body here looks after it almost 95 percent. We do from time to time get involved in it by opening a door up for the company coming to pick up the stuff, or maybe give them a hand with a heavy load. But, other than that, the student body basically looks after it, paper, aluminum cans, drink cans and bottles. They're even into the tabs of the Coke cans, and batteries. They grab all the alkaloid batteries and collect them. They don't do plastic containers yet. But Lisgar was the first. They set the precedent in recycling and all the other schools just followed. And, of course, Ottawa Board is now into recycling and using recyclable products. But what started here at Lisgar just snowballed.

Lisgar is a hard building to work. We don't have an elevator; we have four floors here to look after plus another building on the other side; a lot of heavy stuff has to be carried upstairs, so we try to schedule workloads so that everybody has an equal share, and it's not only a few people carrying the whole load. My staff gets along, and they're respected for what they do, and I think the teachers respect them for what they do, and that helps too. Generally, Lisgar students are considerate. They are. You still have the ones that . . . But this year for the first time the Student Council had a week in recognition of the Care Staff. For a whole week the students would get together in giving a hand in helping the Care Staff and then had a big barbecue for them.

The Care Staff has come a long way, in many years with the Board. They've got uniforms now and they are professionals in their trade. Nowadays they have to be professionals. I, myself, trained through the ranks. But your training never really ends. We have a union. That helps in terms of working conditions and salary, and pensions.

Now the School Board is using a lot of environmental friendly items for cleaning, and everything we do. Our floor soaps and that are biodegradable, We don't use any insecticides in the buildings any more unless it's absolutely necessary and then it has to go to the community to be approved. We don't spray our fields for weeds any more. We basically just try to get a healthy field to kill the weeds. You simply fertilize the grass so that it grows so thick that it crowds out the weeds. All our leaves are raked up in the fall, and we put them into a central depot that composts them. All our bags now are biodegradable. They're like a paper substance. They'll just disintegrate in time. Our tons of paper head off to a recycling plant.

About maintaining the mall. We have an outside person who vacuums it every morning with a special vacuum known as a "Billy Goat" —it eats everything. If there's repairs to be done—the mall is actually owned by the city of Ottawa. As far as the tunnel is concerned there's very little maintenance other than cleaning. Nobody uses it, and they should. The problem with the mall is you've now created an area like parkland where the students can just run across between the buildings. And they do in the winter. It creates a problem for cleaning. We're pretty busy in the winter there. Why don't they like that tunnel? It's kind of out of the way or it hasn't been enforced that they should use it. Someone's got to say "The tunnel's got to be used." I think too, eventually, as time goes by security is starting to become a factor and I think that the tunnel will be used because the exterior of the building will probably be locked up. That's a reality that is coming. Yes. Locked up after the kids are in—to stop people from wandering in and stealing. Gilmour school is already locked up.

L.E.A.F.
(LISGAR ENVIRONMENTAL ACTION FORCE)

During the school terms of 1991 and 1992 students of Dr. Janet Morchain's senior classes submitted researched papers on a variety of subjects having to do with Lisgar's one hundred and fifty years of history. Although it was impossible to use these papers in their entirety on many occasions, pieces of research material were valuable in the compilation and credits are given in the acknowledgements at the back of this book.

However, Manel Silva's paper on L.E.A.F. is an exception. It is a complete history of not only a precedent-setting, but one of the most important and influential student groups ever organized at the school. It might well be said that L.E.A.F.'s ramifications are global.

L.E.A.F. is an organization which promotes environmental action through awareness at the school, home, community, national, and international level. Activities such as paper and can recycling, publicizing through posters, petition-signing, letter-writing, and lobbying of various groups and organizations, have enabled L.E.A.F. to fulfill its purpose.

L.E.A.F. began as a club in the middle of the 1987-1988 school year, headed by its founding members "the two Katies," Katie Jaimet and Katie Brennan. The club consisted primarily of a small group of dedicated young women (as is the case in most environmental organization) who started, and ran the paper recycling program at Lisgar. As well, the two Katies piloted paper recycling for the city at the secondary school level by visiting various schools and giving presentations to interested students. Together, they initiated the OBE Environmental Committee headed by Mr. Dunlop, by insistently persuading the board to switch to unbleached paper. Through their combined effort, and with the help of many environmentally-aware students, L.E.A.F.'s first year was a success as it became a recognized force in the school.

During the 1988 school year, Katie Brennan continued her involvement in L.E.A.F. as chairperson. As well as co-ordinating the paper recycling, L.E.A.F. members attended a board wide conference in April on environmental action through the high schools. This conference attracted new members for the following year, and rekindled the interests of returning members.

The next year's activities coincided with the media's new and global environmental awareness surrounding the first official Earth Day, April 22, 1990. During the first few months, Lien Khan-Ho was the head of L.E.A.F. Through her leadership, she continued paper recycling and began the recycling of aluminum cans and glass bottles. The cans program was a pilot project of the Ministry of Education called the "Star Program," and was instituted in all the OBE high schools. (Later the same year, the Ministry also instituted a board-wide paper recycling program although Lisgar already had one). Unfortunately, Lien Khan-Ho had to step down from her position which was transferred to Kieran Lal. His business-like organizational skills and his hard-drive approach provided structure and enthusiasm to the group. That year, there was a large poster painting campaign that led up to the climax of Earth Day. The purpose of these posters was to make students more aware of environmental problems and to educate them on solutions. L.E.A.F. contributed to the many events on that day by providing a booth about recycling at school and at work.

Along with the many new ideas that became reality was the creation of S.A.N.E., Student Action Network for the Environment. The organization, under the direction of Lal and a Glebe student, was set up as a pool of resources and of people-power, and a network between high schools across the Ottawa-Carleton area. Various speakers came in, and, through their suggestions and our own ideas, a draft of the objectives for next year was laid out.

Nearing the end of that year, Lal brought in an interested and enthusiastic new face—that of Eric Ward who became the chairperson during the 1990-1991 school year. While Ward headed the club, many in and out of school activities were organized by L.E.A.F. These included: can and paper recycling; petition-writing for such causes as the incident at Oka and the destruction of the Borneo rainforest; posters publicizing local environmental problems and educating students how to help solve them; bake sales to raise money for donations to various charities and organizations; recycling cans from Pizza Pizza; and various assemblies and guest speakers.

One of the most memorable assemblies ever held at Lisgar was L.E.A.F.'s presentation of Jeff Gibbs, the founder of E.Y.A. (Environmental Youth Alliance), and Muotang, a native of the Borneo rainforest in Malaysia. Gibbs educated the audience on the problems and attempted solutions concerning the clear-cutting of the Borneo forest, and how it related to the indigenous people who depended on it. Muotang, who had fled from his country in order to gather international help (and was therefore blacklisted by his government), pleaded with the students through his limited vocabulary and simplistic yet incredibly powerful drawings, to the point of bringing tears to many people's eyes. A few months later, another assembly of the S.A.V.E. tour (Student Action for a Viable Environment), touched upon the subject of the rainforest and how we, as Canadians, must also fight to preserve our wildlife. The tour, consisting of twelve young Canadian activists, was and still is travelling across Canada to visit high schools, emphasizing the power of youth as leaders of the next generation.

That year provided much publicity for L.E.A.F. both in Lisgar and in the community. Members Catriona Sturton, Holly Morrison, Erica Murton, Eric and I (Manel Silva) were interviewed at the Sparks Street mall by journalists from

Centertown News concerning the display (entitled "Facts and Fallacies About Recycling") we had set up there for Recycling Week. Also, people from Channel 22 came to Lisgar to film L.E.A.F. in action for their segment on high schools, focusing on environmental issues. Due to these activities and to the publicity, the attendance at L.E.A.F. meetings regularly outnumbered Student Council meetings, with as many as 20 "Leaflets" (as coined by David Lamperd, the teacher advisor for L.E.A.F. during its first two years) coming out. Eric became one of two student representatives on the OBE Environmental Committee, which resulted in, among others, the creation of a grant for graduating students going into environmental studies.

I was elected last year to become head of L.E.A.F., after having fulfilled the positions of secretary, head of publicity and vice-chairperson during my two years as a member. In September, the club officially became an organization after having written its constitution for the Student Council. During this year, L.E.A.F. expanded its paper recycling to include newspaper and to become available in each classroom and staff office. The recycling of batteries began, as did the collection of can tabs. (Through the city, one ton of tabs can purchase a wheelchair, to be donated to someone who cannot afford the cost). Members organized and participated in the first L.E.A.F. camping trip in November, with the help of Larry Wade our teacher advisor for the past three years. One highlight of the year was the many concerts which featured Lisgar bands, in the auditorium and outside. Donations were given to organizations such as Foster Parents' Plan, the Rainforest Conservation Fund, and World Wildlife Fund. Since most students enjoyed these concerts, we felt it proved that L.E.A.F. was an organization working not only towards the betterment of our physical environment, but also of our social environment.

Though many things in L.E.A.F. have changed and expanded over the years, there are many which will always remain true. For example, it is inevitable that, once a month, someone will end up sorting paper in the recycling room until 8 p.m., or painting posters and cleaning until 7:30 p.m., or washing out the dried pop from the can boxes very early some morning. Above all, the one which has remained the truest, is that members who get really involved will always have difficulty balancing school work and environmental activities. Speaking from experience, I know how difficult it is to turn away from the idealistic energy of a young bright student who is also a potential leader in the years to come. May the Force be with you (And no we are NOT the Lisgar Enviro-Active Freaks!).

A History of the Lisgar A.V.A. Club

The Lisgar Audio Visual Club ("A.V.A." for short) is one of Lisgar Collegiate Institute's oldest and most important organizations. A service club of volunteers, it has attended to the lighting and sound needs of both class and club for over five decades. The earliest record of the club's existence is from the 1940 *Vox Lycei*. Founded by teachers A.B. Fallis, R.S. Whittle, and A. Procter, the club was called the Lisgar Film Projection Committee. It remained so named until its mysterious absence from the *Vox*, 1949-1952, after which it re-emerged in 1952 under the present title.

In 1946, not long after the club's founding, geography teacher Don Waddell became the A.V.A.'s advisor. Occasionally, other teachers would later assist him, including Gary Smith and Bill Gorham who stayed until 1974. After Gorham's departure, Doug Arrand (then teaching history) and Neil Petrie, full-time A.V.A. technician, became the club's advisors.

* * *

(Story: Neil Petrie dashed down to the history class of an enraged Doug Arrand whose film projector would not work. Doug was convinced that other teachers had maliciously misused his fine machine. Neil took a look.

"Mr. Arrand," he said a minute later, loud enough for the whole class to hear, "the machine is plugged into the cart but the cart's not plugged into the wall.")

* * *

Student members of the club numbered only six in 1940. This would change however, especially after Don Waddell's arrival. Membership mushroomed in the 1950s when the club averaged 25 to 30 students and continued at this size until the mid-1970s. One reason for the club's popularity was Don Waddell's recruiting technique of showing great films in his Grade Nine geography classes where he urged his new students to join the club. Neil Petrie and Doug Arrand have also recruited new members over the past two decades, making pitches to Grade Ten classes each year.

Any students with a good work ethic and interest in serving the school through the A.V.A. are welcome to join, regardless of their previous technical experience (or lack thereof). Each year, the club takes new members and teaches them how to operate the equipment as professionally as possible.

In the 1940s, if new members of the A.V.A. were not formally trained and tested upon joining the club, they certainly were by the 1950s under Don Waddell's direction. The club's 1957/58 yearbook write-up reads:

"Each new member has to take several hours of instruction in the operating of projectors, sound equipment, spotlights, etc. After this training, each new member must pass a series of practical tests before receiving authority to operate school equipment."

Senior members did most of the training in the 1950s and '60s, and tests would include threading a 16-mm film projector in under 60 seconds, threading a projector in the dark, and carrying the heaviest tape recorder from the basement to the top floor (the latter test being designed to keep girls out of the club!). By the mid 1970s, Neil Petrie was doing most of the training and there were no more formal tests; training today is again done by seniors but the only testing is actually working at the events (i.e., sink or swim!).

* * *

(Story: Senior member Gord Belyea was instructing his junior entourage in the art of carrying equipment. Attempting to lift an extremely heavy speaker on his back, he nearly gave himself a hernia.

"And that's how *not* to do it," he said.)

* * *

Not only has the club's size, leadership, and training methods changed over the past fifty years, but the services it has provided have evolved as well. The Film Projection Committee was originally funded by the Student's Council to show free films such as ski travelogues, cartoons, and some commercial films to the student body. Early yearbook write-ups often note the club's supportive capacity in the classroom, showing films on science, health, and for Lisgar's *Defence Training Program*, information on World War II. In the early 1950s, the A.V.A. was showing movies

at noon, and by 1958 the school had three new portable 16-mm projectors, though these were used mainly by the geography department.

Although the A.V.A. was still responsible for showing films in classrooms through the 1960s, the increasing simplicity of the newer projectors and the arrival in the 1950s of easy-to-use 24-inch black and white television sets substantially reduced the need for the club in the classroom. Furthermore, there was little demand at this point for commercial films since there were many cinemas such as the Elgin, Capital and Regent theatres in the area showing films all day long. The A.V.A.'s origins were in showing films but, had it not provided other services which were in demand, it would have ceased to exist long ago.

* * *

(Story: "Help!" came the little voice of Harry Monsour. "Help!"

Neil Petrie opened the door to the teacher's class but could only see his torso. . .the rest of him was hidden behind a pile of film four feet high! The take-up reel had been pressed against the back wall and no one had noticed in the darkness that the film was just spewing onto the floor.)

* * *

The A.V.A. club has always had a place in Lisgar's auditorium. Morning assemblies were held each day up until the early 1960s, typically requiring an A.V.A. crew of four each time to cover the P.A. system, lighting, and slides. (Incidentially, the old Delineoscope 4-inch slide projector which projected words to school cheers typed in the office on yellow paper is still in use today!)

By the early 1960s, regular morning assemblies numbered only about two per week, and by the 1970s they had become extinct; this explains, in part, the downsizing of the club's membership at this point. The A.V.A., however, was still needed for the annual concert, a large production which was the climax of the year. Taking months to plan, it always required careful integration of performances and audio-visual effects. There was another club during the 1960s called the Stage Crew which also worked on the concerts, taking care of props and sets, and completely distinct from the A.V.A. By the 1970s, however, it no longer existed and Neil Petrie did much of the set-building until the A.V.A. came to share this responsibility too.

Since the 1960s there have been other productions, in addition to the concert, which have showcased the A.V.A.'s talents. These include plays such as *The Diary of Anne Frank*, *The Miracle Worker*, *The Prime of Miss Jean Brodie*. Since the 1980s, Lisgar has also worked on demanding annual fashion and dance shows, all of which have demonstrated the A.V.A.'s professionalism.

All these big productions, as well as the smaller various school assemblies which nowadays average one per month, require many hours of rehearsals. In the 1960s, these were always held after school and often ran past 10 or 11 o'clock at night. With the school no longer open 24-hours a day, however, and with more and more students working part-time or involved in other activities, the trend at present is toward day-time rehearsals; the increased complexity of shows and the resulting workload has also required A.V.A. members not only to sacrifice the odd "spare" but to miss

the occasional class as well (a reality still not universally accepted among the members' teachers!).

* * *

(Story: The Perils of Duty; One fine spring day on the Lisgar mall, students were fund-raising for the "Jump Rope for Heart," skipping to music furnished by the A.V.A. All was fine for the (anonymous!) crew member in charge until behold, from on high, a diarrhetic sea gull christened the sound system and the member's homework!)

* * *

As Lisgar's shows have increased in number and complexity over the decades, so has the equipment used for them. The Film Projection Committee got its first microphone in 1943/44, and improvements have been added gradually ever since. The club made a projection screen for the auditorium in 1947/48, and the school received a new film projector, a better P.A. system, and a permanent film

This is a photo of the 1958-59 Audio-Visual Aids Club, by then six years old. Back row; l to r, W. Maddick, G. Elliott, J. Franklin, J. Batza, T. Lowry, B. Holdham. T. Bond, G. Read, B. Preston. Middle row, l to r: W. Lefresne, P. Lebel, H. York, B. Brassington, B. Berry, C. Beckingham, G. Knee, B. Lowry. Front row, l to r: L. Aubrey, J.E. Fordyce, R. Haas, B. Taggart, L. Jones, F. Blair, B. Switzer, J. Baldwin, E. Hanna. Absent; R, Craig, W. Anderson, C. Ross, B. Gilmore, D. Thorsell.

PRESIDENTS OF STUDENTS' COUNCIL, 1945-1993

George Toller	1945	Alison Brodie, Dave Sadavoy	1969
Bill Extence	1946	Elizabeth Baird, Bruce Laffin	1970
Eric Toller	1947	Grant Buchanan, Victoria Jordan	1971
Gayton White	1948	Cheryl Kardish, Sean Meehan	1972
Bruce Kirby, Pat Lowe	1949	David Robison, Shelagh Rogers	1973
Paul Hudson, Betty Joe	1950	Peter Blaiklock, Christie Laidlaw	1974
Miriam Rainboth, Basil Clark	1951	Adam Shoemaker, Sarita Verma	1975
Sylvia Van Steenburgh, Brian Wherrett	1952	Vince Parkin, Jocelyn Webb	1976
Betty Swerdfager, Bill Thorsteinson	1953	Catherine Drake, Paul Litwack	1977
Sally MacDonald, Fergus Oliver	1954	David Littlejohn, May Zayed	1978
Helen Alexiade, Dick Charron	1955	Eva Bild, Tom Kovesi	1979
Bob Gaudsley, Adrienne Poy	1956	Judy Gorman, John Young	1980
Hugh Hiscox, Pat Young	1957	Chris Parsons, Chak Wong	1981
Charles Bostock, Margery Hayward	1958	Mitchell Anderson, Brian Mitchell	1982
Eric Manning, Phyllis-Anne Payan	1959	Ian Clayton, Lilani Kumaranayake	1983
Bob Green, Anne Groves	1960	Peter Cureton, Steve Tenai	1984
Steve Duncan, Barbara McPhee	1961	Steve Harris, David McFarlane	1985
Bill Hamilton, Judith Schneider	1962	Inez Costa, Chad Hutchison	1986
Dick Leeson, Joanne Schneider	1963	Cynthia Jolly, John Shoemaker	1987
Simonne Dion, Doug Thom	1964	Dan Darin-Zanko, Tracey Tanaka	1988
Heather Buchanan, Martin Hume	1965	Peter Land, Virginia Okolie	1989
Beth MacFarlane, Jack Munro	1966	Cameron Hughes, Leonard Tse	1990
James Benedickson, Joan Fisher	1967	Max Edwards, Lisa Merrithew	1991
Dave Fletcher, Patricia Fulton	1968	David Applebaum, Max Herzog	1992
		Leslie Kriekle, Eric Schouten	1993

booth for the auditorium in 1948/49. By 1952/53, the P.A. system had been improved with a new tape recorder and microphone. By the 1960s, "sound" consisted of a cabinet in the wings with a few mike jacks, an amp, and a home-made mixer for a remote; this system was also hooked into the school's P.A. system so that students not in the auditorium could listen in from the classroom (for only half the school could fit into the auditorium at a time).

Don Waddell writes of the early years of the club:

"The school had very little in the way of audio-visual equipment. Stage lighting consisted of a few sixty-watt footlights [which have since been removed] and one or two 100-watt overhead stage lights. We were not fortunate enough to have any coloured lights to add warmth to the stage. . . For concerts we were able to borrow a 500-watt spotlight from one of the local theatres."

The school's lighting system did improve, however, as it gradually acquired such equipment as the Strand carbon-arc followspot in 1953/54, an item still in use today.

Nevertheless, by 1964 the auditorium light system consisted of only eight to ten good spotlights which were connected to eight or nine big mechanical transformer dimmers located in the wings—there was no remote! David Jeanes, A.V.A. president in 1963/64, worked with Strand Electric for two years to design a new system to suit Lisgar's needs. The new system used thyristor solid state dimmers and was the first of its kind in Canada! The console was also custom-labelled and colour-coded for the school, a feature which was not available once Strand put the unit into mass production. The lights were also upscaled in 1965/66; F.O.H.s were moved from under the balcony to the window wells where their light would not blind performers, and two bars of coloured strip lighting ("X-rays") were installed along with a baton of spotlights above the stage.

While a new amp and six-channel mixer purchased by the A.V.A. were added to the auditorium's sound system in 1986, the light system remained pretty well the same until 1991/92 when it was replaced, again, by state-of-the-art Strand system. The new set-up is a "dedicated system," using one dimmer per outlet, and while the old dimmer racks were over 30 cubic feet apiece with a total capacity of 40 circuits, the new rack is only 20 cubic feet and can handle up to 96 circuits. The new console is programmable, extremely versatile and, unlike its massive predecessor, light enough to be lifted with one hand.

* * *

(Story: "That wasn't very smart," said Chris Parker with an unnatural smile, shaking a little as he walked slowly across the stage, holding a half-cut electrical cord in one hand and a melted pair of scissors in the other!)

* * *

The A.V.A. has not only been indispensable in the auditorium but also in the gymnasium and cafeteria where it has provided music at scores of school dances. The Film Projection Committee was deejaying dances as early as 1944/45, although there is no mention in the *Vox* until 1960/61 of the club ever holding its own dances. The first A.V.A. evening dance was held in 1963/64, when the club's sound system consisted of two tape recorders, a record player, and two small P.A. speakers. Most of the music was borrowed from friends or taped from the radio, although the club tried in vain to get free promo 45s from the distributors. All the same, the A.V.A. continued to keep Lisgar rocking at dances for many years thereafter.

A.V.A. members delivered Bell telephone books to raise some capital which enabled them to start deejaying again, but this time at elementary schools. They started with the old Bogen amp, Courier P.A. speakers, a turntable, members' records and charged about $25 a dance. The dance lights consisted of two "light boxes" which contained coloured flood lights, and an old mechanical chaser which had once run the Ottawa Auditorium billboard.

By the late 1970s the A.V.A. was doing Lisgar dances again, and by the early 1980s, exclusively so. Today, the club's equipment also includes a Yamaha WX200 dual-bay cassette deck which gets considerable use in Lisgar's four to five annual dances.

* * *

(Story: At a dance at Ashbury in the 1970s, the A.V.A. managed to get hold of the sound system used for the Festival of Spring. An experiment to see how well 700 watts of power can fill a small room was soon answered by the police, responding to a complaint called in from half a mile away!)

* * *

Throughout its history, the A.V.A. has shown itself to be innovative, creative, and ready to explore new ways to serve the school's students. In the 1960s, for example, long before light shows were in vogue, the club was already experimenting with black light: in 1964/65 the club held a "Twilight Zone Dance" and at one assembly students were shocked to see a piece of fluorescent chalk "drawing all by itself in the darkness." For another assembly in the early 1960s, when only one Beatles' single was available in North American stores, the club managed to get hold of an entire album, parts of which it played to a bewildered student audience!

By the late 1970s, another innovation known as the "taped announcement" was born and became an instant hit; so much so, in fact, that rules had to be established to regulate for how long and how frequently the announcements would be played. The A.V.A. was also, indirectly, the founder of C.W.L.S., a school radio station which aired in the building during lunch-hours in the early 1980s.

The club has had a history of joint ventures with other clubs. Around 1980, for example, the A.V.A. saw there was a demand among students for a photocopier, so the club joined with the Library Club to rent this expensive new technology for the library; this later led to the school purchasing one of its own. More recently, with contributions from the Dance Club and Lisgar Fund, the A.V.A. was able to buy a $1100.00 Rosco fog machine.

Over the past twenty years, the club has acquired well over $15,000.00 worth of its own equipment, including its sound system. Tascam mixer, Par-64 and Par-38 lights. Rosco fog machine, and even the school auditorium sound and intercom system.

Hopefully the club's next investment with the help of the Lisgar Fund, will be new lights for the auditorium.

* * *

(Story: While working on a Lisgar concert, member Ian Ng had dropped his pencil down the dark cavity behind the catwalk in the flies and had decided to climb down and retrieve it. He didn't realize the area he had stepped down into was the ceiling of the exit for the stage. When he fell through the ceiling Ian broke his ankle and was lying there on his back with people leaning over him saying, "What happened? What happened?" "I dunno," Ian said, "I was just standing there when the ceiling flew past my face!")

* * *

Many Lisgar alumni have used their experience gained in the club to embark on careers in stage, television, or radio productions, people like John Franklin at CBC Parliamentary TV, Dave Midgley with Glen Warren Productions. Nevertheless, even those alumni who have gone into other fields have still benefitted from the unique experience of being a part of the A.V.A., an experience of learning, creativity, and teamwork (along with a healthy dose of pressure!).

Over the past fifty years, technology has made rapid advances, especially in the audio-visual field, with the advent of video tape and CDs, to name a few. From the film projector to the digital lighting console the A.V.A. club has kept abreast of this technology and is sure to continue to do so at Lisgar for another fifty years or more.

Some alumni from the 1950s and '60s may have A.V.A. club pins or even club crests among their memorabilia. Today, however, graduating members are awarded with the coveted Golden Wrench Award, named after that certain ever-elusive tool. Its engraved brass plaque reads:

"GET A GRIP ON IT!"

—Jeffrey Cavill, 1987-1991

HISTORY OF LISGAR LIBRARY

The library at Lisgar Collegiate Institute has been an integral part of the school from the outset. Mr. Robert Stothers, secretary of the Executive Committee responsible for the 1904 publication, *A History of the Ottawa Collegiate Institute 1843-1903* ("the Colonel" to the many history students he taught in his forty years at Lisgar) quotes a "writer of the time" describing the first library space: . . . "on the right and left [on the ground floor] are general classrooms and on one side a library measuring twenty-five by fifteen feet. . ."

In 1992, looking back over twenty-three years, Dave McGougan enumerated some of the changes to the library in his time as music teacher at Lisgar from 1959 to 1964 and later as librarian, 1964 to 1992.

When I joined the Music Department of Lisgar in September 1959 the library was still just one room on the first floor of the North building. Renovations the previous summer had included the addition of oak shelving and new light fixtures. Work that summer also saw the addition, on both sides of the library's entrance, of plaques commemorating the students who had served in both world wars as well as the Korean Conflict. Above the doorway, oak panels with the hand-carved numbers *14-18* and *39-45* were included as another tribute to the soldiers of both world wars. The plaques and oak panels formed the basis of the Memorial Hall, a tribute to military service that graces the school's main entrance to this day.

Upon my arrival at Lisgar, [Mr. McGougan continued], the librarian was Mrs. Lillian Atkinson. In addition to her duties in the library, Mrs. Atkinson also taught history and provided counselling in the Guidance Department for an hour in the morning before classes, and for another one-half hour after school each day. Members of the Library Club helped with a variety of

The Library Club has had a long history of volunteer help in the library. The Library Club of 1974-75, besides duties at the circulation desk and reading shelves, showed a few old silent movies during the year and sponsored a noon-hour lecturer from Carleton University. The library provides displays in the main showcases, archival and literary. In 1974-75 as a result of inflation, overdue fines had to be raised. Back row, left to right; Anmtoni Ogonowski, Pat Power, Lydia Prins, Anthony Burton, Francisco Toro, Howard Mount, Mike Pootmans, Allan Maybe. Middle row, l to r: (space), Susan Li, Pat Whitridge, Sau Lin Leung, Cathy Alexander, Chris Franklin, Terry Berkley, Mike Berkley. Front row, l to r: Bonnie Blair, Karen Tanino, Dave McGougan, Jane Armstrong, Jane Franklin, Stephen Lawrence.

duties including shelving returns, circulation record-keeping, and cataloguing new materials. Because of the library's modest size, seating was limited to only a few students; and all circulation procedures were handled from a small desk situated at one side of the room near the entrance.

The library's collection during this period consisted solely of books, approximately five or six thousand titles. No catalogues were kept; rather, accession books (still in use today) were used and each book was processed for the shelves. A card pocket was glued to the inside cover of each book. A borrower's card was made out and inserted in the pocket of each loaned book. A library stamps and a Dewey Decimal Classification call number were affixed to each book. Since all information regarding the loan of an individual book was handwritten, tracking the collection was a very labour-intensive exercise.

The 1960s brought many changes to the library. In 1960 the library was expanded by incorporating the classroom on its west side. A seminar-study room was built in the northwest corner of this newly expanded space to afford senior students a place to study. By the mid-1960s this seminar room was converted into the library's office as well as a small workroom where books were processed.

During the 1961-62 school year the library's hours of operation were expanded to include one-half hour during the lunch period. Members of the Hi-Y helped to monitor the library during this time. Unfortunately these expanded hours lasted only two years. In 1963-64, due to insufficient help, the library was again closed during the lunch period. It was also during this period that Mrs. Atkinson retired and Mr. McGougan was appointed librarian. For the first time Lisgar's library had a full-time librarian, and students were able to access the library on a daily basis between eight o'clock in the morning and five o'clock in the afternoon.

The growth of the library continued in the late 1960s. A clerk-typist and an assistant librarian, Mrs. Shagufta Rana, were hired in the summer of 1968. Simultaneously, a classroom on the east side of the library—up until that time Mr. Argue's history room—was claimed for the library. The newly expanded library was refurbished with new tables, study carrels, chairs and drapes to complement an ever-increasing book collection. In 1969 there were approximately eighty-three hundred books.

Also during this period the library acquired audio-visual equipment and materials. Film strips, film loops, and recordings, along with the requisite equipment, were acquired. In addition, the library staff began to keep a vertical file, which included a vast array of clippings, pictures, maps, and various pamphlets deemed to be of interest to library users. Mrs. Rana who is responsible for this file, has come to know, in her more than twenty years at Lisgar, what students require in the way of supplementary materials.

Mrs. Rana explains that the vertical file is intended to supplement Lisgar's book collection: "It gives students a current perspective, and different views, on a particular subject. The subjects of most interest to today's students," she observes, "are abortion, free trade, constitutional history, and the environment."

The creation in 1967 of the Library Service Centre by the Collegiate Institute Board of Ottawa had a profound effect on all school libraries under its jurisdiction. Instead of having to catalogue all the new books themselves, school librarians could send them to the Centre for processing, thus giving librarians more time to spend with teachers in promoting the use of library resources in their schools.

In the fall of 1968 Lisgar celebrated its one hundred and twenty-fifth anniversary. The Library Club arranged a display in the library of all extant copies of the *Vox Lycei* stored in the library and dating from 1886 to 1967. The one hundred and twenty-fifth reunion also gave renewed impetus to the library staff's practice of collecting pertinent Lisgar material: articles, photographs, and correspondence relating to the school have been collected and filed in the school's Archives. Teachers have also been encouraged to contribute programmes, lists, reports, photographs, and memorabilia thought to be worth saving for future historical reference as Lisgar matures into its second century. Indeed, the archival record expanded to such a extent that it became necessary to set aside a room specifically for the storage of these treasures. Prior to the one hundred and fortieth anniversary of the Collegiate in 1984, considerable archival material was turned over to the City of Ottawa Archives for storage and safekeeping.

During the 1970s, three floor stacks were installed in the east room of the library to accommodate the growing number of volumes. Floor stacks were utilized to make the best use of available space since it was not possible to expand the library: there were no more adjacent classrooms that could be claimed. These stacks were destroyed during the 1977 renovations, but have since been replaced.

In the 1970s works in French and German were added to the collection to service the needs of the increasing numbers of students studying these languages. At the teachers' request, these books are kept in separate locations within the library, and, to facilitate their effective use, a separate card catalogue denotes the selections available.

Beginning in the spring of 1976 and continuing through the summer, the whole of the North building, including the library, was renovated. During this renovation some floor space was gained by moving the library office and eliminating the workroom. Overhead lighting fixtures were removed entirely and replaced, in all three rooms, by indirect wall lighting. Track lighting was installed in all three rooms when it was discovered that the existing lighting did not meet provincial standards for school libraries. The comfort factor was further enhanced at this time with the installation of air-conditioning.

The early 1980s were a time of growth in terms of both the collection itself and the programmes the library offered. In 1982 the Ottawa Board of Education published a document entitled *Partners in Education*, which outlined practical measures to effect the transition of school libraries to "library resource centres." Teacher-librarians were encouraged to spend more time working in co-operation with teachers and the administration to promote greater use of the libraries and more effective research techniques. In the fall of 1983, as a response to an increase in losses due to thefts, a security system was installed to prevent books that had not been loaned, and recorded as such, being removed from the library. By 1985 the collection had reached approximately thirteen thousand and three hundred books as well as numerous audio-visual materials.

In the spring of 1984, to commemorate the one hundred and fortieth anniversary of the Collegiate, copies of *The Vox Lycei* were again presented for display in the library. By this time all copies of the yearbook had been individually bound to prevent their deterioration. The cost of this undertaking had been subsidized by the Student Council of 1974.

Another development aimed at improving library service during the 1980s was the adoption of the University of Toronto Library Automation Systems (UTLAS Inc.). Participating Ottawa Board of Education libraries were provided with microcomputers to which catalogues were transferred. Since then, all existing holdings and new acquisitions have been catalogued on this computer and the data has been transferred to a central hard disk. As a result, the Library Service Centre is now able to track the collections of all participating libraries and effect inter-institutional loans when necessary.

In the spring of 1992 the Lisgar library acquired CD-ROM technology. Utilizing compact disks, much like those used in stereo systems, CD-ROM technology allows users access to sound and moving pictures, as well as conventional text

Library Technician; Mrs. Shagufta Rana 1968 —

data. The amount of information stored on a single disk is very impressive. For instance, the Time Inc. CD held by the library contains all issues of *Time* magazine from 1920 through 1991! Colour representations of the covers, as well as the articles themselves and a variety of maps, charts, and graphs, provide users with a complete document of the later three-quarters of the twentieth century. The system is interfaced with a printer that allows users to obtain copies of illustrations and text for further reference or inclusion in an essay.

Over the years several collections have been established in the library: the George C. Holland Memorial Collection, the Victor N. Bruce Memorial Collection, the J. Earle Thom Memorial Collection, the J.W. Neil Canadiana Collection, and the Rich Little Humour Collection. George C. Holland attended the Ottawa Collegiate Institute before 1900 and

later became part owner of the *Ottawa Citizen*. The Victor N. Bruce Memorial Collection was established by Principal Bruce's widow shortly after his death in 1960. J. Earle Thom taught biology at Lisgar from 1944 until his death in 1970, when his widow donated many of his personal books to the library in his memory. J.W. Neil joined the Lisgar staff in 1939, becoming vice-principal in 1951 and then principal in 1960; upon his retirement in 1972 a group of alumni established the Canadiana Collection in his honour. Finally, the Rich Little Humour Collection was set up during the one hundred and fortieth anniversary in 1984 by the Student Council to honour one of Lisgar's most famous alumni in the entertainment field.

Several of Lisgar's alumni have become successful writers and the library has always attempted to purchase their books. Included in the collection at present are the works of Peter Abrahams, Adrienne Clarkson, Joan Finnigan, Norman Guiou, Anthony Hyde, Christopher Hyde, Norman Levine, W.F. Lothian, Wilfred Lynch, and Tim Plumtre.

The library's walls are graced with a number of paintings and prints, many of which have been donated. Others have been rendered by students and alumni of Lisgar, among them an ink drawing of Lord Lisgar, crafted by Anne Thackray, to recognize the one hundred and twenty-fifth anniversary of the school, and an original pencil drawing of the school done recently for the book, *Historical Sketches of Ottawa*, a copy of which may be found in the library's collection.

In 1983 the Royal Canadian Dragoons presented the school with a copy of the print, "Saving the Guns at Leliefontein, 7th Nov. 1900." The scene depicted shows the act of bravery that resulted in Sergeant Edward J.G. Hollands being awarded the Victoria Cross. Ben Babelowsky's original oil painting of the one hundred and twenty-fifth anniversary logo of the Collegiate is also on display in the library.

—Dave McGougan

THE CLASSICS DEPARTMENT

For about ten years after the end of the Second World War the Classics Department reflected what the departments in all schools were reflecting—namely that people were coming home and going back to peace again. And the feeling of going back brought about a fair amount of stability so that from about '45 to '55 there were not many changes. Students will remember textbooks like our own one, *Latin for Canadian Schools*, and will remember Latin for five years leading up to Grade Thirteen. In Grade Twelve the reading became a little wider, and then in Grade Thirteen there were those cycles—Cycle One, Cycle Two, Cycle Three for the departmental exam at the end of the year. I'm quite sure that many memories come from the textbook where people plodded through declensions and conjugations, being able to reproduce paradigms of verbs in the third person plural, getting on to such high spots of grammatical activity as the passive paraphrastic without which no educated gentleman dare even think of facing the world.

Luckily for us, a Lisgar graduate, May Hambley, decided that she could put a revision forward. It was accepted and the revision managed to make the learning of the vocabulary, for instance, much more relevant to English vocabulary by derivations. In my opinion this was one of the signs in the late fifties and probably the early sixties that change was coming into the school system whereby curriculum was moving forward into something a little more relevant. At the same time, the Classics Department since 1936 led by Wally Showman, was gaining much credit throughout the scholastic milieu. A very thorough and dedicated scholar, he was assisted by Mary Gemmill and Doug Kennedy. During those years many students of the classics attained high marks, won scholarships. The unfortunate thing was that a lot of people felt the English-to-Latin sentences, for instance, were one of the real "banes of life." And the translation material of those cycles was pretty dull and pretty formal, being almost unchanged cycle after cycle.

267

Doug Kennedy who taught Latin at Lisgar for twenty-eight years.

In 1966 Wally Showman retired and I was appointed to the department, still with Mary Gemmill and Doug Kennedy. We began to institute change again on the level of trying to make the link with the English language, and with English literature in general, a little more the result of the learning of Latin. The textbook changed to *The Cambridge Latin* produced in Cambridge County in England and more oriented around the reading of Latin and not nearly so heavily loaded on memorizing grammar. True, the grammar came, but not in the same way as it had done through the previous textbook and teaching method.

I do believe that the reading material in *The Cambridge Latin* was the reason for Latin holding out at a time when everywhere around us Latin was being dropped. For instance, the first section of the reading concerned Pompeii. Chapter after chapter had to do with real people who lived in Pompeii at the time of the eruption of Mount Vesuvius. These changes that began to take place in the sixties were reflected right across the province, not only in Classics, but in many other subjects. People began to suggest that the departmental examinations might be done away with, and indeed they were in the mid-sixties. No longer did students have to face the examination in Grade Twelve or the annual Latin exam in Grade Thirteen. Schools were left to set their own examinations. Many schools across Ontario and the United States began to use *The Cambridge Latin* and with it there began to be the feeling of reading Latin and seeing its relation to English, thinking widely about the use of Latin,

and other subjects like Greek. Into the curriculum we managed to insert Classical Civilization for one year. This was not, of course, a language course but it was one whereby the students were able to look at the civilizations that led up to the Greek one, and then at Greece and Rome, and then at the civilization of today which inherits very much from the Greek or Roman civilization. And one of the school activities that reflected this wider approach to the classics was the beginning in 1971 of school tours to Italy and Greece.

I think there will be many people who will remember the tour in 1971. After some time in Rome the students went to Pisa. You can imagine the chaperones' delight when—as soon as the people got out of the bus—they shinnied up the Leaning Tower and held onto the pillars—which didn't have guard rails—waving and yelling down at the poor chaperones on the ground.

The ship left from Genoa. As soon as it cleared the harbour, waves began to break over the bow of the ship. Not being a great lover of rough seas, I thought this suggested stormy weather and my stomach agreed! But Doug Arrand who somehow manages to believe in waves as being part of sea travel said, "Oh, it's just a little wave here and there." However, when the ship was heading towards Greece and Istanbul the captain, one night, had to put on full power, turn the ship into the storm, and hope that he wouldn't be blown ashore. Many students were holding on to the rails and wishing that they had never left home. However, in the end, this slight storm got us into calmer weather and through the Corinth Canal over to Turkey and Istanbul.

In Istanbul the sights were duly seen and in the evening students went off in the buses to a night club. Enter Barrie Laughton. Now for customers that night and our party of about ninety people the main entertainment, of course, would be belly dancing. Lisgar students were absorbed in the shapely young lady as she executed some very tricky pieces of her art. And then didn't we see Barrie Laughton at the end of one of the tables trying to pin an artificial flower on the belly dancer! Now there are not too many places available on a belly dancer for pinning anything on, so Barrie managed to raise great shouts of laughter by his attempts to decorate the young lady. When the dance ended she stood up, thanked everybody and suggested that since belly dancing is such a lovely activity, she would be quite happy to teach somebody how to do it. She walked straight forward to Barrie saying, "I wonder, sir, if you would come out and I'll teach you a few steps." Being an excellent sport Barrie went forward for his lessons. She showed him how to gyrate with all her body parts moving. But Barrie was really not built for belly dancing.

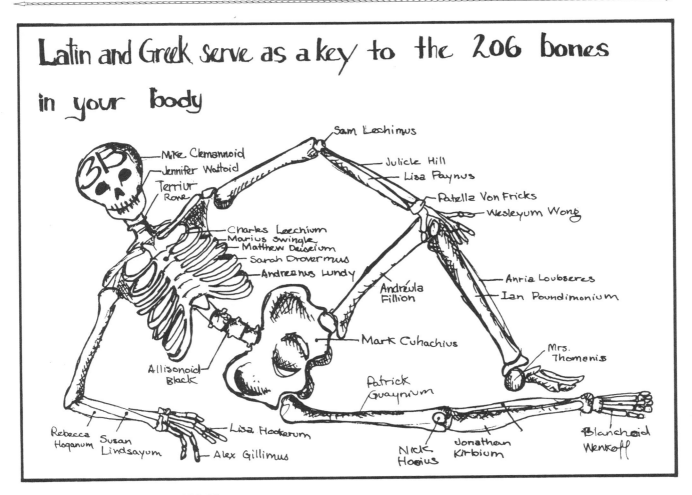

Latin and Greek serve as a key to the 206 bones in your body

Sam Leehimus
Mike Clemannoid
Jennifer Wattoid
Terriur Rone
Julicle Hill
Lisa Paynus
Patella Von Fricks
Wesleyum Wong
Charles Leechium
Marius Swingle
Matthew Deiselum
Sarah Drovermus
Andreanus Lundy
Andréula Fillion
Anria Loubseres
Ian Poundimonium
Mark Cuhachius
Allisonoid Black
Patrick Guaynium
Mrs. Thomenis
Rebecca Hoganum
Susan Lindsayum
Lisa Hookerum
Alex Gillimus
Nick Hooius
Jonathan Kirbium
Blanchoid Wenkoff

A class ad in the *Vox Lycei*, 1982-83.

A short time later a conjurer came on stage—he wanted somebody from the audience and nobody was surprised when Barrie again was asked to participate. Within a minute of being asked where he came from and what he did, the conjurer had removed both Barrie's wristwatch and the belt from his trousers! For the second time Barrie was the hero of that night in Istanbul. It certainly was the kind of thing that gives a wider, deeper understanding of the classics.

From then on about every third year we were able to get a group together and that tour of Italy and Greece almost became a regular feature of the curriculum. On all of these tours an attempt was made to be in Rome at the time of the Papal audience, usually held on a Wednesday, so that the students would be able to have a close-up view of the Pope as he came down the aisle of St. Peter's. Surprisingly, however, one of the students came up to one of the chaperones and said, "Do we have to stay?" When we asked her why she said, "I'm getting my bottom pinched all the time by the Italian boys. They're doing nothing but going around showing the Italian greeting, and I don't like it." We tried to shoo these amorous males out of St. Peter's and make them leave our Canadian girls alone.

A permit was given for the Lisgar students to be sitting right in the front row beside the altar so that when the Pope came down they'd have an excellent view. At the same time a permit was given for one teacher and two students to have a private audience with the Pope, at that time Pope Paul the Sixth. When the service was over and the rest of the students were going back out into St. Peter's Square, the two chosen students were ushered into the Pope's little room where he was standing with an interpreter. But he didn't need any interpreting because his English was very good.

During the eighties prices began to go up and it became difficult sometimes to raise forty-five people to make a bus load. That was when we began to join up with Glebe or Hillcrest and, by linking two schools together, still be able to make a tour group. Back home during the eighties with costs still rising, travel became less possible, and so things at home became more important. In school, the Classics Department did its best to keep the standard up and everybody was very conscious of the discussion going on about having standardized exams, departmentals or otherwise, in some form. Even now into the nineties there is still talk of what to do with standards.

Concerning these standards, I had a very interesting experience when I was attending an Ontario Classical Association meeting at Brock University. A teacher rose and asked me to stand. When I did, he then pointed in my direction and said, "There is the Head of Classics at Lisgar Collegiate in Ottawa, the only remaining Ontario school with Latin for a full five years, Greek for three years, and Classical Civilization at Grade Eleven." There was a good round of applause because, by the time the late eighties had rolled around, there were so many other languages and so many other subjects vying for positions on the curriculum that maintaining a full classics program was regarded as some achievement!

—Robin Wedderspoon

SCIENCE
1940s-1990s

THE FORTIES

World War II overshadowed everything. Lisgar students went to war, some never to return. Those students who were too young to fight could not help but be affected by the absence of their peers or their relatives. Studying the mundane subjects of high school must have seemed irrelevant, even trivial to some. Even when the war ended, the emergence of the antagonisms between communism and democracy did little to renew youths' faith in world order. Germany was split into two separate states, one aligned with the West, one with the East. Western nations sought a common defence against communism in the 1949 creation of the North Atlantic Treaty Organization. The eastern block countries would counter with the Warsaw Pact in 1955. One of the few hopeful signs in the forties was the creation of the United Nations. Somehow, through this terrible decade, education continued.

The mainstays of the Science Department in the forties were Louis Meng (physics), Stewart Felker (chemistry), Andy Fitzsimmons (chemistry) and A.H. "Fuzzy" Irwin. Earle Thom arrived, in 1944, from Markham High school, where he had been for eight years, as teacher and principal. He was to teach chemistry at Lisgar but soon became one of the best-known biology teachers of the time.

Of necessity, Lisgar students were aware of the world around them. The war had driven home the destructive applications to which scientific advances could be put. Just two years after the end of the war, the *Vox* editor made reference to "The imminent peril of an atomic war. . ." This fear would remain a part of students' lives for several generations.

The *Vox* also demonstrated attitudes towards women that were typical of the time and that would remain pervasive for decades to come. On a page headed *For Boys Only*, appeared a parody of a textbook description of a chemical element. The element was Women (Wo) and the text went on to outline its physical and chemical properties ("Boils at nothing, and may freeze easily," "Ages and deteriorates rapidly.") Uses were listed as "Adorning magazine covers" and "Helping men spend money." Such an item, seemingly innocuous by itself, was part of an environment that made subjects like science and engineering male domains, and vestiges of which remain to be eradicated to this day.

This chemistry lab was new in 1903. It remained this way until 1972 renovations.

Probably a biology lab and classroom, new in 1903 and used for sixty-nine years.

Room 307, the old science lecture hall.

While the Second World War dominated the lives of everyone in the realm of science and technology, other events occurred that were to influence students' lives and studies in the years to come.

1940: The Tacoma Narrows Bridge, a suspension bridge in Tacoma, Washington, collapses from resonance set up by wind gusts in the area. The film of the event becomes a staple of physics classes to this day. Important advances are made in the study of fissionable material, and in the separation of uranium-235 from uranium-238. The invention of freeze-drying advances the technology of food preservation. The first experimental colour television signal is broadcast. A Canadian discovers carbon-14, a substance that will become vital in dating ancient materials. An antibiotic is developed from penicillin.

1941: Sir Frederick Banting dies. Aerosol spray for insecticides is invented.

1942: The first controlled chain reaction is conducted by Enrico Fermi. Stephen Hawking, widely regarded today as the most brilliant physicist since Einstein, is born in England. Overcoming the debilitating effects of Lou Gehrig's disease, Professor Hawking has changed our view of the cosmos with his research into black holes and the birth of the universe. The prototype of later electronic computers is developed.

1943: The substance LSD is found to be hallucinogenic. A kidney dialysis machine is built. Streptomycin is discovered. Jacques Cousteau is co-inventor of the Aqualung. Alan Turing produces the first all-electronic calculating machine. Named Colossus, it is used for war-time code-cracking.

1944: A Canadian, Oswald Avery, is co-discoverer of the hereditary role of deoxyribonucleic acid (DNA). DNA is the molecule that is the ultimate and universal controller of life processes. V-1 and V-2 rockets are used in the war. The first tetracycline antibiotic is discovered.

1945: Knowledge of cell structure is greatly increased by electron microscope studies. The herbicide 2,4D is introduced. The first use of fluoridation of water supplies to prevent dental decay occurs in the United States.

1946: A V-2 rocket carries a scientific payload to a height of 55 km. The Electronic Numerical Integrator and Computer (ENIAC) is completed. It is considered to be the first true electronic computer. The power drain during operation is such that lights dim in a nearby town. A serendipitous discovery leads to the first "artificial" snow storm, caused by seeding clouds with dry ice.

The Fifties

The decade began with the Korean War. The cold war between East and West intensified. The Warsaw Pact was formed, the Soviet Union invaded Hungary and the superpowers continued their above-ground testing of thermonuclear weapons. School children were subjected to missile attack drills and the general populace paid more than a passing interest in the home bomb shelters and other possible defences against nuclear war.

Student rebellion against their elders, occurred as usual, in their music. In this decade, however, their defiance resulted in a durable musical form that, with various mutations, would survive until the present. The decadence of Rock and Roll had arrived. Parents, educators and politicians fretted over the evil influence of Elvis, Chuck Berry, Jerry Lee Lewis and Little Richard. Buddy Holly had legions of fans and was less threatening to adults. His untimely death in 1959 was marked by a local radio station playing his last record repeatedly for 24 hours. Pat Boone had full parental approval and therefore was less appreciated by students. Folk music, sung by groups like the Kingston Trio and the New Christie Minstrels, also had a large following. Recording quality improved as the scratchy and fragile 78 RPM disks were replaced by the long-play vinyl album and the ubiquitous 45 RPM single.

The Science Department was anchored, through the fifties, by Louis Meng (physics), Earle Thom (biology), Stewart Felker (chemistry), Andy Fitzsimmons (chemistry). The latter retired at the very end of the decade after a 25-year stay at Lisgar. As the *Vox* noted at the time, when he left, "There wasn't a dry eye in the school." In 1953, A.H. "Fuzzy" Irwin retired after one of the longest teaching careers ever—44 years, with 32 of them devoted to Lisgar. To add to this astounding record, Mr. Irwin was a graduate of O.C.I. in 1907!

Student concern with science in the real world continued to be expressed in the school year books. Fear of the nuclear threat showed itself in phrases like "Perhaps we shall have no tomorrow" and in calls for an end to stockpiling of nuclear weapons as an antidote to "world destruction." Thoughtful editorials pointed out the implications of the space race, started by the Sputnik launch. The editor in 1959 observed, "There is a sudden demand for more, better-paid, better-trained teachers, for more extensive science courses, for fewer 'frills'." Students were also recognizing the world's population problems, with one editor quite accurately noting that the world population would double to almost five billion within 40 years.

Events that would have an impact on the lives of students and on what they studied were many.

1950: The first embryo transplants for cattle are performed. Colour television is available for the home viewer. The first charge card is put into circulation. Cyclamate, an artificial sweetener is marketed.

1951: UNIVAC 1 becomes the first electronic computer to be made available on a commercial scale. It stores data on magnetic tape. The Nobel Prize for Chemistry is given, in part, for the discovery of plutonium.

1952: A hearing aid that uses transistors is introduced. A pocket sized transistor radio is produced by Sony. Chalk River becomes the site of the world's first accident at a nuclear reactor. A study of viruses attacking bacteria is an important first step that would later lead to genetic engineering. The Hydrogen bomb, which generates its energy through nuclear fusion, is developed. The first one is exploded at Eniwetok Atoll.

1953: X-ray studies of DNA help eventually to unravel its structure.

1954: A study of chemical bonds wins Linus Pauling a Nobel Prize. The photovoltaic cell, able to produce electricity from sunlight, is produced by Bell Telephone scientists.

1955: Deep freezers that are able to freeze fresh food are marketed. Artificial diamonds, a practical hovercraft and optical fibres appear, and Velcro is patented. Albert Einstein dies at Princeton, New Jersey.

1956: The first large electrical generating plant, designed for the peaceful use of nuclear power, opens in England.

1957: Earth's first artificial satellite, Sputnik, is launched.

1958: The United States successfully launches its first satellite. Bifocal contact lenses are marketed. In medicine, ultrasound is used to observe unborn babies.

1959: Xerox sells the first copier. The St. Lawrence Seaway opens the Great Lakes to ocean traffic.

THE SIXTIES

A turbulent time for North America. While students here worked to prepare themselves for the "real world," in the nation to the south, political leaders were assassinated, and violence erupted over racial issues. U.S. students no older than our own went to war in the far east, dropped out of mainstream society, and experimented with drugs and new sexual attitudes. It was the decade of Woodstock and the protest songs of Dylan and Baez. Strong feelings and attitudes from south of the border spilled over and influenced a generation of young Canadians.

With the introduction of the audio-cassette in 1963, listening habits began to move away from the record player, towards the more portable cassette tape-recorder. The music of youth progressed from the innocent naivete of the early Beatles' "She Loves You" to their later recordings like "Lucy in the Sky with Diamonds,' and "Magical Mystery Tour" album, from Elvis crooning "Are You Lonesome Tonight" to Strawberry Alarm Clock and "Incense and Peppermint," an anthem to the Flower Children. Surfer songs like those of the Beachboys, the Motown sounds of the Supremes and Marvin Gaye, the dark music of the Doors and the wild sounds of Hendrix and Joplin were also prominent in the musical lives of students in the sixties. And of course, the Stones. Musical theatre ranged from the early *Fiddler on*

the Roof to *Hair* at the height of the Vietnam era.

This was a transition decade for teaching at Lisgar. The changing of the guard. The sixties saw the flame passed to a new generation of teachers. In most departments, the old guard, the pride of L.C.I. and the object of respect and esteem of the teaching profession, ended their 30, even 40 year careers. Names like Mann, Meng, Rentner, Argue, Bishop, Felker, Showman, Rothwell, Fallis, Procter, Thom and Thompson receded into the educational history they had created. Young teachers apprenticed with some of them for a few years, then were left with the heavy responsibility of carrying on the Lisgar tradition of excellence.

Louis Meng, Science Head, physics teacher, and an institution at Lisgar since 1922, retired in 1965, leaving the leadership of the department to Larry Wade. Larry, an intense and dynamic chemical engineer had four years experience at Lisgar at the time of his appointment, and he would guide the often disparate personalities of his staff for the next 27 years.

This period saw the departure of Stewart Felker, author of the Grade 13 text, *Chemistry for the Upper School.* The 1947 *Vox* referred to this popular teacher as a kindly mentor, and stated that "his manner of fire-side philosophizing is as homey (sic) as marmelade (sic) and toast." Biology specialist, Earle Thom, renowned for his meticulous notes arrayed in coloured chalk across every blackboard in the room, retired in 1970. Arriving for lengthy stays were Margaret Herbert (biology and physics) and Terry Prichett (physics). The congenial Roger Brisebois (biology) and jovial Jim Forster (chemistry) each arrived early in the decade, made their marks, but left for other pursuits before the sixties ended.

Textbooks changed during the sixties first as a result of concern over the successes of the U.S.S.R. in the space race, then as a consequence of the Hall-Dennis Report. An example of the former was the appearance of the Physical Science Study Committee (PSSC) physics course. Created in the States, this course produced anxieties in senior physics students at Lisgar for the next 20 years—but prepared them well for future studies. Important changes in the senior chemistry and biology courses also occurred in the late sixties. The Chemstudy course, with its greater emphasis on experimentation, was introduced. Biology changed from its emphasis on classification and anatomy to a study of much of the chemistry associated with biological processes. The Hall-Dennis Report, particularly at the lower school level, resulted in a number of efforts at student-centred learning, some of which are best forgotten. Later attempts accomplished the transition from rote learning to a more self-directed learning that prepared students for the changing world around them.

The year 1967 saw the last Provincial Examination. Some interpreted this as the end of standards. Others saw it as an end to "teaching to the exam," and the restraints that the exams imposed. The truth, as always, lay somewhere between the extremes. Science teachers, like their colleagues in other departments, indeed had more freedom to try new approaches and tailor some topics to the interests and abilities of the class, but there were still courses of study and examination standards still had to be maintained.

New science contests were introduced on the provincial level, offering scholarships as awards. One of the best known of these was the SIN (Sir Isaac Newton) Contest. Lisgar students were encouraged from the start to enter and the first of many hundreds of SINners began a quest for the wages of SIN.

From the standpoint of science facilities, one important change was made at Lisgar in the latter part of the decade. At the instigation of Larry Wade, a new "standup" laboratory, designed solely for chemistry and equipped with a fume cabinet, was installed on the south side of the building. Next to it was built a small walk-in cupboard for storage of hazardous chemicals.

The sixties also saw a host of significant events in the world of science and technology. Many of these had an impact on what was taught in high school, or how it was taught.

1961: A laser is used for the first time for eye surgery.

1962: The first industrial robot is marketed in the States. Niels Bohr dies. In 1913, Bohr, a Danish physicist, developed a model of the atom that is familiar to students of Chemistry and Physics today. John Glenn makes the first U.S. orbital flight. Rachel Carson writes *The Silent Spring*. The Telstar communications satellite is launched.

1963: Valentia Tereshkova-Nikolayeva becomes the first woman in space. Syncom 2 becomes the first satellite in geostationary orbit.

1967: Christiaan Barnard performs the first partially successful human heart transplant. The technology of Dolby sound is introduced. Dolby noise reduction is used to reduce the background hiss on audio tapes.

1968: Irradiation to preserve food is introduced but not used because of fears of possible adverse effects.

1969: Neil Armstrong steps onto the lunar surface.

THE SEVENTIES

Students' musical tastes changed again in the seventies. The visual aspect of concerts and dance music became important. The former resulted in "glam rock," "shock rock," and "glitter rock," as exemplified by the likes of Queen, Alice Cooper and David Bowie. Dance music dominated the late seventies in the form of Disco and the Bee Gees. The nihilism of Punk Rock attracted some students, while Heavy Metal, initiated by bands like Led Zeppelin had devoted followers. And of course, the Stones. Movies ran the gamut

from the bizarre cult favourite *Rocky Horror Picture Show* to the benign *Grease*. (The latter film created an interesting Physics trivia question: which singer and actress had a Nobel Prize winning grandfather? Answer: Olivia Newton-John, star of *Grease* and popular seventies singer, was the grand-daughter of Max Born who won the Nobel in 1954 for his work on quantum dynamics in the twenties.)

Changes in teaching staff continued. Continuity from the sixties was provided by Larry Wade, and Terry Prichett, both of whom remained at Lisgar during the whole decade. Margaret Herbert became Margaret Dawson in 1975 and left to raise her family in 1979. Fortunately she was (and is) frequently available to return and supply teach for ailing department members. 1970 saw David Lamperd (biology), Bob MacMillan (chemistry) and Angus Cameron (chemistry) arrive, and each of them remained stalwart Lisgarites when the seventies ended. Terry McDonald taught biology briefly, left for several years, then returned and stayed into the eighties.

The science department continued to implement the ideas of the Hall-Dennis Report. Various techniques were employed to emphasize process while not eliminating content. Independent learning programmes were used in some courses. Changes in the training of teachers led to a greater awareness of current learning theories on the part of teachers. Higher level thinking skills became more important and the teaching of links and applications to the "real world" was encouraged.

PSSC test booklets continued to terrify senior physics students. These standardized tests asked students to apply what they had learned to situations they had not encountered before. Reliance on the ability to solve "type problems" was reduced. Despite the difficulty of such tests, the number of Grade 13 Physics classes rose from two or three small classes to four or five large ones in the ten-year span. Increases in enrollment occurred in Grade 13 Biology and Chemistry as well. The Ministry of Education document, HS1 or the "credit system," colloquially described as the "cafeteria approach" to course selection, was introduced early in the decade, and raised fears that students would avoid vital subjects like the sciences in favour of easier routes. Advisory efforts by all staff at the school and pressure from universities for more uniformity in applicants' backgrounds helped Lisgar students to continue to choose their programmes wisely. There were also encouraging signs that more girls were entering sciences. In Biology and Chemistry girls made up about half of the classes and their numbers approached this in Physics also.

A science club blossomed briefly in the early seventies, but only lasted two years. Lisgar students continued to distinguish themselves in academic science contests like the SIN and the Chemstudy contests.

Two major societal issues had influence on student concerns and the concerns of those who decided what would be taught in science courses. Rachel Carson's book, *The Silent Spring*, published in the early sixties, brought pollution issues to a head in the late sixties and early seventies. The OPEC oil embargoes of the seventies, however, supplanted pollution worries, replacing them with fears of life without oil. Educators became concerned with familiarizing students with energy issues.

In 1975 the old school was gutted and renovated. Most of the renovations were to bring the building up to fire and safety codes but there was some upgrading of the Science Department. A more efficient use of the available floor space resulted in some changes to classrooms and storage facilities. The washroom on the third floor became a storage closet. The hallway bay between rooms 305 and 306 was converted into a walk-through equipment storage area that led into a still inadequate staff workroom. Small teacher preparation areas were created. The moving of the main staircase necessitated the relocation of one non-science classroom and caused some disorientation of former students who returned to visit the alma mater. Teaching staff were able to introduce some changes to their rooms, in the form of new cupboards, counters, etc. New, supposedly more efficient windows were installed. They looked better, but still iced up in the winter. The ventilation system was improved but it was a number of years before it operated properly. After all this, the old pedestal benches, destroyers of gas and water pipes alike, remained in the lab.

Changes in the world of science and technology continued, but at an accelerated pace.

1970: Data storage for computers is improved with the arrival of the floppy disk.

1971: The first CANDU nuclear reactor goes into commercial service. For about $150 students could buy the first pocket calculator. Unfortunately, it required a strong pocket, since it weighed about 2.5 pounds (more than a kilogram).

1972: In California, law requires textbooks to treat Biblical accounts of creation with the same attention as the evolutionary theory. Landsat, the first satellite designed to survey earth resources, is launched.

1973: A calf is born for the first time from an embryo that had been frozen. Skylab is launched.

1974: A magazine publishes an article on the construction of a "personal computer." The first programmable pocket calculator appears on the market.

1975: The Altair 8800, a kit-form personal computer, is marketed. It has a massive 256 bytes of memory!

1977: The Apple II is now available.

1978: Apple markets the first disk drive for personal computers. Seasat, designed to study ocean currents, goes into orbit.

1979: Partial meltdown occurs in the core of the Three Mile Island nuclear reactor. Personal computer users are able to purchase Visicalc, the first spreadsheet programme.

These and other events were markers for two trends that would have significant impact on education—first, the start of an explosion in computer technology that continues today and affects the way students learn and the information to which they have access and second, the beginnings of a move towards examination of science and social issues.

THE EIGHTIES

Listening habits again underwent a major shift with the arrival, in 1982, of the compact disc and its remarkable sound reproduction. Now into its fourth decade, rock and roll was still youths' music of choice. Appropriately the eighties started with Billy Joel's hit, "It's Still Rock and Roll to Me." Hard driving acoustic rock, exemplified by John Cougar (call me Mellencamp) and Bruce Springsteen, was

In a 1980s science lab, these are the 5D science class composers of the limerick, dedicated to science teacher Larry Wade;

"Mr. Wade, though he's often explosive,
Will sometimes seek spaces enclosive.
When asked, 'Why that be?'
He replied, 'When 5D's
In the lab things get awful explosive'."

A science class ad in the *Vox Lycei*, 1982-83.

well-liked by students. Heavy metal increased its popularity, moving groups like Aerosmith and AC/DC to AM radio play. Canadian artists like Bryan Adams, Tom Cochrane and Alana Miles were favourites at home and became internationally known. All-music cable TV stations, like MuchMusic, increased the importance of the visual to music. For icons like Madonna, Michael Jackson and Prince, videos were as important as their music. Students also rediscovered the music of their parents, and enjoyed the Beatles, Led Zeppelin and the Who. And of course, the Stones.

For the better part of three decades, students had lived with the threat of nuclear war. Surveys had even shown that some youths did not believe that they would grow up, complete a career, have a family, because of the inevitability of a major war. In the eighties, Perestroika, the end of the Soviet Union and the fall of the Berlin Wall, reduced the perceived risk to a great extent. By the end of the decade, the standoff between two superpowers had gone, but regional conflicts and fragmentation seemed to be increasing.

The tendency for teaching staff to remain at one school for an extended time was changing. The eighties were, in all departments, a time of flux. Teachers and department heads were encouraged to move between Ottawa Board Schools. Almost twenty science teachers worked in the department

for various lengths of time during this decade. Larry Wade, David Lamperd, and Terry Prichett continued at Lisgar and logged another decade of service to the Blue and Grey. Angus Cameron completed his career and moved to a well-earned retirement in 1983. The most significant change, and the saddest for his colleagues and students, was the death of Bob MacMillan in 1987.

The definitive Ministry document of the eighties was Ontario Schools: Intermediate and Senior Divisions (OSIS). OSIS introduced levels of study, refined graduation requirements and replaced the old Grade 13 courses with the new Ontario Academic Credits (OAC). General level science courses were designed by staff and introduced, but they were eventually dropped as students showed little interest in taking them, opting instead for the advanced level courses.

OSIS also resulted in the complete dissection and ultimate reassembly of all of the science courses from grades 7 to OAC. Many new texts were written to accommodate the changes. The mid-eighties also saw a growing public concern about the "decline of standards." The Board responded with a return to common examinations in the form of System-Wide Evaluation. These events created pressure on schools to change science texts. Most science courses switched textbooks at some point in the eighties. Even the venerable PSSC course fell victim.

Terry Pritchett's space simulation programme has been one of the most valuable hands-on science experiments in Lisgar's history. Not only have Lisgar science students participated and learned but classes from Ottawa and area also have been welcomed to this live and learn experience. Student Jean Kassie in the space shuttle.

The philosophy of OSIS was incorporated into the new courses. Independent study programmes became mandatory in OAC science courses. More than ever before, teachers developed lessons designed around lists of objectives provided in Ministry Curriculum Guidelines. These objectives were divided into affective, skills and knowledge categories. Applications of learning and societal implications were also required. As the information explosion continued, how to learn and adapt to the changes in the real world became increasingly important.

Advances in technology had their impact on science classes at Lisgar. In the sixties and seventies, experiments on motion and forces had been done with three-wheeled dynamics carts that looked like roller skates, metre sticks and stop-watches. The seventies brought the versatile air table and electronic spark-timer as well as the first linear air-track. In the latter half of the eighties the experiments were being done on a new, precision linear air-track with photo-gate timers and computer timing programmes. The air table continued to give excellent service for two-dimensional motion experiments.

While the large demonstration oscilloscope, purchased around 1970, continues to serve today's physics classes, bulky electrical meters for student use have been supplemented or replaced by compact multi-meters.

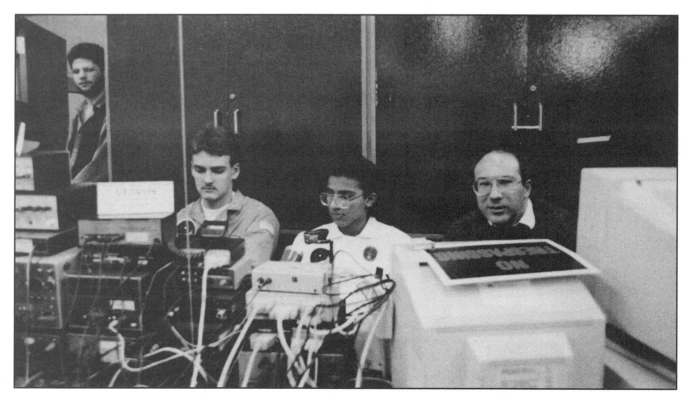

This is the ham radio station set-up at mission control. Left to right; David Junk (standing), former Lisgar student who designed and built space suit used on mission, Pat Harley, South Carolina exchange student; Vikram Bajaj, Lisgar student; Ted Paull, member of local ham radio club, there to offer advice, technical help. The robotic arm was also built by a Lisgar student.

A group of Lisgar astronauts posed against the space simulation longhouse just after completion of a mission. Since the mission is three days long, the longhouse is part living quarters with toilets, showers, fridge, microwave, ventilation system, and part science laboratory. Back row; Terry Cheatham, South Carolina teacher, Terry Pritchett, Lisgar science teacher and co-ordinator. Third row, left to right; Jon Beverly, Michael Ting, Jefferson Dubrule, George Showman, Nicholat Chop, Liam Morland, Ben Lahaise, Scott Padgett, Fletcher Blake, Adam Hucks, Michael Shaver, Jason Sooch, Hilary Myron, Isaac Morland, Vikram Bajaj. Second row, l to r: Tu-Anh Nguyen, Marcus Mah, Smia Sheikh, Xun Wang, Onotole Papadoulos, Mirian Padolsky, Christy Baldwin, Marilyn Brown. Front row, l to r: Neil Fraser, Chris Thompson, Jenn Kassie (Mission Commander), Margaret Jones, Monnie Murray, Mitch Grunsky.

In the sixties, mass determinations were made on triple beam balances or on the enclosed, equal arm pan balances using precision brass mass sets. The triple beam balance gave way to the dialagram balance and ultimately, they were all superseded by the rapid and accurate electronic balance.

In the same 30-year period, microscopes progressed from the difficult-to-use, low quality ones that had a small mirror to illuminate the sample, to better models that had their own built-in light sources. In the seventies a stereoscopic microscope was added to the inventory and in the late eighties, teachers had access to a video microscope that could display sample images on a television screen.

Computers were becoming an integral part of science. Their uses ranged from simple data collection and data manipulation to commercial programmes that simulated experiments that would be too difficult or dangerous to perform at the high school level. Software packages, complete with sensing devices, were now available to measure, record and analyse sound waves, motion of objects, oxygen content of the air, acidity of a solution, temperature, gas pressure and more. A modem connection in the school gave students access to additional research facilities such as the on-line library catalogues of Ottawa University and Carleton. As well, students could log in to various computer networks that allowed them actually to retrieve up-to-date material in science and technology.

In all of the sciences, films have gradually been displaced by videos. The convenience of video has been paid for by a substantial reduction in the quality of video images compared to those on film. Towards the end of the eighties, the department acquired a 40-inch large screen television that improved viewing for students at the back of the room.

1991 Lisgar graduate Elizabeth Caskey with astronaut Roberta Bondar upon her arrival back in Canada after first flight in space. Photo taken Feb. 17, 1992, at a reception hosted by the Prime Minister and the Ministry of State for Science and Technology. Now a second-year science student at the University of Western Ontario, Elizabeth was a National Scholar and a Canadian Scholarship winner at Lisgar. She was editor of the *Vox Lycei* and heavily involved with the International Student Space Simulation Programme. She won the Henry Birks Medal and a Lisgar "L" for her leadership and contribution to student life while at Lisgar.

Changes in the physical character of the third floor were minimal to a casual observer. Carpets appeared and were much appreciated by students lounging or studying. Problems with their maintenance led to the return of tiled floors in the early nineties. The large equipment storage area between rooms 305 and 306 was adapted to include teacher workspace for the whole department. This, unfortunately, reduced even further the already inadequate storage space in the department. The largest storage space now available was the bookroom, hidden under the seats of the auditorium balcony. To this day, those who venture into this gloomy, windowless chamber, risk concussion and permanent brain damage from the low, sloping beams that support the upper balcony.

This decade saw the introduction of a number of special programmes that were designed to address various elements of OSIS. A major school Science Fair was held annually. For many Grade 9 and 10 students the Science Fair project was part of their course work. For others, it was a voluntary enrichment project, for which they could receive some credit in one of their science classes. On the day of the Fair, science classes were cancelled as all classroom space was jammed with student exhibits. Winners of the school Fair were encouraged to enter the Regional Science Fair, where they often won further awards. A number of them also advanced to the National Science Fair, where some have won trophies, cash awards, trips and major scholarships.

Career day was first implemented during the eighties. Over a period of one week every year, one of each science class was given over to a lecture from someone who worked in pure science, engineering, medicine or some other science related field. Particular attention was paid to providing female role models for the young women studying science at Lisgar.

The late eighties also saw the launching of the Student Space Simulation at Lisgar. This multi-disciplinary programme encouraged students to design and build a simulated space habitat, complete with mission control, and then plan and execute all aspects of a 72-hour simulated mission. Partly by luck and partly due to its reputation in the Sir Isaac Newton Physics Contest, Lisgar was the first school invited to join by the Houston school that started the programme. Since its inception in 1989, when the Houston school, Lisgar, and six students from Japan were the only participants, the programme has grown to include over 50 schools. These schools each construct a habitat and launch missions simultaneously. They contact each other and co-ordinate mission events by telephone, fax, computer modem, amateur radio and even slow-scan television. This annual simulation has proven an effective vehicle for interesting students in science and technology, and for broadening the interests of those students who are already science-oriented.

By the eighties, oil concerns had largely abated, and attention was again focused on pollution. This time, society took a broader approach to the problem, and pollution became a sub-heading for the larger issue of the environment. The Greenhouse Effect, the depletion of the ozone layer, and conservation of the earth's finite resources all became topics for science classes and major concerns for the public—including the environmentally aware students who would have to live with the consequences of action or inaction now. Two determined students set up the city's first paper recycling programme at Lisgar. Several years later, recycling of cans was introduced. The Lisgar Environmental Action Force (LEAF) was formed and has been an active organization ever since.

EVENTS THAT HELPED SHAPE SCIENCE EDUCATION:

1980: Voyager I flies by Saturn.

1981: The IBM personal computer, using standard disk operating system (DOS) goes on sale. The space shuttle (Columbia) goes into space for the first time, and is launched again later that year. It thus becomes the first ever reusable spacecraft.

1982: Compaq makes the first IBM PC clone. The Remote Manipulator System (Canadarm) is tested in space.

1983: Sally Ride, the first American woman in space, used Canadarm to deploy and retrieve a satellite. Apple introduces the mouse as a cursor control device on computers. IBM brings out the first computer with built-in hard drive memory storage.

1984: The Macintosh computer hits the market and gains instant acceptance. The technique for "genetic fingerprinting" is discovered.

1986: The Challenger space shuttle explodes after launch, killing all aboard. The Chernobyl nuclear reactor accident occurs, with catastrophic consequences. A U.S. company does trials of genetically engineered plants. A hepatitis-B vaccine, produced by genetic engineering is approved for use in the States. Computer speed increases markedly as Compaq introduces the 80386 chip in its models.

1987: The U.S. Supreme Court rejects the provision of equal time for the teaching of creationism in science courses. In Britain, an accused is convicted on evidence provided by genetic fingerprinting. A Russian cosmonaut returns from the Mir space station after a record 326 days in space.

1988: The highest temperature superconductor to date is discovered. It works at 125K (-148°C). A genetically engineered mouse is patented in the U.S.

WERE YOU THERE FOR:

– war memoirs? A longtime teacher often delivered tales of the First World War during physics classes.

– the flash? A science teacher was nicknamed "flash" because of his speedy locomotion. He once estimated he had logged 16 200 miles on his daily trips to and from school. Since he taught at Lisgar for 27 years, this may have been an underestimate if he walked every day.

– the contraceptive caper? A biology teacher, teaching principles of birth control, inadvertently sprayed himself with contraceptive foam, to the delight of his senior students.

– the 125th anniversary? The science department set up a display on the fourth floor. It was the first (and last) time many visited this legendary location.

– the 140th anniversary? The science department held a major open house. All the new equipment and experiments were brought out for this special event.

– the mouse massacre? A group of students begged to be present for the feeding of the boa constrictor. Although they knew that mice were on the menu, they were still unprepared for what followed. The teacher was loath to feed live mice to the immature boa lest the snake suffer injury, so the mice had to be freshly killed. Poison was out of the question since it too might damage the snake. The most humane method of execution was a sharp blow to the skull. Accordingly, the teacher dropped the mouse into a clear plastic sandwich bag under the watchful eyes of the increasingly puzzled students. A hammer appeared and at the sound of the crunch, many of the audience raced from the room, some retching violently. They did not return to see the denouement of this biological morality play.

– the great snake escape? One morning, to the nervous amusement of classes in room 306, the terrarium holding the boa was found to be empty. The serpent was on the lam! To this day, perhaps 15 years later it has never been found and a curious legend is passed on to new generations of rambunctious grade nines.

– the poison gas affair? A mishap in the chemistry lab resulted in the release of phosphorus pentoxide, a heavy white gas. Students evacuated the building in a quick and orderly manner, and a potentially serious incident ended happily. Lab procedures were, of course, reviewed to prevent any recurrence of such an accident.

– the flame thrower phenomenon? A rookie teacher made an error in a demonstration that caused a glass elbow tube to be blown off, and a two-foot jet of flame to fire for 30 seconds—much to the delight of the Grade 9 students watching in awe. The teacher made a quick-witted but unsuccessful attempt to convince the class that the demonstration was planned to show the consequences of not following instructions carefully.

– the da Vinci expedition? Many classes of Grade 12 Physics students travelled to Montreal to visit the exhibit of Leonardo da Vinci's works—original drawings and writings as well as models and full-scale working representations of his remarkable concepts. A side trip to the Museum of Fine Arts was also on the programme that day.

– the sewage sagas? Many chemistry classes have been treated to visits to the Green's Creek sewage plant to study the chemical processes in the treatment of Ottawa's wastes. The controversy over whether this field trip should be held before or after lunch was never satisfactorily resolved.

– energy escapades? Annual two-day visits to the Toronto area by enriched chemistry classes focused on various aspects of energy. They included trips to the El Dorado uranium processing plant and the Darlington nuclear power station.

– Energy 2000? As an enrichment project, some 50 students took part in this Ontario Hydro sponsored simulation activity. In teams, the students extensively researched various energy options for the province and wrote a comprehensive advocacy report on their findings, which was to be presented to an Energy Board, consisting also of a team of students. The simulation culminated in the Energy Board Hearings, held in the elegant boardroom of the Ottawa Board of Education. Seated in the Trustees' executive seats, and using their individual desktop microphones, the students showed poise and maturity as they argued their respective cases. Student "intervenors," acting as concerned member of the public, "special interest" groups, and the Energy Board members questioned the advocates' conclusions. The responses for the participants to challenges to their reports showed the extent of their research skills as well as their ability to think and debate.

—Terry Prichett

MUSIC AT LISGAR

My 26 years at Lisgar with the Music Department encompassed a number of "firsts." One of these in 1966, the year of my arrival, was the invitation for Toby Fyfe, our tuba player, to perform with the Robin Hood Band at the Rose Bowl in Pasedena, California.

Prior to my arrival in 1966, morning Assembly was convened every day at 9:00 a.m. in the auditorium before regular classes. I remember Assembly taking place each Wednesday only, when the orchestra or band played "O Canada" and at least a march. Over the years even Wednesday Assembly was phased out.

The following year, 1967-68, Lisgar celebrated its 125th anniversary and the Music Night program was dedicated to this major event. Cellist Tony Wallis performed "Canzonetta" by Pergolesi on the program.

Dwight Rudisuida joined the Lisgar Music Department in 1968-69 to teach strings and Latin. We had a successful exchange with Wheable Secondary School of London, Ontario that year when the orchestra featured the "Rossmunde" Overture by Schubert at its performance. In addition, the string orchestra was honoured with an invitation to perform at the prestigious Waterloo Instrumental Clinic with the well-known music educator and clinician Frederick Muller.

The following year, 1969-70, Dwight Rudisuida left Lisgar to teach strings at the elementary level. In that same school year our first experience at fund-raising for the orchestra evolved into an embarrassment. John Roebuck, my assistant for nine years, and the band took it upon themselves to sell coffee mugs decorated with Lisgar logos in order to help finance a band trip to the Alfred Training School.

Lisgar Orchestra, 1954, in the days when morning assemblies were such an important part of school life.
Back row, left to right; Mike MacKay, Bill MacMillan, John Dempsey, Mike Rasminsky, Dave Dod, Pete MacArthur,
Bob de Pencier, Tim Murray. Middle row; Jerry Clute, Syd Cardash, Paul Hertzberg, Solly Gunnar, Dave Alexandor,
Bruce Jackson, Morris Perkins, Conductor Mracek, Bill Roberts, Ray Laws. Front row; Emilya Malihauski, Ann Tolmie,
Janet Swerdfager, Evelyn Feldman, Joyce Harwood, Jo-Anne Boyce.

Many mugs were sold to Lisgar students' families. Unfortunately, after the first washing, the logo-decal washed away! We received many unpleasant phone calls, purchasers had to be reimbursed, and we tried to forget our first capitalistic venture.

By spring of 1971 my first group of students Ellen Henry, Sheila Embleton, Nancy Illman, Cathy Herbert, Andrew McClure to name a few who had started strings with me back in 1966 were graduating after four years of active music involvement.

About graduation time, June of 1971 as I was driving to school, a radio news bulletin announced that an FLQ bomb had been detonated in the window-well of one of the temporary buildings in downtown Ottawa and a woman had been killed. Little did I realize then that the catastrophe had occurred in the building closest to Lisgar and near my music room! I arrived at the school amidst a flurry of activity. As I parked my car, the army and the RCMP were busy cordoning off the street. The bomb blast had broken a pane of glass in my home-room and, as I was about to open the back door to my room, I discovered a piece of the explosive device at my feet. I had worked with dynamite and detonators on my summer jobs in a Timmins' gold mine and immediately walked over to present my find to a gentleman in white coveralls who seemed to be the person in charge of the investigation. Once he realized that I could identify, with some certainty, the components of the bomb I became a prime suspect. After some interrogation by the RCMP and the Attorney General's Department, they were convinced that I taught at Lisgar Collegiate and was to be trusted. In fact, they contacted Wright Neil, the principal, and he released me to assist in the investigation. They were keen to have me aboard because they did not have anyone immediately available who was familiar with this type of explosive device. A further search revealed some pieces of the FLQ bomb on the roof of the Lisgar gym building. I referred to this event afterwards as The Day a Music Teacher Turned Sleuth!

The entire Lisgar staff was saddened when Wright Neil, retired in 1972. The band was busy rehearsing "Samba for Flute" by Osterling that year and violinist Peter Brooks was featured in the J. B. Accolay "Concerto" in A Minor for violin and orchestra. We were shocked by the untimely and unexpected passing of Harvard student Joyce Lu, formerly an active member of our orchestra. In November of 1972, the Joyce Lu Memorial Scholarship Fund was established for the students at Lisgar with the highest achievement in Music and Mathematics, the two areas in which Joyce had excelled while at Lisgar.

The term 1973-74 was one of great musical accomplishment. Carmelia MacWilliam performed the exotic flute "Concertino" by Chaminade, violinist Sharon McMillan featured the "Allegro" by Fiocco, and clarinetist Paul Strazak impressed the audience with "Clarinet on the Town" by Ralph Herman.

The orchestra was busy "Meowing" with the "Waltzing Cat" by Leroy Anderson. In the spring of 1975 the orchestra had a successful exchange with Sherwood Secondary School of Hamilton, Ontario. John Roebuck departed from Lisgar to continue his teaching career at the elementary level, and the band conquered the demanding "Suite No.1 in E Flat" by Gustav Holst.

In 1975 Ed Sullivan came to Lisgar to teach band music. With a strong stage band background, having performed with various groups including Canadian Air Force stage bands during the war years as well as with the late Moxey Whitney band, Ed Sullivan was ideally suited to organize and develop Lisgar's stage band.

The 1977-78 edition of the orchestra was an outstanding performing organization led by musicians such as Don Krishnaswami, Michael Sproule and David Sharpe. It was the year of the exchange with Eastview Collegiate of Barrie, Ontario, and the unfortunate accident to our star cellist, David Sharpe, in the evening—an accident which well demonstrates the teachers' added responsibilities and risks on exchanges, trips afield, and "away" games.

Following our performance at Eastview, Lisgar students and their billets went roller skating, but it was not until we were boarding the bus the following morning was I informed that David Sharpe had broken his wrist at the roller-rink. I was assured by the Barrie Music Director that Sharpe's wrist had been set by the top orthopaedic surgeon in Ontario who just happened to live in Barrie. But I was still uneasy and, since we were returning to Ottawa via Toronto after visiting the Science Centre, I suggested to David that perhaps we should have his wrist examined at a Toronto hospital. He assured me that he was fine and continued with his painkillers. As we headed for Ottawa after the Science Centre tour, David became increasingly uncomfortable. When we arrived in Ottawa, his parents took him to a local hospital where they discovered that the broken bones had been improperly set!

Fortunately, David recovered full mobility of his wrist and went on to perform with the orchestra at Washington State University. That same year the string orchestra performed at McLeod Stewarton United Church to commemorate Education Week. Michael Tevlin, a clarinetist, was an active performer that year.

The following year, 1978-79, the string orchestra combined with the choir of Bells' Corners United Church to present a Bach Cantata at the church. Violinists Michael Sproule and David Mount were soloists in the "Concerto Grosso" in A Minor by Vivaldi and Stephen Mah, a talented saxophonist, performed the "Sicilienne" and "Allegro" by Bach. In the spring of 1980, clarinetist Ian Gray accompanied by Claire Pottinger, was featured in the "Concertino" OP. 26 in E Flat by Von Weber. The orchestra, in the meantime, was enjoying rehearsing and performing "Hootenany," a fun composition with a distinctively country flavour.

The concert band was a very busy performing group and was in need of distinctive attire in order to appear visually homogenous as well as musically so. In addition, we had been planning a performance visit to Disney World in Florida and one of the stipulations for appearing there was to have the band in uniform. The Florida trip did not materialize, but we did get our uniforms!

We decided we needed a uniform for the concert band and embarked on the first serious fund-raising since the ill-fated coffee mug fiasco. This time we sold long-life light bulbs with limited success, but we managed to finance the purchase of eighty-eight used band jackets from a firm in Devil's Lake, North Dakota. A real bargain—five dollars per jacket for a total cost of $533.34. They were in excellent condition and, once we sewed on the Lisgar shoulder flashes and wore our blue ties and grey cords, we were both aurally and visually presentable. Wearing our newly-purchased jackets we had a successful performance at O'Neill Collegiate in Oshawa, Ontario.

While touring one of the Oshawa General Motor plants, one of our students, Chris Brown, made a suggestion to the plant manager which would potentially improve an assembly line procedure. The manager took the concept seriously and was astounded by the ingenuity of the boy!

For Christmas of 1981 the concert band presented the 'Twas The Night Before Christmas production with Lisgar teachers acting out the various parts. Harry Monsour was a big hit as one of the sugar plum fairies and David Lamperd was the ideal little elf for Santa, played by John Boehmer. The narrator, Barrie Laughton was his usual undeniably humorous self. This assembly was a highlight of the year. At Music Night, flutists Sophie Borcoman, and Alexia Zerbinis and cellist Steve Gower performed the Second Movement of the "Trio Sonata" in C Minor by Quantz.

When Ed Sullivan retired in June of 1982 Trudy Bradley entered the Lisgar music scene. Work with strings and orchestra was a condition for her acceptance of a position at Lisgar; and when I took on the wind and band teaching assignment we were to work as a team for ten years until my retirement.

Phong Mach, a talented violinist, who with his pianist sister Tu, had arrived from Vietnam in early 1981, impressed the Lisgar audience by performing the first movement of a Concerto Grosso by Vivaldi. Phong and I enjoyed playing violin duets by various composers during his Lisgar years. This was also the year that Vladimir Radonjic performed his own composition for violin and piano. The concert band and orchestra had a successful combined exchange with a high school from London, Ontario.

Lisgar celebrated its 140th anniversary in 1984 and our music groups were busy contributing to the celebration. The concert band gave concerts at Island Park Lodge, the Rideau Centre and the Children's Hospital of Eastern Ontario while the orchestra performed at Place Bell Canada. In addition, the concert band served as the music pit group for Lorne Greene and Rich Little at the major evening review in our school auditorium. The band premiered composer Glen Morley's commemorative march "Alere Flammam," composed and dedicated for this special anniversary. Many of the overflow audience had to watch the program on video monitors in the gymnasium.

In May of 1984, the concert band and orchestra travelled by bus to Boston, Massachusetts, and performed at two schools in the city. We were well received at both institutions. This was our first experience with inner-city schools in a large U.S. city and for all of us it was an eye opener! Madison High School, the second school we visited, was enveloped in high security. While the students remained on the buses, I attempted to get into the school but the doors were locked from the inside! Someone eventually let me in and I proceeded to look for the music teacher. I found him carrying a heavy chain with which to secure the auditorium doors!

During the performance our students were instructed to keep all personal effects including instrument cases beside them lest they disappear. We were rushed to the cafeteria for lunch while their students were still in their classes lest we face physical confrontations. We were told not to place our hands on our hips at any time because that was an aggressive signal that could provoke an attack! Washrooms needed keys and all mirrors had been removed in order to prevent theft or vandalism. There was a great deal of high fencing around the perimeter of the school and at the end of the day many carloads of police arrived in order to guide all students from the school property. Students had to be off school property twenty minutes after the final bell. A female student leaning against a post after the deadline was immediately detained by police. The music teacher admitted to me that academic standards left much to be desired and that it would be impossible for him to travel with his students. It was a beautiful school and we were jealous of their high quality musical instruments, but Lisgar was like heaven to us after what we had seen!

The tour of Boston following our performances included a visit to the USS Constitution, a walk through old Boston where we saw "Cheers," the bar made famous by the television series of the same name, and a lovely evening cruise in the harbour where we could appreciate the lights of Boston as they reflected on the still waters.

In 1984-85 the band held a fruit sale to assist the financing for a proposed trip to Jamaica. Unfortunately Jamaica ended up having a political crisis of sorts which resulted in violence including arson and looting. The situation was serious enough that we cancelled our travel plans. This third fund-raising project was successful but the trip had to be cancelled in favour of a performance trip to a Montreal high school. Although a visit to Montreal was not Jamaica the members of the band found the excursion one of the most

rewarding ever. We had a very receptive audience and later toured St. Joseph's Oratory and had smoked meat at Ben's.

In 1986 the concert band travelled to Wolfville, Nova Scotia, on an exchange with Horton District High School funded by a grant from Open House Canada. In addition, we required additional funds to supplement the grant. We had a very successful meat sale, even though at the outset many had reservations about selling this particular product. We sold meat from Macgregors Ltd., Toronto. It was an excellent product and included various packaged steaks, chops, etc. Students took orders in advance and then contacted the purchasers as to the specific school delivery date. Purchasers either picked up their product at the school on that date or made special arrangements with the selling student for home delivery. It is understandable that some students would initially have some reservations about selling "raw meat" as a fund-raising project!

On the way to Nova Scotia, we came close to having an international incident. VIA Rail had neglected to inform us that we would be travelling through the U.S. at one point. At about midnight the lights in our coach were suddenly turned on and trench-coated men commenced checking our papers. Five students were found lacking and were herded into a vacant coach in order to be interrogated. I attended in order to defend the students. Nick Futter had been born in East Germany, came to Canada at age one, and was a Canadian citizen. He was the first to be released. Pat Smith, Joanna Patrick and Carsten Podehl were soon set free. Only Argentinean Horatio Alioto remained in detention; he was from Argentina and lacked official documentation at the time when the Falkland's War was in the headlines. He was only released after some bitter exchanges between the officer-in-charge and myself, especially after I refused to turn over our group tickets to his custody. I emphasized that we were travelling under the auspices of the Canadian government and that this was a serious threat to Canada-U.S. relations. I guaranteed that Horatio would not step on U.S. soil and we were free to leave. We were cheered like heroes by our group as we returned to their midst. The coach lurched and once again we were on our way!

David Morrison joined the Music Department full-time in September, 1987. In November the concert band took part in the special Victoria Cross Assembly which honoured Sergeant Edward J.G. Holland. A memorial plaque was unveiled in his honour and the band played "Monsieur Beauclaire," the march past of the Royal Canadian Dragoons. Violinist Patrick Lam was featured soloist as the orchestra performed "Danse Macabre" by Saint-Saens at Music Night.

The year 1987-88 ended up being one of the busiest for Lisgar musicians. Russell Itani dazzled the audience with his flute performance of Chaminade's "Concertino" and Lisgar presented the Ottawa premiere of "A Suite for Synthesizer and Band." The "Suite for Synthesizer and Band" was written specifically for the Yamaha DX7 synthesizer and had its Ottawa premiere at Lisgar in May of 1988. Music purists were reluctant to accept the electronic synthesizer as a serious instrument and we were willing to feature it in a solo with the acoustic instruments of the concert band. The unusual combination of electronic and acoustic instruments in a successful concert performance heralded the acceptance of an electronic instrument as a viable medium of musical expression. In fact, a number of Ottawa schools are now offering electronic piano-synthesizer group instruction labs. The electronic music era has arrived.

In the late fall of 1987, I arranged a school trip to Montreal to see the production of *Cats*. It was such an impressive musical, utilizing the latest computer-sound-light technology and with so many memorable themes. Based on *Old Possum's Book of Practical Cats* by T.S. Elliott, many of our students could relate the literary work to this fine musical having studied in it class.

At the Christmas assembly the concert band and teachers combined forces to perform *'Twas The Night Before Christmas* with Barrie Laughton, of course, as narrator. In early May, a Finnish Youth Choir conducted by Jarmo Kokkonen gave an extraordinary concert for the school. Our concert band performed with them for an evening concert open to the general public in the Lisgar auditorium.

In the fall of 1988, the brass ensemble played at the dedication of the Human Rights Monument at the corner of Lisgar and Elgin. Lucanor Silva was featured at Music Night in Telemann's "Viola Concerto" in G Major, and Adrian Payne performed the smooth alto saxophone solo, "Strawflower" by Herman.

In the spring of 1989, the Lisgar concert band toured Finland and visited the city of Leningrad in the U.S.S.R. Preparations for the trip started the previous September and continued at a feverish pace through February and early March. Mr. Robert Hursti, the conductor, proudly stated that "it was probably the most ambitious program performed by a school organization with such limited rehearsal time." Program numbers included pieces such as the "Italian in Algiers," "Prince Igor" and "Finnish Rhapsody."

The band gave numerous performances in the cities of Turku, Helsinki, and Tampere. A highlight was the concert on Palm Sunday at the beautiful Mikael Cathedral in Turku. The Lisgar students were billeted for the Turku part of the tour in the homes of choir members who had visited and performed at Lisgar in May of 1988. They were perfect hosts and a number of lasting friendships blossomed. Many Lisgarites are now believers and advocates of the Finnish sauna.

Before returning to Canada, the band travelled by train from Helsinki to Leningrad and stayed at the Pribaytiyskaya hotel on the Gulf of Finland. Due to the serious amoeba contamination of Leningrad water, the band was forced to bring their own water from Finland.

After our arrival at the Pribaltiyskaya Hotel in Leningrad we discovered that native Russians were not allowed in the hotel. It was for foreign tourists only and all currencies were accepted as legal tender. I discovered that Paul McCartney had made a recording in the U.S.S.R. prior to our arrival, one that was not available in the West. It would be a valuable collector's item! One of the Russian entrepreneurs who was a source for these records had illegally acquired a room in the hotel. He was also selling other contraband and to have any dealing with him might not be healthy! Leave it up to my students to find him out and make a few purchases, including the McCartney recordings. David Moon, one of my band members, was one of the Lisgar contacts to this Russian wheeler-dealer and after supper one evening he showed me one of the McCartney recordings. Through David's amazing negotiating skills I acquired the recording, as did most Lisgarites. Evidently David had to outbid many European, Japanese, and American collectors for the recording in the "secret store" at the Pribaltiyskaya.

While in Leningrad the band visited The Hermitage, St. Isaacs Cathedral and the Pushkin Palace. Some students also attended a performance of the Barber of Seville (in Russian) at the Maly Theatre and everyone attended an evening of Ukrainian dancing. After returning to Helsinki, the band flew back to Canada. The first European tour by a Lisgar music organization was a success story that will be remembered on both sides of the Atlantic.

In the spring of 1989, Michael Woodside was brilliant as he performed the "Bassoon Concerto" in B flat Major K 191 by W.A. Mozart on the trombone accompanied by the band. Toby Kiesewalter displayed his recorder virtuosity as he played the "Concerto for Soprano Recorder and Strings" in C Major by Babell.

In the fall of 1989, we embarked on another musical field trip similar to the Cats excursion of 1987, this time to the Pantages Theatre in Toronto to see *The Phantom of The Opera*. A total of six bus loads of students and chaperones attended the production on October 4, four buses from Lisgar and two from Glebe. Matthew Shaw had missed the bus in Ottawa, but flew to Toronto and met me outside the Pantages Theatre just as I was scalping his ticket!

The concert band and teachers again entertained the Lisgar audience with *'Twas the Night Before Christmas* at the 1991 Christmas assembly with Dave MacGougan as narrator. Of course, Santa was there to present gifts to well-behaved persons, mostly teachers! By popular request I organized another trip to the Pantages Theatre in Toronto to see *The Phantom of The Opera*. There was some foul-up in the bus reservations and we ended up with four buses, two each from different firms! In addition to this crisis, the buses did not arrive at the specified time and we left an hour late. Unfortunately, our late departure forced us to miss the pre-Phantom tour of the Pantages Theatre and a chat with the cast.

Members of the Concert Band on trip to Finland, 1989. Back row, left to right; Matthew Tunnicliffe, Chris Kinsley, Kamal Gautam, Mark Eatherley, David Browne, Liam Scott, Martin Pergler, Tobias Kiesewater, Marosh Furimsky, David Woodside, Robert Murphy, Michael Woodside, Cameron Read, Adrian Payne, David Moon, Joshua Ramish, Bob Hursti, James Ojaste. Next row; Geralyn Plum, M. Carby-Samuels, Hannah Lovejoy, Lara Mills, Yun Chan, Jennifer Bruce, Robert Montgomery, Megan Lamont, Anne Burbidge, Rosaline Duckworth, Hetta Huittinen, Desmond White, Greg Fraser. Next row; Hilary Gunn, Mikijam Amikazizi, Stephanie Marsan, Leah Box, Sharon Li, Adrienne Lee, Devon Curtis, Katherine Pestieau, Tanya Firman. Front row; Peter Economopoulos, Tina Neimanis, Elsbeth Vaino, Siri Brown, Fiora MacIntosh, Heather Patterson, Elizabeth Pang, Janina Pietrzak. Missing from the photo; Peter Graham, Steve Roberts, Pablo Navarro.

Graduating student Fiona MacIntosh was featured at Music Night in the romantic solo, "Trumpet by Candlelight," composer T.A. Kenny. Mrs. Joy Heft successfully conducted a newly-formed vocal ensemble in numbers such as "The Rose" and "Whispering Hope." Mrs. Trudy Bradley's orchestra performed "Jupiter" from The Planets by Holst and Dave Morrison conducted the Lisgar Stage Band in numbers such as "Nightwatch" and "Summertime" for the last time. Dave Morrison accepted a new position at Laurentian High School for September 1991. I had no idea at the time, but this was to be my last Music Night at Lisgar Collegiate. Little did I realize that "Brandenburg Jubilee," the final number on the program was to be my last podium experience in the Lisgar auditorium.

The Robert O. Hursti music award was established May 1991 and presented for the first time to Tobias Kiesewalter at the final assembly. The award honours the student who has made an outstanding contribution to music at Lisgar and it is to be presented annually.

—Bob Hursti

LISGAR ORCHESTRA

The Lisgar orchestra has been in existence since the First World War when musicians, led by Dr. James Bearder, provided music for the daily assemblies in the Lisgar auditorium.

The 1980s were years of rejuvenation and growth for the Lisgar Orchestra. Conducted by Trudy Bradley, the orchestra of 1982 consisted of probably thirty enthusiastic students. The string players of the orchestra performed a dozen concerts in the public schools and the community, thus promoting and encouraging strings at Lisgar. Players were rewarded after each concert with chocolate cake decorated with Smarties, baked by the conductor. This became a Lisgar tradition which is still in effect today, even though there are now three large performing groups, the Lisgar Orchestra (68 members), the String Ensemble (27 members), and the Intermediate String Orchestra (55 members).

Lisgar musicians giving a concert in the Parliament Buildings. Standing; Music teacher Trudy Bradley, politician Barbara McDougall. Circle, left to right; Sharon Wong, Patrick Lam, Tanya Lana, Bernice Alderson, Sean Tan, Rob Shotton, Dawna Duff, Mag Wong.

In 1983 the Lisgar quartet was formed, consisting of the very talented violinists Phong Mach, Lisa Bromley, violist Robert Shotton, and cellist Dawna Duff. They performed in the community, on Parliament Hill, and in the schools. This led to the creation of the Lisgar octet in 1985 as more talented players enrolled in the Lisgar orchestra including Peter Kerslake, head of the English Department, on the French horn.

By 1986 there were enough string players to create a third group, the Intermediate string orchestra, giving the less experienced musicians a chance to perform in public. This group was now given the task of performing at public schools to entice future Lisgar players, a task which is still carried out today. They have also performed quite a few joint ventures, such as performing with the Alta Vista and Vincent Massey orchestras, the Glashan choir, and various local church choirs.

In 1987 the octet was expanded into the Lisgar string ensemble, a group of highly polished players who perform Baroque chamber music with the choirs of Knox Presbyterian Church, St. Matthew's Anglican Church, St. John the Evangelist and others. Performances have included Handel organ concertos, Vivaldi's "Gloria," Haydn's "Johannes Mass," Eccles Cello Concerto with Stephane Benzekri, many

Vivaldi concerto grosso with Marc and Stephane Benzekri and Mika Kosaki, recorder concertos with Tobi Kiesewalter and trumpet concertos. The String Ensemble and the Lisgar Orchestra have been privileged to work with David Currie, conductor of the Ottawa Symphony, and Gerald Corry, bassoonist with the National Arts Centre Orchestra. Throughout the years the orchestra has been involved with many varied performances as well as the traditional evening concerts at Lisgar Collegiate. They have performed for local cable TV, at the provincial Ontario Music Educators Association conference, accompanied the Lisgar dancers for a performance of "Danse Macabre," at an international dog show "The show of shows" at Lansdowne Park, acted as rehearsal orchestra for a conductor's master class led by Gabriel Chmura, conductor of the NACO, participated in a music exchange with a Scarborough orchestra and in the international exchange with Rickmansworth School in a suburb of London, England.

The 1990 international tour to England by the orchestra was preceded by a great flurry of rehearsals and fund raising. The orchestra and the student council had a garage and bake sale, with various members performing chamber music throughout the day. Extra concerts by quartets and small ensembles played at dinner parties, weddings, and museums, and provided additional money. We also sold citrus fruit to everyone we knew. This tour and the subsequent visit by the Rickmansworth orchestra would not have been successful without the hard work by everyone, especially the work by Doug Arrand, and Barrie Laughton.

The Rickmansworth hosts were most surprised at the many different nationalities represented in the orchestra. The evening concert at Rickmansworth school had been advertised throughout the town, and the entire hall was packed. They provided a wine and cheese reception during the intermission, something we would like to pursue at Lisgar. They were most impressed with Patrick Lam's violin solo, Tobi Kiesewalter's oboe concerto, Natasha Lena's soprano solo, a Vivaldi Concerto Grosso, and orchestral music such as "Marche Slav," " Rosamunde Overture," " Grand March" from "Aida," Scherzo from Dvorak's "Symphony No. 7," and "Russian Sailor's Dance." The Orchestra also travelled and performed at a college in Leicester, Hitching Girls' School, and a secondary school in Reading.

During the fourteen days of music making and travelling throughout England we experienced many enjoyable moments. We attended a concert at the Royal Festival Hall with our hosts, went to the musical, *Starlight Express*, and the play, *The Importance of Being Earnest*. Some of the students managed to slip in a few more performances such as *Miss Saigon*. During our travels we learned that Tobi Kiesewalter could play his recorder concerto through his nose on the bus. Whenever someone made a new purchase it was immediately modelled by the student in the bus. In York, there was a fire alarm in the early hours of the morning and Barrie Laughton was frantically banging on doors to get all Lisgar students out of the building during chaos. In many cases he had to go back in again because students had great difficulty waking up. They emerged in various stages of undress. Fortunately, it was a false alarm and the next day the bus was very quiet. The bus drivers were very friendly and helpful. The larger of the two men, Ernie, could steer the bus with his stomach. He enjoyed playing all the students' tapes, including "Fat Man Waving." We stayed in Trust Forte Hotels and other guests were impressed with the manners and dress of the orchestra members. At the Strand Palace Hotel in London, we celebrated various members' birthdays with a big dinner and a birthday cake. We also visited Canada House with our hosts and were entertained at a reception given there.

The students from the Lisgar and Rickmansworth Orchestras, were very well matched and many lasting friendships ensued. Orchestra members were accompanied by Doug Arrand, Barrie Laughton, Principal Ian Macdonald, their wives, and Trudy Bradley the conductor. The following year the British students and teachers performed and toured in Ontario. This also was an exciting yet hectic time at Lisgar. During the concert at Lisgar, the conductor of the Rickmansworth Orchestra was presented with a pair of Lisgar boxer shorts which he immediately put on over his trousers. Having played all their concerts the Rickmansworth group then went to Camp Tawingo for a few days to experience the wilds of Canada.

Many students have participated in the orchestra for the five years they have been at Lisgar. Some of the students are multi-talented and following graduation from the orchestra have gone to graduate schools; Micheline White (violin), Robert Shotton (viola), Steven Woodside (French horn), into medicine; Lisa Bromley, Sarah Capes, Anthony Luke, Jose Pascual (all violinists), into law; Brigid Luke (violin), and into teaching; Sandra Holowka (violin). The very talented violinist Phong Mach went on to study music at the Toronto Conservatory. Other graduates such as Katherine Butler, now taking a master of music degree, Fiona Macintosh, Paul Butcher, Jason Van Eyck, Martina Smazal, and David Woodside, enrolled in music at university. The very talented Bernice Alderson studies art at the Emily Carr School of Art in British Columbia. Presently two brothers, violinist Stephane and cellist Mark Benzekri are members of the National Youth Orchestra which travels and performs throughout Ontario during the summer. Over the past ten years the orchestra has had three sets of twins; the Bells, the McElmans, and the Malinas. For some, participation in the Lisgar orchestra has become a family affair. All three siblings of the White, Holowka, Woodside, and Shotton families have played in the orchestra.

Members of the present Lisgar Orchestras perform on average some twenty-five to thirty times a year. Performances range from quartets at weddings, dinner parties, and museums, to large orchestral performances in the community. The groups have received recognition from the music community, educators, and parents of the school. Lisgar Alumni should be very proud of the ongoing music making and enthusiasm of the orchestra members. By their participation and achievements they continue to promote Lisgar's tradition of excellence.

—Trudy Bradley

GUIDANCE COUNSELLING

As far back as sixty-five years ago perceptive Lisgar students were aware of the need for Guidance Counselling in the high schools. In this *Vox Lycei* of 1930 the editor makes the case.

Did you ever consider how important a role Chance plays in determining the life-work of the graduate who leaves our halls?

This is made very clear when we look at the question in a negative manner. In this year's Fifth form fully eighty per cent of the boys, whom we may consider as average graduating pupils (average, that is, in this one respect) have decided upon their vocations. There are, for instance, to be four lawyers, two clergymen, one dentist, one medical doctor, one chemical engineer, and, we fear, one professor of Classics. Now the vital question is this: Why is such and such a boy going to be a lawyer, and why is such another one going to be a doctor? How have they reached their decisions? Certainly, in the vast majority of cases, at least, it has not been by a process of calm introspection, of careful self-analysis, and of a thorough examination of the possible fields of endeavour. No, some freak of chance has poured one life into this mold and another into that: the winning of a debate, perchance, has made a lawyer, an inspirational address from the platform has made a minister, and some more or less successful work upon the *Vox* has made a journalist. And the pity of it is that in getting a third-rate lawyer the world may be losing an actor of the first water, that the minister might have rendered greater service as a YMCA secretary and that the talents of a successful business man may lie unused in the brain of a struggling writer. Truly we realize the sadness of the words "it might have been."

Guidance teachers Lionel Rule and George Morrison, former head of the department.

If there is one important decision that we make during our Collegiate years it is the choice of our life-work, and yet this is a subject that is absolutely neglected within the school. When we enter the school almost total inability to think and to reason is presumed by our teachers, yet we are considered capable of choosing our vocation, a matter which demands a sound sense of perspective, a true spirit of service, and a full knowledge of self. It is little to be wondered at that many make false decisions, and that many others, unable to decide, fail to focus their energies in any one direction and leave the school handicapped by the curse of laziness.

The young man's desire to reform the world is proverbial. Novelists laugh at him, preachers pity him, cynics jeer at him, Heaven smiles on him. He has enthusiasm, determination, ability; he lacks—direction. Put each man to the task that suits him; then prepare thyself to live in a better world.

As far as the Collegiate is concerned, the problem, we think, can be solved by the appointment of a Vocational Director as a regular member of the staff. His duties would be to learn the inclinations and aptitudes of each student and to advise him what vocation to pursue, and how to fit himself for it. He would understand and be able to explain the intricacies of the various college curricula (if, indeed, such

a thing be humanly possible); he would tell each students which of the school activities it would profit him to specialize in; he would encourage the development to literary, oratorical or musical talent wherever found; in short, he would be the friend and adviser of every student, boy or girl, first-former or senior.

We understand that Vocational Directors have been appointed in certain American schools and that, where appointed, they have proved their worth in no uncertain manner. Undoubtedly our school is large enough to support a Vocational Director. Undoubtedly, the need is a real one. Then why not have one appointed, even if only as an experiment?

* * * * *

A decade after this editorial appeared in the *Vox Lycei* guidance services were established in the Ottawa high schools by the Collegiate Institute Board in the 1940s. Wright Neil was one of a small group of teachers who played a significant role in the organization and development of Guidance in the Ottawa high schools in its early stages. Neil was put in charge of the new Guidance Department at Lisgar and, although he was appointed Vice-Principal in 1951, continued to direct the programme until 1957.

That year Lionel Rule was transferred from the Ottawa Technical High School to be in charge of Lisgar's Guidance Department. Mrs. Lillian Atkinson and Chuck Watts were other counsellors in Room 113, Mrs. Atkinson also functioning as the school librarian and Watts as a science teacher.

Students who attended Lisgar at that time will recall the group testing sessions that were held early in the Fall, the Grade 9 Occupations Classes and many senior students taking the Kuder Interest Tests. The focus of Guidance Counselling was much narrower then than it is today as it was to meet three needs: first to assist students who were experiencing difficultly in their studies and to challenge students who seemed to be underachieving; secondly, to provide counselling for choices in post-secondary educational programmes; and thirdly, to assist students in career planning. Arrangements were made to have speakers come in to school to give "career talks."

Since the 1960s there has been a gradual but steady growth in the services provided by the Guidance Department. Principals, staff members, parents and students have become increasingly supportive of Guidance services. On the advice of school psychologists during the 1970s the group testing programme was revised and expanded to include a full battery of Differential Aptitude Tests. The results of these tests have been most helpful in counselling students. For a decade now the Ottawa Board of Education has arranged in all of its schools for educational psychologists and social workers to be available to students who might require their services. In recent years the necessity has been recognized for the services of further more specialized professionals; speech and hearing pathologists and teachers, special education teacher diagnosticians and a substance abuse resource teacher.

The period since the end of World War II has encompassed sweeping changes in educational policy, changes which tended to support and enhance the importance of Guidance services in the schools both at the elementary and secondary level.

Before 1970 official student records were kept on office cards in the main office. After 1972 the Ministry of Education required that in all schools both at the elementary and secondary level the Ontario School Record file folder (OSR) be used as the student's official academic record. The responsibility for maintaining and keeping these records was designated to the Guidance Department. If the student transferred to another school in the province, the OSR folder was to be forwarded; otherwise, the school was to keep the OSR for seventy years. All records of courses completed and credits earned were to be entered each year. All other data pertinent to that student was to be put in the file.

The Hall Dennis Report of 1969 introduced further significant changes to the work of Guidance Counsellors. Prior to the adoption of the Credit system students rarely dropped or changed courses during the year. After 1972, students were permitted—with the approval of their parents—to drop courses or make changes in their programme of studies. Requests for these changes were directed to the Guidance Department. As a result there was a marked increase in the number of course changes. Another important change was that Grade 12 diplomas were to be granted to students upon completion of twenty-eight credits.

Throughout the years a very high proportion of Lisgar graduates were admitted to university degree programmes. Lisgar graduates will recall that they had to apply for university admission application forms for the universities of their choice. In Ontario after 1969 the universities adopted a common application form which provided spaces for four choices of university and programme. Copies of these forms were sent to the Guidance Department for all Grade 13 students. It became the responsibility of the Guidance Department to have these forms completed by the Grade 13 students by the end of December. In addition, the Guidance Department supplied to the Grade 13 students their marks in Grades 11 and 12, and their Grade 13 midterm marks. In this way the universities were able to obtain the admission application information much earlier and also reduce the number of application forms to be processed.

For many years scholarship application forms were looked after by Lorne Rentner, head of the Mathematics Department. During the late 1960s this responsibility was taken over by the Guidance Department. Lionel Rule looked after scholarships until his retirement in 1985.

There have always been a number of Lisgar graduates who applied each year for admission to American colleges and universities. They have always been required to write College Board examinations for admission. For several years these examinations were written at Lisgar Collegiate under the supervision of Carl Thom of the Lisgar staff. Later the Ottawa College Board Examination Centre was moved from Lisgar Collegiate to Ottawa University.

In 1964 Frank Vetter, a 1953 Lisgar graduate, took over from Rule the direction of the Guidance Department and was later appointed as head of the department. Rule continued as a full-time counsellor until his retirement in 1985.

There have been, of course, many changes in Guidance personnel over the years. Maurice Raymond was a counsellor and French teacher at Lisgar for many years. He later became head of the Guidance Department at École Secondaire Champlain. Douglas Arrand, a Lisgar graduate of 1961, became a counsellor and teacher at Lisgar in 1967. The following persons have served as heads of the Lisgar Guidance Department over the years: 1964-71, Frank Vetter; 1971-74, Victor Shouldice; 1974-87, George Morrison; 1987-91, Brian Pilgrim; 1991-92, Mrs. Pat Current; 1992-, Yvonne Seier.

Counsellors who have served the department both full-time and part-time include: Louyes Chouinard, Robin Wedderspoon, Barrie Laughton, Bill Fraser, Gary Smith, Carol Sabean, Maurice Raymond.

—Lionel Rule

In the spring of 1952, the dream of one Lisgar Grade 13 student was to go off to university and become a dietitian; however, aware that the family financial situation made this an impossibility, she applied instead to Bell Canada for a job as a customer service representative. She subsequently was steered in the direction of Lisgar's guidance counsellor, Wright Neil, who suggested that her aptitude for math could perhaps lead to a job at the National Research Council. After explaining where and what the NRC was, he produced an application form. The application resulted in an interview, which was followed by a long silence. In the meantime, Bell had indicated an eagerness to hire the young lady; a medical exam was passed and a starting date almost agreed upon, when an invitation arrived from NRC to join its (then) Division of Physics. Had it not been for Neil, a thirty-eight year productive career at NRC would never have happened.

Office Staff. From left to right; Carmen Kingsley, Suzanne Matthews, Darlyne Searle, Phyllis Yourth, Susan Smith. Absent from photo; Brenda Beattie (Head Secretary), Bev Halden, Lynne Labelle.

Lisgar has had a long tradition of dedicated head secretaries in the front office, working to co-ordinate the affairs of the school, everything from late slips to exam timetables. Carmelita Grimes left in 1926 to be married. Jessie Watt, a Lisgar student from 1918-1922, returned as secretary, 1926-29. This is a photo of Oneahta Fillion, head secretary, 1929-1940. She later married Lisgar student Kingsley Cawdron.

Oneahta Fillion Cawdron was followed by Dorothy Parrington. Bernice McLaurin, née Scheunemann, was head secretary from 1952 to 1968. This is a photo of Marjery J. Ferguson, head secretary for one of the longest terms at Lisgar, 1968-1984.

STANDARDS OF EXCELLENCE AT LISGAR

1943-1993

In 1975 at an open Citizen's Forum gathered to save Lisgar from the wrecker's ball, M.J. Weeks, then vice-principal of Lisgar, made a fervent plea for preservation and, in the process, defined Lisgar's long and enduring record of academic excellence as well as its high standards in athletics, drama, music, and languages. The following is excerpted from that address:

The question "Is Lisgar worth retaining?" reminds me of a statement attributed to George Bernard Shaw: "No question is so difficult to answer as the question to which the answer is obvious." I now understand exactly what he meant.

I must begin with some of the academic history of the school. Consider the Rhodes Scholarship Award. From the inception of the award up to 1962 one-eighth of all Rhodes Scholars coming from Ontario, came from Lisgar.

Did you know that 70 percent of our Grade 13 students apply to university? We process more university applications than any other Ottawa school. The school has a basic objective of academic excellence. We provide a solid modern education without the frills. We tend to attract high achieving students with fairly strong motivation.

Proficiency Medal for Marion Masson presented by John Christie, Esq., in 1895. The sterling bar pin was added to the medal for her daughter Marion Gale, in 1926. In addition to Marion's daughter, her granddaughter and great-granddaughter also attended Lisgar.

Graduation on the mall, 1991.

Most of you are aware that Lisgar has always had a very large number of Ontario Scholars each year. It is interesting to note that the year the Grade 13 Examinations became an internal matter instead of being set and marked in Toronto, Lisgar came up with the usual large number of Ontario Scholars, while some Ottawa high schools jumped from three to twenty-eight Ontario Scholars. This is further evidence that Lisgar has always had high but reasonable standards and that they have been maintained.

The high standards set at Lisgar have always given higher institutions of learning and employers confidence in accepting Lisgar students. One of the difficulties in starting with the academic excellence of the school is that one might overlook the excellence attained in other areas.

DRAMA: We have one of the most respected Drama Departments in the city. The play *Johnson* two years ago was the winner of the 1972 Eastern Ontario Intercollegiate Drama Festival.

MUSIC: Lisgar offers one of the finest Music Programs in Ontario. In String Music the students are so advanced that they travelled to Waterloo as a demonstration group for a new string approach introduced into Canada at Lisgar. Speaking of music and a unique school—where else would a student audience burst into applause when a radio disc jockey asks them how many liked classical music?

SPORTS: There are more than thirty-five secondary schools in Ottawa and the surrounding area. To win an athletic championship is a real accomplishment. **BASKETBALL** Ottawa Champions last four years in a row. This year— All Ontario Champions: Champions last four years in a row. **CROSS COUNTRY**: Present City Champions. **TENNIS**: Present City Champions for twenty-two years (1988).

Achievements of this sort demand a dedication to the pursuit of excellence. And that is what this place is all about. Whether it's academics, athletics, or other things— there is a dedication to the PURSUIT OF EXCELLENCE.

The variety of social, racial and ethnic backgrounds provides a tremendous advantage both in class and in the larger social situation. A few years ago, over one three-year period, one hundred and thirty-seven different ethnic and national groups were represented. This year, students from sixty-seven different ethnic and national groups attend Lisgar. Just the other day I was in a Home Economics Class in which nine different countries were represented. Nowhere else does this mixture occur. Nowhere else do we get both ends of the economic spectrum as well.

A word about Lisgar teachers, past and present. There are seven ethnic groups represented on our present staff. The history and tradition of Lisgar have provided a strong basis for high morale among these teachers (and the students). The staff at Lisgar has for years presented high standards of scholarship and professionalism for the newcomer to emulate. Because teachers at Lisgar have been exposed to students from such varied cultural, ethnic and social backgrounds they have acquired a tolerance and skill in handling students—skills not found in every school.

Long before the "English as a Second Language" course became established in this system, Lisgar was taking in and coping with large numbers of students who could not speak one word of English upon their arrival. History records the eventual achievements of many of these students.

Lisgar teachers recognize that we have here a special place of learning—it is not a factory or an assembly line.

Lisgar's location provides many advantages as well. The opportunities for out-of-school educational programs in the core area of the city are unique. Lisgar has one of the most active out-of-school educational programs in the city. Trips out of the school are less disruptive and less time-consuming because of our location, trips to such places as N.A.C.— Theatre Arts and English Classes; Churches—History and World Religions Classes; National Art Gallery; Parliament Buildings; University of Ottawa; the National Museum; the National Library and Archives

The location of this school results in its drawing students of all backgrounds, cultural and social, providing an education in itself. The central location of Lisgar makes this type of academic school more accessible to students from all over the city.

We are one hundred and thirty-one years old. *This school is twenty-four years older than Canada.* I'm reminded of something a student said to me in my office about a year ago. He was a visitor to our country and his education spanned several different countries even though he was only sixteen years of age. He said: "I have noticed that Canadians have a strange custom—as soon as a building becomes old you tear it down. Where I come from *something is not valuable until it is old.* I'm going to enjoy being educated in this old building."

As one enters the building one can only be impressed by the stained glass windows, the oak-panelled walls, the marble-lined staircases. This is a place where the past and the present meet. We are steeped in tradition. The names of those Lisgar students and teachers who volunteered for the First and Second World Wars and who gave their lives for Canada, line the front halls.

Although this building is old, some of our facilities are as good if not better, than those in other schools—the Art room, this Auditorium, the D.A. Room are some examples. This building provides a sense of permanence in a time of change—it provides a heritage of values and customs. [This school] is the very root of the educational system in Ottawa.

Teachers at Lisgar

1843-1993

A Successful Teacher Needs

The education of a college president.
The executive ability of a financier.
The humility of a deacon.
The adaptability of a chameleon.
The hope of an optimist.
The courage of a hero.
The wisdom of a serpent.
The gentleness of a dove.
The patience of Job.
The grace of God, and
The persistence of the devil.

PROFESSOR W.L. LOUDON, JANUARY-SEPTEMBER 1881

I taught mathematics in the Ottawa Collegiate Institute from January 1881 until September of the same year. Mr. John Thorburn was Principal. My duty was to look after the welfare and progress of the Second Form, enforce discipline and attendance! The Principal at that time had not the power he has now. Much was left to the discretion of the teacher who was held responsible for a particular form.

There was little trouble in the School. Although I was only twenty at the time I managed to keep order and teach some arithmetic and algebra, and a little English, to my class. This I did by keeping pupils in when they played hookey or misbehaved, and making them do sums in arithmetic, generally multiplication or long division, and get them correct. I always kept a stock of sums on hand, with correct answers.

My first adventure in Ottawa was on my arrival at the old station near the Chaudière. It was a cold winter night in January. A friend, Hayter of the Audit Office, met me and said that another friend, McMinn, had a horse and buggy waiting to drive me out to Hayter's home, which was on Bank Street. I was much impressed with the limestone cliffs and the piles of snow as we turned at Wellington Street amidst a large grove of pine and hemlock trees. The rocky nature of the road, the piles of snow, the houses closed tight, chimneys black with smoke, the picturesque appearance of the people, the sound of running water and the odor of fresh pine and cedar from the mills—all created in me a strange impression which time has never quite effaced from my memory and clings to me whenever I set foot in the sacred city of the North. Years have altered all this, but the scenery still remains.

We were driving out Bank Street when our horse stumbled, and we overturned in a ditch and might have been stranded in the zero weather had it not been for an important-looking man who appeared in a great sleigh driven by a coachman with a footman by his side. This man ordered his servants to help us out, and we went on our way. I had a good look at him. He was fair and handsome, dressed in furs with a fine sable cap stuck rakishly on his head. McMinn informed me that our friend in need was the Marquis of Lorne who lived at Rideau Hall.

I left the Collegiate in September with much regret. I had spent some of the happiest hours of my life there. Ever afterward, when I had the opportunity, I paid visits to Ottawa in order to fish down the river or up the Gatineau near the Picanock, or to sit on Parliament Hill and admire the river filled with rafts of square timber, or gaze in rapture across the river to the blue Chelsea hills.

DR. NORMAN M. GUIOU, STUDENT 1911-15

"Sky" Morris was a highly respected teacher with a characteristic voice which could be imitated. One of his statements—"This business of a small number of men playing a game, and the rest watching them, is not my idea of things. We need a good physical program which involves every student."

Sis Tompkins, Mathematics, was the most notable character of the time. Her sharp tongue maintained good discipline. Students were called by their last names, which she remembered for years. I was in the store at Manotick one day when I noted Sis (then retired and a local resident) browsing around. I quietly informed the storekeeper about his famous customer. Some years later, (by that time, a senior surgeon at the Civic Hospital), I was making rounds one morning when I heard a sharp, "Guiou!" emanating from a private room. I stopped at the door and was greeted with "Guiou! What did you tell that storekeeper about me?" Cordial exchange followed.

Bill Smeaton, a bachelor, was one of the Science teachers. One afternoon an insurance agent had evidently received permission to canvas the teachers. . . "and how many children have you got Mr. Smeaton?" and—"The returns aren't all in yet." He had 5th Form Biology, dissecting frogs. He announced that if we would provide them, we could dissect cats. We heard that a Sparks Street Grocery store was troubled with cats in the basement, and we were welcome to come and take as many as we wanted. We approached with closed market baskets. The cats became so enraged that they became miniature tigers. One bit right through my shoe. The cat hunt was reluctantly abandoned.

Alexis Helmer was a student at that time. He later became a young artillery officer in World War I. A warm friendship developed between him and the units medical officer (then Major John McCrae). Alexis' death from an enemy shell is said to have so moved John McCrae that it inspired him to write his famous poem "In Flanders Fields."

MISS E.A. "SIS" TOMKINS, 1903-08

When Volume I of the history of Lisgar Collegiate Institute was compiled in 1903, Miss E.A. Tomkins contributed to it from the student's standpoint, 1898-1903. For Volume II published in 1943, she reminisced from her standpoint as a teacher of mathematics, 1902-33.

Many of my memories of the 1903-08 period are by this time rather dim, but not the memory of my joy and relief on finding, when the 1903-04 term opened, that the students had now adjudged my year's initiation well and truly carried out, and that therefore the galling provocations of the previous year were to be discontinued.

History is always more or less mixed with tradition, and O.C.I. tradition had it that the new teacher must be initiated. To quote the student writing for the 1895-98 period of Volume I: "The general idea was that the new teacher was meant to be *harassed*, and we thought it a grand 'score' when we got him angry and off his dignity." I am in a position to rather amplify that statement for I had fallen on evil days. When I was appointed to the staff in October 1902, the only woman then on the staff was Miss B.M. Scott, who had been appointed in 1892, and was therefore by this time established. Here now came a late-entering teacher who was not only new but also a member of the so-called weaker and more easily dominated sex. What fun awaited the harassers!

In these olden days wild stories were afloat of deeds of daring performed within the O.C.I. walls—of disciplinary engagements in which the teacher was always ignominiously routed —and of course such exploits challenged emulation. Also in these days many of those who passed High School Entrance did not go on to high school. Of those who did go on some few felt themselves on top of the world, and it was from these few that nearly all disciplinary trouble emanated. Dazzled by their nearness to the sun, they refused to look or climb higher, and, idling in their time, they found that mischief that awaits the idler. Now mischief that aims at doing the merely "funny" things merits no sweeping condemnation—is indeed often refreshing. Not so the mischief that has lurking within it something of the sadistic element, and it is to be regretted that this type is to be found in higher halls of learning than collegiate institutes, as evidenced by the "initiation" rites in colleges and universities where the most cruel indignities are heaped upon the student whose only crime is that he is *new*.

I feel the chilliness of the atmosphere I am creating, yet no right-minded person can deny that these often brutal rites are anachronisms that have been too long tolerated, divorced as they are from all ideas of British fair play—to say nothing of the Golden Rule.

Having quixotically tilted at a windmill in the higher altitudes of advanced (?) education, I parachute down to our "little wanton boys" of Lisgar, and their exasperating, if rarely malicious pranks. I quote Shakespeare: here in no belittling sense. I have long ago forgiven said boys for my year in the valley of humiliation, expiated as it has been by all the succeeding years during which O.C.I. boys gave me every reason to carry with me through life very happy memories of the vast majority of them.

In these happy memories the girls of course have their place. One slackens tension somewhat in thinking of them. They gave little trouble to the two new teachers of their own sex— their batteries were brought to bear on male teachers, and I am bound to say that their tender mercies were sometimes not far from cruel. A girl of this period when asked why she and her form-mates so tormented one of the men answered, "Well, why doesn't he do what he says he'll do? He is always *threatening*, but never *does* anything." I relate the incident because of the valuable moral involved in her somewhat paradoxical reply.

Miss Aletta E. Marty was appointed to the staff in September 1903 to take the headship of the Department of Modern Languages in succession to Mr. Luther Alexander, resigned. Miss Marty was a woman of much force of character, and of brilliant intellectual, academic, and professional attainments, and I thought that all this would permit her escape from such "harassing" as had been accorded to one whose chief recommendation to the O.C.I. Board had been her reputation as a disciplinarian won while principal of Hintonburg Public School.

Not so however—without fear or favour O.C.I. youth girded themselves to "try conclusions" with a foeman so eminently worthy of their steel; but though they persevered for a whole year, their ultimate defeat could never be in doubt. Alert in mind, Miss Marty's quickness of retort was invaluable—an enthusiastic teacher, she strongly resented being diverted from her true function of teaching by enforced sallies into the field of discipline. A very thorough teacher, she was a firm believer in the efficacy of "detentions" in preventing the laggard from acting as a drag upon the class, and sacrificed much of her time after school on the altar of uniformity of class progress.

(Miss Marty was indefatigable in promoting the interests of her alma mater, Queen's University, and some years later her many friends were highly gratified when that University conferred on its gifted daughter the Doctor of Laws degree.)

Musing a moment at this point on detentions in general and the precious time so many teachers devote to them, there recurs to me, as often happens, the memory of the only detention imposed by me whose details I can clearly recall. This one stands out from the past because of one unique detail. One forenoon young R—- was told to report to me after school for algebra homework neglected. I knew he was absent from school that afternoon, so when he appeared in my room after four o'clock I gazed at him in astonishment and said, "I thought you were absent this afternoon." "So I was," he replied, and added, "*I came to put in that detention.*" Imagine! One of my most cherished pictures of memory, he

stands before me now, as he stood before me then, a tall young stripling of most engaging countenance.

In 1906 a certain sartorially-minded member of the staff agitated for the wearing of "gowns" by all its members. Hitherto only the principal had assumed any sort of toga— Dr. Macmillan had worn his gown unfailingly; Dr. McDougall, as principal, had worn his somewhat irregularly for four or five years, then abandoned it altogether. Our agitator carried his point, and behold an imposing array of gowned teachers! But not for long—the gowns were found to be uncomfortably warm in summer and an inconvenience at all times. They very soon became shabby—were worn only intermittently—were discarded. *Sic transit!*

Mr. Finlay Hood was appointed to the staff in 1906, and under him what had been modestly known as "Drawing" developed into "Art"; and with Mr. Wm. Smeaton's appointment in the same year a witty and invigorating Scotch element was infused into the Science Department. Next year Mr. H.C. Mann entered the English Department, where he began an energetic bolstering up of what has become in twentieth-century secondary schools "a slowly dying cause," viz., the teaching of Formal (English) Grammar.

After the summer holidays of 1908, school did not re-open until October 5, because of unfinished building operations. The east wing of the Lisgar building had been added in 1902, and of it the editor of the Lisgar history (Volume I) says: "It was no sooner built than it was filled," and he went on to predict: "The time is not far distant when the attendance will require a similar wing on the west side to that on the east, and thus give symmetry to this stately pile of limestone."

EXCERPT FROM FINLAY HOOD'S DIARY, 1929

May 10: News reached us that Miss A.E. Marty had passed away in South Africa. She was a public school inspector in Toronto and was on exchange with a South African inspector. For many years Miss Marty was a most popular and successful teacher of Moderns in Lisgar Collegiate.

June 10: Mr. W.D.T. Atkinson has been appointed principal of Collingwood Collegiate.

June 21: An oil portrait of Mr. R. Stothers was presented to the Board today. The presentation address was delivered by Hon. W.L. Mckenzie King, and the portrait was received by Mr. H.P. Hill on behalf of the Board. The portrait, which was painted by Fosbery, has a conspicuous position in the assembly hall.

REMINISCENCES OF LISGAR TEACHER MARY KETTLES AS A STUDENT IN THE 1930s

In the depths of the Depression I found myself in Form 1F of the massive gray stone building I had often seen across the canal and railways tracks. When we came "to town," we came in Nicholas Street from my home in the country. Compared with the one-room rural school at Ramseyville, Lisgar

Collegiate was a formidable maze. The First Formers had an opening Assembly on the first afternoon of School. After that the various teachers visited us in Home Room and told us the books we needed. Armed with this long list, I found my way to Jarvis' bookstore. It was a madhouse. Poor Mr. Jarvis! As he wiped the perspiration from his forehead he barked, "You won't need most of these books for a month." But we had our lists. We had to get books, and get them we did! No text books were supplied in those days.

The next morning I lugged all those books to school and from class to class, until we could get a lock and have a locker assigned. On the way along the hall, someone bumped into me at the foot of the "down" staircase. Down went most of my new books. I've always been grateful to Miss Brown, the young Latin teacher, who rescued me. She took me into her room and let me leave some of my books there until I got a place to put them. We didn't have Gym that first full day of school. Miss Smith and someone else (probably a senior student), were issuing locks. It didn't take too long to master the art of using a combination lock. Success number one in Lisgar!

What do I remember from the early years? Chiefly personalities. All those kids with brains and the wonderful clothes some of the girls wore; one girl's father owned a dress store. The people who made announcements in Assembly. One of them was Lorne Green. The athletes among us. Two girls from the Japanese Embassy were crackerjacks at basketball! We knew our teachers with their quirks and foibles. Mr. Strader's construction problems in Geometry. He'd say, "Imagine it's finished." Then he'd make a diagram on the side board. On the front board he'd begin to build the construction. Back he'd go to the "blueprint" on the side board to find out what to do next.

Mr. Showman's homework assignments! How many work books did we fill with synopses of Latin verbs with all their tenses? We never figured out why he called them synopses. For some reason, Mr. Rentner thought we always had to do his homework. And we did. I had Mr. Nicholls for Geometry three days when Miss Hills was sick. He taught me that a polygon was a dead parrot. We soon learned to recognize Mr. Mann's stride as he came along the hall.

One day Lord Tweedsmuir came to visit our classrooms. The poor teachers! They didn't know he was coming until he got to the school. Miss Meadows was very gracious, but we knew she wished she had known he was coming. If she had, she'd have gotten her hair done. Mr. Felker took His Excellency's visit in his stride. How could anyone be so cool in such a mighty presence? A few years later I met Mr. Felker on a Montreal train. When I told him I was teaching high school now, his remark was deflating— "Languages, I presume?"

I'll never forget my fifth form French class, Miss Muir taught in the room with the big bay window on the second floor. There were fifty-six people in that class and not a dropout all year. Never once did I see her lose her cool. Every class went like clockwork. At the beginning of each lesson she would say, "Si vous n'avez pas ecrit tous les exercises, levez-vouz." If we hadn't finished our homework, we'd stand. As she wrote down our names, she'd say, "Très bien. Je vous verai ce soir" and we went back and finished our homework and did an extra exercise. We were in fifth form, but never thought of not complying. One did not question her quiet authority.

We sat in Home Room groups in Assembly every morning. Dr. Bearder was in charge of the orchestra. On mornings when he went to Glebe, Bill Boss often conducted the orchestra. We usually sang a song. Sometimes we sang, "God Save the King;" sometimes we sang "Dieu protège le Roi." Occasionally we sang "La Marseillaise" and sometimes "O Canada" in either English or French. The great bilingualism tension was all in the future.

Occasionally we had special guests, a film or slides, sometimes a travelogue or a demonstration. In retrospect I think the speaker who impressed me most was Denton Massey, guest at the final assembly the year I was in fourth form. His title: *You Can't Saw Sawdust*; his theme: You can't progress if you just keep doing the same thing over and over. You can't just live on your laurels.

One particular morning assembly stands out in my mind. Everyone was agog that morning. The word was around. Lisgar beat Glebe in the football game. . . for the first time in six years. When the announcement was made, huddles formed as if by magic all over the hall. The cheers were deafening. The excitement generated after six years of waiting for victory electrified us.

There were Senior and Junior Lyceums. These groups presented little concerts after school, for ten cents a person. There were short plays, dancers, songs, piano and vocal solos, drills, other musical offerings, and sometimes elocution numbers. Cartier Square was an extension of Lisgar. The only buildings on the block bounded by Lisgar, Elgin, Laurier and the Driveway, were Lisgar, Ottawa Normal School, The Drill Hall, and the Military Stores Building. Practices for games were held out there in good weather. Cadet practices also took place there. So did Cadet Inspection—quite a military event. The rest of us got out of school to see it. A few days later, Mr. Meng made the rounds of the classes where someone had been so remiss as to forget to return his uniform. With no wasted words, he announced that they were to be returned. . . "Immediately . . . OR." Then he turned his back and strode out.

WALLACE SHOWMAN, 1933-66

From a pioneer's sod house in Alberta, I came via Queen's University to teach Classics at Lisgar in 1933. The 33 years I spent there were the best of my life. Lisgar's distinguished academic tradition, even at that time, went back 90 years. There was a strong and dedicated staff, and a student body that contained, I felt sure, more than the average proportion of able and ambitious young people, many of whom were determined to work and fight their way out of the Depression, and who realized the value of education. But the War came, and the names of some of our boys appeared upon the Honour Rolls which flanked the door of the Library.

My main extra-curricular role was in photography. We formed a Camera Club, using as a darkroom, the tiny storage cubicle at the back of Mr. Smeaton's Science room up on the Third Floor. It was only 4x8 feet in area, but large enough to contain the few items of equipment that we gradually acquired. Using my own darkroom and equipment, I took the photographs for the *Vox Lycei* for many years, including the 1944 Centenary and the building of the Gymnasium.

Most of my Lisgar memories are happy ones, but I recall that sad day in winter when a Grade 9 girl was killed at the Girls' Entrance by a fall of ice from the roof. That was before the protective restraints were out in place.

JERRY DIAMOND, 1931-36

Since my graduation from Lisgar Collegiate 48 years ago memories have dimmed; nevertheless they are still there. One does not forget his school days especially if they were happy ones, and so I will begin my contribution to the proposed booklet which will commemorate Lisgar's 140th Reunion, as the highlights of my years at Lisgar come to my mind, whether they be of our teachers, the extracurricular activities, or of anecdotes.

First I would like to say something about our teachers, the teachers of the Dirty Thirties. There were Sis Tomkins and Minnie Hills who will be fondly remembered by thousands of students as "the yes and no girls" talking to each other between classes. Due to unfortunate circumstances, one shook her head up and down, the other from side to side.

Mr. Rentner was a fighter and real tough; I recall the time he got into a fist fight with a fellow named Jones. This was during our Physics class across from the girls' gym on the third floor; we carried one of the girls who fainted into the girls' gym where young Dorothy Bishop had recently become Phys-Ed teacher.

There were Louis Meng, Mr. Blake, Mr. Irwin and Mike Strader, a real nice guy with a red nose and broad smile. And there is always a love story to remember. Mr. R.S. Whittle, teacher and my Basketball Coach, met his Waterloo during my second year. One Marion McLean had just been added to the teaching staff and her home-room was across the hall from Mr. Whittle's. Marion had a beautiful head of hair and we nicknamed her Clara Bow, one of the current Hollywood beauties. Mr. Whittle must have noticed because day after day he talked to her between classes and before long it was Mr. and Mrs. R.S. Whittle.

One day recently, I telephoned Walter B. Mann and said to him, "Walter, this is Jerry Diamond, a former student of yours at Lisgar; do you remember me?" To which he replied, "Sure I do," and we went on for a long time talking of teachers and students we both knew. After no contact for 48 years!

Hank Ellis, nicknamed Hangman Ellis, because of a namesake at the local jail on Nicholas Street who performed such tasks in the days of capital punishment, was my Arithmetic teacher and one day manhandled me because I skipped class; another day he bought me a beer at a local pub, The Ottawa House, when I handed in a perfect term paper.

I have fond memories of Mr. Drulard my Phys-Ed teacher in my first year. As a 13 year old weighing in at 98 pounds, I came to a try-out for the Cub Team (Basketball), and green as I was, I came unprepared to purchase an athletic support. I had no money. Without Mr. Drulard I never would have made the team. He gave me the support.

Having walked by all the rooms of these memorable teachers we come to the Inner Sanctum where pretty, young Oneahta Fillion handed out the sick slips and her boss, Principal Nosey Stuart ruled with an iron hand. I recall Mr. Stuart walking into the Rialto Theatre on Bank Street one Friday afternoon red-handedly catching some fifth formers skipping classes. You could put nothing over Nosey Stuart.

On Stuart's retirement, Johnny Dunlop became Principal. Johnny was pretty tricky too. In his classes, he continually looked out of the window during exam time and woe to any student who talked or cribbed. He saw the reflection in the window.

G.R. BOWEN, 1940-44

In the fall of 1940, I believe, J.J. Dunlop noticed a very high vacancy level in a few of the classes one afternoon. Being wise in the ways of the students, he immediately went to the Elgin Theatre, had the show stopped, the lights turned on, plucked out about forty students, and marched them back to school. We spent a great deal of time thereafter attending detention classes. I don't remember now what was playing at the theatre—it must have been good.

BOB McDOWELL, 1935-40

As they say. . . Once upon a time . . . we were all in Mr. Felker's lab and working on an experiment from the good manual—we being myself, Mac Richardson, and Leo Heaps. Well! Mac and I were religiously applying ourselves to the experiment in hand, but unbeknown to the two of us, Leo was off on his own on the next experiment in the manual.

So we were not in any way expecting the ensuing near-holocaust. Leo had two test tubes—each over a Bunsen burner and connected to each other via a delivery tube. Not having read the fine print, Leo was supposed to have them loosely stoppered. Leo in fact had them plugged tightly. I think it was sulphuric acid in one tube and silver nitrate in the other. Naturally, as these test tubes heated up, there had to be, and there was, an explosion!

Acid all over the place confusion supreme. Mac and I, although we had a basin in our lab "desk," ignored same and made a dash for Mr. Felker's basin. Our clothes were rapidly starting to fall apart and I had a great blob on the end of my nose. All h—— broke out, and to his great credit, good old Eric Nichols appeared from nowhere, threw us into his car (a maroon two-door Dodge, I think), and took us for medical attention. There was, as it turned out, nothing serious at all—except the sport jacket that I was sure wowed all the girls was now in great shambles and completely finished.

It was therefore somewhat intriguing to note that, when I came back from overseas and visited Lisgar, they had not forgotten this momentous occasion. There on Mr. Fitzimons' board for all to see and take note of was a recapitulation of our "daring-do" and great warning that such things should never happen again. It took the same importance as the First World War and I thought, how appropriate, for really, both should never occur again. It's somewhat rewarding that for a very brief period in Lisgar's history Leo, Mac, and I were cast in roles of "dubious" folk heroes.

THE TOMKINS LEGEND

If half of the epigrams that flashed and sparkled from the lips of the late Miss Elizabeth ("Sis") Tomkins, former mathematics teacher at Lisgar Collegiate, had been jotted down and collected, they would have made a fair-sized volume and, in Ottawa at least, a best seller. Her wit and wisdom were proverbial not only in the classroom but in the world outside and in circles of the Anglican church where she was esteemed and beloved.

The latest issue of the *Ottawa Diocesan News* quotes in part the *Journal's* recent editorial tribute to Miss Tomkins, refers to her as a "great" churchwoman, and the Reverend A.E.O. Anderson recalls two typical anecdotes of "The Tomkins Legend."

A new teller at the Bank of Montreal asked Miss Tomkins for some identification. She looked over her spectacles through the wicket and called, "Boys—"; a number of heads popped up and she was identified.

On a trip to Niagara, as the bus came in sight of the Falls, quite a discussion arose as to the greater grandeur of the Canadian side. An American woman said, "That should belong to us. We should have fought for it." Miss Tomkins nearly stopped the bus with "You did!"

—Ottawa Journal editorial

ISABEL (BROWN) BUCHANAN, 1929-55

I joined the staff of Lisgar Collegiate in 1929, having grown up in Brockville. After graduating from Queen's University (M.A. Classics) I taught Latin and Greek at Cornwall Collegiate for two years before coming to Lisgar, where I succeeded W.D.T. Atkinson, who became Principal of Glebe Collegiate, the new school. Its recent opening had necessitated changing the name of Ottawa Collegiate to Lisgar. Over 26 years I served under three principals—F.A. Stuart, J.J. Dunlop, and J.W. Strader. The staff was predominantly male, especially in the earlier years. Among the women teacher when I arrived were Jessis Muir, Head of Modern Languages, E.A. (Sis) Tomkins and Minnie Hills, both in the Math Department, and Bessie Scott Lewis, Librarian.

Teaching at Lisgar was a stimulating and enjoyable experience. There was a genuine rapport between the staff and student body of over 1000 representing not only Ottawa, but also a cross section of Canada and of the world. There were families of the various Embassies, of the Members of Parliament, of the National Research Council, the Armed Forces, and the Civil Service. Several who enlisted from our classes in World War II did not come back. I think of Cecil and Bob Heeney, Digby Cosh, Tony Coughlin, Alex Grange, Hugh Cairns, Edward Lambart and many others. We experienced sunshine and shadow.

Among those with musical talent, names that pop out are Betty Joe singing at the annual Concert, "There's a Rainbow Round My Shoulder," and Gerry Fink taking the tenor lead in Brigadoon. I cannot forget the faithful young people in the school orchestra, playing each morning at the brief assemblies and on special occasions. I often noted that they were our best students. I remember the scholarship winners, including two Rhodes Scholars who had been in my classes, Boudy Van Oort and Harley Smyth. There was an interesting succession of Head Boys and Head Girls who led the Students' Council, making decisons and taking responsibility for the whole student body. Who could forget the Saturday crowd with John Currie and Dick Barber off to Camp Fortune to ski, and the many boys' and girls' athletic teams and their loyal supporters!

Every other morning Dr. John W. Bearder would come to direct the orchestra, going to Glebe on alternate days. Bill Boss was happy to fill in as maestro. We had a repertoire of about 200 songs from which we sang lustily at the morning assembly, one each day. Every Wednesday students stood at the door of our beautiful Assembly Hall with milk bottles to collect our pennies or small change. An annual cheque for CARE was the result. Favourite visitors from the Collegiate Board were James Warren (Jimmie) York, well known lawyer, also the first woman member of the Board, Mrs. C.H. Thorburn. Special guest speakers at Assembly or Commencement included Gratton O'Leary, Editor of the *Ottawa Journal*, who gave a memorable address on "The King's English," and Denton Massey, who impressed us with his remarks entitled "You Can't Saw Sawdust." Among our favourite singers at Lisgar was George Montgomery, with Evelyn Feldman as accompanist. Some 25 years later they returned to thrill everyone with their number "The Lord's Prayer" at the 125th Anniversary of the school in 1968. I will remember Betty Kennedy and Adrienne Clarkson among my interesting students. They are still my good friends.

The most famous student in my classes was John Buchan, Canada's Governor-General (1935-1940)—Lord Tweedsmuir. This could not have happened anywhere but in Ottawa. An author and keenly interested in education, he arranged to visit Lisgar, and chose to include my Greek class. Asking if he might stay for the rest of the period, he was with us for 20 minutes, and sat with the students. Afterwards he thanked me for taking him back to his school days in Scotland. We were all thrilled.

The two books I have written are in the Lisgar Library, and also in the Ottawa Public Library. One was published in Toronto in 1975. It is entitled *A Time To Cheer*, and was written to celebrate the 100th anniversary of our Canadian Mission in Central India. The other came out in Brockville in 1981, a collection of 60 poems which I have written over the years.

I resigned from the Lisgar staff in 1955 to go to India to be married to a missionary, the Rev. Dr. Thomas Buchanan, whom I had met the year before on a ship crossing the Atlantic. Five years later he retired after serving 40 years in India, and we returned to live in Canada, settling in Toronto, where my husband became Assistant Minister at Fairlawn United Church until his death after a brief illness in 1976. I returned to Brockville to live in an apartment overlooking the St. Lawrence, and just across the street from the house where I grew up.

MARION MEECH, 1943-70

In September of 1943 I was welcomed to the Lisgar staff by Mr. John Dunlop, the Principal. This proved for me the beginning of a long period of growing affection for the school, its long history, its staff and students. It was a particularly fortunate year to arrive, as we were just about to celebrate the 140th anniversary, and it was an appropriate time to discover the history and traditions of the school and to meet former staff and returning alumni.

I was impressed by the handsome building in an architectural style, quite different from any school I had been in either as a pupil or teacher. I realized also that the building was much older than the date of construction—quarried from stone of the Laurentian shield, and given structure and colour by millennia of geologic upheavals. And it was amusing to discover that the original name of the street was Biddy. Does it make you think of clucking hens? They probably had been on the site, as it had been occupied by a farmer before being purchased as a location for the school. Of course if the name had been retained, it might be supposed to indicate the indoor sound effects. But it was fitting to honour Sir John Young, who became Governor-General in 1868 and was elevated to the peerage as first Baron Lisgar, by naming both street and new school after him. Perhaps too, a distinguished name would help lessen the criticism that the school was too far out of the city limits.

The main entrance to the building I found to be gently illuminated by five lovely stained glass windows, with portraits of five of the great intellectuals. We recognize Benjamin Franklin, Beethoven and Sir Isaac Newton, but who are the two figures with laurel wreaths in the narrow

panels in the side walls? Petrarch? Dante? Hardly both of these, but probably one of them.

In the main hallway was the bronze plaque commemorating the names of those students who served in the First World War. It was a moving experience to discover that the young man whose death prompted Dr. John McCrae to write "In Flanders Fields" is honoured there. Alexis Helmer had known McCrae at McGill, and was in the same army unit in France; according to the story McCrae was with him at his death, read the burial service of his faith, and then took a notebook and pencilled those familiar lines.

In the corridor beyond, to east and west, were marble staircases worn into hollow spots by the footsteps of several generations. My classroom had generous sunny window sills where plants flourished; there was a ceiling of pressed metal stamped in floral designs, a material and style that is no longer used, but some of which has been imaginatively preserved in recent renovations. More important than the physical building were the personal contacts within its walls. There were many staff members whose whole teaching career was at Lisgar, and the resulting stability and continuity were a stimulus and source of strength to newer appointees.

JESSIE MUIR, 1920s

In a May 1979 issue of *Federation Update*, the newsletter of the OSSTF, Jack Hutton paid tribute to one of Lisgar's outstanding female teachers.

Here's the story of an Ottawa teacher who scored a victory 59 years ago today on behalf of women teachers all across Ontario. . . Our tale begins the night of April 27, 1920, when a delegation of women secondary school teachers asked the old Ottawa Collegiate Institute Board to be paid on the same basis as men with similar qualifications. The board's response: no. That would have ended the matter except that a slim envelope arrived shortly with a resignation. It came from Miss Jessie Muir, M.A., Head of the Department of Modern Languages at Lisgar Collegiate Institute, and one of the city's most respected teachers. There were hasty telephone calls, including more than one to ask Miss Muir whether she were serious. Could, perhaps, something be done to improve her salary? The redoubtable Miss Muir stood firm.

On the night of May 7, 1920, the school board met again. Its terse minutes report two important decisions. First, the resignation of Miss Jessie Muir, M.A., was refused. Secondly, the school board voted to raise the pay of its women teachers to the level of male teachers. May 7, 1920, became a date for posterity. Jessie Muir didn't halt there. When the fledgling OSSTF (Ontario Secondary School Teachers Federation) held its second meeting in Toronto, Jessie Muir was there to represent Ottawa and that part of Ontario. (The 1920 annual meeting included both men and women, unlike the 1919 one which was exclusively male).

In the middle of the afternoon, she rose with a motion "that the principle of equal pay for equal work be formally adopted into the general policy of this federation and that the adoption of this policy be at once made public through the press."

The delegates had no problem with the first part of the motion but the latter part was a worry. The founding meeting had been held entirely in secret for fear of reprisals. Again, however, Jessie won the day. The result was a two-column story on page four of the *Globe*, Dec. 29, 1920: EQUAL PAY FOR EQUAL WORK RIGHT OF WOMEN IN SCHOOLS. It was the first press release of the Ontario Secondary School Teachers Federation.

In the early years of the federation, Jessie Muir's name blazes through the records like a comet. She served on the provincial executive for at least two years, leaving before she reached the presidential chair. (She would have been OSSTF's first woman president except for her departure.) The records show that she, Walter Clarke and William Mitchell, the first OSSTF president, appeared together on platforms all over Ontario. In 1921, she wrote to the Bulletin urging a program to rebut ill-informed criticism of teachers.

Finlay Hood's diary for April 29, 1939, records: "The school suffered a severe loss in the death today of Miss Jessie Muir. She taught Moderns in the school from 1909 and was head of the Moderns Department from 1919 when she succeeded Miss Marty. The school was closed on May 2 to allow teachers and students to attend the funeral." Tributes came from many levels of the community, including the University of Ottawa which had tried for years to woo Jessie Muir as its Dean of Women. An entire city felt the passing of one teacher.

In 1979 Jack Hutton discussed Jessie Muir with a long-time colleague of Jessie Muir's—the one and only Walter Mann.

"Formidable," said Walter, stressing the French pronunciation. "Jessie was the official arbiter of Manners and Morals at Lisgar, and heaven help you if you fell out of line. She had no hesitation about reminding students in private that the school had certain standards and they were expected to meet them."

One irony is that Walter, a district president in the 1940s, can't remember federation involvement by either Jessie Muir or William Smeaton, a Glasgow-born science teacher who attended the 1919 OSSTF meeting. "I think she felt strongly about women's rights in the early days, but once she felt she'd made her point she directed her energies elsewhere."

The 1843-1943 history of Lisgar Collegiate recalls William Smeaton as a man "who lived with himself on terms he willed," and Walter Mann's recollections seem to bear this out. "I noticed for years that he always walked alone, and finally summoned nerve to ask him why. His reply was unforgettable: 'I can break wind at will'."

"Only one thing puzzled me," Walter added. "I can never recall anyone on staff called Will."

Jessie Muir wouldn't have approved that story. She didn't approve of William Smeaton either, if Walter's memory is accurate. But let's accord her a place of honour in our memories; a remarkable teacher who was years ahead of her time.

SMACKEMS, 1927-1993

The private lives of teachers are really not for public examination. The exception to this piece of common sense arises when some great accomplishment is achieved, far from the field of pedagogy. Just such a success involved eight teachers, all with Lisgar connections, in the year 1927 (prior to the stock-market crash that precipitated the Great Depression). This was the year of the founding of "Smackems" Bridge Club, one of Ottawa's oldest duplicate bridge organizations. This then is a story involving the private lives of people you will all remember.

"Smackems" is an acronym, created from the first letter of the surname of the bridge club's members. S is Mike Strader, mathematician and principal; M is George Mabee, classics head; A is Don Atkinson who moved to Glebe Collegiate as principal; C is Don Clark, later to be vice-principal at the High School of Commerce; K is J. Kaiser, history teacher; E is George Ellis, mathematics teachers whose room has been absorbed today by the library; M is Lou Meng, master of physics and World War I; S is Fred Stuart, the principal (who hired me!).

As the years have passed, replacements have had to be made. The acronym Smackems no longer applies literally. For instance, when the club celebrated it fiftieth anniversary in 1977, the members were Hal Axon, High School of Commerce; Bernie Black, principal at Sir. John A. Macdonald; René Charron, head of French at Lisgar; Patrick David, English teacher and consultant; Walter Mann, retired; Bill McCarthy, principal; Bob McMichael, principal; Wright Neil, retired principal; and Gale Smyth, elementary school principal. Readers will notice the strong continuing Lisgar connection as well as an inclusion of other schools.

As in teaching Smackems had its "occasional" players, some as members and some as substitutes. How many of these names do you recall? John Dunlop, Red Legon, Stu Holmes, Andy Fitzsimmons, Bill Kendrick, Gar Kiel, Harold Rothwell, Jack Quinlan, Vic D'Amico, Maurice Obonsowin, Tom Sparling, John Hussar, John Poggione, Terry Murphy, Frank Turner, and the list goes on.

Smackems still meets sixteen times a year with its unique set of rules. It awards one hundred points (not fifty) for a part or full score; it accepts "honours" because of the competition they make possible; and it insists on keeping "minutes" of the evening's play (we have a continuous record of play, peace time, war time, depression time from 1927 to 1993). We use hand-made duplicate boards, playing three "rounds" of eight hands each session. After sixteen sessions, the winner is given the Smackems cup, a pewter glass-bottom beer stein, engraved with his name and the year and an alphabetical listing of the players.

Like all clubs, in their early days, the serving of refreshments became more and more elaborate. Then sense dawned. The only thing served was beer. This meant that on occasion the third round was somewhat exaggerated in bidding and play. However, by 1993 the host of a Smackems session prepared a bar with its chips and cheese and crackers.

Lisgar Collegiate has been famous for initiating many things. Until this publication, Smackems has been a well-kept secret. Now you all will know one of the private activities that stimulated the minds of your teachers in their extra-curricular hours.

—Walter B. Mann

THE LAST WORD GOES TO WALTER MANN, 1933-68

What other institution has contributed so much to the life of this nation as the school called Lisgar Collegiate? Perhaps McGill, Queen's, the U. of T. come to mind as you try to answer my question. But these are institutions attended by people who have already made their choices, who wish to pursue a field of study already made intriguing to them. Made intriguing by whom? I contend that the significantly formative years are the high school ones. Here, consciously exposed to Mathematics, to Science, to Language Studies, to English and History with their built-in forages into philosophy, religion, aesthetics and even psychology (the poems of Browning, Klein, the plays of Shakespeare) the student chooses his way. The business men, the doctors, the teachers, the economists of Canada all have roots in a high school. And how lucky are those who since 1843 can say "that Collegiate on Lisgar Street was mine."

I cannot make that proud statement even though my teaching career of thirty-three years at Lisgar comprises about 24 percent of Lisgar's life. Yet I dare to hope that I contributed something to the reputation that has made Lisgar so great. Therefore I have the temerity to join you Lisgar graduates, and say, "yes, and Lisgar was mine too (by adoption); some of those old grey stones belong to me."

Washed into teaching by the tide of the great depression of the thirties, I contracted for $1800 per annum, less 10 percent, a cut which had just been extracted from the civil service, and hence was deducted from Ottawa's teachers' salaries. Today $1620, would hardly pay for a week-end in Toronto! Yet I knew I had arrived; the old school had an "air"; it was a place to belong to, with style, with reputation. Situated in a magnificent city, drawing a cross-section of students with varied, colourful backgrounds, Lisgar was, as it still is, a lodestone to draw loyalty from its staff and students.

Fifty-one years later, tiny ludicrous recollections come to me; my two-year struggle to get one electric outlet installed in 114; my introduction of music—via my own radio—into the class room; only to have the caretaker ram a screwdriver through its vernier plates; my longing to unscrew the desks

and make the room into a forum; the 11:30 a.m. mouse which appeared daily in 114's bay window recess, having climbed from the cafeteria below through a knot-hole in the floor; one day I tore the earpiece of the old rotting intercom telephone; my total failure to get the room carpeted ("preposterous and revolutionary!!"). "The good old time—the good old time."

"Wasn't that the best time—that time when we were young—and had nothing?" with apologies to Joseph Conrad, and love to a fine old school.

Great teacher Walter B. Mann addressing the assembly at the 140th celebrations.

TEACHERS

Name	Subject	Years
Adams, Miss Marion	Art	1966-1969
Ade, W. F. C.		1939, 1943-1947
Agnew, A.		1877-1880
Alexander, L. H.	French, German	1894-1903
Ami, Rev. M.	French	1872-1882
Anderson, F.		1915-1916
Anderson, Mrs. Irene	Home Economics	1983-1984
Andrews, Miss Margaret	English	1966-1968
Argue, Douglas	History	1957-Dec. 1971
Armstrong, David	Mathematics	1980-Oct. 1990
Armstrong, W.	English	1901-1903
Arrand, Douglas C.	History, Guidance	1967-Dec. 1985, Jan. 1987-
Arthur, Mrs. Irene		1964-1965
Ashdown, C.		1920-1921
Ashenhurst, Ms.		1975-1976
Ashworth, Paul	Geography	1990-
Atkinson, Mrs. Lillian E. (née Hill)	History, Guidance	1931-1965
Atkinson, W. D. T.		1921-1929
Audet, Rome	Business, Law	1975-1991
Bachelor, Peter	Dramatic Arts	1978-1979, 1980-1981
Badger, Mrs. Margaret	Mathematics, Science	1967-1968
Bailey, Mr.	Science	1979-1980
Bainbridge, Michael	Physical Education	1976-1977
Baldwin, Ms. Julia	Business	1984-1985
Ballantyne, Miss K.		1883-1884
Band, C.		1940-1941
Banevicius, Miss Sigita	Art	1983-1984
Banks Trevor	English	1988-1989
Barnes, C. A.		1876
Batstone, A.	History	1916-1922
Beall, James	English	1968-1971, 1972-1977
Bearder, Dr. James	Music	1919-1938
Beatty, Mrs. Rose	English	1988-1990
Bee, Mrs. Pat	English	1991-1992
Behan, Robert	Mathematics	1965-1976
Belfry, O.		1879
Bishop, Miss Dorothy	Physical Education, English	1934-1966
Black, Bernie	Physical Education, English	1953-1957
Blake, Peter	Modern Languages	1967-1968
Blake, S.		1928-1934
Blonde, Mrs. Louise	French	Sept. 1990-June 1991
Boehmer, John	History	1970-
Boileau, Ms. Karen	Dramatic Arts	Dec. 1989-1990
Borthwick, Rev. H.	Principal	1859-1862 (Ret. 1903)
Bowman, Mrs.	(dec. 1989-90)	1965-1966
Boyce, Hugh A.	Vice-principal	1976-1984
Boyle, Ms. Marie-Lou	Géographie, Histoire	1989-
Bradley, Mrs. Trudy	Music	1982-
Briggs, Miss Beverley	English	1981-1991
Brisebois, Roger	Science (dec. 10/04/90)	1962-1969
Brondex, Mrs. Edmonde	French	1979-1981
Brophy, Pat.	English	1965-1967
Brown, Miss Isabel (later Mrs. Buchanan)	Classics	1929-1954
Brown, Miss Bonnie	English	1965-1967
Bruce, Victor N.	Principal	1956-1960
Bryan, P.		1932-1933
Bryan, Mrs.		1962-1963
Buan, Larry	Science	1986-
Bucens, Mrs. Irene	Science	1989-1991
Buchanan, Mrs. Isabel (née Brown)	Classics	1929-1954
Buchanan, Marc	Vice-principal	1987-1990
Burke, Gary	Mathematics	1980-1989
Burridge, A.	Physical Education	1916-1928
Burrows, Geoffrey	French (dec. 27/02/90)	1984-1985
Butterill, Duff	Mathematics	1958-1960
Calloway, Mrs. Barbara	Physical Education	1967-1968
Caloia, Mrs. D. Louise	Home Economics	1980-1982
Cameron, Angus	Science	1970-1983
Campbell, D. A.	Science	1896-1903
Campbell, T.	Mathematics	1886-1887
Campbell, Mrs.		1957-1958
Carbonneau, Miss		1953-1954
Carroll, Mr.	Science	1957-1960
Carruthers, John C.	History (dec. 03/03/86)	1947-1977
Carson, Miss	English	1979-1980
Carter, W.		1872
Carter, Sgt. Major W.		1927-1933

Cattenach, Mr.		Ret. before 1903
Chambers, Catherine	Physical Education	1988-1992
Charron, Mrs. Marena		
(former Mrs. Compain)	French	1977-1984, 1985-
Charron, René	French	1960-1989
Cheung, Stephen T.	Mathematics	1967-
Chisholm, W. J.	French, German	1887-1889
Chitty, Sgt. Major D.		1903-1909
Chouinard, Miss Louyse	French, Guidance	1979-
Christensen, Miss Diane	Mathematics	1960-1961
Church, Peter	French, Latin (dec. 03/92)	1983-1985
Cillis, Mrs. D. J.	English	1963-1964
Clark, D. M.		1922-1927
Clarke, William	Mathematics	1990-
Cleal, Robert	Music	1963-1965
Cleland, Ted	English	1973-1976
Clifford, Miss Gail	French	1964-1966
Clothier, J.		1919-1921
Cluff, Miss E.		1894
Cochrane, Peter	English	1962-1963
Colbert, Mrs. Heather	Mathematics, Geography	1978-1979
Collins, Frank	French	1965-1967
Compain, Mrs. M.		
(later Mrs. R. Charron, 1981)	French	1977-1984
Conklin, J. D.	Commercial	1894-1902
Connolly, Mrs. Shirley	Art	1975-1977
Conway, Mrs. Dorothy	Mathematics	1975-
Cook, Mrs.		1962-1964
Cope, E. B.		1882-1884
Coughtrey, Bruce	Mathematics	1976-1988
Cowie, Miss Helen	French, German	1920-1922
Cowley, R. H.	Science	1894-1898
Craig, Douglas	Geography	1979-1980, 1981-1982
Cunningham, Robert	Science	1974-1975
Current, Mrs. Patricia	Guidance	1991-1992
Currie, Jean	History	1985-1990
Curtis, J.		1913-1921
Dain, Mrs. Daphne	Art	1990-
Daniel, Pat	English	1968-1970, 1971-1972
Davey, Harvey	History	1981-1982
Davidson, A. B.		1880-1881
Davies, Mrs. Ruth		1947-1964
Dawson, Mrs. Margaret (née Herbert)	Science	1961-1979
Day, Mrs. Mary-Anne	English	1962-1964
Derry, Mrs. Louise	Librarian	1992-
Derry, Robert	French	1987-
Desbrisay, Miss		1949-1950
De Souza, Selwyn	Physical Education	1979-1980
Dickson, Mrs. Janet	E. S. L.	1984-1988
Dillon, Michael J.	Geography	1966-1968
Doherty, Neil	Mathematics	1968-1970
Domineco, Errol A.		1967-1968
Donaldson, W.	Science	1912-1920
Dougall, M.		1927-1928
Dowd, Sean	Geography	Jan. 1985-June 1985
Drulard, E.		1928-1932
Dubé, Normand	French	1978-1979
Dunlop, John J.	Teacher	1921-1951
	Principal	1939-1951
Ecclestone, Mrs. Margaret	French	1974-1979
Ellis, George		1920-1938
Ellis, O.		1913-1917
Elson, Miss Rosland	English	1962-1966
Emmerson, Richard	Mathematics	1984-1985
Emond, Vincent	English	1982-
Endicott, Miss Claire	English	1961-1962
Erskine, Mr.		1956-1957
Everett, Peter	Vice-principal	1986-1989
Ewing, W.		1905-1907
Fader, Ms. Janet	History	1988-
Fagan, Gerald	English	1961-1962
Fair, S.		1932-1933
Fallis, Arnold	Shops	1939-1969
Fallis, Mrs. Frances (née Lee)	Physical Education	1949-1967
Felker, Stuart	Science	1934-1961
Ferguson, Robert D.	Vice-principal	1980-1986
Fink, Bruce	History	1980-1986

Finn, Donald	Business	1970-1975
Fisher, Mrs. Rosalyn	English	1983-1984
Fitzsimmons, Andy	Science	1934-1959
Flett, George	French	1951-1962
Flynn, Bernhard		1939-1945
Forfar, C.		1889-1892
Forster, James	Science	1960-1969
Forward, Mrs. A.		1919-1922
Forward, Miss Isobel	Home Economics	1943-1968, 1969-1974
François, Michel	French	1967-
Fraser, A.		1946-1947
Fraser, William	English	1965-
Fraser, Miss Martha S.		1979-1981
Frazer, Miss		1956-1957
Galilee, Miss Gwen (later Mrs. Terrenoire)	French	1965-1967
Galligher, Hugh	Mathematics	1982-1983
Gaudreau, Ron	Mathematics	1991-
Gemmill, Miss Mary	Latin, French	1956-1968, 1969-1970
Ghantous, Mrs. Catherine (later Miss van Loon, 1984)	Business	1983-1984
Gilchrist, D.		1912-1938
Gilhooly, Miss B.	English	1916-1922
Gillespie, Mrs. Ann	Business	1992-
Glavin, Stephen J.	Principal	Jan. 1977-1987
Glenny, Miss	Art	1973-1974
Goldie, William	Science	1968-Dec. 1971
Graham, W.	English, Mathematics	1895-1906, 1909-1922
Grant, S. Ian	Teacher - Business	1973-1976
	Vice-principal	1989-
Grant, Miss Margaret	Art	Sep.-Dec. 1989 only
Grant, Mrs. Sherri	Art	1990-
Gray, Mrs. Georgina (née Thornton)	French	1969-1975
Green, Robert	Teacher - Mathematics	1963-1968, 1970-1971
	Vice-principal	1975-1980
Greer, Mrs.		1957-1961
Gregor, L.		1886
Griffin, Paul	Dramatic Arts	1990-1992
Guignard, J. A.	French, German	1890
Guillet, C.	French, German	1890-1894
Gurgal, Ms. Roberta D.	Art, English	1977-1983
Guthrie, E.		1923-1927
Hackett, J.		Before 1872
Hagan, Miss Andrea	English	1974-1976
Halbert, E.		1909-1910
Hale, Larry	Physical Education	1964-
Halliday, H.	English	1887
Halloren, Martin	English	1964-1968
Hamilton, William	History	1966-1967
Hardie, William	Latin	1905-1920
Harris, Miss		1956-1961
Harris, Mrs. Sheila	Mathematics	1964-1973
Harstone, L.		1882-1884
Hawkins, Ralph		1933-1934
Hayden, W.		1905-1912
Heft, Mrs. Joy	French	1970-1974, 1990-
Herbert, Miss Margaret (later Mrs. Dawson, 1972)	Science	1961-1979
Hetherington, Mrs. Mary	Physical Education	1960-1961
Hewitt, Miss Susan	Science	1991-
Heymans, Mr.		1957-1958
Higgins, Mrs. Patricia D.	Art	1971-1973
Hills, Miss Ruth (later Mrs. Davis)		1929-
Hislop, T.		1874-1876
Hockey, Dr. David	Vice-principal	1973-1975
Hokkinen, Kal	Science	1949-1958, 1961-1963
Hollingsworth, Douglas	Science	1962-1967
Hollingsworth, William	Mathematics	1968-1973
Holmes, Miss		1951-1953
Holmes, Mr.		1921?
Hood, Finlay	Art	1906-1939
Horreman, Mr.		1949-1964
Howie, J.		1912-1916
Huggins, M.		1911-1913
Hunter, James	Science	1969-1972
Hunter, Mrs.	Science	1971-1973
Hursti, Robert	Music	1966-1992
Hussey, Craig	Mathematics, Science	1991-

Hutchinson, J.		1921
Hyba, Norbert	English	1976-1987
Ichino, Mrs. Shigema	Japanese	1990-1992
Iles, Miss I.		1880-1882
Irvine, Brian	Vice-principal	1984-1987
Irwin, A.		1919-1922
Irwin, N.		1916-1922
Jalitte, O.		1910-1933
Jelinek, Miss Jay	Art	1960-1966
Jenkins, Mrs.		1956-1957
Johnston, Harley	Shops	1962-1966
Johnstone, Miss A.		1884-1905
Joliffe, O. J.	Latin	1884-1903
Jones, Miss	Physical Education	1974-1975
Joyce, Walter	Vice-principal	1964-1965
Kafka, Mrs.	Dramatic Arts	1979-1980
Kaiser, J. B.	History	1922-1933
Kayuk, Miss Linda	Science	1979-1982
Keill, L.	Latin	1922-
Keliher, Tom	Physical Education	1958-1963
Kellock, E.		1918-1919
Kennedy, Douglas	Latin	1957-1978
Kennedy, G.		Ret. before 1903
Kennedy, Peter	Science	1991-
Keogh, L.		1907-1913
Kernohan, Donald	Shops	1972-1975
Kerslake, Peter	English	1968-Dec. 1971, 1976-1988
Kettles, Miss Mary	Geography	1968-1977
Kilpatrick, J.		1918-1927
Korn, Ms. Janet	Mathematics	1984-1985
Kostash, Miss Elizabeth	Physical Education, Law	1981-1983, 1984-
Kuhi, Miss T. A.		1962-1963
Kujala, Mrs. Andrea	Business, Law	1976-1991
Kyle, Robert	Mathematics	1983-1984
Lacroix, Ms. Anna	Special Education	1987-1989
Lafleur, P. T.	French, German	1882-1886
Lalande, Lionel	French	1928-1964
Lamperd, David	Science	1970-
Lane, J.		1911-1922
Lane, Kenneth	French	1966-1968
Lane, Larry	Mathematics	1984-1991
Lapensee, E.		1922
Lapensee, Mr.	French	1943-1947
Lashley, Miss	Home Economics	1951-1959
Latour, C.	French	1915-1927
Latreille, Lloyd	Science	1979-1980, 1983-1984
Laughton, Barrie	Geography, Gifted	1968-
Lawrence, Mrs. Anne	English	1980-1987
Lawrence, Miss		1947-1948
Lawson, Don	Physical Education	1991-
Lee, Miss Frances (later Mrs. Arnold Fallis)	Physical Education	1949-1967
Leggat, Ms. Denise	French	1991-June 1991
Leggett, Joe	Physical Education	1960-1981
Legon, E. F.	Latin	1936?
Letouzel, William	English	1968-1971
Lewis, Mrs. Bessie (née Scott)	English, Physical Education	1892-1906, 1924-1939
Lewis, Wayne	Geography	1967-1976
Libby, W. H.	English	1891-1894
Liebner, E.	Science	1903-1906
Little, T.		1946-1947
Livesley, John P.	Vice-principal	1965-1967
Living, Miss A.		1875-1879
Locklin, E.		1920-1922
Lonsberry, Bruce	History	1982-1984
Loudon, W. J.	Mathematics	1881
Love, Jon	History	1981-1982
Lowe, Miss Beverley	French	1968-1970
Mabee, G. E.	Latin	1910-1936
Macdonald, D. Ian	Principal	1987-
Macdonald, J.		1926-1927
MacGougan, David	Music, Librarian	1959-1992
MacGregor, A.		1921-1922
MacGregor, Ms. Marilyn	Business	1988-1989
MacKay, D.		1917-1934
MacKenzie, Dean	Science	1968-1970, 1992-
MacLean, B. C.		1872-1873

MacLean, Miss Marion		
(later Mrs. Whittle, 1956)	English	1932-1934, 1956-1967
MacMillan, Brian	Business	1991-
MacMillan, H. S.	French, Latin	1897-1903
MacMillan, J.		1897-1903
MacMillan, John	Teacher	1864-1882
	Principal	1882-1904
MacMillan, Robert	Science (dec. 08/87)	1970-1987
MacMinn, M.		1916-1923
MacNaughton, Ian	Science	1986-1989
Maheux, Fred	Art	1973-1974
Manly, C.		1876-1877
Mann, Harold	English	1907-1943
Mann, Mrs. Marjorie	English	1960-1961
Mann, Walter	English	1933-1960, 1961-1968
Manning, Eric	English	1964-1970
Manning, Mrs. Margaret	English	1970-1971
Manson, P.		1882-1887
Makepeace, Ronald	Mathematics	1969-1973
Marshall, Gregory	Science	1985-1991, 1992-
Marty, Miss A.	French, German	1903-1919
Massie, Ms. Holly	English, Dramatic Arts	1987-1989
May, E.		1922-1923
Mayhew, Kenneth	History	1984
Mayhew, Miss Phyllis	French	1968-1969
McArthur, C. P.	History	1941-1956
McCafferty, John	French	1968-1969, 1970-1973
McCamus, W.	Latin	1919-1921
McCarthy, William	Vice-principal	1967-1970
McCormick, Mrs. Phyllisann	French	1965-1967
McCracken, M.		1933-
McCummon, Mrs.		1956-1960
McDermott, I.		1932-1939
McDonald, Terry	Science	1972-1973, 1978-1986
McDougall, Dr. A. H.	Teacher - Mathematics	1889-1904
	Principal (O. C. I.)	1904-1922
	Glebe Collegiate	1922-1928
McDowall, J. W.		1872-1873
McGill, A.	Science	1882-1887
McIntyre, Miss Alta	Mathematics	1947-1967
McKinley, C.	Latin	1920-1921
McLaughlin, John	Mathematics	1973-1979
McLeary, Miss		1947-1948
McLennan, Mrs.	Home Economics	1981-1982
McManus, E.		1906-1918
McMellan, G.		1909-1915
McMichael, Robert	Teacher - Mathematics	1953-1957
	Vice-principal	1960-1964
	Principal	1972-Dec. 1976
McNab, J.		1910-1912
McNamara, D'Arcy	English	1966-1973
McNeil, Miss	English	1961-1962
McNevin, I.	Mathematics	1881-1883
McNulty, Mrs. Bonita	Physical Education	1984-1985
McQueen, J.		1921-1922
Meadows, P.		1930-
Meech, Miss Marion	History	1943-1970
Meiklejohn, A.		1906-1909
Meilleur, Sister Marie	French	1981-1989
Melanson, William	French	1967-
Meldrum, William	Mathematics	1988-
Melvin, Miss Janet	Science	1982-1986,1987-1988
Meng, Lou	Science	1922-1965
Merrill, A.	English	1895
Michel, Miss Norma	Special Education	1977-1988
Michels, Henry	Mathematics	1986-1987
Millar, O. Timothy	Principal	1856-1858, Ret. before 1903
Mitchell, W.		1939-
Moenting, Mrs. Denise	Guidance	1990-
Monsour, Harry	English (dec. summer/84)	1972-1984
Morchain, Dr. Janet	History	1973-
Morrison, David	Music	1987-1991
Morrison, Rev. George	Guidance	1974-1987
Moynihan, Ms. Gail	Business, Library	1987-
Mraceck, Mr.	Music	1955-1959
Muir, Miss Jessie	French, German	1909-1939
Mulvihill, Mrs. Denise	French	1969-1973
Murphy, Dennis	Vice-principal	1991-Jan.1992
Murphy, Robert	English	1970-1976

Murray, Mrs.		1951-1952
Murton, Mrs. A. E.	French, German	1962-1965
Nash, Mrs.		1953-1954
Neil, J. Wright	Teacher - English, Guidance	1939-1951
	Vice-principal	1951-1960
	Principal (dec. '85)	1960-1972
Nichol, W.		1909-1916
Nicholls, Eric A.	Physical Education, Mathematics	1932-1972
Norris, I. T.	Teacher - Mathematics	1898-1922
	Vice-principal	1922-1928
Northwood, Miss B.	Mathematics	1898
Nugent, A.	Mathematics	1883-1887
O'Brien, Miss	English	1961-1963
O'Brien, Pat	History	1967-1973
O'Driscoll, Kevin	Guidance	1986-1989
Orr, A.		1886-1887
Palumbo, Fidel	History	1990-
Park, Miss Lexie (married name: Pettus)	English (on exchange with Walter Mann from Scotland)	1952-1953
Park, Wally	Latin, French	1958-1965
Parsons, John	Vice-principal	1992-
Paryas, Heinz	History, German	1979-
Paryas, Mrs. Phyllis	English	1987-
Passmore, A.		1886
Patterson, Miss		1956-1960
Patterson, A.		1910-1911
Pattison, Arthur	Mathematics, Science	1990-1991
Peters, Lawrence	English	1977-
Phillips, Mrs.		1947-1948
Phillips, F.		1909-1912
Phillips, Rev. T.	Mathematics	1878-1880
Pilgrim, Brian	Guidance	1987-1991
Plummer, Dr. David	Science	1969-1970
Poetschke, Ms. Margaret	English	1988-
Porter, Miss		1958-1959
Porter, Terry	Music	1992-
Poupore, Dennis	French (L.T.D. 1988-1989)	1985-1989
Pottras, A.		1921-1922
Powell, F.		1877-1878
Powers, Mr.	Science	1982-1983
Prichett, Terry	Science	1966-
Priebe, Laurence	English (dec. 23/11/86)	1967-1977
Procter, Albert	English	1938-1966
Prosenyak-Weber, Mrs. Brenda	French	1991-
Proulx, Mrs. Francine	Guidance	Jan.-Nov. 1986
Pulker, Dr. Edward	History	1971-1974
Purdy, Mrs. Diane	Science	1989-1991
Purdy, Michael	Geography	1982-Dec. 1984, 1985-1988
Putnam, Mr.		1947-1948
Qadri, Mr. Rifat	Geography	1962-1990
Ramsay, J.		1909-1910
Rathwell, Mr.		Ret. before 1903
Raymond, Maurice	Geography, French	1962-1970
Readdie, G.		1914-1919
Redwick, C.		1917-1921
Reid, Hugh	English	1973-1979, 1980-1982
Reid, R.		1909-1910
Rentner, Lorne	Mathematics	1923-1965
Ricci, Mrs. Norma Jean	French	1973-1975
Richards, Mrs. Mirka		1982-1983, 1984-1989
Riddell, W.		1923-1927
Rimes, Ms. Anne	Science	1991-1992
Riochet, Miss Leticia (later Mrs. Trevino)	French, Spanish	1985-1987, 1989-
Robb, Rev. J.	Principal	1845-1850
Robbie, John		1954-1955
Roberts, William	Business	1964-1969
Robertson, Miss D.		1947-1948
Robertson, N.		1874-1875
Robeson, W.		1876
Robinson, Mrs.		1947-1948
Roebuck, John	Music	1966-1976
Rogers, J.	Home Economics	1939-1943
Ross, J. R.		1873
Ross, W. A.	Principal	1850-1856
Ross, Mrs. Mary	Mathematics	1970-1977
Rothwell, Mr.		Ret. before 1903

Name	Subject	Years
Rothwell, T. J. Harold	Mathematics, Physical Education	1934-1964
Rouleau, Mr.		1949-1954
Roundell, Jack	Science	1990-
Routhier, Fern	History	1980-1989
Rowat, William	Music	1991-1992
Rowat, Mrs. Margaret	Physical Education	1983-1984
Rudisuela, Dwight	Latin	1968-1970
Rule, Lionel	Guidance	1957-1985
Russell, Fred	Science	1968-1970
Sabean, Mrs. Carol	English	1972-1975
St. Aubin, Gerry	Science	1989-
St. Jacques, H.		1909-1910
Samis, Miss Jane	French, German	1956-1960
Sanderson, W.	Mathematics	1887-1889
Saunders, Sam	Art	1974-1989
Schernerman, Miss		1953-1954
Schmidt, Leonard	French, German	1970-1983, 1984-1989
Schouten, Miss	Home Economics	1968-1969
Schutt, Karl Rosemary	Art	1984-1987
Scott, Miss Bessie (later Mrs. Lewis)	English, Physical Education	1892-1906, 1924-1939
Scott, C.	Science, Art	1887-1894
Scott, Gary	Business	1967-1970
Seiers, Miss Yvonne	Guidance	1992-
Shapiro, Jack	Vice-principal	Jan.-June 1987
Shea, Mel	French	1989-Jan. 1991
Shelton, Mrs. Phyllis D.	Physical Education	1970-1971
Sheppard, David	Science	1986-1990
Sherman, James	English	1971-1974
Shillington, Miss Marilyn (later Mrs. Sloan, 1972)	Physical Education	1963-1974
Shouldice, Vic	Guidance	1971-1974
Showman, Wallace	Latin, Greek	1933-1966
Showman, Mrs. Eva H.	English	1964-1965
Sidey, T.	Latin	1892-1903
Sienkiewicz, Ed.	Geography, History, English	1977-1979
Simard, Mrs.	Art	1974-1975
Simcoe, George	Mathematics	1974-
Simmons, J.		1889
Simpson, A.		1910-1912
Simpson, R.	Commercial	1902-1916
Slaver, M.		1928-1932
Sloan, Mrs. Marilyn (née Shillington)	Physical Education	1963-1974
Small, Darrel F.	Mathematics	1981-1982, 1991-
Smeaton, William	Science	1906-1940
Smith, C.		1912-1913
Smith, Ms. Cathy	Physical Education	1976-1984, 1985-1991, 1992-
Smith, D. E.	French, German	1886-1887
Smith, D. S.		1883-1884
Smith, G.		1920-1922
Smith, Garry	History	1965-1976
Smith, H.		1913-1922
Smith, Miss Jessie	Mathematics, Physical Education	1927
Smith, Miss Lillian E. (later Mrs. Atkinson)	History	1931-1965
Smith, W.		1931
Snell, Steve	Mathematics	1991-
Sobieniak, Mrs. Joan	Physical Education	1970-1971, 1972-1981
Somerville, T. C.	French, German	1892
Sonley, J.		1921-1922
Sparling, Earl	Mathematics	1964-1970
Sparling, Harry	Mathematics	1968-1969
Spriggings, M.	Business	1985-1986
Standing, M.	French	1926-1928
Staples, Miss Helen	English	1967-1968
Starrs, Miss Jean	Mathematics	1972-1976
Stevenson, Robert	Geography	1988-1991
Stevenson, W.	English	1906-1920
Stewart, F.		1915-1939
Stewart, G.		1911-1922
Stinson, Miss	Mathematics	1981-1982
Stitts, Donald	Geography	1978-1979
Stothers, R.	History	1887-1928
Strader, J. W.	Teacher	1923-1951
	Principal	1951-1956
Stratton, Craig	Shops	1969-1972
Strong, David	Shops	1966-1968
Stuart, F. A.	Teacher	1915-1929
	Vice-principal	1928-1939

Name	Subject	Years
Stykes, W.	English	1894-1911
Sullivan, Edward	Music	1976-1982
Summerby, W.		1876
Swann, Mr.		1956-1958
Symons, H.		1917-1919
Syres, W.		1894-1903
Takemura, Mrs. Akiko	Japanese	1989-
Tasse, Mrs. Vicki (née Miller)	Dramatic Arts, English	1980-1981
Tate, Mrs. Susan	English	1969-1970
Taylor, Douglas	Latin, Greek, World Religions	1979-
Taylor, J.	Mathematics	1892
Taylor, D. Timothy		1964-1965
Tennant, H.		1920
Terrenoire, Mrs. Gwen (née Galilee)	French	1965-1967
Thom, J. Earle	Science	1944-1970
Thomas, Mrs. Sandra	English	1981-
Thompson, Miss Erica	French (dec. 29/07/90)	1941-1970
Thoms, C.		1919-1922
Thomson, Mrs. Pat	Home Economics	1974-19820
Thorburn, J.	Principal - Latin	1862-1881
Thornton, Miss Georgina (later Mrs. Gray, 1975)	French	1969-1975
Tilden, G.		1929-1930
Tobin, Myles	English	1972-1973
Todd, Mrs. Eleanor	Mathematics	1956-1971
Tomkins, Miss E.	English, Mathematics	1902-1932
Trevino, Mrs. Leticia (née Riochet)	French, Spanish	1985-1987, 1989-
Trites, Bruce	Mathematics	1976-1981
Tubman, Mr.		Ret. before 1903
Van Jantsch, Miss L.	French, German	1890
Van Loon, Miss Catherine (earlier Mrs. Ghantous)	Business	1983-1984, 1986-1987
Van Scherrenberg, Mr.	Music	1965-1966
Ventresse, A.	English	1888-1890
Vetter, Frank	Guidance	1964-1971
Waddell, Donald	Geography	1947-1972
Wade, Larry	Science	1961-1968, 1970-1992
Wade, Malcolm	Mathematics	Oct. 1990-1991
Wallace, Mrs. Irene	Art	1969-1971
Wallace, J.	Mathematics	1883-1898
Walsh, Mr.		1957-1958
Wang, Zhen-Wu		1989-Feb. 1991
Wardrope, G.		Ret. before 1903
Wardrope, Thomas	FIRST PRINCIPAL	1843-1845
Watkin, Mrs. Bernice	Physical Education	1991-
Watts, Charles	Science	1956-1962
Weaver, M.		1885-1886
Webb, Mrs. Susan	History	1977-1982
Webb, Vernon	Science	1983-1989
Weber, Eugene	Mathematics	1980-1991
Wedderspoon, Robin	Latin, Greek, World Religions	1966-1989
Weeks, Michael J.	Vice-principal	1970-1976
Wen, Yen Kuang		1990-
Whittle, Mrs. Marion (formerly MacLean)	English (dec. 15/05/91)	1932-1934, 1956-1967
Whittle, R.	English	1932-1955
Williams, Brian	French	1980-1987
Williams, Ms. Gloria	French	1984-1985, 1989-1990
Williamson, Mrs. Dorothy	English	1969-1981
Wills, N.		1928-1929
Wilson, Ms. Beverley	English	1987-
Wilson, Ms. Margaret		Sept. 1991 only
Wilson, Michael	Dramatic Arts	1970-1971, 1972-1973, 1977-1979, 1992-
Whol, R.		1876
Woods, James E.	Physical Education	1981-1991
Woodward, Mrs. Olga	Geography	1989-1981, Sept.-Oct. 1983
Wong, Mrs. Sue	English	1982-1983
Wright, Ms. Alison	Art	1989-1990
Young, Brian	History	1964-1968
Young, Mrs. Margaret	Vice-principal	Feb.-June 1992

ALERE FLAMMAM

Since then, ah Lisgar, since you began
How many, for a short, brief span
Have come to delve in knowledge stores.
And then have passed beyond your doors?
What heads have bent in heavy thought
Have studied, learned and soon forgot;
And came exams, what minds in haste
Have cursed the time they had to waste
In loafing, trite and useless things.
What tales appeared writ in lead scribblings
On books. What intrigues have been heard;
What gossip stained the halls by word
Of mouth. What old songs have been sung
In assembly when the rafters rung
"With the glory of the O.C.I."
What crowds have roared out "Phi Chi Psi."
What teams have won—what men,
Ah Lisgar, have fought for you since then;
What knuckles rulers broad have cracked.
These stout old desks,—what knives have hacked
Out letters. The dances—years ago—
What whisperings—when the lights were low;
All things the same—times goes its way,
The youth at school is as yesterday.
In years, ah Lisgar, you are wise,
You have a youth that never dies,
Your heart shall not grow old, feel time
For the spirit of youth is in your rhyme.

—Joan Finnigan, *Vox Lycei*, 1944

Photo by Malak

PATRONS: BLUE AND GREY

Lillian Smith Atkinson
Dr. Colin Henderson Smith
Nigel Stephens
Kathy Early Ullrich
Jeffrey D. White
David Whitfield

BENEFACTORS: ALERE FLAMMAM

Peter and Nenita Clark
Joscelyn V.B. Cosh *
Gordon F. Henderson
W. David Hopper **
E. Peter Hopper **
Wilbert (Bill) H. Hopper **
Walter B. Mann
Dr. Neville G. Poy
John Ruedy

Yvonne Seiers
Erik Spicer
Irving Taylor
George Owen Toller
Peter Ullrich Memorial Fund
(Ottawa Board of Education)

*   in memory of Digby R.B. Cosh and Beverley
   Cosh McLean
** in memory of Wilbert Clayton Hopper
   (1894-1965)

SPONSORS

Dr. Stanley J. Abelson
Daniel Ages
Jeanne D. Ainslie
Elda (Bortolotti) Allen
Thomas C. Anderson
Claire (Bruce) Anfossie
Lynne R. Armstrong
Douglas Arrand
Ariadne Athanassiadis
Gina Athanassiadis
Mirella Athanassiadis
Harry Avery
W.K. (Bill) Bangs
Kathleen R. Barclay
Joan (Windle) Barnes
Herbert W. Beall
Paul M. Bennett
Cynthia (Gora) Blumenthal
John F. Boehmer
Chloe Bouza
Reuben Bouza
Richard C.E. Bray
Grant Buchanan
Charlotte (MacKay) Burgess
Lorna Calderwood
Sarah E. Capes
Sharon L. Cardash
Laleah A. Carscallen
The Rev. Dr. A. Caulfeild
John Chance
Peter Godwin Chance
Beatrice (Wallace) Charbonneau

Kim M. Chung
Hartman P.V. Chung
Elisabeth Anne Cleghorn
Dr. Douglas C.T. Coupland
Sheila (Bowser) Creed
Elizabeth (Nugent) Culley
Ruth (Hills) Davis
Arzu F. Deen
Joan (Klaas) Doubt
Mrs. Carrie-Joy Dover
Eleanor (Bates) Dunn
Maxwell K. Edwards
Michael K. Edwards
W. Kemp Edwards
Mary Evans
Carmen Figueroa
Barbara (Fenton) Fisher
Jane (Thurston) Foley
Sheila (Lamke) Forhan
Betty (Cracknell) Forrest
William R. Fraser
Michael D. Froislie
Sylvia (Abelson) Gellman
Connie Keyes Gibbon
Ron Gibson
Ron Gould
Ted Greenway
Lloyd C. Guest
Rodney, Andrea, Wendy Hagglund
Dr. Bruce Halliday, M.P.
Sarah Hallman
Leith (Ross) Harding

Catherine (Thomas) Harper
Douglas Harris
Mike Herzog
Donald A. Hill
Dr. James H.B. Hilton
Patricia (Pearce) Hood
Marie (O'Callaghan) Hutt
Rochelle Ironstone
Bill Joe
Neil W. Johnstone
Gorman Kerr
Mary I. Kettles
Bruce Kirby
Barbara Joan Fisher Kirk
Joan F. (Duncan) Kirk
Matt Kosaki
Thomas Kritsch
Martin Kusy
Gail Luther Larose
Walter W. Latimer
Barrie Laughton
Jean-Paul Laurin
Ann Tarantour Lazear
Lois (Bourne) Leadlay
John W. Lee
Valerie Delaute Leesing
Saretta (Rill) Levitan
Andrea N. Lobo
Ronald Scott Lyle
D. Ian Macdonald
Maxwell Macfarland
David V. MacGougan

Elizabeth MacIntosh

Dr. Arthur G. Mackey

Jean MacLean

Christopher S. MacNeil

Jim Macpherson

Bill Mann

Nora M. Mansfield

Joan (Toller) Mavor

D. Earl McCullough

Bernice (Scheuneman) McLaurin

Robert G. McMichael

Rachel (Micklethwaite) McRae

Marion Meech

Lois M. Miller

Keith Mills

Bill Mitchell

Jonathan Mitchell

David Molot

Janet B. Morchain

Hisako Mori

Naura A. Mosley

Marjorie Woodburn Mowat

Beryl Murton

Etta Neil

Ronald E. Newman

Gretel Margaret (Bates) Nieboer

Barbara, Brian, Christopher and
  Jennifer O'Brien

Christian (Spence) Ogden

Heinz and Phyllis Paryas

Ann (Abraham) Pepper

Mrs Susan Petric

Alexandra J. (Park) Pettus

Margaret (Lugsdin) Pippy

Isobel (Lockhart) Pitkethly

Cecylia Podoski

Margaret Mary Poetschke

James F. Pratt

Edward A. Pulker

Jon G. Purcell

Dr Charles Ramsden

Catherine Hart Rayment

Sarah Jane Reesor

Ronald J. Reimer

Pamela C. Reynolds

Betty (Fraser) Rhoades

Bill Richards

Terry Rielly

Susan Riley-Guilbault

John Digby Roebuck

Josephine L. Rogers

Beth Roodman

Elizabeth Olmsted Rose

Lionel C. Rule

Charles E. Ryan

Steve Sansom

Russ Sawchuk

Rudy Scarabelli

Albert G. Sculthorpe

Sarah and Milton Shaffer

Colin H. Shaw

John N. Shoemaker

Fairlie (Dale) Sills

Tanis K. Skabar

Jeannie (Ferguson) Smith

Elvins Y. Spencer

Ross B. Stewart

Allan Sutton

Ernest Taylor

Karlheinz Theil

Elizabeth (Hooke) Timleck

Stephanie A.J. Van Vliet

Harold and Alice (Ringrose) Vollmer

Kenneth and Susan Webb

Alden (Al) Weeks

F.W. White

Donald Whittemore

Sylvia J. Wiggins

Douglas Fleetwood Wilson

Heather D. Wilson

Dr Edward Wolstein

Paul K. Woodburn, Sr

Irene F. Woolford

CREDITS

This history would not have been possible without the help and advice of the following people; Doug Arrand, Alumni Consultant; Joan Litke, transcribing and word-processing, Burnstown, Ontario; Pat Hood, copy editing, Nepean; Betty Corson, editorial assistance, Kingston, Ontario; Marion Meech, Walter and Marjorie Mann, Dorothy Bishop; Dave McGougan, archival research; Doug Symington, research; the office staff of Lisgar; Mrs. L. Derry, Mrs. G. Rana, librarians; and Margaret Pippy, Alumni Office Administrator.

Photography credits: Neil Petrie for photography, copying, printing and original photography; Bill Marsh, Doug Brierley, Helen Ogilvie, David Dunlap, Mildred Minter, Joan Coughlan, Fergus Lothian, Marjorie Hall, Arthur Lewis, Gail Hess Casselman, Elizabeth McIntosh, Mike Clarkson, Vince Emond.

Rev. Arthur Caulfeild, Robert McDowall, B.A. Thurston, Dr. McFarlane, Cathleen Scanlon Pedersen, M. Stevenson, Alice Bawden, G.R. Goven, R. Forbes Hirsch, Ken Medland, Tom Greenberg.

JANET MORCHAIN'S CLASS, 1991-92: Luiza Chwialkowska, Tara Dwivedi, Scott Gordon, Catherine Henin, Mike Herzog, Paul Laperriere, Austin Lawrence, Heather Mackinnon, Matthew McCarthy, Virginia Preston, Anand Radhakani, David Reid, Manel Silva, Martina Smazal, Vishnu Som.

JANET MORCHAIN'S CLASS, 1993: Alexandra Bedyn, Stephane Benzekri, Rebecca Carson, Melanie de Groot, Christina Di Gangi, Chris Dodge, Kamp Edwards, Nick Hamilton, Collin Harker, Bob Kennedy, Yakup Krarup, Mike Lawson, Jordan Lynn, Angus McKinnon, Jennifer Peters, Jeff Morton, Patrick Jonathan, Andy Plewis, Geoff Robinson, Janet Rowat, Jill Russell, Azadeh Sabour, Zoe Stikeman, Kate White, Gillian Price, Richard Zayed, Amanda Tomlin.

GRADUATES INTERVIEWED FOR JANET FADER'S CLASS PROJECT, 1992: Dr. Shailandra Verma, David Jeanes, Larry Kane, Meribeth Morris. Dr. Moe Gencher, Doug Brierley, Marion Meech, Miss Jean Maclean, Betty Jane Bolduc, William Telfer and Mary Telfer, James Hilton, Miss Patricia Crossley, Dave Chance, Dr. William Mills, Bill Fraser.

JANET FADER'S CLASS: Christopher Allen, Christina Di Gangi, Chris Cooper, Jeff Hsu, Bonnie Seshadri, Gillian Price, Shannon Dodge, Marlisa Tiedermann, Samantha Ovimet, Jennifer Kingsley, Catriona Sturton, Sarah Taylor, Holly Morrison, Fiona Smith, Claire Tansey, Matthew Stephenson, Mehmet Karman, Tony Jackson, Ray Gardner, Jen Scrimger, Dylan Collingwood, Nancy N. Neill, Elizabeth Legg.

... was probably that ya
... the skin, where it wasn't
... very dirty white we began
... Professor Nolan's feelin
... that color) had come to a
... end and feared that
... be great to the Exec. Co
... cat has been a frequen
... their meetings. However i
... transpired that their
... and continues to bo
... my fur in the coal du
... basement but we would
... three young ladies wh
... not stand a sudden